Rommel's Desert War

At the height of his power in January 1941 Hitler made the fateful decision to send troops to North Africa to save the beleaguered Italian army from defeat. Martin Kitchen's masterful new history of the Axis campaign provides a fundamental reassessment of the key battles of 1941–3, Rommel's generalship and the campaign's place within the broader strategic context of the war. He shows that the British were initially helpless against the operational brilliance of Rommel's Panzer divisions. However, Rommel's initial successes and refusal to follow orders committed the Axis to a campaign well beyond their means. Without the reinforcements or supplies he needed to deliver a knockout blow, Rommel was forced onto the defensive and Hitler's Mediterranean strategy began to unravel. The result was the loss of an entire army which, together with defeat at Stalingrad, signalled a decisive shift in the course of the war.

MARTIN KITCHEN is Professor Emeritus in the Department of History, Simon Fraser University. His previous publications include *The Third Reich: Charisma and Community* (2007), *A History of Modern Germany, 1800–2000* (2006) and *Europe Between the Wars* (second edition, 2006).

Cambridge Military Histories

Edited by

HEW STRACHAN, Chichele Professor of the History of War, University of Oxford, and Fellow of All Souls College, Oxford

GEOFFREY WAWRO, Major General Olinto Mark Barsanti Professor of Military History, and Director, Center for the Study of Military History, University of North Texas

The aim of this new series is to publish outstanding works of research on warfare throughout the ages and throughout the world. Books in the series will take a broad approach to military history, examining war in all its military, strategic, political and economic aspects. The series is intended to complement *Studies in the Social and Cultural History of Modern Warfare* by focusing on the 'hard' military history of armies, tactics, strategy and warfare. Books in the series will consist mainly of single author works – academically vigorous and groundbreaking – which will be accessible to both academics and the interested general reader.

Titles in the series include:

John Gooch *Mussolini and his Generals: the Armed Forces and Fascist Foreign Policy, 1922–1940*

Alexander Watson *Enduring the Great War: Combat, Morale and Collapse in the German and British Armies, 1914–1918*

Mustafa Aksakal *The Ottoman Road to War in 1914: The Ottoman Empire and the First World War*

J. P. Harris *Douglas Haig and the First World War*

ROMMEL'S DESERT WAR

Waging World War II in North Africa,
1941–1943

MARTIN KITCHEN

CAMBRIDGE
UNIVERSITY PRESS

CAMBRIDGE UNIVERSITY PRESS
Cambridge, New York, Melbourne, Madrid, Cape Town, Singapore,
São Paulo, Delhi

Cambridge University Press
The Edinburgh Building, Cambridge CB2 8RU, UK

Published in the United States of America
by Cambridge University Press, New York

www.cambridge.org
Information on this title: www.cambridge.org/9780521509718

First published 2009

Printed in the United Kingdom at the University Press, Cambridge

A catalogue record for this publication is available from the British Library

Library of Congress Cataloguing in Publication data
Kitchen, Martin.
Rommel's desert war : waging World War II in North Africa, 1941–1943 / Martin
Kitchen.
    p.   cm. – (Cambridge military histories)
Includes bibliographical references and index.
ISBN 978-0-521-50971-8 (hardback)
1. World War, 1939–1945 – Campaigns – Africa, North.   2. Rommel, Erwin,
1891–1944.   3. World War, 1939–1945 – Tank warfare.   4. Germany. Heer.
Panzerarmeekorps Afrika – History.   I. Title.   II. Series.
D766.82.K58   2009
940.54′23 – dc22   2009017321

ISBN 978-0-521-50971-8 hardback

FOR ANDRA AND DARRELL

CONTENTS

ILLUSTRATIONS

MAPS

ACKNOWLEDGEMENTS

First and foremost I would like to thank the Social Sciences Research Council of Canada for their generous support. It came as a pleasant surprise at a time when military history is regrettably out of favour in intellectually fashionable circles. It made it possible for me to make lengthy visits to Germany for archival research.

I am grateful to Jonathan Reeve for his interest in the project and regret that, due to circumstances beyond his control, he was unable to see it through to the end. Thanks also to Heather McCallum, who gave me some valuable advice at a difficult time.

I am greatly indebted to Geoffrey Hamm, who gave me invaluable assistance during the early stages of the planning of this book.

I would also like to thank the staffs of the Bundesarchiv (Militärarchiv), Freiburg im Breisgau, the Politisches Archiv of the Federal German Foreign Office, Berlin, and the Bibliothek für Zeitgeschichte, Stuttgart. They were unfailingly helpful.

Vera Yuen at Simon Fraser University's Interlibrary Loan Department tracked down a rich assortment of rare material with exceptional skill.

At Cambridge University Press I have been given every possible assistance by Michael Watson, Helen Waterhouse and Elizabeth Davey. My copy-editor, Carol Fellingham Webb, combined skill with tact. Don Dosset kindly volunteered to design the dust jacket.

Hew Strachan, the series editor, gave me much valuable advice and suggestions for improvements.

ABBREVIATIONS

1a	chief of operations
AA	Reconnaissance Group
ACV	armoured command vehicle
ADAP	Published papers of the German foreign office
Amt Ausl./Abwer	Counter-intelligence
AOK	Army High Command
AP	armour piercing
BAMA	Military Archives of the Federal Archives
BdU	Commander-in-chief of the submarines
BZG	Library for Contemporary History, Stuttgart
DAF	Desert Air Force
DAK	German Africa Corps (Afrikakorps)
Delease	Delegation of the Supreme Command in North Africa
DIPA	German–Italian Panzer Army
DRZW	Das Deutsche Reich und der Zweite Weltkrieg
EK	Einsatzkommando (special unit)
Flak	anti-aircraft gun
GRT	gross register tonnage

HE	high explosive
Ic	intelligence officer
JIC	Joint Intelligence Sub-Committee
Kasta	Main Support Group
KTB	War diary
LRDG	Long Range Desert Group
NFA	Radio Intelligence Company
ObdM	Commander-in-Chief of the German Navy
OBS	Supreme Commander South
OKH	High Command of the Army
OKL	High Command of the Luftwaffe
OKW	High Command of the Armed Forces
PAAA	Political Archives of the Foreign Office
PRU	Photographic Reconnaissance Unit
RAD	Reich Labour Service
RSHA	Reich Security Main Office
SD	Security Service
Sigint	Signals intelligence
Skl	German Naval Command
SiPo	Security Police
Stuka	dive-bomber
VAA	Foreign Office Liaison Officer
WFSt	Armed Forces Command Staff

INTRODUCTION

Hitler's decision to send troops to North Africa was made with considerable reluctance, and his motives for finally agreeing were political rather than military. Right from the very beginning of his political career he was convinced that an alliance with Italy should be the cornerstone of German foreign policy. There were many powerful opponents to such an idea within the National Socialist hierarchy. It would, after all, mean that Germany would have to abandon any claim to German-speaking South Tyrol, which had been awarded to Italy at the Versailles peace conference. There was widespread contempt for the Italians as an inferior race and soldiers pointed to the wretched state of their armed forces, as well as their pitiful lack of natural resources. Conventional wisdom was that in the event of a major European war, Italy would be more of a hindrance than help. Hitler, who thought in ideological and political rather than strategic terms, would have none of this. He shared many of these reservations about Italy as a partner, but believed that the two countries had a common destiny, as well as a compatibility of interests, and saw in Mussolini an outstanding leader, a faithful comrade and loyal partner in a common cause. The relationship became increasingly strained, but Hitler's loyalty to Mussolini never broke, not even when his bankrupt regime lay in ruins.

Italy did not enter the war until shortly before France's surrender, much to the relief of Hitler's senior military advisers. Meanwhile Major-General Erwin Rommel, a highly ambitious soldier who had won the *Pour le Mérite*, Germany's highest military award, in the First World War, had established a close relationship with Hitler. He was attached to Hitler's headquarters during the Polish campaign as one of the 16 officers and 274 men responsible for the Führer's safety. He first attracted attention as the forceful commander of an armoured division in France. The state secretary in the Ministry of Propaganda, Karl Hanke, was attached to Rommel's staff and gave him access to Goebbels, who in turn did much to enhance Rommel's reputation. The unusual appointment of an infantry officer to command an armoured unit was due to Hitler's influence, which gave the grateful and appreciative Rommel the reputation of being a Nazi general. Rommel admired Hitler and was grateful to him for furthering his career, but he had no time for National Socialist ideology and it is highly unlikely that he ever read the signed copy of *Mein Kampf* that Hitler gave him in February 1940. Baldur von Schirach, the head of the Hitler Youth, was perfectly correct when he told Martin Bormann that Rommel 'was in no way to be considered as a Nazi'.

Hitler, who in 1940 was at the very pinnacle of his power, basked in popular adulation. He had crushed the 'hereditary enemy' and made good the 'shame of Versailles'. Germany dominated Europe, from the Bug to the Atlantic coast, from Norway to the Brenner; the 'racial comrades' now began to enjoy the profits gouged from the plunder and exploitation of those outside the 'racial community'. Wilhelm Keitel, in his capacity as head of the High Command of the Armed Forces, proclaimed Hitler to be 'the greatest commander of all times'. The British had ignominiously retreated at Dunkirk, leaving the bulk of their equipment behind, and had virtually nothing with which to resist an invasion that was expected at any moment. Final victory seemed to be only a matter of time. The Security Service (SD) and Security Police (SiPo) got ready for the invasion, drawing up a lengthy list of prominent figures to be liquidated shortly after the arrival of the Wehrmacht on British soil. On 31 July, confident that Britain was already beaten, Hitler issued instructions to the Wehrmacht for planning to begin for a two-pronged attack on the Soviet Union towards Moscow and Kiev. The invasion was to begin in May 1941. The army, ever eager to oblige, had already begun planning such an attack when Hitler first ordered Walther von Brauchitsch, the commander-in-chief, to examine 'the Russian problem' on 21 June.

There was ample reason for the Germans to be so confident that Britain was on the verge of collapse. By late June statisticians were warning Fighter Command that within six weeks they would have no aircraft left. On 12 August the Germans inflicted severe damage on the vital radar stations on the Channel coast. Attention now turned to Operation 'Sea Lion', designed to deliver the *coup de grâce to* Britain;

but for an invasion to be successful Germany had first to gain control over British airspace. It was at this point that Göring's Luftwaffe made the fatal mistake of stopping the attacks on airfields and radar installations in southern England and concentrated on bombing cities and towns. The Germans did not count on Churchill's dogged determination to continue the fight against all the odds and whatever the cost, nor on the gallantry and skill of the fighter pilots in 'The Few', many of whom were exiled Poles. They saved Britain, and ultimately Europe from Nazi tyranny. This was indeed Britain's 'finest hour'. On 17 September Hitler cancelled Operation 'Sea Lion', the invasion plan, but he still clung to a vague hope that Britain would in the end come round to see that an alliance with Nazi Germany would be a wiser course.

The Germans were now faced with an awkward dilemma. Would it be unwise to attack the Soviet Union before finishing off the British, or would an attack on the Soviet Union bring the British to their senses and force them to realise that it lay in their best interests to co-operate with Germany in confronting the Communist menace? Failing this, once the Soviet Union was destroyed, as most experts believed would be achieved with a matter of weeks, the British would have to throw in the towel, and the awkward business of a cross-channel invasion against an overwhelming naval force would be avoided.

It was at this point that the Italians found themselves in serious difficulties and reluctantly admitted that they desperately needed German help to save themselves from defeat in North Africa. Italy had entered the war in June 1940, confident that the war would be over by September. Against the advice of cooler heads, Mussolini imagined that his ragtag army in Libya, now secure from an attack from the French in Tunisia, could take on the British in Egypt. The German military knew full well that their gallant allies could not do it alone, but some were tempted by the glittering prospect of a German–Italian armoured force seizing the Suez Canal which, given Britain's command over the Mediterranean, was still an essential lifeline for the Commonwealth and Empire.

By the end of August 1940, by which time it was clear that an invasion of southern England would not be possible until the following year, Hitler began to think of a strategy for driving the British out of the Mediterranean. The Panzer were not to be used in 'Sea Lion' and would not go into action against the Soviet Union until the following spring.

Therefore two armoured divisions could be sent to North Africa, without which the Italian offensive against Egypt was likely to fail. At the same time Gibraltar would be seized, but this would only be possible were Franco's Spain and Pétain's Vichy regime prepared to co-operate. Both men stubbornly refused and Hitler, who was absorbed with preparations for the campaign against the Soviet Union, was obliged to put the plan on hold.

By this time fundamental differences between the various branches of the German armed forces, as well as between the Germans and the Italians, had become glaringly apparent. The basic issue was whether the attack on the Soviet Union should be launched before Britain was defeated. Grand Admiral Erich Raeder and the navy, thinking in global rather than continental terms, were adamant that Britain had first to be knocked out of the war, and that this goal could best be achieved not by a cross-channel invasion, but by defeat in Egypt and the Mediterranean. Indeed, Raeder went even further by suggesting that with the defeat of Britain the problem of the Soviet Union would take on a quite different complexion.

Hitler took the opposite view. He came to the conclusion that the simplest way to bring Britain to its knees was to smash the Soviet Union in a lightning campaign. With no hope of support on the continent of Europe, Britain would be forced to sue for peace. Within Hitler's military entourage there was a considerable degree of disagreement, until after weeks of cajoling, bullying and tantrums they were all brought into line, albeit with varying degrees of reservation. Some soldiers agreed with the navy that priority should be given to defeating Britain in the Mediterranean. Others were intoxicated by the vision of a vast campaign of conquest in the east. A few cautious souls wondered whether an attack on the Soviet Union might be altogether too hazardous an operation. But the idea of sending armoured forces to North Africa was agreeable to all three positions. Those who wanted to defeat Britain in the Mediterranean were enthusiastic. Those who gave priority to the invasion of the Soviet Union felt that limited operations in North Africa would provide excellent cover for their true intentions. Those with second thoughts welcomed the idea of tying up German forces in another theatre. There were still two outstanding issues. The first was that of how substantial the commitment to North Africa should be. Once the second option was adopted it was clear that it would be modest. Absolute priority had to be given to building up the largest possible reserves of men and matériel for the massive attack on the stronghold of Jewish Bolshevism and the foundation of a vast racially purified eastern empire. The other thorny issue was the attitude of Mussolini.

The Duce was determined not to play second fiddle to the Germans, and to fight a 'parallel war'. In fact he imagined that he might be able to avoid doing much fighting at all. All that was needed was a few thousand Italian dead to earn an honourable seat at the armistice negotiations. He had heard that 'Sea Lion' had been postponed indefinitely and that Hitler was seeking a diplomatic solution, which he was confident in achieving. At the same time he was told that Keitel had announced that the seizure of Cairo was more important than that of London. Encouraged by the success of the Duke of Aosta in driving the British out of British Somaliland in early August, while conveniently overlooking the fact that an overwhelmingly superior Italian force had suffered almost ten times as many losses compared with the British, Mussolini was determined to launch an offensive in North Africa to deliver a final mortal blow to an enemy that appeared to be on the verge of total collapse.

Mussolini's generals were appalled at such aggressive posturing. They knew that the Italian forces in Tripoli were no match for the British and that an immediate offensive would end in disaster. They pleaded for an indefinite postponement. Knowing full well that this was unlikely to happen, they then tried to persuade the Duce to delay the offensive until German units began landing in England. Mussolini ignored all their objections. He turned down the German offer on 6 September 1940 to send Panzer units to North Africa, for fear that his ally would insist on a degree of command and control. On the following day he ordered General Rodolfo Graziani, the commander of the Italian forces in North Africa, to launch an offensive two days later. The British, who were very thin on the ground, prudently retired. Graziani advanced across the empty desert, but all he achieved was to lengthen his lines of communications, while the Western Desert Force took up a defensive position at Mersa Matruh and prepared to strike back.

In late September Hitler began a dramatic and ultimately fatal process of rethinking his grand strategy. Whereas he had hitherto thought purely in terms of a continental strategy, with his Italian partners dealing with the Mediterranean, he now began to think in global terms. It is within this context that the campaign in North Africa, apparently a peripheral affair, played such an important role, even though Hitler never realised its true significance. He knew that Britain's survival depended to a large extent on assistance from the United States. Although he tried to downplay this factor during his meeting with Mussolini at the Brenner Pass on 4 October 1940, he argued that it might be wise to make preparations for a confrontation with the United States. To this end Germany should create a firm foothold in northwest Africa, make use of Vichy's military installations in Casablanca and Dakar, and establish bases in the Canaries, the Cape Verdes and Azores, whence submarines and the long-range Amerika bombers could disrupt Atlantic shipping and raid the United States. At the same time Hitler made yet another dramatic change of tack. Whereas he had previously been strongly opposed to the idea of Germany attempting to rebuild an overseas empire, although he had often used a threat to reclaim the colonies lost at Versailles as a diplomatic bargaining chip, he now saw these new strategic bases as a means of safeguarding a German 'Middle Africa'.

Mittelafrika had been a dream of the German colonial lobby since Bismarck had first made his ill-fated move to enter the race for overseas possessions. It was seen either as complementary or as an alternative to the concept of a German-dominated *Mitteleuropa*. That Hitler made this dramatic switch was due in large part to pleading from Raeder and the foreign minister, Joachim von Ribbentrop, both of whom were anxious to finish off Britain before tackling the Soviet Union. Hitler, believing that the swift defeat of the Soviet Union would force Britain out of the war, saw no urgency in the matter, but was also anxious to keep up the momentum during the hiatus before 'Barbarossa' was launched. Ribbentrop's concept of a 'continental bloc', an alliance of all the countries from the Iberian peninsula to Japan, depended on the active participation of Spain and Vichy France and, since it would include the Soviet Union, would only have been a temporary measure. None of this was possible. Franco chose to remain aloof, thus saving Gibraltar from attack, and denying the Germans use of bases in Spanish Morocco. Pétain also would not commit himself wholeheartedly to the Third Reich, so that Vichy's colonies were denied to Germany. The Soviet Union was naturally wary of joining a revamped version of the Anti-Comintern Pact. Nothing came of this new grand strategic concept, but Hitler's vision of world domination remained vivid. Mussolini was greatly relieved when it all came to nothing, for he feared that an alliance between Germany, France and Spain would be at Italy's expense.

By October Mussolini had come to the reluctant conclusion that he needed German help in order to dislodge the British from Mersa Matruh, but he still hoped to continue with parallel warfare. In other words he wanted the Panzer without the Germans. Franz Halder, chief of the German general staff, knew that the Italians did not have the ghost of a chance in North Africa without help from German armour, and pointed out that it would take at least ten weeks for the troops to arrive, so that an offensive could not be mounted until the New Year. Mussolini accepted the idea of German support in principle, the Germans set to work examining the situation in North Africa, units of 3 Panzer Division were allocated for duty in North Africa, but no further practical steps were taken.

Mussolini, who had managed to convince himself that Graziani had won a great victory, now prepared his next dramatic move. On 28 October 1940 the Italians invaded Greece. They were soon in serious trouble. The Italians were, as the German military had already assumed, no match for the Greeks. A counterattack forced the Italians back into Albania where they remained tied up over the winter. These developments were most unwelcome to Hitler. The British responded to the Italian attack by establishing a base on Crete and sending troops to Greece. This left the Romanian oilfields, which were essential to fuel the armour for 'Barbarossa', vulnerable to attack. Hitler's attention was thus once again drawn to the Mediterranean, where he was determined to strengthen the southern flank of the forthcoming eastern offensive.

The British launched their offensive in North Africa at the beginning of December in Operation 'Compass'. Germany's Mediterranean strategy quickly began to unravel. Franco still refused to co-operate with the Germans in an attack on Gibraltar. Vichy France would not be lured into closer co-operation. The Italians were on the run, and it seemed likely that they would soon be kicked out of North Africa, which in turn could well lead to the collapse of the increasingly unpopular Fascist regime. That this did not happen was due in large part to the decision by the Defence Committee of the British Cabinet on 8 January to send a substantial contingent from the Middle East to Greece in anticipation of a German invasion.

Hitler, who was concentrating almost exclusively on preparations for 'Barbarossa', professed to be interested in North Africa only in as much as were the British to be victorious they would be free to send their troops elsewhere, and an Italian defeat could well lead to Mussolini's downfall. Having convinced himself that the campaign in the Soviet Union would be short and decisive, he failed to grasp a golden opportunity to destroy the only country still at war with Germany. He felt that all that was needed was to ensure that the Italians stayed in Tripoli. For this a modest armoured force would be quite sufficient. Once the Soviet Union collapsed the Germans would sweep down upon the Middle East from the Caucasus, so that there would be no need to face the nightmarish logistical problem of sending a large army across thousands of kilometres of waterless desert. His soldiers, who needed everything available not only for 'Barbarossa', but also for the invasion of Greece in Operation 'Marita', designed to secure its southern flank, were in full agreement.

Mussolini visited Hitler once again in mid-January 1941 and agreed to Operation 'Sunflower', the dispatch of a German force to Tripoli. He did so with considerable reluctance. Although the force was to be placed under Italian command, it was obvious that this was the end of parallel warfare. Having failed miserably in Greece, with his 10 Army in North Africa destroyed, and his East African empire falling apart, he now would have to bend to the exigencies of German strategy. Even though the German forces allotted to North Africa were initially very small, consisting of a light division, a Panzer regiment and an artillery unit, they had in Rommel a forceful commander who basked in Hitler's favour, and who was determined to go his own way. He was certainly not a man who would easily bow to his nominal superiors.

Both the Italians and the Germans knew full well that what was needed were Panzer to enable a mobile forward defence of Tripoli. This alone would allow for sufficient space for manoeuvre to counter an outflanking movement, as well as for an aerodrome for immediate air support. The Panzer was the Germans' key weapon, which they had learnt to master in the interwar years. The British had invented the tank, but apart from a few interesting experiments in the late 1920s had not found a way to integrate the weapon. The Red Army was obsessed with the tank, adopting the English name for it, and the T-34 outclassed all others in 1941. But it was the Germans who found the answer to how best to use the weapon at the operational level. They developed the Panzer division in which the Panzer were integrated with infantry, artillery, signals and reconnaissance, supported by supply columns and specialised engineers, with all units mechanised so as to be able to move at the same pace as the Panzer. Germany's opponents had nothing to stop the Panzer division with its awesome versatility and daunting speed. It is for this reason that Rommel, an infantryman whose first experience of commanding Panzer was in France in 1940, was able with strictly limited forces to deliver such a series of stunning blows against the British forces in North Africa. The British, who were left helpless against such operational brilliance, were painfully slow to learn, and only prevailed owing to sheer guts and an overwhelming superiority in men and matériel.

Prevail they did, thereby scoring the first great victory over the Germans, a British victory that was only to be outshone by General Slim's brilliant campaign in Burma. For this reason the literature on the North African campaign in English, particularly on the Battle of El Alamein, is truly vast. The concentration, naturally enough, is on the British side, on the shifting reputations of the leading personalities, as well as 8th Army's bitter experience of learning on the battlefield how to cope with a highly skilled enemy. The British, from Churchill and Montgomery down through the ranks, were fascinated by Rommel to the point that he came to be regarded as almost superhuman. Goebbels was amazed at the assistance given to him by the enemy in boosting Rommel's reputation. Setbacks could be attributed to his genius, the defeat of his army represented as an extraordinary feat of arms. Early biographies, such as that by Desmond Young, were positively adulatory, while Liddell Hart's edition of Rommel's papers provided further material to enhance his reputation. A much more balanced account was provided by David Irving in his substantial biography, but he is unable to give a full account of the North African campaign in a work that covers an entire eventful career. More recent works in German by Ralf Georg Reuth and Maurice-Philip Remy are far too sketchy to be of much value. American historians have, like their British colleagues, examined the US army's brutal education in warfare after the 'Torch' landings, but are far more critical of the leadership and less triumphant in victory. They only had to deal with Rommel when he was already defeated, although they had a taste of his medicine at Kasserine. Besides they had, in General George Patton, a Rommel of their own.

German historians have largely ignored the North African campaign, not only because it was peripheral, but also because their major

concerns have been with the eastern campaign and the degree of com-
plicity of the Wehrmacht with National Socialist atrocities. This latter
issue simply does not arise in desert war, which was fought according to
established norms, although recent work by Klaus-Michael Mallmann
and Martin Cüppers shows that the SS, assisted by local Arabs, was
ready to set to work slaughtering Jews, once Rommel had cleared the
British out of the Middle East. Obviously the campaign in the Soviet
Union was a far larger operation, and it was there that the war in
Europe was decided, but defeat in North Africa significantly altered the
strategic balance by immediately facing the Germans with the difficulty
of dealing with the threat of a second front, thus draining the eastern
front of valuable assets.

The North African campaign has usually been seen, as in the
title of Rommel's account, as a 'War without Hate', and thus as further
proof that the German army was not involved in any sordid butchering,
which was left to Himmler's SS. While it is perfectly true that the German troops in North Africa fought with great distinction and gallantry,
and that Rommel was ever scrupulous in the observation of the rules of
war, to the point of deliberately ignoring Hitler's orders to the contrary,
it was fortunate for their subsequent reputation that the SS murderers
who followed in their wake did not have an opportunity to get to work.
Hitler saw the Arabs as useful temporary allies against the Jews and the
'English', by which he meant the British Commonwealth and Empire.
There could be no call for ethnic cleansing in the barely populated
Western Desert. The 8th Army barred the way to Egypt and Palestine,
thus denying special units from the SS the opportunity to set about the
mass murder of Jews in close collaboration with the local populations.
In the urban areas of Tripolitania and Tunisia German efforts to exploit
and eliminate the Jewish communities were constrained by the Italians
under whose command they served. Germany's Italian allies did not
approve of their intense anti-Semitism and eliminatory zeal. They were
determined that Jews who held Italian citizenship should be exempted
from any form of discrimination, and with their colonial ambitions did
not approve of German efforts to win over the Arabs to their cause
by apparently supporting their national aspirations and fanning their
anti-Jewish sentiments.

The political dimension of the campaign is ignored in two lively
works of popular military history by Paul Carrell and Wolf Heckmann, the latter providing a stoutly revisionist account of Rommel's

leadership. These books enjoyed considerable success, but they did not inspire historians to dig deeper. For many years the best material on the North African campaign on the German side was contained in specialist journals and the memoirs and reflections of leading figures such as Albert Kesselring, Fritz Bayerlein, Friedrich-Wilhelm Mellenthin, Walter Nehring, Enno von Rintelen, Eberhard Weichold and in Rommel's own incomplete account. Serious studies of the campaign were mostly highly detailed and strictly limited. Adalbert von Taysen's monograph on Tobruk deals only with Rommel's first unsuccessful attempt to take the garrison. Similarly, Ralf Georg Reuth's study of Germany's Mediterranean strategy deals with only the early stages of the campaign. A notable exception is Karl Gundelach's detailed study of the Luftwaffe in the Mediterranean, which provides much valuable material on this essential arm. It was not until the German Institute of Military History began to publish its massive history of the Second World War that anything approaching a full picture began to emerge. Contributions by Gerhard Schreiber and Bernd Stegemann (1984) and Reinhard Stumpf (1990) give an overview based solidly on extensive archival research, although the final stages in Tunisia are given scant attention. Until this present study no attempt had been made to flesh out this excellent pioneering work. This requires setting the campaign within a wider setting.

Rommel's exceptional position was due not only to his forceful personality and military accomplishments, but even more to his unique relationship with Hitler. The key to success in the Third Reich was ease of access to the Führer. Rommel was well aware that without Hitler's support he would not be able to go his own often irresponsible way, and would be obliged to follow orders from Mussolini and the Italian Supreme Command. He had a valuable ally in Joseph Goebbels, who admired his courage, dash and maverick approach and who built him up as a model hero for the new Germany. Hitler's admiration for Rommel further estranged him from the officers at the High Command of the Army (OKH) and High Command of the Armed Forces (OKW), who regarded him with the deepest suspicion. It was generally agreed that he was courageous to the point of folly, but also that coming from a modest background he lacked elementary social graces, was grotesquely self-promoting, and lacked the rigorous all-round training afforded to staff officers, so that there was no restraining influence on his recklessness. Above all it was agreed that he had been elevated well beyond his abilities solely because of his closeness to Hitler, and that he would have achieved precious little had he not had the support of a number of outstanding staff officers. There was much truth in these charges, as this book shows, and once Hitler's favour was withdrawn when Rommel disobeyed orders at El Alamein his star rapidly waned, leading eventually to his enforced suicide.

For these reasons Rommel's temperamental relations with Hitler and with his superiors at OKH and OKW are examined in detail, revealing much about the way in which the Wehrmacht functioned. The fighting on the ground has to be seen within the structure of Hitler's overall strategic conception for the interaction between the various fronts to become clear. Critical here is the question of whether Rommel would be able to do it alone, or whether his should be a holding operation until the Soviet Union was defeated, after which the Middle East would be taken by forces pouring down from the north. Political constraints have also to be given due weight. Hitler's Mediterranean strategy was modified as his attitude towards Britain changed, as well as by the refusal of both Spain and Vichy France to co-operate in his ambitious schemes. Above all, he had to face the problem of the Italians who, with their exotic colonial ambitions, were pursuing diametrically opposed goals in North Africa, and whom he had at all costs to save from defeat.

The desert was ideal terrain for armoured warfare, but the logistical requirements of a German armoured division were extreme. With Tripoli the only sizeable port until Alexandria, OKH insisted that Rommel should remain on the defensive, otherwise he would outrun his supply lines. But Rommel could not be restrained, and his startling successes tempted the less cautious to think that he might be able to destroy the 8th Army, even though the odds were stacked heavily against him. Unaware of the forthcoming invasion of the Soviet Union, he was convinced that he was being deliberately starved of reserves by jealous superiors and tried to force their hand. Then he was given far too rosy a picture of the campaign in the east, so that he was tempted to go for broke. His only hope was that the Soviet Union would soon collapse and the British would fail to recover from the series of setbacks he had delivered. Once the Germans got into serious trouble in the Soviet Union and Montgomery began to lick the 8th Army into shape, Rommel's position became increasingly precarious. When the Allies landed in North Africa it was hopeless, as he well knew. But Hitler's strategy was now reduced to hanging on at whatever cost to whatever had been won, winning back every inch of ground that had been lost, and never giving up anything anywhere. A strong argument can be made that he was correct to insist that Paulus should make a last-ditch stand at Stalingrad. In North Africa he pointlessly lost an entire army, and by continuing to order his armies to stand and fight to the last, he left behind a people bankrupt and starving, amid a pile of rubble. The causes of this catastrophe are exceedingly complex, but a major factor is Hitler's determination, right from the beginning of his political career, to go to war and to do so in alliance with Italy.

1 ✠ NAZI GERMANY AND FASCIST ITALY

Hitler had always insisted, much to the distress of most of his supporters, that an alliance with Italy was an essential precondition for Germany's bid for dominance in Europe and the winning of 'living space' in the east. Initially this had nothing to do with his admiration for Mussolini. As early as 1920 he said: 'We must do everything possible to get Italy on our side.'[1] In *Mein Kampf* he wrote of Italy as a suitable partner with Britain (which he always referred to as 'England') in an alliance against France.[2] Fascist Italy was in many ways an admirable partner. It was a determined opponent of Freemasonry, had banned the 'international Jewish press' and outlawed Marxism, which faithfully serves the interests of the 'Jewish world-hydra'.[3] Such a policy of alliance would naturally involve abandoning the Germans in South Tyrol, an area that had been awarded to Italy in the peace settlement. Hitler even managed to convince himself that Jews were behind the agitation for returning South Tyrol to the Reich, because this could be done only by force, thus ruining any chance of an alliance with Italy.[4]

Goebbels initially felt that Hitler's obsession with an alliance with Italy and Britain was 'ghastly'. Preferring an association with the Soviet Union, he condemned Hitler as a 'reactionary'.[5] He felt that South Tyrol should become part of a greater Germany, dismissing Italy as a 'little big-mouth state' and the Italians as 'swine'. Goebbels was far from alone among the Nazi leadership in holding such views, and Hitler eventually came to much the same conclusion about the Italians, although he continued to admire Mussolini until the bitter end.[6] Such opposition from within the party is part of the explanation why he devoted a considerable amount of space to the South Tyrol question in his 'Second Book', written in 1928. In this unpublished work he insisted that Italy had as great a need for 'living space' as did Germany, and that this would inevitably lead to conflict with France. Italy was destined to become a 'new Rome' with a Mediterranean empire that would find its true place as a largely autonomous entity within a German *Weltreich*.[7] In other words Italy would enjoy a kind of dominion status within a worldwide German Empire.

Mussolini had long believed that war was the essential precondition for Italy to become a great power. As early as 1924 he told the German ambassador, Constantin von Neurath, who was to become Hitler's first foreign minister, that the Treaty of Versailles made war between Germany and France inevitable. Italy would join in on Germany's side, crush France, claim France's North African colonies, and turn the Mediterranean into a *mare italiano*. He would then depose the pacifist king and proclaim himself emperor.[8] But by 1933 he was singing a very different song. Initially he viewed Hitler with the deepest suspicion. In 1934 he perceptively said of National Socialism: 'One hundred per cent racism. Against everyone and everything: yesterday Christian civilisation, today against Latin civilisation, tomorrow, if at all possible, against civilisation throughout the world ... they are drunk with the desire for war.'[9] He was determined that Austria should remain Italy's client state and act as a buffer between Italy and an expansionist Germany. In spite of his enmity towards France, he still saw Fascist Italy as an integral part of western civilisation, as distinct from Germanic neo-barbarism. The first meeting of the two dictators in Venice in 1934 was not a success. Hitler waffled on for hours on end, spouting ideas from *Mein Kampf* in seemingly endless monologues, prompting Mussolini to remark on his return: 'he is like a gramophone with seven records. When they are finished, he starts all over again in the same sequence.'[10] His nightmare vision was of the swastika flag flying on the Brenner Pass, so that when the Austrian chancellor Dollfuss was murdered by the National Socialists, shortly after the Venice meeting, he mobilised two corps on the border. Italy then joined with Britain and France in the admittedly toothless anti-German Stresa Front of April 1935. But by 1936, with the Italian invasion of Ethiopia and the Spanish Civil War, Germany and Italy grew gradually closer, with Mussolini proclaiming an 'Axis' between Rome and Berlin in November, which he described as an affair rather than a marriage. Mussolini had turned his back on his ambitious schemes in the Danubian basin by opting for North Africa, thus opening the way for an agreement with Germany. Italy joined the Anti-Comintern Pact between Germany and Japan in November 1937, but the Italian foreign minister Ciano's announcement that this was a Berlin–Rome–Tokyo triangle of world political significance was a piece of typically empty bombast. By 1938 Mussolini dropped his objections to an *Anschluss* between Germany and Austria and gave his blessing to the invasion, for which Hitler pronounced himself to be eternally grateful. Mussolini was still somewhat uneasy, but was dragged into total dependence on Germany, in part because of Britain's refusal to give him any support.[11] By slavishly courting Germany, the Duce had alienated both elite and popular opinion, which saw a weak Austria as a buffer between Italy and Germany as the greatest achievement of the war. Hitler's visit to Italy in May 1938 did not result in a pact, but Mussolini told Hitler that 'now no power can separate us', whereas two weeks previously he had announced that the border with Austria would be hermetically sealed and that he would lead the world against 'Germanism', holding Germany down for at least two hundred years.[12]

Mussolini could not possibly achieve his ambition of turning the Mediterranean into an Italian sea without the support of Germany. Italy was almost totally dependent on the import of raw materials, three-quarters of which came via the Straits of Gibraltar, the Suez Canal and the Dardanelles. Given the overwhelming strength of the French and British navies, with their powerful bases in Gibraltar, Malta, Cyprus, Corsica, Tunisia and southern France, Italy would have to rely on imports from continental Europe, and that could only mean a firm alliance with Nazi Germany.[13] The 'Pact of Steel', signed by Ribbentrop and Ciano on 22 May 1939, seemed to give him the possibility of realising his wildest dreams, which he had revealed to the Fascist Grand Council some six weeks previously. Italy would at last be able to 'unlatch the prison doors' of Corsica, Malta, Cyprus and Tunisia, and then either march towards the Indian Ocean through Sudan, or reach the Atlantic by driving the French out of North Africa. The preamble to the Pact contained a Mussolinian boast that it would secure both countries' 'living space', but had a somewhat craven postscript saying that the 'inevitable' conflict with the western democracies would have to be postponed until 1943, so as to give the Italians time to get ready for war. This was the work of General Ugo Cavallero, who in the summer of 1941 was to replace Pietro Badoglio as chief of staff in a reorganised Comando Supremo. He had shot his bolt having master-minded the

Vittorio Veneto offensive in 1918 and was now better known for his staggering duplicity and deceitfulness, rather than for his military ability. He had been head of the Ansaldo, the vast state-owned armaments combine, for four years, but was forced to resign when the navy discovered that the firm had delivered substandard armour and defective machinery to it.[14] As a commander in the field he was soon to preside over the Albanian debacle. Hitler simply ignored this rider, professing himself to be delighted with the arrangement. The High Command of the Armed Forces (OKW) was not impressed by Cavallero's military abilities and felt that since he was very close to Ciano the rift between the military and the politicians would grow even wider. Their very worst fears were confirmed with the invasion of Greece in October 1940.[15]

The leadership of the Italian armed forces, as well as most economists, had serious reservations about the Duce's hallucinatory schemes. Italy as a land without raw materials, dependent on supply by sea, would be incapable of conducting a lengthy war against the western powers. Whereas Hitler thought entirely in political and ideological terms, the German military regarded the Italians with undisguised contempt. At the outset of the war the Italian army was going through a process of reorganisation that was far from completion. The artillery was outmoded, most of it captured from the Austro-Hungarian army in 1918. Their tanks were light, poorly armed and notoriously unreliable. The troops were badly trained, the officer corps remote from the men, the NCOs too few and far from impressive. There were no field kitchens, so that the troops were appallingly badly fed, while their officers indulged in substantial three-course meals. Standard food for the troops was tinned meat stamped 'AM' for *Administrazione Militare*. The Italians christened this *Arabo Morte* (dead Arab), the Germans, when they had the misfortune to come across it, *Alter Mann* (old man). Those with a classical education named it *Asinus Mussolini* (Mussolini's donkey) or a literal translation into the demotic. It was therefore hardly surprising that morale was extremely low, rendered even worse by a lack of support at home for the war. A devastating pre-war report on the Italian army by the German general staff had to be withdrawn on Hitler's orders.[16]

Mussolini would have liked to go to war in 1939, but he faced the opposition of the armed forces, the king and public opinion. He now estimated that he needed about four years before realising his grandiose plan, the first phase of which would be either a surprise attack on Malta in order to secure the sea route to the Italian colony in Tripolitania, or to march into Egypt, seize control over the Suez Canal and link up with the Italian colony in East Africa. Hitler, however, had no intention of waiting until the boastful Duce had sharpened his sword, and was determined to strike before Germany lost its relative advantage over France, even though that meant that Italy would not simultaneously mount an offensive in the Mediterranean. A raid on Malta was discussed again in mid-April 1940, at a time when the island was virtually defenceless. The island air force consisted of a small detachment of pretty little biplane Gloster Gladiators in the Hal Far Fighter Flight. Three of these death traps were affectionately known as 'Faith', 'Hope' and 'Charity'.[17] The Axis was to pay heavily for its failure to deny the British this vital base. But since Mussolini argued that the war would not last much longer, it hardly seemed to be worth the effort.

Hitler, disappointed that Italy did not join in the fray when France and Britain declared war, dismissed as a lame excuse Mussolini's insistence that his armed forces were not yet sufficiently prepared. The Germans were anxious to persuade the Italians to participate in the attack on France, but Mussolini refused to budge, announcing that he would act 'not with Germany or for Germany, but only for Italy'.[18] His policy of *non belligeranza* made little difference to the outcome of the German campaign in the west. The Wehrmacht did not have to take account of an unreliable ally, and Britain and France still felt obliged to tie down forces in southern France and the Mediterranean in anticipation of Italy's entry into the war.

With France's surprisingly rapid and shattering collapse Mussolini finally decided to act, declaring war on Britain and France on 10 June, even though his chief of staff, General Badoglio, a profoundly pessimistic and unwarlike soldier, phlegmatic to the point of near inertia, who had once warned that war with Britain would reduce Italy 'to a Balkan level', once again protested that the army was not yet ready. The Italian army consisted of seventy-nine singularly ill-equipped divisions, of which thirty were serving abroad. Only nineteen divisions were deemed to be fully equipped, but their weapons were obsolete relics from the First World War. The army had virtually no tanks, and those in service had proved virtually useless in Spain. The M13/1940, M14/1941 and M15/1942s that followed were all so under-powered, under-armed, under-armoured and mechanically unreliable that British tank crews dreaded being given one of these captured machines. Italian tanks were not equipped with radios until 1941, and were then provided with sets that were so weak as to be virtually worthless. Nor were they provided with the compensated compasses that were vital for navigation in the desert.

The Italian air force consisted of about 3,300 outmoded planes of which only 1,796 were ready for action. Since they were mostly designed for a high-altitude bombing campaign, they were of little use against naval vessels. The SM85 dive-bomber proved more deadly to its crews than to the enemy. Fiat continued to produce the CR42 biplane from 1938 until the end of the war, even though it was outmoded at the time of its maiden flight. Fiat's G50 monoplane fighter is generally considered, in spite of some stiff competition, to be the worst plane in this category during the entire war. Co-operation with the navy was virtually non-existent. The Italian navy was marginally more impressive, largely as a result of its considerable size. On the other hand, there were only two capital ships in service, the *Cesare* and the *Cavour*, both of which were distinctly antiquated. The rest were technically outdated, the crews poorly trained, the senior officers sadly lacking in tactical skills. The navy firmly opposed the idea of aircraft carriers, even after they had been shown to be extremely effective when used by the British at Taranto and again at Matapan. The considerably larger Italian navy was thus no match for the British Mediterranean fleet.[19] Italy produced fewer numbers of the worst weapons at the highest cost, than any of the other belligerent nations. The Italians produced a total of 4,152 armoured fighting vehicles by 1943. In the same time period the Germans built 18,600, the United States 57,585.[20] In addition to industrial incompetence and chicanery, bureaucratic inertia and the fact that one man at Ansaldo designed all tanks, there was a widespread belief, deeply embedded in the Fascist mindset, that it was mind not matter, men not matériel that counted. Even Badoglio, one of the few senior officers who had any experience of armoured warfare, conceded in 1937 that 'the tank is a powerful weapon, but let us not sing hosanna in its praise; let us reserve our reverence for the infantryman and the mule'.[21] It was not until June 1941 that Colonel Giuseppe Cordero Lanza di Montezemolo, the sharpest intellect at the Comando Supremo, where he was chief of operations for Africa, reminded Cavallero that quality counted for more than quantity and that 'a single motorised division, EVEN FOR DEFENCE AND OCCUPATION MISSIONS, has the capability of four infantry divisions, while it eats only a fourth as much and requires only a fourth as much transport from Italy'.[22] Cavallero did nothing about it, and remained stuck in the traditional mould, resulting in the vast majority of Italian troops being left immobile, a millstone around the Afrikakorps' neck. The Italian army's mobility ratio of thirty-eight men under arms for every truck remained virtually unchanged throughout the war.[23]

Mussolini dismissed Badoglio's objections, confidently telling him that the war would be over by September, and all he needed was 'a few thousand dead' as an entry ticket to the peace conference, from which he hoped to make substantial gains in the Mediterranean at the expense of Britain and France.[24] Italy's entry into the war was thus designed as a demonstration of national might, rather than a carefully planned military operation. Italy's German allies were not consulted, there was a desultory bombing raid on the British base in Malta, and on the day that the French sued for peace, units of the Italian army crossed the border to sun themselves on the Riviera.

Mussolini's calculation that once France was defeated Britain would throw in the towel proved to be a serious miscalculation, thanks to Churchill's unwavering leadership and the courage of 'The Few'. Bombing raids on Malta in June were troublesome, in that the island could not be used as a submarine base for a while, but the Italians failed to drive home the attack, so that Malta remained a permanent menace to the sea lanes from Italy to Libya. Meanwhile, the British continued to build up their bases in Alexandria and Suez, providing the infrastructure for a projected nine divisions, twelve bomber squadrons and ten of fighters. The Royal Air Force (RAF) began systematically to raid the airfields in Libya, concentrating on the strategically important port of Tobruk. In one such raid, on 28 June 1940, Air Marshal Balbo, the commander-in-chief in Libya, was shot down by his own anti-aircraft fire on 28 June 1940. It was rumoured in Rome that Balbo, one of Mussolini's earliest supporters, who had become increasingly critical of the Duce, had been deliberately killed, but this was never substantiated. Whatever the reason for his death, this was a severe loss, for his successor, Marshal Rodolfo Graziani, had none of his energy and soldierly ability. Graziani, who had presided over the rapine and plunder of the Fezzan in Libya, handing over their land to colonists, had narrowly escaped an attempt on his life in Addis Ababa, since which time he had become somewhat hesitant and lethargic.[25]

Italy's position was greatly strengthened with the fall of France. There was now no threat of a French attack on Libya from Tunisia, so that the Italians were tempted to contemplate an offensive against Egypt, even though the energetic efforts of the Royal Navy had given the British naval supremacy in the Mediterranean, thus securing the supply routes to Egypt. In spite of the fact that the German military attaché in Rome, General von Rintelen, had sent a devastating report on the Italian forces in Libya after a visit by one of his subordinates in May, by the end of June both the High Command of the Armed Forces (OKW) and the High Command of the Army (OKH) began to gloat over the prospect of capturing the Suez Canal, in an Italian offensive supported by German Panzer.[26]

The Panzer had little to do in the summer of 1940. They were not intended for use in the forthcoming invasion of England, and Hitler's announcement on 31 July 1940 of his intention to attack the Soviet Union the following spring did little to change the situation. On the contrary a campaign in Africa, as the commander-in-chief of the German army, Brauchitsch, suggested, would be a convenient means of diverting attention from preparations for 'Barbarossa', the codename for the attack on the Soviet Union. There was also increasing scepticism about the 'Sea Lion' plan for the invasion of England, which prompted a search for an indirect strategy against Britain. On 31 July 1940 the head of home defence suggested to Hitler that a Panzer corps should be sent to North Africa in support of the Italian offensive.[27] Two days later it was agreed that, if 'Sea Lion' were to be cancelled, the Panzer would definitely not be needed until early the following year, so that it was in the Mediterranean that Britain was most vulnerable. The army and navy were ordered to examine the question in greater detail.[28] To this end the army's chief of staff, General Franz Halder, sent Major-General Ritter von Thoma, the commander of 3 Panzer Division, to North Africa in order to find out the most suitable route for sending Panzer troops to the region, and how they could best be deployed in support of an Italian offensive. Planning for the invasion of England continued, but the alternative Mediterranean strategy was kept on the table, with General Alfred Jodl, chief of staff at OKW, insisting that joint planning with the Italians was essential in order to ensure that the Axis fought shoulder to shoulder in the 'final battle' with Britain.[29] While Hitler dithered, OKH continued to prepare a Panzer brigade for use in North Africa. Halder, who had witnessed the Italian manoeuvres

Suez Canal, he supported Rintelen's suggestion for a military convention with Italy, but Jodl, who was totally beholden to Hitler, was not
prepared to fight for this idea.[36]

A third solution to the problem posed by Britain was proposed
by Ribbentrop, who in the course of a tour of duty as ambassador to
the Court of Saint James had developed an abiding loathing of all things
British, and consequently thought that Hitler's notion of dividing the
world with the British Empire was a total absurdity. He subscribed to
the view of the prominent professor of geo-politics, Karl Haushofer,
that the solution lay in a 'continental bloc' stretching from the Iberian
peninsula to Japan and including Germany, Italy and the Soviet Union,
thus cutting Britain off from the bulk of its empire.

By the end of August it was clear that 'Sea Lion' was very
unlikely to be launched in 1940, and probably not at all, so Hitler
agreed to send two armoured divisions to North Africa to support the
Italian attack on Egypt. At the same time planning was ordered for an
attack on Gibraltar in which it was hoped that the Spanish could be
persuaded to lend a hand. The declared aim of these operations was to
drive the British out of the Mediterranean.[37] Raeder, the commander-
in-chief of the German navy (ObdM), who remained convinced that it
would be a great mistake to attack the Soviet Union while Britain was
undefeated, made representations to Hitler on 6 and 26 September 1940
in which he argued that Britain could best be hurt by seizing Gibraltar
and the Suez Canal, adding that: 'The Russian problem would then take
on a quite different aspect. It would then be questionable whether operations against the Soviet Union from the north would be necessary.' He
repeated these ideas again on 14 November, with the added argument
that the Italians would need German assistance, because they would
be unable to deal with the British on their own.[38] On 5 September
Jodl told the Italian military attaché, General Efisio Marras, that Hitler
intended to make an offer of Panzer units for North Africa, and that
the offensive should go ahead even before they arrived.[39] Jodl made
a formal offer of a German armoured corps for North Africa the following day, but he was given the cold shoulder.[40] Mussolini received
intelligence that indicated that 'Sea Lion' would be postponed indefinitely while Hitler sought a diplomatic solution to the war. He had also
heard that General Keitel was claiming that the seizure of Cairo was
more important than that of London.[41] Mussolini therefore ordered a
limited offensive against the British in North Africa so as to enhance his

bargaining power at the armistice negotiations, which he anticipated would begin within a matter of weeks. Marshal Rodolfo Graziani, the commander of the Italian forces in North Africa, was an old-fashioned and cautious soldier, who insisted that the offensive would have to be postponed. He had warned Ciano that Badoglio was not doing enough to check Mussolini's 'aggressive spirit', insisting that: 'We are heading for a defeat which, in the desert, must inevitably end in a rapid and total disaster.'[42] Graziani added an important rider by ordering the attack on Egypt to begin 'as soon as a German patrol lands in England'. He continued to prevaricate, saying that all his generals were opposed to the idea of an offensive.[43] This made little impression on Mussolini, who was determined to go ahead regardless of German support. He finally lost his patience with Graziani's dithering and on 7 September ordered him to begin an offensive two days later with the objective of seizing Sidi Barrani.

Deployment began on 9 September and the attack was launched four days later, in spite of Graziani's reluctance and the serious reservations expressed by a number of senior officers. The Italians had some of the newer M/39 medium tanks, but most were light tanks, all of them greatly inferior to the British tanks. Their infantry and artillery were not mechanised, so that their mobility was strictly limited, and they had no co-ordinated armoured units. Their advance began on 13 September south of Bardia, meeting with virtually no opposition. The Western Desert Force was very thin on the ground, its commander, General Richard O'Connor, having withdrawn his armour to Mersa Matruh for servicing and replenishment. The Italians had overwhelming superiority in the air. The British abandoned Sollum, where the bulk of their forces were placed, virtually without a fight. They offered some resistance in the Halfaya ('Hellfire') Pass and on 16 September the Italians reached Sidi Barrani, having advanced 90 kilometres.[44] The Italians then adopted a defensive stance, with Graziani announcing that he had no intention of continuing the advance until December, by which time he hoped that the coastal road would have been improved and a water pipeline built from Bardia to Sidi Barrani. It was a somewhat pointless operation, an 'operative torso', that brought the Italians little glory.[45] The British lost a useful airfield in Sollum, but that was more of an inconvenience than a serious danger. Mussolini considered this a great victory, but others saw it as a deliberate move by the British to lure the Italians away from their base and lengthen their lines of communication.[46] But as the Italians continued their advance a mood of euphoria spread. Britain would soon capitulate, and Alexandria would fall into the hands of the Italians.

Meanwhile the British concentrated on strengthening Malta with anti-aircraft guns and fighter squadrons, so that submarines were soon able to operate against Italian convoys to North Africa. When the Italians invaded Greece on 28 October the Greek government offered Crete to the British, thus giving them an important air base in the eastern Mediterranean.

Jubilation soon gave way to anxiety when the British made a stand at Mersa Matruh and Graziani called for a halt while he brought up supplies for a renewed offensive, which he scheduled for November. He did not hesitate to point out that if his supply lines did not function adequately he would have to retreat, to which he added that in the desert a retreat is equivalent to a rout.[47]

At the end of September Hitler began to toy with Ribbentrop's idea of a continental bloc. At this time he held the odious Ribbentrop in high esteem, especially after his pact with Molotov, the Soviet foreign minister, imagining this charlatan to be a true man of the world and a diplomat of international stature. On 26 September the foreign office attempted to assuage Soviet concerns about the Three-Power Pact about to be signed by Germany, Italy and Japan. On 4 October Hitler met Mussolini on the Brenner Pass and told him that the Soviet Union was militarily so weak that it posed no threat whatsoever, that the United States had reacted to the Three-Power Pact in a 'very cowardly' manner, and that Britain was in a 'hopeless situation militarily' since its hopes for aid from the United States and the Soviet Union were unfounded. He boasted about the 'titanic efforts' of the Germans preparing for the 'final battle' against England, stressing that it was in the interests of both states, particularly with regard to the economic reorganisation of Europe, that the war should be ended as soon as possible. He was now simply waiting for the weather to improve to deliver the knock-out punch. Mussolini had the temerity to enquire why it was that, if the British were in such a parlous state, they did not eat humble pie. Hitler replied that they were stubborn and were hoping that the USA or the USSR would come to their rescue. But that was all in vain. The Americans would give material assistance, but they were fudging the books and greatly exaggerating the amount of aid they were sending. According to Ribbentrop the Russians were terrified of Germany and would not get involved. Hitler, thinking it prudent to prepare for a confrontation with the United States, proposed creating a German bastion in north-west Africa, as well as on islands in the Atlantic. This would have the added advantage of guarding the gateway to German colonies in 'Mittelafrika', the overseas counterpart to 'Mitteleuropa', of which German colonialists had dreamed since the late nineteenth century. With the Germans firmly entrenched in North Africa the British would be unable to lure the French colonies away from Vichy. The British and Free French landings in Dakar, which had taken place only a few days previously, designed to persuade the governor-general in West Africa to break with Pétain, had obviously alarmed Hitler, even though Operation 'Menace' was a badly bungled operation. Fears about the French colonies and the loyalty of the Vichy regime were to remain with him throughout the war. He regarded Pétain as a weak old man, the French as fractious, jingoistic and unpredictable. For Hitler Gibraltar was the key to the Mediterranean, but for the moment this could not be taken without Spanish consent. The problem was that Franco was demanding an exorbitant price for his co-operation, and was not even content with a promise that he could have French Morocco. Hitler then expounded at his wonted length on his ideas for a continental bloc. Mussolini pretended that it was an excellent idea, but pointed out that he doubted whether France and Spain would agree. He preferred to await the outcome of Hitler's forthcoming meetings with Franco and Pétain. He also felt that it would be wise to sign a peace treaty with France as soon as possible for fear that there might be another de Gaulle. Mussolini did not share Hitler's concerns about the Free French. He imagined that de Gaulle was discredited after the Dakar fiasco, a military operation that provided rich material for Evelyn Waugh's satirical pen, but that his place might well be taken by a similar figure if a satisfactory agreement were not reached over the future of France.[48]

Mussolini, who had come without a representative of the Comando Supremo, put on an extravagant performance as a great commander and strategist. He announced that he intended to continue the offensive in North Africa in mid-October and take Mersa Matruh, but requested a hundred heavy tanks and several squadrons of dive-bombers. This would amount to the formation of a 'mixed Panzer brigade' or a 'small Panzer division'.[49] Hitler expressed his somewhat gnomic agreement to this request. Mussolini wanted the Panzer, but he did not want the Germans. Halder once again pointed out that without the support of a German Panzer division the Italians had little chance of success, but it would be at least ten weeks before it could arrive in North Africa, so that an offensive could not be mounted before the New Year. Hitler managed eventually to persuade Mussolini of the need for German assistance. In mid-October OKH decided which units of 3 Panzer Division were to be seconded for service in North Africa.[50]

In spite of all Hitler's bragging on the Brenner, Keitel informed the Italians shortly afterwards that the invasion of England would have to be postponed until next year. This plunged Badoglio into a deep depression. He asked Rintelen what was to become of Italy's colonies in East Africa. All would be lost in a lengthy war, even British Somaliland, which he himself had conquered in Italy's only successful operation against the British. At much the same time Mussolini learnt that Hitler was sending military instructors to Romania without first informing him. This made him so irate that he decided to invade Greece on his own, in order to restore the Italo-German balance in the Balkans. Hitler, he complained to Ciano, always presented him with a *fait accompli*; now he would get one in return.[51] For the moment the Germans were kept completely in the dark as to the preparations for and timing of the invasion.

The dictators sought to outplay and deceive one another with extraordinary displays of bluster, boast and braggadocio, with Mussolini trying hard to maintain the pretence of 'parallel warfare'. Hitler made promises of territorial gain at the expense of France, but was reticent about his future plans, in part because they were still inchoate. It was one thing to talk of compensating France, Spain and Italy with the spoils of the British Empire, but it was another to see how this could be done. Hitler reverted to his pre-1933 manner of promising something for everyone, with blissful disregard for his ability to deliver the goods.

Mussolini, in spite of his overt endorsement of the idea, was far from enthusiastic about the suggestion of a continental bloc; understandably fearing that an alliance between Germany, France and Spain would be at Italy's expense, it was with some relief that he heard that this grandiose plan had come to nothing. On 22 October Hitler discussed these issues with Vichy's foreign minister, Pierre Laval, at Montoire and on the following day met Franco at Hendaye. The Caudillo, whom Hitler described as 'a Jesuit pig', refused to be drawn into an alliance, preferring to keep all his options open. Hitler returned to Montoire on 24 October in a towering rage for further talks with Pétain and Laval. They too were inconclusive. Hitler admitted to Halder that the fundamental differences between the three states over the Mediterranean were unlikely to be smoothed over by the formation of a continental bloc, which he now described as 'a giant swindle'.[52] Ribbentrop, whom Hitler once described as a 'second Bismarck', now gradually fell from grace, in part because he was the father of this abortive idea.

While in Montoire Hitler was told that Italy would invade Greece within the next few days. He was furious that Mussolini had acted alone, putting the neutrality of the Balkan states, on which Germany relied for vital supplies, in serious jeopardy. He also doubted whether Italy would be a match for the Greeks, whom he regarded as excellent soldiers, whereas every second Italian, as he was fond of remarking, was either a traitor or a spy.[53] He promptly went to Florence on 28 October to meet Mussolini and decided to make the best of a singularly bad job. In the hope that the Italians would at least be able to cause the British a mild headache in the eastern Mediterranean, he offered to send paratroopers to strengthen the Italian positions in southern Greece, and to help seize the strategically important island of Crete, which left the Romanian oilfields within the range of RAF bombers. Once again Mussolini, believing that he could do it alone and score a cheap propaganda victory, turned down Hitler's offer. He expressed the fear that were he to take Egypt along with the Germans he would never be able to get rid of them, and would always have to dance to their tune.[54] Halder laconically noted in November that 'The Italians don't want us' and were thoroughly fed up with Germany's attempts to become involved in their affairs.[55]

Having been snubbed in France, Spain and Italy Hitler had perforce to abandon the idea of a continental bloc that, since it would have included the Soviet Union, would in any case only have been a strictly temporary affair. The Italian offensive, launched from bases in Albania on 28 October, soon ran into difficulties and Hitler immediately realised that Germany would have to lend a helping hand. On 4 November OKH began planning for the occupation of Greek Macedonia and Thrace.[56] Molotov, who arrived Berlin on 11 November, delivered the final blow. He made it quite clear that the Soviet Union had no intention of being persuaded to threaten the British in the Middle

East and India, but had expansionist ambitions in the Balkans. When Molotov left Berlin the following day, Hitler promptly issued orders to step up planning the deployment against the Soviet Union.

That very same day HMS *Illustrious* launched its torpedo bombers against the Italian fleet in Taranto, putting three of its six battleships out of action. The antiquated Swordfish biplanes, with their open cockpits and maximum speed of 100mph, known to the Fleet Air Arm as 'string-bags', exceeded all reasonable expectations. The Italian navy panicked, withdrawing the bulk of its vessels from the Ionian Sea, leaving the British in undisputed command of the eastern Mediterranean. Italy's supply routes to Libya and Albania were now seriously compromised, calling future operations in North Africa and Greece into grave doubt. Meanwhile, Major-General Ritter von Thoma, who had been sent to Libya to prepare the ground for the Panzer, delivered a devastating report on the performance of the Italian troops that coincided with an independent assessment by a staff officer from OKH, Major Meyer-Ricks. The conclusion was that one Panzer division was not nearly enough to do the job. It would probably need at least four, in an exclusively German operation. More than four would be impossible to supply, given the extended lines of communication from Tripoli to Egypt. Furthermore, an effective Mediterranean strategy would have to include an invasion of Crete, as well as Syria via Bulgaria and Turkey. Such a massive operation would seriously compromise planning for the attack on the Soviet Union.[57] Hitler flew into a fury, ordering that preparations for sending Panzer to North Africa should be suspended, at least until the Italians had taken Mersa Matruh, and even then the main support would come from the Luftwaffe.[58] The Italians proudly announced that they had no need for German support, adding that the discussions on the Brenner had merely been 'theoretical considerations'. Mussolini was still determined to continue with his 'parallel warfare'.[59]

The Italian attack on Greece had led to the British establishing air bases in Crete and Attica, whence they might launch attacks on the Romanian oilfields that were vital to the German war effort. Hitler could also not allow Italy to suffer yet another serious blow to its prestige, while at the same time he was happy to see Mussolini pulled down a peg or two. On 5 December he remarked that Italy's misfortune 'has had the healthy effect of once again reducing Italian claims to within the natural limits of Italian capabilities'.[60] For the moment Greece seemed to be the most threatening theatre, whereas the situation in North Africa could best be served by concentrating on attacks on Malta, which was only ten minutes' flying time from Sicily. To this end he ordered OKW to make plans for an air base in northern Greece to meet the threat from the RAF and moved 10 Air Corps, specialists in attacks on shipping, from Norway to southern Italy and Sicily. Hitler did not want to wait until 'Felix', the attack on Gibraltar, or for the Italians to reach Mersa Matruh. There was no further mention of sending Panzer units to North Africa, Hitler having ruled this out on 5 December. The next day he ordered an air offensive in the eastern Mediterranean to begin on 12 December, followed by an attack on Gibraltar at the beginning of February 1941. 'Marita', the invasion of the Balkans and Greece, would be launched a month later; the attack on the Soviet Union was to begin in mid-May.[61]

Hitler had nothing but contempt for the German military attachés and liaison officers in Rome, whom he claimed did nothing but sit around having prolonged breakfasts with their Italian homologues.[62] Indeed the Luftwaffe's liaison officer, General Baron von Pohl, and the OKW's liaison officer, General Enno von Rintelen, who was also military attaché, initially did little more than pass on snippets of information. Vice-Admiral Eberhard Weichold, head of the naval liaison staff, was a much more ambitious officer who persistently argued that the Italians should be goaded into action.[63] In a series of memoranda to his superiors in Berlin, written before the Italian attack on Greece, he argued that Malta, Crete and the Dodecanese were the key positions for a strategic defence of the Mediterranean.[64] Of these Malta was by far the most important. It provided the Royal Navy with an essential fuelling station for long-range operations in the Mediterranean, as well as a base for flank attacks on the Italian supply route to Libya. Malta was also a valuable base for the RAF, which was inflicting severe damage on Italian shipping. The Italian Supreme Command as well as the Naval Command, faithful to their doctrine of 'parallel warfare', ignored Weichold's arguments and continued to insist that the navy's mission was simply to guard the supply routes to Libya and Albania. Weichold, who was starved of information, gave vent to his frustrations in blistering attacks on the incompetence of the Italian navy with its 'traumatic fear' of the British. He was soon to reach the conclusion that the Italian navy was bent on preserving itself, claiming that it would thus be a diplomatic bargaining chip at the peace table. The fierce argument that raged over Malta was to continue after the war.[65] The central issues were whether it would have been possible to invade the island, and even if it had been, would it have made such a significant difference, given Rommel's grossly overextended lines of communication across 1,500 kilometres of desert. Given optimal conditions it would still have required an unbelievable number of trucks, consuming vast quantities of fuel, adequately to supply a sizeable mechanised army.

Rintelen, in addition to being military attaché, was given the title of German General in the Headquarters of the Italian Army. As attaché he had to report via the ambassador, whereas in his new position he could contact OKH and OKW directly, thus cutting the foreign office out of the picture. Weichold as the German Admiral in Italy and von Pohl as German Luftwaffe General, were similarly free to contact their respective arms of the service directly. Göring requested of Badoglio that von Pohl should, like Rintelen, be fully informed of all that was going on in his headquarters. Raeder immediately did the same for Weichold, but Badoglio replied that he only needed one liaison officer, and that he was perfectly happy with Rintelen.[66]

The German Naval Command (*Seekriegsleitung*, Skl) also ignored Weichold's jeremiads, telling him that he would have to reconcile himself to the present situation and that 'parallel warfare' would soon be crowned with success. Weichold persisted in offering his unsolicited counsel to the Italians, urging them to seize Crete before the Royal Navy moved there from Alexandria, thus threatening forthcoming Italian operations in Greece, as well as placing the central Mediterranean at risk. This unwelcome advice was also ignored. The British began landing in Crete the day after the Italian invasion of Greece, and the Royal Navy stepped up operations in the central Mediterranean, including the attack on Taranto.

Rintelen was every bit as appalled at the miserable performance of the Italians in Greece as was his naval colleague. He expressed his grave scepticism that the offensive, which had ground to a pitiable halt when the Greeks mounted a counterattack on 14 November, forcing the Italians back across the Albanian border, would be able to resume before the following spring. The Italian Supreme Command feared that there would be further setbacks. There was a serious lack of transport, leaving the troops starved of supplies, so that Rintelen was requested to ask OKW for air transport to relieve the situation. The request was met, with Hitler offering to send units of the Luftwaffe to the Mediterranean to harass the British. The Comando Supremo once again turned down the offer, sticking proudly to its policy of 'parallel warfare', even after the Greeks advanced further into Albania, seizing Koritza on 21 November. Mussolini was at last beginning to have second thoughts, which were confirmed when the Greeks occupied Podradec on 4 December and General Ubaldo Soddu, the desk-bound commander-in-chief of the Italian forces in Albania, panicked, pleading that the conflict be ended by diplomatic means. Mussolini now realised that he could not continue in the illusion that 'parallel warfare' was a viable option.[67] He therefore ordered the Italian ambassador in Berlin, Dino Alfieri, who was on sick leave in Rome, to return to his post and ask Hitler for help.

By the time Alfieri met Hitler on 8 December the situation had improved somewhat for the Italians so that General Ugo Cavallero, who had replaced Badoglio as chief of the Comando Supremo two days previously, reported that it would be possible to hold the line, prepare an offensive and thus salvage 'parallel warfare' and Italy's honour.[68] Alfieri, who told Hitler that the situation was 'problematical and critical', asked whether it might be possible for the Germans to mount a diversionary action, such as urging Bulgaria to begin partial mobilisation, or start a press rumour that large numbers of German forces were being deployed in Romania. Rintelen continued to send gloomy reports on the situation, warning that the Italians always painted things in the best possible light, but in fact the front stabilised and Italy was out of immediate danger, at least on the borders of Albania and Greece.

By November 1940 Hitler, having abandoned any idea of a 'continental bloc' and of a 'peripheral strategy', concentrated on planning the forthcoming attack on the Soviet Union. In Order Number 18 of 12 November he suggested that he might consider sending forces to North Africa, but only after the Italians had reached Mersa Matruh. The Luftwaffe would be sent on condition that they provided the necessary air bases. One armoured division was to stand by for service in North Africa. German ships in Italian ports that were suitable for conversion into troopships were to be at the ready. The Luftwaffe was to draw up plans for raids on Alexandria and the Suez Canal so as to close it to British warships.[69] Two further operations considered at this time were the invasion of Greece, codenamed 'Marita', as well as an attack on Gibraltar, which Hitler had already discussed with Franco, scheduled for February 1941, codenamed 'Felix'.[70] Hitler's main concern was with Romanian oil, which would be seriously threatened if the British were to establish positions in Thrace. Operation 'Marita', combined with a strengthening of the Luftwaffe's contingent in Romania, was designed to meet this challenge. With the Germans and Italians firmly established in Greece and with Gibraltar under Axis control, it was considered possible to close off the Mediterranean at both ends. Hitler had already set the timetable. The fleet in the eastern Mediterranean would be attacked from the air on 15 December, Gibraltar seized at the beginning of February, 'Marita' would be launched in early March and be completed by the end of the month, or possibly at the end of April. Thus, as Hitler bragged, the Mediterranean would, 'within three or four months, become the grave of the English fleet', and even if Britain was still not willing to sue for peace, at least the southern flank would be secure, ready for the attack on the Soviet Union.[71]

On 15 November Keitel finally met Badoglio in Innsbrück. The meeting had originally been scheduled for early October, but had been postponed initially until after Hitler's visit to France to meet Laval and Franco, then because of the Italian invasion of Greece. Keitel had not been shown a copy of Order Number 18, so the discussions were very vague. The only decision taken was to remove units of the Italian air force from the Channel coast where they had proved singularly ineffective. Keitel announced, to general astonishment, that 'England' had lost the war, but had not as yet recognised the fact. Rintelen attributed this astonishing remark to his 'lord and master'. Badoglio had a weak hand to play after the fiasco in Greece. Keitel announced that Germany would not send any Panzer troops to North Africa until the Italians took Mersa Matruh. He expressed the need for closer co-operation between the allies, but nothing concrete was settled, so that 'parallel warfare' continued.[72]

On 18 November Hitler told Ciano, during a visit to the Berghof, that Germany would not be able to send troops to the Balkans until early the following year, but he promised to lend Italy material and diplomatic support.[73] Ciano treated this offer in a somewhat offhand manner, and when he met Hitler again on 20 November in Vienna he announced that Mussolini had informed him that the situation in Albania had stabilised, so that Italy had no need of German assistance.[74] Hitler was less sanguine and wrote a carefully worded note to Mussolini stressing the need to send units of the Luftwaffe to the Mediterranean. The Duce, having received reports that the Italians were indeed in difficulties, replied that he was fully aware of the need for close co-operation with the German air force in the Mediterranean. Hitler promptly ordered the Luftwaffe to examine the question of how best to assist their Axis partner.[75]

On 5 December Hitler told Brauchitsch that he intended to send to Sicily and North Africa an air corps made up of two groups of Junkers Ju87 dive-bombers (Stuka) and Junkers Ju88 bombers taken from Norway, which was to be known as 10 Air Corps, in an operation imaginatively codenamed 'Mediterranean'. Field Marshal Erhard Milch, secretary of state in the air ministry and inspector-general of the Luftwaffe, and General Hoffmann von Waldau, chief of air staff, were immediately sent to Rome to meet Mussolini and to discuss forthcoming operations with the Italian air force. The delegation arrived in Rome the same day. Mussolini was once again in a confident and boastful mood, but agreed in principle with Hitler's suggestions. Discussions between Milch, Hoffmann von Waldau and the Italian generals Franceso Pricolo and Giuseppe Santoro were far from smooth. The Germans put forward Hitler's plan that 10 Air Corps should concentrate on the Suez Canal and the Mediterranean between Sicily and Tunisia, whereas the Italians insisted that it was needed for operations against the Royal Navy in the central Mediterranean, which would be tantamount to a declaration of war on Greece, something that Milch was determined to avoid at all costs. After much heated debate it was agreed that the Germans would send forty aircraft, without crews, to Albania and that 10 Air Corps would be stationed in Sicily, to be used against British shipping in the immediate vicinity. Milch also suggested that it might be possible to blockade Malta from the air, but the issue was shelved. The outstanding question was now one of command. The Italians argued that 10 Air Corps would have to be placed under their direct control, whereas Milch insisted that it had to be independent. Milch won the day after lengthy argument.[76] The order to send 10 Air Corps to Sicily was issued on 10 December with instructions to attack Alexandria and the Suez Canal, as well as protecting shipping between Sicily and North Africa.[77] The order had been given, but 10 Air Corps was not operational until 10 January, much to the Italians' aggravation.

By early December all hopes were dashed that Spain and Vichy France might co-operate with the Axis powers in the Mediterranean, helping to seize Gibraltar in Operation 'Felix', while Hitler was becoming increasingly concerned that Vichy France might sooner or later be tempted to change sides. General Maxime Weygand, who was in command over France's colonies, was felt to be particularly unreliable. Operation 'Attila' was drawn up to meet this eventuality, involving the occupation of Vichy France and a subsidiary Operation 'Camelia' for the invasion of Corsica.[78] With Franco remaining adamantly aloof, every effort was made to improve relations with Vichy, but this came to nothing with the arrest of Pierre Laval, the strongest advocate of close co-operation with the Germans, on 13 December. A secret agreement between Britain and France, whereby if Vichy were to remain neutral the British would guarantee its colonies, was a further step away from an alliance with Germany. Hitler was thus left with only one embarrassed, awkward and ineffectual ally in the Mediterranean.

On 8 December Alfieri told Hitler that the situation in Albania was approaching the catastrophic. Hitler drew the necessary conclusion, spelling out the details of 'Marita', the German intervention in Greece, in Order Number 20 of 13 December. As in November, the operations were to be concentrated in northern Greece, but this time it was considered possible that they would push down the mainland all the way to Corinth. The operation could not be mounted until March, but OKW drew up contingency plans in Order Number 22 of 11 January 1941 for immediate intervention in Albania should the Italian front suddenly collapse.[79] The situation once again stabilised, so that this did not prove necessary. Admiral Wilhelm Canaris, the head of German military intelligence, began secret negotiations in an attempt to reach a diplomatic solution to the impasse, failing which 'Marita' was to bring this unfortunate episode to a close.

Whereas the situation in Albania had stabilised somewhat, the Italians soon found themselves in serious difficulties in North Africa. General Sir Archibald Wavell, as commander-in-chief Middle East, had a vast area under his command, stretching from Egypt to the Persian Gulf, from Cyprus to Kenya, so that he did not yet have enough troops effectively to counter threats on various fronts. In the autumn of 1940 his principal problem was the Duke of Aosta, who with 255,000 men had captured British Somaliland, but he still had to keep an eye on Graziani's 10 Army which presented a potential threat to the Suez Canal. To this end he ordered General Henry Wilson, commanding the British troops in Egypt, to hit the Italians head-on should they begin to advance towards Mersa Matruh. Wavell had a poor opinion of

Graziani, whereas the Duke of Aosta was a fine soldier with a number of impressive subordinates, such as General Carnimeo, an expert in mountain warfare. He therefore decided first to move against Graziani before turning on the Duke of Aosta.

His offensive, codenamed Operation 'Compass', began on 9 December, with the Western Desert Force taking advantage of the fact that the Italian forces were widely dispersed to launch a series of hit-and-run raids on isolated positions by General Sir Michael O'Moore Creagh's 7th Armoured Division, soon to be nicknamed the 'Desert Rats', while General Richard O'Connor's unorthodox, caustic and highly controversial staff officer, Brigadier Eric Dorman-Smith, developed a brilliant plan of attack on Sidi Barrani. It was a daring and imaginative plan in which the 31,000 British were outnumbered four to one. The Desert Rats were to cut off the Italians' lines of retreat by driving towards the sea at Buq-Buq, the Italian supply base 35 kilometres west of Sidi Barrani, while 7th Royal Tank Regiment and the 4th Indian Division hit the poorly positioned and widely dispersed Italian forces in Sidi Barrani. The offensive was a great success, even though Graziani had a far larger force at his disposal. In total 38,000 prisoners were taken, while the remainder of the Italian army fled across the Libyan border to Bardia where four divisions, with supplies for only four weeks, were encircled by the Desert Rats. It seemed likely that Tobruk, which was held by only one division, along with the divisions at Benghazi, would soon be in the bag.[80] Mussolini was badly shaken by this setback. Graziani began to talk of retreating to Tripoli 'in order to at least keep the flag flying on that fortress', blaming Mussolini and the Germans for forcing him to wage a war 'of the flea against the elephant'.[81] Mussolini said of Graziani: 'Here is another man with whom I cannot even get angry, because I despise him.'[82] The basic problem for the Italians was that they were cut off by land and by sea from their forces in East Africa, as long as Egypt and the Suez Canal remained in British hands.

Keitel and Jodl, who did not seem to realise that in the desert infantrymen slogging on foot were no match for motorised units, refused to believe that the situation in North Africa was serious. For the moment their sanguine attitude seemed justified. The Italians were given a brief respite when Wavell and 'Jumbo' Wilson decided to move the Indian troops to the Sudan where they played a decisive role in the battle for the heights of Keren that led to the Italians losing Eritrea. It took three weeks to bring the 6th Australian Division from Palestine up to the front where they supported the 7th Royal Tank Regiment in an attack on Bardia, which fell with little resistance. Having reached Tobruk on 12 January, O'Connor decided to press on in order to cut off the Italian retreat to the west of Benghazi. The Desert Rats, armed with a mass of intelligence material gathered from all grades of operational traffic, covered 275 kilometres in thirty-six hours across difficult terrain, establishing a record for armoured mobility and taking the Italians by surprise at Beda Fomm, where a mere 3,000 men took 20,000 Italians prisoner. Operation 'Compass' was a triumphant success. The Italian 10 Army was destroyed, 130,000 prisoners were taken along with 845 guns and 380 tanks, with a loss of 500 dead, 1,373 wounded and 55 missing. O'Connor longed to press on to Tripoli, but the advance had to be halted because of the withdrawal of men to Greece. The energetic efforts of the Royal Navy in support of 'Compass' gave the British absolute mastery of the Mediterranean, so that convoys could pass through the Suez Canal, rather than round the Cape, and the British were now able to supply their troops in the Middle East with little interference.

In December 1940 the German Naval Command (Skl) argued that the British would have to tie up a substantial amount of their air and land forces in Greece, in order to establish a bridgehead in Europe, and to begin a bomber offensive against the Romanian oilfields. This would leave the British off balance, offering Germany the prospect of driving the British out of the Mediterranean, thus achieving a final victory. Then things began to unravel. On 7 December Franco refused point blank to support 'Felix', the attack on Gibraltar. Pierre Laval, the advocate of the closest possible co-operation with Germany, was in prison for precisely that reason. The Italians suffered a series of shattering defeats in North Africa and it looked as though the Fascist regime might collapse. By the end of December Raeder told Hitler that the navy would now concentrate its efforts in the Battle of the Atlantic in an attempt to cut off supplies destined for Britain, but he also stressed the need to take possession of Gibraltar, which he described as a cornerstone of the Atlantic convoy system, as well as being the key to the Mediterranean, and thus to British efforts in North Africa and Greece. Skl thus proposed an all-out offensive in the Atlantic. This was to be combined with a defensive strategy in the Mediterranean, in order to tie up as much British shipping as possible, thus increasing the chances of success in the Battle of the Atlantic. Raeder further proposed urging the Italian navy to go on the offensive.[83]

The Italian navy would not be able to operate freely as long as the British were able to make use of Malta. Skl doubted that the Italians could be persuaded to make a landing in Malta and therefore took up Weichold's repeated suggestion that the island should be heavily mined. Skl turned down Weichold's further suggestion that light units of the German navy should be sent to the Mediterranean on the grounds that they were needed in the Baltic in support of 'Barbarossa' and that all efforts were now to be concentrated on the Battle of the Atlantic. The navy was represented by Vice-Admiral Kurt Fricke, chief of operations, at a meeting at the Berghof on 8 and 9 January. He urged Hitler to make sure that the Italian navy was placed under German command, but Hitler refused on the grounds that it would be insulting to his closest ally.[84] Skl could now only hope that Admiral Arturo Riccardi, newly appointed head of the Italian navy, had more fighting spirit than his lame predecessor. They were soon to be disillusioned. The situation of the Italian forces in North Africa was now critical, and could not be improved without an energetic effort by the Italian navy. That this was not forthcoming made it imperative to seek help from the Germans, without which they faced almost certain defeat.

2 ✠ GERMANY INTERVENES IN NORTH AFRICA

On 19 December 1940 Rintelen had accurately predicted that Bardia and Tobruk were likely to fall, and that the Italians intended to establish a line of defence to the east of Cyrenaica, which he seriously doubted would hold. Mussolini was determined to hang on to Tripoli and to this end requested that the Germans send an armoured division to support this last-ditch stand.[1] The next day Rintelen forwarded a request for the equipment of thirty divisional and twenty corps artillery battalions, almost 8,000 trucks, 750 ambulances and specialised vehicles, 1,600 light anti-aircraft guns, 900 8.8cm anti-aircraft guns, 800 medium tanks, 300 armoured cars, 675 anti-tank guns, 9,000 mules, 300 medium and long-range radio sets, 20,000 bails of concertina wire, 500,000 stakes and 10 million sandbags, along with a host of lesser desiderata.[2] Hitler had not the slightest intention of giving the Italians equipment he needed for 'Barbarossa', but he was concerned to keep Italy going until he had finished off the Soviet Union, after which he could turn his attention to driving the British out of the Mediterranean and the Middle East. On 21 December General Efisio Marras, the Italian military attaché in Berlin, reported to Mussolini that Hitler was prepared to consider sending two divisions to Libya.[3] One week later Marras made an urgent appeal for help, saying that Cyrenaica could not possibly be held without German help. He estimated that even a small German contingent would have a bracing effect on Italian morale, discourage the British and stiffen the Vichy French troops in North Africa to such an extent that the Italian North Africa could be saved. Hitler's New Year's message to Mussolini contained rousing words of encouragement, along with a vague promise of support, but offered nothing concrete.[4]

Also on New Year's Day 1941 Weichold sent a lengthy memorandum in which he once again complained about the supine attitude of the Italian navy and insisted that Malta was the key to Britain's supremacy in the Mediterranean.[5] Having long given up the hope that he could goad the Italians into action, he suggested that the Mediterranean theatre should be placed under German command.

Weichold's ambassador, Hans-Georg von Mackensen, the son of a field marshal and son-in-law of Hitler's first foreign minister, a party member and SS-Gruppenführer, was in broad agreement, having already suggested to Ribbentrop that Germany should have a say in military operations in the Mediterranean. He reported that the Fascist regime was undergoing a severe crisis with the fiasco in Greece on top of the humiliating defeat in North Africa, and that the military attachés agreed that there was a very real danger of Italy losing the war in the Mediterranean. But he disagreed strongly with Weichold's suggestion that a German supreme commander be appointed, arguing that this would result in a further disastrous loss of prestige for the Duce.

General Pricolo, head of the Italian air staff and under-secretary of state in the air ministry, urgently enquired when 10 Air Corps would finally be operational, for it was a whole month since the decision had been taken to send it to Sicily. 10 Air Corps was to be made up of 14,385 men with 307 aircraft and it took a considerable time to get it in place. It was commanded by General Hans Geisler with Lieutenant-Colonel Harlinghausen as his chief of staff. They were the Luftwaffe's leading experts on the use of aircraft against naval vessels. They first went into action on 10 January from bases in Catania, Comiso, Palermo, Reggio di Calabria and Trapani, putting the cruiser *Southampton* out of action and severely damaging the aircraft carrier *Illustrious*, which was saved at the last moment by fighters scrambled from Malta, and just managed to limp back to Valletta for emergency repairs. Expert pilots were brought in to finish the ship off, but they arrived too late and *Illustrious* sailed back to Alexandria unnoticed.[6] The aircraft carrier was then sent to the United States for repairs. 10 Air Corps now concentrated on attacking Malta and defending its airfields in Sicily from the RAF's Wellington bombers. Two further squadrons of fighters were sent in early February to support these efforts.

On 8 January Rintelen forwarded a memorandum from General Guzzoni on the situation in Libya.[7] The tone was slightly more optimistic. The British advance had slowed down because of logistical problems. The Italians would soon have enough troops in North Africa to defend Tripoli. The Italian air force, supported by the German 10 Air Corps operating from Tripoli, Sicily and Pantellaria, would be able to disrupt the movement of British shipping in the Mediterranean. Two of the Italian battleships damaged at Taranto would soon be back in service, ready to lend support to an attack on Gibraltar, for which Guzzoni hoped in spite of Franco's intransigent attitude. Nevertheless, he repeated the request for a German Panzer corps, or at least a Panzer division, for service in North Africa.

On 9 January Hitler professed to Brauchitsch that he was not in the least bit interested in operations in North Africa. Italy's defeat in this theatre would not in his view alter its vulnerability to attack by air. The situation in French North Africa would remain unchanged. But he was very concerned about the psychological effect on Italy. He was also worried that were the Italians to be thrown out of North Africa the British would be free for deployment elsewhere. To avert what seemed to be a distinct possibility, he ordered OKH to make the necessary preparations for sending a mixed unit that would provide the Italians with effective protection against Britain's superior armour. This would include anti-tank guns, pioneers for mine laying, and the latest model Panzer IIIs with 5cm cannons, as well as 7.5cm anti-aircraft guns. The force should be ready to be shipped to Tripoli by 20 February. OKW proposed a force of about 8,000 men with 1,350 vehicles, exclusive of the Panzer Hitler had mentioned, to be ready within three weeks. It would take roughly four weeks to ship them across to Tripoli, using twenty ships.[8]

Hitler, who was concentrating on preparations for the attack on the Soviet Union, failed to realise the vital importance of the Middle East to the British, thus missing an opportunity to deliver a devastating blow to the only country against which he was still at war. He calculated that the campaign in the Soviet Union would be swiftly concluded; the Wehrmacht would then sweep down on the Middle East from the Caucasus, forcing Britain to throw in the towel. For the moment the Mediterranean was little more than the southern flank of 'Barbarossa', the only really vulnerable point being the Romanian oilfields. As long as the Italians could avoid a crushing defeat, he could afford to be relatively indifferent to the North African theatre.

In Operation 'Sunflower' OKH, acting upon Hitler's orders, established 5 Light Division under Major-General Baron von Funck, made up of units from 3 Panzer Division.[9] The operation, with

Mussolini's full agreement, was scheduled to begin in mid-February.[10] Funck promptly left for Libya to prepare the ground. Meanwhile OKW began to consider the political implications of helping out the Italians in North Africa. Lieutenant-Colonel Bernhard von Lossberg, from OKW's planning staff, produced a memorandum on 7 January 1940, in which he insisted that Germany must have control over political developments in the Middle East, making it clear that, in spite of Italy's colonial ambitions, the Axis would have to support the Arabs' struggle for independence. Only by frustrating Italy's aspirations in the region could Germany win Arab support against the British, allowing them to settle the 'Jewish question' in a mutually agreeable manner. Lossberg approached the foreign office on this point, insisting that since the Germans were bailing out the Italians they had no need to worry about their political sensitivities. Ribbentrop, mindful of Hitler's concern not to offend Mussolini, felt that they should move softly, but added that since the Italians were singularly inactive in this area, Germany had a chance to seize the initiative. Ernst Woermann, head of the political department of the foreign office and a man of impeccable anti-Semitic credentials, endorsed his minister's approach, leaving the way open for a proactive policy towards the Arabs.[11]

Hitler reached his decision to send German troops to North Africa after two days of discussions with a select group of senior officers at the Berghof on 8 and 9 January. Ten days later a humiliated Mussolini arrived at Hitler's mountaintop residence, fully aware that he would have to abandon 'parallel warfare' and take full account of Germany's strategic priorities. Hitler claimed that a major problem was the stubborn resistance of Franco, a man whom he described as an average officer, who had become head of state by pure chance, and who was proof that generals had 'unlimited incompetence' as politicians. Thanks to him the Axis did not have control over Gibraltar, and was unable to send two divisions to Spanish Morocco. That would have secured the Axis position in North Africa and put an end to 'de Gaulle's magic'. He assured the Duce that detailed plans had been drawn up for the seizure of Gibraltar, but these could obviously not be put into immediate effect. After further discussion it was agreed that Mussolini should use his 'Latin relationship' with Franco to persuade him of the need to help deliver Gibraltar to the Axis.

Hitler was careful not to wound the Duce's sensibilities and in the course of interminable monologues promised that he would help the Italians in Greece with 'Marita', stressed the vital importance of holding on in North Africa, and undertook to send an armoured group to Tripoli, insisting that the German troops would go into action right away and not behave like the British in France and let their ally do all the fighting. Hitler's main concern was that the British would take Tripoli, press on to the Tunisian border, make contact with Weygand, the 'General Delegate of the French Government in North Africa', and persuade him to break with Vichy.[12]

Mussolini somewhat lamely tried to reassure his host that he hoped to be able to hang on in Tobruk and western Cyrenaica for some time, at least until the German troops began to arrive in mid-February. It was hoped that the Axis forces would be able to go on the offensive in March, and that they would be able to stabilise the situation before the hot weather began in May. Rintelen, who acted as interpreter during this meeting, was struck by Hitler's dismissive remarks about the Russians and Molotov's recent visit to Berlin. It was then that he first heard of preparations for an attack on the Soviet Union. When he asked Jodl why they did not concentrate on cutting the lifeline to the British Empire in the Middle East, the latter shrugged his shoulders and replied that Russian politics were 'opaque'.[13]

The discussions at the Berghof marked the final end of 'parallel warfare'. Mussolini had accepted Hitler's offer of help and would now have to follow German guidelines for future operations. Being careful not to offend Mussolini's sensibilities, Hitler had turned down Mackensen's suggestion that a German field marshal should be sent to Rome as a supreme commander over the Axis forces in North Africa. It was now up to Rintelen to act as liaison officer between the Italian Supreme Comand and OKW. This was a difficult task, owing to Hitler's lack of openness and Mussolini's profound ignorance of military affairs. The Italians knew nothing of the details of Hitler's plans for operations against the Soviet Union. All that had been decided was that Tripolitania should be defended and the Balkans occupied. This was a purely defensive strategy, the success of which ultimately depended on the outcome of 'Barbarossa'.

Meanwhile, the British advance in North Africa continued, in spite of General Guzzoni's claim to Hitler at their meeting in Berchtesgaden on 22 January that they would be able to hang on at Tobruk for some time to come. The fortress fell that very day. The lines of communication for the British forces had become overextended, causing severe supply problems. Hundreds of captured Italian trucks relieved the situation somewhat, but they took a terrible beating and there were no spare parts. A decent port in a forward position was thus imperative, so O'Connor had made the seizure of Tobruk a top priority. The Australians stormed the town shortly after Mussolini returned home from his trip to Bavaria, taking 25,000 prisoners, 208 guns, 23 medium tanks and 200 trucks, at a cost of 49 dead and 306 wounded. The Italians failed to do any serious damage to the port facilities before leaving, so that 13th Corps was well supplied and O'Connor was determined to continue the pursuit.[14] Rintelen, who was unaware that Wavell had been ordered to release four divisions for service in Greece, felt that there was little that could stop the British advance; hence his urgent request to OKW for help to defend Tripoli.

O'Connor gave the Axis a brief breathing space after the fall of El Mechili on 24 January. Needing to bring up supplies, as well as to service his tanks, he decided to await the arrival of two battalions of Cruisers tanks from 2nd Armoured Division in England before resuming his triumphant progress. Nevertheless, on 26 January Rintelen reported that with the fall of Tobruk and Derna, Cyrenaica would be in British hands sooner than expected. That meant that there would be precious little time to prepare the defences in Tripolitania. An effective German anti-tank force was needed to make sure that Tripolitania remained in Italian hands. Given that the Italian plan to defend Tripoli was bound to fail, there would have to be a forward mobile defence in the wastes of the Sirte[15] that only German armour could manage. This would also ensure that the Luftwaffe had adequate space for deployment, which would be impossible were the German forces bottled up in Tripoli.

Rintelen's remarks were based on Major-General Baron von Funck's assessment of the situation, which he had studied the previous day. He had argued that the proposed battle group was not nearly large enough, and that it would need at least an entire Panzer division to avert a catastrophe.[16] Rintelen suggested that OKW should immediately send as many anti-tank guns as possible, followed immediately by a Panzer division. Brauchitsch agreed that a German corps staff should be established to ensure a unified command over all armoured units, so that German influence over the entire operation could be made effective.[17] Opting for a forward defence presented a major logistical problem. The Sirte was almost 500 kilometres from Tripoli, the port through which all supplies would have to be shipped. There was no railway, and the front would be well beyond the 300 kilometres that OKH considered to be the limit for supplying troops by motor transport.[18] If the Afrikakorps were to be effectively supplied it would need an immense amount of motor transport, and would need ever more as it advanced. Even if the Germans were to stay put in the Sirte, they would need twenty times more trucks proportional to the armies preparing for 'Barbarossa'.[19] This was already straining the Wehrmacht's resources to the limit, so that the German commander would have to be restrained from advancing beyond Sirte.

Funck left Rome to report back to the Berghof on 1 February.[20] Keitel, Jodl, Brauchitsch and Halder were present at the meeting, during which Funck painted a bleak picture of an Italian leadership that was so lacking in moral fibre as to 'border on sabotage'. The Italians in the hills west of Derna were in dire danger of being cut off, which would result in the loss of Cyrenaica. They only had four divisions in Tripolitania. They were trying to build a defensive line around Tripoli, but they were without artillery. They were unable to defend Tripolitania further west, because of the danger of bombardment from the sea, plus the likelihood of the flank being turned to the south by motorised units. Funck insisted that the relatively small unit presently envisioned for dispatch to Libya was not nearly large enough. It would need at least an additional Panzer division to save the situation. Hitler's adjutant, Major Gerhard Engel, noted in his diary that 'F[ührer] is shattered and disquieted.'[21] Hitler complained that, on the one hand, the Italians were screaming for help, and on the other, were so 'jealous and childish' that they did not want the Germans to lend them a hand. He had serious doubts whether the situation in North Africa could be saved, while Brauchitsch, who was tremendously impressed by Funck's presentation, warned that it would not be possible to send a substantial armoured group to Libya in time to avert a catastrophe for lack of transport, as well as adequate landing facilities, and also because of the preparations for 'Barbarossa'. Hitler, feeling that the Italians greatly exaggerated the number of British troops they were facing, argued that the idea of a defensive ring around Tripoli was absurd, and poured scorn on their claim that it was impossible to drive across the Sirte to the south of the coastal road. He insisted that a considerable number of troops would have to be sent to North Africa, which would be worthless without adequate air support. He ordered Rintelen to find out exactly what the Italians intended to do, and how long they felt they could hang on to Cyrenaica. He also demanded a report from 10 Air Corps as to whether it would be able to halt the British advance.

The essential question was whether the 132 Armoured Division (Ariete) and the 102 Motorised Division (Trento), supported by Funck's Battle Group, would be able to defend Tripolitania, or whether an entire Panzer division would be needed. OKH was adamantly opposed to the idea of sending a large force to North Africa, while Halder was indifferent to what happened.[22] All that really mattered was to make sure that Italy did not fall apart. The main problem was that the Italians lacked modern weapons, particularly anti-tank guns. Halder saw the need for a small unit, armed with such weapons, which would relieve the Italians of their fear of tanks (*Panzerschreck*). It was for this reason that Funck had been sent to Libya.[23] Funck, however, did not think that such a small unit would do the job, arguing that it would need at least an armoured corps to mount an effective counterattack. The seeds of a major conflict were thus sown. For the time being Hitler ordered the Luftwaffe to examine what it could do to knock out British armoured units in North Africa and their convoys in the Mediterranean. He also called for closer co-operation with the Italian general staff, warning the military liaison officers in Rome to keep a close eye on the Italian leadership to make sure that they remained loyal. The mood in Rome was sombre. The debacle in North Africa confirmed Ciano in his belief that Italy should not have become involved in the war in the first place. He complained bitterly to Mussolini that

> At Sidi Barrani they spoke of surprise. Then you counted
> on Bardia, where Bergonzoli was, the heroic Bergonzoli.
> Bardia yielded after two hours. Then you placed your
> hopes in Tobruk because Pitassi Mannella, the king of
> artillerymen, was there. Tobruk has been easily wrested
> from us. Now you speak with great faith of the escarpment
> of Derna. I beg to differ with your dangerous illusions. The
> trouble is grave, mysterious and deep.[24]

On 3 February Hitler called a meeting of OKW, OKH and OKL (Luftwaffe High Command) at which he announced that although the loss of Libya was militarily of no great consequence, it would probably result in Italy ending the war, leaving the Mediterranean to the British, thus seriously threatening southern France. But he had still not made up his mind whether or not to send German troops to North Africa. For him the main question was whether the Luftwaffe, operating from bases in Libya, would be able to halt the British advance; if that failed the Funck Battle Group would clearly not be enough to turn the tide. In that case a powerful Panzer division would have to be sent to Tripoli. Hitler asked whether it would be possible to spare such a division. For the army Brauchitsch complained that it would seriously compromise 'Marita' and would also mean one less Panzer division for 'Barbarossa'. Milch pointed out that the dive-bombers (Stukas) only had a limited range, and in any case the Luftwaffe was at the moment concentrating on attacking Malta. This prompted Brauchitsch reluctantly to agree to send a Panzer regiment along with Funck's Battle Group. The rest of the Panzer division would follow as soon as possible, the force to be placed under a German commander. Hitler finally gave the go-ahead, the Panzer division to be taken from the troops allotted to 'Marita', adding that success in North Africa might well make 'Marita' superfluous. A report from Rintelen in reply to questions posed on 1 February indicated that the Italians would soon abandon Cyrenaica, and that the Italian navy refused to attack British bases along the North African coast, but that they still felt that they would be able to defend Tripoli with the existing forces.[25]

On the following day Warlimont, head of the Armed Forces Command Staff (WFSt) at OKW, outlined the modifications to 'Sunflower'. 5 Light Division was to be strengthened by a number of Panzer. Preparations were to be made to send an additional Panzer division. Rintelen's staff in Rome would be increased to include a department responsible for the transportation of troops and matériel to North Africa. 10 Air Corps was to ensure the safety of the convoys, in close co-operation with the Italian air force. In addition, the Luftwaffe was to step up the attacks on Malta and attack the British forces south of Djebel el Akhdar, as well as British coastal shipping.[26] On the following day Hitler ordered that the German forces in North Africa would be under the tactical control of the local Italian commander, but would be under the command of a German officer. The German contingent was to act as one group and would not be allowed to be spread out in various different positions along the front. 10 Air Corps was to remain directly under Göring's command.[27]

Rintelen arrived in Berlin on 6 February to brief Hitler. He said that the British would soon be in possession of the port of Benghazi and Agedabia with its generous water supply, thus controlling all of Cyrenaica, so that only a few Italian units would be able to withdraw to Tripoli. In fact Benghazi was in British hands that day, with the remainder of the Italian 10 Army capitulating twenty-four hours later.[28] The Italians now had at most only six divisions with which to defend Tripoli, supported by only 100 aircraft, 400 having been lost in the preceding few weeks. They had lost 150,000 of the 244,500 men deployed in North Africa, along with half of their vehicles. 10 Air Corps now had to concentrate all its efforts on the defence of Tripoli, halting its operations against the Suez Canal, the harbour at Tobruk and the convoys bringing supplies to Egypt. This left the Air Corps stretched to the limit, so that Hitler began to worry that the Fascist regime might topple, Tripoli fall, the British join up with the French North African colonies and Vichy France change sides.

Rintelen insisted that the four Italian infantry divisions, plus the armoured divisions that were on their way, would not be enough to save Tripoli, but at least it would take the British some time to cross the waterless Sirte. There would thus be time to send an armoured division to North Africa that could fight a mobile defence in the Sirte. Otherwise Tripolitania would be lost. Hitler, who had already made up his mind to act, was further convinced.[29] He now felt that Tripoli had to be defended so as to stop the British linking up with the French in North Africa, the consequences of which he painted in the blackest of terms. This was only possible with a forward defence by armoured units.

That same day Lieutenant-General Erwin Rommel was given command over the German forces in North Africa and three days later he interrupted his leave to be briefed by Hitler and Brauchitsch.[30] Baron von Funck replaced Rommel as commander of 7 Panzer Division, which had played a decisive role in the campaign in France. Hitler described Rommel to Mussolini as 'the most exceptional (*verwegensten*) tank general that we have in the German army'. OKH did not agree. They heartily disliked the publicity hungry Rommel, who enjoyed a particularly close relationship with Hitler, and preferred Funck who, as a soldier of the old school, would take his orders from OKH. It was precisely for this reason that Hitler chose Rommel rather than Funck.

Rommel was given command over a force made up of 5 Light Division, a Panzer regiment and an artillery unit, the remit of which to defend Libya was outlined in Order Number 22.[31] Lieutenant-Colonel

Klaus Kreuzwendedich von dem Borne was appointed as his chief of staff. The chain of command was laid out in Order Number 22e of 5 February.[32] Rommel, as 'Commander of the German Troops in Libya', was directly subordinate to Marshal Rodolfo Graziani, the Italian chief of staff, and through him to Mussolini. Tactically he was directly under the command of Graziani in his capacity as Supreme Commander in North Africa. In all other matters, such as personnel, discipline, logistics and the like, he was under the commander-in-chief of the Wehrmacht, thus ultimately answering to Hitler. Mussolini agreed to these arrangements, even though they created a situation fraught with more than the usual amount of difficulties besetting coalition warfare. He seems to have overlooked the important rider which read: 'Should the German troops be given an order that, in the opinion of their commander, would only lead to a serious failure, and thus seriously harm the reputation of the German forces, he has the right and the duty, by informing the German general attached to the Italian high command in Rome to request the commander-in-chief of the army to ask for my (Hitler's) decision.' Rommel was to make frequent use of this clause, and could be certain of a sympathetic hearing. He was not placed under the command of the Supreme Commander South (OBS), Field Marshal Albert Kesselring, but they were ordered to co-operate closely. Kesselring, like Rommel, was under dual command. He was to follow Mussolini's 'guidelines', as relayed to him by the Comando Supremo, while he answered to Göring as commander-in-chief for his Luftwaffe units. Cavallero tactfully agreed that he had the right to countersign all orders in matters concerning Italy and Africa. In spite of these arrangements there were frequent problems over areas of competence, resulting in permanent friction between the Axis partners. Rommel treated the Italians with undisguised contempt, whereas Kesselring, although he was a brutal and callous man, soon to be guilty of appalling war crimes, did his best to smooth the waters and preserve the alliance. Hitler appreciated Rommel's dash and derring-do, but he was ever anxious to prop up Mussolini and needed Kesselring's undoubted diplomatic skills to this effect. There were many disagreements between Kesselring and Rommel, but each admired the other's courage. Kesselring flew two hundred times over territory controlled by the RAF and the light aeroplane that he piloted himself, a Fieseler Storch, was shot down five times.[33] Soon after his appointment Kesselring remarked: 'It was clear to me that in an overseas war it is much more important to ensure that the matériel is brought to the right place, rather than to wrack one's brains whether to attack on the left or the right flank.'[34] It was a pity that Kesselring all too often forgot that operations were impossible without supplies, leaving Rommel stranded, much like Napoleon in Egypt after the Battle of Abukir, with the significant difference that a mechanised army's requirements were infinitely greater than those of an eighteenth-century army. Unlike Napoleon, Rommel was to ignore all logistical difficulties, overextending his supply lines, thus causing an insoluble crisis that he shamelessly blamed on Rintelen and Kesselring.

Rommel did not hesitate to use all available loopholes, using his close relationship with Hitler to make himself a virtually independent commander. None of this disguised the fact that 'parallel warfare' had been replaced by a '*guerra subalterna*' that was to prove every bit as humiliating for the Italians. It was an arrangement that gave Rommel a greater degree of freedom from Hitler and OKW than that enjoyed by any other German general.

Brauchitsch briefed Rommel on 7 February, telling him that his main task was to stiffen Graziani and make sure that he did not retreat to Tripoli without a fight.[35] He was to report daily to the operations division of the general staff, to General Warlimont, as well as to the section for Foreign Armies West. He was told nothing of the planning for 'Barbarossa', so that there was no co-ordination of strategy, leaving Rommel free to make totally unreasonable demands on OKW.

OKW was in a pessimistic mood with the fall of Benghazi. Given that the Italians had nothing to stop Wavell's men marching into Tripolitania, while German troops would not be in full force in North Africa until the middle of April, they concentrated on detailed planning for 'Attila', the occupation of Vichy France, as well as for the invasion of Corsica and Malta, and the crippling of the French navy at Toulon. Göring had already ordered General Kurt Student, commander of 11 Air Corps and the Luftwaffe's expert on the use of paratroops, to examine the possibility of attacks on the Suez Canal, Cyprus, Crete and Malta. Detailed studies were made under the leadership of General Alfred Schlemm, chief of staff at 11 Air Corps, that indicated that large-scale attacks from the air were feasible. A closer examination of Malta revealed that a landing from the air would be exceedingly difficult, but planning went ahead for an operation in the autumn, after the successful completion of 'Barbarossa'.[36]

The German and Italian naval leadership met for the first time on 13 February at Merano. The Italians agreed wholeheartedly with the German insistence on the vital importance of denying the British the use of Malta and of closing off the Mediterranean between Sicily and Tunisia, but that was all. Riccardi announced that the Italian navy would continue to concentrate on protecting the supply routes to North Africa and Albania, and did not have the wherewithal to undertake offensive operations such as Raeder and Fricke suggested. The Italians promised to take a closer look at their allies' suggestions and agreed that a German liaison officer should be attached to the Italian naval staff, leaving the Germans with a faint hope that they might be able to exercise some influence on future naval operations in the Mediterranean.[37] The German delegation returned home in an unrealistically euphoric mood, imagining that Malta would soon be in the hands of the Axis, leaving the Royal Navy in serious difficulties.

OKH issued Rommel and Rintelen guidelines for their discussions with the Comando Supremo, the gist of which was to establish a defensive line at Buerat on the Gulf of Sirte, with motorised units on the right flank, rather than attempting to create a defensive position around Tripoli. The question of command and control remained confusing. The German forces in Libya were to be placed under the Italian commander's tactical command, but were still under the direct command of OKH. Rommel was ordered to work closely with 10 Air Corps, which was subordinate to the High Command of the Luftwaffe (OKL).[38]

The Italians were beginning to panic. Hit-and-run attacks from the Long Range Desert Group (LRDG) and by the Free French were proving demoralising.[39] There were rumours of the formation of an Anglo-French force in Chad that was preparing to attack Tripolitania from the south. The situation in French North Africa appeared to be unstable. On 2 February air reconnaissance revealed that the Italians were in full retreat from Cyrenaica, prompting O'Connor to push forward, rather than wait until the Cruisers arrived from England. The advance was rapid, with the Italians suffering another crushing defeat at Beda Fomm. By 8 February the 11th Hussars were at El Agheila, their reconnaissance moving 70 kilometres forward to the Arco dei Fileni, the monument to Fascist colonialism that stood on the border between Tripolitania and Cyrenaica, known to the British as 'Marble Arch'.[40] The 'Cherry Pickers', who had sent sixty-eight polo ponies to

1. Arco dei Fileni ('Marble Arch')

Cairo in anticipation of some good sport, began to look forward to
the next chukka. But they were to fight so hard during the next few
years that they never managed to get a team together.[41] O'Connor's
men had advanced 1,000 kilometres in two months, capturing

130,000 prisoners, 400 tanks and 845 guns. O'Connor wanted to push on, and had Wavell's support, but on 12 February a message arrived from Churchill that dashed his hopes. Wavell was ordered to form a strategic reserve for service in Greece: 13th Corps was withdrawn from Cyrenaica; 7th Armoured Division was sent back to Egypt for replenishment, to be replaced at the front west of Derna by 6th Australian Division, supported by a weak and inexperienced armoured brigade from 2nd Armoured Division. The battle-hardened 6th Division was shortly to be designated for service in Greece. Further Australian units were left at Ain el Gazala and Tobruk. The British positions in Cyrenaica had thus been stripped bare, leaving the Egyptian border dangerously exposed.

OKW endorsed OKH's plan, which in turn was based on the advice of Funck and Rintelen, for a defensive line at Buerat, with infantry at the front and armoured units under Rommel's command behind the open right flank. The Axis forces would then be in position to meet the British should they decide to advance along the coastal road, or attempt a flanking movement to the south. Mussolini agreed to this plan on 9 February.[42] On the following day OKW ordered that Rommel's mission was to halt the British advance and to destroy them with the offensive use of armour. It was an ambiguous order that Rommel, in defiance of OKW, interpreted as a carte blanche for offensive action.[43]

Rommel arrived in Rome on 10 February where he received Mussolini's approval for OKH's plan. He flew to Sicily the following day, where he conferred with General Hans Geisler, the commander of 10 Air Corps. He suggested bombing Benghazi and the British concentrations south-west of the town. Geisler told an astonished Rommel that the Italians had already begged him not to bomb the town, as many officers and officials owned property there. Rommel, who was travelling with Hitler's adjutant, Colonel Rudolf Schmundt, ordered him immediately to phone the Führer's headquarters to get the go-ahead. This was promptly given, and within hours German bombers were disrupting the British supply lines to considerable effect.[44] After a few anxious weeks the pressure was off. The British offensive in North Africa had ground to a halt because of the movement of troops to Greece.[45] German troops began to arrive in Tripoli, while 10 Air Corps stepped up its bombing campaign.

Rommel landed in Tripoli on 12 February along with a small staff; Schmundt was still by his side as a sign of Hitler's special favour. The initial picture as painted by Major Heinz Heggenreiner, the German liaison officer with the Italian forces in North Africa, was grim indeed. He described the situation as a 'rout', troops had thrown away their weapons and scrambled on to already overloaded trucks in an attempt to escape, Italian officers had packed their bags in Tripoli and were ready to leave. Graziani's successor, General Italo Gariboldi, a man justifiably described by one of Italy's finest commanders, General Giovanni Messe, as 'old and stupid', objected strongly to the idea of a forward defensive line 200 kilometres east of his position at Homs, and had to be brought in line by General Mario Roatta, Rintelen's contact with the Comando Supremo.[46] Agreement was finally reached and Rommel was given command over the joint forces some 200 kilometres east of the Italian lines. After further argument Gariboldi agreed to move the German forces forward to the desert fortress at Nofilia, where they were to make contact with the British.[47] Rommel's tactic was essentially a bluff. He calculated that if some attempt were made to show that the Axis was prepared to stand and fight, the British would pause to regroup and bring up supplies, giving him time to build up a viable force.[48] A note in Goebbels' diary suggests that he had something else in mind. The propaganda minister was overjoyed to hear that Rommel had arrived in Tripoli claiming, contrary to all the orders he had been given, that Mussolini had granted him full power of command and that his aim was to capture Benghazi.[49]

That afternoon Rommel and Schmundt climbed into a Heinkel 111, a slow-moving medium bomber specially fitted as an observer aircraft, and flew across the desert to the Sirte. It was here that Rommel decided that he would make his stand, keeping his armour in reserve. Returning to Tripoli he was relieved to hear that General Roatta had arrived with a message to the effect that Mussolini had no objections to his plan.[50] 10 Italian Corps, made up of the Brescia and Pavia Divisions, was sent up to Buerat. All this took time, and there was not enough transport available to bring the Ariete Armoured Division, with only sixty obsolete tanks that Rommel claimed were only useful for chasing natives around Abyssinia, up along the 400 kilometres from Tripoli.

For the moment the Luftwaffe was the only weapon available to Rommel capable of holding Wavell's army. He flew up again to Sirte, this time to examine the situation on the ground. He found that the town was sparsely garrisoned by one regiment of Italian infantry,

2. Rommel arrives in Tripoli

320 kilometres ahead of all the rest. At least he was impressed by the quality of its commanding officer.

The only port the Germans could use was Tripoli, where it was impossible to unload more than two ships at a time, so that it was estimated it would take at least forty-two days to land the 5 Light Division.[51] The 18,000 men and 4,087 vehicles needed sixty ships totalling 130,000 GRT. In addition there were 10,516 men and 1,672 vehicles destined for the Luftwaffe detachment. The Italians had no shipping available for this task, so lengthy negotiations began between the German and Italian navies. The Germans established bases in Brindisi, Durazzio, Naples and Tripoli under the overall command of a liaison officer in Rome. 5 Light Division was shipped from Naples beginning on 8 February, using sixteen ships divided into four squadrons. Hitler's decision on 3 February to send an armoured force to North Africa meant that five more naval squadrons would be needed. They began work on 25 February, and it was not until the beginning of April that 5 Light Division had arrived in Tripoli in full force. None of these problems stopped Hitler from entertaining fantasies about sending two Panzer corps to North Africa in order to conquer Egypt, admittedly after the successful completion of 'Barbarossa'.[52]

Rommel ordered an Italian division to move up to the Sirte on 14 February, and on the same day a troopship arrived with Lieutenant-Colonel Baron von Wechmar's 3 Reconnaissance Battalion, along with 39 Tank Destroyer Unit.[53] Rommel, who went down to the docks to supervise the disembarkation, ordered the ship to continue unloading during the night, the harbour brilliantly lit, but thanks to the *khamsin*, a desert wind, which caused a sandstorm, they were not visited by the RAF.[54] Wechmar's men were soon on their way to the Sirte, after a brief march past. They arrived there 26 hours later. Columns of German and Italian troops soon followed. In order to create the impression that his was a formidable force, Rommel ordered Volkswagens to be dressed up as dummy tanks.[55]

The British did not seem to be particularly impressed, and Rommel estimated that they were intent on continuing their offensive towards Tripoli. However, air reconnaissance soon revealed that the British had abandoned Nofilia, whereupon on 19 February Rommel sent 3 Reconnaissance Unit, supported by 39 Anti-Tank Unit and the Santa Maria Battalion, to take the oasis with its somewhat salty well. The following day contact was at last made with the British, with an exchange of fire between armoured cars to the west of El Agheila. On 24 February a lieutenant from the 6th Australian Division and two troopers from the King's Dragoon Guards were taken prisoner and an armoured car captured.

On 21 February, the day that Rommel's force was officially named the Deutsches Afrikakorps (DAK), Major-General Johannes Streich arrived with his staff in Tripoli, along with the first units of his 5 Light Division. OKW promised that a further Panzer division would soon be on its way.[56] On 27 February, 8 Machinegun Battalion arrived in Tripoli. This reinforcement emboldened Rommel to change his tactics. Given that the Italian infantry had only limited value, and the Italian commanders in Libya lacked any dash, he decided that his men should no longer be acting as a mobile reserve behind an Italian infantry screen, but be brought up to the front to engage the British as soon as possible.

The Germans were new to desert warfare, but they had already had ample experience with all-arms Panzer divisions in the campaigns in Poland and France that proved ideally suited for this unfamiliar environment. A division comprised a Panzer regiment of two battalions, an infantry regiment of three battalions, an artillery regiment and a reconnaissance unit. Unlike the British army, they were all provided with first-class radio communications, which, combined with a carefully cultivated *esprit de corps*, ensured close co-operation between the different arms and with other units. This enabled the highest possible degree of command and control, which along with a concentration of effort, made the German armoured divisions outstandingly effective.

On 28 February Rommel issued his orders to 5 Light Division. It was to move up to Nofilia, establish a defensive position and send out raiding parties along the coastal road to the east. The following day he revised the order, sending the division to the narrow strip between the salt marshes and the sea at Mugtaa, 700 kilometres from Tripoli and within striking distance of the British outpost at El Agheila, while establishing a defensive line from Nofilia down to the Arco dei Fileni. These positions were taken up and strengthened by the end of March, while 5 Light Division waited for its Panzer regiment and its field artillery to arrive.

The Axis now had enough men for an effective defence of Tripolitania, but the supply problem remained acute. The port of Tripoli had a limited capacity, and was under frequent attack from the RAF. The British dominated the Mediterranean; the front was a long way away. The quartermaster-general had allotted two transport columns for the original detachment, barely adequate to supply them at Buerat, 380 kilometres from Tripoli. Once the second German division, 15 Panzer, had arrived OKH decided that they could not provide any further transport for North Africa without seriously compromising preparations for the invasion of the Soviet Union, so that the Italians would have to help out.[57] Rommel, who was unaware of the true reason, bitterly complained that Brauchitsch and Halder were deliberately starving him of the forces he needed for an effective campaign, and that they were leaving him to rely on sheer luck for a successful outcome.

Fifteen convoys had brought 25,000 men, 8,500 vehicles and 26,000 tons of supplies to Tripoli by the time that Rommel began his offensive in Cyrenaica at the end of March 1941.[58] The transfer of 5 Light Division was completed by the end of April, while 15 Panzer Division began to arrive in the middle of the month. The last remaining units of the division arrived with the twenty-fifth convoy in the middle of May.[59]

The Italian High Command in Libya offered two transport columns, but since the front was now 700 kilometres from Tripoli this was clearly not enough. There was no railway along the coast, and the Italians had destroyed stretches of road during their retreat. 5 Light Division chewed up the coastal route as it advanced, so that it was soon in need of extensive repairs. The Afrikakorps' ingenious quartermaster, Lieutenant-Colonel Otto, brought supplies up by boat, against the advice of the overly cautious Italians.[60] The landings at Buerat, Sirte and Ras el Ali, some 20 kilometres north-west of Mugtaa, were unprotected, often lashed by heavy seas, while the boats were constantly attacked by submarines. Nevertheless, the Afrikakorps was largely provisioned by this makeshift flotilla of small craft, each capable of carrying between 30 and 200 tons of supplies. In spite of all these efforts the Afrikakorps was from the very outset desperately short of essential supplies. The pressing problem of logistics was not one to which Rommel, with his restless ambition and impulsiveness, paid sufficient attention. A further problem was that Italian fuel was of such poor quality that it proved totally unsuitable for use in German vehicles; likewise the food they supplied was not up to standard. As a consequence the Germans were obliged to supply the Afrikakorps with both fuel and rations. Yet in spite of all these difficulties 5 Light Division's energetic quartermaster managed to stockpile sufficient supplies at Arco di Fileni for further operations by the end of March. Fuel may have been in short supply, but it was brought forward in robust 'jerry cans' that did not spring leaks like the flimsy containers used in the British army. Water remained a serious problem. That from four wells at Nofilia was almost undrinkable, so water had to be brought up from Sirte, 140 kilometres away, where it was claimed that it had not rained for three years. In spite of all these efforts the Afrikakorps was never up to full strength, remaining, as Colonel Siegfried Westphal, later to become Rommel's chief of staff, said, 'a torso' throughout the entire desert campaign.[61]

Rommel had ordered his forward units up to the strategically important bottleneck at Mugtaa in accordance with the agreement made with the Italians. The Italians pointed out that there were twenty-two wells at El Agheila, guarded only by a light detachment and no more than 25 kilometres away.[62] The Germans were supported by the Italian armoured division Ariete and the partially mobilised Brescia division. General Geisler's 10 Air Corps in Greece detached two groups of Stukas, a squadron of fighters and a reconnaissance squadron to Sicily. They were under the command of Major-General Stefan Fröhlich, who was given the title of Air Commander (*Fliegerführer*) Africa.

10 Air Corps was given additional planes from western Europe, so that it soon had a total of 510. It took some time for the pilots, who had been trained for naval warfare, to get used to desert conditions, and the detachment was initially hampered by a shortage of fuel, bombs and spare parts. Fröhlich's job was rendered all the more difficult when, at almost exactly the same time as his appointment, Bletchley Park managed to crack the Luftwaffe's code 'Light Blue', and was now able to read all its radio traffic.[63]

Reconnaissance revealed that the British position in Cyrenaica was extremely weak, consisting of part of an Australian infantry division, a raw British armoured division and four squadrons of the RAF. The crack 7th Armoured Division had been withdrawn to Egypt to rest and refit. Wavell had assumed, partly on the basis of misleading intelligence based on 'Enigma' decrypts of Luftwaffe traffic, that the Germans were in no position to launch an attack, and had recalled O'Connor, the finest of his generals, who was suffering from a stomach ulcer, replacing him as commander of the forces in Cyrenaica with Neame, an exceptionally valiant soldier, but one who lacked experience in desert warfare and was definitely not up to the job of facing Rommel.[64] Wavell acted on the assumption that the Germans would not risk sending a large armoured force to North Africa, and certainly would not dare to mount a major offensive. This did not take Rommel into account. He was an overbearingly ambitious general, who now began to think in terms not of defence, but of a major offensive with Egypt and the Suez Canal as the objective. With the British denied the use of the Suez Canal and starved of oil from the Middle East, operations in the Balkans would be superfluous. Rommel therefore deliberately misled OKW, arguing that the British were about to resume their westward drive, in the hope that units designated for 'Marita' would be sent to North Africa to meet this imaginary threat. There was, however, no possibility that OKH would fall for this ruse. Unbeknownst to Rommel the bulk of the German forces in the Balkans were to be used in 'Barbarossa', and could not possibly be diverted to another theatre. He decided to press on regardless. He felt that he could deal with the forward units at El Agheila, even if he did not have sufficient strength to push on to Tobruk.[65] At the end of February he told his friend Lieutenant-General Friedrich Paulus, with whom he had served in the same regiment in the 1920s, and who now served as quartermaster in the general staff, that he intended to attack El Agheila. On

3. Panzer III

7 March he told General Streich that he intended to grab El Agheila and Marada. The following day he informed OKH that he hoped to mount an offensive in the summer that would result in the capture of Cyrenaica after which he would move on to northern Egypt and the Suez Canal. Further details of an attack on Tobruk followed on 17 March, by which time 15 Panzer Division with 120 Panzer, 60 of which were medium Panzer IIIs and IVs, had finally begun to arrive in Tripoli.[66]

The Panzer III had a low-velocity 50mm gun that was in no way superior to the miserable British two-pounder. Its basic armour was only 30mm thick, compared with the 47mm on the Crusader and the Stuart's 44mm. The Panzer IV was a more serious weapon, much feared by the British because of its short-barrelled 'cigar butt' 75mm gun, but it too was of low velocity and lacked sufficient punch for tank penetration. It was far more effective using high explosives against infantry in a close support role.[67] The Afrikakorps thus had Panzer that were on a par with the British tanks and were, except for a few brief moments, at a chronic numerical inferiority. Their successes were due to the superiority of their anti-tank weapons, particularly the 88mm anti-aircraft gun (Flak) which was equally effective against tanks, as well as the 50mm anti-tank gun (Pak 38), which was far superior to the British two-pounder.

4. Panzer IV

5. An 88 used as Flak, 1941

The '88' fired a 10kilogram shell at 1,200 metres per second that could penetrate 150mm of armour at a distance of 2 kilometres. No British tank in North Africa had such thick armour. Only the massive 'King Tiger' (PzKpfwVI Tiger II) with its 185mm of armour would have been a match for such a powerful weapon at this distance. British troops said of the '88': 'anti-aircraft, anti-tank, anti-social'. By contrast the British two-pounder shell weighed 0.91 kilograms, which could only penetrate 56mm of armour at 500 metres. The Panzer IIIs and IVs had 90mm of maximum armour. The British never took up the idea of using their 3.7in anti-aircraft guns against tanks, even though they would have been most effective. This was due in part to the snobbish disdain with which the artillery regarded the ack-ack wallahs. The Flak units were objects of respect, but also of particular envy in the Afrikakorps, because they were provided with portable toilets, whereas others had to make do with a spade in the sand. The close co-operation between armour, infantry and artillery, and above all their exceptional tactical and operational skills, gave the Afrikakorps a distinct advantage over the British, who used the anti-tank gun in a purely defensive role, and failed to use their field artillery to knock out the Afrikakorps' anti-tank weapons. They lacked the Germans' flexibility, as well as their ability to concentrate forces at a decisive point, so as to overcome their overall numerical weakness.[68]

OKW and OKH were appalled by Rommel's totally unrealistic plans for an offensive. Halder, as chief of the general staff, had been paying close attention to the interaction between the projected invasion of the Soviet Union and the campaign in North Africa, and concluded that the logistical problems were such that the most that could be achieved was an advance to Sollum, bypassing the fortress of Tobruk. This would only be possible in mid-May, by which time 15 Panzer Division would have arrived in full force.[69] The Afrikakorps was spread very thin on the ground, and already faced serious logistical problems, with the RAF sinking an alarming amount of shipping destined for Libya, whereas British forces were very well supplied. The troops were all battle hardened, but this was still far from being an elite force. It was a hastily improvised unit. For example, 15 Panzer Division had initially fought as the 33 Infantry Division, but had been remoulded as a Panzer division during the winter. The much-vaunted test for the troops' suitability for service in the tropics amounted to little more than a superficial examination of blood pressure and teeth. They had been given no special training, beyond a few brief lectures on 'tropical hygiene' and 'relations with the Islamic population', with whom they anyway had virtually no contact. This was hardly adequate preparation for the manifold hardships of desert warfare. The Italians were reluctant to share their experiences of fighting in North Africa, so the Germans had to turn to veterans of the imperial colonial forces, and to farmers from Togo and German South-West Africa, in the hopes of picking up a few tips. Rommel, however, considering these to be minor problems, had no intention of remaining on the defensive. Ignoring OKW's orders to concentrate on halting the British advance, he immediately set to work planning an offensive against Tobruk; but for such an operation he needed considerably more than the two incomplete German divisions under his command. OKH insisted that he would have to make do with what he had, and only attack if there was a significant reduction of the fifteen British divisions that they estimated were stationed in Libya and Egypt.

Rommel tried to disguise his real intent by insisting that he was going to conduct a 'tough defence' from forward positions between Buerat and Sirte, and remain in contact with the enemy. This seemed to satisfy the Italians, but OKW and OKH remained suspicious. Captain von Both, whom OKH had sent to North Africa, reported that Rommel's operational intentions were confused and took no account of what was actually achievable. There was considerable confusion over supplies for the Italian and German forces. This clearly had to be brought under a unified command, and the supply routes to Libya secured.[70] Colonel Baentsch from the quartermaster's staff at OKH suggested that Rommel had three options open to him. He could remain on the defensive; attack Agedabia, where Lieutenant Seebohm's radio interception team had revealed that the British were busily strengthening their defences, and press on to Tobruk; or mount a limited offensive along the coast. For the last two he would need a considerable amount of additional transport for supplies, so that he would have to wait until it was available.[71] Rommel was calling for two more motorised divisions, three armoured reconnaissance units and Italian garrison troops for an attack on Tobruk. OKH, seeing no possibility of meeting this request, made a vague promise to send an armoured corps to North Africa, but omitted to tell Rommel that this would only be after the successful completion of 'Barbarossa'. OKH confidently assumed that this would be sometime that winter.[72] On 17 March Hitler told Brauchitsch and

Halder that there could be no question of sending any further divisions to North Africa, and for fear of a hostile French reaction he refused Rommel's request to use ports in Tunisia. Brauchitsch repeated his suggestion that further divisions be sent to North Africa, but only in the autumn, by which time he assumed that operations in the Soviet Union would have been completed. In the meantime Rommel should prepare for an offensive in Cyrenaica, the date to be determined later.[73]

Rommel, refusing to accept OKH's stonewalling, decided to go to Berlin to argue his case. On the way he discussed the situation with Gariboldi in Tripoli, who agreed in principle, but insisted that the offensive should not begin before all the necessary preparations had been completed. Having been informed that air reconnaissance coupled with other intelligence showed that the British were withdrawing south of Benghazi, Rommel telephoned his staff ordering a reconnaissance in force to Mersa el Brega.

Rommel held discussions in Berlin on 20 and 21 March in an attempt to persuade Hitler to change his mind.[74] With some reluctance the Führer agreed that once 15 Panzer Division had arrived Rommel could mount a limited attack on the British outposts at Agedabia and draw up plans for an offensive in the direction of Tobruk to begin in the autumn. Certain of winning Hitler's approval, Rommel had already ordered such an offensive to begin on 24 March. Hitler was full of praise for Rommel and awarded him oak leaves for his Knight's Cross in recognition of his 'exceptional efforts' during the campaign in France, where he had commanded a Panzer division with characteristic panache. Hitler's instructions were issued as a formal order by OKH on 21 March, and on 2 April Hitler told Rommel once again that, even when 15 Panzer Division had arrived, there was to be absolutely no large-scale offensive.[75] Rommel told Halder that if only he were given two armoured corps he could seize Egypt and the Suez Canal and establish a 'German East Africa'. When Halder asked how these two corps were to be supplied, Rommel replied: 'I don't give a damn! That's your problem.'

Goebbels was entranced by Rommel, whom he described as a 'splendid officer'. Rommel complained bitterly to him that the Italians were 'not a warlike race', which caused him 'nothing but difficulties'. He listed the problems that he faced in the desert, but Goebbels assured him that Hitler 'under no circumstances will abandon Africa'.[76] Rommel was thus further encouraged to act as an independent commander, ignoring orders from his Italian superiors. Goebbels' propaganda machine stepped up its efforts to burnish Rommel's image, which was soon to outshine that of another glittering warrior, General Eduard Dietl, who had been at Hitler's side since 1919.[77]

The Italians were excluded from all these discussions and not even informed about what had been decided. Rommel's talks in Rome on 23 March, as well as with Gariboldi in Tripoli the following day, did not go well. He was told not to take Marada, the Italians oblivious to the fact that it was already firmly in his hands, and he was given strict instructions to stop preparations for a further offensive. The Italians complained that most of the shipping going to North Africa was being used by their ally, they were short of transport, and increasingly worried about their forces in Albania, as British troops had recently landed nearby.[78]

That the Germans were able to land their forces in North Africa with relative ease was due in large part to the astonishing passivity of the Royal Navy, which was concentrating on Operation 'Excess', which involved escorting three ships to Piraeus and one to Malta, sending two further ships from Alexandria to Malta, and bringing eight empty freighters back home. At the same time two light cruisers were sent to reinforce the naval force in Malta. These operations were to be protected by the aircraft carriers *Ark Royal* and *Illustrious*, as well as the battleships *Renown*, *Malaya*, *Warspite* and *Valiant*.[79] As already mentioned 10 Air Corps had damaged the *Illustrious* and put the cruiser *Southampton* out of action. On 17 January, eight Heinkel 111 bombers, starting from an airstrip at Martuba, near Benghazi, were sent on a mission to attack a convoy in the Suez Canal. The mission was not a success: the Luftwaffe was unable to find its target, but found some consolation in returning to base unharmed.[80]

While the Germans began sending troops to Tripoli the Royal Navy's 'Force H' attacked Genoa, Livorno and La Spezia. These raids were of little military significance, although serious damage was caused in Genoa, with the Italians suffering a further loss of prestige following upon the loss of Cyrenaica. 'Force H', which included the *Ark Royal*, sailed away undetected by the Italian air force and navy, thus losing a valuable opportunity for which the Germans promptly blamed their Italian allies, even though 10 Air Corps had also failed to spot the ships.

Weichold enjoyed the full support of naval command when urging the Italians to take a more aggressive stance, but it was all to no avail. The new Italian naval leadership, with Admiral Riccardi as chief of staff and Admiral Inigo Campioni as his second-in-command, insisted that with the overwhelming superiority of the Royal Navy there was no alternative to a defensive strategy, and a concentration on securing the supply lines to Albania and North Africa. This they made unambiguous during the Merano meeting with the Germans on 13/14 February, in spite of all Raeder and Fricke's eloquent arguments.

Admiral Angelo Iachino, as commander-in-chief of the Italian navy, had suggested during the Merano talks that it might be possible to attack the British convoys moving men and matériel to and from North Africa, as well as between Egypt and Greece. Operation 'Lustre', the movement of British troops to Greece, began on 6 March with the first convoy from Alexandria to Piraeus, but Riccardi still insisted that he did not have any ships free to intercept. His attempt to sweeten the pill with a lame offer to send a cruiser to help out the Germans in the Atlantic received a frosty reception. On 16 March a couple of Heinkel 111s managed to hit a British battleship, a success that the Germans used to urge their reluctant allies into action. Eight days later, the Italians announced their intention to send a force of one battleship, the *Vittorio Veneto*, six heavy cruisers, two light cruisers and three destroyers in the direction of Crete. They asked 10 Air Corps for air support. This proved fatal. The British, having cracked the Luftwaffe's code, knew that an operation in the eastern Mediterranean was in the offing. Admiral Cunningham, an exceptionally forceful commander, ordered the convoys to Greece to halt and put the Mediterranean fleet out to sea.[81]

The Italian fleet set sail in the night of 26/27 March, but was spotted by a Sunderland seaplane shortly after midday. The Italians picked up the spotter plane's radio message, which was relayed to Admiral Iachino that evening. He saw no alternative to halting the operation. Vice-Admiral Sir Henry Pridham-Wippell's 'Force B' was spotted by a plane operating from the *Vittorio Veneto*, but the Italians were unaware of a much larger 'Force A' under Admiral Cunningham. The Italians withdrew, closely followed by 'Force B', and then turned again in an attempt to attack the British from two flanks. Pridham-Wippell's ships managed to escape in the fog and aircraft from the *Formidable*, supported by RAF squadrons from Maleme and Crete, managed to damage the *Vittorio Veneto* so severely that Cunningham sent in his three slow old battleships, relics from the First World War,

6. 'Enigma' machine in use in North Africa, 1942

for the kill. Further torpedo attacks from the *Illustrious* slowed the *Vittorio Veneto* down even more, but the British lost contact during the night and the wounded ship managed to escape. The remainder of the Italian force was less fortunate. It was caught line-ahead by Cunningham's 'A Force' and submitted to crippling fire. The heavy cruiser *Pola*, already severely damaged and its crew first taken aboard by the British, was sunk, along with two cruisers and two destroyers. The two remaining destroyers in the Italian 1 Division escaped badly damaged. The British lost a total of one aircraft in the Battle of Cape Matapan.[82] It was a significant victory for the Royal Navy and made the Italians even more cautious. The British had cracked one 'Enigma' cipher system in time for the battle, and were to break another used for shipping control during the summer. Information gleaned from 'Ultra' gave the British advanced warning of most of the convoys to North Africa, thus helping to starve Rommel of the men and matériel he needed for his campaign.

Weichold, who attributed the Italians' failure to the incompetence of their naval leadership, once again insisted that German officers should be attached to the Italian naval staff. Skl heartily agreed that the Italians had shown themselves to be totally inept, from which they concluded that it would be unwise to continue urging them to adopt an offensive strategy. Admiral Riccardi responded to German criticism by arguing that faulty intelligence from 10 Air Corps was the direct cause of the disaster. The Luftwaffe had reported that two British battleships had been torpedoed, failed to make contact with the Italian navy on 27 March because of heavy rain, and was only able to protect the Italian fleet for a mere fifty minutes late the following day. Although these mutual accusations were largely justified, the real keys to the situation lay in the British use of carrier-borne aircraft, their use of 'Enigma' decrypts, plus the palpable lack of co-operation between the Italian navy and the Luftwaffe.[83]

Malta remained a major problem for the Axis. OKW concluded that a landing was virtually impossible, either by sea or by air, and that the only hope was that the occupation of Greece and Crete, combined with an offensive in North Africa, would oblige the British to move the bulk of their forces to the eastern Mediterranean. In the meantime 10 Air Corps kept up its bombing raids on the island, which at least forced the RAF to move their Wellingtons and Sunderlands to Egypt, while the fighter support was greatly increased. The Luftwaffe was able to protect shipping destined for Tripoli, but submarines based in Malta sank a number of freighters as well as the Italian cruiser *Armando Diaz*.[84] From the outset British naval and air activity made the crossing to North Africa exceptionally dangerous. This sometimes worked to the troops' advantage. Trooper F.H. of 15 Panzer Division spent eight enjoyable days in Naples, which included a visit to Vesuvius, when the convoy taking him to join his unit was forced to return to port owing to the British blocking the Straits of Messina.[85]

The British were frustrated that they were unable to do more to disrupt Rommel's supplies at a time when their forces in North Africa had been seriously reduced as a result of the decision to help Greece. The Wellingtons were moved back to Malta so as to mount bombing raids on Tripoli, but there was serious disagreement between Admiral Cunningham and his superiors in London as to how best to deny Tripoli to the Axis. Cunningham argued that long-range bombers should be based in Egypt, whereas the Admiralty wanted a blockade by the Mediterranean fleet, which Cunningham realistically insisted would be far too costly an operation. While this debate was going on, the Royal Navy scored a spectacular success when on the night of

15/16 February a group of destroyers spotted a German convoy off
the coast of Tunisia with which 10 Air Corps had lost contact the
previous day. Five freighters, which were carrying the first units of
15 Armoured Division, and two of the three Italian destroyers were
sunk with the loss of one destroyer.[86] Cunningham was ordered to
attack Tripoli and promptly moved the Mediterranean fleet undetected
into position to start a one-hour bombardment in the early morning
of 21 April, supported by bombers from Malta. Cunningham's fears
that there would be serious losses proved to be unfounded. Minimal
damage was done to Tripoli, but he refused point blank to repeat the
raid. More damage was done the following day when some German
bombs exploded in a munitions dump, resulting in a reduction of the
capacity of the harbour by two-thirds, a dire situation that took several
weeks to rectify. Skl once again criticised the Italians for failing to mine
the approaches to Tripoli, in spite of their repeated insistence that this
be done. The Italians finally took this advice on 1 May, by which time
the situation had improved somewhat, because the British were forced
to move the bulk of their ships from Malta to assist in the evacuation
of Greece and Crete. Nevertheless, the Axis lost a total of eleven ships
in May.[87] Continuing bomber raids on Benghazi also greatly hampered
the logistical support of the Axis troops in North Africa, who were left
chronically short of supplies.

Rommel pressed on regardless. After his trip to Berlin he knew
that he had Hitler's support at least for limited operations. He also had
a powerful ally in Goebbels, whose propaganda machine did all that
it could to boost his reputation. Rommel needed Hitler's support were
he to enjoy a degree of independence from OKH, OKW and the Italian
Comando Supremo, and he knew full well that his friendship with
Goebbels would make access to the almighty Führer much easier. But
this did not imply that he subscribed to National Socialist ideology. He
was a fervent nationalist, who shared the Nazis' dislike of the snobbish
old guard, but he had no time for politics or theory. He was grateful
to Hitler for furthering his career, in spite of the opposition of his
military advisers. He was an ambitious soldier, who knew that he was
dependent on Hitler, and to a lesser extent on Goebbels, for his career
to flourish. He was also an honourable man, who refused to comply
with orders contrary to traditional rules of engagement. Once Hitler's
support was withdrawn after the battle of El Alamein, Rommel became
disenchanted and angry that Hitler refused to accept the inevitability of

the Axis' defeat. But this did not mean that he joined the ranks of the opposition.

His decision to push on as far as he possibly could was thoroughly irresponsible. The British had been seriously weakened because of their commitment to Greece, but Rommel did not have the wherewithal to do them any serious damage and it was unthinkable, as OKH pointed out, that he would be able to take Tobruk. Logistics were to prove to be the key to success in the Desert War, so that the transport services are the unsung heroes of the campaign. Montgomery would never have succeeded without the unglamorous self-sacrifice of the Royal Army Service Corps. Rommel failed in large part because of the lack of supplies for his modest forces. Furthermore, the forces at his disposal were far too small for the task he allotted them, and had they been increased, as he persistently demanded, supply problems would have further intensified. But Rommel was temperamentally incapable of playing a passive role, hanging around waiting for the British to attack. He therefore decided to take the gamble, in the hopes that were he to be successful he would overcome the reluctance of his superiors, all of whom ordered restraint, to send him the men and matériel he needed to finish the job. Knowing nothing of preparations for the invasion of the Soviet Union, he attributed OKH's refusal to meet his persistent demands simply to personal dislike and professional rivalry. Strong elements of both were ever present, but the requirements for 'Barbarossa' were the overriding concern.

3 ✠ TOBRUK: THE FIRST ROUND

The Germans had managed to land their forces in Tripoli without any serious problems, and Rommel was sure of Hitler's support for an offensive action, even though this ran against the better judgement of OKH and OKW. The British were unable to do much damage to Tripoli so that Rommel, unaware of the forthcoming attack on the Soviet Union, saw no reason why he should not be given substantial reinforcements that would enable him to seize Tobruk and advance into Egypt. He was angry and frustrated, feeling that he had been starved of men and matériel by jealous and unimaginative staff officers, who had left him with a minimal force that faced seemingly intractable logistical difficulties.

The supply line for the Afrikakorps from Tripoli was now 700 kilometres long, with little relief provided by the limited harbour facilities at Buerat and Ras el Ali. Vehicles were tied up unloading ships in Tripoli, before moving supplies away from the city centre so as to be safe from bombing attacks, leaving insufficient vehicle space available to build up a forward supply base. The Italians provided the Afrikakorps with inadequate supplies of food, most of which was in any case inappropriate for a desert climate, and the fuel could not be used by the Luftwaffe's aircraft. Most vehicles soon proved unsuitable for the desert. Air filters were unable to deal with desert sand, halving the life span of a motor. Tanks could only travel for 1,000 to 1,500 kilometres without a complete overhaul.[1] The Afrikakorps was thus undernourished, plagued with disease, poorly equipped and undersupplied. Such difficulties would rapidly worsen with every step forward, but Rommel simply refused to face the problem. He expected others to look after such tedious details, while he won glory on the battlefield. He was one of the very few army generals who had not been trained for the general staff, having failed the admission examinations for the War Academy. This proved to be a fatal weakness. Whereas most German generals had little strategic ability, they at least had learnt to realise the vital importance of logistics, of meticulous intelligence work, of signals and communications, without which it was impossible to be effective at the operational level. Rommel was a tactician, who had learnt his trade in the thick of battle, who thought it pointless to draw up detailed plans in advance. For him everything depended on swift reaction to unforeseeable contingencies that threw the best-laid plans awry. He was fortunate to have some outstanding staff officers, who kept their eyes on the larger picture, while he dashed around the battlefield making tactical adjustments, frequently getting lost in the process, out of touch with his command post. Field Marshal Gerd von Rundstedt, Rommel's superior during the invasion of France, said of him that he had all that it takes to make a good divisional commander, but nothing higher. It is difficult not to agree with this judgement from an old soldier who was everything that Rommel despised – a staff officer and an aristocrat. There was also widespread resentment arising from the feeling that Rommel owed his rapid promotion not to his soldierly skills, but to the support afforded him by the Führer. He was one of a new breed of senior officers spawned by the National Socialist regime, men of action who were contemptuous of the traditionally conservative, nationalist and 'reactionary' officer corps. Many considered his brusque manner and strong Swabian accent coarse and uncultured. Rommel frequently ignored his superiors in Berlin, while all too often treating his immediate Italian commanders with undisguised contempt.

In an operation described as a 'tactical reconnaissance', 5 Light Division took El Agheila on 24 March without meeting any opposition. That afternoon Rommel again took over direct command of the Afrikakorps. Hearing that the British were moving troops up to Agedabia, he decided to act, even though it was contrary to Gariboldi's orders. The Afrikakorps, although it was still not up to full strength, took Mersa el Brega on 31 March. It was a tough fight. An initial attack in the morning of 30 March was beaten back with heavy artillery fire that caused serious casualties, including a direct hit on General Streich's command post. Undaunted, Streich ordered a night-time attack by Major Voigtsberger's 2 Machinegun Battalion, which was to work its way around the British line of trenches and attack the flank. The plan was successful, showing up the weakness of the British flank that was to be repeatedly exploited in the months to come. The British withdrew, abandoning Agedabia two days later, after two counterattacks had failed.[2] As a result of this engagement Rommel found himself in a completely new operational situation.

Faced with the alternative of attacking with his limited forces before the British built up their defences, or waiting until his own forces were up to strength, by which time he would be faced with a formidable defensive position, Rommel opted for the first solution. General 'Ming the Merciless' Morshead's 9th Division had only just arrived from Australia, relieving the experienced 6th Australian Division that was sent to Greece.[3] Morshead realised that the Mersa el Brega Line could be outflanked to the south, and he did not have enough mines to protect this vulnerable area south of the salt marshes. In fact he only had enough mines to lay a thin line across his front. He would have preferred to move forward to El Agheila, a position that would have been much easier to defend, but he lacked the transport. The British, calculating that Rommel had insufficient logistical support to advance beyond El Agheila, decided to withdraw Morshead's division, replacing it with 2nd Armoured Division, a seriously weakened unit that had lost an armoured brigade for service in Greece. Should the Afrikakorps decide to attack, 2nd Armoured Division was ordered to fight its way back, 'shepherding' the Panzer into the coastal plain where they would be destroyed by attacks on their southern flank.[4] The idea of leading Rommel like a lamb to the slaughter was all the more fanciful, given the shepherd's weakness. The Axis forces appeared singularly inactive after the fall of Mersa el Brega, prompting General Neame to assume as late as 30 March that the Afrikakorps would stay put for the time being. The attack the following day came as a complete surprise.

Taking El Agheila proved to be remarkably easy, with the British hardly reacting, apart from a few raids by armoured cars on Rommel's supply lines. At Italian insistence a joint Operation 'Count Schwerin', named after the commander of 200 Regiment for Special Duties, was already underway in southern Libya, having begun on 15 March from Sirte. The object was to clear the area of the Long Range Desert Group and the Free French. The offensive proper, which began on 31 March, soon threatened to grind to a halt in a heavy sandstorm. Rommel flew over his hard-pressed troops in his Storch, dropping notes that read: 'If you don't get a move on, I'll land – Rommel.'[5] By 2 April the unfortunate troops had covered hundreds of kilometres under appalling conditions, almost without encountering a single enemy, but they had gained invaluable experience of desert conditions. During that day the Panzer finally ran up against some armoured cars in the first armoured engagement in the Desert War. The British withdrew after a fierce fight, crossing the border back into Cyrenaica. Rommel now concentrated on bringing Italian troops up to the front, releasing his armoured units for further operations.[6]

Lieutenant-General Michael Gambier-Parry's 2nd Armoured Division defended the Mersa el Brega Line doggedly, beating back 5 Light Division's initial attack; but it was an inexperienced ill-equipped unit that was dislodged by a daring attack by Lieutenant-Colonel Ponath's 8 Machinegun Battalion across the sand-dunes to the north of the coastal road. Luftwaffe reconnaissance revealed that the British were making a hasty and disorganised retreat. This was confirmed by General Johannes Streich, the commander of 5 Light Division, based on reports from his reconnaissance patrols. Rommel therefore ordered his men to press on to Agedabia, a town of some 6,000 inhabitants and the capital of Cyrenaica, where he established his command post on 3 April.[7] Here even Rommel was obliged to stay put for 24 hours while supplies were brought up from the advance base at Arco dei Felini. Rommel knew full well that he was acting against strict orders, but as he later wrote: 'I simply could not resist this favourable opportunity.'[8] On 1 April Gariboldi had told him not to press on before he had sufficient strength, for fear of a powerful counterattack, but having taken the Mersa el Brega Line with a single machinegun battalion, and with no counterattack in sight, he chose to ignore this pessimistic note.[9] The British had managed to avoid being trapped at Agedabia by a skilful withdrawal, but Rommel was determined to keep on their heels. Ignoring Streich's objections that he needed four days to refuel and rearm and flagrantly disregarding Gariboldi's order to halt, as well as OKH's instructions to await the arrival of 15 Panzer Division, he ordered 3 Reconnaissance Battalion, backed up by 8 Machinegun Battalion, on to Derna, in order to mop up British units as they withdrew from Cyrenaica. Forward units soon reported that the British had already abandoned Benghazi, having set their supply dumps on fire.[10]

The German advance was painfully slow along the old caravan route known as the Trigh el Abd that went to the northwest diagonally across the desert to Bir Hacheim south of Tobruk and on to the Egyptian border. Advancing along this track, which was in an appalling condition, was described by the experienced commander of the Brescia Division as 'suicidal'. Conditions were made even worse by a powerful *khamsin*. The only advantage was that the sandstorm, combined with the clouds of dust thrown up by vehicles as they churned their way through the deep sand, protected the columns from RAF bombers. Petrol soon ran short with adverse conditions doubling normal fuel consumption, while British outposts offered stiff resistance. Old Italian mines along the Trigh el Abd caused a number of casualties, while far away from the coast the daytime heat was unbearable.

Major-General Gambier-Parry, realising that the situation was highly dangerous, withdrew his forces and flew back to Barce for further orders from General Neame. Wavell, assuming that Rommel was mounting a limited attack on Benghazi, ordered him to halt the German advance along the coastal road and to protect the flank of the Australian 9th Division. Although the British were in disarray, the Italians were patently displeased. Rommel's superior in Tripoli, General Gariboldi, dressed him down, pointing out that he had acted contrary to the instructions of the Comando Supremo in Rome. Lack of supplies and transport meant that any further advance was out of the question. On 3 April Gariboldi went up to the front to confront his recalcitrant subordinate.[11] While the two men were locked in acrimonious debate, Gariboldi insisting that Rommel should await his orders before acting, Rommel countering that this would make it impossible for him to take decisive action, a telegram arrived from Hitler congratulating Rommel on his success and permitting him to advance to Benghazi, provided that he kept a close eye on his right flank. Hitler did not seem to be concerned that 15 Panzer Division was likely to be delayed, and even suggested that a further advance would be possible if the British withdrew the bulk of their forces from Cyrenaica. Once again Hitler and his immediate entourage gave a striking demonstration of their unrivalled mastery in counting unhatched eggs. Hitler crowed over Rommel's advance, which showed British propaganda to be nothing but hot air, while expressing his utter contempt for the Italians, who had failed so miserably in Greece and North Africa.[12] Mussolini, eager for any success that might boost his waning prestige, also gave Rommel the go-ahead. On 4 April Rommel ordered Schwerin to reconnoitre as far forward as Tobruk. The mechanised sections of the Brescia Division, mostly consisting of anti-tank guns and light artillery, was brought up to Benghazi, so that 3 Reconnaissance Battalion was freed to continue its eastward advance. Streich was ordered to move 5 Light Division up to the coast between Derna and Tobruk.[13]

Rommel now regarded himself as a fully independent comman-der and immediately ordered his men to press forward. No German gen-eral during the war enjoyed such independence. He wrote to his wife: 'I am sure you can understand that I was so overjoyed that I was unable to sleep!'[14] Benghazi was in German hands by 4 April. Denied a pause to rest, 5 Light Division pressed on to Derna, a charming town with 10,000 inhabitants and an ample water supply, known as 'the pearl of Cyrenaica', as well as to the British base at the desert fortress of Mechili on 8 April, in an attempt to cut off the British as they withdrew along the coastal road to Tobruk.[15]

The British forces in Cyrenaica had been so drastically reduced to meet the commitment to Greece that little stood in Rommel's way, apart from a serious shortage of fuel that worsened as his supply lines grew ever longer.[16] Wavell now sent O'Connor back to Cyrenaica to take over his former command. O'Connor, with characteristic courtesy and consideration, insisted on only acting as an adviser to Neame until the battle was over.[17] Wavell agreed. This was a bad mistake in that it resulted in a dual command at a critical moment. The British forces consisted of two armoured divisions equipped with obsolete and lightly armed tanks. The 9th Australian Division was so lacking in transport that it had had to leave an entire brigade behind in Tobruk. As a result they had not had enough men adequately to defend the Mersa el Brega Line. At the end of March Wavell had sent his only reserves, 3rd Indian Motorised Brigade, to Cyrenaica, where O'Connor ordered them to Mechili, an ancient Turkish fort where there was a major supply base, but where they were soon to be trapped.

Rommel's campaign, which he insisted was based on his deter-mination to maintain the highest measure of tactical and operational flexibility, was irresponsible and highly unconventional, but initially it paid off. He divided up his scant force into three groups, one of which drove along the coast; the second went straight ahead, with a third heading south-east. The three prongs were to join together at Mechili. His lines of communication were overextended. All supplies had to be brought up along the coastal road, which was under incessant fire from British naval vessels. His demands that the Italian navy along with 10 Air Corps should deal with this menace, as well as ensure that not a single ship reached Tobruk, could not possibly be met.[18] As a result he was left chronically short of fuel and supplies, his path forward was littered with broken-down vehicles and isolated units, but the British lacked determined commanders who were prepared to exploit Rommel's glaring weaknesses in a series of counterattacks that would have halted his advance.

Gambier-Parry arrived at Mechili during the night of 6/7 April and assumed that his tanks and artillery would arrive shortly. During the evening of 7 April he was informed that this was not to be, and he was given orders to withdraw. The order came too late. Only a few Indian units managed to escape and Mechili was in German hands the following day. At Mechili, an ancient fort of no military value, but at the crossroads of seven tracks leading in all directions, Rommel proudly reported to OKH that he had taken 2,000 prisoners, among them six generals, announcing with characteristic modesty, that he would soon be in possession of Tobruk after a campaign which would be a combination of Cannae – a favourite analogy among German staff officers since von Schlieffen had proclaimed it to be a perfect battle – and Dunkirk, after which he would mount an offensive against Alexandria in the summer, then seize the Suez Canal.[19] Rommel, who was determined to prove himself to be a modern-day Hannibal, was in the thick of battle, completely out of touch with his staff so that no one knew were he was. His chief of operations, Major Ehlert, suggested to von dem Borne that the Afrikakorps bypass Mechili and press on to Tobruk, but a young officer who took this order up to the front found Rommel directing the attack on Mechili. He had already given Streich orders to advance to Tobruk.[20]

A staff car, a huge white Cadillac inherited from 'Jumbo' Wilson who had been given command over the forces in Greece, in which O'Connor, Neame and Brigadier Combe[21] were travelling, got lost in the dark on 8 April and they were taken prisoner by a detachment of German motorcycle troops from Lieutenant-Colonel Ponath's battle group. There was no one of similar calibre to take their place. This rich prize amply made up for the loss of the Afrikakorps intelligence officer, Captain Count Baudissin, whom the British had taken prisoner. Having bagged Britain's best general, Ponath was emboldened to attack the airfield at Derna in the early morning of 8 April. His first attempt was beaten off, but the bulk of his battle group arrived shortly thereafter and he threw them into battle at 1100hrs. This time he was successful, taking the airfield and blocking the main road. A British

7. Motorcycle troops

counterattack was warded off with heavy losses, and the following day Derna was in German hands, solving all the Afrikakorps' water problems. Ponath's men were almost out of ammunition, the anti-tank guns and light artillery had shot their last rounds, machineguns were down to their last belt, but he had captured four generals, 174 officers and 793 other ranks. Junkers 52s flew in supplies and reinforcements and at 1835hrs Rommel arrived on the scene. Even though Ponath's men were utterly exhausted after their exceptional exertions, they were ordered immediately to advance, arriving in Tmimi at 0200hrs without firing a round. After a brief rest they continued to advance towards Tobruk.[22]

Rommel's advance was supported by the movement of forward supply bases from Agedabia to Mechili via Msus, while coastal shipping began to unload at Benghazi. Since the coastal road from Benghazi to Derna had been rendered impassable, supplies had to be sent via the desert route through Msus and Mechili. Keeping this track open to traffic was exceedingly difficult, and 5 Light Division's engineers and drivers did a remarkable job, keeping 800 trucks constantly on the move.

The British had inferior weapons, an inadequate communications network and poor aerial reconnaissance. Most important of all they totally failed to exploit the possibilities afforded by the desert for a war of movement. If they stayed put they were overrun or bypassed. If they moved it was usually to retreat. At least the stand made by the Indians at Mechili, the result of a last-moment attempt to break out, enabled the bulk of the British forces in Cyrenaica to escape to fight another day.[23] Two Australian brigades, as well as the bulk of the anti-tank and artillery units, had managed to extricate themselves from Rommel's attempt to trap them.

Rommel's campaign had been fraught with serious supply problems, particularly shortage of fuel. There had been all too lengthy delays for refuelling and repairs. Units had got lost, particularly during long night-time marches through the desert, and there was more than the usual confusion characteristic of coalition warfare. But Rommel had pulled off a spectacular coup against the advice of his Italian superiors. Now there was no holding him back. Germany had invaded Yugoslavia and Greece on 6 April, so the situation in North Africa was radically changed in Germany's favour with Churchill's decision to send substantial support to Greece, thus drastically reducing the number of divisions in the Middle East.

A battle group was formed under the command of Major-General Heinrich von Prittwitz und Gaffron, whose orders were to press on to Tobruk. The Afrikakorps was greatly strengthened and encouraged when the first units of its 15 Panzer Division began to arrive at the front. The Afrikakorps was full of confidence. An entry in its war diary read: 'General Rommel decided to continue the pursuit, trap the enemy in Tobruk and destroy them.' They had good reason to be sanguine. The situation for the British was most uncomfortable. Greece had to be defended. The British were heavily engaged in East Africa, taking Keren on 27 March and Asmera on 1 April. A further complication was the seizure of power in Iraq by the pro German Rashid Ali, which resulted in the Iraqi army besieging the RAF's 44 Training Squadron stationed at the Habbaniya airfield. Had the operation succeeded, and had the Germans been able to exploit the situation, the British could well have been denied access to the vital Middle Eastern oilfields. Once the situation in Iraq was stabilised, Wavell had to mount a campaign against French forces in Syria to prevent them from giving the Germans access to their airfields. On 5 April Wavell had felt obliged to rescind the order to send the Australian 7th Division to Greece and ordered its 18th Infantry Brigade to reinforce the Tobruk garrison. The Germans invaded the Balkans on the following day. The same day Wavell met with Sir John Dill, the Chief of Imperial General Staff, and Anthony Eden in Cairo when it was decided to hang on to Tobruk, but abandon the rest of Cyrenaica. The defence of Tobruk was entrusted to General Morshead and his unruly but trusted Australians. The Royal Navy was ordered to bring up ample supplies. Churchill issued orders that Tobruk was to be defended to the last man. Wavell arrived in Tobruk on 8 April and told Morshead that he had to hang on for at least two months while reinforcements were brought up for a counteroffensive, but he did not rule out the need for a withdrawal, in spite of Churchill's order. He regarded Tobruk as a far from ideal defensive position. The land route to the east was lengthy and wide open to attack. The perimeter defences were far too extensive to be adequately manned by Morshead's limited forces, and 2nd Armoured Division having been severely mauled, there were no longer enough tanks to take on Rommel out in the desert. The fortress was also short of anti-tank and anti-aircraft guns.

Morshead was pleasantly surprised to find 18th Brigade in Tobruk, along with his own 24th Brigade, when he arrived on 8 April with two of his brigades that had been withdrawn from Cyrenaica plus an artillery regiment. He already knew the layout of Tobruk's defences, and contrary to Wavell, who had wanted a shorter defensive ring around the fortress, he decided to place three brigades in the perimeter defences, keeping his fourth brigade with a few tanks in reserve. Reinforcements were brought in by sea, unhampered by the Luftwaffe, including an armoured battalion, an artillery regiment and assorted anti-aircraft and anti-tank guns. Lieutenant-General Sir Noel Beresford-Pierse was given command of a newly formed Western Desert Force, made up of two divisions. A mobile force under Brigadier Gott, comprising units from the 11th Hussars, the 3rd Indian Motorised Brigade and 2nd Armoured Division, along with an artillery regiment and an anti-tank unit, was ordered to move to a position south of Tobruk to guard the flank. The 22nd Guards Brigade was deployed along the Egyptian border.

Rommel was unaware of these movements. Imagining that the British were about to abandon Tobruk, he ordered 5 Light Division to move around the town and cut off the line of retreat, while the Italian Brescia and Trento Divisions made a feint attack to the west of the town. Prittwitz's battle group, spearheading the attack from the west on the left flank of the Italians, was therefore uncomfortably surprised on 9 April when they came under heavy fire from the Australians dug in outside the city walls. Rommel ignored this initial setback, sending a reconnaissance unit to Bardia on 11 April and to the Halfaya Pass on 15 April. A further unit was sent to block the coastal road east of Tobruk, thus cutting off the British lines of retreat. The investment of Tobruk was completed by 12 April. Bardia fell to the Axis the following day, Sollum on 14 April, while an advance party pushed on to Mersa Matruh, where they met with stiff resistance.[24]

Rommel continued to bombard OKH with demands that Halder regarded as 'senseless'. For him preparations for 'Barbarossa' had absolute priority.[25] Then Hitler's adjutant, Major Engel, told Halder that the Führer was thinking of sending a motorised infantry regiment to North Africa. Halder was incensed, pointing out that this issue had been discussed at length and that every available unit was needed for 'Barbarossa'. Transport and fuel were simply not available for an additional division. Most important of all there was insufficient air support in the area for major offensive operations, quite apart from the fact that the closer Rommel got to Egypt, the more determined British resistance would become.[26]

Rommel pressed on regardless, leaving the Brescia Division to the west of Tobruk and moving 5 Light Division, made up of 8 Machinegun Battalion, twenty-five tanks and ten self-propelled anti-tank guns, to El Adem to the south. He imagined that he could easily take a town held by 24,000 men, who were well equipped and provisioned and had adequate artillery support, even though he had no information about the layout of the defences. Early skirmishes outside Tobruk did not bode well for Rommel. Prittwitz occupied the positions abandoned by the Australians on 10 April, ordering his men forward along both sides of the coastal road up to Wadi Sahal, 15 kilometres to the west of Tobruk, but the Australians blew up the bridge and forced the Germans back with heavy machinegun fire from emplacements built into the steep slopes of the wadi. Prittwitz withdrew and waited for the artillery. Taking advantage of a lull in the fire, Prittwitz had moved forward to encourage his men, when at midday he was killed by an anti-tank round.[27] It was not until 1630hrs that the artillery was in position to prepare for an assault by a machinegun unit, but this reached the edge of the wadi, only to be beaten back once again by intense artillery and small arms fire. This first major attack, launched

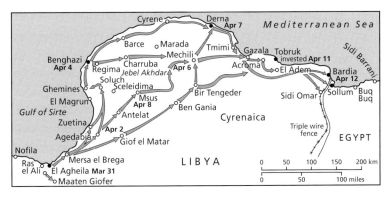

Map 2. Rommel advances to Tobruk and the Sollum Line, April 1941

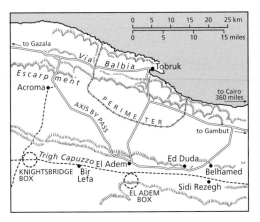

Map 3. Tobruk, 1941

on Good Friday, 11 April, came as a rude awakening. The Germans were beaten back at the first line of anti-tank defences, suffering considerable losses.

Undeterred by this setback, and ignoring the fact that he was fighting virtually blindfold, Rommel ordered a repeat performance the following day. 5 Light Division was ordered to form a battle group under Lieutenant-Colonel Count Schwerin, comprising 2 Machinegun Battalion, a battery of artillery and two heavy anti-aircraft batteries, which was to seize a vital crossroads 8 kilometres south of Tobruk, thereby preparing the way for the mechanised units. The operation was a disaster, with Schwerin calling Tobruk a 'mini Verdun'. Shortages of fuel and ammunition resulted in the force being unable to assemble in time. The Axis lines of supply were now stretched to 1,600 kilometres, forcing them to live hand to mouth. A record amount of supplies had

been shipped to Tripoli and Benghazi, but the major problem now was
to bring them up to the front with round trips of up to 3,200 kilometres,
with appalling road conditions, constantly under attack from the air
and from armoured cars, so that most of the movement had to be
by night. The superb job done by the transport services on both sides
in the Desert War is all too often forgotten.[28] In order to help solve
the supply problem, caused by his strategic blunder of advancing well
beyond feasible limits, Rommel had to take Tobruk, but he simply did
not have enough men to do the job, as in a rare moment of candour he
admitted to OKH; but had he been given the men it would have proved
impossible to supply them. Once in possession of Tobruk, he would
discover that its capacity was minimal, with barely enough coastal
shipping to use it to the full. Further complications were caused by a
severe sandstorm, and with the battle group under intense artillery fire,
the attempt had to be abandoned.

    Rommel continued to insist that the British were far too weak
to stop him from marching to the Suez Canal, and that Tobruk had to
be taken because it blocked the coastal road that he needed to supply
his triumphant advance. He blamed the failure of the first two attempts
on 5 Light Division's insipid leadership, threatened to court-martial for
cowardice any officer who urged caution, and ordered a further assault
on 14 April.[29] He accused 5 Light Division of faintheartedness and pessimism, with its commander, Lieutenant-Colonel Count von Schwerin,
failing to understand modern tactics that were based on concentrating
all forces at one point, smashing through, rapidly rolling up and securing the flanks and pushing on deep to the enemy rear before he had
time to recover.[30] This was only partly true; the major reason was that
Rommel had failed to do an adequate reconnaissance of the outlying
defences, and greatly underestimated both the strength and determination of the British garrison. This was Rommel at his very worst.
Schwerin and Prittwitz were gallant officers who had been allotted
impossible tasks. Their men, especially Lieutenant-Colonel Ponath's
8 Machinegun Battalion, had fought bravely, suffering such heavy
losses that they had almost been wiped out. Although Rommel had
grossly impugned their honour, his subordinates were all to fight on
with unquestioning loyalty and distinction.

    Having delivered this broadside, Rommel was convinced that
the next attack would bring victory. Schwerin's battle group was
ordered to move around the perimeter defences to take up position

across the coastal road to the east of Tobruk. In spite of heavy artillery
fire from the fortress, as well as from the British mobile force on the
high ground at El Adem, the battle group reached its objectives by
1200hrs on 11 April, closing off the coastal road. The siege of Tobruk
had begun. The British troops at El Adem now began to withdraw to
the Egyptian border, pursued by 3 Reconnaissance Battalion, which
advanced partly along the old caravan route from El Adem to Fort
Capuzzo, known as the Trigh Capuzzo, and partly along the coastal
road to Bardia, which was occupied the following day.

To the south of Tobruk another battle group from 5 Light
Division, made up of Ponath's redoubtable 8 Machinegun Battalion,
5 Panzer Regiment and 605 Tank Destroyer Unit, also came under
heavy artillery fire from El Adem, until the artillery was chased away.
The group had no artillery of its own, leaving the south-eastern flank
vulnerable to attack. British hit-and-run units took advantage of this
to launch a series of raids on the rear echelons of the besieging forces.
These, however, were tiresome rather than threatening.[31]

The attack from the south began at 1600hrs. Having advanced
2 kilometres the Germans came under heavy artillery fire. The Panzer
pushed on regardless, but then were halted by a two-metre deep anti-
tank ditch. They then moved east, looking for a gap in the defences, but
now landed in a dense minefield that had been laid during the night.
This forced them to retire south, only to find themselves facing eleven
Cruisers that emerged from the perimeter defences. According to the
Germans six were destroyed, but the Australians claimed only two were
lost. Whatever the score, the Panzer continued to withdraw, and the
Australians now concentrated their artillery on Ponath's machinegunners. They took what cover they could in the stony ground, suffering
forty-four dead and wounded in a merciless barrage, virtually in open
ground. Schwerin's battle group was unable to lend any support to
the southern attack. They were in a dangerously exposed position and
unable to move.

During the night 5 Light Division carried out extensive reconnaissance, trying to find a way across the tank ditch. Pioneers reported
that the ditch ended about 4 kilometres to the northwest, but their activities were spotted by the Australians, who strengthened this area with
reserves from the 18th Brigade, supported by a number of anti-tank
weapons. The division was given orders to seize Tobruk the following day, but the attempt was a disaster. Blinded by a heavy *khamsin*,

pounded by a massive artillery barrage, and without artillery support, the attack had to be called off.

Rommel was still unperturbed, in spite of two disastrous attempts to break through the defences without any artillery support. He managed to convince himself, on the basis of the analysis of intercepted telephone calls, that the Australians in Tobruk were on their last legs. In fact it was the Afrikakorps that was beginning to feel the strain. The men were exhausted after ten days of intense activity. The heat was oppressive, supplies of food and water wholly inadequate, their vehicles in need of repair, reinforcements came in dribs and drabs. On Easter Sunday Ponath reported that he was under such heavy artillery fire that he was simply unable to move, and that an attack across open ground in the face of such overwhelming firepower was out of the question. Nevertheless 8 Machinegun Battalion made two attempts to move to a more advantageous position, where they could at least observe the enemy, but both failed. During the night they finally managed to cross the tank ditch and establish a bridgehead, about 100 metres deep and 400 metres wide. Night-time reconnaissance revealed an opening in the second line of defences to the north-east, but it was questionable whether they would be able to exploit this opportunity. The Australians counterattacked at 2300hrs, and there was ferocious hand-to-hand fighting throughout the night. The Germans suffered heavy losses, but they were able to hang on to the bridgehead, in spite of continuous bombardment. The major problem was bringing in supplies of food, water and ammunition. Supply units either were unable to find the bridgehead in the dark, or were beaten off by intense artillery fire.

Some relief came at 0430hrs when 5 Panzer Regiment with 38 Panzer arrived in the bridgehead, along with a tank-destroying unit. The Panzer had initially broken through the front 3 kilometres to the east of the bridgehead. Realising their mistake they turned left, causing havoc among the Australians. Now they faced the difficulty of command and control. Rommel had given Streich overall command of the operation, but his headquarters were too far to the rear, leaving him out of touch with events at the front. The machinegunners and the Panzer operated separately, with both commanders unaware of the other's intentions. Ponath had a brief talk with a squadron commander, and managed to cadge a lift for some of his men on the forward Panzer, while he joined the infantry and marched on foot. Heavy clouds, mist and dust made it impossible for the Stukas to lend any support.

This disorganised group pushed forward 4 kilometres before dawn broke. They found themselves facing an artillery regiment about 2,000 metres away. The machinegunners were able to take cover in some unfinished bunkers, while the Panzer advanced until the range of the 8.76cm howitzers became suicidal and five Panzer IVs were destroyed. The Panzer then veered off to the east, only to run into anti-tank emplacements and a counterattack by Cruisers, resulting in the loss of four more Panzer. The commander of 5 Panzer Regiment, considering these losses excessive, ordered a withdrawal, during which the regiment was subjected to constant anti-tank fire from self-propelled guns that destroyed another eight Panzer. By 0700hrs the Panzer Regiment was back where it had been at dawn.

The 8 Machinegun Battalion fared even worse. It had been divided into two groups, one left to guard the bridgehead, the other to press forward. The men in the bridgehead were quickly overrun. The others fought on until 1100hrs when they ran out of ammunition. In total 168 men were taken prisoner, most of whom were wounded, and 112 were killed, including the Machinegun Battalion's gallant commander, Lieutenant-Colonel Ponath, who had been awarded the Knight's Cross during the fighting in Cyrenaica.[32]

In April, units from 15 Panzer Division began to arrive, from which Rommel formed the 'Knabe Unit', named after Lieutenant-Colonel Gustav Knabe, commander of 15 Motorcycle Battalion. He was ordered to move immediately from El Adem to Sollum. He joined up with Lieutenant-Colonel Winrich Behr's 3 Reconnaissance Unit, taking Fort Capuzzo, which in fact was nothing but a pile of ruins, and Sollum on 13 April, but they were unable to reach their objective at Mersa Matruh, thanks to stiff resistance from a mobile force.[33] On 14 April Colonel Max von Herff, commander of 115 Infantry Regiment in 15 Panzer Division, a crack Hessian regiment, formally the Grand-Ducal Life Guards, was put in command of all the German and Italian forces in the area from Bardia to Capuzzo and Sollum.[34] He was ordered to take up defensive positions along the Sollum Line and to reconnoitre as far forward as Sidi Barrani.

In the very early morning of 14 April Rommel wrote to his wife full of confidence that he would soon be in possession of Tobruk.[35] To this end Rommel made a desperate attempt to save the situation by ordering the Ariete Armoured Division into the breach, but it failed to appear on the scene until 1700hrs, immediately came under intense artillery fire, panicked and fell apart, scampering away to the south and south-west. General Baldassare had a hard time getting a grip on his division and moving them up into position.[36]

In spite of this disaster Rommel still refused to listen to those officers brave enough to argue that he simply did not have enough men to take Tobruk. Almost half of 5 Panzer Regiment's Panzer had been destroyed. Only a quarter of 8 Machinegun Battalion's men had survived. The Australians had put up an impressive defence, the Germans having to fight in open ground against massed artillery. Rommel did not have nearly enough infantry to take on such a strongly defended position. Two-thirds of his infantry was engaged elsewhere. Heavy artillery was totally lacking, and he lacked sufficient Panzer and engineering equipment, without which he could not possibly take Tobruk. The element of surprise which had accounted for some initial success was now irrevocably lost. It was not until 17 April that the Comando Supremo gave Rommel detailed plans of the defences at Tobruk. Up until then he had been fighting virtually blindfold. Rommel was thus responsible for the first defeat suffered by the Wehrmacht in the war. He stubbornly continued to argue that Tobruk would soon fall, but at least he agreed to a more limited objective for the next attack.

The British had massed artillery on the high ground at Ras el Mdauur to the west of the town, a position that dominated the peripheral road around Tobruk, which Rommel needed to supply his forward units.[37] With no other units available, he allotted the task on 16 April to the Ariete Armoured Division, which had failed so miserably two days previously, strengthening it with two companies of infantry with motorcycles – the sum total of German reserves. It came as no great surprise that the Australians had little difficulty in warding off this half-hearted effort, and in the course of a spirited counterattack took 1,100 Italians prisoner.

In spite of this fiasco Rommel tried again the next day with the Ariete, even though they only had ten tanks left out of the hundred with which they had started out from Tripoli. Co-operation between the infantry and artillery broke down completely, while the Ariete's armour got lost and were out of radio contact. Suddenly tanks appeared on top of the hill, heading for the attacking infantry. Rommel quickly brought in three anti-tank guns, knocking out two tanks that subsequently turned out to be Italian.[38]

Rommel put the blame for these repeated failures on the wretched equipment and inadequate training of the Italian forces. He later wrote: 'Thinking of the equipment with which the Duce sent his troops into battle is enough to make one's hair stand on end.'[39] He conveniently forgot that his German troops, whose training and equipment were far superior, had fared no better, and that he had thrown the Ariete Division against an artillery strongpoint, even though they had already given an adequate demonstration of their incompetence. Now that he was submitted to some robust counterattacks under General Morshead's dogged leadership, he finally decided that he had to wait for reinforcements before attempting another assault, although he still suffered from the delusion that the Australians were about to abandon Tobruk. Had Morshead been provided with better intelligence he might well have inflicted even more serious damage on Rommel. He was led to believe that there were 32,000 Germans in North Africa, almost twice the actual figure. He also assumed that 15 Panzer Division would arrive in full force, with two regiments and 400 Panzer. In fact it had only one regiment with 160 Panzer, about a third of which were light tanks.

That large numbers of ships were docked at Tobruk led Rommel to believe that this was the beginning of an evacuation, when in fact they were bringing in supplies so that Morshead could strengthen his defences. On 22 April the Australians launched a series of attacks outside the perimeter defences, one against the Ariete to the west of the artillery observation spot at Ras el Mdauur, another against the Brescia astride the coastal road to Derna, and a third against 5 Light Division to the west of the road from Tobruk to El Adem. The attacks on the Italians were successful, the Australians taking 400 prisoners, but 5 Light Division managed to beat off the attackers with artillery and anti-tank guns. Rommel, imagining that these attacks were cover for a withdrawal, ordered a series of raids on 24 April to see if the Australians were still holding the front. The result was a resounding affirmative, 150 men from one company of the Trento Division surrendering, the remaining 50 crawling back to the encircling front.[40]

OKH considered the situation to be critical. In an intelligence report for the foreign office they warned that the troops in the Bardia–Sollum area could well be encircled and that 'a change in this extremely critical state of affairs can only be brought about by the rapid dispatch of German troops by air, including bringing 5 Light Division up to strength; also by strengthening the Luftwaffe, particularly fighters, and the deployment of U-boats along the coast from Sollum to Tobruk'.[41] The fighting at Sollum was by far the toughest in the campaign so far, resulting in the troops' morale beginning to crack. Sergeant A. D. serving with 15 Panzer Division wrote home: 'We got to know the English in France. They are very tough customers, well supplied with weapons, equipment and provisions. Their artillery and marksmanship are excellent.' Lance-Corporal S. K., also from 15 Panzer Division, complained bitterly of the sandstorms and the permanently nagging thirst. He wrote: 'I don't allow myself to think of Böblingen. We often got pissed out of sheer boredom, or had one over the eight.' Lance-Corporal H. E., who was with the heavy artillery at Tobruk, like so many of his comrades, longed for the day when it was all over. 'If only the day would come when we are at last at peace... It will be high time once Tobruk has fallen, because there have been far too many losses and the supplies are lousy. Don't get the wrong idea at home, it's easy for the radio to talk.'[42]

Rommel's leadership and abrasive character were the cause of widespread criticism. Colonel Max von Herff, who was serving on the Sollum front, where he had to contend with some fierce counterattacks, said that no one understood the first attack on Tobruk.[43] As soon as a new unit arrived at the front it was thrown into the attack against a greatly superior force with predictable results. Junior officers were at a loss to understand Rommel's orders, resulting in widespread dissatisfaction. OKH were bombarded with complaints, much to the delight of a number of senior officers, since the vainglorious and attention-seeking Rommel was heartily disliked by the army leadership. General Bodewin Keitel, the head of the Wehrmacht's personnel department, summed up these complaints in a memorandum circulated at the top level which concluded that:

> For all [Rommel's] exceptional personal courage and willingness to take tough decisions, it seems to me that he lacks the broad view. Because of this he gives orders that have to be rescinded shortly afterwards, because they were ill-considered and impossible to carry out. The second and even more serious point is the coarse and abrasive manner in which he insults the honour of older and trusted commanders. He is given to making judgments such as: 'I am obliged to remove you from your command', or he makes hasty decisions to dismiss officers and not infrequently calls for a court martial for cowardice.[44]

Brauchitsch, appalled at all the squabbles in the Afrikakorps, asked whether it might be the result of excessive heat.[45]

The Afrikakorps' military courts handed down relatively mild sentences when compared with other units in the Wehrmacht. Soldiers T. and R. stole a vehicle from another unit as a replacement for one that had been lost. When they began to fear that the theft might be spotted they took it into the desert and blew it up. They were given an eighteen-month prison sentence for destroying army property. Infantryman Erich H. left his post and fell asleep while on guard duty at the front. He was sentenced to four years' imprisonment and was declared to be unworthy to serve in the armed forces. Infantryman F. became separated from his unit, hung around the rear echelon, sold some of his equipment, was arrested and escaped. He was given a one-year prison sentence and a dishonourable discharge. Sergeant R. was on a supply ship, where he stole petrol for his own use, as well as some tinned food. He also helped himself to a large sum of money designated for provisions for the troops. He was given the death sentence as an 'enemy of the people' (*Volksschädling*). His accomplices were given prison sentences ranging from four months to six years.[46]

Even though Hitler was clearly in favour of sending a motorised infantry regiment to North Africa and Göring was entranced with the idea of seizing the Suez Canal, and was prepared to give Rommel additional air support, Brauchitsch, who was concentrating on preparations for 'Barbarossa', refused point blank to reinforce a commander whom he regarded as foolhardy. He would have to make do with 15 Panzer Division, which was due to arrive in Tripoli on 5 May. On 14 April Hitler ordered that Rommel should concentrate on strengthening the Sollum Line, and that he should not contemplate anything other than a few raids across the Egyptian border.[47] Halder reacted to Rommel's call for reinforcements after his bungled attack on 14 April by confiding in his diary: 'Now he is reporting that his forces are not sufficient to exploit the "exceptionally favourable" overall situation. We who are far away had this impression a long time ago.'[48]

Major Schraepler, Rommel's adjutant, took the most unusual step of appealing to his commanding officer's wife to bring him to his senses. He wrote:

He [Rommel] will have had little time for writing during the past few days, as they have been very full for him, and very worrying too. His determination and the desire of every one of us to be not only in, but also far beyond Tobruk, is at the moment impossible to realise. We have far too few German forces and can do nothing with the Italians. They either do not come forward at all, or if they do, run at the first shot. If an Englishman so much as comes in sight, their hands go up. You will understand, Madam, how difficult this makes the command for your husband.

The letter ended with reassurances that all was well with her husband and that Tobruk would soon fall. This sounded extremely hollow after such a pessimistic account of the overall situation.[49]

Lance-Corporal H. E., like most of his comrades, shared the major's contempt for the Italians. He wrote home: 'My dear little wife! Don't let anyone tell you that the Italians are soldiers. They are utterly useless. When they screw up we have to sort things out, costing us good German blood for these limp dicks.' He felt that Germany was fighting to regain its African colonies, and therefore had to put up with the Italians. He and his mates felt that a deal should be made about the colonies and peace restored at the earliest possible moment. Lieutenant A. F., an intelligence officer with 15 Panzer Division, was slightly more charitable towards the Italians. In a letter home he said: 'One has to treat the Italians as children. They are utterly useless as soldiers, but at least they make excellent company.'[50]

The Italians lacked the transport needed to supply the two additional divisions that Rommel requested, and his forces on the Egyptian border were increasingly hard pressed. The 22nd Guards Brigade shielded the border while a mobile force harassed them from the high ground to the south. The British attack on the German positions at Fort Capuzzo on 23 April was beaten back, but Rommel became highly alarmed when, as a result of faulty intelligence, he imagined that the British had a force of sixty tanks ready to pounce on the German supply lines. He ordered his forward units to reconnoitre to the south and to adopt a more aggressive attitude. On 26 April they were able to penetrate the British positions on the high ground above the Halfaya Pass, but uncertain of the overall situation they decided to withdraw.

While Rommel floundered at Tobruk the Germans pulled off another lightening coup, this time in Greece. They invaded on 6 April, made a rapid advance and reached Thessalonika three days later. The

Greek army was concentrated on the Albanian border and was unable to offer a serious resistance. The situation was clearly hopeless, obliging the British to begin the evacuation of their forces in Operation 'Demon'. The Greek army in Epirus surrendered to the Waffer-SS Division Leibstandarte Adolf Hitler on 20 April; the remainder of the Greek army capitulated the following day.[51]

This dramatically swift victory prompted the staff officer of 4 Air Fleet, Colonel Günther Korten, to envision an island-hopping operation to Crete, Rhodes and Cyprus, then on to Alexandria, Beirut, Haifa and Jaffa.[52] This would give Germany command over the eastern Mediterranean, opening the way for the German army to advance in North Africa and strike at the heart of the British Empire in India. Korten's commanding officer, General Alexander Löhr, did not get quite so carried away, but he did see the successful campaign in Greece as an 'encouraging step in the direction of Egypt'. Göring was also much smitten by the idea, so that plans were revived to entrust the initial island-hopping to General Student and his paratroopers.[53] OKW still felt that Malta should take priority over Crete, but Student argued the reverse. Hitler agreed.[54] The navy saw Malta as a deadly threat, but was daunted by the difficulties of seaborne landing. The Luftwaffe argued that the walled fields on the island made it impossible to land gliders. Crete seemed to be less of a challenge, and offered the prospect of stepping up operations in the eastern Mediterranean. Bombing Malta therefore seemed to be the only viable option.[55]

The idea of a vigorous offensive in the eastern Mediterranean was warmly endorsed by General Geisler and Lieutenant-Colonel Harlinghausen, who were becoming increasingly frustrated by 10 Air Corps' unproductive raids on Malta, plus the tedious routine patrolling of convoys to Tripoli. They were delighted when on 18 April Rintelen informed them on behalf of OKW that the bulk of their air corps would be moved to the Greek mainland and the Italian-occupied Dodecanese, whence they were to mount operations against the eastern Mediterranean, Alexandria and Suez. On the same day Field Marshal Erhard Milch, Inspector-General of the Luftwaffe, accompanied by General Hoffmann von Waldau, arrived in North Africa to discuss the implications of these changes in air strategy. Rommel's principal concern was for immediate air support for his forward troops. Waldau agreed that Rommel needed considerable additional air support if his plans were to have any chance of success. The two men then travelled back via

8. Local volunteers guard an Me110D, 1941

Rome where agreement was reached with Pricolo on 21 April that only two groups from 10 Air Corps should remain in Sicily – a Stuka group to continue attacks on Malta, and some Me110s to protect shipping destined for North Africa. The Italian air force would have to make up the shortfall.

Shortly thereafter Rintelen brusquely informed the Comando Supremo that these two remaining groups would also be moved to Greece. Pricolo insisted that this would lead to disaster, because the Italians did not have long-range aircraft like the Me110 needed to protect the convoys, and that dive-bombers were also essential. The Luftwaffe's liaison officer in Rome, von Pohl, seconded Pricolo's concerns, adding that the Italian navy was so derisorily timorous that it would probably cease sending convoys to North Africa if it were to be denied German air support. The German navy's man in Rome, Weichold, even though he had always argued vigorously for an aggressive stance in the Mediterranean, agreed with his Luftwaffe colleague's assessment, arguing that German air support was needed to protect the sorely pressed convoys to North Africa: 10 Air Corps had not done a particularly impressive job, but leaving it all to the Italians would lead to a total disaster. Rintelen also raised similar objections, but the Luftwaffe staff in Berlin were not impressed by these jeremiads. On 5 May Baron von

Pohl was given minutely detailed operational instructions for the Italian air force, which he was ordered to give to its high command, Super-aereo. It was requested to confine operations to the western and central Mediterranean, where it would attack British shipping and protect the convoys to North Africa. Malta was also to be kept under constant attack. Predictable Italian objections were to be countered by disingenuously pointing out that in future the forces in North Africa would be supplied from Greece and Crete.[56]

Malta, a group of five islands, British since 1800, is situated only 100 kilometres south of Sicily, 330 kilometres north of Tripoli and 660 kilometres from Benghazi and the Gulf of Sirte. Dominating the entire area by air and by sea, it was of vital strategic importance. Thus 10 Air Corps left Sicily for Greece, having failed to accomplish its mission as laid down in appendix 'd' to Order Number 22. It had neither denied the British the use of Malta, nor closed off the Mediterranean between Sicily and North Africa. It had dropped 530 tons of bombs on Malta, causing the British considerable concern, but traffic had not been seriously disturbed. One warship and six freighters had been sunk – hardly an impressive tally after more than five months. By contrast the losses to Axis shipping were considerable: 33,549 men, 11,330 vehicles and 36,332 tons of supplies for the Wehrmacht were delivered to North Africa between 8 February and 1 May 1941, but 59 per cent of the total shipping was lost in the effort. The Royal Navy's greatest success was when it caught the German Convoy Number 20 off the Kerkenah Islands in the Gulf of Gabes during the night of 15/16 April, sinking five freighters carrying part of 15 Panzer Division, along with three Italian destroyers, itself losing only one ship in the battle.

Meanwhile, OKH were becoming highly alarmed by Rommel's piecemeal and hand-to-mouth tactics, with his troops spread out all over the place with no overall operational concept. Halder complained that he was not being given an accurate and honest account of operations in North Africa and that Rommel was simply not up to the job. By mounting a series of limited attacks with small armoured forces he was incurring unacceptably high losses, while he dashed around, often out of touch with his troops, and continued to bombard OKH with 'insane requests'. Halder decided to send Paulus, one of the Wehrmacht's most skilled and trusted staff officers, to investigate. Paulus was on friendly terms with Rommel and Halder noted: 'Perhaps he is the only one who can exercise his personal influence on this officer, who has gone mad.'[57] In the meantime it seemed to Halder that the real problem was not so much the messy confusion outside Tobruk, as the steady strengthening of the British forces at Sollum. A withdrawal was felt to be unacceptable for propaganda reasons. The situation was thus worrisome, at least for the next few days until 15 Panzer Division's planned arrival on 5 May. Paulus was thus ordered to point out to Rommel that no further reinforcements were available and to force him to make his intentions perfectly clear.[58] At the same time OKH prepared to make five further infantry battalions, a pioneer battalion and two batteries of coastal artillery ready to be sent to North Africa. OKW ordered the Luftwaffe to prepare transport units to move these new units from Naples to Cyrenaica.[59] Once again Hitler butted in to lend his favourite general a helping hand. He ordered air transport to move from Greece to southern Italy, to fly an additional 800 men to North Africa. This merely disrupted transport by sea, because the Me110s accompanying the convoys had now to protect the transport aircraft, while an additional 800 men were hardly likely to make a decisive difference. The Luftwaffe was also required to send a group of dive-bombers from Sicily, along with a group of Me109 fighters from the Balkans, to North Africa to compensate for Rommel's lack of artillery for an assault on Tobruk.

Ignoring the chronic logistical problems that were likely to worsen once 10 Air Corps was moved to Greece, Rommel prepared for a further attack on Tobruk, even though he had at last realised that the British, far from preparing to abandon the fortress, were in fact bringing in reinforcements.[60] He was still short of the transport needed to bring men and supplies forward for the attack. The Royal Navy had command of the Mediterranean, was playing a vigorous role in the land war, and had been ordered by Churchill to cut off supplies to North Africa, whatever the cost. The RAF was causing havoc to airfields and supply lines.

Rommel's initial plan called for a three-pronged attack: the Italians from the east and the west, the Germans from the south. Pointing out that they were being asked to attack across flat open country, 5 Light Division's staff suggested that an attack along the coastal road to the east of Tobruk offered much better cover. On 21 April Rommel had informed OKH that he intended to attack on 1 May, but that this depended on the arrival of two Italian defensive divisions to replace the Brescia and the Ariete, which were needed for the offensive. Comando

Supremo promptly informed him that this was out of the question, owing to lack of transport. The plan had in any case to be abandoned because the Australians mauled both Italian divisions the following day. This obliged Rommel to cancel orders moving the Trento Division to Bardia. The bulk of the division was left at Tobruk to support the Brescia Division, while an infantry battalion was sent to Bardia and placed under the command of Colonel von Herff, who was ordered to deliver the British 'a devastating blow' at Sollum as soon as they arrived.[61]

The men under Herff's command were utterly exhausted and far too thin on the ground to be able to offer any serious resistance to an attack across the Egyptian border. His 3 Reconnaissance Unit had been in action for weeks. 15 Motorcycle Battalion and 33 Tank Destroyer Unit, as well as his anti-aircraft battery, were unaccustomed to the harsh climatic conditions, and had just completed a 1,500 kilometre march, 600 of which were across the desert. The motorcycles with sidecars were unsuitable for desert warfare and were in a wretched state of repair. Much the same was true of the bulk of his transport. He faced a first-rate and experienced mobile force under the forceful leadership of Brigadier 'Strafer' Gott on the high ground, while the 22nd Guards Brigade, freshly arrived from Egypt, manned the coastal strip.

There were only two spots where Herff could reach the high ground. One was at Sollum, close to the coast; the other at Halfaya Pass, 7 kilometres to the south. Herff, determined to keep his men active, concentrated on building a defensive line from Sollum to Fort Capuzzo, while planning an attack on Halfaya Pass. Rommel, who came up to the Sollum front on 19 April, agreed to this course of action, but reserved the right to decide when the attack should be launched. The British landed a force near Bardia on 20 April in an attempt to encircle the town, while the Tobruk garrison was strengthened to the point that OKW felt that the situation there was 'tense'.[62]

Herff was denied any respite. The British moved up to Fort Capuzzo from the south and south-west on 22 April, launching a tank attack from the west the following day. This initial assault was beaten off, but at 1815hrs a second force was spotted to the south heading for the crossroads on the Trigh Capuzzo at Sidi Azeiz. This posed a severe threat to Herff's rear positions at Fort Capuzzo, the more so as an initial report of 'sixty vehicles, some of them tanks' had been transformed into 'sixty tanks' by the time it reached Rommel's headquarters. Rommel reacted with typical derring-do, ordering Herff to keep a close eye on the 'sixty tanks', and should they turn east he was ordered to 'attack with all available anti-tank weapons and destroy them'.[63]

The 'sixty tanks' turned out to be merely a reconnaissance squadron of the 11th Hussars sent to harass the supply lines from Sidi Azeiz to Capuzzo. By the next day they had vanished. Rommel was determined not to sit and wait for the British to attack. On 24 April he issued Herff the following order:

> Control of the triangle Sollum–Bardia–Capuzzo is vitally important for future operations. The Herff Group now has enough troops and modern weapons both for attack and defence, and is able to ward off any attack in accustomed strength. It would, however, be a mistake to remain on the defensive and simply wait for the enemy to attack. The present situation demands that defence along the Egyptian border be conducted offensively. There must be continuous reconnaissance to the south and southeast, and once the enemy is discovered he must be attacked and destroyed.[64]

Herff went into action immediately. His first attack to the south on 24 April was beaten back by artillery. Two days later his men reached the British positions above the Halfaya Pass by nightfall, but as darkness fell he ordered a withdrawal to the frontier fence. Reconnaissance the next morning revealed that the British, grossly overestimating German strength, had abandoned the area and retired to Buq Buq, leaving Herff in control of the triangle. Part of Herff's force went back to Tobruk during the night of 27/28 April; those that remained on the frontier were subjected to a series of limited attacks, none of which was serious enough to endanger the Axis forces at Tobruk.

Rommel's new plan for Tobruk was extremely simple, involving punching a hole through the perimeter defences at Ras el Mdauur to the west of the town, then on the following day sending in German and Italian assault troops from this bridgehead to take Tobruk. The British positions were first to be softened up by Stuka dive-bombers at 1845hrs; at 1930hrs the artillery was to bombard Ras el Mdauur, then at 2000hrs storm troopers from 5 Light Division, under the command of Major-General Heinrich Georg Kirchheim, were to attack on the right flank, while 15 Panzer Division attacked on the left flank. Having been singularly unimpressed by the performance of the Italians in the previous attempts to take the town, he decided to give them only a supporting role. The Ariete Armoured Division was placed to the right of 5 Light Division, the Brescia Infantry Division to the left of 15 Panzer Division, with orders to follow up behind the Germans. In spite of its title, 15 Panzer Division had no Panzer available, while seventy-four Panzer were allotted to Kirchheim's force, which was to bear the brunt of the attack. The infantry were to secure a bridgehead during the night; the Panzer would then be thrown in at first light, heading for the harbour.

Objections were raised to Rommel's plan, particularly from his quartermaster's staff, who argued that supplies were still insufficient for such a major operation. Another problem was that units of 15 Panzer Division were still in Italy and it proved impossible to bring them all up to Tobruk in time. Hans-Henning von Holtzendorff, the commander of 104 Rifle Regiment, who thought that the whole operation was a dubious undertaking, pleaded for a postponement until at least 2 May to await the arrival of 115 Infantry Regiment, and to allow enough time for adequate reconnaissance. Attacking at night in unfamiliar ground, shorthanded and with inadequate logistical support, was not an enviable prospect; but Rommel would have none of this. He argued that time was of the essence: the longer they waited the more the British would strengthen Tobruk. That units would be thrown into battle almost as soon as they arrived, while two battalions of 15 Panzer Division would arrive days late, did not concern him. He also refused to allow any reconnaissance for fear that this would reveal his intentions. He hoped that speed and surprise would do the trick. Fortunately Count Schwerin, who had taken over from Kirchheim, now lying wounded in hospital in Tripoli, ignored Rommel's absurd orders and sent an experienced company commander from his machinegun regiment to reconnoitre on 27 April, accounting in part for the battalion's later success.

Kirchheim had replaced Major-General Johannes Streich, who had been ignominiously relieved of his command by Rommel after the failure of the first attempt to take Tobruk. Streich had objected vigorously to Rommel's hair-raisingly unrealistic plan of attack to which Rommel replied: 'You have gone far too far with your concern for your troops.' Streich, who proudly wore his Knight's Cross, was outraged at this charge of cowardice. Removing the medal that hung around his neck he haughtily replied that he could think of no higher praise for a divisional commander.[65] Streich had in turn outraged Rommel, when the latter discovered that Streich had a huge cardboard Knight's Cross in his command post with a fly in the centre in place of a swastika. The honour was awarded each day to the staff officer who killed the most flies. This was not the sort of thing to amuse a man with a boundless obsession with orders and decorations.[66] General Streich and Colonel Olbricht, the commander of 5 Panzer Regiment, were 'sent for a camel ride' back to Germany as scapegoats, while Rommel continued to hammer away at Tobruk.[67] Back in Sossen at OKH Halder was relieved to learn that the situation had improved on the Sollum front, but doubted that the renewed attack on Tobruk would be successful.[68]

Kirchheim was even more outspoken in his criticism of Rommel than was Streich. In late April he joined the chorus of complaint, writing to Halder deprecating his style of command:

> For days Rommel has given none of us a clear report. I feel, however, that the thing has gone from bad to worse. It appears from the reports of officers coming from the front, as well as from personal letters, that Rommel is in no way up to his command duties. All day long he races about between his widely scattered forces, ordering raids and dissipating his troops. No one at all has a general overview of the distribution of his forces and of their fighting strength ... partial advances by weak Panzer forces have resulted in substantial losses ... Rommel's senseless demands cannot be met by air freight, because we lack enough fuel for the aircraft sent to North Africa to be able to fly home ...[69]

A large number of officers in the Afrikakorps greatly resented Rommel's constant interference at the tactical level, his countermanding of their orders and abusive behaviour. This was very much against the tradition of the German army in which commanders issued broad mission statements, leaving tactical decisions to the men at the front, who could then react quickly to the situation as it developed.

Some years after the war Streich wrote to Kirchheim:

> From my point of view Rommel was turned into a symbol of German military virtues, thanks first to Goebbels' propaganda, then by Montgomery and finally, after he had

*taken poison, by the former enemy powers. His qualities as
a leader were glorified, as were aspects of his character such
as gentlemanly conduct, generosity and humility... Any
open criticism of a personality that had been elevated to
such mystical heights was considered as harmful to the
image of the German soldier.*[70]

Somewhat surprisingly Paulus, who reached Rommel's headquarters on 27 April, felt that the supply situation was adequate, and
having carefully examined the overall situation gave his blessing to
the offensive two days later, even though he had serious reservations
about leaving the Sollum front so weak, troops having been withdrawn
from this section of the front to lend support to the attack on Tobruk.
He reported back to OKH that the Sollum–Bardia front was the key to
maintaining the siege of Tobruk. He pointed out that although previous
attacks on Tobruk had not been successful, losses had been compara-
tively light, although on 14 April 16 Panzer had been lost and a large
part of 8 Machinegun Battalion had been taken prisoner. Nevertheless,
the new plan that called for a mass attack on a narrow front looked
promising. There was plenty of ammunition. The Luftwaffe support had
been strengthened by a fighter group at Ain el Gazala. Although Rommel complained about the Italians, Paulus was particularly impressed
by their corps artillery commander. He was further strengthened in his
optimistic assessment of the situation by the German divisional commanders, who were fully confident that the attack would be a success.[71]
Halder, who felt that Rommel had hoodwinked Paulus, made the following laconic note in his diary: 'I think he is wrong.'[72]

The attack began at 1815hrs on 30 April when Stukas bombed
the southern slopes of Ras el Mdauur. Shortly thereafter they attacked
the northern slopes. The Australians did not seem to be unduly concerned, answering with a brief artillery barrage aimed at the Brescia and
Trento Divisions in the mistaken belief that they were spearheading the
attack. At 1915hrs assault troops from 15 Panzer Division, the Holtzendorff Group, and the Kirchheim Group, supported by 2 Machinegun
Battalion, broke through the Australian defences, reaching the top of
Ras el Mdauur by 2015hrs, but although they managed to beat off a
series of determined counterattacks, they were unable to dislodge the
Australians from their positions on the southern slopes. Further troops
were brought up during the night to support an easterly thrust, but
the Ariete and Brescia Divisions lost their way and did not join in the

engagement. They suffered heavy casualties, largely because they were inexperienced troops who were thrown into the battle as soon as they landed, without being properly briefed and with no knowledge of the terrain. On the left flank the Holtzendorff Group was unable to break through the defences, so that Rommel had to halt Kirchheim's advance towards Tobruk in order to give Holtzendorff's men a helping hand. By dawn they had managed to take Point 182, a crossroads 1.5 kilometres east of Ras el Mdauur. They had broken through the defences, 15 Panzer Division to the left, Kirchheim's Group to the right, and were flailing around in the bridgehead in the morning mist, while subjected to intense artillery fire. Further progress was halted by a minefield as well as heavy fire on the flank. Rommel arrived on the scene at 0900hrs, first ordering the Kirchheim Group to push on regardless, so as to catch up with 15 Panzer Division, which was pressing on in the direction of Pilastrino, about halfway to Tobruk. Almost immediately the order was countermanded. The Kirchheim Group was now ordered to wheel to the southeast to soften up the defences that were halting the advance of the Ariete Division. They managed to clear out several bunkers on the perimeter defences, in spite of a series of tank attacks, but by the morning of 1 May they were exhausted. Neither the Ariete nor the inexperienced and ill-trained Brescia Division was able to contribute much to the attack, even when they finally got into position. Meanwhile on the Sollum front the Herff Group was ordered to carry out an 'offensive defence' to the south-west of Sollum, in order to take the pressure off Tobruk, while the artillery pounded the British positions in the valley below Point 191.[73]

Paulus, who was still at the front keeping an eye on Rommel, was quick to realise that he had been misguided in his assessment of the situation. On 1 May he insisted that a halt be made until fresh troops and supplies could be brought up to the front. The troops were exhausted; there was a heavy sandstorm, and virtually no reserves.[74] Almost half the men were suffering from dysentery. Among the sufferers were Lieutenant Bucher, who was serving in a motorcycle battalion, and his runner, Wievelhofe. They decided to wash their trousers with what was left of the morning coffee and hang them out to dry. Shrapnel from a shell tore the garments to shreds, leaving the two trouserless for two days.[75]

Rommel reluctantly agreed to a pause and waited impatiently to go back on the attack. Although the attack had failed, he insisted on leaving Kirchheim's two battalions inside the British defensive positions, even though they were exceedingly hard pressed. To add to their misery most of the men were sick.[76] The Afrikakorps had made a dent in the British defences 4 kilometres wide and 3 kilometres deep in which they were installed in bunkers that afforded them a much better defensive position. Rommel hoped that he could stay put for three to four weeks, bring in reserves and supplies, and improve the transportation network before continuing with the attack. Then in the afternoon of 2 May Paulus handed his friend written instructions to the effect that the Afrikakorps was far too weak to mount a successful attack, and that the offensive should only resume in the unlikely event that the British withdrew their troops. Gariboldi had complained that he did not have enough transport to bring his rear echelon troops up to the front. Supplies were running short, in large part because the sea routes to Tripoli and Benghazi were far from secure. The Afrikakorps had used up a large amount of ammunition during the offensive and replenishment would take a considerable amount of time. Tripoli was coming under heavy fire as a result of Allied superiority in the air and at sea. The coastal route from Tripoli to Benghazi was also under heavy attack. The Sollum front was so weak that it might well collapse, leaving the Afrikakorps in an exceedingly dangerous situation. Rommel was now told that he was to hang on to Cyrenaica 'with or without Tobruk, Bardia or Sollum'.[77] He was ordered to prepare a defensive line from Ain el Gazala to Got el Ahmer. A further assessment of whether or not to attack Tobruk was to be made once the remainder of 15 Panzer Division arrived at the front. Paulus' memorandum was endorsed by OKH the following day, and Rommel was told that he was not to resume the offensive without the express permission of his commander-in-chief.[78]

Paulus was nevertheless very impressed by the performance of the Afrikakorps. They had managed with relatively weak forces to break through the strongest positions in the defences, and the operation could well have been successful had there been sufficient reserves. Rommel's feints, particularly by creating clouds of dust to suggest a Panzer attack, had done much to fool Morshead as to where the main attack would fall.

For the moment Rommel had his hands full with the Australians launching a robust counterattack in brigade strength in an attempt to regain Ras el Mdauur. Even though the Germans were desperately short

of ammunition they managed to hold on. Paulus, who left the front on
7 May, having discussed the situation with the commanding general
of 10 Air Corps and with the Afrikakorps quartermaster-general, came
to the conclusion, as he reported back to OKH, that: 'The problem
is not with Tobruk or Sollum, but with supplies.'[79] To overcome this
problem the sea lanes from Sicily to Tripoli would have to be secured,
as well as the supply lines to Benghazi, but it was difficult to see how
10 Air Corps could manage this task, given that it was fully committed
in Greece and Crete. As long as Malta remained in British hands the
Mediterranean was under their control, but could this island fortress
ever be taken?

The German forces in North Africa needed 40,000–50,000 tons
of supplies per month, of which the Afrikakorps required about 30,000
tons. In addition the Italians, both civil and military, needed 100,000
tons. This colossal requirement was far beyond the capacity of Libya's
ports. Tripoli could handle about 45,000 tons per month, while Benghazi could only manage 35,000 tons. To make matters even worse,
Benghazi initially had neither anti-aircraft guns nor coastal defences,
so the harbour was left defenceless. It was also impossible to relieve
the supply problem to the front by coastal shipping, because most of
the suitable vessels were in use in Greece. As the German admiral in
charge of transport to North Africa tersely remarked at the end of May:
'All considerations about further operations in North Africa, as well as
the supply of the Afrikakorps, must be determined by the fact that the
eastern Mediterranean will continue to be completely dominated by the
English fleet.' Another major problem was that Libya was a poverty-
stricken colony without an industrial base, so that virtually everything
had to be imported. The workforce was unreliable and undisciplined,
panicking at the first sign of an attack, and often refusing to return to
work when the all clear sounded. Rommel simply refused to address
these problems and persisted in demanding the impossible.[80]

The Afrikakorps' supply difficulties grew steadily worse. An
RAF raid on Benghazi on 1 May put the main dock out of commission
for several weeks. Two days later an assignment of bombs for the
Luftwaffe went off while they were being unloaded in Tripoli, resulting
in the loss of two freighters, the damaging of two others, as well as
serious damage to the docks. A large number of Arabs prudently left
the town, so that there was a shortage of dockers. In the following days
the Royal Navy attacked Benghazi, causing considerable damage and

sinking two freighters. All OKH could do to improve the situation was to offer 1,500 trucks from Tunisia, bought from the Vichy government, plus thirty-six batteries of French coastal artillery ranging from 7.5 to 22cm; 5 Light Division was to be converted into a Panzer division and light shipping would be released for service along the coast.[81] Encouraged by Vichy's response, Hitler invited Admiral Darlan for discussions on 11 May, in the hope that he would agree to let the Axis use the port of Bizerta. Additional port facilities were essential if the Axis troops were to be effectively supplied. Darlan initially agreed, but hastily back-peddled, so that nothing was shipped through Bizerta until the Axis seized the port in late 1942.[82]

Paulus returned home via Rome, where the Comando Supremo was unable to give him any comfort, and he gave OKH a pessimistic assessment of his trip to North Africa. His report, dated 11 May, was sharply critical of Rommel's leadership style and argued that the general had seriously misjudged the situation in North Africa. He found Rommel's publicity-hunting, his courting of war correspondents and cameramen, distinctly distasteful and unsoldierly.[83] He insisted that a renewed attack on Tobruk was out of the question, given the chronic logistical problems and the superiority of the enemy's forces. The most that could be hoped for was to avoid 'a severe crisis'. In order to achieve this, Paulus suggested sending a group of destroyers to protect convoys to North Africa that should now go to Benghazi rather than Tripoli in order to shorten the lines of communication to the front. It took a three-ton Opel 'Blitz' truck fourteen days to make the return journey from Tripoli to Tobruk. With an average fuel consumption of 25 litres per 100 kilometres a truck needed, under the harsh African conditions, at least 75 litres to cover its daily run of 242 kilometres. This meant that the monthly requirement for the fleet of 3,667 trucks amounted to 8,250,760 litres, or 5,776 tons.[84] This was all part of what was to be called the 'rubber band effect' that bedevilled both sides in the Desert War. Forward positions rebounded, because supply lines were overstretched.

Paulus further suggested that a group of Stukas and fighters should be sent to the central Mediterranean to attack British shipping. French trucks from Tunisia should be allotted to the Axis forces in North Africa.[85] Meanwhile, given the strength of the British defences at Tobruk and the blistering summer heat, Rommel should give up the siege and pull all the troops back to a defensive line at Ain el

Gazala, where they could be refreshed and replenished. Paulus placed the blame for the dangerous situation in North Africa squarely on Rommel's shoulders. For him the problem was no longer Tobruk, Sollum or even supplies, but Rommel.[86] Paulus' devastating assessment of Rommel was confirmed when OKH finally obtained a map detailing his positions. His forces were spread out all over the place, indication that he was conducting a campaign that Halder described as 'not to be judged by European standards'. The loss of 53 officers and 1,187 men at Tobruk was considered unacceptably high.[87] Halder, who had developed a hearty loathing for Rommel, having listened to Paulus' report on his trip to North Africa, wrote in his diary: 'By exceeding his orders, Rommel has created a situation which has outstripped his supply capability at this time. Rommel is not up to the job.'[88] It was beyond Halder's comprehension that a commander should send troops into an attack at night without any knowledge of the enemy's positions. Rommel pooh-poohed Halder's remarks, insisting that the Afrika-korps' heavy losses were entirely a result of poor training. He managed to persuade both Mussolini and Hitler that Gariboldi, Paulus and Halder were misguided and that he should stay put on the Sollum Line. Successes there in the battles in mid-May and June were to lend force to his argument, helping to paint his detractors in the dictators' eyes as pusillanimous desk-bound warriors.

4 ✠ COUNTERATTACK

Rommel, who argued that the Italians would be incapable of a fighting withdrawal along a single route under constant attack from the air and from the sea, now decided to use his non-motorised troops to besiege Tobruk, so as to thwart a breakout, hold the Sollum Line and remain in Bardia. His motorised forces would be at the ready to deal with a British attack. But for the moment his troops were far too thin on the ground. The Sollum Line was little more than an outpost. Even though Herff's brilliant attack had succeeded in taking the Halfaya Pass, it was doubtful whether his troops would be able to withstand a concentrated British attack. The pass was only held by a German infantry battalion, a handful of 88s and an Italian artillery battery. Rommel also wanted to establish a defensive line at Gazala to the west of Tobruk, to meet the eventuality of the British breaking through the Sollum defences, but it was difficult to see how he could withdraw non-motorised troops without further weakening the overstretched defences at Tobruk and Sollum. At least he had now been forced to admit that he did not have sufficient forces to take Tobruk.[1]

The situation was also worrisome for the British. Rommel had trumped all Wavell's victories. At the British embassy in Cairo Sir Miles Lampson wrote in his diary on 29 May: 'I don't think I have ever seen our Archie look quite so gloomy.'[2] Even the habitually cool and taciturn Wavell was beginning to feel the strain. His forces were well entrenched in Tobruk, their artillery enhanced by guns captured from the Italians during the recent attack, but they would face serious difficulties if Rommel decided to fight in the desert. The bridgehead through the perimeter defences was a permanent problem, and for weeks to come there was fierce fighting as the Australians attempted to besiege the besiegers. Wavell had virtually no tanks under his command, and those that he had were mostly obsolete models in need of extensive repairs. Wildly inaccurate intelligence reported that 15 Panzer Division had 400 Panzer.[3] Churchill decided to rectify this situation immediately. He gave orders for Operation 'Tiger', a convoy bringing 295 tanks and 53 Hurricanes to Egypt, which was to sail through the Mediterranean, rather than round the Cape, thus saving forty days. The convoy set sail from Gibraltar on 6 May and lost one freighter with fifty-seven tanks and ten Hurricanes when it hit a couple of mines. The Italian navy, licking its wounds after its previous engagements with the Royal Navy, had no stomach for an attack. This left the Stukas of 10 Air Corps to do their best. They managed to hit a British destroyer on the convoy's return voyage.

Life for the Axis troops in the Tobruk bridgehead was sheer misery. Their defensive positions were mostly little more than shallow troughs scraped in the scree that offered precious little protection and increased the danger of injury from ricocheting stones during a bombardment. They were exposed to full sunlight with temperatures of 40 °C at midday, dropping rapidly to 10 °C in the evening. Water, food and ammunition were all in short supply. Lance-Corporal H. E., serving in the artillery at Tobruk, complained to his wife that 'Our food is bad and there is far too little of it. In the morning we get a tin of sardines or a piece of bread and cheese. Then we get nothing for the rest of the day until the evening, when we get a bowl of soup. That's all we get.' Lieutenant A. F. at Tobruk longed for the fortress to fall so that he could lay his hands on some booty. 'Here we have absolutely nothing, not even water.'[4] The wounded and their replacements could be moved only at night. There were no latrines, men had to relieve themselves in situ, resulting in an infestation of flies, so that most of the men suffered from acute diarrhoea. Sand fleas that buried into the flesh were a cause of much misery. But worst of all was the sand that got into every orifice. Combined with filthy clothing it caused serious lesions known as desert sores. Sand under the foreskin was extremely painful, causing an infection that was rumoured to lead to impotence.[5] A New Zealand medical officer performed numerous circumcisions on sufferers, but there is no record of German doctors performing such an ideologically suspect operation.

The British were heartened when they managed to decipher Paulus' report to OKH on the situation in North Africa. Churchill ordered Wavell to go on the offensive as soon as the 'Tiger' convoy arrived, commenting that 'Those Hun people are far less dangerous once they lose the initiative.'[6] Wavell, who also saw the wisdom of attacking before 15 Panzer Division was in full strength, ordered Gott, now promoted to lieutenant-general, to go on the offensive with his armoured force at Sollum, supported by Lieutenant-General Beresford-Pierce's Western Desert Force, in Operation 'Brevity' as soon as 'Tiger' docked, and even before the new tanks could be brought up to the front. Churchill was delighted with this plan, which he hoped would greatly improve Britain's position in the entire Middle East.

Gott had been allotted an exceptionally difficult task. His troops were sparse, his equipment obsolete. On the high ground to the south-west he had 7th Armoured Brigade Group with 29 Cruiser tanks, which was to press on to Sidi Azeiz. To their right, 22nd Guards Brigade Group, with twenty-four support tanks, was to take Fort Capuzzo and seize the high ground above the Halfaya Pass, while a coastal group, consisting of an infantry brigade and an artillery regiment positioned on the low ground by the sea, was to push through the Halfaya Pass and move up to Sollum.[7]

The opposing forces, consisting merely of a company of motor-cycle infantry, an anti-tank company, a motorised reconnaissance group, an anti-aircraft battery and a battalion of Italians, was under the capable command of Colonel Max von Herff. But German field intelligence, having intercepted British signals, knew that an attack was pending, so this modest force was reinforced on 8 May by a Panzer squadron that was held in reserve.[8] Herff followed Rommel's orders to the letter, raiding deep into Egyptian territory, creating the impression that he had an impressive force at his command. At one point a battle group penetrated some 50 kilometres across the border.

Herff was expecting an attack for some days, but his guard was down when it finally began on 15 May, owing to the skilfully dis-guised movement of troops up to the front. The attack was initially a success: 7th Armoured Brigade Group reached Sidi Azeiz, well beyond Fort Capuzzo, which was taken by the Guards, who also took the high ground above the Halfaya Pass as planned. The coastal group moved up to the entrance of the pass. Herff launched a vigorous coun-terattack against the Guards Armoured Brigade at Fort Capuzzo, but he was forced back, having inflicted heavy casualties. His attempt to regain the Halfaya Pass failed. The 1st Durham Light Infantry put up a plucky fight at Fort Capuzzo against 15 Motorcycle Battalion, but

9. Transport column moves up a winding pass

was eventually overwhelmed, losing twenty-nine dead and sixty-four prisoners. Gott then decided to move the Guards to the Halfaya Pass and to keep 7th Armoured Division Group at Sidi Azeiz, thus leaving them in a dangerously exposed situation. After further consideration he felt it prudent to withdraw 7th Armoured and concentrate on the Halfaya Pass. Herff remained deeply concerned about the situation at Sidi Azeiz, having received erroneous intelligence reports of British strength. Rommel was far better informed, telling Herff that the British were much weaker than he imagined, and urging him to attack with everything he had.

Herff was soon in hot pursuit, as far as his petrol supplies allowed, throwing in his reserve armour and catching up with the retreating British forces at Sidi Suleiman, some 15 kilometres west of the British starting line. Although the British were still able to hang on to the Halfaya Pass, Operation 'Brevity' was a failure that lived up to its name. It was decided to wait until the new tanks, Churchill's 'tiger cubs', were ready for service and new divisions had arrived, before attacking again. The secret of the German success was the extremely effective use of 88mm anti-aircraft weapons (Flak), which with their high muzzle velocity were also extremely effective as anti-tank guns (Pak). The Germans had recovered quickly from the initial shock, but were fully cognisant of their own weaknesses. Rommel sent further reinforcements from Tobruk to the Sollum front, including units from 15 Panzer Division, and on 27 May Halfaya Pass was once again in German hands in Operation 'Scorpion', thanks once again to Herff's inspiring leadership. That this key position had been lost placed the British at a severe disadvantage when they launched their 'Battleaxe' offensive in mid-June.[9]

Rommel began to establish strong defensive positions around the Halfaya Pass. The bulk of 15 Panzer Division, now at full strength, was brought up to the frontier and placed in reserve between Bardia and Fort Capuzzo. Three infantry battalions and a couple of artillery battalions remained behind at Ras el Mdauur, while 5 Light Division was moved up from Tobruk to act as a mobile reserve. A key role was allotted to the skilful deployment of the deadly 88 anti-tank guns in concealed emplacements. Italian pioneers and labour battalions built a 75 kilometre long 'Axis Road' along the length of the front in a remarkably short time, considering the gruelling heat. Rommel was a master of armoured warfare, not only in the offensive ('sword'), but also in the defensive ('shield'). He was always at his best when in a tight spot, especially one of his own making. The Afrikakorps reinforced Points 206 and 208 in the desert to the west of the Halfaya Pass, while the Italians strengthened Fort Capuzzo, Musaid and Sollum. The work was greatly hindered as long as Tobruk, which blocked the Via Balbia, was still in British hands. This coastal road, or 'Litoranea', named after the governor-general of Libya, Air Marshal Italo Balbo, which stretched for 1,820 kilometres from the Tunisian border to Tripoli, Misurata, Sirte, Benghazi, Derna and Tobruk, and all the way to the Egyptian frontier at Sollum, was completed in 1937. All supplies had to be brought across the open desert, with light vehicles getting stuck in the sand and trucks making painfully slow progress. The Italians saw the need for a ring road, but did nothing about it.[10]

The forces were deployed so as to tempt the British into an attack, which was expected at any moment.[11] Their armour would be crippled by the 88s, the infantry submitted to heavy artillery fire, and they would be forced to break up into smaller groups that would be picked off one by one in a series of counterattacks by the mobile reserves. The major problem was still that of supplies. Benghazi had to be protected, the coast secured, and the British had to be stopped from reinforcing Tobruk.[12]

10. Soldiers from the Afrikakorps

The Germans, imagining that they would soon be in Egypt, stepped up their propaganda efforts at this time. Konstantin von Neurath, the son of the former foreign minister, who had been appointed liaison officer between the foreign office and the Afrikakorps (VAA) in May 1941, set up a propaganda company that prepared pamphlets on the 'racial question' for the enlightenment of the Arabs. They proclaimed that 'all people are God's people, except for the corrupt and parasitic Jews'. Neurath announced, in Germany's name, that 'We have the warmest possible sympathy for your struggle against the English and the Jews, and God willing will soon give you more than sympathy.' Germany had already shown the way forward, having become fed up with countless Jews, who 'as professors, lawyers, artists, doctors, as well as industrialists and businessmen are like maggots in the national flesh', and had taken appropriate measures to remove this deadly threat to national well-being.[13]

Neurath was assisted by two specialists in Arab affairs, Dr Hermann and Dr Hans Winkler. They acted as intelligence officers, assisting Rommel's intelligence officer (Ic) to whom Neurath formally reported, by analysing British radio traffic, including news reports. They also proved useful by allowing the Afrikakorps to use the VAA transmitter when their codebooks were captured, leaving them without a direct radio contact with Berlin.[14]

The Germans had no reliable agents in Egypt, but German counter-intelligence (Abwehr) was busy trying to smuggle agents into the country. Operation 'Condor', an attempt to drop two Germans into Egypt by air in July 1941, failed, but they tried again in 'Salaam' in early 1942. This time they managed to drop two radio operators from the Brandenburg Regiment, Hanns (John) Eppler and Hans-Gerd Sandstede, known as 'Sandy'. Both men, who spoke excellent Arabic and English, were ordered to contact influential Egyptians who were sympathetic to the German cause, particularly the former chief of the general staff, Aziz Ali el-Misri. To this end they were provided with a letter of introduction from the Mufti. The two men eventually reached Cairo in May, after an adventurous journey over 2,000 kilometres, led by the Hungarian Count Ladislaus Almasy, an outstanding desert explorer,[15] but their mission was a failure. Eppler had spent most of his life in Alexandria, where his German mother had married a wealthy Egyptian. He was made a Muslim and given the name Hussein Gafaar. He therefore reverted to his Muslim identity, whereas 'Sandy' posed as an American by the name of Peter Monkaster. Eppler was more interested in returning to his life as a pampered playboy than he was in espionage, but the two men managed to meet a few prominent Egyptians and to establish radio contact with Berlin, thanks to the help of a signals officer by the name of Anwar Sadat, who was greatly shocked by the whiskey and belly dancers that played a prominent role in Eppler's debauched lifestyle. Eppler's favourite Mata Hari was the voluptuous Hekmat Fahmi, the luscious star of the Kit-Kat Club where prominent Cairenes, including the king, relaxed. In July Eppler and Sandstede were arrested by the British.[16] The Abwehr had provided them with a large quantity of five-pound notes, even though the troops in Egypt were paid in Egyptian pounds. This, combined with the fact that one of Eppler's many girlfriends was in the pay of Field Security, led to their downfall. The two men escaped being shot because Sadat would also have had to have been executed. Killing an Egyptian officer was felt to be altogether too provocative in the tense atmosphere of July 1942, so he was stripped of his rank and sent to jail.[17]

Meanwhile, the Germans were well advised to get a move on rather than wait until November, because Churchill was continually pestering Wavell to go on the offensive as soon as humanly possible. Having captured Crete on 1 June, Germany had air supremacy over the Ionian and Aegean seas, threatening the Levant as well as the bases of the Mediterranean fleet. Benghazi and Derna could now be used to supply Rommel, who had retaken Cyrenaica. In a secret session of the House of Commons the prime minister had warned of the grim possibility of losing Egypt, Palestine, Cyprus and Malta, and thus control over the Mediterranean.[18] On the other hand, signals intelligence (Sigint) had provided details of Rommel's supply difficulties, and the news that he was stocking up with siege artillery in Tunisia suggested that he was not ready for yet another attack on Tobruk. British Military Intelligence therefore assumed that Rommel would not go on the offensive until the end of October.[19] A reconstituted K Force, consisting of the cruisers *Aurora* and *Penelope*, along with two destroyers, began operations from Malta on 21 October. Armed with excellent intelligence they wrought havoc on Axis shipping in the ensuing weeks, further disrupting Rommel's plans. The Photographic Reconnaissance Unit (PRU) based in Malta, using stripped-down Spitfires, was perhaps less glamorous, but it provided more useful intelligence than Ultra, as a result of which between 18 October and 18 December not a single

Axis ship reached North Africa. Rommel was able to keep going only because adequate stocks of fuel, ammunition and provisions had been laid in before the attack on Tobruk began.[20] Yet in spite of Rommel's supply difficulties and intense pressure from above, Wavell felt obliged to procrastinate, much to the prime minister's mounting fury. Most of the tanks delivered in 'Tiger' were still not ready for action. They were mostly the new model of Crusader with which the tank crews of 'Desert Rats' in 7th Armoured Division had to become familiar. Churchill had sent Britain's most modern tanks to the Middle East, but these Matildas and Crusaders were not a serious challenge to the Panzer IVs. The Matilda with its heavy armour was extremely difficult to kill, but it was painfully slow and far too lightly armed. It had a very short range and lacked high-explosive shells to use against infantry.[21] The Crusader was much faster, but more lightly armoured, under-gunned, and was plagued by mechanical failure. Wavell pointed out to Churchill that his tanks were too slow, unreliable and lightly armed to be of much use. Furthermore, the Desert Rats, who had not seen action since beating the Italians at Beda Fomm, had been without tanks during the six subsequent months. Churchill had also ordered Wavell to drive the Vichy French forces out of Syria, clear Iran of German influences, get rid of Rashid Ali and the junta of colonels in Iraq, as well as deal with the situation in Crete. He was thus left short of forces for a major offensive in the Western Desert, so Rommel was given time to improve his defences. Churchill impatiently seized upon some very patchy information from Ultra to goad the reluctant Wavell into action.[22]

Operation 'Battleaxe' was thus hastily improvised and launched with insufficient forces, thanks to Churchill's constant meddling. Once again Rommel's excellent field intelligence served him well, providing him with detailed information of British intentions, gleaned from wireless telegraphy and captured documents.[23] Lieutenant-General Sir Noel Beresford-Pierce's Western Desert Force was made up of two divisions, 4th Indian Division with 11th Indian and 22nd Guards Brigade, supported by 4th Armoured Brigade. Two divisions were lacking: one was in Syria, and the other was in the process of being moved from East Africa. The 7th Armoured Division was also undermanned, with 7th Armoured Brigade consisting of two rather than three regiments, one of which was still equipped with obsolete Crusaders.

Beresford-Pierce's operational plan for 'Battleaxe' amounted to little more than a warmed-up version of 'Brevity', admittedly on a much larger scale. It was precisely what the Germans expected: 11th Indian Infantry Brigade with some armoured support was to move up to the Halfaya Pass, while 4th Armoured Brigade and 22nd Guards Brigade were to seize Fort Capuzzo and Point 206. To their left 7th Armoured Brigade was to overrun Point 208, known to the British as Hafid Ridge, while a support group was to secure the left flank at Sidi Omar. The heavy tanks of 4th Armoured Brigade were first to attack the German forces south of Bardia and then move to the left flank to join 7th Armoured Division at Sidi Azeiz, pressing on to Tobruk. It was hoped that the Desert Rats would tempt the Panzer into a tank battle into which 4th Armoured Division would be thrown. The British had about 100 support tanks and 90 Crusaders while the Afrikakorps only had 50 Panzer at the front, with 67 in reserve at Tobruk. The British had absolute air superiority with 203 machines against 101, although 10 Air Corps was to bring up reinforcements in the course of the battle.[24]

After an initial success in the centre, overrunning two batteries The Afrikakorps was well prepared to meet the attack when it began on 15 June, the British using the same codeword 'Peter' that they had used when launching 'Brevity'. All units were ready at 0500hrs on 15 June, and part of 5 Light Division had been brought forward to protect the eastern flank of the Axis forces at Tobruk. Rommel decided to remain at Tobruk, largely because he was concerned that the Australians might attempt to break out of the fortress. This created a serious problem during the ensuing battle. Rommel and his staff, who were 150 kilometres away from the command post at the front, had little idea of what was going on, because the two divisions only had one signals company apiece.

After an initial success in the centre, overrunning two batteries of artillery south of Fort Capuzzo, and taking point 206, the British were soon in serious difficulties. The coastal group lost fifteen of its eighteen tanks at the Halfaya Pass, and on the left flank 7th Armoured Brigade took a terrible beating at Point 208 where they were left with only forty-eight of ninety tanks still operational. The Italians had built a network of emplacements at Point 208, the site of an Arab burial ground, so that the guns were invisible to within twenty metres. With a battery of anti-tank guns it was a formidable obstacle, blocking the way to Bardia. The 88mms with their 16lb shells could blow the turrets off the new Matilda Mark II tanks in spite of their heavy armour, while a machinegun group picked off the infantry. 15 Panzer Division sent

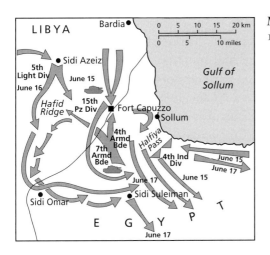

Map 4. 'Battleaxe', 15 June 1941

its 8 Panzer Regiment to strengthen the defence in the centre. It was under the command of Captain Johannes Kümmel, who was to knock out six Mark IIs, thereby earning the Knight's Cross plus the nickname the 'Lion of Capuzzo'.[25] Rommel, sensing that the Australians would remain in Tobruk, sent 5 Light Division to Sidi Azeiz. But it was with considerable difficulty that the Afrikakorps was able to hold a hastily improvised defensive line outside Bardia. This encouraged Beresford-Pierce to order 4th Indian Division to seize the Halfaya Pass and take Bardia on the following day, while 7th Armoured Division, supported by 4th and 7th Armoured Brigades, was to take Point 208.

There was some confusion among the Germans as to how to respond: 15 Panzer Division wanted to concentrate on regaining Fort Capuzzo, while the commander of 5 Light Division ordered an attack along the British left flank by sweeping down to Sidi Omar and Sidi Suleiman. The German counterattack was thus diffused, so that 15 Panzer Division, unable to take Fort Capuzzo, even after three attempts, was withdrawn and joined in with 5 Light Division's flank attack. Rommel later wrote that this was the decisive move that won the battle.[26] Beresford-Pierce was unaware of this threat to his left flank and planned to bring up 4th Armoured Brigade to support 7th Armoured Division, so as to knock out the Panzer, but by the evening of 16 June the British 7th Armoured Brigade had been forced back and was left with only twenty-one tanks, whereupon Major-General Sir Frank Messervy, commanding 4th Indian Division, ordered 22nd Guards Brigade to withdraw from Fort Capuzzo, thus frustrating Rommel's attempt to cut them off. The determined efforts of British armour at Sidi Suleiman held up the Afrikakorps' flanking movement, and covered the withdrawal. Shortage of fuel and ammunition made further pursuit impossible.

Major-General Walther Neumann-Silkow, commanding 15 Panzer Division, and Major-General Johannes von Ravenstein, commanding 5 Light Division, were relatively inexperienced in desert warfare and were partly to blame for allowing the British to escape. The divisions had yet to master the art of marching through the desert, day and night, ready for both offence and defence. This was something they were to perfect during the winter, when their 3.7cm anti-tank guns were gradually replaced by the 5cm model, their artillery strengthened, signals significantly improved and communications at last established with the Luftwaffe. Rommel characteristically placed all the blame on their tactical blunders, whereas he was the real culprit with his refusal to give one of the divisional commanders overall command, plus his insistence on managing the battle from Tobruk, even though his lines of communication were seriously deficient. Rommel imagined that they had missed an opportunity to cut off the British between the Halfaya Pass and the sea, but in fact the bulk of the Western Desert Force had retired to the south. Halder consoled himself with the thought that German losses were considerably less than at Tobruk.[27] Perhaps the most important outcome of the battle was that the Comando Supremo was impressed by Rommel's performance, even though the victory had been a modest one, and began to realise the need for a unified command. This was soon to be reflected in changes in the command structure in Libya.

The British army had managed to avoid a disaster by withdrawing in time, but suffered severe losses. Ninety-one tanks were destroyed while the Afrikakorps lost only twelve.[28] The loss of aircraft was also disproportionate with thirty-six to ten. But the Axis suffered 586 dead and missing and 691 wounded; the British 381 dead and missing and 588 wounded.[29] To add to the misery on both sides midday temperatures on the battlefield reached 55 °C.[30] The key to the battle was that Halfaya Pass, held by a mere battalion, and Point 208, with little more than a company under the command of a lieutenant, had withstood repeated attacks. This in turn was only possible because the Germans' courage and skill, plus the effectiveness of the 88mm guns, led to the destruction of so many tanks. There seem to have been only five 88s at Halfaya Pass, and four at Point 208, but the 50mm Pak 38 anti-tank guns were also extremely effective. The Germans had mastered the art of using their Panzer against infantry and thin-skinned vehicles, leaving their anti-tank guns to destroy tanks.[31] Halfaya Pass, under the command of Captain Wilhelm Bach, a mild-mannered, unflappable, cigar-smoking Swabian, known to his men as 'Father Bach', who was an evangelical pastor in civilian life, withstood repeated attacks, as did Point 208 under Lieutenant Paulewicz. The Matildas of 4th Armoured Brigade were smashed by Bach's 88s, which were dug in, rendering them invisible up to within fifty metres. The hot desert air at ground level reduced everything in size, as if one were looking through the wrong end of a telescope. The Matildas, inexplicably without high-explosive shells, artillery or air support, were helpless against such infantry positions.[32] These two strongpoints held, enabling Rommel to swing around Point 208 with 5 Light Division and 15 Panzer Division and attack 7th Armoured Division from the rear.

Wavell reported to the prime minister: 'I am sorry to have to report that "Battleaxe" has failed.' Churchill, his fortunes at a low ebb and badly in need of a success to save his political career, having presided over a series of disasters and setbacks and with a number of ambitious politicians eager to have his job, was furious and fired Wavell on 21 June, sending him off to India as commander-in-chief. Churchill unfairly blamed Wavell for abandoning Cyrenaica, for bungling the intervention in Greece and for losing 'Battleaxe', an operation designed to 'destroy' Rommel's army and win a 'decisive victory'. To top it off he had lost most of the tanks that had been sent at considerable risk in Operation 'Tiger'. Air Chief Marshal Sir Arthur Longmore, who agreed wholeheartedly with Wavell that the means were simply not available to realise Churchill's grandiose plans and did not hesitate to say so, was also fired. Rommel also held Wavell in high regard, and was full of praise for his 'strategic courage'. He attributed his failure to the slow speed of his heavy infantry tanks that prevented him from reacting quickly to the faster-moving Panzer. The Mark II (Matilda) tank was to be succeeded by the Mark VI (Crusader), which was fast, reaching speeds of up to 42km/h, but, with only a two-pounder gun, seriously underarmed.[33] Wavell was replaced by General Sir Claude Auchinleck, Longmore by Air Marshal Arthur Tedder. On 28 June Oliver Lyttelton, a loyal supporter of Churchill, was sent to the Middle East as the Cabinet's permanent representative, with the title of minister of state. Germany had invaded the Soviet Union on 22 June, and the war entered a new phase.

Back at the Führer's headquarters there was such confidence that 'Barbarossa' would be a resounding and immediate success that planning went ahead for the period after the defeat of the Soviet Union. The results were adumbrated in the draft of Hitler's Order Number 32 dated 11 June 1941.[34] The British positions in the Mediterranean and western Asia were to be destroyed by converging attacks from Libya through Egypt, from Bulgaria through Turkey, and possibly from Transcaucasia through Iran. In North Africa the first essential task was the elimination of Tobruk. The attack should be mounted in about November, assuming that the Afrikakorps had been provided with sufficient men and matériel, and that 5 Light Division had been converted into a fully armoured division. In order that supplies could be brought up as quickly as possible it would be necessary to use the ports in French North Africa, and if feasible the sea routes from southern Greece. French and neutral shipping would have to be chartered. The possibility of moving motor torpedo boats to the Mediterranean would have to be examined. The commander-in-chief of the Luftwaffe was to transfer as many air units and anti-aircraft batteries to North Africa as possible, once they were no longer needed in the east. Goebbels was somewhat less confident, having begun to get concerned about the fighting at Tobruk, which had become bogged down in positional fighting that reminded him of the previous war. He complained about the miserable quality of the Italian officers, but comforted himself with the thought that Rommel was a real inspiration to both the German and the Italian troops, and that whatever the circumstances, he would not shilly-shally.[35]

Lieutenant-Colonel Klaus von dem Borne, the Afrikakorps' chief of staff, had reported to Hitler and OKH at the beginning of June and returned to North Africa with the impression that at least two more German divisions would be sent to North Africa for this offensive. The main outcome of this visit was that Keitel wrote to Rintelen urging him to point out to Cavallero that logistics was the key problem. The Italians would have to make a far greater effort to guard the sea routes to North Africa, and Rommel had to be given more air support and anti-aircraft guns, as well as heavy and coastal artillery.[36] Halder soon put a damper on the Afrikakorps' hopes of receiving more manpower by announcing that they would only be given minimal reinforcements, since the bulk of the shipping was needed to bring in supplies in preparation for an attack on Tobruk, which he estimated should begin in September, and for an offensive against Egypt, to begin early the following year. The quartermaster-general then estimated that it would take until mid-March 1942 to bring in all the supplies needed for the attack on Egypt, only to revise his estimate shortly thereafter to mid-June.[37]

British planners, assuming that the Soviet Union was unlikely to survive for more than a few months, speculated as to Germany's next move. At the beginning of July the Joint Intelligence Sub-Committee (JIC), assuming that it would all be over by August, argued that the Germans would attack the Middle East via Turkey and Syria, rather than through the Caucasus. The attack would come not earlier than November. Auchinleck was therefore more concerned about strengthening his positions in Syria, Cyprus and Iraq than he was about taking on Rommel, but as the Russians continued to resist the German advance, the threat to his northern front began to diminish.[38]

A memorandum by Paulus dated 2 July 1941 shows that JIC was not far from the mark. It gave the outline for an invasion of Egypt by three divisions, two Panzer and one motorised, via Syria and Palestine, provided that the Turkish government granted permission for German troops to cross its territory. The attack was to coincide with Rommel's offensive against Egypt, planned for November, even though the rainy season, which would make large-scale operations difficult, began at that time and lasted until February. To avoid this problem a Panzer corps should be in position in south-eastern Anatolia by the end of September, so as to be able to begin an attack on Syria in October. In co-operation with French troops in Syria the corps would move south to Haifa, the end point of the oil pipeline. Then they would press on through the Sinai peninsula to the Suez Canal. In early 1942 two Panzer corps from Anatolia and the Caucasus would secure the land bridge to India, from the Nile to the Tigris. Enquiries were begun by OKH's operations section as to whether the necessary troops would be available, and how long it would take them to get acclimatised for service in the desert.[39]

This was followed by a more detailed memorandum by Brauchitsch for OKW on operations after the completion of the campaign in the Soviet Union. These included attacks on Gibraltar and Malta to secure the passage of supplies to North Africa, the capture of Tobruk and an offensive against Egypt. They would coincide with an attack on Egypt via Turkey and Syria, as well as an advance to the Persian Gulf from Turkey and the Caucasus. Brauchitsch, who was uncertain about the feasibility of parachute landings on Malta, was inclined to think that it could be bombed into submission. Ignoring Franco's extreme reluctance to become directly involved, he assumed that Gibraltar could be attacked by artillery stationed in southern Spain. German troops might have to be sent to Ceuta and Tangiers, should the British attempt to retreat to Spanish Morocco. Tobruk remained a problem because Rommel's troops were fighting on two fronts: at Sollum and Tobruk. Logistical problems were also so acute that North Africa would always remain for Germany a sideshow, because the British could supply their troops far more quickly. The main weight of the offensive would therefore be from Anatolia and the Caucasus. Since it was doubtful that the Turks would agree to let German troops cross their territory, a major operation would probably be required against Turkey that could not be mounted before 1942. Only when the Soviet Union had been defeated would it be possible to assemble troops in Romania and Bulgaria, ready to attack Turkey. Reinforcements could be brought in from Thessaloniki and Crete, as well as from the Reich. The attack on the Persian Gulf from the Caucasus and Anatolia would be launched in the spring of 1942, regardless of the attitude of the Turks. Gibraltar, Malta and Tobruk would have to be secured in the previous autumn so as to give Germany control over the Mediterranean.[40]

Confident that victory over the Soviet Union was imminent, on 3 July 1941 Halder once again turned his attention to the next phase in the war. Knocking out 'England' was clearly the top priority. The first phase of the new campaign would be an offensive directed against the area between the Nile and the Euphrates. This would be a two-pronged attack through Anatolia, possibly backed by one from the Caucasus, and from Cyrenaica. The offensive in North Africa would mainly be an Italian affair, supported by two Panzer divisions (5 Light and 15 Panzer), plus a few other German units.[41] The fact that the campaign in North Africa was to be left to the Italians was a reflection of the fact that Halder and OKH gave that theatre low priority, and wanted the wild man Rommel placed under a responsible commander on the spot. From the very outset Halder believed that the logistical problems would be so severe that no large-scale operation would be possible in North Africa. This being the case, the best way to attack Egypt and the

Suez Canal was from the north. This view was widely held by the rank and file of the Afrikakorps. Writing home on 27 June 1941, Lance-Corporal S. K., serving with 15 Panzer Division in Benghazi, was confident that 'The war in Russia will soon be over, then we can continue our advance.'[42]

Writing on 6 July Halder noted that 'the situation at Bardia and Sollum remains continually tense', pointing out that although the British had been beaten off, they were likely to renew the attack with overwhelming forces within a few weeks, while the Afrikakorps would still be short-handed. Estimating that the British would field three divisions with 600 tanks, he very much doubted that the Panzer Group would be able to withstand another offensive. 'Battleaxe' had, after all, been a very close shave.[43] Rommel noted that he was unlikely to obtain much help from OKW 'until the Russian affair is more or less over', and did not see much point in going to see Hitler before then to present his case.[44] OKH insisted that the key to the situation was the capture of Tobruk, which stood in the way of the supply lines from Tripoli to the Sollum front, and without which an advance to Egypt would be virtually impossible. Rommel was therefore asked to produce a detailed plan of attack. Rommel sent in a hastily prepared sketch on 13 July, which ignored OKH's suggestion that he wait until infantry and artillery support arrived, insisting that he could do the job with existing forces, depending on supplies, although he did concede that he would be unlikely to be able to mount the attack before October.[45]

At this time Halder also asked Rommel to provide details of his plans for the future. The result was a detailed memorandum entitled: 'DAK's Thoughts on the Continuation of the Offensive Against Egypt', dated 27 July.[46] Rommel took no heed of OKW's gloomy assessment and had no intention of going on the defensive along the Gazala Line as OKH and the Comando Supremo suggested. He firmly believed that he had given the British army a crippling blow in 'Battleaxe' and that it would be a long time before it would be able to regain the initiative. Convinced that 'Barbarossa' would succeed, he still entertained hopes for a two-pronged attack on the British positions in the Middle East which, combined with mounting unrest in Syria and Iraq, would lead to an easy German victory.[47] He therefore announced that he would first take Tobruk and the Giarabub Oasis. He would then destroy the British positions to the west of Mersa Matruh, following which he would advance along the coastal strip between the Qattara Depression and the sea. These operations should take between four and eight days; he would then immediately advance to Cairo, seizing the bridges to the north and south of the city within three days. The Nile would then be crossed and, depending on the situation, a strong DAK force would press on either to Suez or to Ismalia.

Rommel set totally unrealistic preconditions for the success of this plan. He called for the 'destruction or crippling of the enemy fleet', cutting off British supplies to the Middle East; the protection of the convoys to North Africa; blocking the Suez Canal with mines and sunken vessels; the annihilation of the RAF in the Middle East; plus an intensive air reconnaissance in Egypt. The Luftwaffe was to provide paratroopers to help seize the Nile bridges and a commando force, the Homeyer Group, was to blow up the Aswan Dam. The convoys were no longer to be sent to Tripoli, which was now too far from the front, but were to move up along the coast as the DAK advanced from Benghazi, Derna, Ain el Gazala, Bardia, Sollum, Mersa Matruh, the Gulf of Kennayis and finally Alexandria.

Since the harbours in Cyrenaica were unable to handle larger freighters, Rommel argued that smaller swifter ships, such as motor torpedo boats, should be used to bring in supplies. He continually bombarded Hitler, OKH, Mussolini and the Comando Supremo with requests for more supplies, and proposed that Weichold, an officer whose drive and initiative bordered on arrogant contempt for Germany's main ally, should be given overall command of transport to North Africa. The army's quartermaster-general, General Edouard Wagner, was well aware of the supply problems facing the Panzer Group, having been fully briefed by Captain Schleusener, the Afrika-korps' quartermaster. By 19 July, 5 Light division had so little fuel that it would not be able to go into action on the Sollum front should the British attack. He hoped that it would be possible to send 1,000 tons of fuel from tanks in Brussels. Halder turned down the suggestion that oil could be sent from Romania on the grounds that it would take at least four weeks to reach North Africa. The matter was too urgent to wait that long.[48] In Rome both Rintelen and Weichold were increasingly worried that without drastic measures being taken to secure the sea routes before the end of 'Barbarossa', the situation in North Africa would become seriously compromised. At the beginning of July Rintelen had requested that the Luftwaffe be returned to Sicily, but Skl replied that it was 'absolutely out of the question' that 10 Air Corps could be moved before the end of Barbarossa. Skl made a request to OKW for units of the Italian air force to be moved from the eastern front, but without any sense of urgency.[49] The Italians drew the consequences, calling for a retirement from the Sollum Line, abandoning the encirclement of Tobruk and withdrawing to a defensive position to the west. Rommel argued that the best way to overcome the logistical problems was to seize Tobruk. OKW, in spite of many misgivings, was in broad, if reluctant, agreement.

Rommel visited the Führer's headquarters on 30 July 1941. First he reported to OKH, assuring them that the British would not attack before September. Halder was sceptical, saying that he thought August was far more likely. Hitler was in general agreement with his ideas, although he did make the preposterous suggestion that it might be possible to blockade Tobruk, thus making an attack unnecessary, but most of the meeting was taken up by a characteristic monologue on the triumphant progress of the Wehrmacht against the Jewish-Bolshevik hordes.[50] The only thing new that came from these talks was that OKW agreed to send U-boats and motor torpedo boats to the Mediterranean to guard the convoys to North Africa.[51] Halder felt that this would be a serious mistake, because the losses were likely to be unacceptably high. He was perfectly correct. Fifty per cent of these vessels were either sunk or seriously damaged. The navy also opposed the idea, so that all depended on how Hitler would react to the proposal. Rommel obtained no satisfaction from Mussolini during his visit to Rome on 6 August. The Duce was obsessed with the campaign against the Soviet Union and refused to consider sending more troops to North Africa. He did not think that, given the shortage of supplies, an attack on Tobruk would be successful. He therefore revived the suggestion of defending the Gazala Line and waiting until the defeat of the Soviet Union.

OKH had long been thinking how it could best keep the wayward Rommel under control. When Paulus reported back to Berlin after his trip to North Africa in May, Halder reached the conclusion that a German commander should be placed as an intermediary between the Italian High Command in Tripoli and Rommel, so as to form an Army Group Africa directly under OKH. Hitler, who did not like the idea of his favourite general being placed on a leash, argued that a German staff officer attached to the High Command in Tripoli would be sufficient. OKW, well aware that Halder's suggestion would enable OKH to call the shots in North Africa, dutifully supported the Führer.[52]

OKH agreed that a German general should be posted to Tripoli, to act as a liaison officer between Gariboldi, OKH and Rommel, as well as dealing with logistics for the Afrikakorps once they had arrived. Rintelen would continue to be responsible for sending these supplies. The liaison officer would also be made responsible for coastal defences, harbours, oases and the rear echelon forces. Mussolini and the Comando Supremo approved this idea and Major-General Alfred Gause was sent to North Africa to take up his duties on 10 June. Gariboldi refused to accept Gause and his vast staff of 43 officers, 46 NCOs, 110 men and 20 civil servants along with forty-five motor vehicles, one trailer and eleven motorcycles, five of which had sidecars, arguing that neither he nor Rommel had been consulted. Gariboldi, who was also the governor of Libya, was particularly incensed because the Germans loudly proclaimed their support for the Arab cause, reminding them that they had supported the struggle of the Senussi against the Italians in Libya during the First World War. For Gariboldi, Gause and his men were not only superfluous, they were positively dangerous. The battle at Sollum, which Gause followed from Rommel's headquarters outside Tobruk, took attention away from this vexed problem, but on 23 June Rommel addressed the matter once again in a letter to Brauchitsch. He suggested that since he was to be given command over an Italian corps staff at Tobruk and another at Sollum, in addition to the Afrikakorps, totalling six Italian and two German divisions, Gause should become his liaison officer with Gariboldi. This would be a temporary measure until a German supreme commander was appointed.[53]

Gariboldi naturally enough objected vigorously to the idea of a German supreme commander in North Africa, but General Cavallero and the Comando Supremo approved, provided that Rommel was given the job. Halder and Paulus, horrified by the suggestion, suggested creating a Panzer Group Rommel, placed under an Italian commander-in-chief. Brauchitsch was strongly in favour of such a move.[54] Gause was recalled to Berlin to discuss this proposal. He had been in North Africa for only a few weeks, but confirmed Halder's opinion that Rommel suffered from 'neurotic ambition', reporting that no one dared contradict him, or complain about his brutal and callous behaviour, because of the full support he enjoyed from 'the highest office', in other words from Hitler.[55] After lengthy discussion and much hand wringing, Rommel was appointed commander of the Panzer Group Africa in August, comprising the DAK and the Italian 20 Motorised Corps. The Italian

21 Infantry Corps was originally intended to be included, but was placed directly under the command of General Bastico, the commander-in-chief in Libya and former governor of Rhodes. This officer, whom Rommel nicknamed 'Bombastico', had replaced Rommel's rival, General Gariboldi, on 18 July. He was a lively and talkative man, but a soldier of dubious merit, even though he had gained some experience fighting in Spain and in Greece. Gariboldi, a phlegmatic and inept soldier, went on to preside with characteristic lethargy over the collapse of the Italian army at Stalingrad. Rommel was replaced as commander of the Afrikakorps by Lieutenant-General Ludwig Crüwell, an expert in armoured warfare and a portly and charming man of the world, well known for his love of good food. A highly intelligent man, he got on extremely well with the Italians but did not suffer fools gladly. Having fought on the eastern front he thought that by comparison life in the desert was something of a cushy number. This disdainful manner frequently prompted him to resort to the demotic, as when he referred to the hard-pressed 5 Light Division as 'a pile of shit'.[56] When Major-General Gause was moved to Panzer Group Africa as chief of staff on 1 September, OKH no longer had operational control over the war in Libya. Rommel, having regained Cyrenaica and with the support of Hitler and Mussolini, had won the day.[57]

Rommel was, as Major-General von Mellenthin remarked with characteristic understatement, 'not an easy man to serve'.[58] As a fighting soldier who liked to be up at the front he had a low opinion of staff officers, so he was initially resentful of Gause and his large staff. Rommel expected his chief of staff to come with him up to the front, whereas customary staff practice was for that officer to remain behind and act as a deputy commander during his chief's absence. Rommel's preferred arrangement resulted in both Rommel and his chief of staff being absent from the command post, thus placing a heavy responsibility on the chief of operations (1a). During the 'Crusader' battle in November 1941 Colonel Siegfried Westphal was thus left in charge for six days, often completely out of touch with Rommel and Gause. Westphal was a superb staff officer who felt compelled to countermand one of Rommel's orders at the height of the battle; on his return Rommel generously admitted that he had been absolutely right to do so.

Although Rommel was jovial and open with the men, he was frequently outspoken and abusive with his staff officers. He insisted that he and his staff should share the same rations as the men, which consisted largely of sandwiches and tinned food, mostly sardines. When he was told of the old canard about soldiers frying eggs on the hulls of their tanks, he growled: 'Where the hell did the eggs come from?' The Germans had long since been without coffee and had to make do with a concoction delightfully named 'Muckefuck'. The troops claimed it was made from acorns and called it 'nigger sweat'.[59] British troops were amazed to learn that the Germans treated bully beef as a much-treasured delicacy. The lack of fresh food, fruit and vegetables resulted in Rommel's staff suffering from frequent bouts of what the British army called 'gyppy tummy', often in the form of amoebic dysentery, with a correspondingly large number of officers being hospitalised. There were even a number of cases of scurvy. Senior British officers preferred whenever possible to have their food prepared at Shepheard's Hotel in Cairo and sent up to the front.

The benefits of Rommel leading from the front largely out-weighed the problems caused by his long absences from headquarters. He was audacious, quick to react to new situations, courageous and resourceful. Above all the Afrikakorps was ready to follow him wher-ever he led them, in the full knowledge that he shared all their hardships. Private K. B., a signalman with 15 Panzer Division, spoke for the major-ity of his comrades when he wrote home during the withdrawal from Cyrenaica, saying that he had not the faintest idea what the staff was up to, but he was fully confident that 'Rommel will get it right'.[60]

The net result of this reorganisation was the complete reverse of what Halder and OKH had intended. Rommel's position was greatly strengthened and he enjoyed Hitler's full support as well as that of the Comando Supremo. He had warded off the 'Battleaxe' offensive and thus secured Libya from attack, at least for the time being, enabling Hitler to concentrate on 'Barbarossa', which had begun on 22 June. Hitler promoted Rommel to the rank of General of the Panzer Troops as a sign of his special favour.

On 8 August General Walter Warlimont produced a memoran-dum for OKW entitled 'A Short Overall Strategic View of the Continu-ation of the War after the Eastern Campaign' which was incorporated into a further memorandum endorsed by Hitler on 28 August: 'The Strategic Situation in the Late Summer of 1941 as the Basis for Fur-ther Political and Military Planning.'[61] It was reluctantly admitted that Spain was unlikely to enter the war in the immediate future. There was also merely the faintest hope that Vichy France might be persuaded to permit the Axis the use of the port of Bizerta, which was badly needed to supply the Axis troops in North Africa. Similarly, it was extremely doubtful that Turkey would abandon its neutrality. Perhaps the Turks could be bribed into entering the war by offering them the oilfields of the Caucasus. Were this possible Germany would be relieved of anxiety over oil supplies, the British further challenged in the Middle East and an offensive could be launched in March, or more probably in June through Turkey and Syria. None of this was possible without the defeat of Russia, from which it followed that the stabilisation of the situation in North Africa could not be achieved at the expense of the all-important campaign in the east. A further study by OKH in August was based on the confident assessment that operations in the Soviet Union would soon be concluded, so that this gigantic pincer movement could begin in October. Their Middle East expert, Colonel Otto von Niedermeyer, pointed out that this was the only month when the climatic conditions in all operational areas – Libya, Egypt, Syria, Palestine, Iraq and Iran – were suitable. Postponement until the following spring was inadvisable, given the somewhat precarious position of the Axis troops in North Africa. The conclusion of this detailed study was that the Suez Canal would be in German hands within twelve weeks after the commencement of operations.[62]

Mussolini, accompanied by Ciano and Cavallero, visited Hitler in his 'Wolf's Lair' near Krasno at the end of August. The intention behind the invitation was to persuade the Italians to do more to protect the convoys to North Africa. This was not achieved, leaving the participants hoping that a breakthough in the Caucasus would solve the Axis' immediate problems on the southern periphery.

Meanwhile, the German liaison officers in Rome were growing increasingly pessimistic, and began to wonder whether the Axis would be able to hang on to North Africa until the successful completion of 'Barbarossa'.[63] Weichold reported back to the Naval Counter-Intelligence at Tirpitzufer 74/75 in Berlin that it was becoming almost impossible to replace ships that the British were sinking at an alarming rate, and that waiting until the end of 'Barbarossa' might very well be leaving things too late. OKH blamed the critical situation on the failure of the Italian air force to keep up the pressure on Malta after the withdrawal of 10 Air Corps from Sicily. Rintelen was slightly less concerned, but called for two squadrons of Me110s to protect the convoys, as well as an anti-aircraft and searchlight battery to defend the harbour in Tripoli. The Luftwaffe's general staff were also beginning to have second thoughts about the wisdom of sending 10 Air Corps to Greece, but moving it back to Sicily would mean that it would no longer be possible to raid the Syrian coast and the Suez Canal. The only hope was that 'Barbarossa' would soon be successfully completed. Skl was also becoming increasingly concerned about the heavy losses of shipping between Italy and North Africa, and called for more support from the Luftwaffe, but for the moment nothing could be spared.[64] On 18 August Weichold reported that these losses were creating a desperate situation. Between 27 January and 20 August 1941, thirty-three ships totalling 156,819 GRT had been sunk on routes from Italy to North Africa; twenty-six ships totalling 98,676 GRT had been damaged. On the coastal route from Tripoli to Benghazi, nineteen ships totalling 28,064 GRT had been sunk, while twelve ships of 11,372 GRT altogether were damaged. Italian shipyards were totally incapable of building sufficient replacements. A joint shipbuilding programme with the Germans would not be able to begin until 1942, with the first ships going into service the following year.[65]

With attention focused on 'Barbarossa' all these requests were studiously ignored. The bulk of supplies were still sent to Tripoli, so that the convoys were constantly harassed by aircraft and shipping based on Malta, a base that the British were constantly strengthening. At the end of July the aircraft carriers *Victorious* and *Ark Royal* brought sixty-four fighters to Malta in Operation 'Railway'. At the same time bombers were flown directly from Britain, and 40,000 tons of supplies were delivered in Operations 'Substance' and 'Style'. Malta was bristling with 112 heavy and 118 medium anti-aircraft guns, and was thus a formidable fortress, but the Italians made eleven raids on Valletta and twenty-five on the airfields at Halfar and Imkaba in July and August, in an impressive display of their much-maligned courage. None of this had much effect, and with a skilful combination of air and sea forces the British sank 22,330 GRT of Axis shipping in June, 26,437 GRT in July, and as much as 34,768 GRT in August.[66] The Axis remained either unwilling or unable to find a solution to the problem of Malta, while 'Barbarossa' resulted in both Germany and Italy being critically overextended.[67]

The logistical situation was thus becoming dire, prompting Pohl and Rintelen to renew their appeals to the Luftwaffe to send units back to Sicily and to make a serious effort to eliminate the threat from

Malta. Weichold soon joined in the chorus in an urgent appeal to Skl in early September. Skl gave a very pessimistic assessment of the situation in the Mediterranean, arguing that it would be possible to secure the sea routes to North Africa only when Tobruk had fallen. That still left the question open as to whether it would be possible to land supplies further east, which would be essential 'when we get to Cairo'.[68] Even though OKH was concentrating fully on the campaign in the Soviet Union it was obvious that something had to be done. Rommel sent Alfred-Ingemar Berndt, who had been detached from the propaganda ministry to his staff, to plead on his behalf. Berndt was one of a select group of dashing young men in whose company Rommel took particular pleasure, and with whom he enjoyed bathing naked. Otherwise Rommel was emotionally frigid. He had no close friends and his letters to his wife, to whom he wrote almost daily, are totally without even a hint of affection. Berndt had joined the Nazi Party in 1923 at the age of eighteen and had served in a number of senior positions in the propaganda ministry before being posted to Rommel's staff in 1941. He was to be killed on the eastern front in 1945 while serving as an SS-Brigadeführer. Described by Neurath as 'a fanatical Nazi', he was callous and cunning, but he was also exceptionally brave. He was invaluable to Rommel as a link to Goebbels and the propaganda ministry, which had done so much to inflate Rommel's reputation. Well known for his smooth-talking intelligence and diplomatic skills, as well as his impeccable National Socialist credentials, Berndt was able to gain easy access to the Führer. He was backed up by a number of war correspondents, the most prominent of whom was Hanns Gert von Esebeck, who massaged Rommel's ego with effulgent accounts of his heroic deeds. Rommel was always delighted to strike a suitably martial pose for the cameramen, Hans Ertl, who was famous for his films of the Himalayas and had worked for Leni Riefenstahl on the film of the 1936 Olympics, and Eric Borchert, a star photographer from the *Berliner Illustrierte*.[69] As a result of their joint efforts Rommel received thirty to forty pieces of fan mail per day, mainly from infatuated women, asking for his portrait. These were provided by Hitler's court photographer, Professor Heinrich Hoffmann, who sent boxes of photographs to North Africa for signature and dispatch to the hero's devotees.[70]

While in Berlin, Berndt gave a detailed account of the problems in North Africa to his former boss. Goebbels was highly alarmed at what he heard. There seemed no immediate solution to the logistical problem, with British submarines roaming freely, sinking freighters at will. Berndt described the attitude of the German troops as 'somewhat melancholy' as a result of them being permanently at the front, denied leave, suffering from the sandstorms and blistering heat, prone to disease from malnutrition and lack of vitamins, and depressed by the fact that the offensive had ground to a halt with no prospect of regaining momentum. Meanwhile, the enemy was frantically building up their reserves, so as to be able to go on the offensive as soon as the weather improved. The behaviour of the Italian troops, particularly the officers, did nothing to raise the spirits of their German brothers-in-arms. Nevertheless, Rommel was an inspiration to all the troops, both German and Italian, and he was confident that he could withstand an offensive. Berndt complained that Rommel was very upset that Gariboldi had been replaced by 'Bombastico', who tried to compensate for the miserable performance of the Italian troops by behaving in a revoltingly stroppy and arrogant manner. Rommel had complained about Bastico to Hitler, who persuaded Mussolini to make Rommel largely independent from him.[71]

Berndt's intervention had an effect. Hitler was finally persuaded to move aircraft back to Sicily from the eastern Mediterranean to protect the convoys to Tripoli, at the same time moving six U-boats from the Atlantic to the Mediterranean. However, just when things seemed to be going so well a fresh problem arose. Italian Naval High Command, Supermarina, refused to give Weichold detailed maps showing the position of its mines. It was only at the very last moment that the U-boats in the Goeben Group were informed that they were heading for a string of Italian mines, after Weichold had made a frantic appeal to the Italian admiralty staff.[72]

At the beginning of September OKW came to the sorry conclusion that the campaign in the Soviet Union was unlikely to be over by the onset of winter. This meant that the idea of an attack on the Middle East through Turkey had to be abandoned. Turkey was likely to remain neutral and Germany was in no position to risk an attack. The British position in Egypt would thus be further strengthened, since neither Syria nor Iraq presented a serious threat. All Germany's efforts had now to be concentrated on the Soviet Union, and a few minesweepers, motor torpedo boats and submarines were all that could be spared for North Africa. An attack on Egypt was now out of the question. Not only was it highly doubtful whether Rommel had sufficient forces to take Tobruk, but he was also unlikely to be able to withstand a renewed British offensive.

OKH had long since reached the conclusion that the Afrika-korps was in no position to take Mersa Matruh by a *coup de main*. Since it were unable to mount a serious attack on the British, it was highly likely that it would soon come under massive attack. Rommel came to the opposite conclusion, arguing that it was precisely because the logistical situation was worsening, 'Barbarossa' was running into difficulties and the Germans would not be able to sweep down upon the Middle East from the Caucasus, that the British had to be attacked before they were overwhelmingly strong.[73] In mid-August he had drawn up a fantastic plan for an attack on Egypt. First he would seize the oases at Siwa and Giarabub. Then he would take Mersa Matruh, or failing that he would use Italian troops to lay siege to the town. Within four to eight days he would take Sidi Haneish, then push on between the Qattara Depression and the sea. He would use paratroopers to take the bridges across the Nile at Cairo, before destroying all the British forces west of the Nile. Having made sure that the British did not destroy the Aswan Dam he would seal off Alexandria within three to five days, cross the Nile near Cairo and clear the Nile valley within five days. The only major problem he saw was that of building bridges across the Nile should the British destroy the existing ones.[74] Rommel followed up this extraordinary piece of wishful thinking on 6 September by urging the Comando Supremo to exploit what he described as an 'unusu-ally favourable situation' to strike before the British brought in more reserves. After further reflection Rommel began gradually to realise that he did not have sufficient forces to attack Egypt, and that the Panzer Group would be unlikely to be up to sufficient strength for such an operation until early 1942, and then only if the Luftwaffe was strength-ened sufficiently to secure the sea lanes across the Mediterranean.[75] He now proposed yet another attempt to take Tobruk, to be launched in early October, regardless of the situation on the eastern front. The blustering General Bastico, who did not share his predecessor's fixation on the defence, and wished to give a demonstration of Italian military ardour, went even further than Rommel, arguing in favour of bypassing Tobruk and attacking Egypt. This was too much for both Rommel and the Comando Supremo, who felt that Tobruk had to be taken before any further advance, pointing out that this was also the view of OKH, Hitler and Mussolini.[76]

In spite of heavy losses, DAK's quartermaster had done a remarkable job in bringing up reinforcements to the front. On 15 August 5 Light Division was strengthened to be renamed 21 Panzer Division. A new division was formed 'for special use in Africa', soon to be called 90 Africa Light Division. But as a result of heavy shipping losses and the consequent lack of supplies, the offensive had to be postponed from October to November.

A further blow was delivered at the end of September when General Geisler, the commander of 10 Air Corps, visited Rommel's headquarters and told him point blank that he would be unable to provide adequate air support for an attack on Tobruk, or for the defence of the Sollum front should the British attack. Rommel was furious and countered by insisting that Geisler should provide adequate air support for shipping to Cyrenaica, in accordance with an 'Order from the Führer' dated 13 September. Rommel pointed out that eight ships had been sunk between 7 August and 12 September with 12,000 tons of matériel and 332 motor vehicles. During the same time thirty British ships had sailed through the Mediterranean with impunity. Three more ships had been sunk on 18 September, which meant that there was only one freighter left for the route from Tripoli to Benghazi. Geisler replied that this order had been watered down for lack of aircraft, and that he had been given new instructions from Göring, to the effect that he should give air support in the central Mediterranean only in exceptional circumstances. He only had two fighter groups, each with only ten planes operational at any one time. Since he only had enough planes to protect Benghazi, he could not contemplate any further operations such as submarine hunting or support for Rommel's operations at Tobruk. He had no equipment for night fighters and no transport planes. Geisler once again had to point out the fundamental menace from Malta, an unpleasant fact that Rommel refused to take into consideration. Rommel continued to insist that Hitler had promised him strong air support, including bombers capable of dropping 2,500-kilogram bombs. Another question was whether, given the fact that the British consistently attacked field hospitals and dressing stations, even though they were clearly marked, permission should be asked of Göring to take retaliatory action. No decision was made on this delicate matter.[77] Rommel concluded the meeting with the complaint that 'we are only stepchildren', but consoled himself with the thought that the Germans were making good progress in Russia, and that once that was settled he would get what he needed.[78] He was clearly unaware of the situation on the eastern front, and it was almost a year before he received any reinforcements.

Malta had been further strengthened in late September by Operation 'Halberd' which brought in a further 50,000 tons of supplies, along with additional air support that gave the RAF absolute supremacy in the air. This was put to good use. Italian air bases came under continual attack, ports in Italy and North Africa bombed, and the convoys were crippled with 49,373 GRT of shipping sunk in September. Of the supplies destined for the Afrikakorps 76 per cent were lost. In October the total amount of shipping lost was 37 per cent, compared with 30 per cent in September. Convoys virtually ceased by the end of October. The Italians had promised 60,000 tons of matériel that month, but only 8,093 tons had actually arrived.[79] The Italian navy no longer had the oil needed to fuel the escorts. Weichold sent an urgent request to Berlin for assistance, while Rintelen told OKW that the convoys would not be able to resume in the foreseeable future. Without additional support from the Luftwaffe, plus substantial deliveries of oil, the situation would become desperate.[80]

OKW, at the urging of the Luftwaffe's liaison officer in Rome, had thought of sending 10 Air Corps back from Greece to Italy as early as June 1941, but Göring flatly turned down the suggestion, on the grounds that this would leave Crete and the supply lines to the Balkans seriously vulnerable.[81] The Reichsmarschall pointed out that the ports in Cyrenaica, such as Bardia and Derna, were not being used to full capacity, and that in any case the imminent defeat of the Soviet Union would radically change the situation, so that ideas outlined in the draft of Order Number 32, dealing with the period after 'Barbarossa', could then be put in train.[82] In the meantime, the Italians should be told to beef up their air force in southern Italy, Sicily, Tripoli and Benghazi, hammer away at Malta and protect the convoys.

After much further discussion at OKH it was decided that once Malta fell, which they fondly imagined would happen in October, convoys could be protected by 10 Air Corps operating from Greece. Hitler had other ideas. It was not until September that dire warnings about the logistical crisis in the Mediterranean reached Hitler's ears. He complained, with some justification, that he had been kept in the dark. He was gradually persuaded to send U-boats from the Atlantic to the Mediterranean, in spite of fierce resistance from the navy, who correctly pointed out that this would give the British virtually unimpeded access to the United States and Canada. In addition to the six U-boats that Hitler agreed to send to the Mediterranean on 14 September, along with some minesweepers and motor torpedo boats, at the end of October he called for eighteen more to be withdrawn from service in the Atlantic. Grand-Admiral Karl Dönitz as commander-in-chief of the U-boats (BdU) protested vigorously. He wrote: 'I cannot accept responsibility for an increase of the number of U-boats in the Mediterranean. It would weaken our efforts in the main theatre of operations, without a proportionate increase of our chances of success in the Mediterranean.' Hitler ignored these objections, sending four more U-boats to the Mediterranean at the beginning of November. On 22 November he ordered the entire frontline U-boat fleet to operate in the Mediterranean and immediately west of Gibraltar. Finally, on 29 November, fifteen U-boats were sent to patrol around Gibraltar, with ten more in the eastern Mediterranean. Dönitz did what he could to protest against this senseless deployment of the U-boats, but received precious little support from Skl. As a result German naval forces were seriously weakened for the Battle of the Atlantic.[83] In addition to the U-boats, Hitler also favoured the idea of making the protection of the convoys from Naples to Sicily 10 Air Corps's main role. Göring was able to put a stop to this idea, but Skl did not have enough clout to stop the Führer from making a serious strategic blunder. This was another piece of typical patchwork, which merely served as a means of shifting the blame on to other shoulders, should things go wrong.[84]

That this was a serious error of judgement was concealed by some initial successes. Captain Friedrich Guggenberger's U81 sank the aircraft carrier *Ark Royal*, which was returning to base in Gibraltar on 12 November 1941. Only one sailor was killed at the point where the torpedo exploded. On 25 November Captain Baron Hans Diedrich von Tiesenhausen and U331 hit the battleship *Barham* with a salvo of four torpedoes, which exploded with 861 seamen losing their lives. On 14 December U557 with Captain Ottokar Paulsen in command sank the cruiser *Galatea* outside Alexandria. The U-boats sank eight freighters and tankers, along with two escort vessels, most of which were heading for Tobruk. By the end of the year only three of the twenty-six U-boats in the Mediterranean had been lost. The Italians also scored a major success when the swashbuckling Prince Borghese sailed in the submarine *Scirè* to Alexandria, where he released three two-man torpedoes that put the battleships *Queen Elizabeth* and *Valiant* out of action for several months. The minefields also took their toll. Three cruisers and four destroyers in K Force were only 15 sea miles from an Axis convoy when they ran into a minefield. The flagship *Neptune* sank with only one of the 700-man crew surviving, along with the cruiser *Kandahar*, most of whose crew was saved. The cruisers *Aurora* and *Penelope*, which had done such damage to Axis shipping in October and November, were badly damaged.[85] As a result of these successes the amount of Axis shipping to North Africa increased from 36,000 GRT in December 1941 to 59,000 GRT in January, and 25,000 tons of supplies were unloaded for the Germans in Tripoli. It was still far short of what was needed to bring the Afrikakorps up to full strength, but enough to encourage Rommel once again to go on the offensive.

The Italians were anxious to have 10 Air Corps sent back to Sicily, and to this end General Pricolo went to meet Göring at the beginning of October at his vast hunting lodge at Rominten in East Prussia, which had been built by the Kaiser and extensively remodelled as 'Emmyhall', named after his second wife. Göring went immediately on the offensive by categorically stating that 10 Air Corps could not be spared for operations against Malta. He then reminded Pricolo that the Italians' three main duties were to attack Malta, blockade the Straits of Messina and protect the convoys to North Africa. He repeated his insistence that supplies should be sent to Benghazi, Derna and Bardia, the routes to Cyrenaica being far safer than those to Tripoli. Pricolo objected that the capacity of these ports was not sufficient to unload the 5,000 tons daily that the Axis forces required. Göring retorted that it was about time that they learnt to improvise 'like the English navy' does.[86] In the end an unfortunate compromise was reached that was typical of coalition warfare. Part of 10 Air Corps was returned to Sicily, but not enough to make much difference, while raids on Egypt from Greece had to be cancelled for lack of aircraft.

In spite of these difficulties the Germans were in a confident mood. Göring was convinced that the Soviet Union was on the brink of collapse. Goebbels confided in his diary that if only the weather held the campaign would be over within two weeks.[87] OKW was slightly less sanguine. Plans were made for the occupation of the Caucasus oilfields and for an advance into Iraq, but the idea of moving through

Turkey to attack the British in the Middle East was put on hold.[88] On 10 October Warlimont's department at OKW prepared notes for a letter from Hitler to Mussolini, in which it was assumed that the Soviet Union would soon be defeated, so that it would then be possible to send Luftwaffe units to southern Italy and Sicily, protect the convoys, and back up the attack on Tobruk. All the forces in this theatre should be placed under the command of a German field marshal.[89] Kesselring, the commander of 1 Air Fleet, was the obvious choice for this position. Jodl put his name forward shortly thereafter. Göring, who still wanted to concentrate on the eastern Mediterranean, sought to undermine this plan by claiming that these goals could be achieved only by sending such a large force that OKW would begin to have second thoughts about its feasibility.[90]

Hitler wanted greater influence over the conduct of the war in North Africa, but, ever mindful of the sensitivities of his Italian ally, was not at all favourable to the idea of a German supreme commander in the Mediterranean, even though the sorry performance of the Italian forces made such an appointment militarily imperative. He also worried about the effect on Italian morale were the Germans to send reinforcements to Italy. Hitler called Rintelen to the Wolf's Lair on 24 October to discuss this issue. Rintelen assured him that although the Italians found it somewhat wounding to their pride, they realised the necessity of reinforcing air support for the convoys to North Africa.[91] He suggested that Hitler make an offer to Mussolini within the framework of a general overview of the war. Hitler heeded this advice in his letter to Mussolini of 29 October, in which he said that he was prepared to send additional air support, should the Duce so desire.[92] Hitler's concerns proved to be unfounded. Mussolini eagerly took up the offer, and Pricolo sent an urgent request to the Luftwaffe for help.[93] The woeful deficiencies in the Italian air force were a clear indication that Pricolo was not up to the job. The Italians were producing only 300 aircraft per month, the British 1,080 technically superior models, and the Americans, who were not yet at war, passed the 2,000 mark by the end of November. In mid-month Pricolo was replaced by General Rino-Corso Fougier.

When the British further strengthened Malta with K Force, Hitler started to become seriously worried that this was part of a diversionary operation, designed to take the pressure off the Soviet Union. He entertained fantastic thoughts of an invasion of Sicily from Malta, or Crete and the Aegean from Egypt, while awaiting a major offensive against the Axis forces on the Sollum front. All this could well lead to the overthrow of the Fascist regime, which was already tottering, because of food shortages and bombing raids from Malta. Were Mussolini to fall the consequences in Vichy France, Spain and Turkey would be dire. For this reason he told Vice-Admiral Fricke, chief of naval staff, that the Mediterranean was 'a decisive area for the continuation of the war'.[94] In spite of the vigorous objection of the naval staff, Hitler now decided to send even more U-boats to the Mediterranean, and ordered a study to be made for the movement to Sicily and southern Italy of Kesselring's 2 Air Command, as well as 2 Air Corps from Army Group Centre, which was pushing on to Moscow. Kesselring's mission was outlined in Order Number 38 of 2 December 1941, which repeated the points contained in Hitler's draft letter to Mussolini. He was to secure the sea lanes to Libya and Cyrenaica, as well as keep Malta in subjection, co-operate with the German and allied forces in North Africa, and paralyse enemy traffic through the Mediterranean, in close co-operation with the Italian and German navies. Hitler, who did not believe that it would be possible to take Malta by storm, argued that the only viable method of dealing with this vexing problem was to cut the island off from its supplies, while keeping up attacks so that the garrison would eventually run out of ammunition and wear out its guns.[95]

Kesselring was placed under Mussolini's orders, but was subordinate to Göring for all air force matters. He was to report all important decisions to OKW. Hitler attempted to place part of the Italian armed forces under Kesselring's command, but this was frustrated by Count Cavallero, who assured Kesselring that 'no orders from the Comando Supremo on matters concerning the Italian and African theatres shall be issued without [Kesselring's] participation and signature'.[96] Kesselring attended a meeting every day at 1230hrs with the head of the Comando Supremo. Cavallero was accompanied by the chiefs of army, air force and naval staffs, as well as the chief transportation officer. Rintelen and Weichold, or their deputies, also participated. Kesselring also conferred regularly with Mussolini.[97] It was a highly unsatisfactory arrangement that reflected the dictators' determination to play active leadership roles, instead of creating a unified command that could get on with the job unhampered by their capricious meddling.

Given the mounting logistical crisis the Comando Supremo revived the question of using French North African ports. Rintelen told

Mussolini that OKW did not support the idea, because of Hitler's concerns about the reaction of the Vichy government, but the Duce ignored this warning, writing to Hitler on 29 December 1941 to suggest that the Axis request permission to use the ports of Tunis and Bizerta in return for certain unspecified compensation. If Vichy refused, force would have to be used. Hitler replied three weeks later that since the French demands for compensation were likely to be so exorbitant, he had not pursued the matter. He rejected out of hand the use of force, saying that it would have a disastrous effect on all of French North Africa.[98] Cavallero imagined that if only the Axis could obtain the use of the Tunisian ports, the war in North Africa would be won, but the offer he proposed would never have been acceptable. Italy would not renounce its claim to Corsica, and Vichy would not have found southern Belgium and Brussels to be adequate recompense.[99]

5 ✠ WITHDRAWAL

Rommel remained blissfully unperturbed, while the logistical situation grew steadily worse. His eyes were on the eastern front, where Army Group Centre had taken Smolensk in mid-July and Field Marshal von Bock's men were advancing rapidly towards Moscow. On 12 October he wrote to his wife, full of enthusiasm over the 'wonderful news from Russia'. Victory in the east was in sight, so that German troops in the Caucasus would soon launch a two-pronged attack on the Middle East. Once Tobruk fell, the way would be open for a successful offensive against Egypt.[1] Carried away by such euphoria, Rommel ignored warnings from OKH and from his own staff that the British were preparing another large-scale offensive. His quartermaster's staff cautioned that the Panzer Group was living off the reserve supplies needed for an attack on Tobruk, but this also fell on deaf ears. Reports that the supply situation was becoming desperate merely served to goad him into further action. On 26 October he ordered yet another attack on Tobruk, to take place between 15 and 16 November. 'Bombastico' agreed with Rommel's plan, but refused to give him 20 Motorised Corps as requested, instead placing it south of Tobruk to guard the flank. Comando Supremo insisted that it would be impossible to attack Tobruk until the Littorio Division arrived at the beginning of December, but the Italian commander in North Africa accepted the earlier date, even though he had only one division, the Trento, which was of questionable value. Rommel was fully aware that he did not have sufficient airpower, one-third of the artillery he needed had still not arrived and his communications network was substandard; but he still wanted to go ahead.[2] General Fröhlich, Commander of the Air Force in Africa, readily agreed to send substantial air support, although it was difficult to see how he could possibly meet his promise. OKW tried

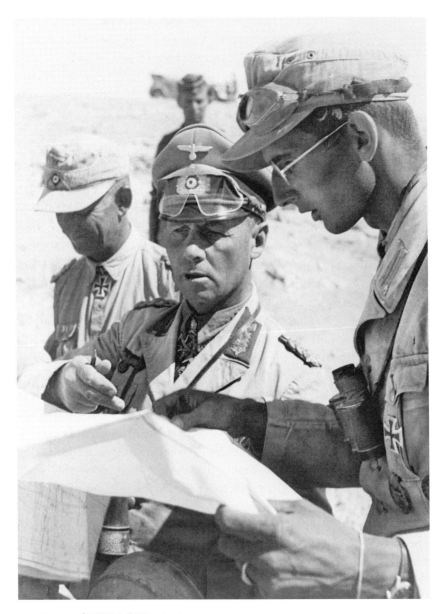

11. Rommel (IWM: HU 5625)

to hold Rommel back by saying that, even if Fröhlich could find these
extra forces, the British would still have absolute air superiority. Keitel asked whether there was a high probability of success, whether the
Sollum front would hold and whether it might be prudent to wait until
next year, by which time Rommel's forces would be up to strength.[3]

Rommel replied with the familiar argument that the longer he waited, the stronger the British would be. He assured Keitel that the Sollum front, with three guns per kilometre, supported by anti-aircraft and anti-tank guns, was amply defended.

Rommel went to Rome on 1 November for final top-level discussions and a few days' rest. He continued to insist that there were no signs of an imminent British attack, even though OKH produced a substantial amount of evidence that this was indeed the case. He therefore concentrated on persuading the Italians to send a further convoy to prime his supplies. He got his way, although the attack had to be postponed for a few days. On the moonlit night of 7 November the 'Duisburg' convoy of five freighters and two tankers, protected by two heavy cruisers and ten destroyers, left Naples. The British, who had cracked the Italian naval code, were fully aware of what was afoot, so that K Force in Valletta, comprising the cruisers *Aurora* and *Penelope* along with two of the latest model destroyers, was immediately alerted, setting sail the following day. In order to create the impression that K Force had been alerted because of air reconnaissance, a long-distance spotter plane was sent from Malta, demonstrably sighting the convoy just after it had passed through the Straits of Messina.[4] The convoy was destroyed during the following night, thanks to the skilful use of radar, with all seven freighters and one destroyer sunk. A further destroyer carrying survivors was sunk by a British submarine the following day. K Force returned to Valletta unharmed.[5]

Bastico continued in his attempts to postpone the attack on Tobruk, while insisting that he agreed in principle that it should take place as soon as possible. He expressed his fear that, were the British to attack, the Sollum Line would not hold. His intelligence indicated that the British were waiting for Rommel to attack Tobruk, so as to catch the Panzer Group on the wrong foot. He stated that the interrogation of British officers clearly showed that a major offensive was in the offing. Rommel's chief of intelligence dismissed this evidence on the grounds that the British were bound to be lying. Bastico also argued that he did not have enough anti-aircraft guns, to which Rommel's staff replied that what his troops lacked above all was not guns, but decent training.[6] A few days later OKW gave Rommel the green light, although Hitler insisted that he must have sufficient matériel, and ensure that his air support was adequate, before launching the attack.[7]

Even though winter had set in exceptionally early in Russia, and the Red Army's resistance was becoming so robust that the Germans were beginning to revise their opinion that the Soviet Union was on its last legs, it was the destruction of the 'Duisburg' convoy that prompted Hitler to order 2 Air Corps, under General Bruno Loertzer, to be detached from Army Group Centre and sent to Sicily. OKH's protests against such a serious weakening of their drive to Moscow at this critical moment were to no avail. The German Naval Staff were outraged at this 'ignominy', and began to think about sending a strong naval force to the Mediterranean. On further consideration it was felt that nothing could be done to avoid a repeat of the 'Duisburg' fiasco until early 1942, so no immediate solution to this extremely serious situation could be offered.[8] The Italians refused to send any more convoys to Tripoli, and those going to Benghazi became extremely vulnerable once the British launched the 'Crusader' offensive on 18 November. Rommel, ignoring these mundane problems, persuaded Bastico that the attack on Tobruk should go ahead on 21 November, as previously agreed.

Once again Rommel's plans came to nothing. On the night of 17/18 November, British commandos mounted a daring raid on what they presumed to be Rommel's headquarters at Beda Littoria, 320 kilometres behind the frontline. In fact Rommel, who had been there in July and August, had handed over the place to the quartermaster staff, but the old signs, which still had the names of various senior staff officers on the doors, had been photographed by a British agent. Four Germans were killed along with Lieutenant-Colonel Keyes, the son of Admiral Sir Roger Keyes, who was awarded a posthumous Victoria Cross for this exploit. The sea was far too rough for re-embarkation in the two submarines used so the remaining twenty-nine commandos disappeared into the night. Only Colonel Laycock, the commanding officer, and Sergeant Terry managed to make their way back to the British lines.[9] An ingenious Carabiniere, familiar with the Arab mind, offered 80 pounds of flour and 20 pounds of sugar for each British commando they handed over. Thus virtually the entire remainder of the force ended up as prisoners of war. Although Hitler had ordered that all commandos should be shot on the spot, Rommel insisted that they should be treated as ordinary prisoners of war. The British dead were buried with full military honours.[10] Rommel admired their daring, but was somewhat insulted that the British had imagined that he would

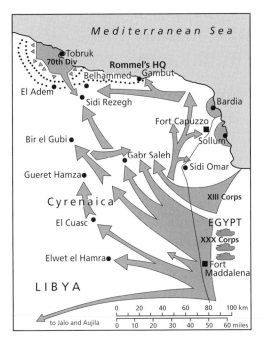

Map 5. 'Crusader', 18 November 1941

be comfortably ensconced so far from the front. The attempt to kill Rommel turned out to be the prelude to a major offensive. Just as Rommel had been repeatedly warned, the British had not remained idle. They struck in full force three days before the date set for Rommel's attack on Tobruk. While K Force cut off his supplies to Tripoli, the British 8th Army was brought up to the front.

At first sight the Axis forces in North Africa facing 'Crusader' seemed impressive. Rommel's Panzer Group Africa was made up of Crüwell's Afrikakorps with 15 Panzer Division, 21 Panzer Division (formally 5 Light Division) and the Division for Special Duties in Africa (soon to be renamed the 90 Africa Light Division).[11] This last division was an odd assortment, comprising 155 Infantry Regiment, 361 Africa Regiment made up of former members of the French Foreign Legion who had changed sides, a battery of artillery, and five 'Oasis Companies' of dubious volunteers of different nationalities. Crüwell also had command over the Italian Savona Division on the Sollum front. The Italian contingent consisted of 21 Army Corps under General Enea Navarini, an enormously popular soldier with a splendid sense of humour and boundless energy, who got on extremely well with Rommel. It was made up of the partially motorised Bologna,

Brescia and Pavia Divisions. General Bastico's chief of staff, General Gastone Gambara, commanded a further motorised corps, the *Corpo d'Armata di Manovra*, made up of the Ariete Armoured Division, along with the Trento and Trieste Divisions. It did not form part of Panzer Group Africa, but Bastico agreed that it would assist should the British attack.[12]

There were 48,500 German troops, but of these 11,066 were on the sick list, mostly because of inadequate or inappropriate diet. 90 Africa Light Division had virtually no signals equipment and was desperately short of supplies. The two armoured divisions had a total of 249 Panzer, but of these 70 were Panzer IIs, which only mounted a 2cm peashooter and a heavy machinegun and were thus worthless in a tank battle.[13] They were still waiting for artillery support to be brought up from Tripoli. Logistical problems were such that the Afrikakorps was never brought up to full strength.[14] The Ariete Division had 137 M13/40 tanks, an unimpressive weapon that was lightly armoured, unreliable, easily caught fire when hit, and had no radio. The crews were given only one week of training. Only half of General Fröhlich's 140 aircraft were ready for combat, but the Italian 5 Air Fleet had 290 planes in Cyrenaica, and 10 Air Corps had more than one hundred ready to send from Greece.[15]

Although he had seriously misread British intentions and had refused to listen to the Italians' warnings, Rommel had excellent field intelligence. By August 1941 the Germans had cracked the War Office cipher that carried much of the traffic to the 8th Army, right down to the divisional level. They continued to do so until January 1942. The Afrikakorps' interception of low-grade traffic was greatly superior to that of the British, in part because of sloppy wireless procedure in the 8th Army. Lieutenant Seebohm, who during the campaign in France had gained valuable experience in 3 Company of 56 Intelligence Section, which had been attached to Rommel's 7 Panzer Division, was an outstanding exponent of radio intelligence. Seebohm's 621 Wireless Intelligence Company (NFA 621), although fully independent and taking orders directly from Berlin, was for administrative purposes attached to 10 Panzer Intelligence Regiment. It was divided into two squadrons: one, which was attached to Panzer Group headquarters, was responsible for decrypting the traffic, while the other was up at the front, listening in to the 8th Army. Lieutenant Wischmann, who was attached to Rommel's command post, deciphered messages relayed directly to him, and immediately passed them on.[16] The average age in NFA 621 was twenty-five. They were highly intelligent and skilled young men, all fluent in English, and it is typical of the German army that junior officers were entrusted with such heavy responsibilities. Their major problem was that much of this communications intelligence, or 'Y', was in almost impenetrable slang, often taken from the arcane vocabulary of the stable and the wicket. It took some time to make sense of such phrases as: 'I shall need a farrier, I've cast a shoe.' 'A chap has retired to the pavilion.' 'Our red friends on ponies, the cherry Ps.' 'My horse and jockey have copped it.' Gradually they realised that 'monkey orange' was the medical officer, and that 'mess tins' were Bren gun carriers. It was not until part of Rommel's field Sigint unit was captured in July 1942 that the British found out the extent to which he was listening in to their radio traffic down to the battalion level and beyond, allowing him to estimate their next tactical move.[17]

The pause in the fighting had given the Afrikakorps a chance to concentrate on training, as far as the fuel and ammunition situation permitted. 15 Panzer Division, which had only recently been motorised, had an opportunity to familiarise itself with its new weapons. 15 Infantry Brigade, which had been at Ras el Mdauur since May, was at last relieved by 155 Infantry Regiment from the Division for Special Duties in Africa. It in turn was replaced by 7 Bersaglieri Regiment of the Trento Division in mid-October. 155 Infantry Regiment, along with the Pavia Division, was given intensive training, in preparation for a further attack on Tobruk. The Savona Infantry Division was brought up from Tripoli to the Sollum front, placed under the command of the Afrikakorps, and set to work improving the defences from Sidi Omar to the Halfaya Pass. The Bologna Division was sent to Tobruk, where it successfully pushed forward its positions to the east and south-east, establishing excellent starting positions for a renewed offensive.

A serious attempt was made to replace weapons that had proved less than satisfactory. These included anti-tank rifles, 5cm mortars and 3.7cm anti-tank guns. The last of the totally obsolete Panzer Is, initially designed for training purposes, was put out of service in October. Trucks remained a serious problem: 15 Panzer Division had 999, but only 45 had four-wheel drive. The remainder were underpowered with rear-wheel drive, a disastrous combination in the desert. More trucks broke down than were damaged by the enemy, and spare parts were a rarity. Captured British trucks mostly had four-wheel drive, a more robust chassis and heavy-duty air filters, but had the disadvantage of being extremely thirsty. Fifteen hundred French trucks from Tunisia brought no relief: fifty-eight different models from seventeen manufacturers could not be used at the front, and were of only limited value in the immediate vicinity of the ports. Replacement Panzer were few and far between. Only forty-four Panzer IIIs and sixteen Panzer IVs had arrived by the end of the year.[18]

In July OKH estimated that if 20,000 tons of supplies could be delivered to the Panzer Group it would be possible to attack Tobruk in mid-September, but shipping losses increased dramatically in September, so the general staff announced that there could be no further attempt to seize the fortress in the foreseeable future. This left Rommel fuming with rage, wildly denouncing the Italians for failing to protect the convoys, while OKH and OKW were accused of ignoring the North African theatre. His interpreter, Wilfried Armbruster, shared his boss's view of their Axis ally, noting in his diary that they were 'a race of shits'.[19]

Auchinleck had a far more impressive force under his command. The fighting in Syria was over; the country left to de Gaulle and the Free French, the British troops withdrew to Egypt. The Germans were unable to give any assistance to the Arab nationalists, so that 'the Auk' could now concentrate on one front. The 8th Army, commanded by Lieutenant-General Sir Alan Cunningham was made up of Lieutenant-General A. R. Godwin-Austen's Western Desert Force (soon to be renamed 13th Corps), which included the New Zealand Division, 4th Indian Division and 1st Armoured Brigade. The bulk of the armour was concentrated in a newly formed 30th Corps under Major-General Willoughby Norrie, comprising 7th Armoured Division, 4th Armoured Brigade Group, 1st South African Division and 22nd Guards Brigade. German and Italian intelligence had gathered accurate information on the strength of British forces, but were unaware of the existence of 30th Corps, which was to play such a vital role in Auchinleck's plan.[20] The 2nd South African Division was held in reserve. Tobruk was under the command of Major-General R. M. Scobie with 70th Division, 32nd Armoured Brigade and a Polish infantry brigade. The 9th Australian Division had been withdrawn at Canberra's request, causing the Royal Navy an additional headache. In total 34,113 men had to be brought into the besieged town and 47,280, including a number of prisoners, moved out. This massive operation resulted in the loss of thirty-four ships with thirty-three others damaged.[21] The 29th Indian Division and 6th South African Armoured Regiment were positioned out in the desert at the Giarabub Oasis, some hundred miles away to the south-east, in order to mislead Rommel into thinking that Auchinleck intended to outflank Tobruk and attack the Axis' lines of communication.[22]

The British also had an overwhelming superiority in weapons. By the end of October 300 Cruiser assault tanks had been brought to Egypt, along with a further 300 American Stuart light tanks, 170 support tanks, most of which were the latest model of Valentines, 34,000 trucks, 600 pieces of field artillery, 80 heavy and 160 light anti-aircraft guns, 200 anti-tank guns and 900 mortars. Thus, 30th Corps had 477 tanks with which to mount the offensive, while 13th Corps had 135, most of which were Valentines. In addition, 32nd Armoured Brigade in Tobruk had 32 assorted Cruisers, 25 light tanks and 69 Matildas, so a total of 738 British tanks were pitched against 386.[23]

The British worked hard to ensure that there were adequate supplies for the offensive. A pipeline was built to bring water from Alexandria as far forward as Mersa Matruh, and a railway now reached Misheifa, some 40 kilometres to the south of Sidi Barrani. Supply dumps, known as field maintenance centres, were established further west. The Germans were well aware of intensified activity in Egypt, but initially they did not think that the British were planning an offensive. At the end of August spotter planes noticed that four supply dumps were being established in forward positions, and on 14 September 21 Panzer Division was ordered to attack 7th Armoured Division, positioned at Bir Habata, some 70 kilometres east of the Egyptian border, in Operation 'Midsummer Night's Dream'. The attack was a miserable failure. The British withdrew rapidly and fuel supplies were not brought up in time, so that the Panzer were unable to give chase. They were soon immobilised and submitted to crippling attacks from the RAF, so the raid had to be called off by nightfall.

The raid failed to reveal the forward supply bases that air reconnaissance had claimed to have discovered, thus confirming Rommel's belief that the British were still not contemplating an offensive. Further reinforcements by the British were attributed to nervousness after 21 Panzer Division's attack. Auchinleck's preparations were so skilfully conducted and carefully concealed that Rommel's staff thought that this was nothing more than an attempt to relieve Tobruk. Given the overwhelming air superiority enjoyed by the RAF they were absolutely certain that the British were well aware that an attack on Tobruk was imminent. In addition, 21 Panzer had not spotted any evidence for an imminent attack. No supply dumps sufficient to support a major offensive had been seen. The British kept absolute radio silence so that the approach march and deployment was not detected by the interception service. Most of the movement was by night, thus remaining undetected by air reconnaissance. By day the positions were skilfully camouflaged. Thanks to such careful preparation, the British achieved complete tactical surprise. The Panzer Group's staff was full of admiration for this skilful deployment, and was thankful that the 8th Army was unable to exploit its advantage.[24]

Throughout September and October OKW, OKH and the Comando Supremo constantly warned Rommel that the British were preparing a major offensive, but his reconnaissance, both by land and air, revealed nothing of the sort, so he was convinced that they were mistaken. He was so focused on Tobruk that he was deaf to any suggestion that the British might make a pre-emptive move. He knew full well that when he attacked Tobruk the British would most likely launch a diversionary attack on the Sollum front, but he assumed that he would be able to take Tobruk within two days, and that his forces on the Egyptian border were strong enough to ward off any such threat. He also assumed that the British would be keeping a close eye on the Caucasus, and would not be so foolish as to get involved in a major operation in North Africa when they might be left so vulnerable. Rommel informed OKH on 4 October that he intended to attack Tobruk in early November. Comando Supremo had given the go-ahead, but High Command North Africa still had certain reservations.[25]

Three weeks later troops on the Sollum front and at Tobruk were relieved in preparation for the renewed attack. The plan called for the Afrikakorps, with the Italian 21 Army Corps to its left, to attack from the south-east, the Germans spearheading the attack. It was to begin between 15 and 20 November. On 6 November OKW gave Rommel a somewhat Pythian order to the effect that he could launch his attack on Tobruk when he had sufficient air power at his command, but he was to let OKW know when he intended to act. Bastico, who remained convinced that the British were about to launch a large-scale offensive, was adamantly opposed to an attack on Tobruk. Rommel's staff agreed that an offensive was a distinct possibility, but that given the importance of Tobruk it was worth the risk. Thus they doctored their intelligence reports to Comando Supremo, so as to make it seem that the British were very unlikely to attack. Rommel decided that the risk was such that he could not spare 21 Panzer Division for the attack on Tobruk, but placed it south of Gambut to meet any threat from 8th Army. In addition 15 Panzer Division, which was to spearhead the attack on Tobruk along with the recently arrived Light Africa Division, was alerted that it might be withdrawn at any moment should the British attack. As a further precaution the Italian Armoured Corps was to cover the approaches to the south.[26] The net result of these moves was that the Panzer Group was left with insufficient forces for a successful attack on Tobruk, while failing to provide adequate security against a British offensive, which was generally believed to be imminent.

It soon became highly questionable whether the attack could start on time. The Panzer Group required 60,000 tons of supplies in October, but by the end of the month only 8,093 tons had arrived in Benghazi.[27] High Command North Africa wanted to wait until another Panzer division arrived, but eventually agreed that time was of the essence and gave the go-ahead, while insisting that Gambara's motorised corps should not be placed under Rommel's command and should be held in reserve. The Luftwaffe and the Italian air force promised only modest support. But Rommel had sufficient ammunition for 7.5 days by 15 November, as well as fuel for 8 days, and could point out that the Sollum front had been greatly strengthened with impressive bunkers modelled on those at Tobruk, a dense minefield and kilometres of barbed wire. Food was in short supply, but it was felt that the troops were so used to reduced rations that this was not a great problem. The problem remained that, with the British sinking so many ships, the Panzer Group was rapidly using up its reserves.

Auchinleck's plan for 'Crusader' was perfectly straightforward: 30th Corps' tanks were to outflank the Sollum Line to the south, push forward in a north-westerly direction, destroy the Panzer and open the way to Tobruk; 13th Corps was to engage the German forces on the borders of Egypt with the New Zealand Division working its way around and behind the Sollum Line, cutting it off from the rest of the Panzer Group. The plan appeared to be reasonable, but it was doubtful whether it could be put into effect, because of a number of serious deficiencies. The British had yet to realise that tanks were useless against Panzer, which could only be destroyed by artillery, or by tanks dug in hull down. Furthermore, Rommel, who was concentrating on an attack on Tobruk, was unlikely to send his Panzer to an insignificant point in the middle of the desert to engage 30th Corps' armour, when all he expected was some minor action on the Sollum front.[28] But that was not all. The 7th Armoured Brigade was an experienced unit, but it was equipped with older models of Cruiser, whereas the new models were given to the inexperienced men in 22nd Armoured Brigade. With Churchill impatiently breathing down his neck, Auchinleck had insufficient time adequately to train these men who had just arrived in Egypt. The 4th Armoured Brigade was equipped with the Stuart, which was an excellent weapon, soon to be nicknamed the 'Honey', but with its 13.5 tons it was a light tank, suitable only as a fast and reliable reconnaissance vehicle.[29] Its 37mm gun was well below an acceptable standard, and its two-man turret was uncomfortably crowded. The 1st South African Division had fought extremely well in East Africa, but its losses had not been made good, so it had been reduced from three to two brigades. The army had strong support from the Mediterranean fleet in Alexandria, which was to play an active role in the battles at Tobruk, Bardia and Halfaya, while the Germans were virtually unable to touch them.[30] Had Cunningham been able to wait until Rommel began his attack on Tobruk, and then attack him from the rear, he might well have had an impressive victory, but Churchill's impatience made this impossible. Rommel was caught partly by surprise, but at least he was not involved in a major operation that would have made redeployment exceedingly difficult.

The Panzer Group ignored all warnings from Army Command North Africa, as well as some disturbing information from its own reconnaissance, while the British were ingeniously deceptive. The weather also helped conceal British intentions. Even the total radio silence on 17 November was not taken to be anything unusual. A severe sandstorm on that day was followed by storms in the evening, that flooded the roads and wadis in Cyrenaica, and put the Axis air forces out of action; whereas the RAF, operating from bases in Egypt, were not so seriously affected. The daring commando raid on Rommel's former headquarters in the night of 17/18 November was not seen as particularly exceptional. On the morning of 18 November troops on both sides of the Sollum Line were mainly concerned with drying their clothes and bailing out their positions, but the long approach march to the south of the Sollum Line in preparation for 'Crusader' had already begun. 30th Corps was able to advance unopposed for 90 kilometres, pushing back the Afrikakorps' two forward positions near Gabr Saleh. 4th Armoured Brigade was then ordered to stay at Gabr Saleh to provide cover for the left flank of 13th Corps to the north-east and the right flank of 7th Armoured Division to the south-west. 22nd Armoured Brigade was ordered to advance and engage the Ariete Armoured Division at Bir el Gubi, some 40 kilometres north of their present position, while 7th Armoured Brigade was to seize the high ground overlooking the road from Tobruk to Sollum. Rommel dismissed this as a reconnaissance in force, but General von Ravenstein, commanding 21 Panzer Division, was very concerned, and wanted to move a battle group forward to meet what he felt was a serious threat. It was even suggested that the British were aiming to link up with the Free French, in an attempt to control the North African coastline, in preparation for the invasion of Europe.[31] Crüwell felt it prudent to alert 15 Panzer Division, stationed on the coast at Mersa Belafarit between Tobruk and Sollum, and to remain vigilant. He then went to see Rommel, who refused to abandon his cherished plan for an attack on Tobruk, saying: 'We must not lose our nerves.' But he did think it prudent to order the Italians to increase their vigilance.

At 1900hrs the Afrikakorps informed the Division for Special Duties in Africa that 1,650 vehicles had assembled in the area between Sidi Omar and Maddalena. The division promptly ordered its two infantry battalions to guard the flanks. Shortly thereafter the Savona Division on the Sollum front reported that a British prisoner said that 7th Armoured Division had already crossed the border, the 4th Indian Division was partially across, while two South African divisions were on their way from Mersa Matruh. This information was largely confirmed by High Command North Africa at 0035hrs. Radio intercepts had revealed a major attack to the south of the Sollum Line around Sidi Omar heading for Bir el Gubi.[32]

Auchinleck's brilliantly prepared offensive caught Rommel in an extremely awkward position. His forces were deployed ready for an attack on Tobruk in 48 hours' time. Completely unaware of Ultra, he concluded that his plans had been betrayed, his finger pointing at the Italians. A heavy sandstorm had made air reconnaissance impossible, and the British had been extremely disciplined in their use of radio traffic. According to the Panzer Group's calculations, excluding the Axis troops in the perimeter around Tobruk and the Allied forces in the garrison, there were 414 Axis tanks pitted against 648 British; 57 armoured cars against 464; 190 artillery pieces against 464; 289 anti-tank guns against 312; 240 anti-aircraft guns against 300; 73 fighters against 200; and 87 bombers against 125.[33]

During the next three days there were a series of armoured clashes in the area west of Sidi Omar and south of Sidi Rezegh. The Panzer Group's reports to OKW showed no great sign of concern. On 18 November it was reported that a British force from south-west of Sidi Omar moving in the direction of Tobruk had been immediately beaten back by German and Italian troops, with heavy losses to the British. The counterattack continued the next day, with Stuka attacks on the concentration of British armour on the Egyptian border. Air attacks were mounted against the military installations at Mersa Matruh, with the RAF losing four aircraft in aerial combat. It was not until 20 November that the Panzer Group reported that it was engaged in fierce fighting with strong British units.[34] The 22nd Armoured Brigade clashed with the Ariete Division on 19 November. Gott's attack was sloppily prepared and poorly executed, and the Italians put up a robust defence, quickly launching a powerful counterattack. Gott lost 40 tanks, including 25 of his 136 latest model Cruisers, whereupon he broke off the engagement, having destroyed 34 Italian M13/40s. Lieutenant-General Crüwell was at first unable to convince Rommel, who had just returned from Rome, where he had had discussions with the Comando Supremo and stayed until 15 November to celebrate his birthday with his wife, that this was part of a major British offensive. At least Rommel did not countermand Crüwell's order to alert 15 Panzer Division, and agreed that 21 Panzer Division should advance south to engage the British 4th Armoured Brigade Group at Gabr Saleh. Rommel went up to the front after lunch to watch the battle. The Panzer pounced on the right flank of the British attack and knocked out twenty-three Stuarts with only three losses, leaving them reeling under the blow, but they were saved by nightfall from an embarrassing defeat. Had 7th Armoured Division remained concentrated, instead of fighting piecemeal, Cunningham could have dealt a deadly blow to 21 Panzer Division.[35]

Even Rommel now had to admit that this was a major offensive. The British, having turned the Sollum front, were clearly heading for the Italian 21 Corps at Tobruk. But 20 November found the Afrikakorps in a confident mood, determined to destroy the British forces in Cyrenaica. Crüwell, having concentrated the Afrikakorps into one compact force, went after the British formations one after another.[36] 15 Panzer Division was ordered to drive the British back to the Egyptian border, supported on the right flank by 21 Panzer Division. Crüwell soon found himself marching through an open door. He imagined that he was on the heels of 3rd Royal Tank Regiment at Sidi Omar, but it had already withdrawn to the south. The bulk of British forces were to the south and west, while 21 Panzer Division was stranded in the desert without fuel. 15 Panzer Division now moved south to hit the British forces at Gabr Saleh, while 22nd Guards Armoured Brigade retired to bolster the defence, but arrived too late. The British lost another ten Stuarts and were forced to withdraw. By chasing around the desert hunting down an imaginary enemy, with Cunningham's forces in disarray, the Afrika-korps lost a valuable opportunity and wasted precious fuel. Once again shoddy reconnaissance work, combined with precipitous action, drew a blank.

The British army was far from passive that day. The South Africans engaged the Ariete Division at Bir el Gubi, while 7th Armoured Brigade continued to hammer away at Sidi Rezegh, an ancient cara-van stop, with its important airfield. Units of 7th Armoured Brigade attacked the airfield at 1800hrs, destroying eighteen fighters, taking a number of prisoners and seizing some trucks. Twenty British tanks then turned back against the Light Africa Regiment at Point 175, 7 kilo-metres to the east of Sidi Rezegh, but the attack was beaten off. Rommel realised that Sidi Rezegh was the key to the British plan, and therefore that evening ordered 15 Panzer Division to stop its wild goose chase at Gabr Saleh, move back to Sidi Rezegh and hit 7th Armoured Brigade from the rear. Cunningham seriously misread this move as a westward retreat. He calculated that the German forces at Sidi Rezegh were so weak that Major-General Scobie, who had taken over command from Morshead on 22 October, would be able to break out of Tobruk the fol-lowing day. He therefore ordered 7th Armoured Division, supported by 1st South African Division, to step up the attack on Sidi Rezegh. In addition, 22nd and 4th Armoured Brigades were ordered to coun-terattack at Gabr Saleh and knock out the Afrikakorps' two Panzer divisions. But once again the British forces were divided, the attacks ill co-ordinated, so that force was dispersed.

At 0400hrs on 21 November Rommel sent a signal to Crüwell telling him that 'The situation in this whole theatre is very critical' and urging him to 'get going in good time'.[37] This proved easier said than

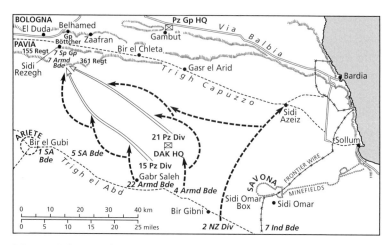

Map 6. Sidi Rezegh, 21 November 1941

done. The Panzer had to break contact with 4th and 22nd Armoured Brigades at Gabr Saleh and advance towards Sidi Rezegh. By mid-day they had shaken off the two British brigades that were pursuing them, but now had to face the 6th Royal Tanks and the 7th Hussars. Once again the British failed to concentrate their tanks and guns, so that most of the 7th Hussars' armour was soon on fire, enabling the Panzer to reach the high ground overlooking the airfield at Sidi Rezegh. Thanks to the superb resistance of Brigadier Campbell's 7th Support Group, and the excellence of the British artillery, the Panzer failed to take the airfield.[38] According to the Panzer Group's Calculations, excluding the Axis troops in the perimeter around Tobruk and the Allied forces in the garrison, Rommel was at a serious disadvantage. By evening the Afrikakorps was under attack from the south-east by 4th Armoured Brigade, as well as 22nd Armoured Brigade from the south-west, but with its central position between the support group and the two armoured brigades, it was able to tackle each in turn.

That evening Rommel ordered Crüwell to stop the Tobruk garrison from breaking out. To this end the Afrikakorps was withdrawn to the east. 15 Panzer Division regrouped south of Gambut, with 21 Panzer Division further north in the Belhamed area, overlooking the Trigh Capuzzo. This left the two Panzer divisions almost 30 kilometres apart, while 7th Armoured Division was at last able to concentrate, with about 180 tanks fit for action.

Scobie's attempt to break out of Tobruk resulted in a heavy butcher's bill on both sides. After two feints, the main breakout began at 0630hrs on 21 November. The weight of the attack landed at the point where the Division for Special Duties in Africa and the Bologna Division joined. The Germans were massed in preparation for an attack on Tobruk and put up a ferocious resistance, even though their 37mm anti-tank guns proved virtually worthless against the heavily armoured British tanks. The Bologna Division was less effective, but managed to hold its ground. The 7th Armoured Division pushed forward across the Trigh Capuzzo, a vital supply route, but was soon halted with one battalion losing 75 per cent of its tanks. Scobie was now obliged to pull his men back and go on the defensive within the bridgehead outside the town. The 7th Armoured Division, which had been forced back 10 kilometres south-west of Sidi Rezegh, now had only two battalions and twenty-eight tanks with which to face 15 and 21 Panzer Divisions, which were heading north-west in the direction of the airfield. The 22nd Armoured Brigade was brought up to attack 15 Panzer Division on its left flank, running into forward units about 10 kilometres south of Sidi Rezegh. They were beaten off, losing 35 of their 114 tanks. The Panzer then moved north-east to establish contact with 361 Africa Regiment at Point 175.

The 8th Army was singularly badly informed as to the severity of its losses, and still imagined that the Afrikakorps was on the run. At Norrie's suggestion, Cunningham ordered Godwin-Austen's 13th Corps, which was still in reserve to the south behind the Egyptian border, to advance westwards. The attack on Sidi Rezegh was to resume, and Tobruk to be relieved.

Hitler was beginning to worry about these developments. Although he considered the North Africa campaign to be peripheral, he was concerned that the Axis troops might well be about to suffer a defeat that would have an unfortunate effect on morale. He therefore ordered Goebbels to soft-peddle the propaganda about Rommel and the Afrikakorps. He still had great faith in Rommel's abilities, but realised that it had not been possible to give him the troops and equipment that he needed to guarantee success. In a fit of uncharacteristic generosity he was full of praise for the Italians, who had done everything possible to help and whose engagement and élan he described as 'truly amazing'. Hitler showed a much greater concern for North Africa than did OKH, but still remained cautiously optimistic.[39]

Rommel visited Ravenstein at midday on 22 November and ordered 21 Panzer to attack the Sidi Rezegh airfield from the north, while 5 Panzer Regiment was to move around the airfield to the north and attack it from the west. The Panzer Group's heavy artillery was positioned at Belhamed, to the north of the airfield, and was to support 21 Panzer's attack with a heavy bombardment. The tank battle of Sidi Rezegh was to rage for the next two days.

The South Africans attacked the Afrikakorps' 155 Infantry Regiment at Sidi Rezegh during the afternoon of 22 November. The attack was initially successful, the South Africans driving the Germans from the high ground to the north of the airfield, but to the west and east they hung on, although with heavy losses. When British armour was spotted heading for the Trigh Capuzzo, Rommel, who was on the spot, ordered 3 Reconnaissance Unit forward, supported by 88s, a move that resulted in 6 Royal Tank Regiment losing all its tanks. 21 Panzer Division's attack on the airfield caught the British completely by surprise. 22nd Armoured Brigade, having lost half its strength, was forced to withdraw. 1st Battalion Kings Royal Rifle Corps was surrounded, with most being taken prisoner. 4th Armoured Brigade was rushed in late in the day in an attempt to save the situation, but by nightfall Gott decided to withdraw, leaving the airfield once again in German hands. Rommel had thus regained the airfield, and had frustrated 30th Corps' attempt to relieve the Tobruk garrison.

Having refuelled and rearmed, 15 Panzer Division received a call for help from 21 Panzer Division, which had received faulty intelligence suggesting that the British were bringing in 180 tanks from the south. Moving up at dusk at 1830hrs, about 8 kilometres south-east of Sidi Rezegh 8 Panzer Regiment ran into the headquarters of 4th Armoured Brigade, along with a battalion of the 8th Hussars, which had been brought up to support the attack on Sidi Rezegh. The British lost thirty-five tanks, several armoured cars, guns, and valuable papers, along with 18 Officers and 150 men taken prisoner, all at a cost of ten Panzer. The brigade commander managed to escape capture by a mere chance.[40]

Meanwhile the New Zealanders and Indians were making good progress against the Italians on the Sollum front, cutting off their lines of communication back to the Panzer Group. The New Zealanders had been beaten back by the Italians in the Savona Division at Bir Ghirba, but were successful at Capuzzo and Musaid, while the Indians took the strong points at Frongia and Sidi Omar. This encouraged Cunningham to order the New Zealanders to advance to Tobruk, so as to join in an attack on Rommel's besieging forces on 24 November.

Rommel, who seems to have been unaware that the Indians and the New Zealanders were moving westwards, had already decided to wipe out the remnants of 7th Armoured Division to the south of Sidi Rezegh, with the Afrikakorps acting as a hammer, driving south against the Ariete Armoured Division forming an anvil. Crüwell, who insisted that the Ariete were not strong enough to take the pressure, ordered 15 Panzer Division and 5 Panzer Regiment to join up with the Ariete and then force the British northwards to the edge of the high ground near Sidi Rezegh that was now held by the infantry from 21 Panzer Division. General Gastone Gambara, in his capacity as chief of staff to the Supreme Commander in Libya, flatly refused to allow the Ariete's motorised corps to take part in this operation, whereupon Rommel sent a telegram to Rintelen instructing him to ask Mussolini to put Gambara under his command, and complaining bitterly that General Bastico had not even deigned to visit his headquarters, and had taken no part in recent operations, which of course was the last thing that Rommel wanted. Mussolini agreed to put the corps under Rommel's command, but Rommel remained formally subordinate to Bastico.

Major-General Neumann-Silkow's 15 Panzer Division moved south without waiting for 5 Panzer Regiment, which had been delayed. It soon ran into the British 7th Support Group with its trucks and artillery, which was caught completely by surprise, so that it was quickly overrun. Neumann-Silkow, wanting to exploit this element of surprise, moved in a westerly direction, destroying a number of 5th South African Brigade's vehicles, but Crüwell intervened, ordering that the original plan should be respected. Therefore, 15 Panzer Division moved south to join up with the Ariete, running into units from 1st South African Brigade, which was moving up to Sidi Rezegh. Facing an overwhelming force, the South Africans were obliged to withdraw.

This was the opening move of what became known in the Afrikakorps as the Battle of Totensonntag (the Sunday before the first Sunday in Advent, the German remembrance day for those who died in the First World War). The British gave it the less portentous title of the Battle of Sidi Rezegh. It was largely Crüwell's battle, since Rommel's directive reached him too late to be followed. At 1300hrs on 23 November 5th South African Brigade's impressive defensive position on the high ground to the south of the Trigh Capuzzo, which overlooked the airfield at Sidi Rezegh, was attacked by the Afrikakorps' 5 Panzer Regiment on the right flank, while 8 Panzer Regiment struck at the centre. Using innovatory tactics, the Panzer were drawn up in long lines, with the infantry following behind in their trucks. The Afrikakorps estimated that the South African position was 10 kilometres deep and 7–8 kilometres wide, with at least a hundred pieces of artillery, as well as a substantial number of anti-aircraft guns. The main attack came from the south, with the Ariete Armoured Division supporting 5 Panzer Regiment's flank attack. Three regiments of infantry from 21 Panzer Division attacked the airfield from the north.

The Ariete were soon in difficulties when 22nd Armoured Brigade attacked its left flank. Earlier that morning the 6th New Zealand Brigade, due to a happy coincidence, overran a large part of the Afrikakorps' staff with their radio command post. Twenty officers and men were taken prisoner, along with their entire radio equipment and valuable papers. They then launched a two-pronged attack from the east, hitting 361 African Regiment, positioned on the left flank of 21 Panzer Division's northerly attack, forcing them back across the Trigh Capuzzo. To the south they engaged 15 Panzer Division's right flank, meeting with an initial success, but were soon forced back. The 5th South African Brigade was doomed, in spite of these stout efforts to help them out. The attempt to bring the two South African Brigades together to the south of the airfield at Sidi Rezegh had failed: 22nd Armoured Brigade lost one-third of its remaining thirty-four tanks, and the New Zealanders' impressive performance was not enough to save the South Africans from destruction. The British continued to hammer away at the Panzer Group throughout the afternoon, but these efforts were uncoordinated and brought little benefit.

The fiercest fight was around the airfield where 15 Panzer Division, backed by units of 21 Panzer Division, was called upon to attack along the entire length of the front. Twice they were beaten back by ferocious anti-tank fire with a heavy loss of life. British armour managed to fight through to the airfield, but was destroyed. By the end of the day 15 Panzer Division bagged 100 armoured vehicles and 2,000 prisoners. A further action resulted in the destruction of 32 more tanks and 400 prisoners taken. But Crüwell's headlong attack resulted in very heavy casualties. Most of the officers and NCOs in the motorised infantry were either killed or wounded, and 70 of the 150 Panzer were lost.

Amid the confusion of battle Crüwell, and what remained of his staff, suddenly found their Mammoth armoured command vehicle

(ACV) surrounded by a number of Mark VI tanks, which fortunately for them had run out of ammunition.[41] The British tankmen walked across to the Mammoth, whose hatches were all closed. They knocked on the hull. Crüwell emerged, to find himself staring in mutual astonishment at a British soldier. At that moment the area was sprayed with gunfire, Crüwell threw himself on the floor, and the Mammoth drove off unharmed. A German 20mm anti-aircraft gun had opened fire on the British crews, who jumped back into their tanks and drove off as fast as they could.[42] Rommel also had a captured Mammoth as a command vehicle. His was nicknamed 'Max', Crüwell's 'Moritz', after Wilhelm Busch's impish young characters.

In the Battle of Totensonntag around the airfield the Germans had succeeded in beating back a serious threat to the Tobruk front, had stopped a breakout, and had destroyed a large part of the British armour, as well as inflicting a severe blow to 8th Army's morale.[43] On the other hand, the Panzer Group had suffered crippling losses, and unlike the British, they had virtually no reserves. They were soon to pay a heavy operational price for this remarkable tactical success. In part this was due to Rommel failing to see the threat posed by the New Zealanders to the north-east of 15 Panzer Division. These were elite troops, experienced in desert warfare, with an outstanding commander in Major-General Bernard Freyberg VC, and armed with the new type of Valentine tanks.[44] They managed to seize Point 175, wiping out 2 Battalion of the Africa Regiment, admittedly at the very high cost of twelve tanks and a hundred dead. Unperturbed by this setback, Rommel turned his attention to attacking the British rear echelons in the area between Sidi Omar and Bardia.

Rommel came up from El Adem to have a look for himself. Encouraged by his tactical success, he ordered 21 Panzer Division to head for the border, finish off the 7th Armoured Division and attack the British troops at the Sollum Line. This was one of the worst mistakes that Rommel made in the course of the entire North African campaign. The Afrikakorps was far too weak to cut off the British as they retired, while it left the forces at Tobruk seriously depleted and in danger of being dealt a deadly blow by the New Zealanders. He thus wasted six precious days, and when the Afrikakorps returned to Tobruk to salvage a dangerous situation, it was worn out after its pointless rush to the wire.[45] Crüwell, who had lost all his radio equipment, was out of touch with the Panzer Group and having spent the day with

15 Panzer Division, now linked up with 8 Machinegun Battalion, intent
on clearing the area to the east of Sidi Rezegh, to secure the supplies captured from the British. It soon became clear that Rommel had greatly
overestimated his success. Panzer Group's headquarters was not yet
able to assess the amount of damage that had been inflicted upon them,
and the situation was still extremely confused. Rommel now had fewer
than one hundred serviceable Panzer, and his infantry had been decimated by the South Africans.

The German navy gave effective support to the ground troops.
OKW ordered all the U-boats operating in the Mediterranean to concentrate on attacking the British supply convoys between Alexandria
and Tobruk. U-boats that had been ordered to the Mediterranean from
the Atlantic began to arrive during 'Crusader', so that by 28 November
there were fourteen U-boats operating in the Mediterranean. By the
end of the year the number had risen to twenty-four. The loss of the
Ark Royal only 25 sea miles from the Rock of Gibraltar was a damaging blow. It is said that in Cairo King Farouk, ignoring the Prophet's
injunction, cracked open a bottle of champagne in celebration.[46]

Cunningham was falling apart under the strain, while Rommel rejoiced in his somewhat pyrrhic victory, once again beginning
to entertain fantastic visions of further triumphs that were impossible
to achieve with the seriously damaged forces under his command. A
more prudent move would have been to stay put and tackle the 2nd
New Zealand Division, which was advancing towards Tobruk along
the Trigh Capuzzo.[47] In the evening of 23 November he ordered the
destruction of the remainder of 7th Armoured Division at Sidi Rezegh,
after which the British were to be forced back to the Egyptian border, enabling 8th Army's supply dumps to be seized as they withdrew.
On the following morning Rommel took over personal command of
the Afrikakorps and the Ariete so as to deliver the *coup de grâce*. He
left his 1a, Lieutenant-Colonel Siegfried Westphal, in command of the
Panzer Group, with strict instructions to stop Scobie from breaking out
of Tobruk, and confidently told his staff that he would be back that
evening, or early the next day. Crüwell, who considered this plan to
be hopelessly unrealistic, suggested a more modest course of action,
which involved clearing the British from the area between the two supply roads, Trigh Capuzzo to the north and Trigh el Abd, an old camel
caravan track, to the south. Rommel refused to listen to what he considered a faint-hearted suggestion. Rommel disappeared with Gause for

several days at this critical stage of the 'Crusader' battle, leaving Panzer Group headquarters without the slightest idea where he was, or what he was doing.

Back in Berlin, Goebbels considered that Rommel had won a great battle and began to plan how to make the maximum propagandistic capital out of a victorious campaign in North Africa. Unaware of Hitler's reservations, he decided that Rommel should be built up into a popular hero. The Luftwaffe and the navy had their stars, but the army was still somewhat reticent, perhaps because the infantry is not nearly so glamorous. Both Keitel and Jodl were in full agreement, and promised to give the propaganda minister every support. Keitel was particularly profuse in his praise of Rommel, who had achieved an astonishing operational success with very limited means. He might not yet have achieved a final victory, but he had withstood a major offensive.[48]

It is difficult to believe that Rommel really believed that he could drive 8th Army 'back to the wire'. He was given to quite extraordinary flights of fantasy, and he is said to have told Major-General Ravenstein that he had an opportunity to bring the campaign to a successful conclusion by nightfall.[49] It was not only the British who were utterly confused. Rommel had no clear idea of how his forces were deployed. He put himself in command of 21 Panzer Division and rushed up to the Egyptian border, with the entire Afrikakorps strung out behind him across 65 kilometres of desert. He charged around all over the place: at one point his armoured command car broke down well inside the Egyptian border so that along with his chief of staff, Major-General Gause and Crüwell, who had been frantically looking for him, he was unable to find a way back through the wire and spent the night surrounded by British troops. His superior, General Bastico, had no idea where he was or what he was doing. At one point he drove through a New Zealand field hospital. On another occasion he drove across a British airfield, narrowly escaping capture, and he was frequently chased by British vehicles.[50] Back at headquarters poor Westphal had to conceal from OKW and OKH the fact that he had no idea where Rommel was to be found. He had lost radio contact, and his reports were outdated, frequently incomprehensible, and gave no hints of his intentions. He thus confirmed all Halder's complaints about his impetuosity, lack of an overall grasp of a situation, inability to issue clear orders, and vainglorious disregard of the achievable.

Rommel ordered 21 Panzer Division to advance along the Trigh el Abd without bothering to find out where the remaining British forces were positioned, and before 15 Panzer Division was ready to move. His intent was to cut off the British retreat by closing the Halfaya Pass. The 7th Armoured Brigade and 7th Support Group spotted this move and swept down from the north, while 1st South African Brigade's artillery opened fire from the south. Rommel continued his advance, having sent 5 Panzer Regiment to deal with the threat to his left flank, reaching the frontier at Gasr el Abid at 1600hrs, by which time the division was stretched out along the Trigh el Abd, leaving it extremely vulnerable to flank attacks. He left a weak covering force behind to the south of Tobruk, under the command of General Karl Böttcher, his artillery commander, who was later to be given 21 Panzer Division. By nightfall on 24 November, 21 Panzer Division, with Rommel urging it on, was straggling behind the staff, who were already across the Egyptian border, to the south-east of Halfaya Pass. It took several days to regain control over the division. Left to its own devices, 15 Panzer Division stuck together, warded off several attacks, and advanced to Sidi Omar where it took up an all-round defensive position.

Rommel gave Crüwell his orders for the following day at 1700hrs. The Afrikakorps, supported by Gambara's motorised corps, was to destroy the British east of the Sollum Line: 21 Panzer Division was to attack from the east, 15 Panzer Division from the south, Gambara's corps from the west, while 33 Reconnaissance Unit was to cut off the coastal road. Crüwell suggested a more limited operation, trapping the British west of the Sollum Line to the south of Bardia. This afforded a better chance of success, given the Afrikakorps' limited forces and the imagined strength of the British positions, but Rommel remained adamant.

In fact both Rommel and Crüwell had no idea what they were up against. They both thought that there were two British divisions on the Sollum Line, when in fact there were only three brigades: 11th Indian Brigade on the coastal plane behind the Halfaya Pass, 7th Indian Brigade at Sidi Omar and 5th New Zealand Brigade to the south of Bardia. Had they known this, it would have been relatively easy to pick off the two brigades to the west of the Sollum Line, one by one.

The British were also somewhat lost, the Afrikakorps' sudden dash forward having caught them by surprise. On 23 November General Cunningham, alarmed by the number of tanks that 20th Corps had lost and worried that the attrition to 7th Armoured Division would be such as to leave the infantry with insufficient protection, had asked Auchinleck to come to 8th Army's headquarters at Maddalena to discuss the situation. The question was whether or not to call off the 'Crusader' offensive.

Rifleman Alex Bowlby's recollections of his experience in the desert reflect the rapid movement and uncertainty that characterised armoured warfare in the vast empty spaces of the North African desert:

> *I'm telling you! It was a different sort of war. There were no civvies mixed up in it. It was clean. When we took prisoners we treated them fine and they treated us fine. The fighting was different too . . . We had a go at them, or they had a go at us. Then one of us fucked off!*
>
> *You fucked off about five hundred miles without stopping, if I remember rightly.*[51]

Auchinleck arrived at Maddalena that evening, to be greeted with the news that 5th South African Brigade had been destroyed. Cunningham, who was completely confused by Rommel's counterstroke, suggested a retreat to the Egyptian border, but Auchinleck refused, ordering a regroupment west of the Sollum Line. Cunningham accordingly went to examine 30th Corps' base at Gabr Saleh the following morning, only to be caught by units of 21 Panzer Division moving along the Trigh el Abd, the supply road to Gabr Saleh. He promptly returned to Maddalena in a state of high alarm, but Auchinleck was adamant that 'Crusader' should continue, the Panzer were to be destroyed, the siege of Tobruk relieved, and the enemy pursued back to Tripoli.[52] There was considerable alarm at 8th Army headquarters during the morning of 25 November, with reports that the Germans were approaching. Auchinleck went back to Cairo for safety's sake, but he insisted that Rommel was acting out of desperation, and that were he to be continuously attacked he would easily be driven back. Auchinleck dismissed any idea of a withdrawal and ordered 'Crusader' to continue, if necessary to the last tank, until Rommel's forces were destroyed. Mellenthin, who was serving as a staff officer at Panzer Group headquarters, was full of praise for Auchinleck's 'fighting spirit and shrewd strategic insight', which, in 'certainly one of the great decisions of the war', saved the 'Crusader' battle.[53]

Cunningham was dispirited and at the end of his tether. He was on the verge of a nervous breakdown as a result of overwork and sleep deprivation. Auchinleck decided that he had to be relieved of his command. On 26 November General Sir Arthur Smith, Chief of General Staff, Middle East Command, arrived at Cunningham's command post with his replacement, his deputy, Major-General Neil Ritchie, who was well versed in all the details of 'Crusader'.

Auchinleck's cool appraisal was absolutely correct. Rommel had completely lost control of the situation, and his glorious campaign quickly degenerated into a series of uncoordinated piecemeal actions, with his unfortunate troops receiving contradictory and frequently incomprehensible orders from himself, Westphal and Crüwell. He managed to re-establish contact with the Afrikakorps during the morning of 25 November, promptly ordering 15 Panzer Division to attack from the west of the Sollum Line, because the Ariete Division had not yet arrived, in an attempt to drive the British back up against their own minefields, while 21 Panzer Division was to do likewise from east of the Sollum Line. As before, 33 Reconnaissance Unit was to cut off the coastal road, but this proved impossible owing to lack of fuel, leaving them as sitting ducks for the RAF.

15 Panzer Division followed orders, only to find itself strung out along a front that was 30 kilometres wide, desperately short of fuel and with strong British forces on both flanks. 21 Panzer Division was also spread out all over the place, spending most of the day trying to establish close contact. 5 Panzer Regiment managed to get lost as it tried to meet up with the division. These were the troops that had caused such alarm at Maddalena. They soon ran up against 7th Indian Brigade and were beaten back. They headed back south for fresh ammunition, only to find that their supply column had been bombed. Rommel came to regimental headquarters at 1300hrs and ordered a fresh attack, even though the Indians were now well positioned behind their minefield. Predictably the attack was a failure. Seven more Panzer were destroyed, the command post lost its aerial and the regiment split into two groups, neither of which managed to establish contact with the division. It was two days before the regiment was once again united.[54]

Meanwhile, Ravenstein waited impatiently to the south-east of the Halfaya Pass for his Panzer and his supplies to arrive, while 15 Panzer Division suffered crippling losses from air attacks. Then came the alarming news that the New Zealanders, supported by eighty-six tanks from 1st Armoured Brigade, had retaken the air-field at Sidi Rezegh and were heading for Tobruk. Scobie ordered another attempt to break out of Tobruk, which this time was success-ful, enabling him to join up with the New Zealanders at the Ed Duda escarpment, south-east of the town. The Bersaglieri to the north of the airfield fought with exceptional gallantry and managed to hold their position against repeated attacks by the New Zealanders, 8th Army's best troops. Westphal reacted promptly: unable to contact Rommel he recalled 21 Panzer to Tobruk, where it was ordered to attack the New Zealanders from the rear. The division was given strict instructions to ignore all orders to the contrary. It was a very courageous deci-sion by an exceptionally intelligent, but exceedingly arrogant subordi-nate. Rommel was furious when he heard of this high-handed action, announcing that Westphal had fallen into a carefully planned trap, and threatened to have him court-martialled. Ravenstein was also severely reprimanded for obeying Westphal's order to pull back his 21 Panzer Division. Rommel continued his floundering operations on the Sollum front, still determined to take Sidi Omar, but finally came to his senses. Realising that Westphal had acted correctly, he ordered his forces back to Tobruk on 27 November. The ensuing second Battle of Sidi Rezegh was to last for five days.

Thus ended Rommel's ill-considered and pointless raid, which had brought no relief to his forces on the Sollum front and in which he had lost irreplaceable assets, largely because of the complete air superiority enjoyed by the RAF now that the New Zealanders denied the Luftwaffe the use of the airfield at Gambut. The British had been able to break out of Tobruk and were given valuable time to bring up supplies and replacements from Egypt. The Boettcher Group at Tobruk was now caught in a pincer movement, one from the south-east and the other from the fortress itself. 16 managed to beat off these attacks, but it was doubtful how long it would be able to hang on.[55] Rommel did not have a single complete German division at Tobruk, and his forces were badly divided and exhausted after almost six months of fighting, against a garrison that was far better defended than it was to be the following year.

Cunningham's successor, General Neil M. Ritchie, was a rela-tively young officer, whose only experience of command in the field had been at the company level more than twenty years ago.[56] It soon turned out to be a very poor choice. Admittedly, Ritchie inherited an extremely

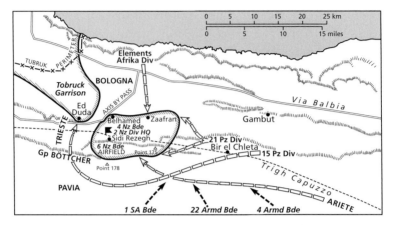

Map 7. Encirclement of 2 NZ Divison, 27–29 November 1941

confusing situation. 'Crusader' had dissolved into an unseemly mêlée, which the Australian journalist Alan Moorehead described as 'an eight-decker rainbow cake.'[57] With British and Axis troops hopelessly inter-mingled, quick decisions had to be made by officers on the spot. Ritchie can hardly be blamed for failing to grasp the overall picture, but suffer-ing from an overdose of self-confidence, he found it exceedingly difficult to delegate authority. Seeing that the Afrikakorps was beating as hasty a retreat as possible from its untenable position at the Sollum front, he ordered Norrie's 30th Corps to cut off its westward retreat. This move failed, in part because both Panzer divisions fought superbly well, but also because the British attack was mismanaged.[58]

Reconnaissance troops from 15 Panzer Division reported that there was a large supply dump at Sidi Azeiz. Major-General Neumann-Silkow, realising that this would be extremely useful for the long march back to Tobruk, ordered an attack at 0830hrs on 27 November. The 5th New Zealand Brigade's staff and assorted troops fought bravely, resulting in 44 dead and 49 wounded, but the brigadier, 45 officers and 650 men were taken prisoner, and the Germans helped themselves to the valuable supplies. This was the only successful operation during Rommel's four days at the Sollum front.[59]

On 28 November the New Zealanders managed to clear a Ger-man strongpoint on the high ground east of Sidi Rezegh, taking 600 prisoners from 155 and 361 Regiments, plus another 182 prisoners from another position, thus temporarily holding up 15 Panzer Division. The division with its fifty Panzer then continued to move westwards back to Tobruk along the Trigh Capuzzo, but was caught unpleasantly by surprise when it found the way blocked by 22nd Armoured Brigade with forty-two Cruisers, and 4th Armoured Brigade with seventy-seven Stuarts on its left flank. Neumann-Silkow only managed to extricate himself from this trap because the British broke off the engagement at nightfall. He then ordered his men to head for the high ground south of the Trigh Capuzzo. The British lacked artillery to dislodge 15 Panzer Division from its new position, while 21 Panzer Division moved westwards along the Trigh Capuzzo to help out. The Ariete was ordered back from the Egyptian border, warding off attacks on its left flank by 7th Armoured Division and 4th Armoured Brigade, while it attacked 22nd Armoured Brigade from the rear. Norrie's 30th Corps had thus failed in its mission, leaving the New Zealanders in an awkward position with the Axis threatening their rear.

They were granted a brief respite, because of yet another disagreement between Rommel and Crüwell on how best to proceed. Rommel wanted to attack the New Zealanders from the north-east, cutting them off from Tobruk, while Crüwell argued in favour of pushing along the Trigh Capuzzo and forcing the New Zealanders back into Tobruk. Crüwell and Rommel were thus at cross purposes, with Crüwell ordering 21 Panzer Division, supported by the artillery from 90 Africa Light Division, to advance along the Trigh Capuzzo, while 15 Panzer Division attacked the New Zealanders at Sidi Rezegh from the south. The Ariete Division was to guard 21 Panzer Division's left flank. Rommel attempted to revise this plan by strengthening 15 Panzer Division's attack, so as to cut off the New Zealanders from Tobruk, but Crüwell simply ignored the order.

Turning north on 28 November, 15 Panzer Division ran across a New Zealand POW camp, where they released 800 German prisoners, at the same time forcing the staff of 13th Corps to retire to the relative safety of Tobruk. A field hospital with 900 wounded New Zealanders also fell into the Panzer division's hands.[60] Crüwell's plan soon ran into difficulties, however. Major-General von Ravenstein, the commander of 21 Panzer Division, was captured on his way back to the division from the headquarters of the Afrikakorps. He was the first German general to be captured in the war. He lost his way and found himself at dawn surrounded by New Zealanders, and ended the war as a prisoner in Canada.[61] Rommel had mixed feelings about losing the general. He appreciated his leadership qualities, but heartily disliked his aristocratic manner, his aestheticism and poetastering, as well as his staff background. Also maps of German minefields and plans for the forthcoming attack found in his possession proved very valuable to British intelligence.[62]

Having managed to take the high ground at Ed Duda, to the north-west of the New Zealanders' positions at Sidi Rezegh, 15 Panzer Division was beaten back in a daring night-time raid by Australians from Tobruk. The Ariete were more successful, taking Point 175, largely because the New Zealanders mistook them for the 1st South African Brigade which had been ordered up from the south, the remainder of the division having been badly mauled on 23 November. The 21st New Zealand Battalion lost 150 prisoners in this operation. It was a significant victory, prompting Rommel to begin dreaming of a major battle of encirclement to the south-east of Tobruk, but the tough New Zealand defences along the perimeter front, combined with some high-grade Sigint, put paid to such an operation.[63] The New Zealanders to the west of Point 175 were firmly entrenched, and the Afrikakorps was far too weak to trap them. 15 Panzer Division launched a successful attack on 6th New Zealand Brigade during the evening of 30 November at Belhamed, taking 600 prisoners, but 21 Panzer Division did less well that day, facing tough opposition from the front and attacks to its flank by 7th Armoured Division. Soon threatened from the rear, the division reported that it would be unlikely to be able to hold its ground, and that there could be no question of a renewed offensive. The division asked Crüwell for permission to fight its way out to the west, but this was refused. It was ordered to stay put, no matter what the cost.

In one of the fiercest engagements in the entire North African campaign, 15 Panzer Division finally dislodged 6th New Zealand Brigade from its positions at Sidi Rezegh. Major-General Sir Bernard Freyberg, a gallant soldier who had had the misfortune to preside over the evacuation of Crete, requested permission to retire to Tobruk, but 13th Corps' commander, Lieutenant-General A. R. Godwin-Austin, refused permission, on the grounds that the South Africans were on their way. 15 Panzer kept up the pressure, hitting 4th New Zealand Brigade with full force, obliging Freyberg to order a withdrawal to the north-east in the direction of Zairian. Rommel's intention to drive a wedge between the New Zealanders and Tobruk was thus achieved, more by accident than design, but the New Zealanders were still far from defeated, even though they had been left badly in the lurch. The

1st South African Brigade was a dispirited force that arrived on the scene far too late, while 4th Armoured Brigade reached Sidi Rezegh when the New Zealanders had already left. With no co-ordinated plan, they headed back south.

The New Zealanders fought with their customary resolution, but were no match for the disciplined skill of the Panzer Group, which also had to contend with a flank attack from the south by British armour. The Afrikakorps had managed to defeat the 8th Army's best infantry divisions, forcing them to retire to the south-east, but the Tobruk front was still largely intact, while 5th Brigade at Bardia had some nasty surprises for the Germans up their sleeves. What at first sight appeared to be a victory for the Afrikakorps was in fact a shattering defeat. The Panzer had fought brilliantly and scored many successes, but they had suffered crippling losses. They were left with just 17 of their 73 Panzer IIs, 31 of their 144 Panzer IIIs and 9 of their 38 Panzer IVs, but Rommel characteristically refused to accept the fact that he had been badly beaten, imagining that he could maintain his investing circle around Tobruk and restore his lines of communication to his men who were cut off at the Halfaya Pass, Bardia and Sollum. Cooler heads pointed out that it was doubtful whether, with the Afrikakorps in tatters, he would be able to stay in Cyrenaica.[64]

The Panzer Group now faced a number of awesome tasks. Contact had to be re-established with the troops marooned on the Sollum front, who had supplies for only two days. The British corridor from Tobruk had to be closed off, the encirclement of the fortress secured. To these ends troops were sent along the coastal road and the Trigh Capuzzo to the Sollum front. During the night of 30 November 90 Light Africa Division unsuccessfully attempted to close the corridor. Another attempt the following day by the 'Kolbeck Battalion', made up of the recently released POWs, supported by the Trento Division, got nowhere. A ferocious counterattack was finally beaten off by 605 Panzergrenadiers, supported by units from 15 Panzer Division, so that disaster was avoided.

Ritchie had not the slightest intention of allowing Rommel time to regroup. On 1 December he ordered 30th Corps to advance to El Adem on the Trigh Capuzzo to the south of Tobruk. The 4th Indian Division was to be brought up in support, having been replaced at Sollum by 2nd South African Division. The New Zealanders were withdrawn, to be refreshed by men from Palestine and Cyprus. Troops were brought in from Egypt and Syria to give additional weight to the offensive, and 1st Armoured Division, which had just arrived from Britain, was brought up to the front. Lieutenant-General Godwin-Austen, anxious not to be left out, let it be known that 13th Corps did not intend to remain purely on the defensive, but had units eager to throw the Germans out of Cyrenaica.

Rommel, determined to break through to the Sollum front, ordered an advance along the Trigh Capuzzo and the Via Balbia, but the forces he allotted to this task, lacking armoured support, were totally inadequate. They were driven back with heavy losses on 3 December. The Panzer Group's reports to OKW continued to put an optimistic gloss on the situation, so that this setback was not reported. On the following day 21 Panzer Division's attack on Ed Duda, where the British threatened the Panzer Group's forces investing Tobruk, was repulsed. 15 Panzer Division, which had been called in to help the push along the supply roads, was initially successful, but soon had to be withdrawn to meet a threat to the south, where the British attacked the German position at Bir el Gubi in the initial phase of a drive northwards to El Adem. Once again Rommel and Crüwell disagreed as to what to do next. Crüwell wanted first to destroy the British forces to the south-east of Tobruk before concentrating on linking up with the Sollum front. Rommel, encouraged by news that units of the 8th Army were retiring to Sidi Barrani, wanted to tackle the British at Bardia and chase the New Zealanders back to the wire. The attack on Bardia was a disaster. 15 Panzer Division did not feel that it had sufficient strength for the task and warned its two forward units not to engage the enemy if they seemed too powerful. In spite of this cautious approach, the 28th Maori Battalion shot to pieces the Afrikakorps' last remaining infantry battalion, which was almost at full strength, at the cost of only nine wounded. An Indian reconnaissance group, supported by heavy artillery fire, halted another German unit, which was pushing along the Trigh Capuzzo. It now seemed that the tide had finally turned.

Ritchie was well aware that the Panzer Group's positions on the edge of the high ground south-east of Tobruk were exceptionally well protected by anti-tank guns and artillery. He also realised that El Adem, to the south of Tobruk, was the vital supply and communications point for the German and Italian forces. He hoped therefore to lure the Panzer out into the open ground around El Adem where his superiority in numbers would bring a decisive result. The 30th Corps, made up of 7th Armoured Division, 22nd Guards Brigade, 1st South African Brigade and 11th Indian Brigade, was ordered to take El Adem, while 13th Corps was to hang on to the corridor from Tobruk. If possible 13th Corps was to join up with 30th Corps to the south. It was now very uncertain whether the Panzer Group would be able to withstand this attack. The Afrikakorps had lost 3,800 officers and men, including 16 commanders, since 18 November. It had lost 25 of its 38 Panzer IVs, 95 of its 144 Panzer IIIs, 25 of its 33 armoured cars, 16 of its 36 light howitzers, 8 of its 12 heavy howitzers and 6 of its 12 10cm cannons. 90 Light Africa Division was below half strength, and some of its units had been completely destroyed. All now depended on the Panzer Group's response to the British offensive to the south of Tobruk. Rommel knew that he had to win this battle if he were to hang on to the Sollum front.

The Afrikakorps moved too slowly to be able to counter Norrie's buildup at Bir el Gubi, largely because Crüwell had to wait for the Italian armour to disengage from the British, before joining in the counterattack. Gambara argued that the Ariete and the Trieste were too weak to fight, but Crüwell insisted that all they had to do was guard the Afrikakorps' flank, leaving the fighting to the Germans. Crüwell bombarded Rommel's headquarters with radio messages in clear demanding 'Where is Gambara?' This was soon to become a popular expression among the men of the Afrikakorps.[65] By this time Norrie had assembled an armoured brigade and four infantry brigades with powerful artillery support. Although the British acted in a very circumspect manner, Crüwell knew that he was hopelessly outnumbered and Rommel, who had just been told by Lieutenant-Colonel Montezemolo, who arrived at his headquarters on 5 December, that the Comando Supremo was unable to send him the supplies and reinforcements he badly needed, and whose urgent appeals for help to OKW and OKH fell on deaf ears, reluctantly agreed to abandon the siege of Tobruk, ordering a withdrawal back to Gazala, on the coast some 60 kilometres west of the town. The Savona Division on the Sollum front was ordered to retire to Bardia where ample provisions were stored.[66]

This setback left Rommel in a towering rage, which was in no way relieved when OKH promised him another 9,000 men, mainly anti-tank units. Confusion reigned in the night of 5/6 December with units of Norrie's 30th Corps floundering around in the dark. The Afrikakorps could have delivered a shattering blow were it not equally muddled and exhausted, with Rommel making the cardinal sin of dividing up his forces in a series of piecemeal attacks. Later he was to denounce Montgomery for time and time again making the same mistake. That the 8th Army won the day on 6 December was due almost entirely to their superb artillery, without which the Afrikakorps might have able to pick off the widely dispersed British units one by one. Major-General Neumann-Silkow died of wounds received during one such massive barrage, standing in the turret of his command Panzer. He was a commander who was immensely respected by and popular with his men, commanding from the front and never losing the common touch. He shared with Rommel what the men in the 8th Army called the 'shit or bust' approach to soldiering that was much appreciated by other ranks on both sides. The withdrawal was further endangered when General Gambara refused to withdraw the Pavia Division from the front, arguing that Comando Supremo had issued orders that Cyrenaica was to be held, whatever the cost. General Navarini loyally reported the incident to Rommel's headquarters, but it took so long to get the order countermanded in Rome that the Pavia Division could not be saved from severe losses of men and equipment when it was attacked by two infantry battalions supported by tanks at 2000hrs.[67]

Field Marshal Kesselring, the newly appointed Commander-in-Chief South, visited Rommel's headquarters on 7 December in an attempt to assuage his aggrieved subordinate, but could only promise him a few additional fighter aircraft.[68] On 2 December Hitler, in Order Number 38, had appointed Kesselring to this new position, having ordered the transfer of aircraft from the Soviet Union to the Mediterranean to meet the renewed British threat in North Africa.[69] 2 Air Fleet was sent to lend support to 10 Air Corps, which had in turn been seriously weakened by having to send aircraft to the east in support of Barbarossa. Kesselring was ordered to secure the sea routes from southern Italy to North Africa, keep Malta in subjection, paralyse British traffic through the Mediterranean, cut off supplies to Tobruk, and co-operate closely with the Panzer Group. He was formally under Mussolini's command, but OKW was to be kept informed of all-important decisions. Rommel was not informed of this new order until 5 December. It gave him hope that with strengthened air power in the Mediterranean he would soon be able to win back all that he was now obliged to abandon. General Bastico ordered Rommel to come to his headquarters, but he flatly refused, whereupon 'Bombastico' swallowed his pride and went to visit Rommel. The unfortunate Italian was treated to a lengthy tirade, during which Rommel threatened to order the Afrikakorps back to Tripoli, after which he would surrender himself in Tunisia.[70] This astonishing performance made a distinct impression on Bastico, who put all the Italian troops in Cyrenaica under Rommel's command, and agreed to a withdrawal to the Gazala positions, while flatly vetoing any further move westwards. The Italians were soon under attack as the British attempted to outflank the Gazala Line from the south, but they managed to ward off the attempt with a counterattack.[71] Rommel hung on at Gazala for three days, before ordering a withdrawal back to Derna and Mechili, in spite of Bastico's order to stand and fight. He now faced the difficult task of fighting his way back across Cyrenaica, a terrain that was exceedingly difficult to defend with such modest forces, because of the ever-present threat of being outflanked.

This still left the question open as to whether to withdraw the Axis troops from the Sollum front. Rommel asked OKH and Comando Supremo for instructions, both of which ordered him to stay put. The problem of supplying the Sollum front was intensified when the Savona Division moved to the Halfaya Pass, rather than back to Bardia. The Bardia garrison managed to ward off attacks by 2nd South African Division on 16 and 17 December, but the situation had become so serious that on 19 December Rommel requested that the Italian navy withdraw all the troops on the Egyptian border. The Comando Supremo, however, insisted that they should remain in place, because they blocked the British supply route along the coastal road, tying up an entire British division.[72] British Sigint prompted the chief of air staff to send a personal message to Auchinleck, which announced with relish that 'It might be deduced that a Dunkirk is to be attempted. In this event, fighter cover might be difficult. This may well be our opportunity to turn it into another and better Crete.'[73]

Meanwhile Ritchie had mounted a massive attack on the Sollum front on 15 December. Kesselring returned to North Africa with Cavallero on 16 December to deal with this threat, to patch up relations between Bastico and Rommel, and to persuade Rommel to defend the fertile area between Derna and Benghazi; but Rommel continued to insist that were he to stay put on the Gazala, he would be encircled and destroyed, whereas a withdrawal would at least enable him to defend Tripolitania. Kesselring stressed the political importance of maintaining good relations with the Italians, while Cavallero argued

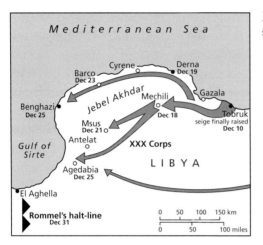

Map 8. Rommel retires to the starting line, December 1941

that now Japan had entered the war the British would be obliged to move forces from the Middle East, thus taking the pressure off the Axis forces. Rommel refused to budge.[74] He wrote to Mussolini saying that the Italian troops in North Africa were so worn out that they would not be able to withstand an Allied offensive. British superiority in the air was causing a number of units to fall apart. He asked for permission to withdraw to the Arco de Fileni, to give his troops a rest and restore their fighting spirit. Announcing that he would not tolerate 'the pointless sacrifice of 15,000 Italian and German soldiers', he told the Duce that he had ordered Generals Schmitt and Giorgis to hold the Sollum Line as long as possible, but if they were unable to do so, they were to surrender.[75] With great reluctance Mussolini eventually agreed that the main thing was to ensure the defence of Tripolitania, but Kesselring continued to insist that Rommel should hold the line east of Benghazi. It was only when aerial reconnaissance revealed that the British army was steadily advancing to the south, thus threatening to cut off Benghazi, that there was general agreement that Rommel should withdraw. An ordered withdrawal from Benghazi began on 22 December.

Rommel had no alternative to a withdrawal, in spite of Bastico's orders to stand and fight, so he sent the Brescia Division, along with the Italian 21 Corps, back along the coastal road to Derna. To the south the Italian 20 Corps, made up of the Ariete and Trieste, along with the Afrikakorps retired to Mechili. Bastico alerted Cavallero to these alarming developments, and immediately went with Kesselring to consult with Rommel. It was then decided to evacuate Cyrenaica

in a slow and orderly manner and to make a firm stand in Tripolitania. Rommel realised that he would have to move quickly in order
to avoid being cut off, opting for a quick dash to Agedabia and El
Agheila. This operation was successful, partly because the pursuing
British soon began to run into logistical difficulties. The Panzer Group
stayed at Agedabia between Christmas Day and Twelfth Night. It was
an unsuitable place to stop while bringing up reinforcements, because
it was extremely vulnerable to flank attack. It was also too far from the
nearest air bases. Rommel was greatly relieved to hear that 45 Panzer
had been delivered to Tripoli and Benghazi. Crüwell promptly threw
them into action, attacking 22nd Armoured Brigade near Agedabia on
28 December, knocking out sixty of its tanks for a loss of only fourteen. In spite of this success, Rommel ordered his troops back to El
Agheila. During the night of 5/6 January, 90 Light Africa Division and
the Italian motorised corps at Agedabia were withdrawn to the new
position, their movement unnoticed by the British.[76] Meanwhile, on
31 December 2nd South African Division, supported by 1st Armoured
Brigade, launched an attack on Bardia with massive support from the
Western Desert Air Force and the Royal Navy. Two days later Major-
General Artur Schmitt surrendered the Bardia garrison of 6,600 Italians
and 2,200 Germans. Radio communication with the troops at the Halfaya Pass was lost, but was restored the following day. The situation
was grim with intense artillery fire and little chance of being able to
withdraw.[77] By 12 January 1942 the first of Rommel's troops were
back in the charming little town of Sirte, once the centre of the saffron
trade,[78] where they had begun their advance to the Egyptian border in
March the previous year. The bulk of the Panzer Group moved back to
the Mersa el Brega between 13 and 20 January, where they improved
the defences while building up reserves, intent as soon as possible once
again to go on the offensive.

In its analysis of the campaign the Panzer Group's staff were
full of admiration for the 8th Army's brilliant buildup for the offensive
and skilful deception, but felt that the operation had been badly bungled by dissipating the forces in small groups rather than delivering one
concerted blow or *Schwerpunkt*. The British were obviously trying to
learn from the Germans but were far too slow, plodding and methodical. Orders from above were far too detailed, and the middle and lower
ranks were given too little leeway to react as the battle developed. The
British soldiers fought well, even though they lacked the Germans' dash.

Their officers were brave and self-sacrificing, but inflexible as a result of the top-down command structure. The NCOs were given very good marks, and the artillery and air force were considered outstanding. The Germans were also full of admiration for the Long Range Desert Group and the SAS. The Panzer Group considered that it had done well against a numerically superior and better equipped army that was used to fighting in the desert. Although beset by logistical problems, compounded by the inevitable difficulties in fighting a coalition war, it had managed to build up its *Schwerpunkte* wherever possible and had never felt inferior to the British while fighting their way back to Libya. The staff insisted that it really did not matter whether Marmarica or Cyrenaica was in British hands or not. Empty spaces of desert were of little account. The object was to preserve one's forces, counterattack and regain all that had been lost. Co-ordination with the Luftwaffe had been excellent, and Kesselring was a frequent visitor to Rommel's headquarters. The Italians remained a major problem. Things improved when they were under the operational control of the Panzer Group, but they could not be trusted on their own. Their leadership was so unimaginative, hesitant and timid that they could not be put in a difficult situation, and they were incapable of withstanding a threat to their flanks. The failure of the offensive was now turned into a major victory. Dr Goebbels' spin machine went into high gear. Germany had been saved from the threat of a second front, the consequences of which 'could not be foreseen'. The British had suffered such a severe setback that they would be unable to go on the offensive for some time to come. The Panzer Group's staff could not resist the temptation to argue that they had thus given Germany a morale boost after the failure of 'Barbarossa', as well as contributing significantly to improved Italian self-esteem.[79]

Rommel placed the entire blame for the failure of his offensive on the Italians, so that relations between the Axis partners were strained to the limit. A few hundred men from the Savona Division under the command of Lieutenant-General Fedele De Giorgis were ordered by Rommel to abandon their position west of the Halfaya Pass and join up with Major Bach's men. Their support was welcome, but placed a further strain on the supplies of food and water. On 17 January De Giorgis, who was now in command of all the troops on the Halfaya Line, starved of supplies and heavily outnumbered, sent out a parleying party. In all 3,800 Italians and 2,100 Germans surrendered to the South Africans, leaving the Halfaya Pass once again in British hands. Major

Bach and his men, like so many of the Axis troops taken prisoner in North Africa, were sent to a POW camp in Canada.[80]

The capitulation was marked by a disgraceful incident. The South Africans treated their prisoners admirably, providing them with food and drink, tending the wounded and prepared to march to the rear. Suddenly some of the German prisoners came under heavy artillery fire from the south. The South Africans were outraged. Eventually a dispatch rider arrived with a message that the fire came from a Free French battery that had acted against explicit orders to hold their fire. A South African officer passed on this information to Major Bach with undisguised contempt for the French.[81]

'Crusader', which preceded the Red Army's counterattack outside Moscow on 5 December, was the first successful offensive against the Germans, forcing Rommel to retire and abandon Cyrenaica. It was celebrated in London as a great victory, for it seemed that the Axis forces in North Africa had been destroyed. But the British had no cause to be self-congratulatory. They had succeeded only because of overwhelming superiority in men and matériel. The Germans had proved to be vastly superior at the tactical and operational level, even though Rommel made colossal blunders by hammering away at Tobruk, making his 'dash to the wire' before taking Tobruk, and by consistently underrating his opponents. The British had lost 600 tanks, the Germans 220, the Italians 120. The operation had been far too long and costly, using up valuable reserves and leaving the British too weak to chase Rommel back to Tripoli and the Tunisian border. The British now faced the problem of long lines of communication all the way back to Egypt, while Rommel had moved far closer to his supply bases. British confidence that they would be able to renew the advance in February was undermined by the destruction of K Force, and by determined efforts by the Axis to frustrate British operations in the central Mediterranean.

The great problem for the Axis was still that of protecting the convoys to North Africa. The Italians did not have any aircraft carriers, which soon turned out to be a serious deficiency. They had also failed to develop radar, so at night they were blind. The British managed to decrypt the Italian naval code, which had been changed at the insistence of the Germans, in the summer of 1941, so that they knew all the details of their movements, and could attack at night with torpedo planes stationed in Malta. The Italian navy put up a miserable performance in the Mediterranean, but the Germans, having lost the *Graf Spee* and the *Bismarck*, and having bungled the operation in Norway, were in no position to criticise their ally. This did nothing, however, to stop Weichold from continually making high-handed suggestions as to how the Italians should conduct their business.

In spite of these difficulties the first convoy to Tripoli in 1942 arrived on time and without loss on 5 January. Along with 'unspecified' Italian supplies, the Afrikakorps received 152 men, 147 vehicles and 3,504 tons of supplies. Even more important were the 51 Panzer, 16 armoured cars and 'a considerable number' of anti-tank guns allotted to the Afrikakorps. The Italians were given three of the Panzer and one armoured car from this shipment.[82]

This was enough to encourage Rommel to launch a second offensive. The overall situation seemed to be propitious. Japan's entry into the war meant that the British were likely to move troops and naval vessels to the Pacific. An air offensive against Malta, which was a constant threat to the supply lines to North Africa, was in full swing. The United States was unlikely to play a serious role in Europe for at least a year. OKW realised that everything depended on victory over the Soviet Union in the summer of 1942, but this was of no concern to Rommel, who never saw the campaign in North Africa in terms of Germany's grand strategy. Estimating that his forces were at least equal to the British, he was determined to strike at once and win a glorious victory that would silence his many critics and further enhance his reputation as a master of modern warfare.

6 ✠ ON THE OFFENSIVE AGAIN

Rommel now concentrated on strengthening his defences at Mersa el Brega, converting them into the '*Ostwall*' in Tripolitania. He could afford to take his time because the British offensive had run out of steam, operating with supply lines that stretched back for 1,000 kilometres, and with the withdrawal, as Cavallero had predicted, of Australian and New Zealand units to fight the Japanese: 7th Armoured Brigade was sent to Burma, 70th Division went to India. Two Australian divisions were moved to the Pacific, along with four RAF squadrons. Part of the Mediterranean fleet was also moved to the Pacific, including six Australian warships. K Force was eliminated. U-boats sank the cruiser *Galatea* and the corvette *Salvia* along with six freighters they were trying to protect off the coast of Crete, while Prince Valerio Borghese's 'human torpedoes' (*maiali* – pigs) had entered the harbour at Alexandria putting the two remaining British battleships in the Mediterranean out of action for several months.[1]

On 19 December the Luftwaffe mounted its first raid on Malta from Sicily after a pause of six months. Pending Kesselring's return 2 Air Corps in Sicily was under orders from Colonel Ernst-August Roth, flying 400 missions against Malta by the end of the year, with 950 in January. These initial attacks were made from a great height and did relatively little damage. Between 18 December 1941 and the end of January 42,000 tons of cargo were landed in Malta, while in the first two weeks of 1942 the RAF flew 107 bombing missions from its bases on the island, in one raid on Castelvetrano destroying forty-nine Axis transport planes. Nevertheless, the Axis managed to protect their convoys to North Africa successfully, losing only one troop carrier in January.

Thus, in spite of all this effort, what Colonel-General Hans Jeschonnek, the Luftwaffe's chief of staff, described as Britain's 'unsinkable aircraft carrier', was still very much in business. Chief of staff of 2 Air Corps, Colonel Paul Deichmann, completed a study for an air offensive against Malta by the end of December. He called for a continuous attack, night and day, that would destroy the RAF on the ground and in the air, while dummy raids would force the anti-aircraft batteries to use up their ammunition. The second phase of the operation called for the destruction of the port facilities and airfields, along with a number of major infrastructural targets. Kesselring ordered Weichold urgently to request the Italians to back up the air offensive against Malta by laying mines outside Valletta and other lesser ports, blockading the island, as well as the Straits of Messina. As usual Weichold seized the ball and ran with it, developing a naval strategy for the entire Mediterranean. He wanted the Italian navy to concentrate on the central Mediterranean, while the U-boats would deny the British access to Tobruk and Malta. The sea lanes to Malta and the Straits of Messina were to be mined. Somewhat later he added Alexandria to the list. Weichold and Kesselring agreed that the mines should be laid between 10 and 20 February, during which time 2 Air Corps would complete phase one of Roth's plan, with phase two to begin on 16 February.[2]

The German navy entertained exotic hopes that Japan's entry into the war would radically alter the naval war in the Atlantic and the Mediterranean. The fundamental error was the assumption that the United States would be obliged drastically to cut back supplies to Britain, while the Royal Navy would have to transfer significant assets to the Pacific. This would give the Germans an opportunity to throttle Britain by sinking 800,000 to 1,000,000 GRT per month. The major problem was that the navy was desperately short of fuel, and there was little chance of solving this problem before the end of March 1942.[3]

On 18 January 1942 agreement was reached between Germany, Italy and Japan on a joint naval strategy, but it was soon shown to be an empty concept.[4] The German navy concentrated on sinking freighters, whereas the Japanese were concerned with purely military targets. It was obvious that the Japanese were not going to help out in the Atlantic. Contrary to earlier hopes, the situation in the Mediterranean did not change significantly, at least not until Rommel was once again on the move. The German Naval Command (Skl) therefore continued to insist that they should concentrate on the Atlantic, where capital ships were once again to be deployed along with the U-boats, as soon as the fuel crisis was mastered. In the Mediterranean it was a question of more of the same. The navy's mission was still to protect Axis convoys to North Africa, and to disrupt British convoys to Malta and Egypt. An apparent agreement on these issues was reached with the Italians at a meeting in the Bavarian resort of Garmisch-Partenkirchen on 14/15 January 1942, but this merely papered over fundamental differences between the allies, and the proceedings were overshadowed by the fuel crisis.[5]

Japan's entry into the war did, however, have a dramatic effect on the situation in North Africa. The British had to withdraw substantial resources in order to meet the threat in the Pacific, so that for the Axis the logistical situation in North Africa greatly improved. During November British naval and air forces managed to destroy 12 of the 46 ships leaving Italian harbours, accounting for one-third of the total tonnage. In December they destroyed 8 of the 30 ships, in January 2 of 35, in February 3 of 33 and in March only 2 of 37. This meant that the destruction of the Axis positions at Sollum and Halfaya on 17 January, and the withdrawal to the Mersa el Brega Line, was of little operational consequence. The Panzer Army Africa had lost 33 per cent of its German troops and 40 per cent of its Italians since 18 November, but these losses could now be made good, the army re-equipped and replenished, so that by 21 January Rommel was once again on the offensive.

Rommel argued that the British were now about equal in strength, and in some respects weaker, but the Panzer Group staff's reports did not bear him out. There were admittedly 192 German and Italian tanks to 188 British, but in all other respects the British were superior. In armoured cars the relationship was 24 to 292; in artillery 118 to 280; in anti-tank guns 151 to 216; anti-aircraft guns 107 to 144; in fighters 57 to 200 and bombers 75 to 125.[6]

The Italians wanted to concentrate on the Mediterranean, knocking out Malta so as to obviate the need for escorts for the convoys to North Africa, which consumed far too much precious fuel. They were supported by Weichold, who was pursuing his own private agenda, while Skl argued that the Atlantic was the key area of operations.[7] Cavallero thought that an offensive against Malta had the additional attraction of providing an effective means of holding Rommel back, by further strangling his supplies.[8] The Germans insisted that the situation in North Africa had stabilised after Pearl Harbor, so that the existing naval and air forces in the Mediterranean were sufficient to do the job of keeping up the pressure on Malta, and ensuring the supplies to the Axis forces in Tripoli. Skl was also strongly opposed to the Italian suggestion that permission should be sought from Vichy France for use of the harbour in Bizerta, on the grounds that this would almost certainly result in the British and Americans seizing the French colonies in North and West Africa.[9]

The Germans were beginning to live in a fantasy world, with Hitler still imagining that he could achieve his outlandish plans for world domination. 'Barbarossa' was already in serious difficulties by November with the onset of winter and a Soviet counterattack at Rostow. The plan to defeat the Soviet Union in a swift campaign was in ruins with the counterattack before Moscow on 5 December. Hitler was already clutching at straws, imagining that social tensions in Britain were growing so intense that a political arrangement was in the realm of possibility, or that were the Japanese to enter the fray there would be a decisive reversal of Germany's dwindling fortunes. At times Hitler hinted that the war was lost, and that he was preparing for a kind of national suicide in a colossal Götterdämmerung. But he also imagined that Britain's overriding determination to preserve its empire would lead to a rapprochement with Germany, leaving him free to finish off his campaign in the east. He was quite right in believing that Churchill's main war aim was to hang on to the empire, but failed to understand that the Middle East, as the gateway to India, was a key area. He was fully confident that Rommel would soon once again go on the offensive and win back Benghazi; then, when the situation stabilised, he intended to use his 'most proficient general' elsewhere, handing over command in North Africa to Crüwell.[10] Mussolini was also living in a world of fantasy, announcing that the United States was a country of niggers and Jews run by a paralytic, which was both too feeble and too distant to pose any threat to Italy's grandiose ambitions.[11]

OKW took a more realistic approach. They acted on the reasonable assumption that the United States would not be able to open a second front in Europe before 1943. In the meantime they would concentrate on building up forces in Britain, North Africa and the Middle East. In order to be ready to meet the threat of an Anglo-American invasion, the campaign in the Soviet Union would have to be brought to a satisfactory conclusion by the summer of 1942. The main aims were to seize Murmansk and Archangel, through which Allied supplies were channelled, to secure the oilfields of the Caucasus, then to establish a securely defensible front line. This would leave Germany economically secure in a Europe that would be militarily and politically defensible.[12] On 14 December 1941 OKW expressed the intention of creating a 'Western Wall' (*Westwall*) from Norway to the Atlantic coast that would repulse any attempt by the Allies to open up a second front.[13]

Hitler had recovered from his bout of pessimism by the end of December. In his New Year letter to Mussolini he said that Japan's entry into the war placed Britain in an exceedingly difficult position so that it should be possible for Rommel to hang on at Bardia and the Sollum front and once again go on the offensive.[14] He announced that their combined navies and air forces should be able to deny the British access to the Mediterranean, while an increased number of U-boats going into service in January would seriously disrupt Allied shipping in the Atlantic. He urged Mussolini to use his U-boats to send supplies to Tripoli: 'Even if sailors are unwilling to do this, because they consider it to be dishonourable to carry tinned food, petrol and ammunition on board, rather than torpedoes.' If they were able to provide the troops in North Africa with a sufficient number of tanks it could very well lead to a dramatic change in the situation and give Herr Churchill something to think about.[15] On 3 January he told the Japanese ambassador, Hiroshi Oshima, that as soon as the weather improved he would continue the offensive in the direction of the Caucasus, then press on into Iran and Iraq. This would inspire the Arabs to revolt against the British and provide the Reich with adequate oil supplies.[16] At much the same time he dusted off Order Number 32 for a two-pronged attack on the Middle East, pointing out to his entourage at the Wolf's Lair that the 'English' were in a desperate situation, having to deal with North Africa, Russia, India and Australia. As soon as the British started to move troops out of North Africa he would send Rommel everything that he needed, then they might finally be brought to the negotiating table. For the time being it was important to hang on, and make every effort to ensure that supplies reached North Africa safely.

The Grand Mufti, Haj Amin al Husseini, had assured Hitler in November that the Arabs longed for a German victory, since in the English, the Jews and Communists they had the same enemies. Victory for their cause was certain, not only because of Germany's large army with its valiant soldiers, led by a military genius, but also because the Almighty would never allow an unjust cause to triumph. The Arabs were fighting for the unity and independence of Palestine, Syria and Iraq. Hitler refrained from giving such a guarantee, but promised that once the German army crossed the Caucasus all the Jews in the Arab world, including those protected by the British, would be 'annihilated'.[17] The Afrikakorps was anxious not to get involved in the 'Arab question', which necessarily involved the 'Jewish question', insisting that this was exclusively an Italian concern. There was a mounting problem in that the Arabs were obtaining a large amount of weapons and there had been a number of attacks on Germans. Gause ordered that all drivers should have an armed escort, and that any Arab who was caught red-handed should be immediately handed over to the Italians. Above all there should be no reprisals. It was assumed that Arabs were simply after plunder, and that various sabotage raids were the work of irregular British units such as the LRDG.[18]

The Italians were still keen to persuade Vichy to give the Axis access to Bizerta. Mussolini even suggested that it might be taken by force. The German liaison officers in Rome seconded this proposal, but Hitler was less than enthusiastic. The German ambassador in Paris, Otto Abetz, arranged for Göring to meet Pétain on 1 December at Saint Florentin-Vergigny and again in Berlin on 20 December, but the talks led nowhere. Hitler was never enthusiastic about the idea, feeling that the price that Vichy would demand would be far too high, and with Japan's entry into the war his hopes that he could reach an agreement with Britain were once again high. Perhaps the French colonies could be thrown in as a sweetener. Hitler therefore ordered Göring to take a hard line with Pétain during the Berlin talks, so that the unfortunate French delegation, which included General Juin and Jacques Benoît-Méchin, Laval's secretary of state, both of whom were known to be pro-German, was reduced to appearing as pitiful beggars, offering all manner of concessions to the imperious Reichsmarschall. A few days after this meeting Vichy went so far as to promise that, should the British army cross the borders of Tunisia, the French forces would be ordered to open fire. This note was left unanswered.[19] It was an empty threat. Months before the Italian consul in Tunis had told Ciano that in Tunisia 'even the stones are Gaullist', and 80 per cent of the middle classes firmly believed in a British victory. Whereas most Tunisians hated the Germans, although they had a sneaking admiration for them, they had nothing but contempt for the Italians.[20] On 29 December Mussolini wrote to Hitler stressing the need to use the Tunisian ports, but the price he was prepared to pay to Vichy France was far too high for Hitler even to consider. Mussolini suggested that the cost to the French of the German occupation could be reduced, the French government should return to Paris, and that a large number of French prisoners of war should be released. Mussolini argued that if the Axis had access to the Tunisian coast the situation in North Africa would change radically in their favour. If they were only able to use Tripoli the supply situation would become critical. The price, in Mussolini's eyes, was well worth paying, but Hitler in his strangely optimistic mood would not agree.[21] A few days later Ciano told the German ambassador, Hans-Georg von Mackensen, that the idea of armed intervention in Tunisia came from Cavallero, who thought in purely military terms. He assured the ambassador that he had had nothing to do with drafting Mussolini's letter to Hitler, and that he disagreed with the whole idea.[22] With that the issue was forgotten for the next several months, until El Alamein and the 'Torch' landings made it of decisive importance.

On 5 January 1942 a convoy arrived in Tripoli with fifty-five Panzer and twenty armoured cars, as well as anti-tank guns and sundry other supplies. For Rommel this was the equivalent of a victory in battle, so he immediately thought that now he could put into effect the plans he had already drawn up for the reconquest of Cyrenaica.[23] Once again Rommel was ignoring major logistical problems that had yet to be solved. German U-boats operating in the Mediterranean scored a number of successes against the Royal Navy in the first three months of 1942, but the Italians did not seize the opportunity significantly to increase the amount of supplies being sent to North Africa. In February and March they fell far behind the minimal requirements of the Panzer army. There was a slight improvement in April, but most of the supplies were still sent to Tripoli, far away from the front. By the end of May Rommel had sufficient supplies of fuel for twenty days of operations, but he lacked reserves and it would not be long before the British hit back with a vengeance.[24]

On 12 January 1942 Rommel climbed into an aeroplane with Lieutenant-Colonel Siegfried Westphal to have a look at his defences. Both men were appalled at what they saw. The Italians were strung out in a thin line with wide gaps between units, so that they could easily be overrun. Westphal ordered the general staff's senior intelligence officer, Major Friedrich Wilhelm von Mellenthin, to report on the strength of the British army facing them. This study showed that 7th Armoured

Division had been so badly mauled that it would have to be withdrawn and replaced by 1st Armoured Division, which had no experience of desert warfare. The 4th Indian Division was positioned near Benghazi and 200th Guards Motor Brigade at Agedabia. This meant that the Panzer Group had a numerical superiority for the moment, but that would soon be lost when the British brought up their reserves. Westphal concluded from this report that the Panzer Group should go on the offensive as soon as possible to exploit this advantage. There was a widespread feeling among the men in the Afrikakorps that they would never be able to regain what they had lost in the past few weeks. Lance-Corporal W. S. from 15 Panzer Division's supply column wrote home: 'For a long time he [the enemy] has had superiority over us in aircraft; also in tanks, of which he has put huge quantities into action. By contrast we have had far too few. Unfortunately we have had to retreat a long way, and I doubt very much whether we will be able to win it back again. They are so much stronger than we are.'[25] Rommel was also initially sceptical, but soon changed his mind and began planning the attack. It was to prove to be Rommel's most brilliant offensive.[26]

Hitler's prediction that the British would be obliged to reduce their forces in the Middle East proved correct, so Rommel was soon raring to leave the Mersa el Brega defences and go on the offensive once again. Further encouragement was offered by the mounting political crisis in Egypt where the British felt obliged to force King Farouk, who was known to be pro-German, to appoint a new pro-British government under Nahhas Pasha, the leader of the Wafd Party. Zulfikar Pasha, Farouk's father-in-law and a close friend of the Mufti, forwarded a letter from the king to Hitler announcing that he was 'full of heartfelt admiration for the Führer and respect for the German people, and sincerely wish that they conquer England, and am one with my people in the hope that German troops will be victorious in Egypt as soon as possible, for we see them as liberators from the unacceptably brutal English yoke'.[27] The French doctor Schrumpf-Perron, who acted as an informant for German counter-intelligence, wrote that: 'The Führer is seen as a supernatural power in the Islamic world. People are convinced that he has a jinnee, that is to say a guiding spirit that tells him what to do and when to act. Besides, the Prophet is against the Jews.'[28]

Farouk's entourage, including Asal Bey, the Egyptian chargé d'affaires in Bern, Hafiz Amir, the consul-general in Istanbul, Prince Mohammed Ibrahim and Zulfikar Pasha, had all been in contact with

German diplomats.[29] These, and other Egyptian diplomats, gave ample expression of Farouk's sympathies for Germany and his hopes for a British defeat. This sympathy did not extend to Germany's Axis partner, whom they regarded as a colonial oppressor. They had every reason to think this way. The Italians, having reconciled themselves to the loss of their East African colonies, hoped to seize Egypt and turn it into an Italian colony.[30] In April 1941 Ribbentrop had the gall to send a message to King Farouk assuring him that Germany wished to create a new order in the Middle East 'based on the principle of respect for the rightful interests of all nations'. This was at a time when Germany had already decided that Egypt was to be in the Italian sphere of influence after a victory over the 8th Army. On the other hand, the Germans were anxious to maintain contacts with the nationalist Wafd, which was in opposition to the pro-British government of Hussein Sirri Pasha. These contacts were sustained when the Wafd formed the government under Nahhas Pasha in February 1942, protected by a detachment of infantry and three light tanks, and continued after Farouk's deposition.

As the Axis troops moved eastwards, Neurath's propaganda unit stepped up its efforts. Hans Winkler, who was temporarily in charge, produced a report on the situation on 10 April that was packed with every imaginable anti-Semitic stereotype. The Jews of Libya, who were said to be equipped with radio transmitters, were busy forwarding information on troop movements to the British, who were fighting on behalf of world Jewry. Winkler was, however, pleased to report that the Arabs were united in their detestation of their Jewish oppressors and exploiters.[31]

Meanwhile Rommel once again began to entertain fantastic visions of conquest, imagining that the British army could easily be crushed, leaving the entire north coast of Africa in German hands, so that all logistical problems would finally be solved. He would then advance into Persia and Iraq, seize the oilfields and establish a firm position from which Russia could be attacked. Rommel imagined that he would be able to do in 1942 what von Leeb, von Bock and von Rundstedt had failed to achieve in 1941.[32] For the moment he felt it prudent to keep these extravagant ideas to himself. Since he did not trust the Italians to keep a secret, he told neither Bastico nor Cavallero of his intentions, but he also kept OKW and even Kesselring in the dark. On 17 January he wrote to his wife: 'The situation is developing to our advantage and I'm full of plans I daren't say anything about

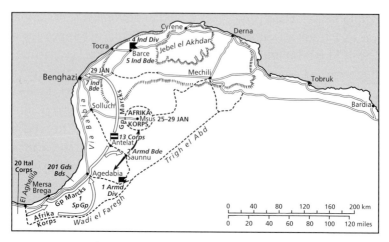

Map 9. Rommel's counterattack, January 1942

round here. They'd think me crazy.'[33] Four days later he launched his offensive, without even informing either Comando Supremo or OKW. Rommel ignored his orders from Berlin, Rome and Tripoli, pushing forward with blissful disregard for present or future logistical problems, determined to exploit his temporary superiority over the 8th Army to regain all that he had lost in 'Crusader'.[34] Private K. B. from 15 Panzer Division was thrilled to be on the move again. As he phrased it in a letter home: 'Once again we are rommeling ahead!'[35]

Ritchie was caught completely by surprise. He was in Cairo, where he busied himself with putting the finishing touches to an offensive into Tripolitania, while C-in-C Middle East was in Palestine. British air reconnaissance was hampered by gales, rain and sandstorms. Forward troops failed to notice any untoward activity. The British were temporarily unable to crack the Wehrmacht's 'Chaffinch' code, and Luftwaffe decrypts did not provide any valuable intelligence. The Italian air force ciphers also became increasingly difficult to read.[36] Rommel was better informed. He knew from Mellenthin's reports that he faced 1st Armoured Division, freshly arrived from England, new to desert warfare. Rommel was now beginning to receive valuable information on the 8th Army's condition and intentions when the Axis was able to read the cipher of the US military attaché in Cairo. On 21 January he therefore hit hard, catching inexperienced troops on the wrong foot.

Rommel's plan was typical for desert warfare. The Battle Group Marcks, made up of three regiments of German infantry, an Italian artillery regiment, an anti-tank section and an anti-aircraft battery, was to advance along the coastal road, supported by 90 Light Division and an Italian motorised corps, while 15 and 21 Panzer Divisions were to attack from the south, the two meeting at Melah en Nagra where they were to advance further in the direction of Benghazi.

The outflanking movement was slowed down owing to the soft sand-dunes, in which the Panzer found it difficult to find a grip, and which used up a great amount of fuel as the tracks whirled around in the deep sand. This enabled the British to withdraw with minimal losses. Rommel was surprised that the British were so weak and decided to continue the advance along the coastal road, the Via Balbia. Marcks, with Rommel and Westphal up at the front, having reached Agedabia at 1100hrs on 22 January, moved away from the Via Balbia, taking the wretched little village of Antelat with its clay buildings at 1700hrs. The Afrikakorps, still stuck in the dunes, limped far behind.[37] On the following day a British concentration to the south tied up Marcks' Battle Group, enabling the bulk of the British forces to withdraw safely and avoid being encircled.

The Comando Supremo in Rome and the Comando Superiore in Tripolitania, who were every bit as surprised as Ritchie by this offensive, were singularly displeased with their headstrong subordinate. Cavallero, convinced that Rommel would soon run out of supplies and would face disaster, visited his headquarters on 23 January armed with orders from Mussolini to stop the offensive.[38] He insisted that shortage of fuel combined with acute logistical problems made it imperative for Rommel to wait until he had built up sufficient reserves. He added the highly implausible warning that there was a distinct threat that de Gaulle's Free French might attempt a landing in Libya and Tunisia. There was also the slightly more believable danger that the British would renew their offensive in Libya. Rommel was therefore ordered to stay put at Mersa el Brega. The infantry was to stay on the defensive, while the motorised units could launch limited attacks in order to disrupt the enemy's preparations for a renewal of their offensive. Kesselring, who accompanied Cavallero, gave him his full support.[39] Rommel, whose chief of staff, Major-General Alfred Gause, had just visited the Wolf's Lair, knew that he had Hitler's full support, and could afford to ignore Cavallero's objections that the overall situation in the Mediterranean was such that it would be imprudent to leave the Mersa el Brega position. Cavallero insisted that Rommel's planned offensive should be nothing more than a sortie, but Rommel would not stand for this, arrogantly announcing that he intended to destroy the British south of Agedabia. If all failed he could always fall back to the Mersa el Brega Line. Kesselring tried to mediate, but to no avail. He left Rommel's headquarters 'growling'. Rommel, haughtily announcing that 'only the Führer can make me change my mind', made it abundantly clear that he intended to continue the offensive, come what may.[40] Rommel noted: 'Cavallero took his revenge by holding back part of the Italian corps in the Mersa el Brega area and part in Agedabia, so that it was more or less removed from my command. In spite of this, German troops retook Cyrenaica.'[41] Goebbels, who was overjoyed at the news that his favourite general was once again on the move, was delighted to hear that the British press was working energetically on his behalf by building up Rommel into an almost mythical figure, making him the world's best-known general. He mistakenly believed that Rommel was such an outstanding personality that he would not let this go to his head.[42] Hitler was also unable to fathom why Churchill and the British press did so much to inflate Rommel's reputation.

The fighting around Agedabia was over by 24 January. Between 21 and 24 January the British lost 143 tanks and armoured cars, 80 guns and 14 planes.[43] On 25 January the 8th Army lost another 96 tanks and armoured cars, including a number of the latest American and Canadian models, 38 guns, and a large number of trucks along with 13 planes. Captured supplies and ammunition enabled Rommel to push on to Msus. Rommel's daring offensive had got off to a spectacular start. For all of Comando Supremo's anxieties and concerns, it was turning into a rout, and it soon seemed that the British were preparing to abandon Benghazi.[44] As a sign of his approval Hitler promoted Rommel to the rank of Panzer-General on 24 January, although Rommel did not know of this until he reached Benghazi on 29 January.[45] Mussolini's signal authorising him to advance to Benghazi only arrived as he was entering the town.[46] Rommel's amazing tenacity had been rewarded with a rich prize.

In spite of these triumphs, Cavallero was determined to do everything he could to rein in Rommel. He let it be known that he would only release the Italian motorised forces when a strong forward position had been established at Agedabia, the infantry divisions had been refreshed and the logistical problems solved. Rommel regarded this as cheap revenge for his disobedience.[47] He did, however, call

Marcks back to finish off mopping-up operations around Agedabia. Everything now depended on the success of his next move. Ritchie, an inexperienced general who had been appointed well beyond his abilities, completely misread the situation. He imagined that Rommel's offensive was little more than a reconnaissance in strength, but he soon woke up to the fact that he was hoping to encircle the entire 1st Armoured Division. Major-General Eric Dorman-Smith, Auchinleck's caustic chief of staff, an arrogant, energetic, undiplomatic and ferociously scathing member of the Anglo-Irish ascendancy known as 'Chink', who was perhaps the most brilliant staff officer in the British army and did not hesitate to let others know it, once remarked that 8th Army's main problem was 'un embarras de Ritchie'. The troops were more succinct. They sang: 'Ritchie – his arse is getting itchy.' Ritchie was well known for his intense dislike of life in the field, as well as for his insistence that his shirts be laundered in Cairo and sent up to the front. Such behaviour did not endear him to his troops.

Rommel's move was poorly executed, so that the British were able to extricate themselves, retreating in somewhat unseemly disarray. Once Marcks' operation around Agedabia was complete the Afrikakorps chased after them in hot pursuit on 25 January, knocking out tanks with concentrations of anti-tank guns and Panzer. The 1st Armoured Division rapidly fell apart and fled, leaving the ill-fated Ritchie at a loss to know what to do. The Afrikakorps advanced rapidly until it ran out of fuel in the afternoon, by which time it had reached Msus where it was in a excellent position to trap the few remaining British forces to the west of Benghazi. Mellenthin accurately reported that the British were confused and uncertain what to do next, so that they would probably abandon Benghazi. His intelligence revealed that the British expected Rommel to advance in a north-easterly direction from Msus to Mechili. Rommel therefore ordered the Afrikakorps to make a feint in that direction, while making a north-westerly swoop on Benghazi.[48] Mussolini, who was greatly encouraged by Rommel's success in this operation, was inclined to let him continue as he saw fit. Rintelen was in full agreement, but Kesselring, still anxious to patch up the differences between Cavallero and Rommel, urged caution, pointing out that the Afrikakorps would soon run short of supplies.

On 28 January the quartermaster in Rome sent an urgent message to OKH saying that any further advance in Cyrenaica was a logistical impossibility. The further the Panzer Army Africa advanced,

the longer the supply lines, and the greater the need for trucks and fuel.
Rommel had already requested 8,000 trucks to meet his supply needs
and these were simply not available.[49] Shortage of fuel, as Kesselring
had predicted, not the Comando Supremo, forced Rommel to call a
halt. He had assumed that the British would calculate that he would
go to the high ground around Mechili that was the strategic key
to Cyrenaica, but he simply did not have the fuel to carry this out, quite
apart from the fact that by continuing the pursuit to Mechili the threat
to his rearward communications in the Benghazi area would be too
great.[50] He therefore ordered 21 Panzer Division to feint an advance
in this direction, while Marcks went north-west to Benghazi, 90 Light
Division and the Ariete moving up along the coastal road. Rommel
seized Benghazi on 29 January with two understrength motorised
brigades, the British having weakened the garrison to meet the supposed
thrust towards Mechili. In Benghazi the Germans discovered ample
supplies that had been stockpiled for the advance into Tripolitania. The
Axis troops were given a warm welcome by the Arab and Italian population. Their losses were minimal. Between 27 and 29 January, Marcks'
Battle Group lost only one dead and thirteen wounded; the Afrikakorps five dead and ten wounded.[51] Bastico was jubilant, expressing his
warmest congratulations to Rommel, and telling the Axis troops that
they would soon win the war.[52] Hitler awarded Rommel swords and
oak leaves to his Knight's Cross as a sign of his special favour, making
him the first army officer to receive this high honour. The 8th Army
retreated all the way to Gazala, but Rommel lacked sufficient supplies
to follow with anything but light forces. Cavallero now ordered Bastico
to make sure that Rommel remained in Benghazi and did not move
further east, except to launch some limited raids; but he had no need
to worry.[53] By 6 February the Axis was once again in possession of
Cyrenaica.[54] There followed several months of preparation, training
and waiting, with the German–Italian forces deployed along the border
between Cyrenaica and Marmarica, the motorised forces to the rear.

Göring, who arrived in Rome on 28 January, was so carried
away by Rommel's rapid advance towards Benghazi that he lost all
sense of reality. Mussolini was infected by this blustering optimism,
announcing that the war in North Africa was already won, because
three convoys had landed safely with Panzer, ammunition and fuel that
were now in the hands of an outstanding commander who combined
daring with circumspection. Göring once again brought up Hitler's

suggestion to use submarines as freighters, arguing that thirty submarines could move 40,000–50,000 tons of supplies to North Africa
per month. Heavily protected convoys could bring tanks, artillery and
other such bulky weapons. Of the United States he said: 'A lot of noise,
but little action.' Mussolini pointed out that sending supplies to Tunis
now made little sense, because of the distance from the front. Tobruk
was now the key for further operations against Egypt, to which Göring
heartily agreed. While in Rome the Reichsmarschall did little but talk
about all the jewels he owned, and calmed his nerves by playing with
a handful of diamonds contained in a small vase. He left on 4 February wearing to the railway station a sable coat that made him look, in
Ciano's words, like a high-class prostitute on her way to the opera.[55]
Mussolini was so overjoyed by the news that Benghazi had fallen that
he too became absurdly optimistic, extolling Rommel's military genius
and giving vent to his contempt for his own generals, while Cavallero
and the Comando Supremo remained coolly sceptical. Rintelen also
remained with his feet firmly planted on the ground, warning that a
hothead like Rommel needed to be reined in, not encouraged.[56]

By early February Rommel's two motorised brigades had
reached Tmimi, some 40 kilometres west of the British defensive position at Gazala, but they were exhausted, their fuel tanks empty, their
ammunition spent and they were subjected to constant harassment
from the plucky rear echelons of the retreating British. The Comando
Supremo, already angered by Rommel taking all available fuel for his
advance to Tmimi, remained resolutely deaf to his entreaties that at
least three of the five infantry divisions at Mersa el Brega, Agedabia
and Benghazi that were outside his command be brought forward.[57]
By now Cavallero not only had to deal with Rommel, but was locked
in battle with Mussolini, who had fallen completely under the German
general's spell, and was accusing Cavallero of being a desktop general,
unlike the dashing Rommel, who was always up at the front urging
his men forward. The Duce claimed that by holding back the Italian
infantry divisions Cavallero was ruining a promising opportunity to
seize Tobruk, on which his heart was set. The Comando Supremo was
by now becoming increasingly disillusioned with Mussolini, whom they
accused of having sold out to the Germans. They were given powerful
backing against the dictator by OKW, which continued to be highly
critical of Rommel's wilful antics.[58] Rommel had been successful, but
the price was extremely high. During the winter of 1941/2 the British

had suffered 17,700 losses, the Axis 36,472, of which 21,712 were
Italians, 14,760 Germans.[59] The Panzer Army Africa was now in the
position at Ain el Gazala, west of Tobruk, that Paulus and Gariboldi
had recommended a year ago.[60]

Rommel was determined to push on, arguing that he had
inflicted such damage on the British that they would be unable to go
on the offensive. In his view the 8th Army's men, with the exception
of a South African brigade that had fallen apart under attack, were
excellent soldiers. The NCOs and junior officers were good, but the
senior commanders were rotten. Thirteen German and thirty-three Italian battalions faced forty British, but the enemy now had superiority
in almost all forms of weaponry. In tanks the proportion was 238:318;
in armoured cars 31:306; artillery 352:414; anti-aircraft guns 247:259;
fighters 54:170; bombers 47:60. Only in anti-tank guns did the Panzer
Group have the superiority with 323:293. Rommel's argument that the
Luftwaffe was qualitatively superior to the RAF was not particularly
convincing, given such numerical superiority. Rommel was full of praise
for the performance of the German troops, and thought it a positive
sign that two of his three divisional commanders had been killed in
action, a third taken prisoner. The Italians had fought well, although
their officers were very much a mixed bag. He attributed the higher
losses suffered by the Italians to a lack of motorised transport.[61]

Mussolini was thus forced into a corner, suffering a serious loss
of prestige and authority. He finally decided to fight back against accusations that he was Hitler's lickspittle by demonstrating his independence from his powerful ally, and by mending his fences with Comando
Supremo. In February he cancelled a meeting with Hitler, scheduled for
the following month, on the palpably dubious grounds of ill health.
He presented an outline of his views on the future of the campaign in
North Africa on 11 February that was remarkably close to the defensive posture of the Comando Supremo. The bulk of the Axis forces
should remain behind at Mersa el Brega, guarding the Tripolitanian
frontier, while light forces were to operate in Cyrenaica. Once supplies
and fresh forces were brought in, Cyrenaica was to be occupied and
Tobruk taken; but given the pressing logistical problems this would not
be possible until 1943. OKW enthusiastically endorsed this analysis,
whereupon Rommel promptly visited Mussolini on 15 February and
Hitler three days later, but to no avail. Rommel had hoped to persuade
Mussolini to give him an absolutely free hand over all the forces under

his command, and to greatly increase air transport to North Africa to bring in fresh troops. From Hitler he requested a reorganisation of the German forces into a Panzer corps and a light corps, more shipping and air transport, increased supplies of oil for the Italian navy, plus a large number of reconnaissance aircraft.[62] Hitler, ever anxious to help Mussolini out of his domestic political difficulties, refused to give Rommel the go-ahead, telling him that 'under no circumstances whatsoever' was there to be an offensive aimed at the Suez Canal in 1942.[63]

Rommel's advance might have been foolhardy, but it did at least bring some distinct advantages. The Luftwaffe could now use the airfields at Derna and Benghazi, from which they could attack British convoys on their way to and from Egypt, as they travelled through 'Bomb Alley' between Crete and the North African coast. Although 2 Air Corps in Sicily did not yet have its full compliment of aircraft, it stepped up operations against Malta. Instead of ineffectual bombing from a great height, they now used Junkers 88b Stukas against specified targets, such as battleships in Valletta, the docks and warehouses, but this proved to be a costly tactic. The Stukas were painfully slow, particularly when pulling out of a dive, and were relatively easy to pick off with anti-aircraft fire. Malta was bristling with ack-ack, resulting in heavy German losses, such that operations against Malta had to be temporarily halted on 8 February.

Far away from the action, Göring and Jeschonnek still insisted that the dive-bomber was the appropriate weapon. Deichmann and 2 Air Corps argued that since the Stukas could only operate in small groups that were terribly vulnerable to concentrated anti-aircraft fire, even the bravest pilots were helpless, whereas conventional bombers were less vulnerable. They therefore argued that a 'horizontal' rather than a 'vertical' approach offered better chances of success. Kesselring dithered between these alternatives, ordering a halt to all but mock raids for one month in order to have time to work out a viable plan of action.

Kesselring then suggested to Comando Supremo that he be given command over an invasion force against Malta, but Cavallero, who was determined that any such operation should be an Italian affair in which he would earn great glory, turned down the suggestion. Kesselring then approached Hitler for support. He was brushed off with a vague assurance that the matter needed further consideration.[64] In February Comando Supremo, anxious to gain the full co-operation of their powerful ally, graciously invited Kesselring to take part in C3, the planning staff for the invasion of Malta. He was asked to forward a request to OKW for help building landing craft, as well as training para-troopers under the supervision of Student's right-hand man, General Bernhard Ramcke, who had close ties to senior Italian officers. A group of Japanese officers who were visiting Rome were quizzed about their experiences of amphibious warfare in the Pacific.[65] Kesselring came to the remarkable conclusion that in spite of all earlier assessments, the invasion would be a relatively straightforward operation, certainly considerably easier that the invasion of Crete. Everything depended on training the Italian paratroopers, which it was assumed could be completed by the summer.

The German navy did not share this optimistic assessment. Given the desperate shortage of fuel and the need to protect the con-voys to North Africa, there was simply no shipping available for an attack on Malta. Furthermore, the mines that had been laid in the Straits of Messina and outside Valletta had proved to be utterly use-less. Raeder ordered that the motor torpedo boats that had recently been sent to the Mediterranean via the Rhine–Rhône Canal should be used against British convoys to Tobruk, not for mining operations at Malta. This left Weichold with only a few U-boats to offer as support for an invasion. His vision of denying the British access to Malta by sea was now in ruins, and with the failure of the air offensive he had to confess to Skl that Malta was once again a major menace to Axis operations in the Mediterranean.[66] He was actually somewhat overly pessimistic in his assessment. The British had felt obliged to move their Blenheim bombers from Malta to Egypt, Air Vice-Marshal Lloyd's RAF contingent on the island had drastically cut back operations and the submarines, lacking air support, remained in harbour. Axis convoys and single freighters were able to reach Tripoli and the ports in Cyre-naica unharmed, bringing Rommel the supplies he so badly needed. For the time being the Axis had been able effectively to neutralise Malta, Britain's major asset in the effort to cut off Rommel's supplies. But in spite of this, British intelligence continued, at least until the middle of April, grossly to underestimate Rommel's strength, and to discount his ability to conduct a serious offensive.[67]

The German navy was so intoxicated by Rommel's advance that they also began to fantasise about the imminent collapse of the British Empire. Captain Hansfrieder Rost from Skl's operations department produced a memorandum in February 1942 that combined National Socialist racial theory, geo-politics and wishful thinking in roughly equal proportions, announcing that 'the situation on the ground is characterised by a colourful racial mixture. South Africans, Indians, Frenchmen and Poles stand beside severely damaged British tanks. Behind them is Alexandria with its badly battered battleships, with rumours of the collapse of British world power on the eastern edges of the Indian Ocean, and the fact of the fall of Singapore.'[68] Such fantasies were fanned by the visit to Berlin of a Japanese delegation under Admiral Nomura in early February. He insisted that victory over Britain was the top priority, after which it would be a simple matter for Germany and Japan to combine together to knock out the Soviet Union. This was music to the German navy's ears. They had always pleaded for a 'Britain first' strategy, and now that they saw a chance to deliver a fatal blow in the Mediterranean, they revived the plans they had developed in the previous spring.

Raeder promptly reported to Hitler on the outcome of these talks. He argued that the Suez Canal and Basra were the 'western pillars of British domination in India'. Were these to be smashed the strategic consequences would be devastating for the British Empire. It was thus of the utmost importance that the Axis forces in Libya should attack the key British position in Suez. This would lead to a 'clearing up of the situation in the Mediterranean', open up the use of the oil supplies from Mosul, radically change the state of affairs in Turkey, encourage the Arab and Indian nationalist movements, strengthen the eastern front and give Germany control over the Caucasus.[69] Hitler did not appear terribly convinced, retorting that his main concern was recommencing the offensive in the Soviet Union.

Skl were undeterred by Hitler's lack of enthusiasm for their global strategy and his continued adherence to his 'continental concept'. They did not go as far as the Japanese, who were calling for a halt to operations in the Soviet Union, but they did suggest taking up defensive positions along a line from Lake Lagoda to the Don and Volga, combined with operations around Leningrad to secure naval domination in the Baltic, as well as against Murmansk to put an end to the British PQ convoys.[70] While the Japanese navy was to dominate the Indian Ocean, wipe out the naval base at Trincomalee and close off the entrance to the Persian Gulf, Axis forces would advance to Suez and join up with the Germans advancing through the Caucasus, Iran and

Iraq. All German naval forces in the Mediterranean would concentrate on supporting Rommel's thrust towards the Suez Canal. Their immediate priorities were the 'capture or total neutralisation' of Malta along with the seizure of Tobruk.[71] After further consideration Skl decided that neutralisation of Malta would not suffice, since Weichold insisted that it would only last as long as the Axis was able to keep up the pressure. Captain Rost, encouraged by Admiral Nomura's visit, noted on 22 February that 'when Germany and Japan join hands in the Indian Ocean, final victory will be near'.[72]

Ribbentrop received a visit from Giuseppe Bottai, the Italian minister of education, in mid-February 1942, whom he treated to a truly astonishing performance.[73] Bottai was told that the war in Europe would soon be over and 'can be considered as already won'. Britain was heading for a crushing defeat, and could only be saved by suing for peace. There was absolutely no doubt that the offensive in Russia would be crowned with success. Ribbentrop totally discounted the Americans, saying that even if they succeeded in building 125,000 aeroplanes and 80,000 tanks, as they promised they would, the Axis could build four times as many. Bottai listened to this tirade with fascinated attention, carried away by Ribbentrop's overbearing confidence, hardly able to get a word in edgeways about the cultural exchanges that were the ostensible reason for their meeting. The Italian ambassador Alfieri was given a repeat performance the following day, but when he asked about an offensive in North Africa, Ribbentrop told him that he was unable to make any comment on military affairs.[74]

Hitler, who was singularly unimpressed by these fantastic notions, continued to concentrate on operations on the eastern front. He had no intention of withdrawing forces from the Soviet Union at this critical stage in the campaign, and still saw no likelihood of an offensive in North Africa in 1942. Nomura's offer of close co-operation by the Japanese navy, and Rost's vision of hands across the ocean, were fully dependent on an Axis offensive against the Suez Canal. Nomura had made it quite clear that the Japanese had no intention of advancing into the Indian Ocean if the Germans were not determined to move up to the Suez Canal. For this reason Skl asked OKH what was required of them for an offensive in North Africa. The curt reply was that they did not have the necessary forces or supplies for such an operation. Skl did not believe this, and insisted that an offensive was still possible under the present circumstances. In early March Raeder urged Hitler to agree to an offensive against the Suez Canal, arguing that 'the present situation was exceptionally favourable and was unlikely to recur', assuring him that the transport problems for such an operation were solvable. He also gave Hitler a memorandum that had been prepared by Captain Heinz Assmann, a senior staff officer at Skl, arguing for the absolute priority of keeping up the raids on Malta.[75] Raeder continued to believe that a landing on Malta was the only viable solution, but knew full well that Hitler was violently opposed to the idea. He therefore kept up the pressure on OKW and the Italians to push ahead with plans for an invasion. Hitler blew hot and cold on the topic. On the one hand, he liked the idea of hitting the British when they were in an exceedingly awkward position, in the hope of persuading them to come to the negotiating table. On the other, he wanted to concentrate on the eastern front, as well as show due respect for the sensitivities of his Axis ally. Raeder was thus treated to a lengthy and contradictory monologue that left him none the wiser.

Hitler's relative lack of interest in North Africa was in part due to his belief that with the Japanese entry into the war the British were doomed. The British were ignominiously driven out of Malaya, then on 15 February Singapore, the linchpin of British defences in the Pacific, fell almost without a fight. The Japanese reached Rangoon on 7 March, so that the Burma Road, the essential supply route to China, was closed. General Wavell's command over the American, British, Dutch and Australian (ABDA) troops fell apart, leaving the East Indies open to the invaders. For Hitler it was only a matter of time before the British threw in the towel. He eagerly awaited the day when the British changed sides, telling the Romanian dictator Antonescu that he was extremely upset to see so many white men being killed, and that should the British come to their senses he would happily send his new partners twenty divisions 'to chuck the yellow people out again'.[76]

Believing that Britain was on its last legs, deliberately misled by Rommel as to the seriousness of the logistical situation, and unaware of the acrimonious squabbles with the Italians, Hitler thought that his favourite general could easily take Tobruk, after which he should advance as far as possible with his existing forces. He relayed a message to this effect to General Nehring, who was on his way from the eastern front to take over as the Afrikakorps' chief of staff.[77]

Hitler was eventually put fully into the picture thanks to reports from Rintelen in Rome as well as from military intelligence, which revealed the intense friction between Rommel and the Italians. It was then clear that Rommel had to be restrained in order to preserve the alliance with Italy. OKW was still kept in the dark as to the actual logistical situation and did not know quite how to react. Rommel was ordered to go to Rome to smooth the waters with Mussolini, thence to the Führer's headquarters at Rastenburg. Hitler sat uneasily on the fence. He neither held Rommel back, nor did he urge him on, but merely remarked that 'When we decide in favour of further offensive operations in the Mediterranean... nothing will be good or expensive enough to ensure a healthy foundation.' Rommel's chief of staff, Westphal, received a similarly ambiguous response from Jodl in the course of a lengthy interview.[78]

OKH had never shown much enthusiasm for the North African campaign. The sea routes from Italy to North Africa were too long, Malta remained an intractable problem, the Royal Navy and the RAF dominated the Mediterranean, and the British forces in Egypt were still impressive. They stuck to their continental strategy, insisting that it would be easier to move through the mountain passes of the Caucasus than to supply an effective campaign in North Africa, and concluded that Suez should best be attacked from the north, once the campaign in the Soviet Union was brought to a successful conclusion. Westphal's glowing account of the situation in North Africa, during which he admitted that serious mistakes had been made at Tobruk and on the Sollum front, did nothing to change their minds.[79] The quartermaster-general in the general staff estimated that Panzer Army Africa required 25,000 tons of supplies per month under normal circumstance, rising to 45,000 tons during an offensive. Given the existing transport capacity it was possible to supply up to the normal level, but without a significant improvement of the transport situation an offensive was absolutely out of the question.

Hitler came to much the same conclusion. Unlike OKH he approved of the idea of an offensive in North Africa in principle, but agreed that for the moment the means were simply not available. He then promptly changed his mind, announcing that an offensive was feasible in 1942, provided that 2 Air Fleet could remain in the Mediterranean. OKW scotched this idea when it stated that most of these Luftwaffe units were urgently needed on the eastern front to support the renewed offensive. Hitler reluctantly had to abandon the idea of a limited offensive in North Africa. Bitterly disappointed that the British showed no signs of wanting to reach an agreement after the fall of Singapore, he devoted his attention almost exclusively to the campaign in the east. Order Number 41 of 5 April 1942 called for the destruction of the Soviet Union, Britain's only remaining hope on the continent of Europe, after which a political arrangement with Germany would have to be reached.[80] Towards the end of March he warned Goebbels not to count on Britain giving up, just because the Japanese were moving into the Indian Ocean.[81]

Skl, disregarding the objections of OKW and OKH, along with Hitler's misgivings, continued to press for a major offensive in North Africa. To this end Raeder had asked Hitler on 12 March to authorise substantial German support for the planned Italian operation against Malta. Hitler, knowing full well that there was nothing to spare from the forthcoming offensive operations in the Soviet Union, avoided making any such commitment.[82] The ever-optimistic Kesselring argued that Malta could be taken by a *coup de main*, once it had been seriously weakened by the air offensive, but Cavallero announced that he could not consider an invasion until August, because he needed the time to train his airborne forces. General von Rintelen begged him to reconsider. Kesselring pointed out that by August he would almost certainly be obliged to send a large part of his air force to support the renewed offensive in the Soviet Union, leaving him with insufficient planes for a successful invasion. Cavallero countered that even if they managed to seize the island they still did not have the wherewithal to occupy it; but after lengthy argument he graciously agreed to consider the possibility of a surprise attack in May.[83] Kesselring met with little enthusiasm for his plan when he visited the Führer's HQ on 21 March. Since Hitler saw no pressing need for an offensive in North Africa, the question of Malta was no longer of great importance. In order to assuage the Italians, Kesselring was instructed to offer them two parachute regiments and a handful of other men to assist in their attack on Malta, provided that the Allies did not attempt a landing on the Continent in 1942.[84] Confidentially, Jodl confessed to Kesselring that one might as well tell the Italians to forget about the operation, as it was bound to fail.[85]

Colonel Deichmann was finally able to persuade Kesselring that his 'horizontal' approach to the bombing of Malta had the best chances of success. But before starting the operation Kesselring wanted to involve the Italian air force. There were serious difficulties to overcome in this regard. General Rino Corso Fougier, who had replaced

Pricolo in November 1941 as chief of air staff, was every bit as sensitive as his predecessor about Italian prestige. Italian aircraft were markedly inferior technically to the German machines, and were therefore unsuitable for joint operations. Kesselring was well aware of this problem, because Fougier had commanded the Italian units that had operated under his command during the Battle of Britain. Their contribution had been less than satisfactory. He therefore proposed first to give the Luftwaffe the task of knocking out the fighters and ack-ack batteries on Malta, and then to bring in the Italians in a second wave. Fougier regarded this suggestion as insulting to the honour of the Italian air force. Kesselring, who had overall command of the operation, ignored these objections, and proposed using the Italians largely to protect convoys and search for submarines.

The battle for Malta began on 20 March 1942 according to Deichmann's plan. During the first three days the Luftwaffe concentrated on the airfield at Takali, where the bulk of the RAF's fighters were stationed, and on the anti-aircraft emplacements. On 23 March Kesselring ordered an attack on the MW10 convoy that had warded off an attack by the Italian navy, and was heading for Valletta. The Luftwaffe managed to sink three of the five freighters, destroying the remaining two in harbour. The results of this loss were catastrophic. Malta depended on at least one convoy per month; the last had arrived in January, so the island had been kept going by a trickle of goods brought by submarines. By April the situation was desperate with General Dobbie[86] cabling London that it was a matter of 'life and death' that he get flour and ammunition as quickly as possible.[87] British reconnaissance planes spotted glider aircraft near Catania, and the news that General Student, Germany's paratrooper specialist who had masterminded the daring landing on Crete, was in Italy pointed to an imminent invasion. The island braced itself for the worst, its morale boosted by the collective award of the George Cross for bravery.

Fortunately Kesselring had no idea that the situation in Malta was so desperate and still imagined that an invasion was the only solution. He ordered attacks on Malta to resume, often up to two hundred missions in 24 hours, so that by the beginning of April the bulk of the RAF's fighters had been destroyed, either on the ground or in the air, and a substantial number of anti-aircraft guns put out of action. The Italians were now invited to join in the destruction of the harbour in Valletta. The RAF brought forty-seven of the latest model Spitfires on board the US aircraft carrier *Wasp*. They landed in Malta on 21 April, but were spotted by the Luftwaffe's radio range-finding devices on Pantelleria. Kesselring promptly sent virtually all available aircraft to hunt them down, resulting in the vast majority of the Spitfires being destroyed within twenty minutes of landing, while they were being refuelled and rearmed. The offensive continued until 28 April, with an average of 286 aircraft attacking per day, roughly the same amount as in the Battle of Britain.

Malta suffered severe damage in these six weeks of the 'Großkampf'. In all 6,557 tons of bombs fell on the island. There were more than 1,000 dead, 4,500 wounded, with 15,500 buildings destroyed. Food shortages were so severe that the population had to be fed in communal kitchens. The submarines and surface vessels had been obliged to leave, the RAF only had six fighters left, and the anti-aircraft guns were rationed to fifteen rounds per day. The island was no longer a threat to the Axis, the 'unsinkable aircraft carrier' put out of action. But Kesselring was grimly aware that he had lost 177 aircraft, merely to win a breathing space. The island's infrastructure was virtually unharmed, because power plants, communications, hangars and workshops were deep underground where they could not be damaged, even by the best that the Luftwaffe's bombardiers had to offer. On 9 May the *Wasp* returned to Malta undetected, bringing with it sixty Spitfires. On the following day the minelayer *Welshman* reached Valletta. Malta was on the way to recovery. An invasion was out of the question with Cavallero dragging his feet, and when 10 Air Corps was sent to the Soviet Union and the eastern Mediterranean in May, the Maltese knew that they had been saved.[88]

Meanwhile, Rommel still dreamed of invading Egypt, and was held back only by the chronic lack of supplies, occasioned by the shortage of fuel for the Italian escorts to the convoys. In a temporary fit of practicality he decided to concentrate on tackling the British armoured forces in Marmarica in June, preparing the way for an attack on Tobruk once the weather got somewhat cooler.[89] Even though he was desperately short of fuel, he ordered the Panzer Army Africa forward at the beginning of April, without bothering to inform his nominal Italian superiors, using as an excuse the need to counter an imaginary imminent attack, and once again complaining bitterly that he was being starved of supplies.[90] He pretended that he had made this move so as to protect his southern flank, although aerial reconnaissance revealed that the British were retiring and posed no threat whatsoever. Rommel, assuming that they would go all the way back to Mersa Matruh, revised his timetable, announcing that he would destroy the British forces remaining around Tobruk, and seize the town 'either by a *coup de main* or a brief attack' before the crippling summer heat began. It remained unclear what was the distinction between these approaches. Comando Supremo continued to insist that supplies had to be built up before there was any further advance, but Rommel argued that the 8th Army would not be finished with replacements until the end of May, and that by the autumn it would probably have a large number of new American tanks, by which time the Panzer Army would no longer be able to count on support from the Luftwaffe's 2 Air Fleet. Mussolini was in agreement in principle, having said that Rommel should concentrate on taking southern Cyrenaica as a springboard in preparation for a further offensive. But he thought it prudent to add that the British had far better logistical support, as well as alarmingly large numbers of armoured cars and tanks back in Egypt.[91] General Barbasetti, chief of general staff to the Italian forces in North Africa, enthusiastically seconded Rommel's proposal, promising him to do everything in his power to ensure that he obtained the logistical support he needed.[92]

Barbasetti, who had recently replaced the energetic and forceful General Gambara, was an officer, courtier and diplomat of the old Piedmontese school, a courteous bureaucrat and meticulous administrator. He soon uncovered a number of severe irregularities within the administration, particularly in the quartermaster's department. Four million lire had been misappropriated, and two officers were arrested. Part of the blame was placed on Gambara for failing to failing to keep a close watch over his subordinates. General Mannerini had been sent to Tripoli to weed out scrimshankers (*imboscati*) in the quartermaster's department, resulting in a number of Gambara's subordinates being replaced. Cavallero was beginning to regret having replaced Gariboldi with Bastico, who seemed to concentrate on his purely representative functions, and had little contact with the troops. Cavallero had therefore urged Barbasetti to persuade him to play a more active role. The Italian headquarters were beset with petty rivalries and jealousies, but the German liaison officer reported that Cavallero was determined to get on with the job, while Rommel was pleased to have in Bastico a hands-off superior.

Part of the problem was that the Italian quartermaster's staff (*Intendenza*) was enmeshed in red tape. The Italians were well aware of the problem and appointed a Colonel Gaipa with special powers to get the task done. He did an excellent job, but he soon fell foul of his superiors, because he tended to deal directly with the Germans, providing them where possible with whatever they required. In late January 1942 he was given a week in detention, after which he was posted elsewhere. He had acted on Rommel's instructions, which were contrary to those of the Intendenza, giving the Germans brand new trucks, rather than trucks in need of repair. Rommel, who was lavish in his praise of the colonel, announced that were he to be punished it would lead to a serious breach of trust between the allies. The Gaipa case was well known in the Afrikakorps, with the colonel regarded as something of a hero, but his reinstatement did not solve the fundamental difficulties, which were mainly due to the difficulty of securing the sea lanes to North Africa and the failure to deal with the persistent problem of Malta.[93]

Rommel had a soulmate in Weichold, whose exotic plans for joint operations along the North African coast were favoured by Kesselring and Rintelen. Weichold confessed that he did not think that an attack on Egypt and the Suez Canal was feasible without first dealing with Malta, but this would have to wait until the autumn, and above all had to exclude the Italian navy, which was bound to mess up the entire operation.[94]

Rommel had little difficulty in persuading Kesselring that he should get moving before the intense summer heat began. The Supreme Commander South (OBS) was in an optimistic mood, buoyed up by the satisfactory results of the attacks on Malta, and readily agreed when he visited Rommel's headquarters at the beginning of April. Both men thought that it would be infinitely preferable to take Malta in a swift attack before the Panzer Army advanced, but feared that the Italians would continue to insist that it be done by a major operation at a later date. Shortly after this meeting Kesselring flew to Rome in an attempt to persuade Mussolini to overrule Cavallero's mulish objections to a *coup de main*. He left it to the airborne specialist General Bernhard Ramcke to present the rationale. Cavallero seriously damaged his own case by claiming that the air offensive had left Malta virtually defenceless, and it proved relatively easy to persuade the Duce that a concentrated attack would put an end to the island threat. He agreed that such an attack should be launched at the end of May.[95] Shortly afterwards he told the commander of the U-boat fleet, Admiral Doenitz, who was visiting Rome, that Malta was ripe for the picking.

The problem remained that the Italians had only two or three parachute battalions, which had not completed their training, and the Germans offered only two of their own. Kesselring returned to the Wolf's Lair on 18 April in an attempt to gain Hitler's support for his plans. He treated the Führer to a heavily embroidered picture of the situation in the Mediterranean, and gave a glowing account of the Italians' preparations for a surprise attack on Malta. Hitler was entranced, put aside all his previous objections and gave the go-ahead for Kesselring's plan, now codenamed 'Hercules', as well as to Rommel's proposed offensive that was to begin before the onset of high summer. He regretted that, given the situation on the eastern front, he would be unable to meet all Rommel's requests for supplies, but agreed to send him fifty-two Panzer and to allot Luftwaffe and Wehrmacht units for the attack on Malta.[96]

Kesselring gave Rommel a report on his visit to Hitler's headquarters, announcing that he would take Malta by the end of May. 2 Air Fleet would provide two parachute battalions for this operation. Hitler was in full agreement that the 8th Army should be destroyed as quickly as possible, because they could build up reserves far quicker than the Panzer Army Africa. However, Rommel should not attack before the fall of Malta, because four groups of fighters, three of Stukas, plus one group of fighters and the training squadron from 10 Air Corps were needed for the Malta operation. Were the British to launch an offensive before the attack on Malta, these air units would be placed immediately at the disposal of the Panzer Army.[97]

Cavallero was bitterly disappointed at the level of German support for 'Hercules', but had no alternative but to take part in the hectic preparations. Kesselring ordered Student to come to Rome and take part in the joint planning. A draft plan was hastily produced that envisaged an airborne landing in the south of the island, the establishment of a bridgehead, followed by a landing by sea. The longer the discussions continued, the greater were the Italians' reservations. Cavallero raised all manner of objections, while senior officers from all three services muttered about Malta's bristling coastal defences, the appalling dangers involved and the high level of casualties likely to be incurred. At the end of April the Comando Supremo sent Keitel a memorandum on

12. Me109, 1941

'Hercules' that stressed the vital importance of taking Malta, while heavily underlining the difficulties involved. It made impossible demands on the Germans that included an entire airborne division, Panzer and anti-tank guns, 150 landing craft, 200 Junkers, 52 transport planes, and 40,000 tons of bunker oil, 12,000 tons of petrol and 500 tons of lubricant. This effectively torpedoed Kesselring's plan, although he still imagined that it might be possible to mount 'Hercules' before Rommel went on the attack.[98] Hitler did not regard this as a matter of pressing importance. Malta was effectively put out of action, so Rommel could go ahead before the island was invaded. Rommel now worked very closely with Kesselring to make the most of what they had. Kesselring, who now felt that the Italians would be able to deal with Malta on their own, promised one Stuka group, plus two fighter groups, one of Me109s, and an anti-aircraft section. Initially he hoped to include two parachute battalions, but this was soon vetoed by OKW. He also made a bold promise of 40,000 tons of supplies to be sent to Benghazi in May. Cavallero, Bastico and Barbasetti were in full agreement with Rommel's plans.[99]

On 25 June Neurath sent a telegram to the foreign office saying that Rommel had requested an 'immediate propaganda initiative in Egypt' and requested information from Ernst von Weizsäcker secretary of state at the foreign office on German–Egyptian relations.[100] He was told that a state of war did not exist between the two countries, that King Farouk was 'thoroughly' anti-British, and that there was considerable sympathy for Germany in all ranks of Egyptian society. Weizsäcker suggested that propaganda should be based on presenting the Axis forces as liberators of the Egyptian people from British imperialism, and was confident that this would meet with an enthusiastic response.

Hitler's optimism that Japan's entry into the war would force the British to come to terms gradually turned into a mounting fear that Anglo-American forces would soon open a second front. He realised that Churchill was in serious difficulties at home, having suffered a series of shattering setbacks, and that far from trying to reach an agreement with Germany he might well be tempted to go on the offensive. He regarded the British commando raid on Saint Nazaire on 28 March 1942 as a presage of worse to come. The Allies might try to land in northern, western or southern France, Portugal, Spain or North Africa. Vichy France would promptly change sides.[101] Intelligence reports showed that the 8th Army was preparing for a renewed offensive in order to take the pressure off Malta. Hitler was adamant that only if Rommel took Tobruk and moved up to the Sollum front could this threat adequately be countered. Victory in the desert would keep Vichy down, and possibly encourage the Arab nationalists to throw off the colonial yoke. With their hands full, the British would no longer be able to open a second front.[102] Perhaps it might also be possible to press on into Egypt, seize the Suez Canal and inflict as severe a blow to British prestige as the shattering loss of Singapore.[103] Given the situation on the eastern front, the Mediterranean was still a minor concern, and there could be no grandiose thoughts of a pincer operation as outlined in Order Number 32, but it was a theatre in which the Germans might still achieve a significant success.

Hitler and his military entourage made some serious miscalculations. They took no account of the astonishing resilience of the British when faced with adversity. Malta was back in business astonishingly quickly. They grossly overestimated the capacity of the harbour at Tobruk, even though it was out of range of the RAF from Malta, and could be protected by the Luftwaffe on the Greek mainland and Crete. Hitler conveniently overlooked the fact that it was within the range of aircraft from Egypt. This meant that the Panzer Army Africa would still need to be provisioned largely via the lengthy and highly vulnerable route to Tripoli. Furthermore, they credulously swallowed Kesselring's assurance that the Italians would be able to take Malta with minimal German assistance, even though Hitler had serious reservations about airborne operations such as Operation 'Mercury', the invasion of Crete, where losses had been unacceptably high: 4,000 men had been killed and 2,500 wounded, putting Germany's airborne forces out of action for a long time. At least there was general agreement on this last point by the end of April, when it became clear that the Italians were thinking in terms of a massive operation that required a totally impossible level of German support. After their experience in Crete, the Germans felt that marching and driving were infinitely preferable to swimming and jumping.[104]

These issues were discussed when Mussolini met Hitler at the Obersalzberg on 29 and 30 April 1942. Hitler took the opportunity offered by a relative lull in the fighting on the eastern front to suggest a meeting. The invitation was sent by Ribbentrop to Mackensen, the ambassador in Rome, on 24 April.[105] Mussolini promptly accepted. He and his entourage were housed at Klessheim Castle, the former residence of the Prince-Bishop of Salzburg. The military agreed that 'Hercules' could not possibly be mounted in May, and that given the climatic conditions in the desert, the offensive in Cyrenaica leading to an advance to the Suez Canal, codenamed 'Theseus', could not be postponed. Keitel and Jodl agreed with Rommel and Kesselring that the Panzer Army Africa should attack before the invasion of Malta. Cavallero, with no little reluctance, finally agreed. It was agreed that were Malta to be attacked, the British would mount an offensive in North Africa to take the pressure off the island. The Panzer Army would then be left with insufficient air support. Hitler was in full agreement, arguing that the British could quickly bring reinforcements to Egypt via the Cape, even if Malta were smashed to smithereens. This totally overlooked the fact that Malta, the Axis' 'thorn in the flesh', was principally used as a base for offensive operations, not to protect convoys through the Mediterranean. Hitler then began to ramble on about the possibility of a revolt in Egypt, and even suggested that the Japanese would not object if the Axis reached an agreement with Britain, since they had already got all that they had set out to achieve, having conquered most of the Pacific.[106] This marked the end of 'Hercules', although Hitler smoothed the Italians' ruffled feathers by professing great interest in the details of an operation that he knew full well was dead in the water, all the while promising additional German support. The Malta offensive was postponed, possibly indefinitely, and the Panzer Army was given the go-ahead for an offensive.[107]

Cavallero saw through this pretence, and pertinently enquired whether the Luftwaffe units would remain stationed in Sicily and southern Italy until July or August, to provide support for 'Hercules'. Hitler tried to avoid this issue by saying that if these units were needed elsewhere they would be returned in ample time for the invasion of Malta. The Italians took cold comfort from this remark, especially as they were informed in the course of other discussions that four groups were earmarked for withdrawal from 2 Air Fleet. Neither OKW nor the Italians were particularly convinced by Kesselring's assurance that for the foreseeable future the British in Malta were no longer a threat.[108] Mussolini suffered greatly during these talks. He was used to talking at length, but now he had to sit and listen to Hitler's interminable monologues. All he could do was to consult his wristwatch frequently in the hope that the Führer would get the message. His efforts were all in vain.[109]

Orders for 'Theseus' and 'Hercules' were issued four days after the final meeting in Klessheim. Hitler issued instructions that some additional equipment should be sent for 'Hercules', so as to maintain the illusion that the operation was still feasible, as well as to keep the Italians happy. It proved increasingly difficult to hoodwink his allies as well as his own generals for much longer, but it did not seem of pressing importance when Kesselring announced that Malta's defences had been destroyed. Göring ordered the withdrawal of the bulk of 2 Air Fleet. Hitler complained about the 'historical experiences' of the pathetic timorousness of the Italian armed forces, which made it unlikely that 'Hercules' would succeed. He went on at length about the problems of supplying Malta once it was captured, but still refused to put an end to speculations about whether an invasion was still on the books. Using a familiar tactic in such awkwardly ambiguous circumstances, so as to avoid making a clear-cut decision, he ordered General Student, along with other senior officers involved in 'Hercules', to come to his headquarters for further discussions.[110] This meeting took place on 21 May.

The planners at 2 Air Corps had already fleshed out their plans for the invasion of Malta, presenting them to Kesselring on

19 May 1942.[111] In addition to the C3 (Malta) planning staff's idea of establishing a bridgehead in the south of the island using landing craft, they proposed landing gliders in the south, so as to seize the airfield and knock out the coastal defences, thus enabling a landing on the beaches the following day. A landing was also to be made on the island of Gozo on the first day of operations. The Axis naval forces were to concentrate on keeping the Royal Navy at bay.

Two days later Cavallero presented the Comando Supremo's plan, to which Student and Ramcke had made significant contributions, at a meeting attended by the heads of services – General Vittorio Ambrosio for the army, Admiral Arturo Riccardi for the navy and General Rino Corso Fougier for the air force – along with Kesselring. It did not include the idea of a glider landing, because the joint planning staff reckoned that the beaches in the south were suitable for landing tanks and heavy equipment. Kesselring insisted that they would have to face up to the difficulties of a seaborne landing in the south without first landing troops by air to soften up the coastal defences. The Italians were horrified at this proposal. Weichold's suggestion that there were suitable landing spots in the north-west of the island was rejected by the soldiers, who dismissed it as the harebrained scheme of a sailor who had no conception of the art of fighting on land. In private Fougier described Cavallero as 'a dangerous clown, ready to follow every German whim without dignity, and a liar'. He was already plotting to secure his dismissal.[112]

Hitler became increasingly sceptical about 'Hercules' in the course of the conference duly held on 21 May. He seized upon Crüwell's description of the lamentable state of morale among the Italian troops in North Africa to place all the blame on his ally.[113] He paid a compliment to enemy intelligence by saying that the British would have a clearer picture of the operation than the Italian commanders, who in the war so far had failed 'to take a single bunker'. The Italians would never be able to make a successful landing in Malta, their fleet would run away as soon as the Royal Navy set sail from Gibraltar or Alexandria, and the German paratroopers would be left to do all the dirty work. The idea of a landing by sea was a 'stillborn child'. Working himself up into a towering rage, Hitler treated Student to a lecture on the many shortcomings of the 'Romance race', chief among which were sloppiness and unpunctuality.[114] Hitler was also mindful of the very costly operation against Crete, which had made him very dubious about parachute landings. Furthermore, he worried about the problem of supplying Malta once it had been taken, arguing that it would be a constant drain on Germany's limited resources.[115]

Göring fully endorsed Hitler's remarks, emphasising the heavy losses sustained in Crete. Jodl remained silent. Jeschonnek defended 'Hercules' on the grounds that if it were cancelled the whole air offensive against Malta would have been in vain, because the British would soon repair the damage, bring in fresh supplies and once again harass the convoys to North Africa. Hitler dismissed this argument, insisting against all evidence to the contrary that Tobruk would handle most of Rommel's needs. The conference ended with an agreement to go ahead with 'intellectual planning' for 'Hercules' so as to avoid the unpleasantness of having to tell the Italians that the operation was off.

Student telephoned Kesselring shortly after the meeting ended, in order to relay the Führer's curious formula about 'intellectual preparation', and told the Supreme Commander South that he had been ordered not to return to Rome, and not to have anything further to do with the planning for 'Hercules'. Kesselring was furious, but he did not believe that Hitler, having given the plan the green light, would really treat the Italians in such an insulting manner. He therefore decided to go ahead with the planning, regardless. Comando Supremo and Kesselring's staff continued separate planning. On 31 May they conferred together and agreed in principle to Kesselring's plan, which was broadly similar to 2 Air Corps' original draft. It called for a force of 100,000 men, supported by all available naval and air force units in the Mediterranean, with a sizeable German contingent including three parachute regiments, an airborne artillery regiment, anti-aircraft regiment, tank group, machinegun battalion and pioneer battalion, and one or two airborne mortar batteries, plus massive support from the Luftwaffe. There was one significant rider to the plan that the Italians called 'Hypothesis EN'. Everything depended on whether or not it was possible to land heavy equipment on the south coast. This was never established, because a commando raid by the frogmen of the crack San Marco unit never took place.

The invasion was scheduled to take place on 18 July and Kesselring went ahead with his detailed planning and preparations. A further specialist for airborne operations, Colonel Gerhard Conrad, was transferred to Sicily to prepare the glider contingent. He brought with him from 11 Air Corps his quartermaster, Colonel Conrad Seibt, who was given charge over the logistical arrangements for the operation. Cavallero had overall command of 'Hercules', Kesselring was responsible for the air forces, Student for the airborne units, and at Kesselring's insistence Weichold was put in charge of the actual landing.

Planning thus went ahead, but it soon became apparent that the operation would not have the wherewithal to succeed. There was such a chronic shortage of fuel that it would be impossible to stockpile the 40,000 tons of oil needed for 'Hercules', and they were desperately short of landing craft. Cavallero made urgent appeals to Rintelen to beg OKW for help, but none was forthcoming. But the major cause of all these difficulties was that on 26 May 1942 Rommel was once again on the march, so that the Luftwaffe was concentrating on supporting his advance to Tobruk, the convoys to North Africa were using up all the oil and the navies were in support, leaving precious little left for 'Hercules'.

Planning continued in a desultory fashion, but when Rommel took Tobruk on 21 June the two dictators agreed that he should press on to Egypt. At the beginning of July Cavallero dropped planning for the invasion of Malta (C3) and ordered its staff to draw up plans for C4, the invasion of Tunisia. 'Hercules' was now postponed until after the completion of 'Theseus', the capture of the Suez Canal. The 8th Army was soon to ensure that these plans were never revived.

Lying between Italy and Tripoli, Malta was a potential threat to the supply of the Axis troops in North Africa, as the German navy constantly reminded OKW. The British initially considered the island to be too close to the Italian mainland to be defensible, and therefore moved the headquarters of the Mediterranean fleet from Valletta to Alexandria, leaving Malta weakly defended. The Italians, who were preoccupied with their foundering campaign in Greece, missed the opportunity to seize this valuable asset during the initial stages of the war. By managing to survive some 3,000 bombing raids, which caused heavy casualties and serious damage, the island was eventually built up into a powerful base that helped cripple the routes to North Africa by sea and by air. By refusing to press for the elimination of this mounting threat, in spite of all the difficulties involved, Hitler contributed significantly to the strangulation of the Axis forces in North Africa and thus to their defeat.

7 ✠ TOBRUK

Rommel's surprisingly rapid advance into Cyrenaica left both sides gasping for breath, so that the next four months were spent in recuperation, reorganisation, building up supplies, training and planning for the next move. Immediately after the conference at the Obersalzberg, Cavallero and Rintelen went to North Africa to discuss the plans for the summer with Bastico and Rommel.[1] Rommel was given orders to move up to the Egyptian border and take up a defensive position along the line from Sidi Omar to the Halfaya Pass and Sollum. Part of his air support would then be withdrawn to take part in 'Hercules'. It was agreed that taking Tobruk was an essential precondition for the success of the new offensive, now codenamed 'Alpha'. The Panzer Army Africa was to destroy the British at Bir Hacheim, Acroma and Gazala and then take Tobruk. Rommel was very concerned about all the rumours floating around of an impending offensive and ordered that all this 'waffle and blather' had to stop. Any offenders were to be court-martialled.[2]

This was an extraordinarily audacious plan given the strength of the 8th Army. The front from Gazala to Bir Hacheim was protected by a vast minefield, behind which were the impressive strongpoints of Tobruk, 'Knightsbridge' and El Adem. 8th Army's staff officers were experienced in desert warfare and morale was high. The infantry was far better equipped than that of the Italian 10 and 21 Corps, though not as mobile as the German 90 Light Africa Division. 8th Army had an overwhelming numerical superiority in armour, with a ten to one advantage in armoured cars, a weapon that was of great value in the desert. The British had considerable superiority in field artillery, whereas the Axis had greatly superior anti-tank guns. The Desert Air Force gave the 8th Army impressive support, although the Messerschmitt 109s completely outclassed the Hurricanes and the Kittyhawks. Most important of all,

13. Tobruk

the British had almost limitless supplies, pouring men and matériel into Egypt. That Rommel was to reduce the 8th Army to a state of complete rout, under such circumstances, was a truly outstanding achievement. It was perhaps fortunate that Rommel greatly underestimated the 8th Army. Had he known its true strength, he might have hesitated before launching this audacious offensive. He had no idea of the extent of the minefields, did not know of the existence of 'Knightsbridge', and was in the dark as to the dispositions of the brigades behind the Gazala Line.[3]

The British had done their very best to fortify the Gazala Line, which marked the border between western and eastern Cyrenaica. The Germans called the sparsely populated desert of eastern Cyrenaica Marmarica. Tobruk lay 59 kilometres to the east along the Via Balbia. It was 200 kilometres from the Egyptian border. The Gazala Line was on a narrow strip of land between the sea and the high ground, where the British hoped to close off the Via Balbia, as well as the two southerly routes, the Trigh Capuzzo and the Trigh el Abd. Auchinleck was determined to hold this line, both as a forward defence of Tobruk and as the starting line of a fresh offensive to drive the Germans back to Tripoli and beyond. He ordered that if it proved impossible to hold, Ritchie was to abandon Tobruk, destroy all the defensive installations, and retire to the

Egyptian border. Rommel caught Ritchie on the wrong foot at Gazala. The defences were impressive, now with 100,000 men, 849 tanks and 604 aircraft, protected by a vast network of 'mine marshes', but he was preparing for a major offensive, Operation 'Acrobat', designed to drive the Axis forces out of North Africa.[4]

Gazala was only one point in a complex of defensive positions around Tobruk. There were also the impressive perimeter defences around the town that had frustrated Rommel the previous year. There were a series of strongpoints peppered about the desert in a broad arc to the south that included the heavily fortified oasis of Bir Hacheim at its southerly point, the apex of a roughly equilateral triangle based on the line from Gazala and Tobruk. The British defences in the Marmarica appeared to Rommel to be skilfully laid out, presenting, in his words, 'a tough nut to crack'; but they had an essential weakness. Owing to constant pressure from the War Cabinet they were designed as a springboard for a westward offensive, not to meet an offensive by Rommel. Furthermore, the need to protect the huge supply dump to the north of Sidi Rezegh meant that British commanders were severely restricted in their ability to manoeuvre, for fear of uncovering this vital base.[5]

The basic problem of defence in the desert was the lack of natural obstacles. This meant that extensive use of mines was the only solution. The 8th Army established 'boxes' along the Gazala Line. These were forts without walls, sizeable square positions covering several square kilometres, surrounded by minefields and barbed wire, the artillery able to fire in any direction, including the new six-pounder anti-tank gun, which was at least as effective as the German 5cm Pak 38.[6] The boxes were further strengthened by a few tanks, and provided with ample supplies of water, food and ammunition. The British now had an effective anti-tank weapon in the six-pounder. The ground between the boxes was patrolled by armoured vehicles, with two to three armoured brigades with Grant tanks, ready to meet an enemy attack. The bulk of the British armoured divisions were positioned behind the periphery, with Rommel often uncertain where precisely they were.

The boxes were fine in theory, but of limited value in practice. Once a box came under attack it was virtually impossible to supply and reinforce. The brigades in other boxes were too far away and virtually immobile, so were unable to offer any assistance. The tactic was yet another example of the British frittering away valuable assets in dribs and drabs.

The M3 Grant I, which first went into battle at the Battle of Gazala, was superior to the Panzer IIIs and the short-barrelled Panzer IVs.[7] It was a very tall tank, with some referring to it as a typically American skyscraper, but it was the first tank used by the British that fired both high-explosive (HE) and armour-piercing (AP) shells. Attacking anti-tank guns head on with AP shells had resulted in unacceptable losses. Now at last the British could shell anti-tank positions from a distance, just like the Germans. With its 75mm gun the Grant could hit a Panzer III at 1,500 metres, but the gun was mounted on a sponson that could be swivelled only a few degrees. A major problem was that the American M72 AP steel shell simply disintegrated when it hit the face-hardened armour on the Panzer. This problem was partly overcome by replacing the M72 shells with captured German 75mm AP shells, using the original American charges. Unfortunately stocks of this hybrid ammunition were lost during the retreat from Gazala, so that the Grants had only the old M72 shells at El Alamein. The Germans soon found out that the way to deal with the Grant was to engage it at the front and hit it on the flank. The standard Panzer III with its 50mm gun was no match for the faster Grant, but the Afrikakorps had only nineteen Panzer III Specials with a high-velocity 50mm gun that could take on the Grants.[8] The short-barrelled Panzer IV was faster and more manoeuvrable than the Grant, but it could be out-shot at a distance. The long-barrelled Panzer IV could penetrate the heavily armoured American tank at a far longer range, but Rommel had only four of these new Panzer when he began his offensive at Gazala, and they had no ammunition.[9] The prime requirements for a tank in the desert were speed, manoeuvrability and the gun's range: the larger the gun, the longer the arm. This could not be made up by heavier armour, for that inevitably led to a loss of speed and manoeuvrability. At last the British had a tank that, despite all its shortcomings, could take on the Panzer. It was hardly surprising therefore that tank crews soon called it the ELH, standing for 'Egypt's Last Hope'.

On paper Lieutenant-General Ritchie's 8th Army had impressive forces at Gazala. 13th Corps (the former Western Desert Force) under Lieutenant-General Gott was made up of the 1st South African Division under Major-General Dan Pienaar and the 50th Division under Major-General William Ramsden, which were positioned along the western perimeter. Major-General Hendrick Klopper's 2nd South African Division was in Tobruk. He also had command over 32nd Armoured Brigade, placed immediately behind the Gazala Line, as well as 1st Armoured Brigade at Tobruk. Gott's headquarters were to the south of Tobruk, outside the encircling defences. To the south Lieutenant-General Norrie's 30th Armoured Corps, made up of Major-General Herbert Lumsden's 1st Armoured Division and Major-General Frank Messervy's 7th Armoured Division, covered the area from the Gazala Line to Tobruk, including the critical strongpoint at Bir Hacheim, which was held by a Free French Brigade Group under Brigadier-General Marie-Pierre Koenig. The 5th Indian Division under Major-General Rawdon Briggs, a naturalised US citizen and much-underrated soldier, was held back in reserve. Four Indian infantry brigades and a British armoured brigade were on their way up from Egypt. There was one essential weakness in these defences. Between the Free French at Bir Hacheim and 150th Brigade to the north there was a 21-kilometre gap, which meant that the Gazala Line was far from continuous. The Italian Trieste Division was to pass through this position on 27 May 1942.

The 8th Army had the enormous advantage that Sigint from Bletchley Park gave them a fairly clear indication of Rommel's intentions.[10] As Auchinleck wrote to Ritchie on 26 May: 'Do not forget that he [Rommel] does not know that we know as much as we do.'[11] But the Axis troops had one extremely valuable new asset. General Cesare Ame, the head of Italian military intelligence, masterminded the theft of the Black Code from the US embassy in Rome. Mussolini did not give the Germans a copy of the book, but passed on some decrypts that enabled them to crack the code and read the messages from the United States military representative in Cairo, Colonel Bonner F. Fellers. They were thus very well informed as to 8th Army's plans and dispositions. British Sigint eventually managed to spot this leak, but too late in the day. Rommel struck before Bletchley Park could warn Cairo.[12] By early May Whitehall was convinced that Rommel would attack by the end of the month. Cairo was initially sceptical, which did nothing to help the already seriously strained relations between Churchill and Auchinleck, but by 19 May both agreed that an attack would begin within a matter of days. There was a false alert on 22 May and again on the 25th. On 26 May 8th Army was warned that Rommel would attack that night. Sigint picked up the codeword 'Venezia' during the afternoon, correctly assuming that this was the codeword for the attack to start.[13]

It was one thing to know that an attack was imminent, but they did not know the precise time, nor did Sigint reveal the details of Rommel's operational plan. Auchinleck and Ritchie disagreed as to how he was likely to proceed. It still took too long for Bletchley Park to decrypt messages and relay the information back to Cairo for it to be of much immediate use to commanders in the field. By the middle of June, when certain other codes had been broken, they reduced the turnaround time to a mere twelve hours. Rommel was thus lucky that he attacked early enough to catch the British partially in the dark, for partial intelligence is very often worse than no intelligence at all. Had he waited another couple of weeks he would have been unpleasantly surprised.[14]

What seemed impressive at first sight was in fact an outdated deployment. The boxes were isolated and mostly could be either picked off or bypassed. Ritchie's mobile mass of manoeuvre in 30th Corps was scattered all over the place in isolated armoured brigades. His immobile infantry and artillery were stuck in their boxes, fighting separately from the thinly spread armour. The general consensus in 8th Army's staff was that it would be impossible for Rommel to head for the strongest position at Bir Hacheim, at the southern end of the Gazala Line, in order to turn the British left flank. They were convinced that he would hit the Gazala Line head on. Thus it was not until 2300hrs on 26 May, when the offensive was well under way, that Ritchie finally decided that Rommel was out to turn his left flank. Auchinleck was still expecting a frontal attack on 27 May, and was still not ruling it out on the following day.[15] Thus only 7th Armoured Division guarded the left flank, while 1st Armoured Division was miles away to the north, near Tobruk, waiting to see where Rommel's main blow would fall. The result was what 7th Armoured Division's commander, General Messervy, described as 'an awful muck of a battle'.

The Panzer Army did not have the advantage of Britain's superb Sigint, but their intelligence was remarkably good under the circumstances. Rommel somewhat predictably decided to deliver a right hook to Tobruk by sending the Afrikakorps to the south of Bir Hacheim and then up to the sea. This move was to be concealed by a feint attack to the north of the Gazala Line by the Italian infantry and at the centre by 90 Light Africa Division, supported by three reconnaissance units, in the direction of El Adem. In order to create the impression that sizeable armoured units supported these two thrusts, trucks equipped with aero-engines drove around to the rear, stirring up huge dust clouds. Rommel did not realise that he would meet Norrie's 30th Corps to the

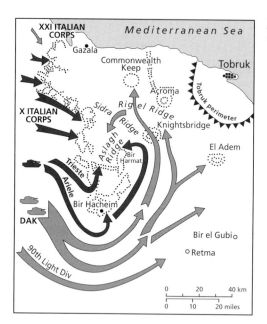

Map 10. Rommel attacks the Gazala Line, 26 May 1942

west. Rather than attempt to outflank them, he opted to begin his swing towards Tobruk further east, thus accounting for the fierce fighting on his right flank and rear on 27 May. The other major failure of German intelligence was that they seriously underestimated the strength of the British forces. They assumed that the British had only 85 more assault tanks, when in fact they had 284, 167 of which were Grants.[16] In spite of all these problems Rommel's final plan was a brilliant feint. It looked as if he was intent on chasing the 8th Army back to Egypt, as he had done in 1941, but then he swung back to take Tobruk.

The offensive began at 1400hrs on 26 May with the feint attack by the German 15 Infantry Brigade along the Via Balbia and 10 and 21 Italian Infantry Corps to the south against the Gazala Line. The Trieste Division, the Ariete and the Afrikakorps then began their right hook. The 'Hecker Group' was ordered to make a landing on the beach about half way between Gazala and Tobruk and cut off the Via Balbia.

Initially all went according to plan. Crüwell's group to the north had no difficulty in overrunning the British forward positions and by 2000hrs he had reached the day's objectives. The British were still not very perturbed. The strongly fortified Gazala position had not been attacked and a crippling *khamsin*, the hot south-westerly wind with its sandstorms that blows for some fifty days from March to May, seemed to offer added protection, but they were caught unpleasantly by surprise when the Afrikakorps attacked in the night of 26/27 May. They had moved forward under the protection of a sandstorm during the afternoon. When reconnaissance units detected a strong concentration of British armour to the north-east of Bir Hacheim, Rommel ordered 'Venezia', a modification of the original plan, calling for the Afrikakorps to make a more southerly sweep.[17] Ten thousand vehicles began to advance in a south-easterly direction at 2100hrs, with a position due south of Bir Hacheim, known as 'Position B', as their objective. Greatly helped by bright moonlight, this vast force covered the 50 kilometres so quickly that the Afrikakorps and the Ariete were in position by 0300hrs on 27 May, an astonishing achievement that was testament to the Afrikakorps' superb staff work. Rommel was extremely tense, charging way ahead and frequently losing touch with the forces under his command. Whereas the 90 Light Africa Division on the right arrived on schedule, the Trieste Division on the far left limped behind, losing contact with the Ariete Division.

Having refuelled, Rommel's group was on the march again at 0430hrs, beginning their swing to the north some 15 kilometres away from Bir Hacheim. At 0700hrs 15 Panzer Division ran into some sixty tanks from 4th Armoured Brigade. They attacked immediately, but the engagement held up their advance. General Walther Nehring, a man whom Rommel described as 'a cold fish', was seriously worried that his two Panzer divisions would lose contact with one another, and ordered 21 Panzer to halt. Rommel arrived at Nehring's headquarters twenty-five minutes later and immediately countermanded this order, because 21 Panzer, having not met with any serious opposition, was advancing rapidly. Rommel, as a modern Hannibal, was determined to push on and fight a classic battle of encirclement. Nehring, who said of Rommel that he was 'a bit like Hitler', in that he always imagined that the enemy would react exactly as he had anticipated, was outraged at Rommel's imperious attitude.

It soon transpired that Nehring had been perfectly correct to urge caution. 15 Panzer Division made quick work of 4th Armoured Brigade, battering the 8th Hussars, crippling the 3rd Royal Tank Regiment and forcing the remnants of the brigade to retire to the 5th Indian Division's strongly held box around the airfield near Tobruk at El Adem, which had been so hotly contested the previous year. But at 0830hrs 21 Panzer Division was attacked by eighty tanks, an engagement that held up the transfer of an artillery regiment and a Panzer group to strengthen 15 Panzer Division on the right flank. The Afrikakorps was once again on the move at 1000hrs after a stiff fight that beat off the Mark IIIs, crossing the Trigh Capuzzo at 1240hrs just east of the British strongpoint 'Knightsbridge', a dreary dump in the desert named after the Household Cavalry's barracks in London, which guarded the strategically important east–west, north–south crossroads on the Trigh Capuzzo, It was manned by 201st Guards Brigade. In spite of a series of plucky attacks by British tanks, Rommel ordered the exhausted 15 Panzer Division to press forward on the right flank, up to the edge of the high ground before the narrow coastal strip, with raiders to move forward to close off the Via Balbia.

The operation had been slowed down by several hours. The Grants came as an unpleasant surprise for the Afrikakorps, which lost a considerable number of Panzer in a series of fierce engagements. The Afrikakorps gave as good as it took, but should have been in a position to begin its westward drive, so as to complete the encirclement by 1200hrs. To make matters worse, 90 Light Africa Division to the north had lost contact with the rest of the Afrikakorps. Now it seemed unlikely to reach 'Position C' by nightfall. At 1415hrs Rommel once again visited Nehring's headquarters to urge his men forward, but by this time the Afrikakorps was stuck, facing vigorous attacks around the Trigh Capuzzo from 1st Armoured Division from the north-east and north, as well as from 'Knightsbridge' to the west. Rommel ignored this little difficulty, ordering the Afrikakorps to advance half an hour later. 21 Panzer Division moved on time, but 15 Panzer Division came under heavy artillery fire from the east, was embroiled in a tank attack from the south-west at 1515hrs, and faced a further sixty tanks with massive artillery support on its right flank at 1600hrs. Norrie was now attacking the Afrikakorps on three sides in a carefully co-ordinated and vigorous action. 22nd Armoured Brigade, which had lost thirty tanks earlier in the day, regrouped to mount a robust attack from the north-east. 15 Panzer Division's right flank came under a ferocious attack, which could be warded off only by calling in the Luftwaffe and thanks to Colonel Alwin Wolz's speedy deployment of three batteries of 88mm anti-tank weapons from his 135 Flak Regiment.[18]

In spite of all these difficulties, 15 Panzer Division advanced along the road towards Acroma at a remarkable pace. By 1700hrs it was within 15 kilometres of the village, hotly pursued by 2nd Armoured

Brigade, which inflicted some damage on the right flank. 21 Panzer Division made much slower progress under heavy artillery fire. Norrie unleashed 1st Armoured Brigade's lumbering old Matildas against 104 Infantry Regiment, cutting off its supply lines and destroying one of its two battalions. The 104 was a colourful mob from the Palatinate, who went into battle with five barrels of red wine, a truckload of Löwenbräu Export, and two calves trailing behind them.[19] It was not until 1700hrs that 21 Panzer Division was once again able to catch up with 15 Panzer Division. At 1810hrs the two divisions were ordered to halt and dig in. They had little time to rest. 21 Panzer Division came under tank attack at 1900hrs from the south-east. They were able to ward this off, and in a counterattack advanced to the high ground to the north of the Trigh Capuzzo.

The Trieste Armoured Division did not follow the 'Venezia' order, probably because they were out of radio contact with 20 Armoured Corps; therefore they did not swing south of Bir Hacheim, and instead passed through the gap in the Gazala Line to the north. The division was thus completely isolated, initially running into a dense minefield; then in the evening of 27 May it suffered severe losses when subjected to a tank attack. Radio contact with corps headquarters was briefly established the following morning, only to be lost again at 1100hrs. The division somehow managed to extricate itself from the minefields and reached the Trigh el Abd. It was a badly bungled operation, but the Trigh el Abd proved to be a vital supply line that was absolutely essential for further operations.

Even though it had close support from 21 Panzer Division, the Ariete fared no better, coming under heavy artillery fire from 3rd Indian Motorised Brigade at 0630hrs on 27 May. Supported by a Panzer group the Italians responded quickly, and by 0800hrs the Indian brigade in its box was overrun. The Indians lost 500 killed and wounded, along with 600 prisoners. They proved to be such a burden to the Axis troops that the officers were released.[20] The Ariete now faced the task of wresting the Bir Hacheim box from the Free French Brigade. Two attacks were launched by 132 Armoured Regiment, but without artillery and infantry support they came to nothing. The French put up a vigorous defence, inflicting a severe toll of killed and wounded and taking ninety-one prisoners, among them the regimental commander. Another attempt to take the box was made in the afternoon, but the Italians were cut off by a minefield and subjected to heavy artillery fire. During the night they were ordered to abandon the attempt, and advance as quickly as possible to 'Position C'.

On the right wing of 'Venezia', 90 Light Africa Division made the fastest progress. At 0830hrs on 27 May it ran into 7th Motorised Brigade in a box south-east of Bir Hacheim, but the hopelessly outnumbered British withdrew eastwards. The division moved rapidly north, overrunning 7th Armoured Division's headquarters and taking General Messervy and two of his staff officers prisoner. They had prudently removed their badges of rank and were able to escape, Messervy pretending to be the general's batman. As a result 7th Armoured Division was leaderless until the afternoon of 29 May.[21] Although 90 Light Africa Division continued its rapid advance, helping themselves to various British supply dumps along the way, it still arrived at 'Position C' three hours later than planned. British resistance then began to stiffen, with refreshed units of 4th Armoured Brigade denying the German troops access to El Adem. The division was divided into three groups to the east, west and south of El Adem, and had failed to join up with the rest of the Afrikakorps as Rommel had ordered. The Marcks Group to the west was soon in serious trouble, surrounded on three sides and under an intense artillery barrage. It was able to extricate itself only with great difficulty and with serious losses. Having failed to take El Adem the divisional commander, General Ulrich Kleemann, ordered his men to form a defensive 'hedgehog' some 4 kilometres to the south.

The two reconnaissance units to the right of 90 Light Africa Division were ordered to dash up to the Trigh Capuzzo, the road that supplied El Adem from the east, so as to cut it off. The British, determined to keep this vital route open, sent in a force of some seventy tanks from Tobruk which succeeded in routing the Germans, who vanished into the desert in complete disarray.

The results of the first few days' fighting were disappointing for Rommel. He had failed to reach his primary objective as laid down in the orders of 20 May: the destruction of the British army in the area of Bir Hacheim–El Adem–Acroma–Ain el Gazala. The northward swing was slower than expected, so that a number of units failed to reach 'Position C' and 90 Light Africa Division had failed to reach 'Position D' as planned. Rommel had achieved tactical surprise, doing what the British had deemed to be impossible, but he was in a very vulnerable position. He was stuck between the remaining boxes to his left and the remains of British armour to his right. His supply lines were dangerously stretched, with his armour too far ahead and the Free French still a major threat at Bir Hacheim. The Afrikakorps was in serious difficulty, with the British mounting attack after attack. If only the British armour had been able to deliver a co-ordinated strike against his flank, Rommel would have been in very serious trouble indeed. The British threw themselves on his right flank with great courage and determination, but it was a typically piecemeal and haphazard effort. The Afrikakorps had lost one-third of its Panzer, the remaining armour was stuck in the desert with empty fuel tanks, but at least it did not have to worry about the pathetic two-pounder British anti-tank guns.

Rommel had hoped to finish the whole operation within four days by destroying the bulk of the British forces by the evening of the second day, then taking Tobruk either by a surprise attack or by a co-ordinated effort from the south-east and south. Two additional days would be needed for this second option, so that the Panzer Army could be on its way to the Sollum Line after six days. Cavallero had ordered that the greater part of the Panzer Army should not go beyond the Sollum Line, but Rommel once again twisted this to mean that he could push on into Egypt with light mobile forces. All this was now merely hypothetical, as Rommel looked for a way out of the precarious position into which he had managed to manoeuvre himself. He confessed that he was 'deeply worried'. Westphal wrote in his memoirs that it was generally agreed that the offensive had failed. Gause talked things over with Nehring, and suggested that they should tell OKH and OKW that the operation had been designed as a reconnaissance in strength, so that they could withdraw without losing face with their superiors.[22] But Rommel soon recovered his habitual cocky self-assurance, pointing out that Ritchie had no idea how to deploy his armour, so that the Panzer Army could afford to let the British wear themselves out with their clumsy hit-and-run raids, then resume the offensive. Once again he was to be proved right.

The top priority was now to move the Afrikakorps and supporting units up to the coastal road, then to break through the northern part of the Gazala Line, so as to shorten their lines of communication. To this end 90 Light Africa Division was moved up towards the sea north of Acroma during the night of 27/28 May. The Afrikakorps was also ordered to move north, with 15 Panzer Division to take Acroma.

228 / Rommel's Desert War

Crüwell's group was to mount a frontal assault on the Gazala Line during the morning of 28 May and quickly secure a breach in the British
defences.

These operations did not go well, largely owing to lack of supplies and a shortage of serviceable Panzer, and quickly degenerated into
a disorganised mêlée. 15 Panzer Division had a mere twenty-nine Panzer
available, its artillery had only twenty rounds per battery, so Nehring
decided to leave the north-westerly thrust to 21 Panzer Division with
its seventy-five Panzer. They managed to overrun Point 209, known to
the British as 'Commonwealth Keep', which overlooked the Via Balbia.
But 90 Light Africa Division met with stiff resistance and became stuck,
while Crüwell's group made precious little progress through the dense
minefields.

On 29 May the Ariete Armoured Division, which had been
straggling far behind, finally managed to move up to re-establish contact
with the Afrikakorps, while 90 Light Africa Division moved westwards
to join up with the Afrikakorps. The Trieste Division also managed
to find its way through the minefields and joined up with the Ariete,
so that Rommel finally had his forces together. Crüwell had to call
off his offensive when the South Africans smashed their way through
the Italian Sabratha Infantry Division. Shortly afterwards Crüwell was
reported missing. It soon transpired that he had been shot down in his
Storch that morning, when lost behind the British lines, and had been
taken prisoner. He was lucky to have survived the crash. The pilot was
shot dead while still in the air, but the plane miraculously made a near-
perfect unassisted landing. Crüwell was treated well by his captors, the
hospitable East Yorkshire Regiment. First he was served a huge gazelle
steak, then driven off to Cairo for interrogation. When being driven
past Shepheard's Hotel he cheekily remarked that it would make an
admirable headquarters for Rommel when he arrived in a few days'
time. The story was relayed to Hitler, who was much amused.

Kesselring, who happened to be at Crüwell's headquarters, was
given command of the group at the insistence of Mellenthin, the staff
officer in charge of operations, even though this created the rather odd
situation of a field marshal in the Luftwaffe, with no experience of a
higher command in the army, being subordinate to a mere general of
whom he was highly critical.[23]

With the coastal road still blocked, logistics remained the major
problem. The route around Bir Hacheim was far too long, the convoys

constantly harassed by the British, while there were only slim pickings
to be had from raids on British positions. Some convoys managed to
find their way with great difficulty through the minefields to the west,
but they brought only scant relief. Rommel had hoped to take Acroma
on 29 May, so as to control the peripheral road around Tobruk, but
warned of a strong British force advancing from the east, he prudently
cancelled his orders. The Afrikakorps soon had more than enough
problems when faced with a robust attack by 2nd Armoured Brigade
from 'Knightsbridge', advancing along the Trigh Capuzzo, supported
by 22nd Armoured Brigade from the east. 4th Armoured Brigade, which
was also ordered to take part in this operation, was held up by a
sandstorm, enabling 15 Panzer Division to ward off the attack and
establish contact with the Ariete.

The Afrikakorps had now turned south in an effort to create
a position that was strong enough to enable supplies to be brought
through the minefields from El Cherima to Mteifel el Chebir. Kesselring, who had only intermittent contact with Rommel, gave the Hecker
Group, whose landing on the Via Balbia had been cancelled, the tricky
task of escorting a convoy through the minefields, Crüwell having
failed to make a breakthrough. None of this improved the situation,
which was rapidly becoming chronic owing to continued attacks on
the Afrikakorps. Nehring suggested retiring to be closer to the route
through the minefields, thus ensuring supplies. Rommel reluctantly
agreed, ordering his forces east of the Gazala minefields to form a
vast 'hedgehog' to guard the supply line through the minefields to the
Italian 10 and 20 Corps. The Germans failed to notice 150th Infantry
Brigade's box on the edge of the minefields. This was to cause them
serious problems in the days to come.

The Afrikakorps moved south during the night of 29/30 May
and were in position by 0600hrs. The quartermaster, Major Willers,
was given the difficult task of organising the shipment of supplies from
the Italian 10 Corps to the west of the Gazala Line through the minefields. His task was made even more difficult by powerful tank attacks
from the north and the east that severely damaged the Italian 10 Corps
units east of the Gazala Line, particularly the Ariete. 15 Panzer Division
was stopped in its tracks as it advanced towards the opening through
the minefields during the morning of 30 May, but one Panzer regiment
from 21 Panzer Division managed to establish contact with 10 Corps'
Brescia Division. The Italian 20 Corps signalled that it was in serious

trouble when it seemed that the British were about to launch a tank attack, and urgently requested help in the form of 88s.[24] In spite of all these problems, compounded by intense artillery fire, Major Willers managed to get all the supplies through the minefields. Most of the trucks arrived by 1800hrs. Two further shipments of water and ammunition were made on 31 May and on the following day the first delivery of provisions was greeted with general jubilation by the dog-tired and half-starved troops.

The logistical problem having been solved, the Panzer divisional commanders announced that they were ready to go on the offensive again. Major Willers had done a splendid job, the only remaining problem being a shortage of water in 90 Light Africa Division, due to a lack of transport. The problem now was what to do next. Rommel had not attained his objectives, and had only escaped disaster because of the British army's inability to co-ordinate an effective response on 28 May, when his forces were scattered all over the desert, desperately short of supplies and completely surrounded. As is so often the case in warfare, a badly bungled operation did not end up as a complete debacle, thanks to a truly astonishing display of military incompetence on the part of the adversary. Rommel had set out to encircle the British and had in turn been encircled, but the British lacked the skill to exploit this golden opportunity. For the next twelve days Rommel acted responsibly, concentrating on strengthening his position, bringing in supplies and knocking out the British strongpoint at Got el Ualeb and the Free French who still held Bir Hacheim. This phase of the battle is known in English as 'The Cauldron', whereas the Afrikakorps, true to their national proclivities, called it 'The Sausage Pot'. Both the 8th Army commander and the C-in-C now concluded that Rommel had no intention of withdrawing, but that he would make a stand, and possibly resume his advance. From this they deduced that they would have first to liquidate the 'Cauldron' bridgehead to the south of Knightsbridge before mounting a counter-offensive.[25] Rommel was to fight a brilliant defensive battle that was to prove to be one of the decisive engagements in the desert campaign.

On 30 May Rommel reported to Bastico that having destroyed two-fifths of the British tanks, he intended to attack at 0600hrs next morning. He was fully confident that he would be successful.[26] The box at Got el Ualeb, an important position between the Trigh Capuzzo to the north and the Trigh el Abd to the south, which was relatively well protected by minefields, as well as by 150th Infantry Brigade, proved to be a very hard nut to crack. Rommel attacked with a massive force on 31 May, throwing in the Afrikakorps from the north and north-east, the Trieste Armoured Division from the south and south-west, the 90 Light Africa Division from the south-east and with the support of a massive attack by Stukas. The British fought with great gallantry, winning the Germans' respect, but they were completely outnumbered and the box was overrun within a few hours. Westphal was seriously wounded during this operation, when a large chunk of shrapnel lodged in his thigh, and he had to be invalided home. The fact that this was the result of friendly fire from a battery of 88s was carefully concealed. Westphal was so badly injured that he was delivered directly to the mortuary, but somehow managed to survive.[27] Rommel sorely missed his invaluable chief of operations in the days ahead. His chief of staff, General Alfred Gause, was also wounded, having been thrown against a Panzer when a shell exploded nearby, resulting in a severe concussion. He was replaced by the highly gifted, but unattractively obsequious ex-ranker, Colonel Fritz Bayerlein.[28]

Got el Ualeb having fallen, Rommel immediately ordered an attack on Bir Hacheim to be launched the following day by 90 Light Africa Division, supported by the Trieste Division. Bir Hacheim was of vital operative importance as the strongly defended southern corner of the Gazala Line. If Rommel succeeded in smashing it, he would be able to open up the Cauldron to the south, secure his supply lines and begin to roll up the entire Gazala Line. Given the strength of the position and its importance, it is surprising that Rommel allotted far fewer forces to the task than he had used at Got el Ualeb, but he insisted that with its deep surrounding minefields it could not be taken by the Panzer. Kesselring, who was furious at the heavy losses sustained by the Luftwaffe during the recent fighting, violently disagreed, but Rommel would not budge, dismissing this argument as an example of the ignorance of a mere airman.[29]

The two infantry divisions marched south during the night of 1/2 June and began their attack at 0600hrs on 3 June. It was a concentric assault with the Italians attacking from the north-east and the Germans from the south-east. Three reconnaissance groups attacked from the west, thus completing the encirclement. The attack failed miserably. The troops were exhausted after a long march, the operation was extremely badly co-ordinated, reconnaissance had failed to note the extent of the barbed wire entanglements and minefields, and the Free French and their anti-fascist comrades fought courageously. Rommel later commented that this was one of the toughest battles in the entire North African campaign.[30] The Italians soon found themselves on the defensive, while the Germans made precious little progress in the face of intense artillery fire. The Axis troops were forced to retire, regroup and lick their wounds, all the while subjected to constant attacks by the RAF and Free French artillery. A British relief force moving on both sides of the Trigh Capuzzo was beaten back by 21 Panzer, which managed to encircle the Guards Brigade and 10th Indian Brigade. Many tanks managed to escape, but 4,000 prisoners were taken, 86 tanks destroyed and 110 guns lost. The Germans had only minimal losses, thanks in part to Kesselring overcoming his earlier reservations and throwing in all the Luftwaffe units he could muster.[31] On 6 June 90 Light Africa Division once again went on the attack. This time they advanced to within 700 metres of the fort, but found themselves without cover, facing a minefield, so the attempt once again failed. Back in Rome Cavallero proclaimed the situation to be 'logical', a favourite phrase that no one understood, but generally was assumed to mean that all was not well.[32] Bastico sent a frantic note to Rommel saying that he had no idea what was going on, and insisting that Rommel was not to go on slogging away until his army was totally exhausted.[33] Rommel joined in the fray on 8 June in a attempt to finish off the resistance at Bir Hacheim, first sending in the Stukas and following up with an attack from the north by an assorted force that include Colonel Wolz and his redoubtable 88s.[34] This new attack was supported by 90 Light Africa Division to the south, but it was hit during the afternoon by 4th Armoured Brigade coming from the east. Later in the evening a couple of hundred infantrymen managed to penetrate the first line of defences, but they soon got stuck and had to withdraw.

The Panzer Army was frustrated that it had been unable to take Bir Hacheim, but it was encouraged by the fact that the British had done so little to help the beleaguered Free French. In fact the DAF bombed the fortress on several occasions, friendly fire adding to the defenders' misery and doing little for Allied solidarity.[35] Operation 'Aberdeen', launched in the early hours of 5 June, which was designed to destroy the Axis troops in the Cauldron, was a badly bungled affair, with the artillery pounding away at a stretch of empty desert and two divisions attacking a phantom enemy. From this the Afrikakorps concluded, with

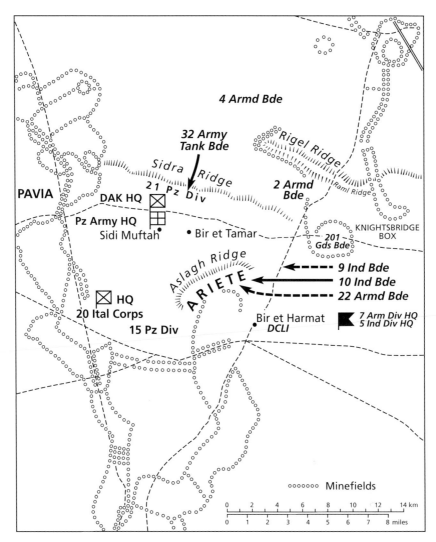

Map 11. The 'Cauldron', 5 June 1942

unconcealed contempt, that the British were concentrating on securing their supply lines and were prepared to sacrifice their courageous
allies.[36] These sentiments were heartily endorsed by the Free French.[37]
They were not far off the mark. Auchinleck had been urging a counterstroke against the Panzer Group's supply lines, but Ritchie, feeling
that this was far too risky, preferred to consolidate his armour around
Acroma to protect his own rear, arguing that he did not have enough
forces to do both. The British Motorised Group 'August' was sent to

harry Rommel's supply lines, causing him a severe headache, indicating that Ritchie had missed a opportunity seriously to disrupt Rommel's offensive. As it was, he wasted his assets hammering away at the Panzer Group's salient to the north.[38] Rommel had Kesselring breathing down his neck, insisting if he did not take Bir Hacheim soon the entire plan would be in jeopardy, and pointing out that the Luftwaffe, having lost a large number of machines, was forced to ignore other vital points in the battle. With no British relief operation in sight, Rommel decided to make a final attack on 10 June.

He took personal command of the Battle Group Baade, attacking after a heavy bombardment by the Luftwaffe, breaking into the box and by the evening succeeding in taking the heavily fortified position at Point 186.[39] The 90 Light Africa Division and the Trieste were less successful. A fierce air battle raged, during which Spitfires saw action for the first time in the desert. The following night the 7th Armoured Division south of Bir Hacheim began to withdraw, making it clear that the British were abandoning the Free French to their fate. Between 2200 and 2300hrs that pitch-black night, in General Koenig's words, the garrison 'tip-toed' away to the west and south-west, a daring move that earned him Rommel's respect. He wrote: 'Once again it had been shown that, however desperate the situation, there is always something that can be done by a resolute commander who is not just prepared to throw in his hand.'[40] Koenig, along with most of his officers and men, managed to escape, making contact with 7th Motorised Brigade, but he lost the bulk of his vehicles, stores and equipment.[41] Among the survivors was an Englishwoman, Susan Travers, who was Koenig's driver and mistress. She was the only woman to become an officer in the Foreign Legion.[42] By the early morning of 11 June Bir Hacheim was finally in German hands.[43]

Among those whom the odious Berndt described as the 'criminals of twenty different nations' who were captured at Bir Hacheim was Edward Tomkins, Koenig's liaison officer with Ritchie, who had became lost in a *khamsin* on his way between HQ and the box.[44] As an excellent linguist he had the unique opportunity of witnessing both Ritchie and Rommel at work. Whereas Ritchie had some thirty ADCs rushing around amid piles of paperwork, Rommel operated with two signals vehicles, for incoming and outgoing messages, and appeared to do virtually everything on his own. Tomkins, who could understand everything that was going on, was enormously impressed.[45]

The capture of Bir Hacheim placed Rommel in a difficult predicament. On 6 June the Panzer Army received a message from OKW saying that Hitler had issued an order that the 'large number of German refugees' who were fighting alongside the Free French were to be 'pitilessly eliminated' in the course of battle. Those who survived were to be immediately shot by the nearest German officer. Exceptions should only be made if it were thought that valuable intelligence might be gained. Furthermore, the armistice agreement between Germany and France stated that Frenchmen were forbidden to bear arms against the German Reich and that 'French citizens who contravene this agreement will be treated as insurgents.' It is much to the credit of Panzer Army's HQ that this order was burnt, and there were no such summary executions. The 'Red Spaniards, Swiss, Czechs, Poles, Niggers and other riff-raff', along with the anti-fascist Germans, were treated as ordinary prisoners of war. There are no reports of there being any Jews among them, although there were rumours that a fanatical 'Jewish Brigade' was fighting to the death in defence of the box.[46] Much was later made of the fact that a man said to be General Alexander's nephew, Lieutenant Michael Alexander, was captured behind the German lines, along with Corporal Henry Gurney, in August 1942. Both were wearing Afrikakorps' caps, but although Hitler had ordered that all commandos (defined as any enemy troops behind the German lines) should be shot, and although Alexander was wearing a German uniform, he was initially treated as any other prisoner of war.[47] It was not until October 1942 that Hitler gave additional orders that all British perpetrators of 'terror and sabotage' acts were to be treated as 'bandits'.[48] Hitler was then asked how the two men should be treated. He ordered them to go before a military court, making it quite clear that he expected them to receive the death penalty. Rommel, who insisted that he confirm any sentence passed by a military court, did not want to accept the responsibility for Alexander's fate. He therefore agreed that he should be sent to Germany for 'special treatment'.[49] Both men were sent by a military court for trial in Germany, charged with being *franc-tireurs*, but they got off relatively lightly. They were interned at Oflag VII/B in Eichstätt in Bavaria, a camp whose famous prisoners included Douglas Bader, Airey Neave and David Stirling. Alexander, who claimed to be the general's nephew in order to avoid the death penalty, was in fact only a distant cousin, but he counted among the *Prominenten* in the Oflag, which included Viscount George Lascelles, the king's nephew, and Tadeusz Bór-Komorowski, the leader of the Warsaw uprising.[50]

Whilst the infantry and the Luftwaffe were tied up for nine days dealing with Bir Hacheim, the Italian troops in the 'Sausage Pot' were subjected to a fierce attack from 5th Indian Division and 7th Armoured Division from the east, and from 13th Corps from the north, in an offensive designed to knock out the 'Cauldron'. The Ariete took a terrible beating and were forced to retire, but the Afrikakorps came to their assistance, halted the British and mounted a counterattack under Rommel's personal command on 6 June. The British attack was once again a piecemeal affair, lacking in a concentrated effort at one point, and was, in Auchinleck's view, 'the turning point of the whole battle'.[51] Mellenthin was somewhat blunter, justifiably describing this inept operation as 'one of the most ridiculous attacks in the campaign'.[52] Some 4,000 prisoners were taken, the 10th Indian Brigade was wiped out, but 201st Guards Brigade managed to hang on to Knightsbridge, thus bringing Rommel's counterattack to a halt, but his exceptional skill, coolness and indomitable spirit had saved the Axis from a shattering defeat.

The capture of Bir Hacheim solved Rommel's logistical difficulties and enabled the Panzer Army Africa to concentrate on mobile warfare, so that Knightsbridge was soon threatened with encirclement by his two Panzer divisions. It also unhinged the British defensive position, although 1st South African Division and the Geordies in 50th 'Tyne and Tees' Division at the northern end of the Gazala Line had been left virtually untouched. Rommel then decided to move north, with the main weight of the advance on El Adem, some 25 kilometres south of Tobruk, then wheel to the left so as to attack the Gazala Line from the rear. It was too late to cut off the South Africans, so the move was designed to stop the British from building up a new front to the south of Tobruk and to isolate the town from the east.[53]

The advance on El Adem began at 1500hrs on 11 June, and 90 Division took the town in the afternoon of the following day. Rommel's next move was to cut off the British lines of communication between the Gazala Line and Tobruk. To this end he ordered his two Panzer divisions north in an attempt to cut off the Via Balbia, whereupon the 1st and 50th Divisions were ordered early in the morning of 14 June to retire to the Egyptian border. The South Africans managed to escape before the Afrikakorps blocked the coastal strip on the evening of 15 June, and fought their way past the German forces at Acroma.

The Geordies broke out to the south and south-east, smashing their way through the Italian 10 Army. The bulk of what little remained of the British armour had now been withdrawn, leaving Tobruk thinly defended by 29th Indian Brigade and 7th Motorised Brigade to the south of El Adem.[54] Rommel was now master of the battlefield, with an overwhelming superiority in armour. Ritchie had made another fatal mistake in continuing to hammer away at the northern flank of the Gazala Line, instead of withdrawing his forces and preparing for a mobile defence against an advance by Rommel's armour.

The Gazala Line having been abandoned in an unseemly retreat known as the 'Gazala Gallop', after a two-week slogging match that destroyed 8th Army's armour and drove it out of its defensive positions, the Italian infantry was able to advance on a broad front towards Tobruk without opposition.[55] 21 Panzer Division suffered serious casualties from the RAF as it moved eastwards. 90 Light Division was halted on 15 June by 29th Indian Brigade in its strongpoint at El Hatian, although the latter broke out and retired to the south during the night of 16/17 June. On 18 June, 7th Motorised Brigade (formerly Jock Campbell's Support Group) was ordered to follow the Indians. Rommel was now free to encircle Tobruk and prepare to deliver the final blow.

Ritchie's decision on 14 June to withdraw Godwin-Austen's 13th Corps, made up of the 1st South African Division and the British 50th Division, meant that Tobruk would have to fend for itself and keep Rommel's men busy, while the badly battered 8th Army had time to be refreshed and return to the fray. The Panzer Group's air reconnaissance noticed the withdrawal along the Via Balbia on 14 June. Rommel immediately issued orders to the Afrikakorps to descend the escarpment and cut off the South African retreat, but after three weeks of intense fighting the corps was utterly exhausted, and the order was ignored. It was not until the following day that 15 Panzer started to move, managing to cut off some of the rearguard, but the bulk of 1st South African Division escaped.[56]

On 14 June Churchill sent the following note to Auchinleck: 'Presume there is no question in any case of giving up Tobruk. As long as Tobruk is held no serious enemy advance into Egypt is possible.'[57] Auchinleck, who in February had argued that Tobruk should be abandoned rather than face a siege, now ordered Ritchie to use two divisions to keep the lines of communication open between Tobruk and the Egyptian border, and hang on to Tobruk come what may. Ritchie replied that he could give no guarantee that it would be possible to hold the line to the east of Tobruk, but argued that the town had enough supplies to survive a siege for two months. The perimeter defences had been strengthened by the arrival of the 3rd Battalion of the Coldstream Guards from 201st Guards Brigade, which had been withdrawn from Knightsbridge on 13 June, and by 32nd Armoured Brigade. Rommel said of the Guards at Knightsbridge: 'This brigade was almost a living embodiment of the virtues and faults of the British soldier – tremendous courage and tenacity combined with an inflexible lack of mobility.'[58] Tobruk could not possibly be defended for two months with such weak forces, commanded by an inexperienced young South African general, with insufficient anti-aircraft and anti-tank guns. Ritchie failed to tell Auchinleck that although he had the supplies, he did not have the men.

Ritchie was persuaded by Gott to ignore Auchinleck's order to hold a line east of Tobruk, so that 13th Corps was not recalled. Ritchie and Gott then went to Tobruk, leaving General Hendrik Klopper with the impression that he would not have to face a siege, and that his perimeter defences, concentrated in the west and south-west, were ideally positioned to meet an attack. Meanwhile Cavallero warned that a lengthy siege of Tobruk was out of the question, because of the need to concentrate on 'Hercules', the attack on Malta, now scheduled for the beginning of August. He added that the fall of Tobruk would mark the end of the campaign, rather than be the first step of an attack on Egypt.[59]

The Battle of Gazala was over, 8th Army in full retreat to the frontier, and Rommel now turned his attention to Tobruk. He decided to attack the fortress from the south-east, where the perimeter defences were weakest, thus reviving the plan he had devised in 1941, but which had been frustrated by Cunningham's offensive. A feint attack was to be launched from the south-west to tie down the garrison. The attacking force was to march eastwards, creating the impression that Rommel was heading for the Egyptian border as he had done the year before, but was then to switch back and attack from the south-east.[60] The first stage of the main attack was on Gambut, some 60 kilometres east of Tobruk, by 21 and 15 Panzer Divisions, along with the Ariete Armoured Division. The attack on Gambut was designed to clear the British airstrips in the area, secure the Via Balbia and complete the encirclement of Tobruk, but it was also to create the impression that Rommel was heading for the Egyptian border.[61] The advance, codenamed Operation 'Four-poster' (*Himmelbett*), began on 17 June. The 7th Armoured Division was forced back and the airfield at Gambut secured. The British were taken in by Rommel's easterly move, imagining that this was indeed a repeat performance of the 'dash to the wire' in 1941, which would leave Tobruk surrounded but intact. First he ordered a halt, helping himself to the ample provisions the British had left behind, then he turned his troops around on 19 June, and at 0520hrs on the following day launched his attack. Meanwhile, the Italian infantry in 10 and 21 Corps, along with the Trieste Division and the German 15 Infantry Brigade, completed the encirclement of Tobruk. The Panzer Army reported to OKH that the British had retreated, leaving their strongpoints at Belhamed and Sidi Rezegh without a fight, and with their divisions 'only partially fit for action.'[62]

Tobruk was a formidable obstacle standing on high ground and surrounded by a double ring of defences built by the Italians. The perimeter was some 15 kilometres from the town and ran for 54 kilometres with 128 defensive positions, each for thirty or forty men, dug in deep and virtually invisible to the attacking forces. There was an elaborate network of tank traps, lightly boarded over and covered with earth. That it fell so easily was largely due to the skilful co-ordination of air and land forces. The Luftwaffe flew a total of 588 missions on 20 June, the Italians 177. Making full use of aircraft from Greece and Crete, 10 Air Corps flew 7,035 missions in North Africa in the month of June. Never again was Rommel to be given such a level of air support.[63]

The attack began with the Stukas destroying the barbed wire entanglements and badly shaking the 11th Indian Division, positioned in the perimeter to the south-east. The artillery softened up the narrow gap through which the Afrikakorps was to pass, while engineers bridged the tank traps. Klopper's men were caught completely by surprise when the Afrikakorps reached the perimeter defences at 0730hrs. One hour later the Panzer began crossing the tank traps, establishing a bridgehead some 2 kilometres deep. Recovering somewhat from the initial shock, resistance began to stiffen, but after fierce fighting 21 Panzer Division crossed the Via Balbia at midday; 15 Panzer Division followed two hours later.[64]

The Italians in 20 Motorised Corps were less successful. They failed to cross the perimeter defences, so that the Ariete Armoured Division and the Trieste Motorised Division had to follow ignominiously behind 15 Panzer Division, before deploying to the west and north-west. 21 Panzer Division was in command of the harbour and the eastern part

14. Rommel at Tobruk

of the town by 1900hrs. Klopper was at a loss what to do. His troops were inexperienced, the defences nothing like they had been the year before, the minefields having been dug up to strengthen the Gazala Line. Should he hang on at whatever cost, attempt a breakout, or surrender?

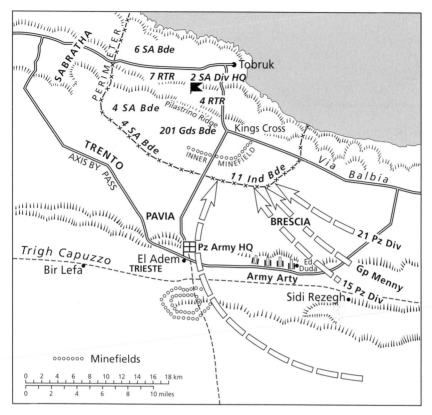

Map 12. Assault on Tobruk, 20 June 1942

Soon Rommel left him no choice. The citadels at Pilastrino and Solaro fell, 25,000 prisoners had been taken, and the remaining defenders hung on desperately in the west. 21 Panzer Division renewed the attack at 0530hrs the following day, and at 0940hrs Rommel met Klopper on the Via Balbia about 6 kilometres west of Tobruk to accept the capitulation of the fortress that was already firmly in his hands. Panzer Army Africa took a total 33,000 prisoners, among them five generals, and helped themselves to a vast amount of weapons and ammunition, including several hundred guns, twenty anti-tank guns, a hundred trucks, thirty serviceable tanks, fuel, clothing and provisions. About one hundred tanks were destroyed.[65] The British had failed to destroy the harbour, which was immediately put into service by the Axis. The British envoys for the surrender of Tobruk first ran into the Italian 21 Corps who told them to go to Rommel's headquarters. This prompted Mussolini to publish an account of the surrender of Tobruk in the morning of

21 June that created the impression that this was essentially an Italian victory. Hitler was furious and to demonstrate to all the world that this was a triumph of German arms, he promoted Rommel to field marshal.[66]

For Rommel and his 'Africans' 21 June 1942 was the high point in the North African campaign. He issued the following order of the day:

Soldiers!
   The great battle in the Marmarica has been crowned by your swift conquest of Tobruk. We have taken in all over 45,000 prisoners and destroyed or captured more than 1,000 armoured fighting vehicles and nearly 4,000 guns. During the long hard struggle of the last four weeks, you have, through your incomparable courage and tenacity, dealt the enemy blow upon blow. Your forceful spirit has cost him the core of his field army, which was standing poised for an offensive. Above all, he has lost his powerful armour. My special congratulations to all officers and men for this superb achievement.
   Soldiers of the Panzer Army Africa!
   Now we must assure the complete destruction of the enemy. We will not rest until we have shattered the last remnants of the British Eighth Army. During the days to come, I shall call on you for one more great effort to bring us to this final goal.

Rommel[67]

The commanding officer of the Afrikakorps, Nehring, and his chief of staff, Bayerlein, celebrated their victory by going for a swim. The expedition almost ended in disaster. Sergeant Voller pulled up the staff car at what appeared to be an abandoned house, whence two half-starved British soldiers emerged, each with a pistol in his hand. The general, the colonel and the sergeant were unarmed, but Nehring saved the situation by engaging the 'Tommies' in conversation until his radio car with an armed escort arrived. Loath to spoil his day at the beach by taking the two men prisoner, he disarmed them and sent them back to Tobruk. Lieutenant Bailey and Sergeant Norton, determined to avoid captivity, made an epic 38-day march along the coast, eventually regaining their unit.[68] Later that day Nehring was quietly relieving

15. German soldiers beside the sea, 1941

himself behind a building when he was joined by Kesselring, who said
to him: 'There you are, you see it could be done after all, yet Rommel
kept saying he couldn't do it. I kept having to push him.' Nehring
thought that this was a bit much, even for Kesselring.[69]

Hitler was ecstatic over the capture of Tobruk, announcing that this was 'destiny's gift to the German nation' and 'an absolutely incredible success'.[70] Ernst von Weizsäcker, secretary of state at the foreign office, was equally euphoric. He wrote: 'The sudden surrender of Tobruk and further developments during Rommel's advance raises the question whether the English are on the verge of collapse. Will Britain's social framework and alliance structure, made up of such diverse parties, begin to fall apart?'[71]

With the British being steadily pushed back, Ribbentrop called upon the Neurath group to step up its propaganda efforts in Egypt. Britain was to be exposed as the country that had robbed Egypt of its freedom, turning the country into a battlefield upon which the Egyptian people were to be sacrificed for its imperialistic ends. 'Rommel's victorious soldiers' were coming to free the Egyptians from the British yoke. They came as friends, with the sole object of driving out the British and the 'people who supported them'. The Axis powers were the friends of the entire Arab world, who were awaited as liberators in Iraq, Syria and Palestine. The Egyptians should do everything in their power to help Rommel and to make life difficult for the British.[72]

The fall of Tobruk could hardly have happened at a worst time for Churchill. He received the news on 21 June while conferring with Roosevelt in the White House, and smarted under the humiliation of yet another disaster. At first he did not believe it could be true, and ordered Ismay, liaison officer between the war cabinet and the chiefs of staff, to check with London. The confirmation was, as Churchill later wrote, 'one of the heaviest blows I can recall during the war'.[73] Britain had suffered a series of disasters since 1940 at Narvik, Dunkirk, Dakar, Greece and Crete. Singapore with 85,000 men had fallen in February to a greatly inferior Japanese force almost without a fight. The Japanese seized Rangoon on 7 March, Rommel had smashed his way through the Gazala Line, and now Tobruk had capitulated to an army half its size. As Churchill wrote in his memoirs: 'Defeat is one thing; disgrace is another.'[74] Roosevelt was fully aware of the gravity of the situation and was determined to do all he could to help his ally. At a meeting of the combined chiefs of staff on 25 June it was agreed that 300 M4 Sherman tanks would be sent to Egypt, along with a hundred 105mm self-propelled guns with 150 specialists for their use, and 4,000 men from the US air force (USAAF), to be convoyed immediately. It was an act of exceptional generosity in that the Shermans, which had only just gone into production, were badly needed by the Americans' own armoured divisions with their obsolete tanks. The Sherman was soon labelled by the Afrikakorps as the 'Tommy Cooker', because its fuel tank could easily be set on fire, and for the same reason the British acerbically called them 'Ronsons', after the famous make of cigarette lighters. However, there were an awful lot of them,[75] and the Sherman did have the advantage of a rounded turret, which was a difficult target for German gunners to hit, the shells often making a glancing blow. It was also well armed with a 75mm gun.[76] Modifications reduced the danger of 'brewing up', and the tank's reliability and endurance was greatly appreciated. The Allies had already agreed on 21 June that six air groups would be sent to the Middle East, three of them immediately. The first of these additional aircraft arrived in Egypt at the end of July, the tanks and artillery at the beginning of September.

Churchill was to face a vote of no confidence in the House of Commons. The motion was supported by erstwhile supporters, such as Sir John Wardlaw-Milne, chairman of the finance committee, Admiral Sir Roger Keyes, former head of combined operations, and the former minister of war, Hore-Belisha. The prime minister blamed Auchinleck for a defeat that was 'unexplained, and, it seemed, inexplicable'.[77] Sir Stafford Cripps, leader of the House and member of the War Cabinet, who was strongly tipped as Churchill's successor, summed up the case against the military in a memorandum he handed to the prime minister on 2 July. He argued that Auchinleck and the senior commanders in the Middle East had been overly optimistic and, had failed to master Rommel's armoured tactics, and that the British armed forces were in all respects inferior to the Germans, in spite of three years of experience fighting in the desert. Churchill rose to the occasion, arguing that Auchinleck had been every bit as surprised as he had been by the fall of Tobruk, and gave a glowing account of the massive support promised by Roosevelt. The vote of no confidence was defeated by 475 votes to 25.

The fall of Tobruk plunged Churchill into deep despair. There was near panic in Cairo, with a mass exodus to Palestine during what was known as 'The Flap'. It had quite the opposite effect on Hitler and Mussolini. They were so carried away that they ignored all previous planning and concerns, imagining that the Panzer Army Africa would soon be in command of the Suez Canal. They thus ignored the massive support given by the United States to the British forces in the

Middle East, which prepared the way for the crushing defeat of the Axis forces in North Africa. Walter Schellenberg, as head of the Security Service's foreign intelligence department, paid close attention to Egyptian affairs. He reported to the foreign office that there was widespread panic as Rommel advanced, with runaway inflation, a mass exodus to Palestine and Lebanon, a transport strike, and mounting unrest as a result of the food shortages. The pro-German King Farouk was now a virtual prisoner in his palace. Schellenberg claimed that the Axis declaration on Egypt had made a deep impression and had fuelled anti-British sentiments.[78] Although it seemed that Egypt would soon be in the hands of the Axis, Cavallero still hoped that the operation against Malta would go ahead. On 20 June he prepared a letter for Mussolini to send to Hitler, which called for his full support for an attack on Malta in August. He had serious misgivings about a thrust into Egypt, pointing out that the Allies might well be tempted to mount an operation against Tunis, which would gravely threaten the Axis. But General Giacomo Carboni, the commander of the assault divisions designated for 'Hercules', who was well known for his detestation of the Germans, was convinced that the operation would end in disaster, arguing that the planning was 'childish', the equipment unsuitable, the oil supplies inadequate.

On 23 June Hitler's reply arrived, in which he assured Mussolini that the fall of Tobruk was 'militarily a historic turning point' that called for the 'ruthless exploitation' of the advantage gained. The 8th Army was 'as good as destroyed'. Tobruk was an excellent harbour with a railhead to Egypt. The vital thing was to strike now before the Allies could build up their forces in the Middle East and American long-range bombers stationed there capable of reaching Italy. The eventual prize was glittering. Combined with operations in the south of the Soviet Union it would lead to 'the collapse of the entire oriental structure of the British Empire'. There was, however, a note of uncharacteristic caution in this outpouring of optimism. Hitler wrote: 'Under certain circumstances Egypt might be wrested from England.' Quite what these 'circumstances' were remained unspecified, and there were a number of assumptions that were soon to prove false. Tobruk was not a particularly suitable harbour, and convoys were still open to attack. The 8th Army had taken a terrible beating, but it was not on the verge of collapse.[79] Just as Hitler had imagined that 'Barbarossa' would make the hazardous invasion of England unnecessary, he now assumed that the capture of Egypt and the Suez Canal would render 'Hercules' irrelevant. The choice was between giving Rommel the go-ahead, and launching 'Hercules'. Mussolini preferred 'Hercules', but Hitler wanted Rommel to be given a free hand, which would mean postponing 'Hercules'.[80] Imagining that the 8th Army was on its last legs, Hitler made no mention of 'Hercules' in his letter to Mussolini. Instead he offered the glorious prospect of 'the collapse of the entire Eastern part of the English Empire', ending his letter with the words: 'The goddess of victory only approaches a leader once. He who does not seize the opportunity will never have it again.' Dreams were revived of a gigantic pincer movement south from the Caucasus, with Rommel driving east into Egypt and across the Suez Canal. It was to be codenamed 'Fredericus II'.[81]

Mussolini agreed with Hitler's euphoric assessment of this 'historic moment', but he had to take Cavallero's concerns into consideration. In his reply to Hitler he therefore argued that the time was ripe for an attack on Egypt, but cautioned that the problem of supplies by sea was still acute, as long as Malta had not been 'neutralised', adding that the lack of oil was still a major concern. With the dictators in broad agreement, all Cavallero could do was to limit the damage by trying to rein in Rommel, hoping that he could count on Kesselring's support in this endeavour. On 21 June Cavallero had announced that it was the intention of the Comando Supremo to take the defensive positions along the Egyptian border and then withdraw aircraft and shipping for the attack on Malta. Bastico was ordered to take the Sollum–Halfaya Line along with the Giarabub oasis and to prepare to transfer his air force. Rintelen managed to secure Cavallero's agreement to allow mobile forces to pursue the British into Egypt, thus leaving Rommel on a dangerously loose leash.

Cavallero's worst fears were confirmed when Rommel sent a message to Rome on 22 June announcing that he had captured enough supplies in Tobruk to enable him to advance 'deep into Egypt' and asking Mussolini to 'remove all restrictions on the freedom of movement'.[82] On the following day Bastico agreed with this assessment. Kesselring, having seen Hitler's letter to Mussolini, had no alternative but to concur. Thus in the very early hours of 24 June Rintelen sent a message to Rommel: 'Duce agrees to Panzer Army's intention to pursue the enemy into Egypt,' but warned that the Luftwaffe would have to be withdrawn in preparation for the attack on Malta, because as long as Malta

16. Rommel and Kesselring

remained in British hands the supply problems could not possibly be solved.[83] Rommel, who had been appointed field marshal 'with immediate effect' on 22 June and was, at forty-nine, the youngest incumbent of this highest military rank, knew that he had Hitler's full support for his unconventional style of warfare. He now was superior in rank to Cavallero and Bastico and the equal of Kesselring.[84] Rommel told his wife that he would rather have had two more divisions than this premature promotion, and forgot to change his shoulder badges until Kesselring gave him his own during the battle of El Alamein.[85] Kesselring, angry that Rommel was now his equal, remarked sourly after the war that 'diamonds would have been enough'.[86]

Rommel had already acted with total disregard for his superiors, on 19 June ordering 90 Light Africa Division to push on east of Tobruk. The division entered Bardia unopposed on 20 June, and then continued its eastward advance. On the afternoon of the following day 21 Panzer Division was ordered to move to the south-east of Tobruk and take the airfield at Gambut. This operation was completed by 0930hrs on 22 June. 15 Panzer Division was ordered to move to the south-east of Gambut, take a couple of days rest, and then to move further south before wheeling eastwards, crossing the frontier wire and thus cutting off Sollum. The Ariete, Littorio and Trieste Divisions were to follow behind the Afrikakorps, while 90 Light Africa Division moved south to join this eastward thrust, their places between Bardia and Sollum taken by units from the Italian 21 Corps.

Rommel was impatient to move, the rest period was cancelled, and the Panzer Army was once again on the march on 23 June, with orders to destroy the remaining British forces in the area between Sollum and Sidi Barrani, This amounted to a massive attack on the frontier positions, which were thinly held by units of 7th Armoured Division and the 5th Indian Division. 90 Light Africa Division reached the wire at 1815hrs on 23 June and the pioneers began the work of clearing a way through the minefields. 21 Panzer Division arrived an hour later, advancing about 5 kilometres across the border before nightfall. Rommel, assuming that the British would withdraw from the Sollum Line and make a stand at Mersa Matruh, ordered a 'ruthless pursuit of the enemy forces' during the night, to continue the following day. The 'ruthless pursuit' was hampered by a lack of fuel, with the Afrikakorps limping behind 90 Light Africa Division, which reached a position south-east of Sidi Barrani by the evening of the following day. Ritchie had indeed intended to defend Mersa Matruh, but was relieved of his command. Auchinleck and Dorman-Smith wisely decided to maintain mobility. This move frustrated Rommel's plans to cut off and destroy the remnants of the 8th Army, and ultimately decided the outcome of the campaign.[87] But it was also a hazardous gamble. Auchinleck and his deputy chief of staff were appalled when they received details of Ritchie's dispositions at Mersa Matruh, which left huge gaps open through which Rommel could drive and force him to fight on a reversed front. They knew that the only viable move was to retire to El Alamein, a position where Rommel would have great difficulty in executing one of his characteristic outflanking attacks, but they did not want to move back without a fight. Mersa Matruh might be an insignificant fishing village, but its loss would be symbolic of yet another disaster which, following closely on the Tobruk fiasco, might well have a shattering effect on morale, and would provoke another storm of outrage from Churchill. But this presented the problem of disengaging from the enemy in the midst of an offensive, which would leave the 8th Army dangerously exposed. The worst was soon to happen, with the withdrawal degenerating into yet another fiasco, in which the 8th Army lost two invaluable infantry divisions.

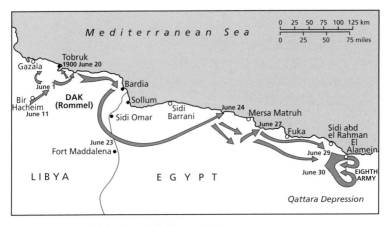

Map 13. From Tobruk to El Alamein, June 1942

Rommel's advance was so rapid that the Luftwaffe was unable to keep up, so he was denied the air support that had been the secret of his earlier successes. The British Desert Air Force was now beginning to inflict severe damage on the Panzer Army, but Rommel pressed on regardless. General Baldassare, an exceptionally courageous and effective commander of the Italian 20 Corps, was killed during clashes with British rearguard forces, along with many of his staff officers.[88] Rommel's reconnaissance units reached Mersa Matruh by the evening of 25 June, whereupon he decided to attack the following day, even before adequate information had been gathered as to the British positions.

On 26 June Cavallero met Rommel near Sidi Barrani and passed on Mussolini's orders for an attack on Egypt.[89] The meeting was ironically known as the 'Meeting of the Field Marshals', because when Hitler promoted Rommel, Mussolini, not to be outdone, elevated both Cavallero and Bastico to the same rank, prompting Ciano to remark that while the first appointment amused people, the second made them indignant. Cavallero said that he had to be promoted because he had found himself 'between Rommel and Kesselring like Christ between the thieves'.[90] Not surprisingly the first operational goal was to capture the area between the Arabian Gulf and the Qattara Depression. True to Italian principles Rommel was then to form a defensive line; his next move would be dependent on the overall situation in the Mediterranean. Rommel refused to be tied down in this manner, and on the following day Cavallero conceded that if the enemy were on the run the advance should continue. Rommel was then to advance to the Suez

Canal from Suez to Port Said, so as to stop the British bringing in reinforcements from the Middle East. Cairo was to be invested, along with
the surrounding airfields. Mussolini was in an ecstatic mood after the
fall of Tobruk, even though he was still indignant that this had been
very much Rommel's show. He was determined that the capture of the
Suez Canal should be a joint Axis affair, issuing orders to this effect on
27 June.[91] Bastico repeated this order, adding that Mussolini insisted
that the Italians should play a prominent role in the capture of the Suez
Canal, and that the Germans should not hog all the glory as they had
done at Tobruk.

    The dictators would have been even more euphoric had they
had a glimpse behind the scenes in London. On 29 June Eden took the
unprecedented step of showing Ivan Maisky, the Soviet ambassador, a
series of classified telegrams from Cairo that painted a grim picture of
the situation. His motives for doing so were to persuade Stalin that a
second front in 1942 was out of the question. Eden told the ambassador
that the most that could be hoped for was a delaying action at Fuka,
and that it might just be possible to hang on at El Alamein. Maisky was
horrified. The 160 generals who were said to be in Cairo could talk of
nothing but evacuation, retreat and abandoning positions. There was
no mention of a counter-offensive. Auchinleck admitted that the British
army were amateurs fighting against a highly professional enemy. This
gave rise to 'anxiety, anger and agitation' in Britain with the widespread
belief that something was seriously wrong with the military machine.
After all, the 8th Army was 'Churchill's darling' which had been built
up over two years, yet had gone down to a humiliating defeat. Maisky,
whose remit was to secure a second front a soon as possible, told
Churchill on 2 July that the best place to defend Egypt was in France,
but the prime minister relapsed into his 1940 mode, talking of fighting
on the Nile, and at Haifa and Beirut. Although this was partly theatrics,
designed to show that a second front in 1942 was impossible, it is clear
that Churchill was far from confident that the El Alamein position could
be held, and this at a time when he desperately needed some success,
however modest, to shore up his political position, which had been
severely weakened, despite his recent rout of his critics in the House of
Commons in a brilliant performance.[92]

    In Cairo Dorman-Smith tried to reassure reporters with talk
of the 'diminishing power of the offensive', the changing fortunes in
the 'pendulum swings' and the 'see-saw' of desert warfare, but this

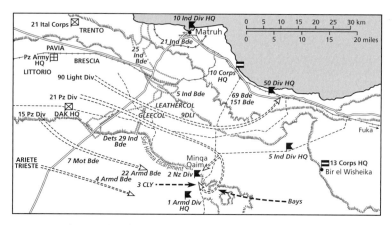

Map 14. The Battle of Mersa Matruh, 26–27 June 1942

did little to disguise the grim truth that the 8th Army had suffered a humiliating defeat which had shown up its tactical ineptitude and operational bankruptcy. There had been a miserable failure to co-ordinate the various arms, reaction to a rapidly changing situation had been alarmingly slow, and there was the catastrophic collapse of morale.[93] Back in Germany it was widely believed that victory in North Africa was imminent. Rommel's splendid victories seemed a guarantee of success.[94] OKW reported on 2 July that 'In Egypt German and Italian divisions, support by several squadrons of dive-bombers, have broken through the El Alamein positions. They are pursuing the defeated British forces, which have retreated to the Nile delta.'[95] On the following day the Axis issued a joint declaration that 'The armed forces of the Axis have entered Egypt... with the aim of driving the English out of Egyptian territory and continuing operations against England so as to free the Near East from English domination.'[96] Rommel knew the extent of 8th Army's losses from the Fellers' decrypts. It was left in disarray, with precious little to halt the Panzer Army's advance. Fellers' reports to Washington were overly pessimistic, but they were enough for Rommel to know that he had to strike now before it was too late.[97] Given the acute logistical difficulties it was a risky but calculated move, not a foolhardy all-or-nothing gamble. At first everything seemed to indicate that he was amply justified, but within a few days Auchinleck was to seize the tactical initiative, forcing Rommel to admit that the chance to seize Egypt by a *coup de main* was 'irrevocably lost'.[98]

Rommel's chief of operations, Mellenthin, later wrote that the attack on Mersa Matruh was made virtually blindfold, and only

succeeded because of the poorly deployed British forces, evidence of
what he called the British 'craving for dispersion'.[99] 10th Corps, made
up of the 10th Indian and 50th Indian Divisions, was placed in front
of the fortress to the north and protected by a dense minefield. 13th
Corps, supported by 2nd New Zealand Division and the British 1st
Armoured Division, both of which had recently arrived from Syria,
was positioned to the south, protected by an impressive minefield. In
between these two positions was a gap of some 15 kilometres that was
lightly mined. The attack began in the afternoon of 26 June. According
to Mellenthin it was quite by chance that it was concentrated on this
weak centre. On the following day 90 Light Africa Division, supported
by 21 Panzer Division, broke through the 10th Indian Division, seized
the coastal road, and thus cut off the fortress from its supply lines. 21
Panzer Division then began to encircle the British to the south. Rommel
fondly imagined that he was facing one armoured division when in fact
it was an entire corps. His 23 Panzer and 600 infantrymen were thus
pitched against 159 tanks, 60 of them Grants. Small wonder then that
21 Panzer was in serious trouble by evening, the situation made worse
when 22nd Armoured Brigade managed to hold up 15 Panzer Division so that they could not lend any support. Rommel was saved from
further embarrassment by 'Strafer' Gott's decision to retire. The New
Zealanders managed to break through 21 Panzer in a night attack. It
was a brutal engagement in which extensive use of bayonets and knives
caused heavy casualties on both sides, and during which a number of
wounded Germans were killed in clear violation of international law.
Rommel's headquarters was surrounded by burning vehicles and submitted to intensive artillery fire, so that he felt it prudent to move to
the south-east out of harm's way.[100] 10th Corps also broke out during the night. German troops, supported by the Bersaglieri from the
Italian 21 Corps, stormed the fortress, taking 6,000 prisoners, along
with a considerable amount of supplies. 21 Panzer Corps chased after
the British forces retiring to Fuka, bagging a further 1,600 prisoners.[101]
Rommel sent the Italian 20 Corps the following message, which was
contemptuous of both his ally and the enemy: 'Hopefully the Corps
will be able to deal with this absolutely pathetic enemy.' Four hours
later the Italians proudly reported that the British were on the run.[102]
Once again Rommel had been extremely lucky. Having won another
brilliant victory, in spite of making a number of serious blunders, he
was confident that he could dislodge the 8th Army from the El Alamein
Line.

Rommel was saved from disaster by Gott's precipitous with-drawal. He had only a handful of Panzer, was virtually without air cover, and was desperately short of supplies. 8th Army had missed yet another chance to destroy the Panzer Army, had abandoned Mersa Matruh, the last fortified port in western Egypt, and further enhanced Rommel's reputation as a soldier of genius. But both sides failed to see that the tide had turned, and that Rommel, by ordering an advance to El Alamein, was heading for disaster. His lines of communication were now stretched beyond the limit, 21 Panzer Division only had enough water for one day, the artillery was desperately short of ammunition, the men were exhausted, having covered 500 kilometres in ten days of heavy fighting. Now, on 1 July, they were ordered to begin their offensive against the British positions in the narrow coastal strip by El Alamein, only 130 kilometres from Alexandria, where the British had decided to make their last-ditch stand. Hitler began to gloat over the prospect of the fall of Alexandria, agreeing with Keitel that this would be a worse blow to the British than the loss of Singapore, and would prompt a revolt against Churchill.[103]

Rommel, insisting that he had 8th Army on the run, argued that he had to deny them the chance of building a new front and of bringing up fresh troops from the Middle East. He told OKW that there were virtually no troops between the Qattara Depression and the Arabian Gulf, so that he would be unlikely to meet with any serious resistance.[104] The German forces were too weak for seriously heavy fighting, but they were still capable of manoeuvre. If he could outflank the 8th Army and attack from the rear, he would force it to flee back to the Suez Canal in disarray.[105] He had seized vast quantities of supplies in Tobruk and Mersa Matruh, and had been assured by the Italians that these two ports were adequate to supply the Panzer Army. This proved to be an illusion. Both were far too small for his needs, and were within the range of British and American aircraft stationed in Egypt. Rommel's strategy was thus risky to the point of foolhardiness, but in his defence he had no real alternative. Comando Supremo's plan for the Panzer Army after taking Tobruk, which called for it to take up defensive positions along the Egyptian border from Sollum to Halfaya and Sidi Omar, and then concentrate on attacking Malta, would have led to disaster. The Panzer Army would have been left immobile, its lines of communication overextended, without air cover, while 8th Army, with its infinitely greater resources, would be left free to build up in preparation for a massive offensive that almost certainly would have destroyed the Axis forces. The outcome of the operation against Malta was highly dubious, the planning in a dreadful muddle.

Rommel, although with no viable alternative to a *va banque* strategy, still held a number of trump cards. He knew that his only hope of defeating a stronger opponent lay in exploiting its weaknesses. The British army was slow, methodical and heterogeneous, whereas the Germans were masters of armoured warfare, tactically adventurous and with a smoothly co-ordinated leadership at the tactical level, for all Rommel's wilfulness and vainglorious derring-do and the confusion higher up the chain of command. Admittedly Rommel made a virtue of necessity, but as he went from success to success his superiors imagined that he could continue to do so, and that they could ignore his persistent requests for more Panzer, men and supplies. Mersa Matruh was the point at which Rommel, OKW and the Comando Supremo failed to realise that the desert war had indeed reached the culminating point, but in the opposite sense to that imagined by Hitler and Mussolini. Rommel had been able to take the town because of Gott's blunders, not as a result of his own sterling military virtues. The Panzer Army had moved so rapidly that it had neglected to do thorough reconnaissance, so that it had no idea of the extent of the El Alamein defences. Rommel saw an 8th Army in disarray, reeling back in confusion, and had no idea that it was ready to meet him, fully aware of his movements and intentions, thanks to the Ultra decrypts. With the support of Hitler, OKW and OKH, Rommel stuck to his principle that the only means of defence was to attack. But at the back of his mind was the regret that he had allowed Freyberg and his New Zealanders, whom he had learned to respect in the course of several fierce engagements, to escape. He wryly noted that he would have been so much happier had they been 'safely tucked away in our prison camps'.[106]

8 ✠ EL ALAMEIN: THE FIRST ROUND

There was nothing at El Alamein but a minuscule railway station with a single track, 3 kilometres from the sea, hundreds from anywhere. The road from Alexandria to Sollum is built along an embankment to the north of the station, beyond which are the salt flats and lagoons that make up the coastal strip. The Qattara Depression to the south, which runs for 300 kilometres, is 134 metres below sea level. With its salt marshes and quicksands it is almost impassable, even for loaded camels. For one hundred of these kilometres the Depression is between 60 and 100 kilometres from the sea, and these narrows form the only route to the Nile Delta. Rommel had no alternative to attacking the British head on. He could not outflank them through the Qattara Depression, nor could he move further south through the waterless sand-dunes. El Alamein may have been, in John Strawson's words, 'the only line in the desert with a top and a bottom', but it was not a continuous line. It consisted of four boxes: a well-fortified position around the station manned by 3rd South African Brigade; another with the 18th Indian Infantry Brigade at Deir el Shein 20 kilometres to the south; a third 12 kilometres further south in the centre for the 6th New Zealand Brigade at Bab el Qattara with a few trenches, but no minefield; and a few scratches in the sand 24 kilometres to the south, on the edge of the Qattara Depression at Nagb Abu Dweis, with the 5th Indian Brigade. Infantry and armour covered the gaps between these boxes. It was a deployment that was excellent in theory, but seriously flawed in practice. It depended on close co-operation between infantry and armour, which was something that the 8th Army was never able to master. The infantry frequently accused the armour of being Cinderellas who left before the ball was over, while the cavalry accused the foot soldiers of failing to clear away Rommel's formidable anti-tank screens.

Equally serious was the fact that Auchinleck was out to defeat Rommel, whereas most of his commanders thought this was an impossible undertaking, owing to intelligence reports that seriously overestimated his strength.

It was a wretched place. With the exception of Alam Halfa, which was 132 metres above sea level, the ridges that were so important for the defence were so low as to be virtually indiscernible. The Miteiriya Ridge was only 31 metres above sea level, that at Ruweisat 66 metres.[1] They were made of limestone so that it was exceedingly difficult to dig in. In addition to the characteristic extremes of blisteringly hot days and freezing nights, over and above the persistent pangs of thirst that made desert warfare so hard to bear, there was the added torture of swarms of persistent flies that came from the Nile delta. Stripped of layers of glamour and myth, El Alamein was one of the most frightful battlefields in the entire war.

Auchinleck had been forced to interrupt the fortification of the El Alamein position when 'Crusader' was launched, and there had been no opportunity to resume serious work. His troops were alarmingly thin on the ground on 1 July. Lieutenant-General Norrie's 30th Corps was responsible for the northern sector, Lieutenant-General Gott's 13th Corps for the south. Two brigades from 1st Armoured Division had to protect the gap between the El Alamein box and the centre, while 7th Motorised Brigade covered the gap to the south of the central box. Assuming that intelligence reports on Rommel's strength were reasonably accurate, Auchinleck could not possibly count on holding the line at El Alamein with his seriously weakened forces and shortage of tanks and artillery. He therefore established Delta Force under Lieutenant-General William G. Holmes to the east as a backstop. Should that fail, Auchinleck planned to fight his way back to the Nile, which *in extremis* would be flooded.

The British position was rendered even more insecure by increasing friction between the partners in the Anglo-Egyptian alliance of 1936. King Farouk was known to be pro-German and the Egyptian government had not declared war on the Axis. The German foreign office announced that it was determined to free Egypt from British tutelage, and on 3 July Mussolini, having consulted Berlin, disingenuously proclaimed that the aim of the Axis was to create an 'Egypt for the Egyptians'.[2] As the Panzer Army advanced across the desert the Germans tried to renew their contact with Farouk, to warn him of British intrigues, and in the hope of luring him either to Rommel's headquarters or to Crete. They made quite sure that the Italians, whose colonial ambitions in Egypt were thinly disguised, were kept in the dark. Farouk thanked the Germans for their support, but decided to remain in Egypt, adding that he would go into hiding when the Germans tipped him off that he was in danger of being abducted by the British.

The Panzer Army reached the area south of Fuka on 28 June. The Afrikakorps headed south-east on the following day, so as to appear to be in a position for an attack on the south end of the El Alamein Line, while the bulk of the Italian 10 Corps, supported by 90 Light Africa Division, advanced along the coastal route. After a fierce engagement with 1st Armoured Division, the Afrikakorps continued its advance during the night of 29/30 June, and in the early morning received orders to attack at 0300hrs on 1 July. The British were to be given the impression that the Afrikakorps intended to attack in the south, but the real intention was to smash through the British positions in the north while it was still dark. At daybreak the Afrikakorps would head south, thus forcing the British to fight on a reverse front.[3]

The Panzer Army's staff was in a confident mood on the eve of the attack. On the evening of 30 June Mellenthin received an encouraging decrypt of a message from the American ambassador to Egypt to the US state department. It read:

> *Fellers considers that within the next few days it will be possible for Rommel to arrive at Cairo and Alexandria unless the British can obtain immediately reinforcements of anti-tank and artillery. Fellers considers that the situation could be redeemed if hundreds of bombers with anti-tank guns were being flown in.*
>
> *In my opinion, I cannot escape the feeling that the scales might be turned even now by some supreme effort.*[4]

This message further convinced Rommel that he had been correct in pressing on into Egypt. He had to strike now before the 8th Army recovered from the shattering blows he had delivered it at Gazala and Mersa Matruh and had time to replenish its armour.

As at Mersa Matruh, Rommel was unaware of the wide gaps between the boxes at El Alamein, so that the *Schwerpunkt* of his attack was unnecessarily heavy. Had his reconnaissance done the job, and

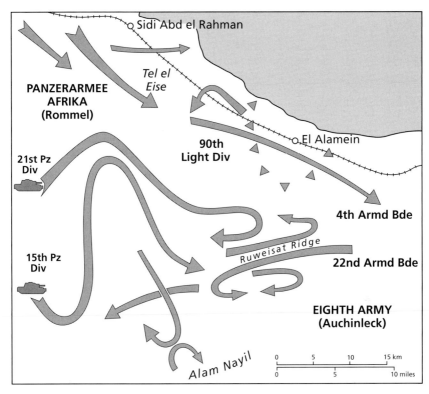

PANZERARMEE AFRIKA (Rommel)

Sidi Abd el Rahman

Tel el Eise

El Alamein

90th Light Div

21st Pz Div

15th Pz Div

Ruweisat Ridge

Alam Nayil

4th Armd Bde

22nd Armd Bde

EIGHTH ARMY (Auchinleck)

| 0 | 5 | 10 | 15 km |
| 0 | | 5 | 10 miles |

Map 15. Auchinleck halts Rommel's advance to the Nile

were the British not in possession of Ultra, Rommel could have encircled the boxes and pulled off yet another brilliant victory in a repeat performance of Mersa Matruh. As it was the Afrikakorps was beset with a host of Clausewitzian 'frictions' that threatened the outcome of the operation. First there was a heavy sandstorm that reduced visibility to a minimum. Combined with a ferocious heatwave this slowed down the northward movement, and seriously affected the troops' morale. 21 Panzer Division was attacked by British forces moving back to El Alamein, but here the sandstorm provided some protection. The descent down the deeply creviced slopes towards the coastal plain proved to be exceptionally difficult, and caused further delays. The Afrikakorps' attack began three hours late.

On 1 July, 90 Light Africa Division to the north attacked on time, but it went straight up against the El Alamein box and were halted by 0730hrs. It then began to work its way round to the south, intent on reaching the coastal road, but it was far too weak to make any

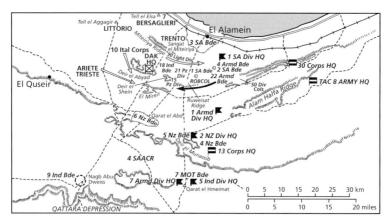

Map 16. The crisis, 1 July 1942

progress, and came under such blistering artillery fire that its advance was halted with some units panicking. Order was soon restored, but the fact that German infantry had cracked for the first time was an ominous sign for the Panzer Army. At the extreme north end 7 Bersaglieri, from the Italian 21 Corps, advanced along the coastal road, cutting off the El Alamein box from the west, but with 90 Light Africa Division pinned to the ground Rommel's attempt to encircle the El Alamein box had failed.

Only fifteen minutes after its assault began, 21 Panzer Division came under heavy attack from the air but the Afrikakorps pressed on against the 18th Indian Brigade in the central box at Deir el Shein, which it reached at 0900hrs. The box fell by the evening and 1,200 prisoners were taken, but the Afrikakorps lost eighteen of its fifty-two Panzers, blunting its fighting edge, and thus compromising the outflanking movement. During the night the Italian 20 Motorised Corps was brought up into the gap between the El Alamein and central boxes. That evening the Panzer Army reported that the 'break in' would become a 'break through' the following day, but there was considerable doubt that this would be possible, and a growing fear that they would become stuck in a battle of attrition that they could not possibly win.[5] The Panzer Army would have been in even worse straits had Auchinleck been able to pull off a flank attack, which never materialised, because signals were unable to contact Gott's headquarters.[6]

Rommel's chief of staff, Colonel Fritz Bayerlein, and his chief of operations, Lieutenant-Colonel Friedrich-Wilhelm Mellenthin, who had replaced the seriously wounded Gause and Westphal, had completely false information about the deployment of the 8th Army at El Alamein, and imagined that the central box was 5 kilometres west of its actual position. Their idea of moving around the El Alamein box and attacking from the rear, as they had done so successfully at Mersa Matruh, did not take account of three South African brigades positioned to the south and south-east. The Afrikakorps' move south to the central box began too soon, so it hit the box head on. Most serious of all, British Sigint was so effective that the Panzer Army was unable either to surprise or to deceive. Coupled with overwhelming airpower, Auchinleck was thus able to anticipate Rommel's every move.[7] That evening the Panzer Army reported to OKH that 8th Army's resistance was extremely strong.[8] The inexperienced 18th Indian Brigade, although left virtually without support, stuck in the Deir el Shein box and burdened with a highly dubious tactical doctrine, had fought doggedly. By blunting the Afrikakorps' ferocious attack, thus denying Rommel another Gazala or Mersa Matruh, the Indian Brigade had saved the day.

On 2 July Rommel did what he could to sort out the mess. It was now clearly out of the question for the Afrikakorps to press on in a southerly and south-easterly direction, but he was still determined to attack the El Alamein box from the rear. To this end he ordered the Afrikakorps to advance eastwards for about 7 kilometres and then turn north and head for the coast. The El Alamein box would come under attack by an advance on both sides of the road and railway. The Italian 20 Corps was left to guard the southern flank.

This new phase began at 1500hrs and immediately ran up against stiff opposition. By 1630hrs it was clear that 1st Armoured Division was intent on encircling 15 Panzer Division from the south. The Ariete was therefore ordered forward to protect the division's southern flank. Meanwhile, 21 Armoured Division was stuck, its supplies running desperately short, virtually without air support, continually pounded from the air and running up against a determined defence. By evening it had only managed to move forward about 4 kilometres. To the north 90 Light Africa Division made no progress against murderous artillery and machinegun fire. Auchinleck no longer relied on static infantry boxes and was beginning to inject some movement into his defence by using mobile brigade groups, a change in tactics for which Rommel was generous in his praise. He had also managed to establish

centralised control and direction of 8th Army's artillery, prompting
him to make a modest and amply understated claim to Brooke that 'the
boche does not like our shell fire at all'.[9]

The Afrikakorps continued its advance on 3 July, but the troops
were exhausted, the leadership increasingly doubtful of success. Rommel threw the Afrikakorps, 90 Light Africa Division and the Littorio
against the El Alamein box, in spite of the New Zealanders' shattering
attack on the Ariete. At 0500hrs the Ariete Armoured Division, the
elite Italian unit, had been attacked by the 2nd New Zealand Division
from the central box and by armour positioned to the rear. The Ariete's
artillery had been left to tag behind the armour, which had moved ahead
on 21 Panzer Division's flank. The Kiwis were quick to exploit this situation: the Italians were overrun, panicked and fled north, leaving behind
the bulk of their artillery. A breakthrough having proved impossible,
Rommel ordered the Panzer to dig in. Only twenty-six Panzer were
operational, ammunition was running short and they had virtually no
air cover. Rommel bitterly complained in his order of the day that
'The battle worthiness of the Italian troops is so insignificant that on
3 July 360 men from the Ariete Division surrendered to a small number
of tanks, without offering the slightest resistance.'[10] The Afrikakorps'
southern flank was now left unprotected, forcing 15 Panzer Division to
go on the defensive. At 2256hrs the Panzer Army ordered a halt. This
was the turning point in the battle. Auchinleck exploited the advantage
of his short lines of supply, while the DAF strafed Rommel's overextended and highly vulnerable communications. There was now no hope
for a breakthrough, and the campaign in North Africa had reached a
defining moment. Rommel was forced to take up a defensive position,
something that he had fought against ever since he arrived in North
Africa, and it remained to be seen whether he would be able to get back
on the move within the next few weeks.[11] He had now been stopped
and dragged into a battle of attrition, which he was bound to lose.
The British had been given a day to reorganise, and draw up armour
along the Ruweisat Ridge. The overwhelming strength of the Desert
Air Force made any further advance virtually impossible. That night
Rommel signalled to Kesselring that he had been forced to suspend his
attack 'for the time being'. News that the Royal Navy had abandoned
Alexandria, and that leaders of the Egyptian nationalist movement had
arrived by air to consult Rommel, did nothing to relieve the gloom at
Panzer Group Africa's headquarters.[12]

Auchinleck realised that he had to seize the chance to attack. Rommel was in a desperate situation. The Afrikakorps only had thirty-six Panzer in running order, the men were exhausted, and ammunition was perilously low: 15 Panzer Division's fifteen Panzer had only two rounds per gun with which to counter a hundred tanks in 1st Armoured Division, supported by the fresh 24th Australian Brigade, on the Ruweisat Ridge. But 8th Army's corps commanders failed to react, apart from some uncoordinated skirmishing by punch-drunk units. Perhaps this was the point at which the Auk should have taken over personal command, for the preconditions were there for a dynamic leader to achieve a major victory, but 8th Army had also fought itself virtually to a standstill and desperately needed time to recover. Auchinleck was still unable to concentrate entirely on the Western Desert, because he also had to keep a close eye on the volatile situation in Persia and Iraq.

In the next phase of the First Battle of El Alamein, 90 Light Africa Division, along with the Italian 20 Motorised Corps, were moved south so as to form a defensive line extending to the Qattara Depression. Italian infantry from 10 and 21 Corps were brought up from the border to relieve the utterly exhausted Afrikakorps around El Alamein, so that it could be refreshed and replenished ready for a fresh large-scale offensive. Thanks to Sigint, 8th Army was fully aware of Rommel's intentions and ordered the armoured brigades to attack, but their efforts lacked any serious punch.[13] They ran up against the Panzer Army's formidable anti-tank cover with its deadly 88s, whereupon 8th Army made piecemeal attacks, most of which were beaten off without too much difficulty. By 9 July the Panzer Army Africa had established a continuous defensive line down to the Qattara Depression, but 21 Panzer Division was left somewhat vulnerable in a salient in the centre, where it was threatened by the 2nd New Zealand Division. Rommel was determined to rectify this situation. A reconnaissance group reported that a strongpoint at Qaret al Abd had been abandoned. This proved to be not quite accurate, but 21 Panzer Division had little difficulty in seizing the concrete bunkers and adjacent airfield, so that the front was now straightened. Panzer Group's headquarters' staff were somewhat perplexed as to why Auchinleck should have given up such a well-fortified position.[14]

Rommel, mistakenly assuming that 8th Army was withdrawing, ordered his southern flank to attack in the early hours of 10 July.

Initially excellent progress was made, but at 0600hrs that day 8th Army mounted a massive counterattack to the north.[15] The 9th Australian Division, which had replaced the South Africans in the El Alamein box on 3 July, supported by 1st Armoured Brigade, broke through the Italian Sabratha Infantry Division, positioned along the railway to the west of El Alamein, after an intense barrage lasting one hour. The inexperienced and undermanned Italians, having lost all their artillery, fell apart and fled in panic. There were an increasing number of reports of Italian soldiers fleeing the field of battle without fighting. Italian courts martial were ordered to take action and not to fear ordering the death penalty.[16] Most of those fleeing were taken prisoner at Tel el Aisa, along with Captain Alfred Seebohm's 621 Radio Intelligence Company (NFA) which was the ears of the Panzer Army. This was a serious loss that was never made good. They were in constant movement up at the front, listening in to British radio messages and relaying information immediately back to Rommel's headquarters.[17] Seebohm was seriously wounded, having attempted to defend his post with a machinegun, and he died a few days later in a British dressing station. The survivors of NFA 621 were interrogated before being sent to a POW camp in the Canal Zone. This was a tremendous coup for British intelligence, but it came as a nasty shock to discover the extent to which Rommel's staff knew of 8th Army's intentions, as well as the appallingly sloppy wireless discipline that had enabled Seebohm's men to learn so much. Coupled with the stopping of the Bonner Fellers source on 29 June, the loss of NFA 621 on 10 July meant that Rommel lost his most important intelligence assets and with them much of his exceptional tactical ability.

The situation was temporarily saved when 382 Infantry Regiment, supported by machinegun and anti-aircraft units from Rommel's staff contingent, was brought up along the coastal road and halted the Australians' advance. 15 Panzer Division launched a flank attack on the Australians, but facing massive artillery fire from El Alamein, made only modest progress at considerable cost.[18] The attack started again on the following day, this time to the south of the railway. Two defensive positions of the Bersaglieri, which had held their ground the previous day, were overrun, and one battalion of the Trieste Division was destroyed. Other units from the Italian 21 Corps dropped their weapons and fled.[19] The Panzer Army had to bring in virtually its entire artillery to help plug the gap, and Rommel was obliged to halt the offensive in the south so that Panzer divisions could go over to the counterattack. The southern sector was now placed under the command of the Afrikakorps, so Rommel could concentrate entirely on the precarious situation to the north, where the British had succeeded in greatly extending their bridgehead. The British advance was finally halted, and the Panzer Army prepared to counterattack.

Supported by massed artillery and the Luftwaffe, 21 Panzer Division attacked from the south at midday on 13 July, intent on breaking through to the coastal road. Although the Stukas had softened the defences, the infantry failed to exploit this situation, and the Panzer once again got stuck under a massive artillery barrage. The South Africans had been alerted by information gleaned from Ultra and were ready and waiting for the Germans.[20] The attack had to be called off at 2100hrs. The bulk of 21 Panzer Division was withdrawn during the night. The division tried again later the following day, this time against the salient that had been made as the Australians advanced, but they got nowhere, and the Panzer Army came to the sorry conclusion that it would perforce have to go on the defensive again until it was brought up to strength. The attempt was nevertheless repeated at 1830hrs on 14 July, but once again co-ordination between the infantry and the Panzer was bungled, so that the attack soon ground to a halt.

The Afrikakorps was now in an awkward position, strung out along the front with 21 Panzer Division in the north, 15 Panzer Division in the centre and 90 Light Africa Division to the south. There was a particularly weak spot in the centre where the Italian 10 Corps, consisting of the Pavia and Brescia Divisions, was positioned. It was here that Auchinleck decided to attack at 0430hrs on 15 July with 5 Indian and 2 New Zealand Divisions, supported by 1st Armoured Division, in Operation 'Bacon'. The offensive was an initial success. By nightfall 8th Army had broken through the Brescia Division and was attacking the Pavia Division to the north from the rear, but the Afrikakorps was soon on the move with 15 Panzer Division, supported by 3 and 33 Reconnaissance Units, mounting a daring counterattack that destroyed 4th New Zealand Brigade, the worst defeat suffered by the New Zealanders in the entire North African campaign.[21] 21 Panzer Division hurried down from the north to the critical point where the British had broken through the Brescia Division. But this was all too late to save the situation. Several units surrendered without a fight. Both the Brescia and the Pavia Divisions were destroyed, with most of the survivors taken prisoner, while 8th Army kept up the pressure with a series of well-timed blows.[22] Auchinleck had shown his tactical mastery, but his troops were proving not quite up to the job. The New Zealand infantry brigades had been left without their supporting arms on the rocky terrain of Ruweisat Ridge, where it was impossible to dig in, and they had failed to destroy isolated pockets of Axis troops, who made access to their positions exceedingly hazardous. They were left without any support when the Panzer attacked from all sides. Those who were unable to fight their way out were left with no alternative but to surrender. 'Bacon' showed up the limitations of intelligence gathered from Ultra. The ever-shifting intelligence picture on which Dorman-Smith depended was an inadequate basis for deliberate planning, and had led to 'Bacon' being cancelled on three occasions.[23] Combined with 8th Army's ineffective command structure and inability to share information at army, corps and divisional levels, it was a recipe for failure.

The Afrikakorps managed to plug the hole left by the destruction of the Brescia and Pavia Divisions, but a counterattack on 16 July made painfully slow progress, 8th Army's 'Y' having intercepted the German orders, and had to be called off during the afternoon.[24] The next day units from 9th Australian Division with tank support moved 6 kilometres down the north–south Qattara Road, broke through the Trieste Division and seized a stronghold manned by the Bersaglieri. Units from 90 Light Africa Division were able to halt the Australian advance and push them back, taking 500 Australians prisoner; but the Trieste had lost an entire battalion, the Trento Division a considerable amount of artillery. A somewhat feeble attack against the Afrikakorps in the centre resulted in the destruction of twenty-five British tanks. 21 Panzer Division managed to plug the gap, seizing the high ground at Points 23 and 25, and defences were improved during the night, but the Panzer Army Africa was now in serious trouble, saved only by 8th Army's dissipation of effort in a series of piecemeal attacks.[25] The British had greatly improved their defensive skills, but still had to master the offensive. The Panzer Army reacted quickly to each attack, so that hard-won gains were quickly lost; but the Italians were falling apart, leaving the exhausted Germans to do most of the fighting. German units had to be interposed with the Italian divisions as 'corset stays' to hold them together. Kesselring and Cavallero, who came up to the front on 17 July, were told by Rommel that the Axis forces would not be able to hang on, unless something drastic was done to rectify the supply situation. The Italians had lost four divisions, so not only were further offensive operations out of the question, but were the British to achieve a breakthrough, the entire Alamein position was in danger of collapsing.[26] But 8th Army was running out of steam and was unable to press home the advantage, resulting in a lull in the fighting from 18 to 21 July.

Bastico took exception to Rommel's constant complaints about the performance of the Italian troops in his messages to OKH. He pointed out that the men were utterly exhausted because of his insistence on constantly attacking. They needed a rest, and their units needed to be brought up to strength. He produced a message from Mussolini to back this up. It called for a pause for the Panzer Army to be refreshed and strengthened in preparation for further operations.[27] Rommel complained bitterly that the Italian units were falling apart, often giving up without offering any resistance. He was particularly incensed by their inability to stand up to bayonet charges, which he considered to be the least threatening form of infantry attack. The British were quick to recognise this weakness and concentrated their attacks on the Italians. Rommel told Neurath that he could not understand why the Italians were giving in 'shortly before the final victory'. Neurath suggested this was because of 'general exhaustion', an inferiority complex with regard to the German troops, and a fear that the Germans would grab all the booty in Egypt. He added that British propaganda played very skilfully on this last theme, thereby suggesting to Rommel that he should reconsider his attitude towards establishing a joint commission to deal with Egyptian property. Rommel did not take the hint.[28]

Auchinleck, realising that Rommel's forces were at the end of their tether, decided that the time had come to finish them off. He planned to begin with the Afrikakorps, before dealing with the Italians. The task was allotted to Lieutenant-General Gott's 13th Corps, the attack to begin on 21 July. The plan, somewhat optimistically code-named 'Splendour', called for 2nd New Zealand Division to force its way through the narrow space between the hillocks of Deir el Abyad and Deir el Shein and then proceed westwards. 5th Indian Division was to cross the Ruweisat Ridge, which ran from east to west, roughly in the centre between the Qattara Depression and the sea, and take Point 63 to the south. 1st Armoured Division, under the deputy command of Major-General Alec Gatehouse, a hard-nosed tank man and outstanding expert in armoured warfare, was to support the New Zealanders' left flank. Meanwhile 8th Army kept up the pressure with a series of limited attacks that, although they were warded off, caused the Panzer Army's supplies and ammunition to run short, the supply ships *Brook* and *Storia* having been sunk, and oil tanks at Tobruk having been destroyed in a bombing raid.[29]

The attack did not go as expected. Poorly trained troops found themselves facing rugged German units. The Indians managed to take Point 63 by 1900hrs, but were soon driven back. The New Zealanders made good progress, with the Afrikakorps unable to make an adequate response, because its communications had broken down as a result of the RAF's continuous bombing raids. Lieutenant-General Walther Nehring, commanding the Afrikakorps, felt it prudent to cancel a night-time counterattack on the New Zealanders and wait until daybreak for a clearer picture. At 0415 hrs on 22 July, 21 Panzer began to move south, while 15 Panzer with infantry support moved north-east, so that the New Zealanders were under attack on both flanks.

Afrikakorps' counterattack was brilliantly executed. The New Zealanders were trapped, with 6th New Zealand Brigade crushed by 21 Panzer for a loss of nearly 700 men. By 0700hrs, 15 Panzer reported that they were back in their original positions, but the New Zealanders had plenty of fight left in them. Supported by 23rd Armoured Brigade, they pushed westwards to the south of the Ruweisat Ridge, reaching the Qattara Road, the Italians at Point 63 having surrendered. 23rd Armoured Brigade charged 5 Panzer Regiment in what has been described as 'a real Balaclava', meeting with ferocious anti-tank fire, followed by a courageous counterattack, which forced them to retreat, having lost 203 men and 40 of their 100 tanks. Of the remainder, 47 limped back, having been badly damaged.[30] They were thrown in against the 88s without infantry support and with no high explosive shells for their pathetic two-pounders. One officer said that it came as a very rude awakening when they discovered on 22 July that the Germans had a gun capable of piercing the lumbering Valentine's heavy armour.[31] Their unfortunate commander, Brigadier Lawrence Misa, was relieved of his command and ignominiously posted to the rear, even though he had bravely carried out his orders, which called for obsolete infantry tanks to perform in a cruiser role. The Afrikakorps destroyed 118 tanks that day, with a further 28 tanks wiped out in the northern sector; 1,400 prisoners were taken.[32] The massacre did nothing to tarnish the reputation of the corps commander, 'Strafer' Gott, who was clearly exhausted and out of his depth. Nor did it rebound on Churchill, whose impatience and ignorance of the exigencies of modern mechanised warfare was mainly responsible for this disaster. 'Bacon' and 'Splendour' were rushed jobs, in which sketchy tactics, hasty planning and a vague command structure were a certain recipe for failure.

The 8th Army failed, both at 'First Ruweisat' on 14/15 July and 'Second Ruweisat' on 21/22 July, to break through to Deir el Shein, destroy the Italian 10 Corps and unhinge the entire enemy front.[33] In spite of overwhelming airpower and artillery, superb Sigint, and courageous troops they still suffered heavy losses. 13th Corps lost two experienced infantry brigades: 6th New Zealanders and 161st Indian. 23rd Armoured Brigade was made up of green Liverpudlians, who had only just arrived from England, having been two months at sea. They had had two years of intensive training, but were totally inexperienced in desert warfare. No match for the veterans in 21 Panzer, they lost two-thirds of their men and equipment within a matter of minutes. As one captured British officer remarked to his German interrogators: 'Two years of training, a sea journey half-way around the world – and in just half an hour it's all over for us!'[34] 23rd Armoured Brigade had failed to co-ordinate with the infantry, turned up at the wrong places at the wrong time, refused to fight at night, drove at 10mph straight through a minefield with open flanks, then turned tail leaving the infantry in the lurch once the German 88s began to pick them off. Günther Halm, a shy and retiring nineteen-year old, in civilian life a mechanic, laid the sights of an 88, positioned in a wadi near the Ruweisat Ridge. Although badly wounded he stayed at his post, knocking out eight British tanks. For this he was awarded the Knight's Cross and became a national hero. He was soon given a commission, and ended the war as a prisoner in the United States.[35]

Panzer Army Africa had also suffered heavy losses, ones that they could ill afford, given the relative strength of the two armies. Even more serious was the embarrassing fact that it was not only the Italians who were beginning to crack. Two understrength battalions of 104 Infantry Regiment had fallen apart on Point 63 on 22 July, while a company of 155 Infantry Regiment on Point 21 was quickly overrun by the Australians. 23rd Armoured Brigade's attack was badly bungled, but it nearly succeeded in overrunning the Afrikakorps' battle headquarters, and had caused an initial panic among troops that stood in its wake. Rommel had interspersed German units among the Italians as 'corset stays', but some of them where beginning to lose their rigidity. On the other hand, the recent fighting had shown the Afrikakorps' superiority in the art of armoured warfare. Although the Qattara Depression made it impossible for the 8th Army to deliver a left hook, the line was very thinly held. An effective mobile defence to the rear was only possible when 164 Division, which OKW had promised to send from Crete, finally arrived. The Germans now had only 30 per cent of their manpower, 15 per cent of their Panzer, 70 per cent of their artillery, 40 per cent of their anti-tank guns and 50 per cent of the heavy anti-aircraft guns. The Italians had 30 per cent of their full complement of men, 15 per cent of their tanks, 25 per cent of their artillery, 30 per cent of their anti-tank guns and 20 per cent of their heavy anti-aircraft guns. The Panzer Army's staff estimated that the 8th Army was not in a position to launch a major offensive until it had brought up its reserves, but it was likely to keep hammering away at the Italians. The plan was to go on the defensive for the next four weeks to allow time to bring in men and matériel in preparation for a fresh offensive.[36]

Rommel was by now beginning to show signs of strain and was unaccustomedly plunged into fits of foreboding. The British were persistently making deep penetrations into his pitifully thin front. Losses were unacceptably high. A breakthrough might well force the Panzer Army Africa to capitulate. If there was a possibility of a breakthrough, then there was no alternative to making a fighting withdrawal. In a reversal of their usual roles, Bastico insisted that the situation was 'strained', but not critical. He was now convinced that the Panzer Army could push the British back. Comando Supremo was more cautious. With fresh Italian troops moving up from Tobruk and Mersa Matruh and with the air force still largely intact, they ordered a defence along the existing line.[37]

Auchinleck, prodded persistently by Churchill, was determined to make one final attempt to break through, but he faced fierce opposition from two of his senior commanders: the Australian Morshead and the New Zealander Freyberg, both of whom had fought with distinction at Gallipoli. They felt they had been let down by the miserable performance of the armour. Morshead warned Auchinleck that if the latter insisted on yet another attack he would have to consult his government. After an angry altercation, the Auk agreed that a British brigade from 50th Division, which had recently been brought up to the front, would tackle the most dangerous phase of the attack. Auchinleck was full of praise for the Australians and assured Morshead that he appreciated the difficult situation in which he had been placed. Morshead grudgingly consented to co-operate.[38]

The renewed attack, Operation 'Manhood', was somewhat more carefully planned than Auchinleck's two previous attempts, but given the chronic shortage of resources was seriously flawed. It was launched in the northern sector on the moonlit night of 26/27 July. After a preliminary artillery barrage a powerful force of infantry and armour, made up of units from the British 50th Division and the Australian 9th Division, supported by tanks from 1st Armoured Division, went into action. Some initial successes were scored during the night, but the Panzer Army reacted quickly, sending in reserves, plugging the gaps and launching a powerful counterattack the next morning, inflicting severe casualties. Brigadier Fisher, commanding 1st Armoured Division while Lumsden was recovering from his wounds, made the all-too-frequent mistake of sending his infantry through the gaps in the minefields without support from his armour, leaving them unable to defend themselves against an attack by a battle group from the Afrikakorps, supported by 200 Infantry Regiment.[39] Thirty-two British tanks were destroyed and a thousand prisoners taken, while the Germans and Italians each lost the equivalent of two companies of infantry. To the south a raid was mounted from the Qattara Depression on the German airfield at Casaba West, during which a number of aircraft were destroyed. The raiders were driven back by a reconnaissance unit that hurried in from Mersa Matruh.[40] Once again the 8th Army had failed to co-ordinate its efforts, the armour was poorly deployed, and effort was dissipated in piecemeal attacks that left the Panzer Army with an excellent opportunity to counterattack. The Panzer Army had shown that it was every bit as skilled in defence as it was in the offensive. Whenever the 8th Army managed to penetrate its 'Devil's Gardens' it was subjected to blistering fire from flanking infantry and artillery. The British were trained to operate in small independent units in the open desert; now they had to fight together closely in operations reminiscent of the 'bite and hold' tactics of the western front in 1918, which Ramsden described as the 'tight battle' as opposed to Wavell's notion of the 'loose battle'.[41] At least they were remarkably quick in learning from their mistakes, soon making the necessary adjustments that made the El Alamein victory possible. The Panzer Army proudly reported to OKW that between 26 May and 25 July it had destroyed or captured 2,514 armoured vehicles.[42] The

Panzer Group had failed to reach the Nile, but had won important defensive victories on 15, 22 and 27 July and the balance of losses was in its favour. From 26 May to 30 July the Panzer Group had taken 60,000 prisoners and destroyed 2,000 tanks and armoured cars; 2,300 Germans had been killed, 7,500 wounded and 2,700 taken prisoner, leaving only 34,000. The Italians had lost 1,000 dead, 10,000 wounded and 5,000 taken prisoner. This left both sides exhausted, so there was a further lull in the fighting until reinforcements were brought up to the front. Bayerlein was later to confess that, had Auchinleck been able to keep up the pressure after 26 July, the Panzer Army would have been defeated. But 8th Army still had to learn from Rommel that infantry unsupported by artillery and armour were nothing but tank-fodder, and that throwing armour against well-placed anti-tank guns was to invite a replay of Balaclava. Auchinleck was not granted enough time to perfect his style of command, and Montgomery had the advantage of inheriting an army whose fighting spirit had not been broken, in spite of taking a severe battering, the latter due in large part to poor training and uninspiring leadership.

Churchill fumed at what he considered to be Auchinleck's 'inexcusable inertia', but Rommel saw things in a truer light. He wrote: 'Although the British losses in the Alamein fighting were higher than ours, the price to Auchinleck was not excessive, for the one thing that mattered to him was to halt our advance, and that, unfortunately, he has done.' Rommel's chief of staff, Bayerlein, was even more generous, describing Auchinleck's achievement as 'marvellous' and confessing that the Afrikakorps knew full well that they had suffered a serious setback.[43]

Rommel, who all too often blamed the Italians for any setback, paid generous tribute to their fighting spirit during the First Battle of El Alamein. The Italian soldier

> *was willing, unselfish and a good comrade, and, considering the conditions under which he served, had always given far better than the average. There is no doubt that the achievement of every Italian unit, especially in the motorised forces, far surpassed anything that the Italian Army had done for a hundred years. Many Italian generals and officers won our admiration both as men and soldiers.*[44]

In his view, the shortcomings of the Italian army were due to an incompetent high command, poor equipment, inadequate training and an excessive differentiation between officers and men. While the men had to make do with wholly inadequate rations, the officers tucked into several courses of fine fare. Rommel was thus gradually changing his opinion of his allies. In the past he had been overly critical of them, using them as convenient scapegoats for his own mistakes. By now he had learnt to appreciate the enormous difficulties under which they were fighting, and was ready to give credit where credit was due. His principal complaint now was that the Italians were hogging the supplies. Although there were about two Germans for every one Italian, 82,000 to 42,000 in the month of August, the German element in the Panzer Army received only 8,200 tons of supplies, whereas the Italians obtained 25,700 tons. The Luftwaffe was allotted 8,500 tons.[45] Rommel attributed much of the blame to Rintelen, whom he considered to be too much of a diplomat to address the problem with due force, and who lacked sufficient rank to throw his weight about. Hitler was of much the same opinion, and regarded Rintelen as utterly spineless in his refusal to stand up to the Italians.[46]

Mussolini had arrived in Libya on 29 June with a vast entourage of Fascist functionaries and journalists, in preparation for his triumphal entry into Cairo. The visit did not begin well. His plane crashed on landing, killing his barber and his cook. A magnificent white charger was shipped by air for the Duce to ride in triumph through the streets of Cairo.[47] He suggested to Hitler that Rommel should be made commander-in-chief in Egypt under an Italian political adviser, to be known as the 'Delegato Politico'.[48] Serafino Mazzolini, the former Italian ambassador in Egypt, was given the position and ordered to act in close co-operation with Rommel. On 3 July Mazzolini flew to North Africa in anticipation of his new role.[49] Back in Rome Ciano's chef de cabinet, Marquis Blasco Lanza D'Aieta, told Mackensen that the appointment of Rommel as commander-in-chief of the occupation forces in Egypt was extremely unpopular in Italy. Off the record he felt that the designation 'Political Delegate' was unfortunately reminiscent of 'High Commissioner', and had distinct colonialist overtones. He felt that the appointment of an ambassador would have been more appropriate, with the Germans sending an envoy, thus recognising Italy's primacy.[50] Hitler, who was in basic agreement that Egypt should be within the Italian sphere of influence, rejected the idea that the foreign office should send a resident to Egypt. This would be insulting to Rommel, who should act as a generalissimo, and it might tempt the Italians to send a diplomatic representative to the Caucasus. Ribbentrop finally decided that Neurath should act as a liaison officer to the Delegato Politico, as well as being the foreign office's delegate to Rommel, in his capacity as commander-in-chief of the occupation forces in Egypt.[51] But the seeds of acrimony had been sown. The Italians had already set up the Cassa Mediterranea di Credito par' l'Egitto to deal with military expenditure in occupied Egypt, and the Germans had reluctantly agreed, with Rommel objecting strongly to Rome having any say in Egypt's finances. He refused to be restricted in what he could grab from the land, as he was in Libya under the terms of an Italo-German agreement.[52] Whereas Hitler felt that the Germans should help themselves to war loot, Mussolini was anxious not to alienate the Arab world by allowing the soldiery to plunder as they saw fit. He wanted to inherit a prosperous colony, not a land stripped bare. Hitler had issued instructions to the foreign office that King Farouk should be offered full protection, but this was to be kept secret from the Italians, as were contacts between the Germans and Egyptian officers such as Gamal Abdel Nasser, a devout student of the Protocols of the Elders of Zion, and Anwar el-Sadat, an active supporter of the Axis cause, both of whom were later to become president of Egypt. After weeks of bickering the Marquis d'Ajeta told his friend Otto von Bismarck that Germany's recognition of Italian primacy in Egypt was little more than an empty phrase.[53] In the course of further arguments and the issuing of a number of vacuous statements, the Germans avoided any commitments or obligations towards Egypt, and clearly intended to act in the same brutal manner as they had done in all those countries that had the misfortune to come under their heel.[54]

The Italians soon began to have misgivings about the Cassa Mediterranea, whose coupons were based on economic principles worthy of the Emperor Seth's Azania in Evelyn Waugh's *Black Mischief*. The coupons were to be issued based on an exchange rate of one Egyptian pound equalling 72 lire and 9.50 Reich marks. As the Italian minister for foreign trade, Riccardi, pointed out to Ambassador Mackensen, since this took no account of the large number of pounds sterling circulating in Egypt, it would result in yet another instance of Germany exporting its domestic inflation to an occupied country. If the coupons were used indiscriminately the Egyptian economy would soon be ruined, leaving the Italians with another Greece on their hands.[55] Such misgivings were somewhat late in the day, because Bastico had already issued coupons for use by the Italian troops in Egypt.[56]

The Italians made repeated efforts to persuade the Germans to agree to a joint commission for Egypt, but to no avail. Rintelen summed up the German attitude in the following message to Clodius at the German embassy: 'With respect to Italian wishes regarding finance and the settlement of other economic issues in Egypt, the Reich Minister of Foreign Affairs asks you to continue treating the suggestion of an Italo-German organisation in such a manner that there be no question of such a body.'[57]

Hitler announced to his entourage that he had no interest whatsoever in the 'Egyptian Sphinx' and that the country should be left to the Italians. He was also opposed to appointing a political representative, insisting that this would lead to a dual government. A military representative would be sufficient to safeguard German interests.[58] But the Germans had not the slightest intention of allowing themselves to be told by their allies what to do in Egypt. After all, had they not done most of the fighting? Were they not entitled to the pick of the prizes? Hitler announced that 'the booty should go to those who take it' and the foreign office was in full agreement.[59] The Italians were understandably suspicious of the Germans, and therefore suggested a joint commission to discuss the future of Egypt. Hitler, who felt that Rommel as a general crowned with 'immortal fame' should help himself to whatever he needed, was adamantly opposed to the idea of such a commission.[60] As so often when faced with uncomfortable decisions, Hitler ordered that the entire matter should be treated in a 'dilatory' fashion, so that the foreign office was continually bombarded with urgent requests from the Italians to settle the issue. They only stopped when their dreams of conquest were shattered at El Alamein.[61]

Hitler's trump card in his negotiations with Mussolini was Rommel, of whom he spoke as 'wrapped in immortal fame and . . . already widely seen as one of the foremost figures in the history of warfare'. He was amazed that Churchill had made frequent references to Rommel's genius as a military leader in a recent speech in the House of Commons. He argued that enhancing the reputation of a commander in this manner was worth several divisions, and could only attribute this to Churchill's stubborn refusal to admit that the British had been whipped by Italian soldiers.

It seemed that it would not be long before Crüwell's prophecy that Rommel would soon be installed in Shepheard's Hotel was realised. John W. Eppler, the German agent in Cairo, sent lurid and exaggerated reports of fear and trembling among the British community in Egypt during 'The Flap'. Wives and children were being evacuated. Jews were fleeing and smuggling gold out of the country. Taxi drivers murmured: 'Today I drive you to Groppi's, tomorrow you drive me!' The British embassy had begun to burn its files on what was instantly called 'Ash Wednesday'. Preparations were being made to blow up the Aswan Dam.[62] Plans were drawn up to withdraw to Palestine and beyond, leaving the Jews to the mercy of the SS murder squad that was waiting in the wings. Demolition teams were assembled to destroy the oil fields of Saudi Arabia.[63] Egyptian troops were confined to barracks, and it was rumoured that King Farouk and the Egyptian government had been ordered to leave the country, but the king announced that at this critical moment his place was with his people, who eagerly awaited the arrival of the Axis troops.[64] Hitler had announced that Farouk should be encouraged to flee, so as to be able to conduct a campaign against the British from a safe place. The Axis would reinstate him on his throne after the defeat of the 8th Army. Hitler expressed his admiration for Farouk on the somewhat strange grounds that he had married the most beautiful woman in the country, which he took as evidence of his sound judgement.[65] The Security Service (SD) chief, Walter Schellenberg, wrote of 'an atmosphere of complete helplessness and the blackest pessimism' among the Allies in Egypt. An informant reported that 95 per cent of Egyptians were pro-Axis and anti-British. All the Jews had left Alexandria, along with the rich Greeks. The Gaullists were fleeing, Baron de Vaux hiding in the lavatory of the train to Kantara. Salvator Cicurel, owner of the famous Cairene department store Les Grands Magasins Cicurel and leader of the Sephardic community, was reported to have paid £25,000 for a flight to Cape Town. Neurath ordered a number of books so as to study Islam and the Near East in preparation for the tasks ahead.

In the Soviet Union the German offensive at Voronezh had begun in late June, with troops advancing towards Stalingrad and the Caucasus. On 9 July Ribbentrop told the Japanese ambassador Oshima that if the Wehrmacht managed to push south from the Caucasus, while Rommel attacked Egypt from the other side, the war would be won. 'In any case, during the last four weeks we have come much closer to achieving this goal than the German leadership, even at its most optimistic, had ever imagined.'[66] Ribbentrop's optimism matched the gloom among the chiefs of staff in London, who entertained the possibility of losing the oil reserves at Mosul and Kirkuk and being forced to fight a two-front war in the Middle East. The crushing victory of the Wehrmacht over the Red Army at Kharkov in the spring did not inspire confidence that the Russians would be able to halt the German advance. If they failed to do so, Auchinleck had precious few troops to defend his northern front. Small wonder then that he spent much of the time anxiously looking over his shoulder.[67]

Himmler was much smitten by Arab anti-Semitism and anti-imperialism, while the Mufti of Jerusalem, Haj Amin Muhammad el-Husseini, warmly appreciated the Reichsführer's robust efforts to deal with the Jewish question. As el-Husseini had said to SS-Brigadeführer Erwin Ettel, the former German ambassador in Teheran, who after his expulsion from Iran became the foreign office's expert on the Middle East: 'Germany is the only country in the world that does not simply concentrate on fighting the Jews at home, but has proclaimed an uncompromising struggle against world Jewry. All Arabs feel themselves to be at one with Germany's struggle against world Jewry.' On Himmler's forty-third birthday in 1943 the Mufti presented him with a handsome gift with the following inscription: 'May we work even closer together in the coming year, and may we come closer to our common goal.' Himmler in reply spoke in the name of 'our comradeship and our common struggle'.[68] He promised the Mufti that once the war was over he would send experts from Eichmann's department to help with 'practical matters' concerning the Jewish question. To this end the Mufti had numerous meetings with Eichmann. The two men were in complete agreement over the tasks ahead. The Mufti also set about organising a giant international anti-Semitic conference to be held in Cracow in 1944, for which he had Himmler's enthusiastic support, but the Red Army's advance put paid to this event. Himmler was so convinced of the similarities between National Socialism and militant Islam that in May 1943 he ordered Gottlob Berger, head of the SS Main Office, to set experts to work in the hope of finding a justification in the Quran for the idea that Hitler was divinely appointed to complete the work of the Prophet. Berger had to report back a few months later that his scholars had been unable to discover Quranic verses to support this contention. Ernst Kaltenbrunner, head of the Reich Security Main Office (RSHA), was not to be put off by these unimaginative pedants. He insisted that the Quran spoke of the 'return of the Light of the Prophet' and that the Führer could be represented as such. Furthermore, Muslims believed in a Mahdi 'who would come at the end of time, to help the faith to secure the triumph of righteousness'. Unfortunately even Kaltenbrunner came to the conclusion that Hitler could be seen neither as a prophet nor as the Mahdi, but he was perhaps 'Isa (Jesus) whose return is forecast in the Quran as a kind of Saint George, who will defeat the giants and the Jewish King Dadjdjâl who would appear at the end of the world.' None of this nonsense had any effect. The Axis had been thrown out of North Africa and defeated in Stalingrad, so its influence in the Arab world was now minimal. The Mufti had nothing much to offer beyond a promise to kill Jews, and the recruitment of some Muslims in Yugoslavia, who happily set to work massacring alongside their German allies.[69]

In anticipation of the occupation of Egypt a special unit of the SS (Einsatzkommando, EK) was made ready to murder the Jews. Walter Schellenberg first discussed the matter with Himmler at the beginning of June 1942, and the Reichsführer mentioned it to Hitler later the same day. SS-Obergruppenführer Karl Wolff, Himmler's chief of staff, immediately approached the Wehrmacht and an agreement was shortly reached that an EK should be attached to the Panzer Army Africa, but that it should take its orders from the Security Police (SiPo) and the Security Service (SD). It was thus fully independent from the Wehrmacht, as were similar murder squads in the Soviet Union, although it was to work in close co-operation with the soldiery. The SD bemoaned the fact that there were no accurate statistics on the number of Jews in Egypt, but was able to report that in 1927 there had been 63,550 'religious' Jews, of whom 22,192 were said to be illiterate. There was no way of telling how many 'racial' Jews there were, nor could the influence of the Jews on Egyptian banking and the press be accurately assessed.[70]

On 20 July Obersturmbannführer Walther Rauff was sent to Tobruk where he was to receive orders for his Einsatzkommando from Rommel. It is highly unlikely that he actually met Rommel, who was 500 kilometres away, fully occupied with fighting the critical First Battle of El Alamein. No documents have survived about Rauff's visit to Tobruk, but it can be assumed that he met a number of staff officers from the Panzer Army. The hastily formed EK travelled from Berlin to Athens at the end of the month, ready for shipment to Egypt and Palestine where their mission was kill as many Jews as possible.

The leader of the group, Walther Rauff, had been a naval officer until he was dismissed from the service for adultery. He joined the NSDAP in 1937 and the SS two years later. He was closely involved with the mass murders in Poland and in 1941 he was appointed head of Section IID (technical matters) in the RSHA. As such he was responsible for supplying the Einsatzgruppen with portable gas chambers, for he felt that shooting victims placed too much of a strain on the men who had to carry out this exacting task. He also accompanied Heydrich to Prague, where he acted as Deputy Reich Protector of Bohemia and Moravia. Rauff curried Heydrich's special favour by allowing his superior always to win at cards.[71] Back in the Prinz Albrecht Straße 8, section VI, he busied himself with Egyptian affairs, but to no great effect. He was contacted by Hussain Said, who said that he was the uncle of the Egyptian queen. He also claimed that King Farouk would be forced against his will to declare war on the Axis. Hussain Said asserted that Farouk had asked him to form a government-in-exile in such an eventuality. Rauff was asked whether the German government would recognise such a government. He forwarded this suggestion to the foreign office. Woermann promptly replied that no one had ever heard of Hussain Said, there was no mention of him among the aristocracy listed in the Almanach de Gotha, and that the Security Service should have nothing to do with the man.[72]

Rauff, a cold-blooded murderer, was given expert assistance by SS-Sturmbannführer Wilhelm Beisner, head of the Section VIC13 (Arabia) in the RSHA, and SS-Obersturmführer Hans-Joachim Weise, who had acted as liaison officer between the RSHA and the Mufti. Weise had initially been appointed to command the Einsatzkommando, but it had then been given to Rauff, who held a higher rank. His future task was to establish contacts with influential Arab collaborationists, who were said to be legion. Weise had been with an Einsatzkommando in Czechoslovakia, while Beisner had previous experience as a commander of an Einsatz unit in Yugoslavia.

SS-Sturmbannführer Franz Hoth was the Einsatzkommando's intelligence officer. He had been a party member since 1931, joining the SD in 1934. He had taken a course in colonial affairs at the Security Police Leadership Academy in Berlin Charlottenburg and had studied at the Italian Colonial Police School in Tivoli. He owed his appointment in part to his friendship with Rauff. He had gained previous experience in the SD in the Sudetenland and with Einsatzgruppen 1 in Poland under Bruno Streckenbach, a man who after the war was to be charged with a million murders, but who was to escape justice because he was suffering from the characteristically German complaint of 'weak circulation'.

The chief executive was SS-Obersturmführer Herbert Werth, a lawyer who had played a prominent role in the Nazi student movement. Prior to joining the Einsatzkommando Rauff he had been a commissar in Gestapo headquarters within the RSHA. SS-Obersturmführer Karl Luba was in charge of administration. He had gained considerable administrative experience in the RSHA, and had taken courses in colonial affairs. The seventh and last officer in the Einsatzkommando Rauff was Waldemar Menge, a sadistic brute who was an expert in radio communications. He was later to play an enthusiastic part in the massacre of Jews in Minsk. He said of one SS officer who became a trifle queasy during a mass shooting: 'The little limp-dick has fallen apart, the cowardly sissy.'

The officers were all young – from their late twenties to early thirties – and active members of the NSDAP. Four of them had been party members before Hitler came to power, thus qualifying as 'old warriors'. There were only twenty-four men in the Athens group, drawn from the police and the SD. This was far too small a number to fulfil the group's appalling mission, even though, as in the east, it would certainly be able to count on the enthusiastic support of much of the local population. After all, SS-Obersturmführer Joachim Hammann with a ten-man Einsatzkommando had managed to kill 137,346 Lithuanian Jews thanks to such assistance. It must therefore be assumed to have been a sort of expeditionary force, an advance guard for the major task ahead. When it was eventually sent to Tunisia it was increased to a hundred men.

Ribbentrop had ordered an intense propaganda campaign in preparation for the occupation of Egypt. A number of highly dubious characters, who professed to be familiar with Egyptian affairs, were called up to assist. The result was predictably crude. Along with heavy doses of exceptionally primitive anti-Semitism, there were indignant denunciations of the evils of British imperialism and heartfelt assurances that the Axis powers were the true friends of the Egyptian people and would drive the British out, thus freeing the Egyptians from those who had bled them white and dragged them into a war, while treating them with a haughty arrogance and unconcealed contempt.[73] Weizsäcker pointed out to Neurath that, although Germany was not at war with Egypt and Egypt was formally neutral, Germans had been interned in Egypt and their possessions sequestered. Germany had done the same to a number of Egyptians in retaliation. Farouk was considered to be pro-German, as was the Egyptian army, but the British had made sure the latter was not properly armed, so it was of little consequence. The Wafd Party was made up of nationalists and *Realpolitiker*, who would pursue their interests under the Axis just as they had done under the British. Some radical students were pro-German, largely because they were anti-British, but, according to Weizsäcker, most Egyptians were non-political opportunists, who were solely concerned with their material well-being.[74]

The Germans considered Wafd leader and premier Nahas Pasha to be thoroughly pro-British, a dyed-in-the-wool democrat, firmly in the camp of the democracies.[75] King Farouk appeared to be enthusiastically pro-German. Zulfikar Pasha, Farouk's father-in-law, who was the Egyptian ambassador to Teheran, had passed on a message from the king to Hitler, but with the British clamping down on Rashid's Ali's nationalist regime in Iraq it became almost impossible for Zufikar to continue discussions with a special envoy from the eastern department of the foreign office, Werner von Hentig. Hitler sent a profuse note of thanks to Zufikar for his message from the king.[76] The Germans were greatly encouraged when they heard that King Farouk had demonstrably refused to go the baptism of the British ambassador's son, and had not even deigned to send flowers. He had then gone to Luxor and Aswan, but in his absence the British had managed to oblige the Egyptian foreign office to break off diplomatic relations with France, which left the king even more ill disposed towards the British.[77]

In July 1942 Walter Schellenberg reported that the British were planning to move King Farouk to the Sudan or South Africa, where he could form a government-in-exile when Egypt was lost. In the meantime Farouk was held as a virtual prisoner in his palace. Ideally the British would have liked to replace him with their willing tool, Mohamed Ali, but the king was very popular, so they feared a reaction were they to force him to abdicate. Nahas Pasha had become so unpopular that the British were thinking of replacing him with someone less obviously their stooge. Schellenberg claimed that the British were caught between a mighty enemy at the front and a hostile population in Egypt. The

British military, he confidently claimed, seriously reckoned with the loss of Egypt and the Suez Canal. 'All Jews and intellectuals hostile to the Axis' had fled to the Sudan, leaving the British utterly demoralised.[78]

The Axis advance to El Alamein was accompanied by a massive propaganda campaign. Neurath, who was responsible for the propaganda offensive in Egypt, most of which was in the form of leaflets dropped from the air, had no interesting ideas. Rommel showed very little interest in such matters, so the net result was negligible.[79] Mellenthin, who had received reports of increased anti-British sentiments in Egypt, was anxious to step up the propaganda effort. He therefore appealed to the foreign office for help. It came in the form of Dr Winkler, a man who knew Egypt well and was attached to Neurath's staff. He wrote a series of propaganda leaflets of staggering crudity that were unlikely to have made much of an impression on illiterate Egyptians. The major problem with such propaganda was that the Italians were very unpopular and no one believed their expressions of solidarity with Islam, so Winkler was careful not to mention them in his leaflets.[80] Alarm bells rang in the Wilhelmstraße when an article appeared in the semi-official journal *Relazioni Internazionali*, which asserted that 'the Egyptian bastion will remain completely under Italo-German control and Egypt's destiny will be determined in Rome and Berlin'.[81]

German and Italian bombers dropped tons of leaflets on Egypt, Palestine, Syria and Lebanon. On 25 June, the day that the Panzer Group reached the Egyptian border, 1.1 million pieces of propaganda were shipped to North Africa to be dropped on Egypt. Neurath soon reported that vast numbers of these leaflets had been dropped. On 12 July a further 760,000 leaflets were delivered from Germany, including 200,000 appeals by the Mufti of Jerusalem, el-Husseini, and the Iraqi nationalist Rashid Ali al-Gailani. El-Husseini, one of the leaders of the Arab revolt in Jerusalem in April 1920, had become Mufti as a result of an election that was rigged by the British in an attempt to appease the Arab nationalist movement. In the following year he was made president of a Supreme Arab Council, established by the British, and as such was a man of enormous influence in Palestine. Al-Gailani, who had been prime minister of Iraq in 1940, but who had been deposed the following year, led, along with the Mufti, the Iraqi revolt of April 1941, which included a pogrom in Baghdad, and had appealed to the Axis for support.[82] Among the total of 1.3 million leaflets dropped by mid-July a large number were directed at Arab youth, who were urged not to serve in the British army. If they did so they would only be supporting the 'occupying forces' and their policy of 'colonisation and tyranny, under the same banner as Bolsheviks and Jews, who want to throw you into the slaughter so as to offer up your youthful blood'. Three hundred thousand leaflets entitled 'Egypt for the Egyptians' were made ready to be delivered after the Battle of El Alamein, calling for a general revolt against the British and co-operation with the Axis forces. The pamphlet claimed that the Axis powers had made a solemn declaration that they would respect and secure the independence and sovereignty of Egypt.[83] They had, of course, done no such thing. The Italians intended to turn Egypt into a colony. The Germans felt that all Arabs were good for was to kill Jews. A singularly inept postcard was distributed with barely recognisable caricatures of Roosevelt, Churchill and Weizmann pointing out the frontiers of a Zionist state that included Palestine, Syria, Transjordan and chunks of Iraq and Saudi Arabia. A leaflet offering further explanation claimed that 'American-English-Jewish statisticians' reckoned that 17 million Jews could settle in this new state. The Arabs already living there would be removed 'by well-known Jewish methods'. Yet another appeal was made to the Arabs to help Rommel's struggle to 'destroy the oppressive English-Jewish-American domination' over their countries. On 3 July the Mufti, whose 'vulpine craftiness' and robust stance on the Jewish question Hitler greatly admired, gave a talk that was transmitted by the powerful shortwave transmitter in Zeesen, just south of Berlin.[84] He announced that the Arabs marvelled at Rommel's strategic genius and at the courage of the Axis troops. They were fighting against their common enemies – England and world Jewry – as well as protecting the Arab peoples from Bolshevism. When the Nile and the Suez Canal were securely in the hands of the Axis, the British Empire would collapse, Egypt would be free, the Suez Canal secure and the Axis would remain a close and loyal ally.[85]

Mussolini spent three weeks in North Africa waiting impatiently for Rommel to smash his way through the 8th Army. Tobruk was the nearest he came to the front 800 kilometres away, and he was much offended that Rommel did not deign to visit him. He returned to Rome on 20 July in a foul mood, complaining that his generals had once again spoken too soon of victory and cursing Rommel for his high-handed and insolent behaviour. He made pretence of optimism by leaving his baggage in Libya and by pestering the Germans about the details of the future administration of Egypt. His return persuaded the Italian public that their rosy dreams about Egypt had been delusional, and a number of senior officers in the Comando Supremo began to think in terms of a withdrawal.[86] On 22 July Mussolini wrote to Hitler giving an account of his impressions during his visit to North Africa. He said that the 'deadlock at Bir el Alamein' was caused by the total exhaustion of the Italian infantry who had been in Africa for up to forty months, marching for hundreds of kilometres across the desert. Under such circumstances it was hardly surprising that the Sabratha Division had fallen back on 10 July when attacked by fresh Australian troops. He hastened to add that this setback was 'of marginal local consequence, without any significant outcome'. The British attacks on 15 and 17 July had not led to any alteration of the front. He thus made light of the situation in North Africa, which caused him such a bitter disappointment, and concentrated on pointing out the appalling conditions in Greece, caused by the horrendous costs of the occupation, in other words by the Germans' ruthless exploitation of the country.[87]

As early as 2 July the German military celebrated Rommel's offensive as a great victory in which the Axis troops had smashed their way through the British positions at El Alamein, forcing them to retreat to the Nile delta. This was based on the Panzer Army's report that 90 Light Africa Division had penetrated the British line, but the report was soon shown to be wildly optimistic. There had been a break-in rather than a breakthrough, and it had been repulsed. Hitler's press chief, Dr Otto Dietrich, reported that the British press was saying that the loss of Egypt would not be nearly so serious as the loss of India, from which Hitler concluded that the British were reconciled to the imminent loss of Egypt.[88] Further published reports spoke of 'a fierce battle', of British attacks being repulsed, which continued for the entire month of July. SD reports indicated that the German public was very sceptical about the situation in North Africa and OKW had to admit by the end of the month that Auchinleck had managed to bring Rommel's advance to a halt.

Cairo was abuzz with rumours in July. News that Admiral Harwood, the commander of the Mediterranean fleet, had ordered his ships to leave Alexandria and sail to Port Said, Port Sudan, Beirut and Haifa, caused widespread alarm, particularly in the Jewish community. The British authorities feared that, were Rommel to break through at El Alamein, there would be a nationalist uprising in Egypt, and that King Farouk and the Wafd Party would welcome the Germans. In fact this was largely an illusion. The Wafd were nationalists rather than pro-Axis, the vast majority of Egyptians were indifferent, most of the educated preferred the devil they knew to one they did not. Preparations in the royal palace to greet Rommel as a conquering hero ceased in July, while the Muslim clergy, headed by Sheik el-Azhar, who were determined to greet the Desert Fox with even greater pomp and ceremony than their predecessors had afforded to Napoleon, felt it prudent to await the outcome of the future battle.

The German naval staff was very concerned about the fate of the French ships that remained in Alexandria. There was a battleship, four cruisers, three destroyers and a submarine, all of which had been disarmed by removing the breechblocks. These had been locked away in the French consulate and the key given to the Swiss consul. The ships were of little value to the German navy because they were of a totally unfamiliar type, but they should not be allowed to fall into British hands. The French promised that if the British left Alexandria, the ships would sail to a French port.[89] The matter was discussed in greater detail with the French at the Armistice Commission, which remained in permanent session in Wiesbaden, as well as at the Franco-Italian Armistice Commission. It was finally agreed that the ships would head for Bizerta; failing that they would enter Greek waters. The American government intervened with the suggestion that they should go to Martinique, but Laval rejected this proposal. Hitler also had his say. Pointing out that Raeder had no use for the ships, he resorted to a familiar formula. He ordered that the whole affair be treated in a 'dilatory' manner.[90]

Hitler replied to Mussolini's note of 22 July on 4 August. He agreed that exceptional demands had been made of the Italian infantry, but he pointed out that the important thing was that the 'English' had been able to dislodge the Axis forces from their positions at El Alamein at a time when they were utterly exhausted. He promised that he would do everything possible to ensure that the troops were given the latest models of Panzer and anti-tank guns, and that they would be adequately supplied and reinforced, so that they would soon be able to go on the offensive. The major problem was to ensure that Rommel obtained what he needed, without compromising the offensive in the Caucasus. With regard to Mussolini's remarks about the excessive costs of the occupation in Greece, Hitler flatly denied that there were any such charges, and that the only costs were for repairing war damage.[91] Two days later Ribbentrop told Alfieri that the Germans would soon be able to withdraw large numbers of troops from Russia and use them to clean up the situation in the Mediterranean and North Africa, also to prepare to meet any Allied landing, and free large numbers of workers to build fighters, heavy bombers, anti-aircraft guns, Panzer and U-boats.[92] On 12 August the Italian ambassador was admitted to the presence. Hitler told him that the Battle of Stalingrad would decide the outcome of the war. As far as North Africa was concerned the important thing was to ensure that Rommel could once again go on the offensive. Alfieri mentioned how popular Rommel had become in Italy, to which Hitler replied that he had first thought of sending Manstein to North Africa, but then decided that Rommel, like Dietl, had the ability to inspire his troops, something that was absolutely essential when the men were called upon to fight in exceedingly difficult conditions, as in North Africa.[93]

The fighting in July confirmed Churchill's opinion of Auchinleck as an indecisive commander. Alan Brooke, the Chief of Imperial General Staff, decided to go to Cairo at the end of the month to see what had gone wrong, but as he was about to leave Churchill announced that he would go to Cairo himself, from thence to Moscow. This involved a dangerous flight over Gibraltar and the North African desert, but Churchill was determined to 'settle the decisive question on the spot'.[94] The prime minister arrived in Cairo on 3 August. Auchinleck virtually ensured his own dismissal by announcing that it would not be possible to go on the offensive before 15 September. After several days of heated discussion it was decided to divide Middle East Command in two. Egypt, Palestine and Syria would be covered by Near East Command, to which General Sir Harold Alexander was appointed, Brooke having turned down the offer. Auchinleck was given the Middle East, comprising Persia and Iraq, but he was unhappy with this demotion and asked for a posting, whereupon he was sent to India as commander-in-chief in place of Wavell who was made viceroy. The case for Auchinleck's dismissal was exceedingly weak. Churchill had dismissed him not when Tobruk was lost, but when he had just halted Rommel. The claim that he had been forced to take this action because of the need to 'restore confidence in the Command, which I regret does not exist at the present time', was both blatantly untrue and exceptionally mean spirited. Dorman-Smith sued him for libel for this remark. The matter was settled out of court. 'Strafer' Gott, whom Churchill unjustifiably regarded as an independent and energetic spirit, was given command over 8th Army, in spite of Brooke's serious reservations and his own express desire to remain with his 13th Corps.[95] He was a very nice man, a former army boxing champion, who was very popular with his troops, but he was tired and dispirited after his poor performance at El Alamein. A man of limited intelligence, he lacked both O'Connor's dash and Auchinleck's ability as a tactician, but was endowed with a magnetic personality. To his credit he had accurately predicted Rommel's next move in an appreciation written on 1 August, but it is not clear how far this was the work of two principal staff officers, Brigadier 'Bobby' Erskine and Major Freddy de Butts.[96] Auchinleck had been impressed and gave Gott the task of using Dorman-Smith's defensive tactics to prepare for the next blow, which he expected within the next couple of weeks. This Gott did with skill and determination. He was killed on the day after his appointment when his plane was shot down by a couple of Me109s that had just disengaged from a dogfight. He died a horrible death. Unable to escape from the rear of the plane, he was burnt alive after a crash landing. Brooke was now able to secure the appointment of his favourite, Lieutenant-General Bernard Montgomery, who was in command of the Home Forces in South Eastern Command. Montgomery was known for his energy, his boundless (if unjustified) self-confidence, as well as his genius for self-promotion. He arrived in Cairo determined to make his mark.

Montgomery was certainly a breath of fresh air, a brilliant administrator and trainer, but the notion that he galvanised an army sunk in despair and defeatism – 'a dog's breakfast' as he put it – and revolutionised 8th Army along the lines of the Panzer Army, is pure myth. He was wise enough to take over plans devised by Dorman-Smith, even though he had a hearty dislike for the man. As a star pupil Dorman-Smith had had the effrontery to criticise Montgomery's teaching of tactics when he was a lecturer at the Camberley Staff College, saying that his idea of tactics was to take a sledgehammer to crack a nut.[97] Dorman-Smith had been ousted along with Auchinleck, with whom he had had a most harmonious relationship, and who had rescued him from the obscurity of teaching at the Staff College in Haifa. His subsequent career was that of a wasted asset. He briefly commanded a brigade at Anzio, but was declared unfit to command a brigade, was demoted to colonel and retired six months before the armistice. He vented his spleen for this affront by changing his name to O'Gowan, a clan of which he was the head, and by acting as a military adviser to the 'official' IRA.[98]

Montgomery inherited a situation that was far more favourable than he was later to claim. Any army that had suffered defeats such as those at Tobruk and Gazala, delivered by numerically weaker forces, with far less in the way of armour, artillery, aircraft, transportation and reserves, was bound to suffer a crisis of morale. Churchill's brusque across-the-board command changes, which left 8th Army leaderless for almost a week, caused further confusion and concern. Why, it was widely asked, had their commander been sacked immediately after he had achieved a major success, when he had survived the humiliation of Tobruk? Auchinleck had managed to halt Rommel's advance at El Alamein, but the British army's confidence had not yet been restored. In large part this lack of confidence was due to Lieutenant-General Thomas Corbett, Auchinleck's deputy commander-in-chief, and his staff in Cairo, who concentrated on plans for the worst case. While Auchinleck and Dorman-Smith thought in terms of a renewed offensive, Corbett concentrated on how to save the 8th Army by withdrawal behind the Suez Canal and back to Palestine, and sent detailed reports to this effect to his man at 8th Army staff headquarters, Brigadier 'Jock' Whitely, who was still Brigadier General Staff, but who had fallen apart after two agonising defeats, and in whom Auchinleck had lost confidence.[99] It is a sad reflection on Auchinleck's hold over his staff that he knew nothing of the detailed planning for a withdrawal that was going on behind his back, and which was quite contrary to his own ideas for the future. Rumours filtering down through the ranks that the army was in effect beaten, and would soon have to fight its way back to save what was left of it, contributed significantly to the collapse of morale. The 8th Army's new Brigadier General Staff, Brigadier Freddie de Guingand, was appalled when he saw these plans, as was Montgomery when he took over command. Knowingly or unknowingly, he attributed them to Auchinleck and ordered them to be immediately burnt.

Montgomery knew that his army would no longer have a reason to exist were the Suez Canal to be lost. He therefore made it perfectly clear that whatever happened there would be no withdrawal. This was to be a last-ditch stand, a predicament that was once said to be the 'spiritual home of the British army'. As he put it in a speech in Cairo on 13 August: 'If we can't stay here alive, then let us stay here

dead.' Coupled with Montgomery's remarkable morale-boosting visits
to the troops, a 'do or die' order of the day lifted spirits, and the army
quickly recovered much of its old confidence. This was a considerable
achievement. Morale had been largely restored, the 8th Army felt that
it had a forceful and energetic new commander, and its mission was
unambiguous.

The 8th Army was an angry rather than a disheartened army,
which was determined to show its worth, having narrowly won the last
round. Field censorship revealed that other ranks put the largest share
of the blame on those higher up. It was widely felt that the staff and
field commanders had failed miserably, and many longed to serve under
a British version of Rommel, whose brilliance was both respected and
feared. Montgomery's tireless self-promotion did something to fit the
bill, even though he never managed to match Rommel at the tactical and
operational level, nor was he ever as widely admired and respected by
his troops. The Germans shared much the same view of the 8th Army,
their assessment remaining unchanged until the bitter end in Tunisia.
They had enormous respect for the dogged courage and endurance
of the average 'Tommy', but felt that the officer corps was second
rate, the command structure inflexible, staff work laboriously slow and
unimaginative, senior commanders hesitant, over-cautious and slow to
react. They learnt to admire and respect the artillery and the air force,
but they were astonished at the lack of co-ordination between armour,
infantry and artillery. There is no indication that they saw any sign of
a problem of morale among the plucky amateurs in the 8th Army.

Montgomery inherited an army that had been reorganised by
Auchinleck and Dorman-Smith, so that his plans for a *corps de chasse*
to match the Afrikakorps, which he considered to be so innovative,
were a duplication of 30th Corps, which had been formed in September 1941, but reduced to an infantry role having lost most of its armour.
This was just one of many instances of Montgomery claiming original-
ity for something that his predecessors had already tried and tested.
Furthermore, his pet *corps de chasse*, even if it had ever been properly organised, would have not amounted to much, because he totally
misunderstood the role of the Afrikakorps. He imagined it was an
elite unit held in reserve for lightning strikes, while others engaged
in holding operations, whereas it was made up of hardened combat
troops, ready for any role allotted to them, rapidly adjusting to changing
circumstances.

Although Montgomery was to insist to his dying day that the dispositions at Alam Halfa were his own, they also had been initiated, developed and approved by his predecessor. He was soon to have an absolutely overwhelming superiority in men and matériel, along with complete command of the air. His lines of communication were enviably short. Equally important, unlike Auchinleck, he knew how to handle Churchill. He knew as well as Auchinleck that time was needed to prepare for an offensive, but he understood much better how to deal with Churchill's constant meddling in affairs that he barely understood. By always maintaining the initiative in professional matters, flattering him, spoiling him and, although himself a teetotaller, pouring vast quantities of wines and spirits down his parched throat, he managed to avoid dismissal. Churchill, although temperamentally poles apart from Montgomery, learnt to respect him, and was greatly impressed by his accurate predictions of Rommel's intentions, which were based on Auchinleck and Dorman-Smith's assessments, as well as on information gleaned from Ultra decrypts.

Two days after Montgomery's arrival in Egypt four merchant ships from the 'Pedestal' convoy managed to reach Malta. On the following day the tanker *Ohio*, although badly damaged and kept afloat by two destroyers, hobbled into the harbour with 12,000 tons of precious fuel. Malta had been saved, at least for a few months.[100]

OKW attributed the fact that Rommel had had to call a halt to his offensive to an acute shortage of fuel, but Hitler, unlike Mussolini, showed no signs of being particularly perturbed that there was scant chance of being able to resume the offensive for some time to come. Failing to see any signs that the fortunes of war, both in the desert and in the east, were about to run against him, he imagined that Rommel would be able to stay on the defensive at El Alamein.[101] The campaign in the Soviet Union was not going well, in North Africa Rommel's advance had been halted, and the Luftwaffe was clearly losing the air war, which was having disastrous consequences on the U-boat campaign – the only area in which the German armed forces were having a degree of success. Hitler ignored all Halder and Warlimont's warnings to this effect, continued in his over-confident, high-handed manner, and removed those who expressed concerns about the way things were going. But there are also signs that Hitler, in his heart of hearts, may well have seen that all was not well, and was already thinking of the apocalyptic downfall of the Third Reich.

On 8 July Rommel had urgently requested that, in addition to bringing his existing units up to strength, he should be given two more defensive divisions with sufficient anti-tank weapons and pioneers, as well as more artillery. Hitler replied that the Panzer Army should be brought up to strength, but refused to send Rommel two divisions from the Balkans. Instead 164 Division was sent from Crete, renamed 164 Light Africa Division, along with a parachute brigade under Colonel Bernhard Ramcke, known as 1 Luftwaffe Light Infantry Brigade. This was certainly not nearly enough to turn the tide.[102] Fuel was still a permanent headache, and remained so until the bitter end of the North Africa campaign.

Ramcke was a colourful character with a chequered past. He had been a merchant seaman, had served in the ranks during the First World War, had been active in the Freikorps and ended up as one of Student's senior officers. He was of a somewhat bizarre appearance, his false teeth being made of stainless steel after he lost most of the originals in a parachute accident. He had fought in Crete and had spent the past year training a new Italian parachute division, the Folgore (Lightning), in preparation for the landing on Malta. Ramcke turned the Folgore into an elite unit with an excellent *esprit de corps*, and a close relationship between officers and men. It was by far and away the best unit in the Italian army, and a clear demonstration of the appalling lack of training, lack of competent NCOs, the disastrous effects of a clear separation between officers and men, and the poor officer selection in the rest of the army. Admittedly the Folgore had received an exceptionally long training period of eighteen months, while replacements were sent to the Ariete Armoured Division who had never driven a tank, or had only fired at most three rounds with the main gun. The landing in Malta having been cancelled, the Folgore were to fight with great distinction in the desert. Although Rommel appreciated Ramcke's courage and dash, he remained deeply suspicious of his brigade. They were from the Luftwaffe, not from the army; hence he called them 'Göring's agents'.

Rommel was forced on to the defensive by 21 July because in the previous ten days he had suffered losses equivalent to four Italian divisions, and the three German divisions had also suffered heavy losses. He had lost 70 per cent of his manpower, 85 per cent of his Panzer, 60 per cent of his anti-tank weapons, half his heavy anti-aircraft guns. This left him with only 45 Panzer in service, facing 160–180 American M3s, while his decimated army faced, in his words, the best that the

British Empire had to offer. Urgent requests for thirty-six 88mm and one hundred 5cm anti-tank guns, plus twenty 10cm K17 fieldguns and a thousand trucks remained unanswered.[103]

Rommel, forgetting his recent reassessment of his allies, attributed much of this desperate situation to the incompetence and cowardice of the Italians. On 11 July he issued an order to all Italian units under his command that soldiers 'who cowardly leave the battlefield without fighting' should be brought before a court martial and that 'death sentences should be meted out without compunction'. On the following day he reported to OKH that there had been an alarming collapse of morale among the Italian troops. None of this had much effect, because Rommel did not have any disciplinary authority over the Italians. On 15 July he complained that the Brescia and Pavia Divisions had been wiped out because the troops could not withstand artillery fire and ran away, while the officers were incapable of getting them to stand and fight. He called for more German troops in place of these worthless Italians. Such remarks did nothing to improve German–Italian relations, and the Duce became ever more disenchanted with his arrogant ally.[104]

Bastico reacted to this criticism by pointing out a number of instances where Italian units had fought well, and attributed much of the present malaise to Rommel's thoughtless leadership.[105] When Mussolini wrote to Hitler on 22 July, ostensibly to report on his recent unfortunate visit to Libya, it was mainly to express his outrage at Rommel's accusation that the Sabratha Division had fallen apart on 10 July. He pointed out that the Italians had been fighting in the desert for 30 to 40 months, marching hundreds of kilometres across the desert, and were exhausted.[106] To some of the Duce's staff this amounted to a craven apology to the Germans, and his authority suffered a further blow.

It was not only the Italians who were exhausted. Rommel's nerves were strained to the breaking point, his health ruined. He pulled himself together and made an attempt to mend fences with Bastico. He pointed out that the situation was serious in all respects. The front was so thin that, were the 8th Army to achieve a breakthrough, the Panzer Army Africa would be faced with the choice between going down to certain defeat by fighting to the last round, or withdrawing back to its bases in Libya, thereby 'saving North Africa'. Bastico promptly replied that the situation was 'serious but not critical' and that Comando Supremo had ruled out any thought of a withdrawal. Reinforcements were on the way, and the Luftwaffe still 'a fighting force'.[107] In Rome Cavallero attributed Rommel's pessimism to 'a momentary state of depression'.[108]

The situation was now reversed. The impetuous and reckless Rommel was urging caution, while Kesselring and the Comando Supremo, who previously had been trying to hold him back, were calling for a speedy resumption of the offensive, with extravagant promises of generous logistical support, in spite of the persistent difficulties of sending supplies by sea and the realisation in some quarters that it would not be possible to conquer Egypt without first taking Malta.[109] Rommel now felt that the most that could be hoped for was that the Panzer Army would be able to hold the line. Particularly vulnerable was 164 Division, having lost nearly all its anti-tank guns and being without its own transport tail. It was a matter of the utmost urgency that new weapons should be brought in from Italy. The paratroopers, who were just beginning to arrive from Greece, were also desperately short of transportation. Rommel's chief of staff reported that there were not nearly enough supplies for an offensive, or even to fight a major defensive battle. Transport remained a major problem. The British had destroyed or captured 85 per cent of Rommel's trucks. Owing to the harsh conditions in the desert, 30 per cent of those that remained were under repair at any one time. On 29 July Rommel issued an order to stand fast, threatening that anyone who left his post would be charged with cowardice, and in certain cases face a court martial.[110]

The chain of command in North Africa was once again changed in August 1942. Operationally the Panzer Army Africa was placed under the direct command of the Comando Supremo. Bastico's command was now confined to Libya under the impressive title of 'Superlibia'. For all other matters the Italian troops were placed under the Delegazione del Comando Supremo in Africa Settentrionale known as 'Delease', under Bastico's former chief of staff, General Curio Barbasetti di Prun. Rommel had to report to him for all but operational matters, and he was responsible for all disciplinary matters concerning Italian troops under Rommel's command.[111] Rommel did not allow this in any way to cramp his style.

Both the Panzer Army Africa and 8th Army had been reorganised, both prepared frantically for the next round, both fearful that the other would be ready first. Rommel still had the initiative, but he had to move quickly, before massive reinforcements for the 8th Army arrived

in Egypt. He had received ample assurances that his army would be
brought up to strength, but it became increasingly doubtful whether
these promises could be realised. Thanks to the increased activity of
British submarines and aircraft, the amount of supplies landed fell by
almost one half in August compared with July. There followed a familiar round of recriminations. Rommel's chief of operations complained
that the Afrikakorps had been doing all the fighting for the past few
months, while it was the Italians who were receiving most of the supplies and reserves. The Germans had not yet received a single truck.
Rommel accused the Italians of hogging the transport and was furious
when they sent the Pistoia Division, an inexperienced unit of dubious
value, instead of German troops and matériel. He was also outraged
when he heard that the Pistoia had been given 300 trucks, while the
164 Infantry Division had been issued only 60. He once again complained that Rintelen was not looking after German interests, and was
allowing himself to be short-changed. He began to wonder whether it
might be possible to put Kesselring, who was at least a very forceful
personality, in charge of logistics. This did not happen, but Kesselring
did his impressive best to stiffen Rintelen during their meetings with
Cavallero. Rintelen's staff in Rome countered that the major problem was that Rommel had told the Comando Supremo that the Italian
troops needed trucks for supplies of food and water, whereas the Germans' top priority was for more 88s. Rommel sent his chief of staff,
Alfred Gause, to Rome in an attempt to persuade Cavallero to be more
even handed. Rommel told Gause that new Italian divisions were of no
use to him at all. He needed German troops with German equipment,
since they would have to do all the fighting. Knowing full well that he
would receive a dusty answer from OKW, Rommel preferred to deal
with Rome rather than Keitel.[112] Undeterred by Hitler's point-blank
refusal, he continued to request another motorised division, insisting
that the 164 Light Infantry Division should be fully motorised, and
arguing that men who had served for more than a year in Africa should
be exchanged.[113]

Panzer Army's staff no longer believed that it would be possible
to break through to the Nile. By August the Germans had cracked the
war office code used by the 8th Army down to the divisional level, so
they knew all about its strength and deployment.[114] Rommel was as well
informed as was his counterpart, thanks to Ultra, and he received the
information faster. The British, with their seemingly limitless supplies

and their superiority in numbers, were superb in static warfare, whereas Rommel was the master of mobile operations. Rommel's staff estimated that the British had about 3:1 advantage in tanks, in air power 5:1.[115] This meant that the Panzer Army could not allow itself to be tied down. Movement could only be achieved by retiring, thus luring the 8th Army forward. Rommel was initially impressed by his staff's arguments, but when Kesselring promised him lavish supplies of fuel he decided to go ahead with an offensive at Alam Halfa during the night of the next full moon. Any further delay would leave the British in far too strong a position to contemplate an offensive.[116]

Rommel reassessed the situation and outlined his future plans in a memorandum on 15 August. In spite of the many difficulties, the Panzer Army had been somewhat refreshed, defensive positions had been greatly improved and the Panzer were at last able to go over to mobile defence. The men were well fed, supplies of ammunition adequate, and by the end of the month Rommel had 250 Panzer and between 200 and 250 Italian tanks under his command. Fresh troops had been brought in by air, the Italian divisions had been refreshed, and the Panzer situation had greatly improved. The Panzer Army estimated that 8th Army had only 400 tanks up at the front and that the Axis had a 50 per cent superiority in heavy artillery.[117] In fact when the battle began 8th Army had 700 tanks. Time was now clearly of the essence. Rommel had to attack while he imagined that he had an advantage, and before the British brought up reinforcements. He suggested that the offensive should begin during the night of 30/31 August. Waiting until the next full moon would be fatal, because by that time the British would have strengthened their defences and brought up reserves. The plan was to deliver a powerful right hook, the only way to fight another Cannae when moving eastwards. He was to attack on a broad front, while delivering a massed armoured blow to the south, swinging up towards the Alam Halfa Ridge, driving up to the coastal road and cutting off 8th Army from the rear, while the forces to the north held the line. The Panzer Army would then continue its march towards the Suez Canal.[118]

Rommel was grasping at straws, and was well aware of the enormous risks involved. Given that 8th Army was on a relatively narrow front, protected on its left flank by the Qattara Depression, the attack to the south was extremely risky. The estimate of relative strengths was wide of the mark. The British had absolute superiority in the air, almost limitless supplies, an excellent plan inherited from Auchinleck and Dorman-Smith, and the intelligence provided by Ultra decrypts.

Cavallero appeared to share Rommel's optimism, announcing on 17 August that the Panzer Army would be ready for successful offensive action within a few days. He pronounced Alexandria, Cairo and the Suez Canal to be the operational goals, promised adequate supplies, and asked the Duce for a final decision. Mussolini gave the go-ahead on 17 August, leaving the date open, while urging that additional supplies should be sent to North Africa with every possible haste. He called for the destruction of all British forces to the west of the delta, as well as the seizure of Alexandria, Cairo and the Suez Canal.[119] Five days later he agreed to Rommel's suggested date, but Gause added the rider that this would only be possible if the supplies arrived in time.

Rommel's forces were still not up to strength. On 17 August he was short of 15,000 men. Three days later the Panzer Army reported that it needed 210 Panzer, 130 anti-tank guns and 1,400 trucks, along with a host of armoured vehicles. The British continued to sink shipping at such a rate that it became clear that Rommel would not have enough fuel to mount a major operation, but he still decided to go ahead, in the hope that somehow sufficient fuel would arrive in time. The new objective was limited to beating the British forces at El Alamein, after which, if he had the fuel, he might be able to continue his advance to the Suez Canal. There was no longer any braggadocio about the 'annihilation' of 8th Army; the most that could be hoped for was a limited success.[120]

The situation for the Panzer Army was desperate, but the situation looked even bleaker when Rommel's health took a severe turn for the worse. On 19 August he had a heavy cold, on 20 August he collapsed and spent the day in bed. An internist, Professor Hermann Horster, diagnosed 'low blood pressure and fainting fits, resulting from a gastro-intestinal disorder and from exceptional physical and psychological pressures and unfavourable climatic conditions'. Horster insisted that Rommel should undergo a lengthy treatment back home in Germany, whereupon Rommel sent a message to Hitler's headquarters calling for the immediate appointment of General Heinz Guderian, a leading expert in armoured warfare, as his deputy. Rommel then went to Mersa Matruh for an extensive check-up, from which Horster concluded that he was suffering from nasal diphtheria. This

17. Petrol barrels flown in by heavy transport plane

was almost certainly a false diagnosis, and when Rommel received word that Hitler intended to appoint the commander of the Afrika-korps, General Walther Nehring, as his successor rather than Guderian, with Kesselring as supreme commander over the army and air force in North Africa, he suddenly recovered his health, and returned to his headquarters, sending a message to OKW to the effect that his health had improved to such an extent that he would, under close medical supervision, command the forthcoming offensive.[121]

It could be that Rommel used his undoubtedly serious medical condition as an excuse to escape responsibility for what his staff considered to be a disastrous undertaking doomed to failure. Four of the five supply ships for the offensive were sunk, but on 27 August Kessel-ring arrived at Rommel's headquarters, assuring him that two ships were about to dock in Tobruk and urging him to get a move on. Rom-mel's staff was appalled at the idea of mounting an offensive before the necessary fuel had actually arrived. Kesselring made wholly unrealistic promises to send fuel by air, and became increasingly belligerent when Rommel's staff officers, Westphal and Mellenthin, urged him to call off the offensive, raising all manner of objections and pointing out that his promises could never be realised. Finally Kesselring insisted on talking privately with Rommel and persuaded him to go ahead. It was agreed that, provided the tanker arrived on 28 August, the offensive would begin two days later. It had already been agreed that 'X-Day' would be announced with 30 hours' notice, with all movements to be completed during the night. Meeting with his commanding generals the next day Rommel said that further operations after El Alamein would depend entirely on the logistical situation.[122]

Kesselring's behaviour is a further mystery. He had been against an advance into Egypt after the fall of Tobruk. Now he was arguing the opposite, even though Rommel clearly had serious reservations because of the lack of supplies, as well as the realisation that the campaign had almost certainly passed the Clausewitzian culminating point. The simple answer is that the dictators had lost all sense of reality. Hitler imagined that his campaign in the Caucasus, where Kleist's 1 Panzer Army had already crossed the Kuban and symbolically planted the flag on the highest peak, would be crowned with success, and dreamed of Rommel pushing on through Egypt and Palestine, joining up with German troops in the Soviet Union. Mussolini entertained similar fantasies of riding in triumph on a white charger through the streets of Cairo. Rommel felt that he really had no viable alternative. He could either make a last throw of the dice and hope that his fortunes would change, or take Westphal and Mellenthin's advice and gradually retreat, thus postponing the final inevitable defeat. The problem with a retreat was that there was no position between the El Alamein front and the Tunisian border that could not be outflanked to the south, quite apart from the fact that Hitler would not hear of any retreat. Kesselring was hoping against hope that if the situation in Egypt were cleared up he could then concentrate on the perennial problem of Malta. He agreed with Rommel that this was the absolutely last chance to go on the offensive, but was considerably more sanguine. On the morning of the offensive Rommel said to Horster: 'Herr Professor, the decision to attack today is the most difficult in my entire life. Either we succeed in Russia to advance to Groznyy, and here in Africa reach the Suez Canal, or . . .', whereupon 'he made a dismissive gesture with his hand'.[123] Nehring knew that this was a desperate gamble. With only 1.5 units of fuel the German Panzer divisions could only drive for at most 150 kilometres, after which they would be left immobile.[124]

Rommel placed the 164 Light Africa Division on his left, along with the Italian Bologna and Brescia Divisions, stiffened by part of Ramcke's Light Infantry Brigade. Their task was to make a diversionary attack on a broad front. The Trento and Pavia Divisions along with two battalions from Ramcke's brigade, positioned in the centre, were to lend support to the attack in the north. To the south the Afrikakorps, the 90 Light Africa Division and the Italian 20 Motorised Corps were ordered to attack at 2200hrs on 30 August, cross their own minefield, move eastwards behind the 132-metre high Alam Halfa Ridge, well to 8th Army's rear, then swing westwards and hit 8th Army from behind. The Ariete, Trieste and Littorio Divisions, with a unit from Ramcke's brigade, were to follow behind to guard the flank. Speed was essential for the plan to work, with Rommel assuming that the British would be customarily slow in reacting, while counting on the tactical superiority of the German forces. There was the very faint hope that having delivered the 8th Army a severe blow, 15 Panzer Division and 90 Light Africa Division would be able to march on to Cairo and the Suez Canal, with 21 Panzer Division moving to Alexandria, but it is doubtful that any responsible German officer felt that this was anything other than wishful thinking.

The 8th Army was divided into two corps. To the north 30th Corps was commanded by Lieutenant-General W. H. Ramsden, who had temporarily commanded 8th Army before Montgomery arrived, and whom Monty's chief of staff, squash and tennis partner, Brigadier Francis ('Freddie') de Guingand, pronounced to be 'bloody useless'.[125] Auchinleck, who had a low opinion of Norrie's performance at Gazala, had replaced Norrie with Ramsden. Rommel, who appreciated a good opponent, was also severe in his criticism of Norrie's lack of tactical skill. De Guingand's assessment of the new corps commander was heartily endorsed by South African Major-General Dan Pienaar, who had had the misfortune to serve under him at Gazala, and whose 1st South African Division was positioned under him at the front, along with 9th Australian Division and 5th Indian Division. 13th Corps was to the south and commanded by Lieutenant-General Brian Horrocks, one of Montgomery's acolytes whom he had brought out from England. Horrocks was a faithful disciple, who had no sympathy for the old school of tally-ho cavalry officers charging around the desert in their tanks and armoured cars in corduroy slacks and suede chukka boots. He dug his tanks in hull down and let, as Montgomery told him to do, 'dog eat rabbit'. He commanded 2nd New Zealand, 7th and 10th Armoured Divisions, as well as the 44th. Lacking experience in commanding an active corps he wisely relied on the advice of Erskine and de Butt, whom he inherited from Gott. It was a difficult command, the corps having performed poorly in July and with the New Zealanders bitterly contemptuous of the armoured units, whom they felt had left them in the lurch, with Freyberg constantly 'bellyaching' on this account.

Whereas the Panzer Army seriously underestimated the strength as well as the positioning of 8th Army, and failed to realise that the Desert Air Force now dominated the skies, Montgomery agreed with Auchinleck's assessment that Rommel would opt for an attack to the south. It did not need great imagination to reach this conclusion. Rommel, lacking the strength to pierce 8th Army's front, was almost certain to opt for an outflanking movement as he had done at Gazala. But in any case there was no need for guesswork. The Government Code and Cipher School at Bletchley Park had deciphered Rommel's situation report of 15 August within two days and forwarded it immediately to the Ultra Intelligence Team at headquarters staff in Cairo.[126] Montgomery took his time, carefully positioning his armoured units to parry Rommel's thrust, and meanwhile rushing around giving pep talks to the troops. He did not change 8th Army's basic approach, but he did create a new atmosphere of confidence and determination.

Rommel's order of the day for 30 August read:

> *In the last few months you have driven our opponents out of Libya in an incomparable victory march. In relentless pursuit you have driven eastwards far beyond the Egyptian border. Our opponents went over to the offensive with fresh units. You have beaten off their attempts to break through with heavy losses, in a number of difficult but successful defensive engagements*
>
>   *Today the army, supported by new divisions, will attack once again in order finally to destroy the enemy. I expect every soldier in my army to give his all in these decisive days.*
>
>   *Long live Fascist Italy!*
>   *Long live the Greater German Reich!*
>   *Long live our great Führer!*[127]

Rommel issued the final order to attack only in the afternoon of 30 August, so that with a twelve-hour delay for decryption there

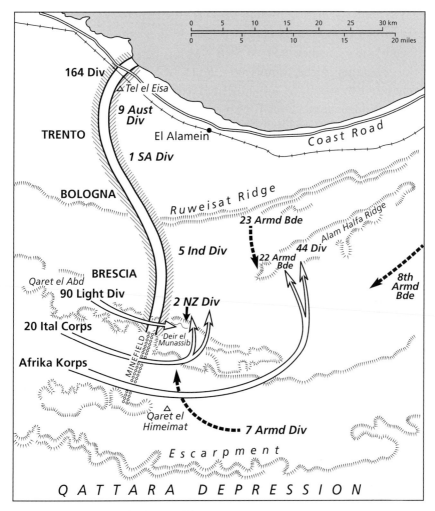

Map 17. The Battle of Alam Halfa, 30 August 1942

was not time for Montgomery to receive the message. Allied reconnaissance spotted 15 Panzer Division moving south and by last light
a troop concentration in the south was clearly visible. As usual it was
the Afrikakorps that spearheaded the attack with 237 Panzer and a full
complement of artillery, including self-propelled heavy howitzers that
had recently arrived. Whereas the infantry in the northern sector managed to advance according to schedule, the armour to the south became
stuck in minefields that were far more extensive than had been imagined.
British intelligence had planted a phoney map of the minefields, which

the Germans deemed to be genuine. Yet again the Panzer Army paid a heavy toll for poor reconnaissance. The Afrikakorps was pounded by Allied bombers as they wended their way through the gaps in the minefields, resulting in the commander, Panzer-General Walther Nehring, being seriously wounded and obliged to hand over temporary command to Bayerlein. General Ulrich Kleemann, commanding 90 Light Division, was also seriously wounded and put out of action. The commander of 21 Panzer Division, who bore the illustrious name of von Bismarck, was killed by a mortar shell. He was a brilliant and energetic soldier, holder of the Knight's Cross, who personally reconnoitred the inner minefields in a motorcycle sidecar, showing the way to his Panzer.[128] Rommel described him as 'this brave and chivalrous officer'.[129] Major-General Gustav von Vaerst, who had commanded 15 Panzer, took over command of the Afrikakorps pending Nehring's recovery. Seven officers in the Afrikakorps' staff were killed that day, causing a serious problem of command and control at a critical juncture.[130]

By daybreak on 31 August the vanguard of the Afrikakorps had only advanced 4 kilometres beyond the British minefield, and it was not until 0800hrs, after ten hours of bombardment, mine clearing and scrapping, that the first Panzer units began to get out into the open where they could disperse to avoid massive losses from the air attacks.[131] Rommel had half a mind to give up the offensive, but Bayerlein and his Afrikakorps managed to get through the minefields and pressed forward at an impressive rate, encouraging Rommel to continue.[132] The original plan had foreseen that they would be about 50 kilometres east of their present positions by daybreak, and then begin their swing to the north. Rommel, having lost the element of surprise, was far behind schedule, and had now to decide whether to go ahead regardless, find some alternative objective, go on the defensive behind the minefields, or call the whole thing off. He hastened up to Afrikakorps' headquarters and after a lengthy debate opted for a modification of the original plan. The Afrikakorps was now to head straight for the high point on the Alam Halfa Ridge known as Point 102, rather than going round behind it. The Italian 20 Corps, which was stuck in the British minefields for lack of mine detectors, was to follow up to the left of the Afrikakorps and to the right of 90 Light Africa Division, also in the direction of Alam Halfa. Kesselring ordered all available Stukas to support this thrust.[133]

At 1300hrs 15 Panzer Division was on the move according to the revised plan, followed an hour later by 21 Panzer Division and the

Littorio Armoured Division. 20 Corps limped behind at 1500hrs. 8th Army could not have foreseen this development, and the Afrikakorps made swift progress against a very weak opposition, only to become stuck in deep sand, which resulted in an alarming wastage of fuel. Nevertheless, 15 Panzer Division reached the Alam Halfa Ridge at 1950hrs. Having failed to dislodge the British, it took up defensive positions. 21 Panzer made slower progress: the new Mark IVs with their high-velocity 7.5cm guns killed twelve tanks and destroyed six anti-tank guns, but the division was soon engaged in heavy fighting against a British strongpoint, where the anti-tank guns of the 1st Rifle Brigade and the 4th County of London Yeomanry knocked out a large number of Panzer. 21 Panzer was forced to go on the defensive at 1830hrs some 10 kilometres from Alam Halfa. 20 Division was straggling far behind, as was the Littorio. The British had withdrawn to the north, suffering minimal losses. Rommel had failed to take the Alam Halfa Ridge, and could expect a massive counterattack on the following day. Montgomery, who was fearful of going on a 'wild goose chase' straight into the 88s, was soon to show him that his fears were groundless.

Rommel discussed the situation with Vaerst that night and decided to remain on the defensive and refuel. Earlier in the day he had seriously considered breaking off the battle.[134] Bayerlein's suggestion that the Panzer should withdraw, move east and attack the Alam Halfa Ridge from the flank was ruled out for lack of fuel. 15 Panzer made a further attempt to reach Point 102 at the height of the Alam Halfa Ridge on the morning of 1 September, but were attacked by a force of between 100 and 150 tanks. At last the British had learnt to concentrate their armour, rather than dispersing it in piecemeal attacks. Tackling this overwhelming force resulted in the Panzer fuel supplies running so dangerously low that the attack on the ridge had to be called off. Under continuous bombardment from the air throughout the day, the Afrikakorps suffered heavy losses. Rommel's headquarters was bombed six times in the space of two hours, a reminder that using 88s as anti-tank weapons seriously depleted the defences against air attack. Rommel realised that Allied supremacy in the air severely limited the possibilities of action on the ground, especially in the desert, where all but night-time movements were in the open. Then Rommel was given the shattering news that the two tankers he had been promised had not yet landed. This was another triumph for Ultra, which deciphered the sailing dates and routes of most of the ships on which the Panzer Army depended. Rommel's army now sat without fuel in front of 8th

Army's heavily defended positions, constantly attacked from the air and by armour. They were saved from disaster only by Montgomery's inability to plan a concentrated counterattack.

Rommel immediately ordered 15 and 21 Panzer Divisions to close the gap between them and concentrate on refuelling and rearming. A limited offensive by 20 Motorised Corps had to be called off for lack of fuel. The situation became critical when news arrived that the tanker *Sanandrea*, one of the two that were on their way, had been sunk, while the other, the *Abruzzi*, had been seriously damaged. When Rommel heard that yet another tanker, the *Picco Fascio*, had also been sunk he knew that he would have to retire behind the British minefield and go on the defensive.[135]

The first of September was a black day for the Panzer Army. It was out in the open without cover, immobile for lack of fuel, a sitting duck for the Allied air forces and artillery. An added problem was that the RAF had changed its radios from short wave to ultra short wave, which the Germans were unable to intercept. Their anti-aircraft guns were either of too small a calibre, or in the case of the 88s had inaccurate sights. Air Commander Africa, Lieutenant-General Hans Seidemann, had precious little to offer against the Allied bombers. On 2 September he flew 252 missions against 806 of the Allies, on the following day only 171 against 902.[136] A number of counterattacks were beaten off, but morale was running very low indeed, largely owing to Allied air supremacy, compounded by the fact that the Panzer Army had no night fighters, thus leaving the troops unprotected for the seven to eight hours of darkness. The Panzer Army had hardly any searchlights and the flight detection devices did not work properly.[137] On the morning of 2 September Rommel decided to withdraw, but he still lacked sufficient fuel to move the bulk of his forces. Kesselring called upon the Luftwaffe to do its utmost to help out the army, ordering attacks on 10th Indian Division during the nights of 3 and 4 September. Montgomery failed to take advantage of this dangerous situation, contenting himself with a few harassing operations by 7th Armoured Division north and west of Qaret el Himeimat.[138] By the following day the Panzer Army was in full retreat, leaving behind fifty tanks, fifty field and anti-tank guns and about four hundred vehicles. This was a decisive turning point in the Desert War, with Rommel finally losing all hope of ever breaking through to the Suez Canal. On 5 September Rommel's chief of staff informed OKH that the Panzer Army was pulling back to its original defensive positions, with the Afrikakorps as a mobile defence, behind the Italian 20 and 21 Corps.[139] Montgomery had showed himself to be a competent if overly cautious commander in the defensive, but he had missed the opportunity to cut off and destroy the Afrikakorps when it lay immobile for 48 hours.

The Allied air forces were mainly responsible for the Axis defeat at Alam Halfa, but ground forces also did their bit. On 3 September German air reconnaissance spotted 200 tanks on the move to the north of Alam Halfa, and a further 150 to the west. Facing such an overwhelming force, the Afrikakorps had to use its remaining fuel to beat a hasty retreat, along the lines suggested by Rommel the previous evening. Montgomery hesitated to throw in his armour, opting methodically to prepare a massive counterattack. In the meantime, an attempt by General Freyberg's 2nd New Zealand Division along with 132 Infantry (Kent) Brigade to cut off the Panzer Army as it retired to the minefields, known as Operation 'Beresford', ended in disaster with a loss of 1,140 men. Much of this damage was inflicted by Ramcke's elite Parachute Brigade, which had another chance to take on the New Zealanders as they had in Crete, as well as by the outstanding Folgore Division. Montgomery was furious. To be beaten by the Afrikakorps was just about acceptable, but to be thrashed by Italians was intolerable. To rub salt in the wounds the Germans awarded the Folgore eleven Iron Crosses. 'Beresford' had been poorly planned and Horrocks had made the serious mistake of sending the green 132nd Brigade, which he had brought with him from England, into the fray before it was anywhere near ready. The New Zealanders fought exceptionally well, with Brigadier Weir's concentrated artillery causing considerable damage, and setting an example for 8th Army's use of artillery in the months to come. 'Beresford' was a miserable failure, but at least the British learned some valuable lessons, from both their successes and their failures.

Among the prisoners taken by the Italians was Brigadier George Clifton, the commander of the New Zealand 6th Brigade. He confessed to Rommel that he was thoroughly ashamed to have been captured by Italians, for whom he had nothing but contempt. When Rommel complained about the number of atrocities and violations of international law committed by the New Zealanders, Clifton attributed them all to the Maori. Rommel, who found Clifton to be 'a courageous and likeable man', acceded to his request to be sent to a German rather than an Italian prisoner of war camp, but this was later countermanded by

OKW. During this exchange Clifton asked to go to the lavatory, where he escaped through a window. He was picked up in the desert some days later by one of Rommel's staff officers who was hunting gazelles. Rommel congratulated him on his daring exploit, but felt it prudent to have him shipped off to Italy for internment.[140]

On the extreme right flank, on the edge of the Qattara Depression a special battalion under Major Otto Burckhardt tried out some of the Wehrmacht's latest weapons under battle conditions. These included fully automatic rifles, an appallingly destructive mortar that spread shrapnel at chest height, a recoilless 75mm field gun with a flat trajectory, a magnetic anti-tank bomb with a delayed fuse and pistols that could fire a high-explosive charge. Their finest weapon, with which Ramcke's brigade was also armed, was the MG-42 belt-fed machinegun which was lightweight, seldom jammed and fired at the amazing rate of 1,200 rounds a minute. The British Bren gun had a relatively small magazine, fired 500 rounds per minute and was notoriously unreliable.[141] Burckhardt had fobbed off a large number of older weapons, many of which were rusty, on to the newly formed Battle Group Borchart, along with some tanks that were in a terrible shape, and deemed beyond repair.[142] This had done nothing to enhance his already tarnished reputation in the Afrikakorps. He was an odious mixture of the arrogant and the lickspittle. He was captured by a unit from the Household Cavalry whose officer, coming from an outfit expert in such matters, declared him to be a 'phenomenal snob'. While being led off for interrogation he turned to his men, saying: 'I am Burckhardt. They want me. Farewell lads, look after yourselves and remember, you have known Burckhardt.'[143]

The 'Six Day Race' of Alam Halfa ended back at the starting line, its failure a result of a lack of fuel and the overwhelming superiority of the British in armour and in the air. For Rommel it was airpower that was decisive. Command of the air gave the 8th Army complete and continuous reconnaissance reports. Even more importantly it left his supply columns extremely vulnerable, thus suspending the tactical rules of mechanised warfare. There was only one answer to the problem. The Axis air force had to be equally strong. This was a virtual impossibility, but it took yet another costly battle for Rommel to draw the necessary conclusions. At least he had been able to avoid a crushing defeat, owing to the fact that Montgomery had fought an unimaginative defensive battle, refusing to let his armour at Alam Halfa be drawn out, for fear that it would be outmanoeuvred. He thus missed an opportunity that would have saved him a costly second battle at El Alamein. But for the 8th Army the battle was a much-needed boost to morale, the legendary Desert Fox had been beaten back, confidence in the new commander was high, and they could look to the future with renewed assurance.

Rommel's chief of staff reported to OKH that the Panzer Army had destroyed 124 tanks and armoured cars, 100 vehicles, 10 guns, 22 anti-tank guns and taken 400 prisoners during the Six Day Race at Alam Halfa. But the Germans suffered 1,804 casualties, the Italians 1,051. The Germans had lost 26 tanks and armoured cars, the Italians 11. The bulk of the total losses were due to heavy aerial bombardments and artillery fire. The Panzer Army now only had sufficient fuel for eight days, ammunition for a fortnight, and food for twenty-three days. Rommel urgently requested that 22 Infantry Division be sent to North Africa immediately. OKW replied five days later that the decision whether to send an additional division had not yet been taken.[144]

On 9 September Mellenthin, who was suffering from a severe bout of amoebic dysentery, reported off duty to Rommel. He was given an appreciation of the situation to hand to OKH that contained yet another urgent plea for supplies and reinforcements. It ended with the words: 'If the absolutely essential supplies cannot reach the Panzer Army, the latter will not be in a position to resist the united forces of the USA and the British Empire, i.e. of two world powers. Despite its bravery the Panzer Army will sooner or later suffer the fate of the Halfaya garrison.'[145] Rommel followed this up with a lengthy memorandum for OKW and OKH, in which he claimed that the battle had had to be broken off because the Comando Supremo did not deliver the supplies that they had promised. Heavy losses were a result of Allied superiority in the air and in artillery. Stressing that the German troops had shown their superiority, in spite of so many difficulties and grossly unequal treatment, he launched into a long litany of complaint about the Italians, whom he claimed had failed in every respect. They were incapable of fighting in the desert, because they were unable to make quick decisions. Their tanks had weak motors and limited range. Their artillery was also limited in range. Their officers were inexperienced, the men poorly led and badly fed. They were useless in defence, unless supported by German 'corset stays', and were incapable of standing up to a British bayonet charge. The Germans had to bear the whole load on the offensive. The British now had a significant superiority in numbers and were likely to attack in October. The Panzer Army would be incapable of standing up to such an attack, unless 22 Infantry Division was sent to prop up the Italians on the highly vulnerable southern flank. The supply problem remained acute. The bread ration had had to be halved, leaving the troops undernourished. Seventeen thousand men were needed to replace those who were utterly exhausted, having served in the desert for more than a year. Rommel ended by repeating that the Panzer Army was facing the best troops the British Empire had to offer, and therefore urgently needed support.[146] The only viable course of action was for Rommel to fight his way back to Tripolitania, but Hitler would hear nothing of this. During the fighting in July, Warlimont had been sent by OKW to impress upon Rommel the importance of standing fast at El Alamein because Kleist was about to invade Iran from the Caucasus and the British in the Middle East would soon be caught in a massive pincer movement. Both Kesselring and Cavallero were adamantly opposed to a withdrawal from El Alamein. They argued that were the British to advance, the ports in Cyrenaica, particularly Tobruk, would come under intensive attack from the RAF, rendering it impossible to send supplies by sea. The German admiralty also insisted that any 'movement to the rear' by the Panzer Army would result in serious loss of prestige that would have a disastrous effect on Turkey, France and Spain. OKW agreed that there was no reason at all to move back from El Alamein. All this reinforced Hitler's stubborn refusal to move one step back as he headed not only for a Stalingrad, but also for a 'Tunisgrad', which was to mark the end of the Desert War with a shattering defeat that could well have been avoided.[147]

9 ✠ EL ALAMEIN: DEFEAT

Rommel knew that with his failure at Alam Halfa the desert campaign had reached a turning point. From January to the end of August 1942 he had had to make do with a mere 40 per cent of the supplies he needed, while the British had ample logistical support, along with absolute superiority in the air. Without secure supplies and massive air support he had precious little chance of survival.[1] He had made the colossal error of mounting an offensive before he was absolutely certain that he had enough fuel. Instead of accepting responsibility for this blunder, he blamed Kesselring for his defeat. A year later he told the German envoy in Italy, Rudolf Rahn: 'I not only think, I know that Field Marshal Kesselring consciously and deliberately delayed sending supplies of weapons, ammunition and above all petrol to Alamein, because he was jealous of my fame as a military commander.'[2] This was a preposterous accusation that disguised the fact that Rommel was no longer the over-confident swashbuckler, full of dash and derring-do, but was worn out, exhausted and depressed.

The Naval Staff argued that Rommel's failure at Alam Halfa marked a significant turning point in the war. OKH did not share this view. They argued that the British would be unlikely to go on the offensive until the following spring, and Halder argued that this would enable 'Field Marshal Rommel, thanks to his outstanding leadership, to seize the initiative and once again go on the offensive'. Warlimont's Armed Forces Command Staff (WFSt) insisted that the navy's concerns were exaggerated and that 'OKW does not consider that the Egyptian offensive has irrevocably failed, but counts on it resuming later . . . The Führer believes that our opponents will hardly be able to break through the Alamein position.'[3] Halder, who was to be fired only a few days later, may well have been speaking tongue in cheek about a man for whom he had scant regard, but WFSt's was undoubtedly a considered opinion.

The Panzer Army Africa reported to OKH on its strength as of 6 September 1942.[4] The German contingent comprised 82,000 men with 11,400 motor vehicles, 1,200 guns of greater than 4cm calibre, along with 12,000 men in the Luftwaffe and 1,500 from the navy. The Italians had 48,000 soldiers with only 2,500 vehicles, and 800 guns greater than 4cm. The Wehrmacht had received 8,470 tons of supplies and the Luftwaffe 8,447 tons during the month of August, whereas the Italians had received 25,672 tons. A strong protest was lodged that not only were the Italians hogging most of the supplies, the Luftwaffe was taking more than its fair share of those going to the Germans, the implication being that Kesselring, who was responsible for supplies, was favouring his branch of the services. The German contingent, including the Luftwaffe, needed at least 30,000 tons per month. Once 22 Division arrived it would have to be increased to 35,000 tons. A similar discrepancy existed with respect to trucks. The Italians had recently received 524, the Germans only 162. This overlooked the fact that the Italians were so short of motor vehicles as to be virtually immobile. Cavallero pointed out the central problem when he wrote to Rommel: 'I can promise you that the supplies will be sent, but I cannot guarantee that they will arrive in Africa.'[5] He might have added that even if they did arrive, there still remained the intractable problem of bringing them up to the front.

The next three weeks were spent in strengthening defences along the El Alamein Line and planting extensive minefields. By this time Rommel's health was the cause for considerable concern. By the beginning of September he was prepared to give way to the urgings of his doctors and go home for lengthy treatment.[6] On 21 August his personal physician reaffirmed his diagnosis, certifying that he was suffering from low blood pressure and a tendency towards fainting fits, as a result of gastro-intestinal problems caused by excessive physical and psychological stress in difficult climatic conditions. Treatment would necessarily be lengthy. It was not until 22 September that Rommel finally gave way to medical advice and began a lengthy cure in Wiener Neustadt. He left with very mixed feelings, for he imagined that Churchill would prod Montgomery into action within the next few weeks, at a time when a number of his best men were either on the sick list or on leave. Gause and Mellenthin had returned home for treatment, Westphal stayed in office, but was far from well, suffering from severe jaundice. Bayer-lein went on leave. Lieutenant-General Baron Wilhelm von Thoma replaced Vaerst as commander of the Afrikakorps, and all the divisional commanders were changed.[7] The Afrikakorps' new commander was a thin, ascetic soldier of the old school who had been wounded twenty times during the First World War. He had been with the Condor Legion in Spain, and had fought in the Soviet Union. Rommel left Panzer General Georg Stumme in charge of the Panzer Army. He was an experienced Panzer expert, who had been Rommel's predecessor as commander of 7 Panzer Division during the Polish campaign, but he was a man with a blot on his escutcheon. In July 1942, when he was commanding 40 Panzer Corps in Army Group Centre in the Soviet Union, Major Reichel, the staff officer in charge of operations in 23 Panzer Division, was shot down between the lines with plans for the first phase of Operation 'Blue', the advance to Stalingrad, in his possession. Hitler ordered Stumme, his chief of staff, Colonel Franz, and the divisional commander, Major-General von Boineburg, to be brought before a court martial under Göring, charged with a serious breach of security. The court found Stumme guilty and condemned him to five years' imprisonment, but Göring pleaded with Hitler for mercy. This was granted, Stumme was posted to Africa, and thus given the chance to save his reputation.[8] The unfortunate result was that, quite unlike Rommel, he was ever anxious to show his ideological fervour, much to the distress of the hardboiled old hands in the Panzer Army. Rommel's parting words to Stumme were: 'If the battle begins, I'll end my cure and return to Africa at once.' Stumme was a crimson-faced man, half strangled in a uniform that was a size too small, a monocle screwed into his eye, but he was also a jovial, level-headed man, far more congenial than Rommel, known with some affection as 'Fireball' on account of his complexion which strongly suggested an imminent cardiac arrest. Rommel's corps commander in France, General Hermann Hoth, had said that, compared with Rommel, Stumme was a 'tired old carthorse', a remark that further inflated Rommel's already excessive self-esteem.[9] Rommel conveniently forgot Hoth's assessment of his performance in France, which he felt showed a lack of judgement and an unattractive discounting of the contributions of others.[10]

While Rommel travelled to Rome to report to Mussolini and Cavallero, Stumme rushed around by land and air, looking into every detail of the defences, following closely the guidelines laid down by

Rommel.[11] All this was to little avail, because supplies in October were significantly lower than in the previous month, even though more ships had been sent from Italy. Nine freighters were sunk, six of them by submarines, for a total loss of 40,012 register tons. Stumme was soon exhausted, deeply worried about the supply crisis, suffering from the familiar German complaint of a 'circulatory disorder', and longing for Rommel to return.[12] Ambrosio also feared they were heading for a battle of attrition that would oblige the Axis to retreat.[13] Shortages of flour resulted in the bread ration being reduced to 375 grams per day, and the troops bitterly complained about their monotonous diet.[14]

The El Alamein Line was held by the infantry: 164 Light Africa and the Brescia Divisions to the north, Ramcke's Brigade and the Bologna Division in the centre, the Trento, Folgore and Pavia Divisions to the south. Armour was positioned to the rear, 15 Panzer Division and the Littorio to the left, 21 Panzer Division and the Ariete Division to the right, with 90 Light Africa and the Trieste Divisions held in reserve to the north behind Sidi Rahman. The artillery was spread in groups along the length of the front. Further to the rear mixed units watched the flank, in response to some badly bungled commando raids on Tobruk and Benghazi on 13 and 14 September, and there was increasing concern that coastal defences were not adequate should the British attempt another such operation. In fact the disastrous results of these two raids meant that the 8th Army did not even consider another attempt. The Tobruk raid, Operation 'Agreement', resulted in casualties of 300 Royal Marines, 280 sailors and 160 soldiers. The cruiser *Coventry* and the destroyer *Zulu* were sunk. The Benghazi raid, Operation 'Bigamy', had to be called off because the German defences had been alerted. Another raid by the Long Range Desert Group (LRDG) on the airfield at Barce was highly successful, resulting in the destruction of twenty-five aircraft.[15] The Panzer Army was positioned with its 'corset stays' in place, but German and Italian units were still under different tactical commands, thus presenting virtually insurmountable problems of command and control, the situation further complicated by their having separate logistical support systems. Supplies were still chronically short and unevenly distributed. There was an increase in sickness due to undernourishment. Ammunition was in short supply and the lack of fuel greatly restricted mobility.[16] Ramcke's paratroopers and 164 Light Africa, desperately short of vehicles, were left to slog away on foot. The troops' morale was low. Lance Corporal K. B., a signalman with 15 Panzer, wrote home: 'Lads come here and after a couple of weeks they keel over. Most of them get sent back to Germany. Still, they don't grumble about this being: "All for a Greater Germany."'[17]

Rommel went to Rome determined once again to stress the vital importance of improving the supply situation upon which everything depended. The Italians promised to send 3,000 men from Libya to build a proper road along the length of the Alamein front. The existing track was so full of potholes that trucks were often badly damaged because, in the field marshal's words, the drivers 'drove like the clappers'. The men were to come from the command of General Barbasetti, who had recently been appointed to act as an 'elastic band' between Cavallero and Rommel, but he announced that he could only spare four hundred men. In the end just over one hundred worked on these improvements, so that the road was not finished before the 8th Army attacked. The Italians also promised to send 7,000 tons of railway track to improve the movement of supplies up to the front, but nothing came of this. In spite of an initial agreement, Cavallero and Barbasetti refused to attack the British commando post at the Kufra Oasis, 100 kilometres south of Tobruk, where the LRDG was proving to be a tiresome thorn in the flesh.[18]

Rommel met Mussolini on 24 September. He made it quite clear that if supplies did not drastically improve, the Axis would be 'chucked out of North Africa'. Try as he might, he gained the impression that Mussolini failed to realise how precarious the situation was. He was flattered by the Duce's confidence in his leadership, but complained bitterly that he would prefer more supplies. Although Mussolini admitted that the Axis had lost the battle in the Mediterranean, and regretted that he would be unable to provide much in the way of weapons, he was adamant that the Nile delta had to be in their hands before the Americans arrived. Quite how this was to done under such circumstances remained a mystery. Rommel said that he planned to make a feint offensive in October, but argued that a major operation in midwinter would be exceedingly difficult. The only ray of hope was that the Axis had a considerable amount of French shipping at its disposal under the energetic aegis of the Gauleiter of Hamburg, Karl Kaufmann, who had recently been appointed Reich Commissar for German Shipping.[19]

18. Hitler awards Rommel the Field Marshal's baton

Hitler presented Rommel with a field marshal's baton in Berlin at the end of September. Rommel had asked Goebbels to find him accommodation during his visit to the capital. Determined to exploit the glamorous young field marshal's propaganda potential to the full, the latter was more than happy to oblige. Goebbels was much taken by his guest, who gradually dropped his reserve and gave a spellbinding account of the fighting in North Africa. The ceremony took place the following morning in the Reich Chancellery, with Rommel shaking hands with the Führer without removing his gloves, an uncouth breach of etiquette that confirmed a number of more conservative officers in their opinion of this upstart. Immediately following the formal proceedings Rommel gave an extensive and pessimistic report on the situation in North Africa.[20] Once again he stressed that he had failed at Alam Halfa because of lack of fuel, Allied superiority in the air, 8th Army's skilful use of its artillery and its seemingly endless supply of ammunition. He also pointed out that British armour, although numerous, was not much of a problem, but that the fighting quality of the 8th Army as a whole had improved considerably.

He was outspoken in his criticism of the Italians, accusing them of having inexperienced leadership, an elderly officer corps, insufficient training and poor weapons. Their tanks were underpowered, had a

limited range and were unreliable.[21] Their artillery was immobile with
a range of only 8 kilometres, and there was a chronic shortage of
anti-tank guns. Morale was low, in part because of insufficient food
supplies and a lack of field kitchens. Ignoring the fine effort by the
Folgore, he proclaimed the Italians to be useless during an offensive,
while they were only any good on the defensive when interspersed
with German units. He insisted that he could not possibly go on the
offensive until his army had a full complement of men and matériel, the
supply problem having been solved. To this end he suggested appointing
a German plenipotentiary for transport between Europe and North
Africa.[22]

The additional demands Rommel made bordered on the fantastic. He called upon the Italians to send 5,200 additional men, 2,000
trucks and 70 guns. The Germans were asked to send 6,000 men in
addition to the thousands required to bring all units up to strength, as
well as 1,080 trucks and 120 Panzer; 17,000 men were also needed to
replace those who had fought for more than a year in North Africa.
164 Light Infantry Division would have to be increased to nine battalions, and an additional division was needed to cover the southern
flank. 2 Air Fleet would need to be strengthened so as to achieve parity
with Air Vice Marshal 'Mary' Coningham's Desert Air Force, as well
as denying the British the use of Malta, thus securing supplies. The
number of freighters would have to be greatly increased, submarines
and motor torpedo boats used to bring especially valuable supplies, and
additional bases for supplies established in Crete and southern Greece.
He demanded 30,000 tons of supplies in September and 35,000 in
October, by which time he hoped that 22 Division would have arrived.
This would give his troops eight units of ammunition and thirty units
of fuel and provisions.[23] OKW had neither the men nor the matériel
to meet such extravagant demands. Even if they had, it would by this
time have been impossible to ship it all to North Africa. Finally, there
was the virtually insurmountable problem of bringing such supplies as
did arrive up to the front, given the distances involved, the appalling
condition of the roads, as well as persistent attacks from the air and by
armoured cars, plus the chronic fuel shortage. Rommel's presentation
ended with the words: 'Only if these conditions are met will it be possible for the German troops, who bear the brunt of the fighting in Africa,
to withstand the British Empire's best troops for any length of time.'
Rommel must have known from previous experience that his demands

19. Tiger I

were unlikely to be met, and that his failure at Alam Halfa marked the end of the campaign in North Africa.

Rommel was surprised to find that the atmosphere at Hitler's headquarters was extraordinarily optimistic. Göring felt that he had been exaggerating the difficulties. When Rommel told him that Allied fighter-bombers could shoot up tanks with their 4cm cannons, Göring dismissed this as nonsense, adding that: 'Americans can only make razor blades!' Rommel replied: 'Herr Reichsmarschall, I wish we had such razor blades!' Hitler offered the facile suggestion that ships with a minimal draught would solve the supply problem, because they would be difficult targets for submarines. They were to be heavily armed with anti-aircraft guns. He also showed Rommel details of a new multi-barrelled rocket launcher, the *Nebelwerfer*, based on the dreaded 'Stalin Organ', promising to send them to the Panzer Army in the immediate future. Forty of the gigantic new 'Tiger' Panzer would soon be on their way.[24] This monster Panzer, the *Königstiger*, was an impressive weapon, with a top speed of 46 kilometres per hour, in spite of its heavy armour. These huge 'furniture vans', as their crews called them, were difficult to conceal and their 700 horse-power Maybach engines were hideously thirsty, requiring up to 900 litres of fuel per 100 kilometres.[25] Taking Rommel aside for a moment Hitler told him of a Münchhausian 'wonder weapon' that was under construction, which could knock a man off a horse, sending him flying through the air for 3 kilometres.[26] The field marshal was left speechless.

Rommel produced some alarming figures in an effort to persuade Hitler and his entourage to make a more realistic assessment of the situation. In the eight days from 30 August to 6 September the Panzer Army had lost 2,910 men (1,859 Germans and 1,051 Italians); 38 Panzer and 11 Italian armoured vehicles had been lost, along with 395 trucks and 55 pieces of artillery, including anti-tank guns. These losses had been made partially good by bringing up infantry to the front, but without the trucks they needed for mobility. This meant that the Panzer Army would have to go on the defensive for the foreseeable future and prepare to meet a massive onslaught by 8th Army.[27]

Goebbels was determined to make full use of Rommel's legendary fame. He was dragged off to accompany Hitler to the opening of the charitable drive 'Winter Help' in the Sports Palace, where he was somewhat alarmed to be greeted by an ecstatic crowd. In his heart of hearts he knew that his star was on the wane, and that the hopes invested in him were no more than wishful thinking. On 3 October Goebbels presented him to representatives of the international press. His heart sank, but he put on a show of optimism and bravado in the hope that it might make the British postpone their offensive a little longer. He began his short speech by saying: 'We are now one hundred kilometres from Alexandria and Cairo and have the gateway to Egypt in our hands. We intend to go into action! We did not go all the way there in order sooner or later to be pushed back. You can be certain of one thing: we shall hang on to what we have.'[28]

Goebbels, who had always admired Rommel, was delighted with his performance, confiding in his diary, after the field marshal left for Semmering to begin treatment for his blood pressure problem, that he was 'just the sort of National Socialist general that we need. We would be much better off in this war if we had a dozen more of this sort.' Goebbels additionally reported that Hitler also admired his 'solid world view', speaking of him as 'a National Socialist, a commander with a gift for improvisation, personal courage, and exceptional imagination. We need this sort of soldier. Rommel is the future commander-in-chief of the army.'[29] It is difficult to say at this stage to what extent Rommel was a National Socialist. He greatly admired Hitler, and enjoyed his support, but he was not politically engaged, and concentrated on purely military matters. It was only when he realised that Hitler and his entourage were living in a world of fantasy that he began gradually to rethink his position.

It was obvious that Montgomery would soon go on the offensive, so both Rommel and Stumme wanted to disrupt his preparations by attacking first; but once again the supply situation meant this was out of the question. Writing to Cavallero, Stumme made something of a virtue out of necessity by proudly claiming that, once 8th Army's offensive began, he would mount a counterattack, the aim of which would be the 'destruction of the 8th Army and the capture of Alexandria'.[30] Stumme was obviously putting an optimistic gloss on the situation, in the hope of encouraging the Italians to make every effort to send more supplies. On the other hand, 8th Army's attempt to take the Munassib Depression on 29 September, in which the Folgore fought with great distinction, was seriously mishandled, indicating that the British had learned very little from their previous attempts. Rommel scribbled a note in his barely legible handwriting to Stumme two days later to the effect that the dictators agreed that the Panzer Army should go on the defensive, build up its strength and prepare once again to mount an offensive. Hitler, he said, had promised 'all the reinforcements possible'.[31]

By 7 October the Panzer Army's intelligence estimated that the 8th Army was up to strength with 8,000–9000 tanks and would attack at any moment.[32] On 9 October a reconnaissance group reported that there was strong indication that the main blow (*Schwerpunkt*) of the offensive would be to the south, but Stumme's staff did not agree. They argued that the 8th Army would attack all along the front, with strong forces to both the north and the south.[33] There was thus no argument that the 8th Army would soon attack, but there was a widespread difference of opinion about where the main blow would fall. Further study on 15 October suggested a number of possibilities. The British might attack to the south, along both sides of the Ruweisat Ridge, or to the south of the coastal road. In any of these eventualities (the third proving to be the correct guess) it was feared that the British would be able to break through the front line of defences. Should this happen the intruders would have to be nipped off in an armoured pincer movement.[34] With inadequate Sigint and unable to make thorough air reconnaissance, because of the Allies' air superiority, Panzer Army was totally in the dark as to what Montgomery had in mind.

The Italians were becoming increasingly nervous about the imminent possibility of an Allied landing in North Africa, which would almost certainly be the preliminary to an invasion of southern Italy. During the summer both Hitler and Mussolini had dismissed the idea of a 'second front' in North Africa as an absurdity. In July Mussolini wrote a memorandum for Cavallero in which he suggested that the Allies might build a new front in Egypt, Palestine, Syria or Iraq, at 'the crossroads of the British Empire', but not in Europe. Hitler smugly wrote to Mussolini at the beginning of August: 'Duce, I consider this second front idea to be totally insane.' If the Allies were mad enough to risk such an operation they would receive such an unpleasant 'technological surprise' that they 'would no longer have any desire for a repeat performance on the European continent'.[35] While the dictators stubbornly refused to face the possibility of a landing in North Africa, both the German diplomats in Rome and some of the Italian military saw this as a distinct possibility. On 10 October Rintelen reported that the Comando Supremo insisted that troops should be sent into Tunisia in such an eventuality, rather than be used to invade Vichy France. Mussolini had ordered that three divisions be sent to Tripoli before the end of the year that would be ready to march into Tunisia. On the same day Weichold reported that Admiral Riccardi felt that, although there were signs that the Allies were preparing a landing in North Africa, he did not think that there was any danger for some time to come. The German Naval Command (Skl) agreed with this sanguine assessment.[36] OKW suggested that more French troops should be sent to North Africa, but Hitler ruled this out for fear of an unfavourable reaction by the Italians. Believing that the Allies would not be ready for a landing until early the following year, he did not think there was any urgency, and instructed Rintelen to tell the Comando Supremo that they should hold off before sending a large number of troops to Tripoli.[37] OKW reconsidered the situation when the 8th Army launched its offensive at El Alamein, and came to the conclusion that the Allies would probably land in Dakar, or possibly on the Atlantic coast of Morocco. They thought that a landing in Algeria or Tunisia was unlikely. In spite of Hitler's earlier concerns, they now insisted that the French should be given arms and supplies, so as to be able to ward off the invaders. They feared that were the Italians to move into Tunisia, the French would resist.[38]

On 17 October Mackensen reported to the foreign office that the Italians felt that, given the disastrous raid on Dieppe, the Allies would not attempt an invasion of occupied Europe, but would opt for a landing in French North Africa, in collaboration with Gaullist and nationalist elements, with the object of driving the Axis forces out of North Africa. They did not feel that it would be possible to resume the offensive against Egypt, but although the Comando Supremo and the general staff thought that the Axis forces at El Alamein were strong enough to withstand another offensive, there were certain factors that gave cause for alarm. Principal among them were the 3:1 air superiority of the British, the continuing shortage of supplies, the possibility that the British might attempt an outflanking movement through the desert far to the south, and the threat of an American landing in Dakar. For these reasons the Comando Supremo made preparations for the occupation of Tunisia. On 10 October Mussolini ordered the Council of Ministers to draw up contingency plans for the occupation, should the Allies make a landing in West Africa. Mackensen spoke of the characteristic pessimism of the Palazzo Chigi, hinting that Italy was indeed in a vulnerable situation should the Allies establish themselves in North Africa.[39] The pessimistic Italians thus made a far more realistic analysis of the situation than could their German allies, who were blindly heading for the fall.

The head of the Department for Western Foreign Armies in OKH, Colonel Ulrich Liss, visited the Panzer Army on 20 October to give it the benefit of his expertise. His assessment came as something of a surprise. He was of the opinion that given the clear indication that the Allies were planning an imminent landing in North Africa, 8th Army was unlikely to attack before that was completed. When the blow came on 23 October Liss, who was still in Africa, calmly announced that this was clearly a feint, but Stumme's staff prudently decided otherwise, and braced themselves for a tough struggle. Panzer Army had done the best it could to improve defences and stockpile its limited supplies. The situation had improved somewhat, but was still far from good. There was a shortage of trucks, water supplies had been affected by a number of storms, and fuel supplies were inadequate for an effective mobile defence.[40] On 19 October the Panzer Army had 273 Panzer and 289 Italian tanks. Of these only the 88 Panzer IIIs and 35 Panzer IVs were modern weapons; the remainder of the Panzer were obsolete, while the Italian tanks were useless.[41] The 8th Army had about 1,029 tanks, among them 170 Grants and 252 Shermans, both armed with 75mm guns, the Shermans with long barrels. The latter

20. The air ace Hans-Joachim Marseille

tank, a vastly improved version of the Grant with a fully rotating turret and an armour-piercing shell capable of penetrating all the enemy's armour, was a match for any Panzer, with the exception of the handful of IV specials. The 8th Army also had a further one thousand tanks under repair or undergoing modification.[42] When the battle began the 8th Army had a fighting strength of 195,000 against the Panzer Army's 90,000.[43] The relative strength of the air forces was similarly greatly in the Allies' favour. Tedder had 1,500 aircraft ready for duty, whereas the Luftwaffe had 528 in the entire Mediterranean theatre. Kesselring made another attempt to knock out Malta in October, but lost a number of valuable assets in the process and only inflicted minimal damage on the island. In the course of the campaign the Spitfires showed their superiority over the obsolete Junkers 88s, the mainstay of the Luftwaffe in the Mediterranean. Wellington bombers continued to wreak havoc on supply ships in the Mediterranean, further starving the Panzer Army of fuel. On 30 September the highly decorated air ace Captain Hans-Joachim Marseille, who had more than one hundred 'kills' to his credit, in part due to a novel technique of cutting back the throttle so as to make a steeper curve when attacking, leaving him virtually motionless when taking aim, had been killed when his plane caught fire and crashed. While bailing out of the cockpit of his brand new Me109F he was

21. Marseille chalks up another kill, 1942

knocked against the fuselage, lost consciousness and was unable to open his parachute.[44] Stumme's order of the day, paying generous credit to this popular hero, was seen by many as an obituary to the Luftwaffe in North Africa.[45]

It did not need any exceptional insight to realise that the British would attack, but the how and the when were open questions. Stumme assumed that the British would make several landings along the coast as well as a frontal attack. He was particularly concerned about Benghazi, which was extremely vulnerable, because Barbasetti's forces might well prove incapable of warding off an attack. Stumme agreed with Rommel that the best solution would be for the Panzer Army to hit hard before 8th Army's preparations were completed, but he seriously doubted whether this would be possible. He did not believe that the avowed aim of taking Alexandria and Cairo and then moving up to the Suez Canal was feasible, but he did think that it might be possible to parry a British attack, destroy the 8th Army and take Alexandria. He added modestly that he doubted whether the Panzer Army could do much more than that.[46] Montgomery was to deny the Panzer Army the opportunity to fight in the open, and in doing so Stumme's hopes and dreams were dashed.

Stumme was quick to address the problem of the Panzer Army's poor reconnaissance. Not only did he stress the importance of improving the quantity and quality of patrols, he also ordered that more prisoners should be taken to gather information. To this end British patrols were not simply to be beaten off; they should be either captured or destroyed. In the course of the next few days these efforts revealed that there were increasing indications of an imminent attack. It was assumed that this would probably be at Ruweisat, as well as along the coastal road.[47] The major problem still remained that of supplies. The Panzer Army bombarded Rome with urgent requests for more matériel, men and equipment, but as the British continued to sink Italian freighters at an alarming rate, there was precious little that could be done. Nine freighters had been sunk in September, with disastrous consequences. Inadequate and monotonous food resulted in a sharp increase in the sick list. The medical officer of 1 Light Infantry Brigade reported that in September he had 174 wounded and 1,041 on the sick list, suffering from gastro-enteritis, dysentery and jaundice. The men were mostly seventeen or eighteen year olds, who were thrown into battle before they were properly acclimatised. They were eager young men, who only reported sick in extremis, by which time it was too late to treat them at the front. A large number of the sick had to be sent home, because there were not enough hospital beds in Africa. In such conditions it was hardly surprising that there was a marked decline in morale, particularly among the Italians. On 20 October Stumme announced in his order of the day that seven men from the Brescia

Division had deserted to the enemy. He described them as 'riff-raff, who did not deserve the honourable name of soldier', who would get 'a bullet or the noose' when the war was over.[48] Further ammunition against the Italians was provided when the Panzer Army's intelligence chief reported, with evident relish, that the new Italian pay books had a space to indicate whether or not the soldier was literate. Almost the only good news that the Panzer Army could report as it braced itself to meet 8th Army's offensive was that, in spite of all the shortages and difficulties, the pioneers had succeeded in planting 445,358 mines in the 'devil's gardens' on the El Alamein front.[49]

There was yet another unfortunate incident at this time. It was reported that the Desert Air Force had bombed a clearly marked field dressing station, resulting in a number of deaths and wounded. This was by no means the first time that such accusations were made against the DAF, and a careful investigation was made. It was reported that the red cross was not visible from the air, and that the Storks used as ambulances also were not marked with red crosses, so were fair game.[50] This may not have been a 'war without hate', as Rommel claimed, but it was on the whole fought according to the Geneva Convention, with an unusual degree of mutual respect, and, with a few unpleasant exceptions, relatively free from the excesses in which soldiers so often indulge.

Montgomery and de Guingand's plan, codenamed, with morbid levity, 'Lightfoot', was essentially a repeat performance of Auchinleck and Dorman-Smith's. This was indeed what the Panzer Army expected, but owing to shoddy intelligence work, admittedly hampered by the plugging of the Fellers leak at the end of July and the loss of Seebohm's unit, it was uncertain when it was likely to begin. The main weight of the offensive was to be in the north, where movement was easier, and where the Allies could best take advantage of their massive superiority in men and matériel. The infantry of Lieutenant-General Oliver Leese's 30th Corps were to work their way through the minefield, followed by Lieutenant-General Lumsden's 10th Armoured Corps, 8th Army's elite unit which had been given the dashing title of 'Corps de Chasse'.[51] Lumsden was an immensely tall and colourful figure in his immaculately tailored uniforms and brightly coloured neckerchiefs, and widely known as a daring horseman who had won the Grand National. He was an arrogant snob, but had acquitted himself well as commander of 1st Armoured Division during the 'Gazala Gallop', and enjoyed

Alexander's favour. He was precisely the sort of person Montgomery detested, but as he had brought in his own disciples, Horrocks and Leese, as corps commanders, he thought it prudent to let him have his way for the moment.

Lumsden's armour was 'to exploit success and complete the victory' by moving through the minefields, breaking through the line of defence and then cutting off the north–south road known as the Qatarra Track. Meanwhile, Lieutenant-General Brian Horrocks' 13th Corps to the south was to fight a diversionary action to tie up as much of the Panzer Army as possible. Montgomery insisted that there would be no question of the old 'hit and run' tactics; this was 'a killing match'.[52]

Montgomery modified this plan somewhat at Lumsden's insistence. Lumsden did not like the idea of his 10th Armoured Corps merely offering support to the infantry, but wanted to be up there at the front, fighting side by side. Montgomery agreed, in spite of the difficulties involved in two corps fighting closely together, but felt that the armour could take up defensive positions hull down as the infantry advanced, giving them substantial cover, and tempting 15 Panzer Division to attack. It was an unimaginative plan that could only hope to succeed because of the glaring superiority of the 8th Army in every respect, except for audacity, tactical skill and operational ingenuity.

On 19 October the Allied air forces mounted a series of attack on the Axis airfields at El Daba and Fuka which had had been flooded in the recent rains and where the aircraft were grounded. For the next four days groups of about twenty bombers, escorted by up to fifty fighters, attacked day and night, with the result that the Luftwaffe was pulverised, leaving it virtually unable to play any role in the battle of El Alamein, which began in the moonlit night of 23/24 October.

The attack came unexpectedly. Skl had come to the conclusion that the war in North Africa had reached a turning point when Rommel's offensive had been halted at El Alamein and Alam Halfa. OKH did not agree. They felt that the British would not attack until early in 1943, that Rommel would be able to stop them, once again seize the initiative and go over to the offensive. The planning staff at OKW agreed. A memorandum written shortly before the 8th Army attacked read: 'OKW does not consider that the offensive in Egypt has failed, on the contrary it reckons with its resumption.'[53] Cavallero noted in his diary on 22 October that the habitually optimistic Kesselring did not think that the situation in Egypt had changed substantially, and that if the British attacked it would be for political rather than military reasons. On 24 October he wrote that dispatches indicating that an offensive had begun were mere rumours, just as Kesselring had said the day before.[54] Hitler firmly believed that the 8th Army would not be able to break through Rommel's positions at El Alamein.

Apart from persistent aerial attack, the Panzer Army enjoyed a relatively quiet day on 23 October. Then, at 2040hrs, a massive barrage began along the entire length of the front, which gradually concentrated on the northern sector.[55] It was of an intensity and accuracy that the Panzer Army had hitherto never experienced, and the damage caused in the initial five and a half hours was considerable. The artillery was supported by massive air attacks, resulting in communications between the forward positions and the rear being severed. The 5.5 inch howitzers and 25-pounders, along with the Wellingtons and Halifaxes of the Desert Air Force, played a decisive role in the destruction of the Panzer Army. The Germans were unnerved by what they called 'Tommy's arty-magic' (*Ari-Zauber*). One NCO wrote: 'The English have artillery that really should not be allowed. Full stop.'[56] The 25-pounders, onomatopoeically called '*Ratsch-bums*' by the Germans, were particularly feared, because it was impossible to hear the shell coming.[57] Stumme blundered badly by refusing to bombard the British positions to disrupt their preparations, arguing that he had to save ammunition. The silence of the German guns was due more to the lack of ammunition than to the efficacy of 8th Army's counter-battery fire. The Panzer Army's artillery failed miserably to realise the vital importance of counter-battery (CB) work. Brigadier Sidney Kirkman's superb artillery was left virtually unscathed by counter-battery fire during the months of fighting around El Alamein, so that they could hammer away with little hindrance and to devastating effect.

This initial attack was by 30th Corps infantry, comprising 9th Australian, 51st Highland, 2nd New Zealand and 1st South African Divisions, who went into action in the north at 2200hrs. Each of these divisions was supported by an armoured regiment, the New Zealanders by an armoured brigade. Their objective was the 'Oxalic Line', behind the minefield some 5 to 8 kilometres beyond the starting line. The outposts 'J' and 'L' were quickly overrun by the Australians and the Highlanders, the men either killed or taken prisoner. The Italian 62 Infantry Regiment and two battalions of the 164 Infantry Division were wiped out by the British artillery in the early hours of the morning.[58]

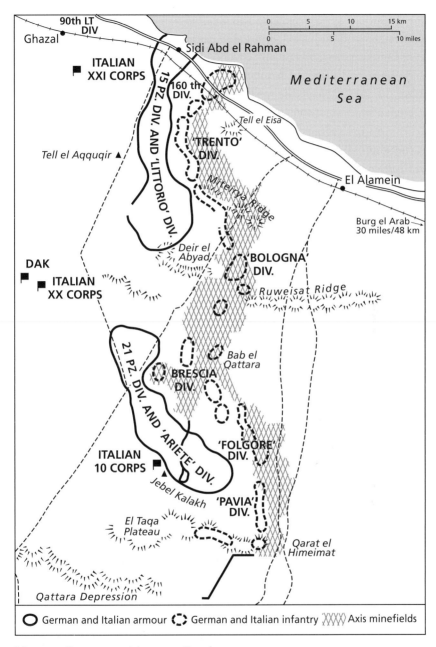

Map 18. German positions, 23 October 1942

The division was substandard and well below strength, made up mainly of Silesians and Sudeten Germans of dubious quality. By 0100hrs, 30th Corps had overrun all the forward positions and was through the minefields on a 10-kilometre front, but Stumme still had no idea what was going on, and was unable to decide whether this was the long-awaited offensive or some lesser action.[59]

Shortly after dawn the following morning Montgomery awoke to the news that about half the infantry had reached their objectives, while the remainder were not far behind. Casualties had been mercifully light. A major cause of concern was that Lumsden's armour had put up a pathetic performance, had failed to back up the infantry and had not formed the screen needed to protect against the inevitable counterattack from the Afrikakorps, orders for which were issued at 0615hrs.[60] In Lumsden's defence it is difficult to see how Montgomery's call for more 'pep' and 'drive' could realistically have helped him move through the minefields any more quickly without unacceptable losses.[61]

Stumme knew that the Italian 62 Infantry Regiment from the Trento Infantry Division had fallen apart under the barrage that was, as Rommel later put it, of First World War proportions, and that its position had been quickly overrun. But in order to obtain a clearer picture he drove up to the front with his signals officer, Colonel Andreas Büchting.[62] Stumme acted with characteristic impetuosity, taking off with neither an escort nor radio communications, in spite of Westphal's energetic protests against such foolhardiness, which was all too reminiscent of Rommel. On his way to visit 90 Light Africa Regiment he ran into an ambush and dropped down dead from a heart attack. Büchting was shot through the head, and the driver, Corporal Wolf, failed to notice that the general had scrambled out of the vehicle and drove off in panic. Initially Stumme was reported missing and temporary command was given to Thoma, who still remained at his command post with the Afrikakorps.[63] It was feared that the Australians might have captured Stumme, but his body was discovered the following day by a patrol.[64]

Stumme had confided in Westphal before he set out on this fatal trip that he did not feel up to the job, and that Rommel should be recalled.[65] Within a few hours of Stumme's disappearance Rommel and Kesselring were on their way to the front.[66] Hitler was not particularly perturbed when he heard of the British offensive. He was confident that the El Alamein positions could be held, and that Rommel was a guarantee that the Panzer Army Africa would be a match for the 8th Army. OKW showed no interest whatsoever in a battle which was to prove of critical importance. They concentrated entirely on the campaign in the Soviet Union, where the battle for Stalingrad was reaching the culmination point, so there is no mention of North Africa in OKW's war diary, and scant mention in that of OKH. There was considerably less confidence at the front. The army only had fuel for three days, supplies for one of which were still in Benghazi. It took seven days for a truck to make a return trip from Benghazi to the El Alamein front.[67]

While Stumme drove off into the desert, 15 Panzer Division mounted a counterattack, supported by tanks from the Littorio Armoured Division, which largely succeeded in pushing back the British intruders to the main line of defence. But this meant that the Panzer Army was forced to bring its mobile reserves up to the front line, throwing in everything it could to back them up. On 25 October the Highlanders inflicted severe damage on a battalion of the German 382 Grenadier Regiment, while a battalion of the Italian 61 Infantry Regiment surrendered; but another counterattack by 15 Panzer that lasted throughout the day managed to stop the rot, and push the Jocks back to the 'Mine Box' L. At 2145hrs the British once again attacked from 'J' and 'L', by which time 15 Panzer Division was running desperately short of fuel.[68]

In the south 7th Armoured Division gave the Folgore a nasty shock, attacking with 160 tanks; but it was pushed back by a skilful counterattack by 21 Panzer Division, supported by the Ariete Armoured Division, backed by massive artillery fire. They were ordered to hang on to the 'commanding position at Himeimat' at any cost, and were successful in beating back an attack on the following day.[69] Here too the front line defences had been destroyed, the mobile reserve thrown in to plug the gap.

Göring had arrived in Rome on 23 October for talks with Mussolini. He too was concerned about the possibility of an Allied landing in the French African colonies, Libya, Sardinia or Crete, but he did not think that Italy was in any imminent danger. The perennial problem in North Africa was logistics. Here the Reichsmarschall repeated Hitler's request that the Italians use their submarines as freighters, since surface vessels were easy targets for British submarines. He promised that he would discuss Malta with Cavallero, but insisted that Gibraltar

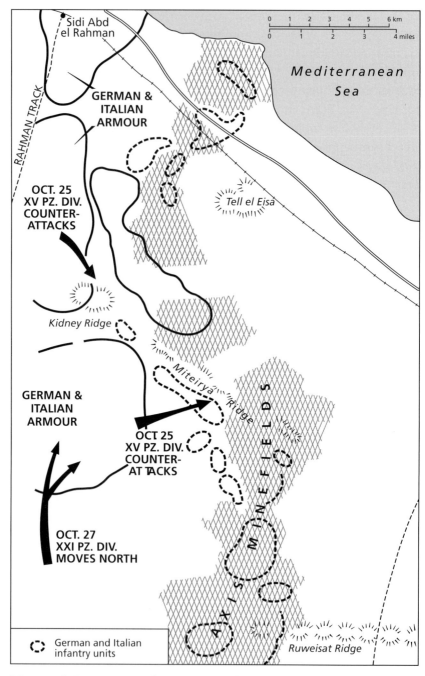

Map 19. Axis counterattacks, 25–27 October 1942

and the eastern Mediterranean were more important, thus echoing Hitler's lack of enthusiasm for an attack on Malta. He argued that whether or not the El Alamein Line could be held depended almost entirely on supplies. Göring made the extravagant promise to send three more divisions to North Africa, along with the latest Panzer, the Tiger I with an 88mm gun.[70] The division that was already on its way could ward off any attempt by the British to outflank the Panzer Army. The other two, a Panzer division and a motorised division, would be sent to the Tunisian border to meet the threat of an Allied landing in North Africa. With singular lack of tact, Göring told Mussolini that all the French treated 'the Germans with respect, the Italians with contempt'. They might make token resistance to an Allied landing, but all the officers in North Africa were Gaullists, the civilians fifth columnists, so they would rapidly change sides if the Allies were successful. He asked Mussolini why on earth the Italians had not demanded Tunisia during the armistice talks in Wiesbaden. Mussolini admitted that this was a grave mistake, since the possession of Tunisia would solve the problem of supplies.[71] The meeting ended on an upbeat note, with Göring announcing that 'on the whole, the war is already won', in part because the Allies lacked leaders. Roosevelt and Churchill could not possibly be even compared with the Führer and the Duce.

In the afternoon of 24 October Rommel received a telephone call from Keitel telling him that the British had attacked during the night and that Stumme was missing. He was asked whether his health was such that he could return to North Africa and take charge. Rommel promptly replied in the affirmative.[72] Keitel promised to keep him in the picture and he would soon know whether or not he would return to his command. Rommel waited impatiently until Hitler phoned. He said that Stumme had been reported missing and asked him whether he could return to North Africa at once, adding that he would call again to make sure that the situation was so critical that he could ask Rommel to interrupt his course of treatment. Rommel, having ordered a plane to be ready at 0700hrs the following morning, drove from Semmering to his residence in Wiener Neustadt. Hitler called again shortly after midnight ordering him to return immediately, because the situation was now critical. Rommel set out within hours, conscious of the fact that he 'was not going to earn any laurels', largely because of the chronic supply situation.

Rommel arrived in Rome at about 1100hrs and was met by Rintelen, who painted a grim picture of the fuel situation. The Panzer Army only had three 'units' between Benghazi and the front, whereas it had had eight when Rommel left. Ideally it should have had thirty. This meant that the Panzer Army was tactically hamstrung. Rintelen bitterly regretted the fact that he had not been able to do more, but he had been away on sick leave. Rommel arrived at headquarters in his Fieseler Fi 156 'Storch' at sundown on 25 October with a heavy heart.[73] He only managed to have a few hours of troubled sleep, while the British pounded away with their artillery and sent in wave after wave of bombers, all the while moving men and equipment to the northern sector in order to extend their bridgehead west of the minefield. In the face of overwhelming artillery and a robust defence, an attack on this salient by 15 Panzer Division, the Littorio and the first battalion of the Bersaglieri achieved very little. During the night the Australians succeeded in taking the strategically important northern part of Point 28 (known to the British as Point 29), and brought in reinforcements, so as to be able to push on in the morning. Their task had been substantially helped when a German reconnaissance group was captured, among whom were the acting officer commanding 125 Panzergrenadier Regiment and the acting commander of its second battalion. They both had detailed maps of their defences and the tracks through the minefields.[74] The Panzer Army's attempt to win back Point 28 the following day failed. Lacking the ammunition seriously to disrupt the build-up and having failed to seal off the penetration, Rommel ordered 90 Light Africa Division to attack, moving the Trieste Division behind so as to secure an eventual breakthrough. Meanwhile, German and Italian aircraft attacked the British supply columns, but they ran into intense anti-aircraft fire, and were no match for the Spitfires, which shot down a large number of the slow-moving dive-bombers. Italian pilots fled the scene, increasing their speed somewhat by dropping their bomb loads on their own troops.

The Australians, working their way northwards to the coast, succeed in seizing some high ground at Point 80, to the north of 'J'. The 8th Army concentrated on the northern sector, gradually extending its bridgeheads. The large numbers of the new M4 Sherman tanks, along with the American Bell P-39 Airacobras equipped with 4cm cannon, used as an anti-tank weapon, proved extremely effective, inflicting heavy losses on the Panzer Army.[75] By now there was a critical shortage of supplies. Fuel was sufficient for only 36 hours of normal fighting. Ammunition was running so short that the Afrikakorps estimated that the British had a 500 to 1 superiority.[76] Supplies were clearly the critical issue and the familiar merry-go-round began again. The Panzer Army's staff appealed to Kesselring. Smiling Albert passed it on to Rommel. Rommel insisted that it was all Rintelen's responsibility. Rintelen called upon the Italians to do more to protect their convoys. But precious little could be done in this regard, given the virtually total command of the Mediterranean enjoyed by the Allies, so that the counterproductive round of reproaches and recriminations continued. The Panzer Army had suffered serious losses, with 15 Panzer and the Littorio division the worst affected. The former, which had had 100 Panzer on 20 October, now had only 39. The Littorio had lost 56 of its 116 tanks. The massive artillery barrages and aerial attacks were also beginning to have a serious effect on morale.

During the day the shattering news broke that the tanker *Proserpina* had been sunk. The Panzer Army immediately contacted OKW, OKH, Kesselring and Rintelen, informing them that it was no longer able to fight a mobile battle, so if the fuel situation were not immediately rectified it would have to break it off. The shortage of ammunition was also chronic. When the transport officers in Rome were asked what could be done to remedy the situation, they shrugged their shoulders and said that all available transport was currently being used to move fuel. An urgent appeal was sent to OKW that at least 47 Infantry Regiment from 22 Division, designated for North Africa, should be sent as soon as possible. WFSt replied that its training was not completed and that it was not yet fully equipped.[77] This was followed by a sardonic message from Hitler asking whether the Panzer Army would agree to allotting the necessary transport to move the regiment, given that the supply situation was so serious.

That evening Rommel decided to move 21 Panzer and his artillery north in the anticipation that it was here that Montgomery was concentrating his offensive. It was an irreversible move, owing to the chronic shortage of fuel. The night-time movement was hindered by concentrated attacks by the Desert Air Force, so that by daylight it was still far from complete. Rommel knew that the battle had reached a decisive point and in his order of the day announced that there would be 'at any moment an enemy attack along the entire front, with the *Schwerpunkt* north of Ruweisat'.[78] Rommel knew that his only chance was to retire and force the 8th Army to fight in the open. The Allies would then not be able to use their air power when their armour was engaged at close quarters, and the Afrikakorps' tactical skill might outweigh their numerical inferiority. But he simply did not have the fuel to make this possible, so he had no alternative but to stand and fight.[79] This meant that he was locked into a battle of attrition that he could not possibly win. Rommel fully realised that his chances were extremely slim. In a letter to his wife on 28 October he wrote:

> The battle is raging. Perhaps we will still manage to be able to stick it out, in spite of all that is against us – but it may go wrong, and that would have very grave consequences for the whole course of the war. For North Africa would then fall to the British in a few days, almost without a fight. We will do all we can to pull it off. But the enemy's superiority is staggering and our resources very small.[80]

On 27 October the main weight of the British attack, spearheaded by the 51st Highland Division, was concentrated on the bridgehead to the south of Point 28, where 3 Battalion of German 382 Panzergrenadier Regiment from 164 Light Africa Division had taken a terrible beating the day before. The Germans collapsed and the British broke through in a south-westerly direction. With superhuman effort, 15 Panzer and the Littorio had managed to push the Highlanders back, thereby losing sixty-one Panzers for fifty-six tanks. In the early morning Rommel ordered a counterattack by the Afrikakorps, the Littorio and units from the Ariete, to begin at 1500hrs, while 90 Light Africa Division was to keep up the pressure on Point 28 to the north. The aim was to retake points 'J' and 'L' and return to the original front line.

The Panzer came up against a formidable defensive line of anti-tank guns and tanks dug in hull down. Having made no progress, they were obliged to withdraw with heavy losses. The new British six-pounder anti-tank gun, which was gradually replacing the worthless two-pounder, was to prove its worth.[81] 90 Light Africa Division, which came under heavy artillery fire and air attack, initially made some progress in its attempt to retake Point 28, but by evening the division had to be withdrawn to help out at another point on the front. The Desert Air Force had ensured that the attack went ahead without the support of the Stukas and their covering Me109s, thus denying the

Panzer a vital component of earlier successes. But the main reason for the success of the defence was the skilful use of artillery, made possible by excellent communications and the astonishing bravery of the forward observers.[82] By evening the Panzer Army had to concentrate on plugging holes in the front, while Rommel sent frantic messages to Rome and Hitler's headquarters for supplies, but realising that there was little chance that they would be heeded, he began to reconcile himself to the idea that 8th Army would gradually grind him down.[83] He now began discussions with Westphal about a withdrawal to a temporary defensive position at Fuka.

Montgomery's original attack was a badly bungled affair with two corps fighting two separate battles in the north, where 30th Corps' infantry and 10th Corps' armour were mixed up in confusion on too narrow a front. Lumsden violently objected to his tanks being called upon to clear minefields and attack anti-tank units in defile, an appalling misuse of armour. Montgomery insisted that what Lieutenant-Colonel Charles Richardson called a 'scene of chaos' that was 'absolutely unbelievable', was largely due to the cowardice and inertia of 10th Armoured Division.[84] This was a gross slander on the divisional commander, Major-General Alec Gatehouse, who was an exceptionally courageous and experienced soldier. Placing his Grants and Shermans hull down may have lacked 'pep' and 'ginger', but they beat back 15 Panzer Division's attempt to take Miteiriya Ridge. Even if 8th Army's armour tended to break off an engagement far too early, reckless courage risked unacceptable losses. Contrary to his later assertion that the entire battle went according to plan, Montgomery was quick to realise that he had to try a fresh approach. Gatehouse's 10th Armoured Division was withdrawn and ordered, along with 9th Australian Division, to push north to the coast. Montgomery thus moved the direction of his attack by ninety degrees: 10th Corps was now to push in a north-westerly direction from the bridgehead formed by 1st Armoured Division.

Both of these two thrusts became stuck because they had to deal with Rommel's renewed attack on Point 28, forcing Montgomery once again to regroup his army. The New Zealanders were withdrawn to form a reserve. The bulk of 7th Armoured Division was detached from 13th Corps and moved north. 9th Australian Division was ordered to persist in its attempt to break through to the north-west. The Panzer Army lacked the fuel and the ammunition to mount any counterattacks, so it was being gradually worn down by constant aerial attack

and artillery fire. On 29 October Churchill's son-in-law Duncan Sandys
arrived in Cairo with a message from the prime minister that the Allied
landing in North Africa was scheduled for 8 November, and that Montgomery had better get a move on, so as to link up with the invading forces. On the same day Montgomery heard that 90 Light Africa
Division had moved north, from which he assumed that Rommel had
realised that this was where the main attack would come. De Guingand
promptly suggested that the main thrust should now be further to the
south of Point 28, fondly imagining thereby that he could fool Rommel.
Once again Montgomery changed his plans.

Operation 'Supercharge' ordered units from 2nd New Zealand
Division under Lieutenant-General Bernard Freyberg, supported by
151st (Tyneside) Brigade and 152nd Highland Brigade, to punch a
hole through the Axis positions between Point 28 and Kidney Ridge,
through which Lumsden's 10th Corps would pass.[85] Lumsden's armour
was then to head for the sea, closing the Qattara Track and cutting off
the Panzer Army from the rear. Originally scheduled for the night of
30/31 October, the operation was postponed for 48 hours at Freyberg's
request.[86]

The Panzer Army, whose staff had already noticed the steady
build-up of forces in preparation for a renewed offensive, obtained
a copy of the plans for 'Supercharge' from a captured British officer
and braced itself for an attack that it assumed was imminent. The fuel
situation had deteriorated seriously. By 28 October the Panzer Army
Africa only had enough fuel for 1.3 days. In spite of using all available transport planes to bring in fuel, it had only been possible per
diem to bring in enough for 0.6 days.[87] This meant that there was
no transport available to bring in fresh troops to replace the large
number of killed, wounded and sick. Rommel knew that he could
not possibly win the battle of attrition on which the British seemed
intent. The only straw at which he frantically grasped was that the
Japanese might mount a major offensive that would oblige the British
to remove troops from the Middle East, thus forcing 8th Army to halt
its offensive.[88] Failing this unlikely eventuality, all Rommel could do
was to continue to demand more supplies, ask Kesselring for more air
support, urge the Italians to give better protection to their freighters and
threaten with court martial anyone, regardless of rank, who disobeyed
an order or failed in a mission during the course of this 'life and death
battle'.[89]

For the next few days the main fighting was to the north, where Morshead's 9th Australian Division was ordered to attack, while Freyberg prepared for 'Supercharge'. A fierce attack during the night of 28/29 October was warded off, but a battalion from 164 Light Africa Division and a battalion of Bersaglieri from 31 Army Corps were wiped out. The attack resumed in the morning, but was successfully countered by 90 Light Africa Division. The tanker *Morandi* had docked at Benghazi, but that was 1,500 kilometres from the front, so it would be at least a week before the fuel arrived. In the morning of 29 October Rommel had received the shattering news that the *Luciana*, which had been sent as a replacement for the *Proserpina*, also had been sunk, leaving the Panzer Army high and dry. Rommel promptly urged Kesselring to make sure that more fuel was sent by air. At that moment only one-tenth of fuel supplies were flown in. He backed up this request with a furious letter to Rintelen in which he pointed out: 'Over and over again the army has pointed out the absolute necessity for sufficient provisions, fuel and ammunition. Responsibility for the present acute crisis rest squarely on the shoulders on those who are in charge of supplies.'[90] Rintelen calmly replied that the fuel situation was likely to worsen as long as the problem of Malta was not seriously addressed. There was also no point in sending any more troops to North Africa if they could not be supplied.[91] The unfortunate General Barbasetti, who visited Rommel's headquarters later in the day, was also submitted to a ferocious tongue-lashing. News that two divisions had broken through in the south, where Rommel had virtually no troops, did nothing to improve his foul mood, but this soon turned out to be a false alarm from the Comando Supremo.[92] One piece of good news was that Göring had agreed to release an air transport group from Russia to bring fuel to North Africa.[93]

The 8th Army took a pause on 29 October, but the Panzer Army doubted that this would last for long. The following day was also quiet, but Rommel knew that his army was by now far too weak to be able to withstand a major offensive. He therefore sent Krause back to Fuka to decide where to establish a defensive position.

On 31 October 8th Army launched a limited attack in the north with the Australians reaching the coast, thus trapping 125 Grenadier Regiment from 164 Light Africa Division. Rommel promptly ordered General von Thoma to counterattack with units from 21 Panzer and 90 Light Africa Divisions. Thoma was initially dumbfounded by this

order which sent him off to an area of the front with which he was
unfamiliar, but quickly realising the seriousness of the threat to 125
Panzergrenadier Regiment in the coastal salient, he re-established contact with them, and managed to drive Morshead's Australians back
south across the railway line, taking 120 prisoners and destroying 18
tanks.[94] Rommel had survived another day, but he knew that it would
not be long before Montgomery mounted a full-scale attack, and that his
position at El Alamein was untenable. His main concern now was how
to withdraw to Fuka with as few casualties as possible. The major problem was the sizeable Italian infantry units stuck out in the middle of the
desert without transport, which constituted, in Rommel's words, a 'ball
and chain'. When he withdrew from Cyrenaica, the Italians at Tobruk
had been so far west of the front so that he had been able to move them
out of the way, covered by his motorised and armoured units. This was
no longer the case. He obtained little comfort from a message from
Cavallero on 1 November relaying Mussolini's congratulations for his
magnificent counterattack, and expressing his confidence that he would
bring the battle to a triumphant conclusion.[95] He bemoaned the fact
that his reputation was such that he was expected to perform miracles,
and any setback was attributed on high to sheer maliciousness. The
loss of yet another tanker, the *Tripolino*, was a further blow, seriously
limiting his ability to manoeuvre.

The fighting in the north was the most ferocious of all the
engagements in the El Alamein battles. The Panzer Army had launched
counterattack after counterattack that had reduced the immensely
tough and determined Australian 19th Division to a mere shadow of
its former self. But the Diggers, by bearing the brunt of the Axis counterattacks, had drawn them away from the point where Montgomery
planned to launch his next major offensive.

'Supercharge' began at 0100hrs on 2 November with seven
hours of attack by air and a 300-gun barrage lasting three hours.[96] This
was followed by an unimaginative frontal assault on the Panzer Army
immediately north of Kidney Ridge, which the commanding officer of
the 3rd Hussars, the dashing 'Colonel Push On', Lieutenant-Colonel
Sir Peter Farquhar, described to Montgomery with admirable candour
as 'suicidal'. Montgomery replied: 'It's got to be done. If necessary,
I'm prepared to accept one hundred per cent casualties in both personnel and tanks.'[97] That was almost what he had to accept. Tanks
with pathetic two-pounders were left with no alternative but to charge

anti-tank guns. Some overran the guns, but only a tiny handful of tanks survived the attack. Dust, smoke and freezing cold added to the infantry's misery and made a coordinated attack virtually impossible. The few who managed to reach their objectives found the ground so hard that they were unable to dig in, so that they were pounded remorselessly by the Panzer Army's artillery. 9th Armoured Brigade fought heroically, but failed to reach its objectives and was reduced to a smoking remnant in what amounted to a repeat performance of 23rd Armoured Brigade's Balaclava on 22 July. Leese's 1st Armoured Division was slow to follow up and profit from this fearless if misguided sacrifice. 9th Armoured Brigade had failed to break through the anti-tank screen so that 2nd Armoured Brigade following behind prudently decided to go on the defensive rather than make yet another suicidal charge.

The weakly held positions of 200 Panzergrenadier Regiment from 90 Light Africa Division were overrun within fifteen minutes. Further to the south, units of 155 Panzergrenadier Regiment from the same division along with 115 Panzergrenadier Regiment from 15 Panzer Division, as well as 9 Bersaglieri[98] and 65 Infantry Regiments from the Trieste Motorised Infantry Division, put up a stiff resistance, but were unable to halt Freyberg's New Zealanders, who pushed on towards the Telegraph Track (known to the 8th Army as Rahman Track). At daybreak 15 Panzer Division counterattacked from the north, 21 Panzer Division from the west, and the Littorio Armoured Division from the south in an attempt to cut off the 4 kilometre wide bridgehead. Montgomery poured in men and matériel and succeeded in breaking out to the south-west where the Trieste and Littorio Divisions had failed to get into position in due time. By 1600hrs Rommel had to bring up the Ariete to help plug the gap, but this left the southern flank wide open and bereft of motorised units.[99]

In spite of the overwhelming strength of the 8th Army, the Panzer Army had managed to contain the bridgehead, thus ensuring that 'Supercharge' had failed, but it was now at the end of its strength, having suffered crippling losses, including 20,000 men, most of whom were Italians. It had used up its reserves of ammunition and Rommel was fighting blindfold. The telephone lines were severed and the British had managed to jam most of his radio sequences. The situation at the front was chaotic, and everything depended on the tactical skills of local commanders.[100] Italian 4.7cm and German 5cm anti-tank guns proved to be worthless against most British armour, resulting in Italian units falling apart. The Littorio and Trieste Divisions panicked and fled to the west, their commanders no longer in control. The Panzer Army had used 450 tons of ammunition, but warships had delivered only 190 tons to Tobruk. Ritter von Thoma reported that the gaps in the front had been mostly stopped, and that the British infantry was extremely cautious, but he estimated that the British had a three or four to one advantage in tanks. The Afrikakorps was left with only thirty to thirty-five serviceable Panzer, a mass attack by 8th Army's armour was expected on the following day, and he doubted whether they could avoid a breakthrough, particularly as the Italians were utterly useless in defence. He said that he would begin to withdraw, fighting his way back. Rommel endorsed this assessment, pointing out that the Panzer Army was exhausted having fought for ten days against a vastly superior adversary. He did not have enough transport to move the six Italian and two German non-motorised divisions back, so they would almost certainly be overrun. Even the motorised units would be lucky to escape, since they were running short of ammunition. The shortage of fuel meant that it would be impossible to retire for any great distance, so he decided to move about 100 kilometres to the west to the Fuka Line, which had been carefully examined and replenished, meanwhile bracing himself for heavy losses from enemy aircraft on the way back.[101]

The Panzer Army was now in a desperate situation. Orders were given on 2 November for a partial withdrawal to shorten the front, but the move was also designed as the first stage of a withdrawal to Fuka. It was obvious that given the chronic shortage of fuel and vehicles, the bulk of the non-motorised troops would be overrun. The motorised troops would find it difficult to disengage. Those that were able to do so would be harassed, day and night, by the Desert Air Force. Panzer Army's staff concluded that, 'in spite of its heroic resistance and the outstanding morale of the troops, it is highly likely that a large part of the Army will gradually be destroyed'.[102]

On the following day 8th Army managed to advance to about 9 kilometres south of Sidi Abd el Rahman, where 125 Panzergrenadier Regiment had been withdrawn from its exposed position to behind the Telegraph Track. 90 Light Africa Division, the Afrikakorps and the 20 Italian Corps began a gradual withdrawal. But 8th Army failed to push home its advantage, enabling the Panzer Army to disengage in an orderly fashion. There were numerous armoured car raids on the rear echelons that proved very troublesome, disrupting supplies and making staff work even more difficult. The rear was dangerously exposed, because all available troops had been thrown into the main battle. Supply columns were under constant attack from armoured cars from the Royal Dragoons who had wormed their way through the Panzer Army's anti-tank defences and were causing severe damage in the manner of the LRDG and the Jock columns. Westphal reported that 'The already serious situation leaves us stretched to the limit.'[103] The whole nature of the war in North Africa had radically changed. What had been something approaching a colonial war was now a war of matériel, in which tactical skill, courage and morale were no longer significant. It was a war that the Axis could not possibly win. Rommel knew this, and Cavallero wrote on 30 October 'I have the impression that this is the end of the army,' adding that if the enemy continued their offensive it could only survive for two or three days.[104] Henceforth Cavallero closed his eyes, refusing Rommel's repeated requests to come to the front and discuss the situation. Kesselring did likewise. Urgent warnings from Skl that the situation in the Mediterranean was critical were dismissed by OKW as overly pessimistic. Hitler, who was suddenly obsessed with a possible threat to Crete, prepared to depart for Munich to celebrate the anniversary of his attempted putsch in 1923.

During the evening of 2 November Rommel wrote to OKW saying that although the troops had fought splendidly and spirits were still high, given the overwhelming superiority of the British in infantry, tanks, artillery and in the air, he would have to begin a withdrawal the following night to Fuka. The Panzer Army had fuel for 1.7 days and was running short of ammunition, with precious little in dumps to the west, having lost the *Brioni* in Tobruk harbour with 300 tons of ammunition on board. There was also a serious lack of trucks that would render the withdrawal all the more difficult. He concluded his report on a sombre note: 'In this situation I have to reckon with the gradual destruction of the army, in spite of its heroic resistance and the troops' exceptional spirit.'[105] Rommel's message came as a bombshell. OKW had been concentrating on the campaign in the Soviet Union, and with its absolute faith in Rommel's invincibility, had almost completely ignored the fighting at El Alamein.

A second message from Rommel arrived at 0300hrs on 3 November informing OKW that he had begun to withdraw at 2200hrs. The officer who received the message, a fifty-year-old major

on the reserve, a man well known for his reliability, failing to understand its importance, did not report it to his immediate superior. It was
not until 0900hrs on 3 November that Warlimont read it as he prepared
for his daily conference. He immediately passed it on to Hitler, at the
same time warning the unfortunate major to get everything ready for
the thorough investigation of the incident that was bound to follow.

At 1200hrs Hitler's adjutant Major Engel stormed into Jodl's
office where Warlimont had just begun to give his daily report, and
demanded to know at what time Rommel had made his end of the
day report in which he announced that the withdrawal had begun.
Hitler had noticed that he had only received this message shortly before
Rommel's next message, sent at 0800hrs on 3 November, had been
given to him. Hitler then arrived on the scene in a towering rage,
placing all the blame on Keitel for the failure of his staff. He then calmed
down somewhat and the midday conference proceeded normally. When
it was over he ordered Keitel to stay behind, lashing out at him in
such a hysterical tone that his words could be clearly heard through
double doors.

Warlimont went back to his office where he almost immediately
received an order to appear before Hitler with the duty officer. He found
Field Marshal Keitel, who had come to collect the hapless major, in an
extremely agitated state. Hitler, who obviously thought that there was
a conspiracy to withhold vital information,[106] leaving him with a fait
accompli, told the major that if he did not tell the complete truth he
would be a dead man 'within ten minutes'. Warlimont was removed
from an office he had served with great distinction for four years,
without even being given the chance to tell his side of the story. Jodl
did nothing to defend Warlimont. He briefly attended his farewell party,
where all he could say was that the Führer's will was 'definitive'. The
major was reduced to the ranks and posted to a detention battalion.
Hitler's adjutant, General Rudolf Schmundt, a fanatical anti-Semite
who was killed in the 20 July bomb plot, at least had the decency
to intervene in an attempt to have the major's punishment reduced
and Warlimont's dismissal reversed. He succeeded in the latter, but
Warlimont was so incensed at the way he had been treated that he
asked for time to think it over, remarking that he would not tolerate a
repeat performance.[107]

The Panzer Army was exhausted and it was difficult to see how
the infantry could possibly be withdrawn in an orderly fashion given the

chronic lack of transport. By 1942 the Italians had a ratio of vehicles to men of 1:19, while the Germans had 1:3 or 4.[108] Rommel had to reckon with the gradual destruction of his painfully slow-moving army and was obliged to inform OKW and OKH of this dire situation. He described 3 November as one of the most unfortunate days in history. He now knew that the desert campaign was lost, and complained that the desperate situation facing his troops was made even worse by constant meddling from Comando Supremo and OKW. That day he wrote to his wife: 'the battle is going very heavily against us. We're simply being crushed by the enemy's weight. I've made an attempt to salvage part of the army. I wonder if it will succeed. At night I lie eyes wide open, racking my brains for a way out of this plight for my poor troops.'[109]

At 1330hrs he received the following message from Hitler:

> *The German* Volk *and I are following the heroic defensive battle in Egypt with absolute confidence in your abilities as a leader, and in the bravery of the German and Italian troops under your command. In the situation in which you find yourself there can be no other thought than to stand by your post, not to take even one pace back, and to throw every available weapon and every available soldier into the battle. Substantial reinforcements of air force units will be sent in the next few days to the Supreme Commander South. The Duce and the Comando Supremo will also do everything possible to ensure that you get the necessary means to continue the fight. The enemy is worn out, in spite of his superiority. This is not the first time in history that resolute willpower shall prevail over the enemy's stronger battalions. There is only one alternative that you can offer your troops: victory or death.[110]*

A second message from Mussolini ordered him to hold the line and not to think of retreat.

Rommel was shattered by this senseless order from the Führer. He muttered to a junior staff officer: 'The Führer must be mad!' Hitherto he had enjoyed a close relationship with Hitler, had been able to get his way, and had an exceptional freedom to act as he saw best. Now he was being asked to do the impossible. He and his entire staff were left speechless. Rommel saw no alternative but to obey. He expected absolute obedience from his subordinates, and felt that as a soldier he had to carry out the orders of his superiors. He promptly issued an order to all units to stand fast and fight until victory in the present battle was won.[111] At the same time he reported directly to Hitler that Italian divisions to the south had been moved back to shorten the front. The losses of German infantry, anti-tank units and pioneers now amounted to about 50 per cent; 40 per cent of the artillery had gone, and the Afrikakorps was left with only twenty-four Panzer. The Littorio and Trieste Divisions had been virtually wiped out, but Rommel still assured the Führer that 'the utmost is being done to ensure that we hold our ground on the battlefield'.[112] He was later to recover his self-confidence and attributed this temporary weakness to shock and amazement. At the same time he sent a message to Hitler saying that if he stayed put the Panzer Army would be lost, as well as the whole of North Africa. He promised to obey, but detailed the heavy losses he had sustained. Hitler's order had a shattering effect on the entire Panzer Army, which knew it was doomed if it stood and fought. Rommel was given only a temporary respite, thanks to 8th Army's astonishingly sluggish and hesitant behaviour that left him utterly amazed.[113] The Afrikakorps reported during the evening of 3 November that were the British to continue the attack the next day, they were certain to break through. If the Panzer Army did not begin a 'flexible withdrawal' it would be destroyed. The 8th Army's lethargy that day offered an excellent opportunity to withdraw safely, but now this was denied.

Four reasons were given for the lost battle: the enemy's superiority in the air and with armour, incessant bombing with virtually no response from the Luftwaffe, the pathetic performance of the Italians, and the 8th Army's overwhelming superiority in modern weapons. The Afrikakorps did not even have enough fuel for the pitifully few remaining Panzer to withdraw as far as Mersa Matruh.

Rommel was still fuming about Hitler's senseless order, complaining that 8th Army's lethargy during the night of 3/4 November had provided an excellent opportunity to withdraw safely that had been lost, when Kesselring arrived at his headquarters. There followed an ugly exchange, with Rommel accusing his visitor of being responsible for Hitler's order to stand and fight to the last man, by having painted far too optimistic a picture of the situation. Kesselring denied this, and agreed that Rommel should be given freedom of action, regardless of Hitler's order. He promised to report to Hitler to this effect.

That evening Westphal, knowing that he had Rommel and Kesselring's support, told the Afrikakorps that if they could no longer withstand the pressure they were free to retreat. Hitler remained convinced that if his will had not been frustrated by the incompetents in Sperrkreis II, Rommel would have held fast at El Alamein, where he would have ultimately prevailed. In London Brooke read the decrypt of Hitler's order, which made him feel as if he was 'treading on air'.[114]

Rommel was disdainful of the usual assurances that massive reinforcements were on the way, the assertion the British were on their last legs, and the habitual guff about willpower being of greater importance than battalions. He therefore decided to send his well-connected and impeccably National Socialist aide, Alfred-Ingemar Berndt, on yet another visit to Hitler's headquarters with orders to put all the cards on the table, point out that the desert campaign was almost certainly lost, and to ask that Rommel be given complete freedom to act as he saw best.[115]

Berndt arrived at Hitler's headquarters in East Prussia on 4 November and reported to the Führer that evening. He found great favour in Hitler's eyes by pointing to Rintelen as the villain of the piece. Berndt insisted that it was owing to his incompetence, and his failure to impress upon the Comando Supremo the urgency of Rommel's requests, that the Panzer Army was starved of supplies. This was, of course, utterly preposterous. The problem was due entirely to the fact that so many cargo ships had been sunk, the harbours in North Africa bombed, the lighters shot to pieces by the RAF and the Royal Navy. Berndt reported that Rommel claimed that the positions at Fuka and Mersa Matruh could not possibly be held. The best that could be achieved was for General Nehring to bring fresh troops up to the Libyan/Egyptian border and establish a defensive position to which the Panzer Army could retire. Hitler ordered that 47 Infantry Regiment, both battalions of the 5 Parachute Regiment plus, if possible, 7 Parachute Division, be sent to North Africa as quickly as possible. Furthermore, twelve Tigers and twelve Panzer IIIs that had been sent to Italy should be shipped to Tripoli immediately. Two groups of fighters were to be moved from the eastern front, along with a Luftwaffe Battle Group from Norway, to be sent to Sicily. Ten 88mm anti-aircraft guns, model 41, were to be sent from Thessaloniki to North Africa. Henschel in Kassel had produced fifteen Tigers in the past month, destined for North Africa. However, all this was hedged about with words such as 'immediate transport', 'some' heavy Panzer, 'at once' and 'soon', long since shown to be nothing but empty promises that betrayed a complete lack of understanding of the precarious position of the Axis troops in North Africa.[116] Berndt returned several days later with the news that Hitler had airily announced that Rommel was not to worry about Tunis, and that he should stay put at Mersa el Brega. This merely confirmed Rommel's belief that the Führer was out of touch with reality. Berndt also said that Hitler had been noticeably moody and unfriendly, although he sent a message to Rommel assuring him of his 'very special confidence'.[117]

Back in Rome Ciano's confidant, Otto von Bismarck, painted a very bleak picture of the situation in Libya, a view that was endorsed by Cavallero, who had known for some time that all was not well. Mussolini talked in terms of retreating to Fuka, but Cavallero now argued that the only position that could be defended was at Sollum–Halfaya. As a withdrawal seemed in danger of turning into a rout, Mussolini felt that Libya was lost. He put a brave face on this, claiming that they could now concentrate on the defence of the homeland. Responsible figures such as the industrialist Alberto Pirelli, Generals Fougier and Gambara, as well as Admiral Mancini, realised that the game was up, whereas those lower down the ranks imagined that this was just another episode in the back-and-forth chase across the desert.[118]

On 4 November Horrocks' 13th Corps took the positions to the south that had been abandoned by the Italians the previous evening. Rommel's staff, seeing this as an attempt to turn the flank to the south of Fuka, sent their 500-man Main Support Group (*Kasta*) to try to plug the gap, but in spite of an arduous night march they arrived too late to save the situation. The Kasta then returned to take up its usual duty of protecting Rommel and the Panzer Army's command post. This proved to be an arduous duty, as they were frequently under attack from the Long Range Desert Group, whose courage and skill they had long since learnt to respect. Their lives were also made all the more miserable by sickness, with sixty-six of their members suffering from jaundice and kidney infections.[119] In the centre, units from 7th Armoured Division attacked the Italian 21 Division which had already begun to withdraw. Rommel promptly issued orders that the Trento and Bologna Divisions should about turn and face the enemy, as both Hitler and Mussolini had ordered the previous day. The Ariete Armoured Division got into serious difficulties when attacked from the south by about a hundred tanks.

A substantial part of the division was destroyed, large numbers of prisoners taken, in spite of a courageous counterattack, while the remnant just managed to fight its way north to link up with the Afrikakorps. This left the Panzer Army's right flank dangerously exposed, so that the Afrikakorps and 90 Light Africa Division were in dire danger of being encircled. The Littorio Armoured Division and the Trieste Motorised Division were decimated, so that virtually all that was now left was the Afrikakorps and the remains of 90 Light Africa Division, placed in a thinly manned reversed crescent, with 90 Light Africa Division dangerously exposed in a forward position to the north, about 15 kilometres south of the railway. They were eventually joined to the south by the remnants of Ariete, the Littorio and the Trieste Divisions from 20 Italian Armoured Corps, who had fought their way back with exceptional bravery in their wretched tanks, against a host of heavy tanks. Rommel generously reported this exceptional achievement by his much-denigrated allies.[120] The disaster on 4 November was due in large part to Hitler's order to stand and fight, which meant that the Italians had not been able to withdraw in a timely manner.

At 0800hrs the Afrikakorps faced a frontal attack by about 150 tanks aimed at the point where 21 and 15 Panzer Divisions joined. Initially Thoma managed to hold the line, but during the afternoon 1st and 10th Armoured Divisions broke through to the north at five different points, surrounded the Afrikakorps command post, and Thoma was taken prisoner.[121] The circumstances of Thoma's capture are a matter of dispute. Bayerlein claimed that he was standing by a burning Panzer in a hail of fire, while others insist that he was cowering in a trench, waiting to be taken prisoner.[122] Whatever the truth, Thoma was an exceptionally gallant officer and gentleman, who commanded his men from the front. He had donned his medals, an unusual habit in the desert, and gone to the front, remarking sourly 'as Rastenburg had ordered', thus underlining the futility of Hitler's order, even though it was one that as a soldier he felt he had to obey. He surrendered to an equally admirable soldier, Captain Grant Washington Singer of the 10th Hussars, who had directed the fire that disabled the Panzer besides which Bayerlein claimed to have seen him standing. Thoma went up to Singer, saluted, handed over his pistol and shook hands. He gave his binoculars to Singer's driver, Trooper Lindsay, who drove Singer and his captive off to 8th Army's Tactical Headquarters, where he dined with Montgomery. He told Montgomery that the Germans

were convinced that they had lost the war, and that the Wehrmacht
was solidly anti-Nazi, because it was Hitler who had got them into this
mess.[123] Singer was killed in action the next day, whereupon Thoma
wrote an exceptionally sensitive and moving letter of sympathy to his
widow.[124] Rommel, fearful of Hitler's reaction were he to hear that
Thoma had surrendered, wrote in his account of the North African
campaign that he had fought in the front line, intent on dying at his
post.[125] The daily report to OKW underlined that Thoma had fought
with great distinction and gallantry.[126]

Assured of Kesselring's support, Rommel decided that 90 Light
Africa Division, which was putting up a tremendous fight against the
Australians, as well as the adjacent left flank of 21 Panzer Division,
should pull back if necessary. Bayerlein, who commanded the Afrikakorps, in place of Thoma, passed on this order shortly after 1400hrs,
stressing that there should be 'no unnecessary sacrifices'.[127] Major-
General Raymond Briggs' 1st Armoured Division broke through the
centre of the Afrikakorps' position at 1500hrs and headed north-west.
The right flank of 15 Panzer Division to the south was broken, while
the New Zealanders in Major-General A. F. Harding's 7th Armoured
Division broke through the Italian 20 Armoured Corps further to the
south. Montgomery was at last out in the open, in a position to trap
the entire Panzer Army by pushing up to the coast to the north-west.
The Panzer Army Africa took a terrible beating that day, with the
8th Army's overwhelming superiority reducing it to a series of isolated
battle groups.[128] When he heard that the Ariete had been overrun,
Rommel ordered a general withdrawal to the Fuka Line at 1530hrs,
without waiting for Hitler's reply to his request for freedom of action.[129]
He concentrated his forces on the high ground to the south so as to
frustrate the attempt to outflank the Panzer Army. Rommel was at last
beginning partially to rethink his attitude towards the Italians. He said
of Italy's best armoured division: 'In the Ariete we lost our oldest Italian
comrades, from whom we had probably always demanded more than
they, with their poor armament, had been capable of performing.'[130]
Rommel's message to Hitler asking for permission to withdraw read:

> *During the last few days the enemy has succeeded in*
> *breaking through the front line on a 10 kilometre front to a*
> *depth of 15 kilometres, with 4,000–5,000 tanks and strong*
> *infantry units, thereby destroying our defences and almost*

wiping out our frontline troops. Everything possible was done to hold the front, but the losses are so high that it is no longer possible to hold an unbroken front.

We cannot expect any fresh German troops. Given the enemy's overwhelming superiority in the air and on land the Italian troops have no fight left in them. Some of the Italian infantry has already begun to abandon safe positions against orders.

I am fully aware of the need to hold on to the bitter end, and not take a single step back.

But I also know that the English tactic of destroying our units one after another, by maintaining constant artillery barrages and aerial attack, is using up our last ounce of strength.

I therefore think that mobile warfare, in which we fight over every inch of ground, is the only way of hitting back at the enemy, and of avoiding the loss of the North African theatre.

I request permission to do so.

If this is granted I intend to make a fighting withdrawal to the Fuka Line. This front, about 70 kilometres long and 30 kilometres deep, is almost impossible for armoured units to cross.[131]

It was not until 2045 hrs that Rommel learnt that Berndt's mission had been successful, and that Hitler had agreed to a withdrawal. The message read: 'The situation is such that I accept your decision. The Duce has given the necessary orders via the Comando Supremo.'[132] This was a rare instance of Hitler giving way against his instinctive judgement. With his absurd belief in fanatical willpower, he never believed that it was necessary for Rommel to withdraw from El Alamein. On 12 December he ranted on about Rommel, insisting that he had had enough fuel, after all he had retreated hundreds of kilometres and 'had not done that on water'. He claimed that both Kesselring and Ramcke argued that there had been no reason whatsoever to withdraw, because 'the English were completely routed; all we had to do was to push on and attack from some flank'. The only possible explanation was that Rommel had completely lost his nerve. Göring fully agreed with him.[133] Hitler had lost faith in Rommel, and realised that he was no

22. Abandoned German position at El Alamein (IWM:E 18657)

longer a loyal myrmidon. Rommel was bitterly disillusioned by Hitler's attitude. Not only was he outraged at Hitler's order to stay and fight, he now realised that the campaign in North Africa was lost, and that given the overwhelming superiority of the Allies in men and matériel the war could not possibly be won. He wrote to his wife in November 1942: 'What will become of the war if we lose North Africa? How will it finish? I wish I could be free of these terrible thoughts.'[134] Rommel realised that the decisive battle in North Africa had been lost. He attributed this to the lack of supplies, the overwhelming Allied superiority in the air and the absurd order to stand and fight to the last man and the last round. He wrote: 'The bravest of men cannot fight without a gun, the best guns are worthless without ammunition, and in mobile warfare guns and ammunition are virtually worthless if they cannot be moved around in vehicles with enough petrol.' Air superiority was also a vital component of victory because the lines of communication could

351 / El Alamein: defeat

be destroyed from the air. This was now to a large extent a battle of
attrition fought from the air, with overwhelming air power seriously
limiting operational and tactical options. The 'gabardine swine' from
GHQ and other members of the 'Short Range Shepheard's Group' might
poke fun at the 'flying fairies' of the Desert Air Force as they sipped
their cocktails on the hotel's riverside terrace, but theirs was an essential contribution to the defeat of the Panzer Army at El Alamein. The
8th Army had avoided a fight in the open, and opted for an unimaginative battle of attrition that, with its overwhelming quantitative and
qualitative superiority in matériel, it was almost bound to win. Rommel was generous in his praise for the disciplined training of the British
infantryman, the speed and accuracy of the artillery, and the skill and
courage of the air forces. The use of armour was still the 8th Army's
greatest weakness. Indeed the British army never came anywhere near
matching the Germans or the Red Army in its use in the exploitation
phase after a breakthrough or in the 'deep battle'. Rommel was outraged that his old enemies and rivals, whom he dismissed as 'desktop
strategists', began to suggest that he was a defeatist and implied that
his men had thrown down their weapons and run away. He felt that
his only fault had been not to have ignored Hitler's ludicrous 'death or
victory' order 24 hours earlier.[135] Even after the Panzer Army had narrowly escaped a crushing defeat at the Fuka Line, and was desperately
hanging on to the Mersa Matruh position, OKW was still out of touch
with reality. On 7 November its war diary reported that the situation
could be 'regarded with greater confidence', even though the battered
remnants of a small army, desperately short of fuel and ammunition,
faced ten British divisions, a brigade of Free French and two regiments
of 'Greeks and Levantines'.[136] The withdrawal from Mersa Matruh
to Sollum was a nightmare for traffic control. The roads were packed
nose to tail, with traffic jams up to a hundred kilometres long that were
constantly strafed by the Desert Air Force. The Panzer Army had to
find its way back along the narrow coastal strip, sown with minefields,
with the 8th Army constantly threatening an outflanking movement.
The Afrikakorps reconnaissance group (AA), the Menton Regiment
and the Italian 20 Army Corps fought desperately to ward off any
such attempt.

OKH attributed 8th Army's success at El Alamein to a number of factors. The shortage of ammunition made it impossible for
the Panzer Army to lay down counter-battery fire, thus at least partly
overcoming the tremendous superiority in artillery. As soon as ways

were cleared through the minefields, heavy tanks were brought to act as mobile artillery, closely followed by the infantry. The 8th Army was particularly skilled at night-time attacks, in which heavy tanks were also used. Attacks were usually spearheaded by heavy tanks, which came to within 1,800 metres, where they were out of the range of the Axis anti-tank guns, then picked off anti-tank and anti-aircraft guns as well as Panzer. Once they had achieved a breakthrough, they promptly sent in armoured cars that caused havoc to the rear echelons and supplies.[137]

November 1942, the month of doom in modern German history, was a major turning point in the war. Rommel had been beaten and forced to retreat at El Alamein. The Allies landed in North Africa and the Red Army completed the encirclement of Stalingrad. The Germans still had a great deal of fight left in them, but they had finally lost the initiative.[138] Precious few saw that the writing was on the wall, least of all Hitler and his sycophantic entourage. Or were his senseless orders to stand and fight, and his dreams of winning back what had been lost, preparation for a national suicide, the Third Reich's Götterdämmerung?

10 ✠ TORCH

During the summer of 1942 rumours of an Allied landing began to circulate, but it was never clear where this would be. North Africa was an obvious possibility, but it was one of many. Perhaps they would opt for Portugal or Spain, maybe in Spanish or French Morocco, the Azores or even Cape Verde. The German embassy in Stockholm reported that a large force of British and American troops, possibly up to five corps, was being assembled in Scotland. The news that Eisenhower had been promoted to Lieutenant-General on 7 July was taken by the Budapest embassy to be indication that a second front under his command was envisaged. After some further reflection the ambassador, Dietrich von Jagow, felt that it would likely be in North Africa. The badly bungled Dieppe raid in August was taken as further evidence that an invasion was on the books, with North Africa as the most likely spot. At the end of August Eberhard von Stroher reported from Madrid that the Spanish air minister, Juan Vigón, had hinted that there would be a landing in Tunis or Algeria, probably in October. This was confirmed in Paris on 25 September by Otto Abetz, the ambassador to Vichy, whose sources in the Vatican indicated that the invasion would be sometime between the middle of October and the middle of November.[1]

The volume of rumours increased, fed by British deception, indicating a landing in Belgium, Holland, Denmark, other places in Africa and even the Middle East. Hitler was particularly worried that there would be an invasion of Norway, but the main weight of the evidence was that it would be in North Africa.[2] By October Comando Supremo was convinced it would be in French North Africa, but Kesselring assumed that increased activity in the Mediterranean was in order further to strengthen Malta, rather than in preparation for an invasion.

Cavallero, arguing that precautionary actions against such an eventuality should take precedence over preparations for the occupation of Vichy France, insisted that several divisions should be sent to North Africa to meet the threat.[3] Kesselring finally agreed with the Italians' assessment, while Skl thought the landing would be further east between Tripoli and Benghazi. Hitler and Jodl agreed. On 17 October, the day that the first troopships left British ports, there were eight U-boats positioned along an east–west line, 70 sea miles long, west of the Bay of Biscay, but Dönitz ordered them south, assuming that this convoy was heading for West Africa. On 31 October air reconnaissance spotted two aircraft carriers 280 sea miles west of Cape Finisterre, but there were not enough aircraft available to follow their course, and Dönitz failed to send the twelve U-boats stationed to the west of Cape Saint Vincent to engage these two ships, because they were attacking a convoy off the coast of West Africa. Even when this operation was successfully completed the commander-in-chief of the U-boats (BdU) failed to send them to cut the carriers off at the Straits of Gibraltar. The huge 'Torch' convoy across the Atlantic was also not spotted by U-boats.[4] As late as 4 November OKW imagined that the armada assembled in Gibraltar, which included one battleship, two aircraft carriers, five cruisers and twenty destroyers, was probably designed for the protection of another convoy to Malta. They showed no concern about the possibility of an imminent landing.[5] On 6 November Göring took it upon himself to pass on Hitler's views to Kesselring. He dismissed out of hand the idea of a landing in French North Africa. Blissfully disregarding the fact that the Luftwaffe was exhausted and the Italian navy barely seaworthy, he ordered that the armada with 190 escort ships should be 'attacked and destroyed by day and by night.' This was followed by a message from the Führer to all German naval vessels in the Mediterranean: 'The existence of the Africa Army depends on the destruction of English forces. I expect a ruthless and victorious action.'[6] The following day Hitler twice ordered Rintelen to urge the Italians to make preparations for the defence of Tripoli and Benghazi, including the erection of roadblocks.

Hitler was now on his way to Munich for the annual jamboree with his old comrades to celebrate his 1923 putsch. He received news of the Allied landings while his train was in the middle of Thuringia. He could do little but remind the French of their promise to defend their overseas possessions against any attack. They initially obliged, resisting the Allied landings at several points. A message from Hitler's headquarters, the 'Wolf's Lair' in East Prussia, to the effect that the Panzer Army was now threatened on two fronts and could not possibly survive, was ignored amid a torrent of geo-political and strategic obfuscation from the Führer.[7]

In Rome Anna Maria von Bismarck told Ciano that at the German embassy everyone was 'literally terrified' by this blow, and that her husband's dire forebodings were once again confirmed.[8]

No adequate preparations had been made to meet the threat of an Allied invasion of North Africa, beyond the decision that Vichy France would have to be occupied. Even as late as October 1942 OKW imagined that the French would defend their overseas territories, but Hitler was becoming increasingly dubious. The Italians were in no position to master the situation, as they readily admitted. Rome was plunged into gloom, faced with the prospect of an invasion once the Panzer Army had been destroyed. This temporary reprieve was unlikely to last more than a couple of months. Hitler was in a state of extraordinary helplessness: short of issuing a blustering order to the navy and urging the Italians to do what they could to defend Tunis, he did absolutely nothing. He gradually woke up to the fact that with the Allies firmly established in Tunis, the next likely step would be the invasion of the Balkans, southern France or Italy, which would leave the enemy with a base in continental Europe, and probably lead to the destruction of his closest ally. It is for this reason that he would not listen to the likes of Rommel and Colonel Baron Horst Treusch Buttlar-Brandenfels, head of operations in Warlimont's Armed Forces Command Staff (WFSt), who were arguing that North Africa was lost, and that the Panzer Army should be withdrawn.[9] He now imagined that with the occupation of Vichy France and Tunisia the situation could be stabilised. The Allied forces in French North Africa would be stopped, rendering an invasion of southern France impossible, Rommel's rear echelons would be safe, and the Axis navies and air forces would still be able to operate in the Mediterranean. All this was well and good, but how could it possibly be realised? As Warlimont remarked of Hitler: 'His every thought and action became increasingly centred on holding what had been won, winning back what had been lost, and never giving up anything anywhere.'[10] Whereas Rommel called for an African Dunkirk, Hitler ordered, as he told Mussolini, a 'Mediterranean Verdun'. Jodl argued that 'North Africa is the glacis of Europe and must be held under all circumstances. If it is lost we must expect an Anglo-Saxon attack against south-eastern Europe via the Dodecanese, Crete and the Peloponnese; we must therefore pacify and secure the Balkans.'[11] By the end of December 50,000 German and 18,000 Italian troops were sent to Tunisia, to be followed by 100,000 more Germans and 10,000 Italians.

November 1942 was a decisive month. The Panzer Army had been smashed at El Alamein, the 'Torch' landings were successful, and in the Soviet Union the Wehrmacht was heading for crushing defeat at Stalingrad. The Wehrmacht had 260 divisions in the field, of which 230 were on the defensive, but Hitler still dreamt that a mere seven divisions was all that was needed for a renewed offensive in North Africa that would destroy the 8th Army, and leave the Germans in possession of the Suez Canal. Tunisia was for him the 'cornerstone of the southern flank of the European war'. The sea route to Tunisia had to be secured, armoured units poured into this bridgehead, U-boats were to destroy enemy convoys, and the Panzer Army would once again drive east.[12] It is truly amazing that the sycophants in OKW failed to realise that this was all pure fantasy, and that Hitler had long since lost touch with reality.

Roosevelt had managed partly to overcome his innate distrust of Churchill, had overruled the united opposition of the military to a landing in North Africa, had flown in the face of widespread sentiment that America was being duped into pulling British chestnuts out of the fire while they dawdled along the North African coast, to order an exceedingly complex and hazardous operation that achieved almost complete strategic surprise. The Germans were not only caught off balance, they failed to realise that the war had now entered a new phase. Here at last was a combined strategy that was to impose its pattern upon the rest of the war. The American military were frustrated that 'Torch' had taken precedence over 'Sledgehammer', a landing in northern France. The Soviets were furious that they had not got a second front. But the Normandy landings would never have been so successful had valuable lessons not been learnt in North Africa and Sicily. Roosevelt had two powerful arguments for postponing 'Sledgehammer'. Unlike his overly optimistic service chiefs, he knew it would be a singularly hazardous operation; it would also be a largely British affair. Within a year or so the United States would be very much the senior partner in the alliance. Dwight D. Eisenhower was in command of 'Torch' and it was hoped that an American general would pull off a relatively easy victory, after a series of setbacks and defeats, in a year of Congressional elections. Churchill, who was more concerned about shoring up Britain's imperial pretensions than he was about defeating Germany, was in favour of delaying a cross-channel invasion. Roosevelt wanted a delay so as to ensure American predominance over the Atlantic Alliance.

The landing craft for 'Torch' were in position on 7 November and by midnight the first units were ready to go ashore. The Americans had already established contact with the group of French dissidents known as 'les cinq' who planned to create an independent French North Africa, should the Germans occupy Vichy. The Allies had chosen to ignore de Gaulle, putting their money on General Henri Giraud, who had made a spectacular escape from a prisoner of war camp in Königstein in Saxony and had managed to return to Vichy, where he received a hero's welcome. The Germans reacted to Giraud's escape by arresting Weygand and taking him to Königstein as a suitable replacement.[13] Giraud, tall, moustached and swaggering, soon turned out to rival de Gaulle in arrogance, self-assurance and high-mindedness. He even had the gall to inform the Allies that the price of his co-operation was to be put in command of the Anglo-American invasion of North Africa.[14]

OKW seriously misread the situation. They imagined that 'Torch' involved only American troops. They failed to notice that landings had also taken place at Oran. They assumed that the French would offer stiff resistance to the invaders. Buttlar clearly realised that North Africa was lost, but he was in East Prussia at the Wolf's Lair, while Hitler and his entourage were in Munich, so he played no part in the conference with the Italian and French foreign ministers, Ciano and Laval, at which vitally important political matters were discussed.[15] Hitler claimed that the 'Torch' landings were not a serious threat, certainly not as dangerous as the British landing in Norway, where the population had been solidly on their side. The conclusion of these talks was that the Germans and Italians would no longer send weapons as 'friendly support' to Vichy, because France had ceased to be 'well disposed and co-operative', and was now 'ambiguous in its attitude towards the Axis'. Hitler, refusing to consider a withdrawal, even though the attempt to persuade the French to join in the war came to nothing, ordered a strengthening of the German forces in Crete to help guard the sea lanes to North Africa. A bridgehead was to be built in Tunis in cooperation with the local French forces. Should the French refuse to cooperate they were to be disarmed. With the flight of Giraud, the lack of clarity over Darlan's stance, plus the fact that the French in Algeria had already laid down their arms and Laval had been singularly contrary during the discussions in Munich, this seemed to be more than a distinct possibility. Orders were given while Laval absented himself for a moment to smoke a cigarette, so that the claim that Vichy France was occupied and a joint bridgehead in Tunisia was established 'at the request of and with the consent of the French government' was a barefaced lie.[16] Operation 'Anton', the occupation of Vichy France, was to begin at 0710hrs on 11 November, significantly the date of the armistice in 1918.[17] To underline the importance of hanging on in North Africa, Rommel was ordered to establish a defensive position 'as far east as possible'.

'Anton' began ten minutes earlier than originally planned with the Italians hobbling five hours behind their allies. They were also obliged to postpone the occupation of Corsica because of high seas.[18] The operation was completed within a couple of days, although the naval base at Toulon was not taken until later in the month. The vast majority of the ships were sunk by their crews, much to the annoyance of the invaders. The Italian 4th Army occupied southern France up to the Rhône valley. After some altercations between Hitler and the Comando Supremo, it was placed under the command of Gerd von Rundstedt, commander-in-chief in the west.

The situation during these critical days was highly confused. Hitler was in Munich, uncertain where to go next, completely out of touch with his headquarters, without even a liaison officer to the chief of general staff. Warlimont had been recalled, initially to act as a liaison officer with the Vichy army, but when that project floundered he agreed to take back his old job. He sat in a special train in Munich station, where he tried to pick up the threads. His situation was made all the more difficult because Jodl ordered him not to attend any conferences with Hitler, who was still angry over the El Alamein incident. He was not allowed back into Hitler's inner circle until 19 November. At the Wolf's Lair the headquarters' staff were all at sea without their all-powerful Führer.[19] Eventually Hitler decided to move his headquarters from East Prussia to Salzburg, while he retired to his mountain home in Berchtesgaden to regain his strength and clear his mind. This led to further confusion. OKH remained in East Prussia and Zeitzler, who had replaced Halder as army chief of staff in September, seldom appeared at Berchtesgaden. The differences between OKW and OKH thus grew wider. Keitel and Jodl, along with Major-General Walter Buhle, chief of army staff at OKW, and Colonel Walter Scherff, OKW's official historian, were lodged at the house of Hans Lammers, Hitler's Cerberus and assiduous chief of chancellery, twenty minutes' drive away from the Berghof. The staff at Salzburg had their offices in a special train that was three-quarters of an hour away. The confusion and inefficiency resulting from these arrangements had a disastrous effect on military decision making, worsening the already serious November crisis.

The German navy managed to sink four warships and twelve transport vessels in the Atlantic and Mediterranean once they realised the Allies' intent. Between 8 and 15 November the Axis air forces sank a cruiser and five troopships, and bombed the ports of Algiers and Bougie, but since the troops had already landed this was something of a wasted effort. None of it seriously disrupted the Allied landings. Subsequent attacks of supply ships to North Africa resulted in the loss of eight U-boats, prompting Dönitz to argue that his men should concentrate on sinking freighters in the Atlantic. Hitler would hear nothing of this, insisting that top priority should be given to disrupting Allied operations in North Africa.[20] This conflict was a reflection of the fact that the U-boat fleet was now far too weak to be effective in either theatre.

The German Naval Command agreed with Rommel and Buttlar that with the defeat at El Alamein and the Allied landings, North Africa was lost. Skl suggested to Hitler that the Allies' next step would possibly be a landing on the Iberian peninsula, in order to deal with the submarine threat, an invasion of Italy or of the Balkans. Therefore the Axis should occupy the Iberian peninsula as well as Vichy France, because it was here that the Allies could move most easily 'once the French resistance in North Africa ceased'.[21] A plan for landings on the west coast of Spain and Portugal, codenamed 'Isabella', had already been drawn up on 9 May 1941, but the forces needed to carry this out were no longer available. A modified plan, 'Ilona', called for closing off the passes across the Pyrenees should the Allies be tempted to land on the Iberian peninsula. The Spanish government was not informed, but when an SS officer reported in September 1942 that he had lost his briefcase with detailed plans for 'Ilona', OKW thought it prudent to change the codename to 'Gisela', without making any changes in the plan.²² At the end of November three reserve divisions in southern France were ordered to move into position for 'Gisela', but lacking transport they stayed in place. Then 7 Panzer Division was made ready for 'Gisela', but on the next day it was sent to join Army Group Don. None of this made any sense. It was merely a sign of the Axis' dwindling resources and alarming lack of realism. As long as the British hung on to Gibraltar the Allies had no need to secure a foothold in Spain.²³

Meanwhile, Ribbentrop phoned his Italian homologue Ciano on 8 November, inviting him to come to Munich with Mussolini to discuss the situation in France with Hitler.²⁴ Laval had also been invited to attend. Mussolini had assumed that the Allied landings would be in French North Africa and that after a token resistance the French troops would lay down their arms. Hitler was of a contrary opinion. Even on the day of the landings he insisted that they would be at Tripoli or Benghazi, in order to cut off Rommel's line of retreat. On 8 November Jodl had ordered Rintelen to relay Hitler's assessment to Mussolini. The Duce stuck to his guns, so that Rintelen was sent a second time to persuade him otherwise. Hitler continued to insist that the Allies would not be so foolish as to land in French North Africa, because they knew that they would meet with fierce resistance. Mussolini proved to be absolutely correct. He now argued that the Allies would soon be in the position to invade Italy and that Germany should go on the defensive in the east, so as to concentrate on the dire threat in the Mediterranean.²⁵

Mussolini, who claimed not to be feeling well, ordered Ciano to go alone to meet Hitler. The meetings were far from cordial. Ciano referred to Ribbentrop as a 'tramp' and Hitler as a 'criminal'. Hitler 'played his gramophone record', which Ribbentrop parroted. He assumed that the long since agreed-upon plan to occupy Vichy France and Corsica, in conjunction with building up a bridgehead in Tunisia, would now go into effect. Ciano reported in his diary that he was relieved to find that Hitler and Göring were well aware of the serious-ness of the situation, but this seems to have been wide of the mark.²⁶ Hitler imagined that sending two Stuka groups and one fighter group to Tunisia was sufficient to give the Axis time to build up their forces. The German navy was far less confident, calling for 'the inclusion of the Iberian peninsula in the European power base'. This request was ignored. Hitler seemed largely unconcerned by the Allies' 'second front' in Tunisia. He discounted all apprehensions, announcing that Germany had suffered many military setbacks in the past, but had always emerged victorious. He was confident that Rommel would once again turn the situation around, as he had done in the winter of 1941/2. Hitler dismissed with a barrage of empty phrases Mussolini's pleas for a separate peace with the Soviet Union, or at least a halt to offensive operations so as to meet the threat in the west. The meeting reached no conclusions whatsoever, in spite of Ciano's final communiqué to the contrary. Rather in the eyes of many influential figures in Italy it marked an important stage in the dissolution of the Axis partnership. The meeting was described by Hitler's shrewd interpreter, Paul Schmidt, as 'shadow boxing in the obscurity of the Rastenburg forest'.[27]

The German position in Tunisia was made all the more difficult by the passive resistance and sabotage of French civil servants which caused serious disruptions in the electricity works, railways, tramways, mines and bakeries. The German envoy, Dr Rudolf Rahn, who had hitherto been responsible for propaganda in occupied France, tried to counter this by calling mass meetings attended by representatives of elements that were loyal to Vichy, including the French Popular Party (PPF), the veterans' organisation SOL, the youth group 'Companions de France' and the labour service 'Chantiers de jeunesse'. They were treated to rousing lectures on European solidarity, the struggle against Bolshevism and denunciations of the treacherous Gaullists.[28]

The Vichy minister of information, Marion, sent an energetic former Communist and experienced agitator, George Guilbaud, to support Rahn's efforts. Realising that it was pointless to try and play the Germans off against the Italians so as to preserve France's sovereign rights in Tunisia, he concentrated his propaganda on the struggle against Bolshevism and the Allied armies. He established a political police force that worked in close collaboration with local representatives of the SS and Security Service (SD), and began systematically to purge the administration of all untrustworthy elements. He uncovered an espionage network on the docks, a Gaullist radio transmitter, caches of arms, as well as an underground postal service. Funds were sent via Rauff's Einsatzgruppe to enable Guilbaud to take over the local newspaper and run 'Radio Tunis'. Control committees were established to deal with such matters as civil defence, public works, refugees, provisions, finance, economic affairs and policing. They managed to secure a certain degree of resentful co-operation between the various groups and factions in Tunis.

The situation in Bizerta was far more tense. On 11 November Admiral Derrien issued the following order:

After two days of restiveness and uncertainty I have been given the clear and unambiguous order as to the enemy against whom we are to fight: the Germans and the Italians are the enemy. Soldiers, sailors and airmen defend Bizerta and march valiantly against the enemy of 1940! Now is the time to take our revenge!

Later that day General Nehring, the French resident-general, Admiral Jean-Pierre Estéva, a dyed-in-the-wool collaborationist, who was Vichy's official representative, and Rahn met Derrien and persuaded him to rescind this order and declare his loyalty to Vichy. This he did without a murmur.

This complex political situation, in which opportunists and collaborators of every stripe wondered when was the best moment to abandon ship, was rendered even more difficult by the presence in Algiers of Admiral Darlan, the commander-in-chief of the French armed forces. He was visiting his son, who was being treated for polio. Darlan was an unprincipled opportunist and intrigant, whose Anglophobia was confirmed by Britain's 'betrayal' at Mers el-Kebir. He had twice met Hitler, to whom he had made offers of close co-operation, but like so many in Vichy France, he was undecided as to which way the wind was blowing. He had nothing much to offer in the way of resistance to the Allied invasion, but he also did not want to provoke Hitler into occupying Vichy France. This left the French forces uncertain how to react to the invaders. Initially, the French resisted them, inflicting severe casualties. The Armée d'Afrique killed about a thousand Americans before it prudently gave up the unequal struggle. Initial talks with General Barré, the commander of the 10,000 French forces in Tunisia, got nowhere, so Hitler and Mussolini agreed on the necessity of building a bridgehead in Tunisia. It was not until 10 November, when the Allied forces were safely ashore, that Darlan issued the order to all French units in North Africa to lay down their arms. The Germans marched into Vichy France on the following day, leaving Pétain powerless. No resistance was offered, so Pétain's assurance to Roosevelt that France would resist any invasion applied to the Allies, rather than to the Germans.[29] Pétain's authority was passed on to Darlan, who promptly appointed

Giraud commander-in-chief of the army, and Marshal Juin as head of the army in North Africa.

The Germans sent Captains Schürmeyer and Behlau on 9 November to discuss a common strategy against the Anglo-American invasion with Admiral Estéva and General Barré. General Péquin, commander-in-chief of the air force in the region, also attended the meeting, so that all three services were represented. The French delegates, having received no instructions from Vichy, were at a loss to know what to say.

Barré was left sitting extremely uncomfortably upon a fence. The following day he announced that the Germans could use the airfields at El Aouina and Bizerta, but were they to attempt to land military aircraft elsewhere they would be fired upon. He also issued a stern warning that Italian units should not be used in Tunisia. The Italian 23 Fighter Squadron landed in El Aouina regardless. The French protested, insisting that they should be sent back to Italy, and refused to allow them any provisions. The Axis studiously ignored this empty gesture. By the evening Barré, having been in touch with his government, was decidedly conciliatory. He agreed to withdraw his troops from Bizerta and Tunis, leaving the two ports to the Germans. This action proceeded slowly, prompting a rumour that the Tunis garrison would go over to the Americans.

On the morning of 9 November Hitler had personally given Kesselring 'a free hand in Tunisia' in order to strengthen the bridgehead. The same day Luftwaffe units were sent to Tunis under the command of Colonel Martin Harlinghausen. His group landed later that day and met with no resistance.[30] They were followed by units from 5 Parachute Regiment forming the 'Battle Group Schirmer', which secured the airfield and town of Tunis on 12 November. In the night of 13/14 November Colonel Harlinghausen posted guards at the exits to the town, seized the post office and all public buildings, in an action that prompted a protest from Estéva, who threatened retaliatory action. Estéva was given a dressing down the following day, when Admiral Platon arrived from Vichy. Platon complained that Estéva had not been cooperating with Barré and the Tunis garrison, and was not following Vichy's instructions. Estéva, who had not been given any clear orders, and who had to deal with a highly confusing situation, was exceedingly anxious and made a solemn declaration of his undying loyalty to Vichy. He repeated this assurance to Rahn, who described his attitude as one of 'benevolent neutrality'.[31] But he soon began to lodge a series of protests, so as to cover his rear should the Allies succeed in taking Tunis. Meanwhile, Platon ordered Barré to come to Tunis for discussions, but he refused on the grounds that he was far too busy, and suggested that the admiral come to his headquarters in Beja. Platon swallowed his pride and set off to meet Barré, but when he heard from the advance guards that they had been ordered to fire on the Germans, he suspected that a trap had been set for him. He discreetly returned to Tunis, having first issued an appeal to Barré's troops to resist the 'Anglo-Saxons', and making the empty gesture of relieving the rebel French generals in Algeria, Juin and Giraud, of their commands. Platon then requested that Vichy replace the 'apathetic' Estéva as well as the unreliable Barré. Their replacements were delayed, but were soon no longer relevant.

The Germans still had too few troops in Tunisia to resist, had Barré's men seized the mountain passes and guarded the main bridges. They were also fully dependent on French officials in Tunis for the port to function, as well as for electricity, gas, water and provisions. 'Incorrigible elements' who refused to co-operate would therefore, in Rahn's view, have to be 'neutralised or terminated'. Rahn immediately began negotiations with Barré, appealing to his soldierly duty and his honour as a Frenchman to follow Marshal Pétain's orders. He also obliged Estéva, a man whom he described as a feeble creature of liberal Christian views, who was regrettably under the influence of 'Jewish, Anglo-Saxon, and Masonic' elements within his administration, to issue an appeal to the French troops and the civil population to resist the invaders. He also wrote to Barré, repeating his argument that he should strictly enforce the instructions he received from Vichy. Barré assured Rahn that he had ordered his men not to fire on German troops, but warned that he would resort to force were the Germans to enter the area to which he had withdrawn his coastal garrisons, in accordance with the agreement reached between the Vichy government and Berlin over the use of the Tunisian ports. He stressed that he was particularly outraged that Italian troops had entered Tunisia without an agreement between Vichy and Rome.[32]

General Nehring, who arrived in Tunisia on 16 November, sent one of Rahn's staff to Barré to arrange a meeting. This eventually took place after a somewhat hair-raising journey. Barré gave the impression of being very confused, as he was obviously waiting for the Americans to arrive before openly siding with General Juin and the renegades. On 19 November a German reconnaissance aircraft was fired upon by his troops, whereupon Rahn demanded of Laval that Barré be dismissed, and that an appeal be made to all French troops in North Africa to desist from firing upon Axis troops. Pétain replied to Estéva the following day calling for a ceasefire, but he pointedly did not relieve Barré of his command.

The problem for the Germans now was that Barré's men were positioned in such a manner as to enable the Anglo-American forces to advance unhindered, and he not only refused to move, but had his guns trained on the Germans as Juin had ordered.[33] Another note was fired off to Laval, who replied that all French troops in North Africa had been ordered to resist the Anglo-American invasion, and those who refused to do so were guilty of disobeying orders. Pétain made a radio broadcast to this effect on 21 November that ended with the words: 'I am still your leader. You have only one duty: to obey. You have only one government: that to which I have given the power to govern. You have only one fatherland, which I incorporate: France.' Thousands of leaflets were printed with this message. Kesselring arrived on 20 November and promptly issued an ultimatum to Barré to lay down his arms and move out of the way. Barré did not reply. Kesselring was not perturbed. All French units were disarmed and demobilised on 8 December without any show of resistance, the officers having been subjected to a series of pep talks from Admiral Estéva and the redoubtable Guilbaud. All potential resistance having been broken, a labour service for building defences was peacefully instituted in February 1943, conscription beginning at the beginning of March.

Panzer General Walther Nehring, the former commander of the Afrikakorps, was placed in command of the army units in Tunisia, with Kesselring as his immediate superior. He was ordered to build a bridgehead that he was to extend as far west as possible.[34] The operation was given the codename 'Brown'.[35] Quite how he was to do this remained a mystery. All he had was the 'Battle Group Lederer' made up of one battalion of infantry, a company of Panzer, one artillery and two anti-aircraft batteries, along with a battalion of Italian infantry. This small force was called upon to carry out reconnaissance as far as Bône, resulting in an engagement with the British on 16 November, while building up his bridgehead as far east as Bizerta. Rudolf Rahn from the foreign office came with Kesselring as political envoy. He soon had his hands full when Communists and Gaullists went into action.[36] Nehring was given extravagant promises. He was to receive 10 Panzer Division from Marseille, which was in the process of replenishment, the Hermann Göring Division from Cognac, and the Kriemhild Division (334 Infantry Division) from Germany. Hitler ordered 47 Panzergrenadier Regiment and 190 Anti-tank Section (Pz Jäg Abt.190) to go to North Africa to make up for deficiencies. Each was to move as soon as it was ready. In fact the Kriemhild Division was as mythical as the vengeful woman after whom it was named. It existed only on paper. Only 10 Panzer Division and units from the Hermann Göring Division arrived in time to meet the Allies. 190 Anti-tank Section hung around in Italy for months and in spite of frequent requests from the Afrikakorps, it failed to arrive before the campaign was over.[37] Nehring's staff was soon renamed 90 Corps and in early December given the grossly inflated nomenclature of 5 Panzer Army. For the moment Nehring was preoccupied with wondering how he could possibly hold up the British advance before reinforcements arrived. Mussolini, who regarded Tunisia as one of Italy's 'aspirations', insisted that Italian troops should be sent there, so that this would be a joint operation. OKW was opposed to the idea, but gave way for the sake of maintaining the Axis alliance. The Germans imagined that the forces in the Tunis bridgehead would be able to drive the invaders out of Africa, while the Italians were more sceptical. They felt that the major task ahead was to cover Rommel's retreat from Cyrenaica.[38]

Pétain's broadcast, plus the announcement two days after Kesselring's arrival in Tunisia that a 'Falange des volontaires pour l'Afrique' had been formed, failed to impress the Germans.[39] When Darlan was assassinated on Christmas Eve by an aristocratic young royalist, whom the Germans were convinced was working for the British secret service, Eisenhower insisted that Giraud be appointed his successor.[40] Few Allied tears were wept for Darlan, who was widely considered to be a Quisling or a Judas, but although an unattractive character he had put an end to French resistance and thus saved a few Allied lives, at the cost of enraging the Free French and the indignation of principled anti-Fascists. Giraud soon revealed himself to be a well-groomed, reactionary windbag, singularly lacking in political nous. Admiral Derrien remained in Bizerta, determined to fight the Germans if they dared set foot in Tunisia, but was dissuaded from this rash action by Estéva.[41] He hardly needed to have bothered. When faced with a German ultimatum Derrien handed over the coastal batteries, the arsenal, his artillery, three motor torpedo boats, one destroyer, nine submarines and two reconnaissance ships, along with 10,000 troops, after which he collaborated dutifully with the occupation forces, running the port for them.

Hitler wrote two letters to Pétain explaining why he had been forced to occupy southern France. The first was sent on 10 November, explaining that the Anglo-Americans were intent on invading southern France and Corsica so Hitler was obliged to make this pre-emptive strike. On the following day the Abwehr, fearing an imminent Allied landing, called for detailed maps of Corsica. Hitler's second letter to Pétain, a seven-page screed dated 27 November, was a detailed reply to the marshal's protest note. Hitler claimed that 'treasonable French officers' had co-operated with the Anglo-American invasion force in French North Africa, thus rendering the Franco-German treaty null and void. Germany had nothing against France, and sincerely hoped that good relations would soon be restored when France had an army that obeyed its own government. Once this happened Germany would guarantee all France's colonial possessions. Working himself up into a frenzy of righteous indignation, Hitler continued in an all too familiar vein:

> *I have to represent the interests of a people that has been forced to go to war, and that is obliged to go on fighting for its self-preservation against those who started this war, and continue to fight with the aim of destroying all of Europe in the interests of a European, and partly non-European, Jewish-Anglo-Saxon clique.*
>
> *I have been forced in the last resort to continue this war in the name of those millions of people who want to free not merely their own country, which has managed to escape from the pressure of ruthless capitalist plundering, and which is not prepared to be an eternal victim, facing not only international exploitation, but the final destruction of its national identity* (Volkstums).[42]

Resistance to the landings by the French army was largely symbolic, the air force remained on the ground and only the navy offered any serious defiance. The Americans had to fight off a naval attack at

Casablanca, suffering a certain amount of damage in the process. The fighting at Port Lyautey to the north was even fiercer, involving land forces as well as the navy. The Centre Task Force that landed near Oran and the Eastern Task Force near Algiers were virtually unopposed. An Abwehr report suggested that news of the Allied landings was toasted in champagne, with people imagining that they would be liberated within three weeks. The report claimed that although the French still had great respect for the Wehrmacht, they detested the Nazi Party, could not understand Germany's racial laws, and pitied the fate of the Jews, particularly that of the children. Such indirect criticism of the Third Reich is indication that for some at least the writing was on the wall.[43]

Eisenhower's main problem was how to reach Tunisia before the Panzer Army arrived. It was an extremely difficult task to move an army through the rugged terrain of the Atlas. The supply problems were daunting. The British, who had wanted to land further east, felt vindicated. On 11 November they moved troops forward to Bougie, 150 kilometres east of Algiers, then to Bône on the following day. They were now only 100 kilometres from the Tunisian border, in possession of an adequate port and airfield. Axis planes caused some disruption, but it was not enough seriously to compromise the operation. On 16 November British paratroopers first exchanged fire with the 'Battle Group Lederer' at Djebel Abiod in Tunisia.

Once it was clear that the French would offer no serious resistance, Nehring ordered the formation of forced labour groups to build fortifications. Leaders of the Jewish community were ordered to organise such groups and to place them at the service of the occupation army. Unlike other groups they were treated as hostages, were unpaid, and the Jewish community services had to provide their food and equipment. The Italians soon raised objections, as they had done in Tripoli. They continued to insist that Jews with Italian citizenship be exempted from forced labour. In October 1942 the German consulate in Tripoli had given a detailed report to the foreign office on the effects of the Laws on Jewish Business Activities of 2 May 1942 and the Civil Mobilisation of Italian and Libyan Citizens of Jewish Race of 28 June 1942. The major obstacle was that the Italians did not have a Jewish census, so it was not possible to identify all the Jews between the ages of eighteen and forty-five. From the initial cull of 6,000, all of whom were under the age of thirty-one, only 600 were found to have the necessary skills. They

23. Jewish forced labour in Tunisia

were sent to work for the army in Cyrenaica. Since they were so few, they could not be employed as a separate group, which was seen to be a serious problem. A special commission was established to examine the issue, which decided that the Jews should be forced to work building the railway. They were to be given a medical test to see whether they were fit to undertake such onerous work, but this also proved highly unsatisfactory, because the doctors readily accepted bribes, so that a number of perfectly healthy men were exempted. The medical boards were then replaced by a lottery that resulted in 4,000–5,000 of Tripoli's estimated 16,000 Jews being forced to work. Payment was on the same miserably low scale as that for the Arabs. The consul bitterly complained that the two racial laws in force in Tripoli were not as comprehensive as those in Germany. They were not designed to isolate the Jews, nor were they an integral part of a systematic war on Jews. They were simply designed to overcome the chronic lack of manpower. This meant that the vast majority of Jews in Tripoli were able to go about their business as usual, with the inevitable harmful consequences for commerce and the civil administration. Jews managed to worm their way into military installations where they presented a serious potential danger. They also worked in offices where there was ample scope for corruption. The consul concluded his report by regretting that most of the local bourgeoisie were not particularly anti-Semitic. He assumed that this was because they imagined that were they to express strong anti-Jewish sentiments, they would be faced with certain commercial disadvantages.[44] It was not until the end of March 1943 that the French in Tunisia were forced to perform obligatory labour service for the Wehrmacht and the Reich Labour Service (RAD). Admiral Estéva organised this mobilisation in three age groups, and his residency was called upon to foot the bill.[45]

Obersturmbannführer Rauff's Einsatzgruppe, comprising six other officers and seven men, which had been withdrawn from Athens when it became clear that they would be unable to set to work in Egypt, was now sent to Tunisia, arriving on 24 November.[46] Three other officers – Obersturmführer Theo Saevecke, Sturmbannführer Georg Best and Untersturmführer Heinrich Harder – joined the group, which worked alongside units of the Security Police (SiPo) and the Security Service (SD).[47] The group was rapidly expanded to one hundred men, including sixteen German nationals who had been serving in the French Foreign Legion.

There were about 85,000 Jews living in Tunisia, of whom about 5,000 had Italian citizenship. The majority of them lived in Tunis.[48] The Jewish leadership in Tunis had been arrested before Rauff arrived, but they were soon released after pressure from the French authorities. Rahn, who later styled himself as the saviour of the Tunisian Jews, ordered the confiscation of all radio sets owned by Jews, claiming that they were used to spread Allied propaganda, and called for intensified anti-Semitic propaganda via the Arab radio. At a meeting between Nehring, Rahn and Rauff it was decided that Jewish forced labour should be employed to build the frontline defences. Rauff called the Jewish community leader, Moishe Borgel, and the chief rabbi, Haim Bellaïche, to his office and informed them that Borgel's council was to be abolished, and that Jews were to be forced to work for the Axis. A nine-man council was appointed with instructions to ensure that all German orders were promptly implemented. The council was ordered to find 2,000 Jewish labourers, failing which 10,000 Jews would be arrested. The labourers were to wear a large yellow Star of David on their backs, so that they could be easily identified and shot should they be tempted to desert.

It proved impossible to carry out Rauff's orders within the time allotted, whereupon he ordered his Einsatzkommando to go to the main synagogue where all present were arrested and sent to a camp at Cheylus, 65 kilometres south of Tunis. One handicapped young man was murdered on the way. Rauff then told Borgel that he had killed a number of Jews in Poland and the Soviet Union and would not hesitate to mete out similar treatment on their co-religionists in Tunisia if they did not fully collaborate. The Einsatzkommando then went to the Jewish community centre and arrested all present, demanding that a list should be made of one hundred prominent Jews, who would then serve as hostages to ensure that in future all German orders were promptly carried out. The council gave way to this pressure, ordering that all males between the ages of eighteen and twenty-seven were to present themselves for labour service.[49]

That Rauff did not set about murdering the Tunisian Jews is due in part to the opposition of both the Italians and the French, but the Tunisian bridgehead was a relatively confined space that only the wildly optimistic imagined would hold out for long. Shipping space was simply not available to send tens of thousands of victims to their death in the camps in Poland. Denied the opportunity to murder the Tunisian Jews, Rauff nevertheless made their lives as miserable as he possibly could during the five months of German occupation. All forms of chicanery, ranging from forced labour, to plunder and imprisonment, were employed. Conditions in the more than thirty labour camps were appalling. Those who were not eligible for labour service were heavily fined, on the pretext that 'international Jewry' was responsible for the bombing raids on Tunis. 'Compensation', totalling 50 million francs, was extracted, most of which was handed over to Arabs who professed support for the Germans. The Jewish community on the island of Djerba was ordered to pay a fine of 10 million francs. When this proved impossible, they were ordered to hand over 50 kilos of gold. In all 43 kilos were collected.

In neighbouring Morocco, Giraud set about reversing Vichy's racist legislation, removing all the pictures of Pétain in public buildings and sacking Vichy loyalists.[50] The German consul in Tangier, Rieth, was horrified to report that an Alsatian Jew by the name of Weill had been appointed to the constituent assembly, and that confiscated Jewish property was being restored to the rightful owners. Freemasons were given back their jobs in the civil service, while loyal Vichy supporters, German civilians and prisoners of war were being systematically tortured to death, and forced to work in chain gangs on the trans-Sahara

railway.[51] Laval made General Guillaume responsible for Pétainist propaganda in North Africa in order to counter Giraud, but it was far too
late in the day to be of any effect.[52]

The day after the Allied landings the Mufti gave a broadcast
address to the Tunisian Arabs, calling upon them to co-operate with
the Axis and create a 'Maghrebian Liberation Army'. The Mufti
assured the Germans that 'They [the Maghrebi] sympathise with the
Axis because of its previous enmity to France and its opposition to the
Jews, and because of the submission of the Anglo-Saxons to Jewish
influence. These feelings are well known...'[53] OKW were keen to
encourage the North Africans to fight against the Allies, and were
heartened by the Mufti's bland assurances that they would. Rahn
supported this initiative, even though it was bound to be anathema to
the Italians, to say nothing of Vichy France, but warned that it would
probably result in pogroms and the plunder of French property. This,
he thought, was an acceptable price to pay. The German foreign office
calculated that even if it would not be possible to win over the urban
middle class to the Axis side, propaganda might be effective among the
mountain tribes. Even if this were to fail, at least it might make it more
difficult for the Allies to recruit them to their cause. Whereas the Mufti
was keen to go to Tunisia to drum up support for the Axis, Hitler felt
that this would be unacceptable to Mussolini, who entertained colonial
ambitions in the area.[54] The foreign office had no objections in principle
to the Mufti's call for independence for Algeria, Morocco and Tunisia,
provided that the Axis was permitted to maintain military bases, but
it had to reassure the Italians. The head of the political department
in the foreign office, Ernst Woermann, tried to persuade Casardi
from the Italian embassy that there would be no open declaration of
independence, but at the same time asked what was the precise attitude
of the Italian government to this question.[55] The German ambassador
in Rome, Mackensen, warned that the Italians regarded Tunisia as
their 'Lebensraum' and were horrified at the idea of the Mufti making a
declaration of independence.[56] The army regarded the Mufti with deep
suspicion, and Nehring asked his envoy to leave Tunis so that he could
concentrate on fighting a war, leaving political matters to the bureau-
crats in Berlin. OKW were by now in full agreement and wanted to keep
the Mufti out of Tunisia. Rather than sponsoring Maghrebian guerrilla
bands, it was now agreed that Admiral Canaris should send a sabotage
group from the Abwehr to Tunis that would work behind the Allied
lines.[57]

The idea of a Maghrebian Liberation Army having been dropped, greater attention was now paid to the German-Arab Training
Section, comprising 6,000 men. Of these 5,200 were Germans from
outside the borders of the Reich, with a mere 800 Arabs. The Germans
had been given a rapid course in elementary soldiering before being
shipped off to the Kalmuk steppes south of Stalingrad in August 1942,
on the assumption that the fighting would soon be over. They were soon
to be wiped out. Ribbentrop did not see the point of sending the Arabs
off to be slaughtered, while the army thought them militarily worthless,
so they were posted to winter quarters in Crimea. By now there were
four companies of Arabs, one made up of Palestinians, Syrians and
Iraqis, the other three by Moroccans, Tunisians and Algerians. The
Palestinians, most of whom had already gained valuable experience
killing Jews, were by far the best of the bunch. The Italians objected
vociferously to the Arab Legion. They had not been consulted, they
were angry that they wore German uniform, and saw this as yet another
instance of the Germans acting counter to crucial Italian interests.[58] In
spite of the miserable failure of this experiment Lieutenant-Colonel
Meyer-Ricks continued with the thankless task of turning reluctant
Maghrebi into soldiers in a training unit under his command in Tunis.
Most deserted when the first rounds were shot, and General von Arnim
only found use for the remainder as navvies. A low-flying aircraft killed
Meyer-Ricks in February 1943, and after North Africa was lost there
were only 600 luckless Arabs, mostly Moroccans, undergoing training
in Greece. Considered to be thoroughly untrustworthy, they were used
to guard railways.[59]

Faced with Italian opposition and ever suspicious of the Mufti's
value as an ally, the Germans concentrated on propaganda in which
virulent anti-Semitism played a key role. A representative from the
foreign office worked closely with the propaganda unit of 5 Army
Command, churning out all manner of propaganda material. Amulets
with swastikas were handed out, quotations from the Quran were
mixed with words of greeting from the German troops, tea bags with
swastikas and 150 kilograms of sugar lumps individually wrapped
in paper that read 'With Allah's help a German victory is certain'
were widely distributed. Rahn worked closely with Kesselring, resulting in piles of leaflets being dropped from planes based in Catania and
Toulouse.[60]

The bulk of this material was predictably crude. The empha-
sis was on anti-Semitism, anti-capitalism and the threat to Islam from

Bolshevism. The Allies, who were fighting on behalf of world Jewry, were intent on handing over North Africa to the Jews. Jews and capitalists were responsible for the war and its prolongation. As a foreign office memorandum put it, this was a case of 'rich man's war, poor man's battle'.[61] Whereas the war in the west had been fought in a chivalrous manner, in the east it had been marked by Bolshevik atrocities. Much was made of the anti-Semitic measures already taken by the Germans in Tunisia. Jews had been obliged to do forced labour. Jewish property had been given to Muslims who had been bombed. Members of the nationalist Neo-Destour Party in Morocco had been released thanks to the Axis powers, who had also permitted the formation of the Red Crescent. Whereas the Allies requisitioned everything in sight, and dragged off Muslim women into their tents, the Germans had doubled the oil ration in Tunisia and treated women with due respect. 'New European Socialism', based on National Socialist economic principles, was said unambiguously to reject capitalist imperialism and offered the prospect of fair trade, with neither exploiter nor exploited. Thanks to the Axis, wages in Tunisia were now based entirely on the 'achievement principle'.[62]

Arabs were to be encouraged to attack Jews. Americans would then rush to their defence, thus showing themselves to be pro-Jewish. The evils of French colonialism in Morocco were roundly denounced. They had made use of the Jews to bring the country economically under their control. The population had been ruthlessly exploited by being reduced to wage slaves. The colonial administration was systematically venal, and would now be replaced by an equally vicious Jewish-American administration that would seize the new harvest. The Americans had absolutely nothing to offer the people of Morocco. They were racists, seeing themselves as crusaders and missionaries, who had had no respect for Islam. The Germans, by contrast, would ensure that the Jews were forced into ghettos, and made to wear distinctive traditional costumes. Co-operation with a German-dominated New Europe would ensure general prosperity.[63]

One such leaflet read: 'Listen, noble Arabs! Free yourselves from the English, the Americans and the Jews! Protect your families, your possessions and your faith! The English, Americans and Jews and their allies are the worst enemies of the Arabs and of Islam!' Another pamphlet, addressed to the Moroccans, read: 'What do the Americans want? They want to help the Jews. The Americans are the enemies of Germany, because we want to eliminate the Jewish menace for you, and all mankind. Moroccans! If you work for the Americans you are working for the Jews and will enslave yourselves more and more ... You know that Adolf Hitler and his soldiers are your powerful friends ... Take up arms wherever you find them. Hurt the enemy wherever you can with sabotage actions.'[64] The Moroccans were told that the 'heroic resistance of your Palestinian brothers' had frustrated England's attempt to hand over Palestine to the Jews, but that Roosevelt intended to turn Morocco into a Jewish state. A Jew hid behind every American soldier and would stay behind when the soldiers left. Moroccans were called upon to show themselves worthy of their Palestinian brothers. The Quran was liberally quoted for denunciations of Jews and other infidels.

Hitler eventually dropped his objections to sending the Mufti to Tunisia and the latter prepared to go with Admiral Canaris in mid-December to meet up with an estimated five hundred saboteurs, who had been recruited by OKW's counter-espionage unit (Amt Ausl./Abwehr) to co-operate with the Germans.[65] Meanwhile, in the hope that the authorities would take a more robust attitude towards the 'Jewish question', Rauff ordered work to begin on the building of a concentration camp at Sfax. As the Tunisian bridgehead gradually shrank, Rauff decided that at least the leadership of the Tunisian Jews should be deported to Poland, but they were forewarned. A prominent Muslim hid Borgel in his house, but some twenty Jews and resistance fighters were rounded up and sent to Germany, where most were murdered.[66] Rauff's Einsatzkommando left Tunisia four days before the capitulation of the Axis forces, to set about their brutal work in northern Italy.

The Germans imagined that the Tunisian Neo-Destour Party, a nationalist organisation founded in 1934, was a strong supporter of the Axis. The party leader, Habib Bourguiba, was imprisoned in Marseille, along with other prominent Neo-Destourians. The German foreign office secured the release of Bourguiba along with six of his party friends, whereupon Klaus Barbie, the murderous Gestapo chief in Lyon, went to Marseille on 18 January and accompanied them back to Chalon-sur-Saône, where they were briefed. In January they were handed over to the Italians. On his arrival in Tunisia Bourguiba promptly went underground. Unlike so many other Arab leaders, Bourguiba had no intention of submitting to the Axis, particularly at a time when their North African adventure was clearly about to come to a sorry end.[67]

The Tunisian Arabs had initially welcomed the Germans, whose anti-Semitism they applauded, and whose half-baked anti-capitalist ideology they found sympathetic.[68] The release of Neo-Destourian prisoners was extremely popular, but this began to turn slightly sour when Bourguiba spent some time in Rome of his own free will. This seemed to indicate that the Germans were intent on handing over Tunisia to the Italians. Tunisian nationalists were horrified at the idea of their country becoming an Italian colony, overrun by land-hungry foreign peasants, and preferred to remain in a French protectorate. The Axis powers tried to get Bourguiba on their side and made an open statement of support, but knowing that Tunisia had a far better chance to gain independence were the Allies to win the war, he avoided all such traps.

Bourguiba reassured his followers, quickly regaining his popularity, so that his extreme form of nationalism, combined with his opposition to the Axis, was a real threat. The Germans therefore tried to build up the Bey as a counter to the extreme Destourians, but there was precious little room for manoeuvre. The Bey was counting on an Allied victory, and the fact that his oldest son, who was married to an Italian, was openly opposed to the Allies as well as to the Gaullists was little more than cold comfort.

German efforts in Tunisia were greatly hampered by the fact that their Italian allies were heartily disliked by French and Arabs alike. The Germans were also outraged that the Italians succeeded in protecting Jews with Italian citizenship, so that not only did their property remain intact, they were also exempted from compulsory labour service. This did not go down well with the local Arabs. There was also disagreement between the Germans and the Italians over volunteer Arab army units. The Germans argued that they had to take anyone they found; the Italians feared that armed Arabs would eventually turn their weapons against them. German optimism and Italian fears both soon proved unfounded. Efforts to recruit volunteers for the German army in North Africa brought meagre results. A pompously named Légion Impériale was founded in November, soon to be renamed the Phalange Africaine. There were virtually no volunteers. Eventually a company of 150 men was formed in January 1943, now called the Légion des Volontaires Français. It was made up of sundry riff-raff, mainly Arabs, and was virtually without military value. A company of exceedingly dubious French was finally fielded alongside the remnants of the German 334 Infantry Division at the beginning of March, and the French military mission managed to scratch together a pioneer battalion. Three of the French Legionnaires were awarded the Iron Cross second class on Hitler's last birthday. Most of the handful of Arabs under arms deserted at the first signs of danger; those who remained were posted to labour battalions.[69]

Major General V. Evelegh's British 78th Division, known as the 'Battleaxe Division', was painfully slow in advancing towards Tunis from the west, taking its time to bring units up to strength before moving. This enabled Kesselring to bring fresh troops into the Tunis bridgehead, strengthen the defences and launch a series of limited attacks to keep the Allies off balance. Lieutenant-General Walter Koch, a daring and independently minded commander of 5 Parachute Regiment (FJR5), who commanded a battle group, managed to dislodge the 1st Guards Brigade from Majaz el Bab, some 40 kilometres west of Tunis, after heavy fighting.[70] German paratroopers landed to the south at Gafsa and succeeded in taking the town. Airborne American troops landed at Gabes, but were driven back and the town was occupied by Italian troops from Libya. Incidents such as these prompted hardboiled and contemptuous British troops to describe their gallant allies as 'our Italians'. It was not until 25 November that 1st Army's commander, Lieutenant-General Kenneth Anderson, was ready to move. Supported by the US 1st Armoured Division he made a three-pronged advance. The group in the centre, known as 'Blade Force', was stopped by a Panzer Group commanded by Walter Barenthin. To the south, where Anderson's attack was concentrated, the British 11th Infantry Brigade succeeded in surrounding the Koch Battle Group. Nehring ordered all available aircraft to attack in a desperate effort to halt the Allied advance, but to no avail. Part of Barenthin's Battle Group was surrounded, the Allies passed Majaz el Bab and advanced towards Djedeida. Nehring saw no alternative to a general withdrawal, so by the late afternoon American armour had managed to take the airfield at Djedeida, less than 40 kilometres west of Tunis. Twenty Stukas and Bf109s were destroyed on the ground by the Stuarts from 1st (US) Armoured Regiment, but the latter were soon driven back, with the 88s killing three of the twenty tanks.

The Allied attack on Djedeida resumed the following day. 78th Division continued its advance, while to the north the British 36th

Infantry Brigade advanced towards Mateur. Nehring quickly rear-ranged his defences to meet the threat but Kesselring, feeling that Nehring had lost his grip, relieved him of his command on 8 December. Kesselring was a swashbuckling airman, a man of enormous energy, who whenever there was a slight improvement in one area or another, was given to fits of exaggerated optimism. Nehring, a level-headed and cautious soldier, was quite the opposite. Jodl felt that the changeover was due to excessive concern for the sensitivities of the 'don't touch me' Italians. Göring had argued in Rome for a unified command in North Africa under the Italians.[71] Hitler, who was torn between his contempt for the Italians and his concern to keep them on board, did not have a firm opinion on the matter, and let his underlings fight it out among themselves. Kesselring had visited Nehring's headquarters on 28 November and ordered him to expand the bridgehead, insisting in all too familiar language that he had to play for time, adding the famil-iar argument that morale and willpower were every bit as important as purely military considerations. Nehring issued orders for an 'offensive defence'. 10 Panzer Division, commanded by a hardened veteran from the eastern front, Wolfgang Fischer, managed to push 'Blade Force' back to Tebourba and beyond, in what soon became an unseemly rout. Anderson felt obliged to apologise to Eisenhower for this debacle as the Germans, with their Tigers making their first battlefield appear-ance in North Africa, chased the Americans over the high ground until they eventually ran out of steam east of Majaz el Bab.[72] He had a lot more apologising to do in the weeks ahead as his men gradually learnt how to fight experienced troops in unfamiliar terrain. Ander-son's performance served to confirm the fears of those who felt that he had been appointed well beyond his abilities. Indeed, almost the only thing over which Montgomery and Patton were in agreement was that the taciturn and gloomy Anderson was at best well meaning, at worst incompetent.

It was at this point that Hans-Jürgen von Arnim, the comman-der of 39 Panzer Corps on the eastern front, arrived in Tunis with his second-in-command, Heinz Ziegler, to replace Nehring. Arnim, an aris-tocrat of the old school, was promoted to the rank of colonel-general and was given command of a new 5 Army Command (AOK 5), as sug-gested by Kesselring, supported as usual by Jodl.[73] Hitler's adjutant, Major-General Schmundt, put forward Arnim's name and Hitler read-ily agreed, even though Arnim had no experience of desert warfare.

24. General Von Arnim

He was placed directly under Kesselring, and mindful of Rommel's difficulties in delegating command, was given General Ziegler to act as his deputy, the first time that such an appointment had been made in the German army.[74] The ideologically resolute Berndt described Nehring to Goebbels as a pessimist who had given up all hope of victory, and thought that Arnim was of a higher calibre. Goebbels bemoaned the fact that little had been done before the war to ensure that there were enough 'solid National Socialists' in the army.[75] Hitler promised Arnim and Ziegler that three new divisions would soon be on their way to North Africa, but like most of the Führer's promises it was in vain. This meant that there were now two armies in North Africa, with no unified command. This was a situation fraught with difficulties until 23 February 1943 when Rommel was given command over the Army Group Africa, but for the moment the front was stabilised and for the next two months the Allies concentrated on defending what they had gained, and preparing for a further offensive. All attention was now on Montgomery's advance from the east in preparation for his assault on Rommel's force at Buerat.

11 ✠ THE RETREAT FROM MERSA EL BREGA

Shortly before the 'Torch' landings, Rommel's army had begun its withdrawal from the El Alamein front at nightfall on 4 November. It was a pitch-dark night so that vehicles frequently strayed away from tracks and became stuck in the sand. The British managed successful to jam the Panzer Army's radio communications, so that the staff had no idea how the situation was developing. They were relieved to discover that it was not until the following morning that British armour took up the pursuit along the coastal road, where the situation was chaotic, traffic was jammed and constantly bombed by Allied aircraft. The staff knew that it would be impossible to establish a temporary defensive position before Fuka, and seriously doubted whether it would be possible to get back to that place in one piece.[1] Hitler's pig-headed order had made the Panzer Army lose a critical 24 hours that could well prove fatal. To the south 13th Corps chased the Italian 10 Corps which was soon in serious difficulties owing to an acute shortage of fuel and ammunition. The Afrikakorps, positioned in the centre, was soon in danger of being outflanked by 10th Corps. 90 Light Africa Division managed to get back to Fuka in safety at 0800hrs on 5 November, but an estimated 400 British tanks pushed forward to the south in an attempt to cut off the remainder of the Afrikakorps. 21 Panzer Division simply did not have the fuel to counterattack, so during the afternoon 7th Armoured Division succeeded in breaking through at the highly vulnerable point where 21 and 15 Panzer Divisions joined. Rommel hoped to be able to hang on to Fuka until he had managed to bring back all the slow-moving units, but this soon proved impossible because his forces were far too weak for a viable defence, so that he was forced to abandon the idea and order a withdrawal to Mersa Matruh. Cavallero had already told him that Mussolini had agreed to a withdrawal and that the Pistoia

Division, along with anti-tank units, would be sent up to strengthen the Sollum–Halfaya Line. If a further withdrawal were necessary the Giovani Fascisti (young fascist) Division would be brought up from Siowa to strengthen the southern flank.[2] By the early evening it was once again clear that the 8th Army had failed to drive home its advantage. The Panzer Army managed to disengage, with two reconnaissance units under the command of Captain Friedrich Wilhelm Voss, Rommel's former ADC, covering the general withdrawal, attacking from the rear a British force of some sixty tanks that was intent on destroyed the virtually immobilised 21 Panzer Division.[3] By the next evening the bulk of the Panzer Army had reached Mersa Matruh. 21 Panzer Division, which had suffered a terrible beating and had run out of fuel, was still 22 kilometres to the south-east and had to abandon and destroy a number of empty Panzer. The remnants of the Panzer Army at Mersa Matruh huddled together in a 'hedgehog', waiting anxiously for fuel. The Italian 10 Corps and Ramcke's crack unit, 1 Luftwaffe Light Infantry Brigade, appeared to have vanished. OKW assumed that they had been wiped out. Ramcke suddenly reappeared, reporting to Rommel on 7 November: his 600 exhausted men had marched on foot across the desert for three days, without supplies and constantly harassed by 8th Army's reconnaissance units. It was a remarkable feat, for which Ramcke was mentioned in OKW's daily report and awarded the oak leaves for his Knight's Cross.[4] Ramcke's relations with Rommel were often strained. As a paratrooper he was from the Luftwaffe and constantly demanded special treatment. He was singularly indignant that he had not been given sufficient vehicles for his retreat. Rommel, who was impressed by his outstanding leadership qualities, simply pointed out that there were none available, short of leaving the Italians totally in the lurch.[5] There had been ugly scenes between Italian and German troops, and even exchanges of fire, as they scrambled for transport. Some Italian units were abandoned in the desert to die of hunger and thirst, when German troops seized the few remaining trucks.[6]

In the afternoon of 6 November Rommel received a visit from General Antonio Gandin, who had been sent by Cavallero to be briefed on the overall situation and to hear of Rommel's plans. Rommel did not mince his words. He intended to head back to Libya as quickly as possible, as he was in constant danger of being cut off. There was simply no time to restore even a semblance of order before then, for speed was of the essence. Under no circumstances would he accept

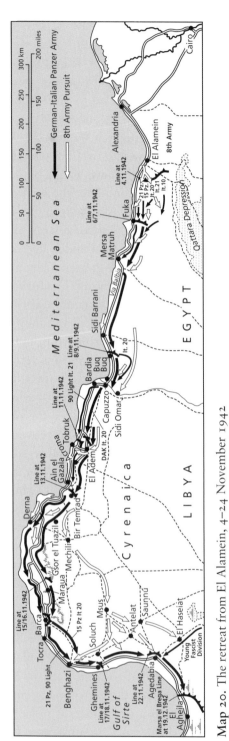

Map 20. The retreat from El Alamein, 4–24 November 1942

battle, for that would mean the total destruction of the remainder of his mechanised units. Gandin was horrified at this grim account and was at something of a loss to know what to tell Cavallero, who from the safety of his office in Rome refused even to contemplate the idea of a retreat.[7]

As at Fuka, Rommel hoped to be able to remain at Mersa Matruh for a few days and to sort out the Panzer Army which was rapidly declining into a demoralised shambles. However, fearing that 8th Army would attempt to outflank him, he felt that he had no alternative but to continue westwards. 8th Army indeed had such a plan, Operation 'Grapeshot', a left hook aimed at Tobruk, but Montgomery constantly took units from the 'Grapeshot' reserve to push forward on a broad front.[8] That evening, at 1855hrs, Rommel received orders from Mussolini that he was to make a stand at the Halfaya Line. Given that he had lost the bulk of the Italian infantry, most of his armour and artillery, he was still desperately short of supplies and heavy rains had rendered the roads dangerously soft, it was unthinkable that he could possibly halt the 8th Army, which could easily outflank the position to the south.[9] 21 Panzer Division had lost almost all its Panzer during the fierce fighting in the afternoon of 6 November.[10] On 7 November the Afrikakorps and the Voss Group were ordered back to Sidi Barrani along the coastal road, which, because of the heavy rains, was the only track that could be used. 90 Light Africa Division was to guard the retreat and follow next day. Rommel imagined that Montgomery would deliver a left hook aimed at Tobruk, thus trapping all his units in Sollum, Bardia and Tobruk, but once again the British outflanking movement was too slow to cut off the retreat from Mersa Matruh in the night of 7/8 November, although a couple of battalions of the Pistoia Division and a German heavy artillery battery were overrun at Halfaya. The Young Fascist Division, having arrived late, did not have enough time to take up defensive positions there, and was ordered to withdraw to Bardia. By the evening of 8 November the bulk of the Panzer Army was between Sidi Barrani and Buq-Buq, but it had to move on the following day. It was calculated that the narrow winding road near Sollum would be the scene of massive traffic jams that would hold up the withdrawal for two days, but thanks to the energetic efforts of a number of transport officers the traffic initially moved smoothly, although it was soon disrupted by constant attacks from the air. It was then that Rommel was informed that an Allied invasion force was on its way. When Westphal told him that it had landed, Rommel knew that this spelt the end of the Panzer Army in Africa.[11] He also finally received an order from Hitler, written on 18 October, to the effect that all enemy 'commandos', even if they were in uniform, should be shot on the spot.[12] Colonel Westphal burnt the order with Rommel's approval. By now OKH realised that Rommel was in serious trouble. The Italians had been decimated, he had lost most of his Panzer, anti-tank and anti-aircraft guns as well as the bulk of his artillery, he was chronically short of fuel and ammunition, so that it was unlikely that he would be able to hold the Sollum–Halfaya Line against the 8th Army's awesome strength.[13] Rommel was gradually losing control of the situation because he had lost so much of his means of communication and the British were very successful in jamming radio transmissions. At one point he even asked General Count Barbasetti di Prun, the head of Delease, to take over command, while keeping in close touch with him, but nothing came of this attempt to shift responsibility for defeat on to the Italians.[14]

On 10 November, by which time the Panzer Army was behind the Sollum front, Rommel asked Kesselring and Cavallero to come to North Africa, since the situation had worsened significantly, clearly calling for some important decisions at the highest level, but neither saw any urgency in the matter.[15] Meanwhile, Mussolini reconsidered his order to make a stand at the Halfaya Line and gave Rommel freedom of action. At first he hoped that the Panzer Army could hold on Tobruk and Gazala for a while, but this also proved to be impossible, with the British 2nd Armoured Division at Sidi Omar and Sidi Barrani poised to swoop down on the fortress. Now Rommel's only hope was to make a stand at Mersa el Brega, which would be somewhat more difficult to outflank. When the British 1st Army Tank Brigade attacked the Halfaya Line from the east and south-east at daybreak on 11 November the Panzer Army had already begun to withdraw. 90 Light Africa Division reported that 1 Bersaglieri Battalion in Tobruk had run away in the direction of Gazala, creating a chaotic situation that made an orderly withdrawal impossible.[16] Rommel had done his best to follow Cavallero's order to protect the Italian infantry divisions during the withdrawal from the Sollum–Halfaya Line and at Bardia, but the lack of discipline among the Italian troops made this impossible.[17] A regiment of the Pistoia Division was overrun on 11 November, three German batteries were taken, and the British were in command of 'Hell

25. German retreat – abandoned vehicles (IWM: E 19360)

Fire Pass' which had been so fiercely contested when Rommel had made his previous withdrawal. Meanwhile the British 7th Armoured Division moved around the Halfaya Line to the south, swung up to the Trigh Capuzzo and advanced rapidly. The only positive result of this debacle was that Rommel now had Hitler's and Mussolini's consent to an orderly withdrawal from Cyrenaica.[18]

Rommel's position was made even more desperate by the arrival of 1,100 fresh troops, rather than the fuel he had so frequently demanded.[19] There were no provisions for the new arrivals, and it was almost a miracle that stragglers from the Panzer Army could be withdrawn before British armour reached the Via Balbia in an attempt to cut them off. Rommel persistently blamed Kesselring for the shortage of supplies, so relations between the two field marshals grew steadily worse, with Rudolf Rahn's attemps to bring about a rapprochement between the two men at their meeting at Fasano on Lake Garda having failed.[20] By the afternoon of 12 November the British were at El Adem on the ring road to the south of Tobruk, forcing the Afrikakorps and what was left of the Ariete to retire, while the British took Tobruk almost without a fight. The Germans now had only 0.4 of a daily fuel ration, in spite of frequent and urgent requests for help.[21] Rommel sent Berndt back to see Hitler. He arrived at the Berghof on 12 November, with a list of complaints about the unfortunate Rintelen having failed to secure supplies for the Panzer Army. Berndt also pointed out that the situation was made all the worse by increasing tension between the ever-optimistic 'Smiling Albert' Kesselring and Rommel. Kesselring tended to make promises that he could not fulfil, leaving Rommel in the lurch. Hitler responded by making Rintelen subordinate to Kesselring, but only in the areas for which Kesselring had direct control, while he remained in his capacity as military attaché with the German quarter-master in Rome still answerable to him. Gause, Rommel's former chief of staff, in whom he had great confidence, was placed under Kesselring's command and made responsible for ensuring that Rommel's requests to him were made clearly and forcefully. Hitler assured Berndt that he had absolute confidence in Rommel, and that he would give him every possible support.[22]

None of this shuffling had any real effect, nor could it have had. The real problem lay elsewhere – the complete domination of the Mediterranean by Allied forces at sea and in the air.[23] During the month of November 178,000 GRT of shipping was sent to North Africa, more than half of it going to Tunisia. Although this was a record amount for the entire year, 32,000 GRT were sunk and 25,000 GRT damaged. The Panzer Army and air force needed at least 47,000 tons per month, but in November 1942 only 6,300 tons arrived in Tripoli for the German units.[24] Urgent steps were needed to remedy the situation, but precious little was done. The Axis navies were now chronically overextended. They not only had to protect their own convoys to North Africa; they also had to interdict the Allied convoys to Bône. Their air forces were short of fuel and thus unable to undertake adequate reconnaissance in support of naval operations. They had precious few minesweepers and were painfully slow to adapt naval vessels for anti-submarine warfare. As a result the 2.8 million GRT of Italian merchant shipping at the beginning of the war had been reduced to 1 million by the end of

1942.[25] The damage done to Allied shipping was relatively minor and was rapidly made good.

Rommel decided that the best he could do was to hold up the 8th Army in Cyrenaica for as long as possible, so as to have time to build up the defences at Mersa el Brega. On 11 November he sent a message to Mussolini to this effect.[26] On 12 November he ordered the Panzer Army to fight its way back to the Gazala Line, starting at 0500hrs the following morning.[27] The withdrawal went smoothly, apart from some traffic jams on the winding road near Barce and Tocra, but it was obvious that the Gazala Line could not be held for long. The Afrika-korps and 90 Light Africa Division did their utmost to hold the line, but the 8th Army's advance was so rapid, the right flank so danger-ously exposed, that Rommel had to order the immediate evacuation of Cyrenaica, with defensive positions to be established at Mersa el Brega as ordered by Mussolini. Owing to the shortage of fuel they could not take the desert route via Msus, but had to stick to the coastal road. The Afrikakorps and the motorised 20 Corps were to move as quickly as possible, 164 Light Africa Division was to defend Agedabia before falling back to Mersa el Brega, while 90 Light Africa Division guarded the rear. On 14 November Mussolini issued orders that the Panzer Army was to fight its way back to Mersa el Brega, but it was not per-mitted to retire further west because 'the destiny of the Axis in Africa' depended on it standing fast. The Panzer Army lumbered back along the coastal route, but the rains made it virtually impossible for 8th Army's armour to dash across the desert and cut it off. Montgomery's decision to concentrate on the Derna–Tmimi–Mechili triangle so as to secure the aerodromes at Martuuba, which he felt to be a prime objec-tive for the RAF in securing the Mediterranean and guarding the Malta convoys, also allowed Rommel once again to escape.[28] It was not until 17 November that armoured cars from the 11th Hussars and the Royals began to threaten the Panzer Army's southern flank. By 15 November the fuel situation was so critical that the Afrikakorps was rendered immobile, while 90 Light Africa Division in eastern Cyrenaica had only enough for one day. Rommel's chief of staff was outraged to learn that the Italians were abandoning Benghazi and were busy destroying supplies of ammunition and water that would be needed as the bulk of the Panzer Army retreated. The water and electricity works were saved from demolition at the last minute.[29] 90 Light Africa Division was ordered to stay in Benghazi as long as possible, so that supplies could be unloaded. Precious little arrived. The eagerly awaited tanker *Hans Arp* was sunk en route for Benghazi, rendering the fuel situation even more precarious. Fuel had to be flown in to enable 90 Light Africa Division to leave on 19 November, having begun to blow up the harbour at 1300hrs the previous day, but shortages of transport and fuel made it impossible to retrieve the substantial amount of supplies stored in the port: 2,500 tons of badly needed ammunition had to be destroyed. The movement of the infantry and the supply situation were made even more difficult by low-flying aircraft that knocked out an alarming number of trucks.[30] The withdrawal across Cyrenaica was exceptionally difficult, with the ever-present threat of an outflanking movement to the south over Mechili. The fuel situation remained chronic, with transport columns left immobile with empty tanks, sitting ducks for the DAF. The Panzer Army was now living hand to mouth, barely able to survive.

Having heard that Allied troops had taken Bône on 12 November and were advancing eastwards, Rommel wrote to his wife on the following day: 'The battle in North Africa is nearing its end. This will make the odds even higher against us. Here too, the end will not be long for we're being simply crushed by the enemy superiority. The army is in no way to blame. It has fought magnificently.'[31] Hitler, however, still placed the blame for the defeat at El Alamein on the failures of his staff and on Rintelen, and did not seem to be particularly concerned at the amazing rapidity with which Rommel was retreating, in spite of his assurances to the contrary and orders from both OKW and the Comando Supremo to hold on as long as he could at each step of his withdrawal. Rommel was particularly incensed with Cavallero, who had come to Libya on 12 November, but had not seen fit to visit his headquarters. He demanded an explanation as to why he had not turned up for an arranged meeting, thus keeping him waiting.[32] The fuel situation was now worse than ever. The Germans were virtually immobile in Cyrenaica. Those fortunate enough to have some fuel in their tanks were unable to move because of the heavy rains and muddy roads.[33] As early as 16 November Jodl heard that Rommel intended to retreat all the way back from Mersa el Brega to the Tunisian border. At the same time the Wehrmacht's Command Staff, the navy and Gerd von Rundstedt's staff at Supreme Command (OB) West were annoyed at the way Hitler had alienated the French, all because of his undue concern for the Italians' interests and his exaggerated suspicions of the French.[34]

Rommel knew that his position was desperate and that he could only play for time. Reporting to the Comando Supremo and OKW on 17 November he pointed out that almost the entire Italian 10 Corps with the Pavia, Brescia and Folgore Divisions had been taken prisoner at Fuka. They had been constantly attacked by an overwhelming number of tanks, and in spite of some determined and courageous counterattacks, were unable to avoid defeat owing to lack of fuel and transport. The Italian 21 Corps with the Trento and Bologna Divisions had been reduced to one and a half battalions and two batteries during the retreat from Fuka. There was precious little left of the Italian 20 Armoured Division. The Ariete had been wiped out, and the Littorio and Trieste Divisions had been reduced to one regiment without tanks. The Afrikakorps had the strength of one armoured regiment. 90 Light Africa Division was down to about one and a half battalions. Only two of 164 Light Africa Division's nine battalions were left intact and the division had lost two-thirds of its artillery. Ramcke's brigade had been halved. At Mersa el Brega Rommel only had the equivalent of one weak German division, three Italian infantry divisions – the Spezia, Pistoia and Young Fascists – and the Centaurio Armoured Division. They would soon have to withstand an anticipated two armoured and four motorised British divisions, all richly supplied and with massive air support.[35] The Young Fascists (Giovani Fascisti) was a volunteer division that like the Folgore proved to be extremely effective, thus winning the Germans' respect. But that was not nearly enough to turn the tide. Rommel made it plain that unless he was given ample supplies of anti-tank weapons, fuel and ammunition, plus greatly improved air support, he could not possibly hold the Mersa el Brega Line. He was incensed when 5 Parachute Regiment, which had been originally intended to be sent to strengthen the Panzer Army Africa, was sent to Tunis. This in turn only made sense if the Tunis bridgehead was intended as an assembly point for a general withdrawal of the Axis troops from North Africa. Hitler's refusal to withdraw anywhere and under any circumstances simply meant that he was sending men and matériel that he could ill afford into a sack that the Allies were bound to tie up within a few months at the latest.[36]

None of this seemed to make much of an impression on either OKW or the Comando Supremo. Cavallero, via the German air attaché, Baron von Pohl, issued orders from Mussolini to hold the Mersa el Brega Line for at least a week.[37] This prompted Rommel to write: 'Marshal Cavallero was a type of intellectually semi-qualified and feeble-willed desktop officer. Logistics, leadership and everything creative require not intellect, but above all energy and the absolute determination to tackle a job without consideration for one's own problems. Theoreticians see warfare as a purely intellectual problem and demand energy from those whom they describe in somewhat contemptuous terms as "troupiers".'[38] Rommel was quick to point out that it was virtually impossible to hang on at Fuka. There was now practically nothing left of the Afrikakorps. The 90 and 164 Light Africa Divisions were reduced to little more than a couple of below-strength regiments. The four Italian divisions were of little value because they were so poorly armed. 8th Army would be able to attack this pathetic force within two to three weeks with its two armoured and four motorised divisions.[39]

Hitler sent a message to the Panzer Army asking that it list its needs, but this was a pointless gesture, given the virtual impossibility of shipping supplies to North Africa.[40] Even if they had arrived there was a shortage of transport and fuel to supply the front. Two destroyers from Italy's fair weather navy loaded with fuel were turned back because of high seas, so the Afrikakorps and 90 Light Africa Division were now entirely dependent on fuel brought in by air, but Kesselring announced that this was no longer possible.[41] Rommel appealed to Bastico for 500 tons of fuel from Tripoli, stressing that the army was 'desperate', down to its last drop. Bastico responded immediately.[42] But this brought only temporary relief. As Rommel pointed out in an urgent message to Rintelen in Rome, if the Italian troops at Mersa el Brega were not motorised they would suffer the same fate as their comrades at El Alamein.[43]

On 20 November Rommel sent General De Stefanis to Rome. He was the highly intelligent and effective commander of 20 Corps, who was greatly appreciated for his coolness under stress, his laconic wit and his politeness.[44] His mission was to protest against the decision to make a stand at Mersa el Brega, pointing out that his 'decimated' army, strung out along a 160-kilometre front, could not possibly withstand 8th Army's armour. Indeed it would probably prove impossible to hang on to Tripolitania. Rommel had hoped to make this clear to Cavallero when he came to North Africa, but he had been denied the opportunity. De Stefanis was told to call for a move back to Homs that would bring the Panzer Army closer to its supply base in Tripoli, and stretch the

British lines of communication across 'the waterless Sirte'. He was also given a message to hand to Mussolini telling him that the Italians had fought well in the last few weeks and adding: 'Both nations have carried out the withdrawal in close comradeship, and there was not a single discordant note during the entire time.'⁴⁵ Shortly after sending De Stefanis on this mission, Rommel drove to see General Navarrini, who was now commanding 21 Corps, consisting of the Pistoia, Spezia and Young Fascist Divisions. He agreed that it would be sheer folly to accept battle, and was reassured by Rommel's promise that he would do everything possible to avoid losing the Italian infantry a second time during a further retreat.⁴⁶

Still without a reply from Rome, on 22 November Rommel presented an even more drastic version of these ideas to Bastico, who had once again been given command over the Panzer Army. In the course of these discussions he suggested a compromise whereby the infantry, which were in dire danger of being overrun thus leaving the road to Tripoli open, should withdraw to Buerat. Navarrini was in full agreement. Rommel stated that he would of course carry out Mussolini's orders, which had been endorsed by Hitler, but felt obliged to make his views clear. In conclusion he said that he doubted whether it would be possible to remain in North Africa, and he was convinced that if the Panzer Army Africa made a stand at Mersa el Brega it would be destroyed.⁴⁷ This left Bastico in an awkward position. He avoided giving Rommel an answer and muttered that he would pass on his misgivings to the Comando Supremo. On the following day Rommel assured Keitel that he would do his best to hold the Mersa el Brega Line, but it had a front of 160 kilometres, with virtually no depth. The German motorised troops were exhausted after fighting continuously for one whole month, across 1,300 kilometres of desert. He had only 32,000 mines for his 'devil's gardens', whereas at El Alamein he had had 500,000. Even if he concentrated all his forces to the north, where the main attack was likely to come, he would have only one battalion per 3 kilometres of front. The strongpoints were few and far between and could easily be infiltrated. The Italians had proved themselves to be incapable of standing up to the devastating artillery and bombing that was bound to come. The Germans had only 45 Panzer to pitch against 420 British tanks, 300 armoured cars, 360 pieces of light artillery, 48 heavy guns and 550 5.7cm anti-tank guns, so he must 'reckon with the destruction of the remains of the army in its defensive position'.⁴⁸

By now Rommel realised that he would only be able to hang on in Tunisia for a limited time. Faced with overwhelming Allied forces he could gradually shorten his front, step by step evacuating his troops by air and by sea, so that when the Allies had completed their conquest they would find nothing much there except for a few prisoners. They would 'thus be robbed of the fruits of their victory, just as we had been at Dunkirk'.[49] Not all of his men shared this pessimistic assessment. Some still entertained Hitler's illusion that forces could be built up in Tunis so that the Panzer Army could once again go on the offensive. Without Tunis, Tripoli would have been the Axis' Dunkirk. With Tunis a 'final victory' (*Endsieg*) was still possible.[50]

The first units of the British 7th Armoured Division reached Agedabia on 22 November. The Panzer Army immediately came under intense artillery fire that caused serious damage to the supply lines. Lacking ammunition for a counter-battery response the forward divisions of the Panzer Army were forced to move back behind the Mersa el Brega Line, which was thinly defended by the Spezia Division to the north, the Pistoia Division to the south, with a battery from the Young Fascist Division in the centre. Most of the Italians lacked battle experience and were likely to crack under intense artillery fire, being unable to withstand a major offensive.[51] Two days later the bulk of the Panzer Army was in position, anxiously awaiting the arrival of the British 7th Armoured Division and the 2nd New Zealand Division. OKW promised to send reinforcements, but Rommel had heard such promises too often. A major problem was that the individual strongpoints were 2–3 kilometres apart, so that the gaps could not be covered by fire, making it easy for the British to slip through. Furthermore there was neither a continuous barbed-wire entanglement nor minefield along the length of the front. There were simply not enough reserves to meet the threat of an outflanking movement to the south. Since all fighting units were up at the front there was no possibility of manning effective defences east of Tripoli to which the Panzer Army could retire.[52]

On 24 November Kesselring, Cavallero and Bastico arrived at Arco dei Fileni to discuss the situation.[53] Rommel, accompanied by Westphal, did what he could to open their eyes to the gravity of the situation, but to no avail. He began by saying that his army had suffered a crushing defeat at El Alamein. He had been 30,000 men short, his supplies were inadequate, the superiority of the enemy, particularly in the air and with heavy artillery, was overwhelming. He described in detail the difficulties encountered during the withdrawal after the battle. He was very doubtful whether he could hang on at Mersa el Brega, and were that position lost it would be impossible to defend Tripoli. Neither Kesselring nor Cavallero would agree to the evacuation of Libya. Kesselring insisted on the strategic importance of Libya for the air war in the Mediterranean. Cavallero continued to live in what Rommel described as 'a neurotic fantasy'.[54] He suggested making a stand at Buerat, but Rommel pointed out that it would be impossible to defend Mersa el Brega while building up the defences at Buerat. Rommel then said that he might be able to hold off the 8th Army for a while provided that he was given fifty 7.5cm anti-tank guns, fifty long-barrelled Panzer IVs, an assortment of seventy-eight guns, 4,000 tons of fuel and another 4,000 tons of ammunition. The Luftwaffe also had to be significantly strengthened. Rommel knew perfectly well that these conditions would not be met, while Kesselring and Cavallero remained adamant, creating the impression that Rommel was faint-hearted, a commander who was vainglorious in victory, a naysayer when the tide had turned. The meeting ended inconclusively, leaving Rommel irate and frustrated.

After lengthy discussions with Rommel, Rintelen climbed into a Savoia 79 in order to fly to Bastico's headquarters in Misurata. When the aircraft reached an altitude of 30 metres it crashed into a German fighter and was completely destroyed. With the exception of the rear-gunner, an Italian NCO and Rintelen, all passengers and crew were killed. Rintelen was severely wounded and was out of action until the following spring, while his chief of staff, Colonel von Waldenburg, acted as his deputy.[55]

Two days after this unsatisfactory conference the entire Panzer Army was behind the Mersa el Brega Line, where they were given seventeen days' respite while Montgomery prepared to attack with characteristically methodical caution. Mussolini continued to demand that the Mersa el Brega Line be held, and called for an offensive, which he claimed would be backed by massive Luftwaffe support. Rommel's staff knew from experience that this was an empty promise. Bastico was told that he could permit a retreat only in the direst of emergencies. This was designed to stiffen Rommel's back, but he did have the decency to pass on the order.[56]

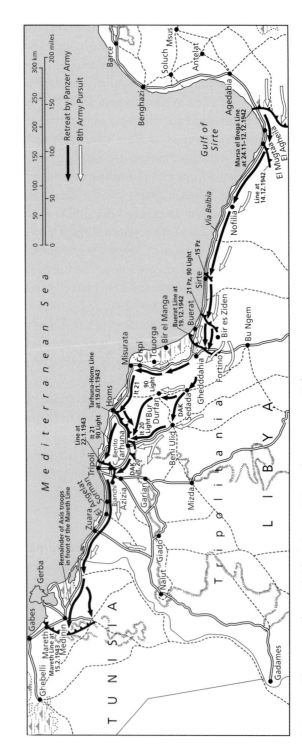

Map 21. The retreat from El Alamein, 24 November 1942–15 February 1943

Perhaps it was to counter the charge that he was altogether too pessimistic that Rommel shot off a broadside at Bastico, complaining that the latter had ordered 20 Corps back to Buerat without telling him and contrary to Mussolini's orders that the Panzer Army was to stand and fight. He demanded of the Comando Supremo that Bastico not be allowed to make tactical decisions without consulting him.[57] Bastico replied that there would be no withdrawal, except at his express orders, and repeated the Duce's order that the Mersa el Brega Line should be held. He suggested that the rainy weather should make this an easier task and that limited attacks should be made on 8th Army's vanguard.[58] During the next few days Rommel alternated between discussing details of a withdrawal and insisting that Hitler and Mussolini's orders be strictly obeyed. He told Bastico that there was simply not enough transport available to withdraw the army quickly enough in the event of a breakthrough: 10,000 Germans would have to make use of returning supply trucks, which would take several days; 17,500 Italians would need at least 48 hours using their existing transport. 21 Corps needed 500 more trucks immediately if a catastrophe were to be avoided.[59] A somewhat humbled Bastico then asked Rommel for permission to remove 20 Corps' battle group, as well as the Ariete and Littorio Armoured Divisions from Mersa el Brega back to Buerat. Rommel refused, repeating Hitler and Mussolini's order to stand and fight. He added, somewhat lamely, that he would like to make some limited attacks, but he did not have enough men and equipment to do so.[60] Meanwhile, the 8th Army was steadily building up its forces, with 7th Armoured and 51st Highland Divisions already in position.

Relations between the Germans and the Italians were steadily worsening under the strain. A man from the Heydte Battle Group reported that he had talked to a group of Italian soldiers who had said that they much preferred the idea of a few years in an Allied POW camp to being dead. Their officers had told them that the Germans took all their food, and that they were responsible for the war because of their ridiculous desire to play soldiers. They saw no reason why Rommel should boss them around; after all they had far more experience of fighting in the desert. These complaints were confirmed by an Italian who had asked to join the German army.[61]

Rommel, who was growing increasingly impatient and bitter, decided to visit Hitler in an attempt to get him to see reason. The

Italians were incensed that Rommel had not first consulted them. The German assistant military attaché in Rome was told that if an Italian general had acted in like manner he would have been instantly hauled before a court martial.[62]

Rommel set off at 0200hrs on 28 November accompanied by his amanuensis, Lieutenant Berndt, leaving the Panzer Army in the hands of Panzer General Gustav Fehn, the commander of the Afrikakorps.[63] Flying via Sicily and Wiener Neustadt, he was met by Jodl at Rastenburg airport at 1520hrs and was admitted to Hitler's presence at 1700hrs. Hitler was outraged at what he considered to be a flagrant act of insubordination. Not only had Rommel come of his own accord, without an order, he had abandoned his post in North Africa at a critical time without the permission of the Comando Supremo, who were extremely angry at this high-handed behaviour. He had withdrawn to Mersa el Brega without permission, and now he had come to announce that he intended to retreat all the way to Tunisia. Rommel countered that the waterless Sirte was a nightmare for friend and foe alike.[64] Tripoli was now worthless as a base. Precious few Italian ships managed to reach the port, there was no industry, and nothing but dates to feed the army. The Panzer Army had no alternative but to retire to Gabes, where some Italian troops were already stationed, relieve the Tunisian bridgehead, and prepare for a renewed offensive. Against his better judgement Rommel suggested that he could transform the shattering defeat at El Alamein into a brilliant preliminary move in building up a strongpoint in Tunis. The loss of Tripoli would soon be forgotten once the Panzer Army again went on the offensive. Victory in Tunis would inspire the Italians to renewed effort, while the 8th Army would face serious logistical difficulties with the overextended lines of communication under permanent attack from the air. Rommel presented his demands for the necessary reinforcements, as he later wrote, 'somewhat brusquely' and concluded his presentation by saying that the campaign in North Africa was definitively lost. His remarks acted like 'a spark in a powder keg', Hitler launching into a furious tirade. When Rommel said that only 5,000 of the 15,000 men in the Afrikakorps had weapons, Hitler accused them of having thrown them away. With blissful disregard for tactical and logistical realities, Hitler insisted that the Mersa el Brega Line had to be held and that a major bridgehead in North Africa was essential to the preservation of the alliance with Italy. He made the usual promises to send supplies and ordered Göring to go to Italy with plenipotentiary powers to sort out the logistical difficulties, and to smooth feathers that had been ruffled by Rommel's visit to Hitler's headquarters.[65] Hitler, who treated Rommel with a coolness bordering on contempt, had no intention of honouring his commitments. According to Hitler's orderly, Heinz Linge, Rommel left the room after a three-hour ordeal, looking 'like a drowned poodle'.[66] Jodl, who had made the unusual gesture of meeting Rommel at the airport, probably as a gesture of his support, remarked that evening: 'North Africa will be lost all the same.'[67] This from a man who only a few days before had announced that 'North Africa, as Europe's front line, must be held at all costs.'[68] Rommel sent an order to the Panzer Army after his interview with Hitler to the effect that all available troops in the rear echelon should be brought up to the front, which was to be held at all costs. Exception was made only for men working in various harbours, along with those responsible for the defence of Tripoli.[69] Army Command (AOK) passed on this order, only to be told by Comando Supremo that Mussolini had given his permission for a withdrawal.[70]

Rommel and Göring travelled to Rome in the Reichsmarschall's luxurious private train that evening. The atmosphere during the long journey was tense, with Rommel incensed that Göring refused to accept the fact that the situation in North Africa was desperate. The monomaniac Göring now began to imagine that he could win glory and honour by pulling off a splendid victory in the desert by sending in the Luftwaffe along with his praetorian guard, the Hermann Göring Division. He announced that he would promise the Duce no fewer than three crack divisions, the Leibstandarte Adolf Hitler, the Hermann Göring and the Deutschland: 'three names that mean so much to German honour'.[71] Just as the 8th Army felt that it was fighting Germany's finest general and in the Afrikakorps the cream of the Wehrmacht, Rommel argued that the British and Americans, with their superior leadership, better trained men and superior equipment, were a more formidable adversary than that faced by any other German commander. The fact that the Germans had a far better understanding of modern warfare counted for nothing without the necessary supplies. Göring dismissed all this as defeatism, hinting that Rommel was a fair-weather sailor, while Rommel argued that things looked different at the front than from a well-appointed Pullman car. Rommel became so angry that he was unable to talk reasonably to Göring and eventually decided that he would once again make use of Lieutenant

Alfred-Ingemar Berndt, whose diplomatic skills he greatly appreciated, to persuade Göring that the 'Gabes Plan', a withdrawal to Tunisia and the defence of the Gabes Line, was the only viable solution.[72] His confidence in this silken-tongued Nazi seemed to be fully justified. Berndt managed to convince Göring, at least for a moment, that by concentrating all the Axis armour in Tunisia it would soon be possible to launch an offensive into Algeria, the propaganda effects of which would be considerable. Göring, who had not been present when Rommel presented this plan to Hitler, imagining that he would thus be able restore his tarnished reputation and win his way back into the Führer's favour, eagerly swallowed this preposterous suggestion.

Rommel arrived in Rome somewhat encouraged, but Kesselring immediately put a damper on the proceedings. He continued to insist on the strategic importance of Tunisia for the air war and rejected the Gabes Plan out of hand. Göring as an airman immediately reverted to his earlier objections to the idea of a withdrawal to Tunisia and began waffling on about the danger of a triangle from Malta to Algeria and Tripoli, whereupon Rommel lost his temper, pointing out that it did not matter whence the Allied aircraft started, it was the bombing that mattered. Quite apart from this, the idea that the Panzer Army could possibly hang on in Libya was an absurdity that could not be concealed by talk of willpower, grit and sanguinity.

The party arrived in Rome at 1400hrs on 30 November. They met Mussolini, Cavallero and Admiral Riccardi three hours later for lengthy discussions. The ill feeling between Rommel and Göring reached a new low when the Reichsmarschall told Mussolini, in Rommel's presence, that the Italians had been left in the lurch at El Alamein. An ugly scene was avoided when Mussolini promptly remarked that he knew nothing of this, and that the withdrawal after the battle was a 'masterpiece'.[73]

Rommel managed at least partially to persuade the Italians of the wisdom of the 'Gabes Plan', but for the moment had to follow Hitler's orders to stand and fight on the Mersa el Brega Line. Göring, remembering the Führer's orders and retracting his agreement with Berndt, insisted that the line had to be held. Mussolini stated categorically that he would only permit the Panzer Army Africa to stay put as long as losses were acceptable. The Italians at least were sensible enough to realise that, were Rommel to make a last ditch stand at Mersa el Brega, it would eventually lead to the total destruction of the

Panzer Army, not least because of the long stretch of waterless desert that lay behind the line. Much to Göring's disgust, Mussolini granted Rommel permission to begin building defences at Buerat.[74] The news that the number of ships sunk en route to North Africa was increasing rapidly made Hitler's assurances to Rommel empty, while greatly weakening Göring's hand during the discussions in Rome. Hitler was reduced to frustrated fury over this serious setback.[75] The clash between Mussolini and Göring once again showed that the Duce at least had an inkling of conditions in North Africa, while Hitler and Göring had absolutely none.

Otto von Bismarck, chargé d'affaires at the German embassy, confided in the Marquis d'Aieta, chief of cabinet at the Italian foreign ministry, that the Germans knew perfectly well that North Africa was lost and the 'nonsense' that Göring had been talking was pie in the sky, designed to place the blame on the Italians for failing adequately to supply the Panzer Army. Colonel Montezemolo, who had acted as secretary of the meeting between the four marshals – Göring, Kesselring, Rommel and Cavallero – confirmed this opinion, referring to the Reichsmarschall's 'proud ignorance'.[76] None of this had any effect on Cavallero who continued to grovel at Göring's feet, to the utter disgust of most of the younger officers present.

Mussolini had come to an even more drastic conclusion. When Rommel began his retreat after El Alamein, even before the Allied landing in North Africa, he began to think that the war in the east had to be stopped. On 6 November he told Rintelen that a separate peace with the Soviet Union was essential. On 1 December he told Göring that the war in the east 'no longer made any sense', and made the fantastic suggestion that Germany could pull off a repeat performance of the Treaty of Brest Litovsk, by offering the Soviet Union compensation in the Middle East. Failing that the Axis should set up a defensive line that would require fewer troops. He ordered Ciano to visit Hitler and put forward these suggestions.[77]

Rommel returned to North Africa at 0700hrs on 2 December frustrated and depressed. Westphal described him as 'a broken man'.[78] It would need enormous skill to avoid the annihilation of his army as a result of some senseless orders, and his staff was appalled to hear of the blindness of the high command to the reality of the situation at the front. Immediately upon his return Rommel conferred with Marshal Bastico at the airfield at Uadi Tamed.[79] Bastico announced that Mussolini had granted permission for the Panzer Army to retire to the Buerat Line and once again to go on the offensive against an army that would be facing serious logistical problems across the Sirte. Rommel replied that his recent trip had shown that neither Hitler nor Mussolini had the slightest idea about the situation in North Africa. Bastico pointed out that he had told Mussolini that there was simply enough fuel to withdraw to Buerat. If fuel were brought up to the front there would be none left for the trucks to return to Tripoli. The only possibility was to wait until there were sufficient reserves of fuel available for two to three days of operation. This would take some time because air raids on Tripoli were seriously slowing down the unloading of such ships as managed to reach port. Bastico kept repeating his catchphrase: 'no petrol, no movement'. Rommel suggested that the Italian troops start to move back regardless, to avoid abandoning the Italians to their fate once again. All movements were to be during the night, beginning with 21 Army Corps during the night of 3/4 December, provided that the fuel was available, leaving the Afrikakorps and 90 Light Division to hold the line. Rommel now repeated his arguments in favour of the Gabes Plan, managing thereby to persuade Bastico. Bastico said that he had been thinking about Gabes for several days and agreed with Rommel that the two armies had to link up, otherwise the road to Tunis would be cut off. He added despairingly: 'Hardly a single aeroplane reaches Tripoli, not to mention a ship.' Rommel urged Bastico to repeat this assessment to the Comando Supremo. Rommel had dropped the truculent pose he had adopted while smarting under the charge of faintheartedness, and admitted that the Mersa el Brega Line could not possibly be held. Detailed orders were issued as to how they were to fight their way back, but whether this was possible depended on a solution to the fuel problem. The *Gualdi*, *Veloce* and *Audace* had all been sunk, resulting in a serious shortfall in fuel supplies.[80]

Since Rommel was directly under Mussolini and the Comando Supremo, he could afford to continue ignoring Hitler's orders. On 4 December he ordered the infantry to move back from the Mersa el Brega Line and their replacement by motorised units, but he had to wait for the fuel to arrive before making the move.[81] The Allies had wisely concentrated their attacks on freighters carrying fuel, thus rendering the Panzer Army virtually immobile. During the month of November 4,879 tons were of fuel was landed, 8,110 tons sunk, whereas 2,331 tons of ammunition arrived and only 295 tons were sunk, 3,044 tons of provisions were unloaded and only 175 tons sunk.[82] The Germans were desperately short-handed. There were only 1,938 officers (1,120 short of a full complement) and 40,532 men (35,529 short). The Afrikakorps should have had 353 Panzer, but only had 86. It had just 29 armoured cars instead of 120, 140 anti-tank guns instead of 724, and so on down a long list.[83] Rommel told Bastico that he could not carry out the withdrawal as he had hoped during the night of 5/6 December because of a lack of fuel and transportation: 21 Corps needed 500 trucks and had only 280. He wrote an urgent note to Kesselring saying that the Panzer Army was a sitting duck, unable to move because of lack of fuel and trucks, and complaining that once again the Italians were not pulling their weight. Faced with a steady build-up of British forces, which indicated that an attack was imminent, Rommel decided that he had to move, with inexperienced Italian troops the first to be withdrawn.[84] This began during the night of 6/7 December, the major problem still being the chronic lack of fuel.[85] Axis shipping was being sunk at an even higher rate, and most of the available fuel had to be given to reconnaissance units needed to watch out for the Allies' next move. Moving the Italian infantry back to Buerat, where Westphal and the 164 Light Africa Division were preparing the defences, left the Afrikakorps and 90 Light Africa Division at Mersa el Brega virtually without fuel, while further frantic appeals for help brought no relief. Fortunately for the Panzer Army it seemed that the 8th Army had not noticed the Italians' withdrawal, even though it had been a noisy affair using headlights. Hitler reluctantly agreed that Rommel should stay put 'as long as possible', while the defences at Buerat were prepared, thus leaving the initiative with Rommel.[86] On 7 December the Operations Staff War Diary noted: 'just now the Führer considers it a positive advantage that for the moment Rommel's army has insufficient fuel to enable it to withdraw further'. But the Führer had now, at least at the back of his mind, given up the idea of defending Tripolitania and was concentrating on building up the Tunisian bridgehead in preparation for a major offensive that would drive the Allies out of North Africa. The sheer fantasy behind such an idea was underlined when he ordered the '999 Africa Brigade', the other ranks made up of convicted criminals, to be sent to Tunisia rather than Crete.[87] It would be difficult to imagine a unit less suited to the task, particularly as desertion would be extremely easy. Jodl did his best to persuade Hitler that Rommel was completely justified in acting as he did, but Hitler had not forgiven him for letting him down at El Alamein, so Rommel could now do nothing right in his eyes.[88] The result was general confusion and a failure to lay down clear guidelines, all made worse by Hitler taking up an inordinate amount of time ranting on about historical, psychological, military and sundry other topics to the intense frustration and tedium of all but the toadyish members of his entourage.

Shortages of fuel and transportation made Westphal's task of improving the defences at Buerat singularly difficult. Superlibia offered 5,000 picks and shovels and 3,600 Italian labourers, which gave some relief, but had no fuel to spare. There was still a serious shortage of manpower and matériel, as well as a series of frustrating arguments with Delease, which was ultimately responsible for all such matters.

The remains of 21 Army Corps were withdrawn during the night of 7/8 December. The German troops at Mersa el Brega braced themselves for a massive attack that they knew was imminent.[89] Orders were issued that they were to avoid the mistake made at El Alamein of allowing the 8th Army's artillery to smash the forward positions by withdrawing to a rear defensive line and prepare to retire to the west once the codeword '333' was issued. The German–Italian Panzer Army was in the unenviable position of being unable to disrupt 8th Army's preparations for an offensive, while at the same time being starved of essential supplies thanks to the Allies' overwhelming command over the Mediterranean. A special envoy from Kesselring's headquarters, Captain Genzow, arrived on 10 December with the alarming news that there would be no appreciable improvement of the fuel situation for at least eight to ten days. Rommel pointed out that this was far too late, given that 8th Army was likely to strike at any moment. Genzow insisted that nothing could be done, whereupon Rommel sent yet another urgent message to OKW and Kesselring, pointing out that if the fuel situation did not improve drastically the Panzer Army would be left high and dry somewhere between Mersa el Brega and Buerat, where it would be destroyed.[90]

The long-awaited attack by 8th Army came during the night of 11/12 December, when the British began a massive artillery barrage and brought troops up along the coastal road at 0300hrs.[91] Rommel quickly realised that Montgomery was about to launch another of his frontal assaults to the north. He knew that it would be suicidal to remain at the Mersa el Brega Line, also that he simply did not have enough fuel to counter any outflanking movements. He had no alternative to an immediate withdrawal back to Merduma, where perhaps the 8th Army might be held for a while. During the morning British armour attacked in the south with strong artillery support, but 15 Panzer Division counterattacked and plugged the gap, but in doing so used up an alarming amount of precious fuel. It was not until the early afternoon that 7th Armoured Division attacked General Cantaluppi's Ariete Battle Group with some eighty tanks. The Italians put up a stout defence until the early evening, when the Centauro Division counterattacked, driving the British back with a loss of twenty-two tanks and two armoured cars. Rommel congratulated the general on a splendid achievement.[92] At 1740hrs the order '333' was given for the withdrawal to begin.[93] The Panzer Army was now being followed by two divisions along the coastal road, along with an armoured division to the south. Fuel supplies were rapidly running out, prompting Rommel to tell Kesselring that the situation had 'never been so serious'.[94] The Panzer Army continued to retreat along the Via Balbia, skilfully managing to avoid being cut off by the New Zealanders. Rommel was extremely frustrated that the lack of fuel made it impossible for him to exploit frequent opportunities offered by 8th Army to counterattack, leaving him with no alternative but, as he put it, 'to get out of the bag'. By the next morning 21 Panzer Division had taken up defensive positions on the narrow coastal strip at El Mugtaa, while the remainder of the Panzer Army continued its withdrawal westwards.

Rommel was most indignant when the RAF bombed his command post, which he had established roughly halfway between El Mugtaa and Nofilia. He blamed this unfortunate incident on the presence of General Hans Seidemann's Fieseler 'Stork'. The Air Chief Africa had come to visit Rommel, bearing the bad news that the British were advancing rapidly, whereupon Rommel ordered the formation of a battle group made up from units of 15 and 21 Panzer Divisions. Its mission was to keep the Via Balbia open for the Afrikakorps, so that it could disengage from heavy fighting and retire safely. As the pressure on 21 Panzer Division increased, Rommel ordered a withdrawal to the high ground at Arco dei Fileni.[95] The battle group on the Via Balbia was unable to halt the British advance, so the Panzer Army was pulled back to Nofilia that evening. Shortage of fuel made it impossible to bring 15 Panzer Division back until the next morning.[96] The Panzer Army had been in a most precarious situation on 15 December, with 8th Army attacking the front and penetrating deep into the flank, leaving the Afrikakorps in serious danger of being encircled. The chronic shortage of fuel had made a counterattack impossible, and it was only when additional fuel was brought in during the afternoon that they were able to escape to the west.

During the morning of 16 December British infantry managed to secure the high ground overlooking 90 Light Africa Division's positions at the arrière-garde, while other British units cut off the Via Balbia. 15 Panzer Division extricated the Panzer Army from this dangerous situation by parrying the 8th Army's forward units, enabling the remainder of the Panzer Army to return safely to Nofilia.⁹⁷

Once again Rommel was saved by Montgomery's unimaginative plan. He should have known by now that the Panzer Army would not stand and fight against such overwhelming odds. His only chance of defeating Rommel would have been first to launch an outflanking movement to the south, thus cutting off an escape route, followed by a frontal assault to finish him off. Once again the British seemed to have failed to notice the withdrawal. By the time they attacked, the Panzer Army's infantry had been withdrawn to Nofilia and the Buerat Line. The Panzer Army reached Nofilia on 16 December, saved by the sluggishness of 8th Army's pursuit.⁹⁸ OKH, fearing Hitler's reaction on hearing of the withdrawal, were careful to point out that it was according to Mussolini's instructions to withdraw to the Buerat Line, which Hitler had implicitly seconded. Hitler was furious, once again insisting that Rommel should have stayed put at El Alamein, and asking when he was ever going to make a stand.⁹⁹ Goebbels, however, was much amused to hear that Montgomery had called the war correspondents out of bed only to announce that Rommel had once again slipped through his fingers. He felt that this was hardly an occasion over which to make such a to-do.¹⁰⁰

Shortage of fuel and other supplies obliged Rommel to make a stand at Nofilia for as long as possible, but he knew full well that the position could not be held in the long run. At 0900hrs on 17 December he went to see Bastico and presented him with a familiar litany of complaint. The reinforcements he had been promised had not arrived, lack of fuel made mobile warfare impossible, since his motorised forces had to be mainly to the south to counter an outflanking movement, leaving the positions along the coastal route extremely thin. He was desperately short of anti-tank guns, artillery and mines. The Italian infantry had no experience of desert warfare and he had absolutely no mobile reserves. If the British had made a serious effort to break through there would have been no possible way that he could have stopped them, and the Panzer Army Africa would have been destroyed, Tripolitania lost, the way to Tunisia wide open. Rommel insisted that there was no alternative to fighting his way back to Tunisia, where he would attempt to make a stand at the Gabes Line, which had already been partially fortified by the French.[101] There he could link up with Arnim's Operational Group. The mountainous terrain would be secure against any outflanking movements, so that he could replenish and prepare for a fresh offensive, in either an easterly or westerly direction. Although he had been kept in the dark as to the situation in Tunisia, he was deeply concerned that the Allies would attack the Gabes bottleneck from southern Tunisia, thus driving a wedge between the two armies. Rommel forwarded this assessment to OKW, OKH, Kessselring and the Comando Supremo, having secured Bastico's partial agreement to an eventual withdrawal from the Buerat Line to Homs, thus guarding the coastal road to the east of Tripoli.[102]

Bastico was extremely concerned about the 'political repercussions' were Tripoli to be lost, not the least of which would be that he would lose his job as governor. He argued that the Panzer Army could not afford to lose the munitions dumps and vehicle parks in Tripoli, but Rommel pointed out that there was no position that could be adequately defended east of the Tunisian border. Any attempt to defend Tripoli would inevitably lead to the total destruction of the Panzer Army. He admitted that the Gabes position presented a serious problem in that the Panzer Army would be crammed into a very narrow space, but unlike the Buerat Line it was virtually impossible to outflank. Rommel insisted that the Buerat Line could not possibly be held, pointing out that Cavallero had agreed that Tunis was more important than Tripoli when they discussed the matter at Arco, and that Mussolini was in full agreement. Bastico finally agreed with Rommel's assessment, ending the discussion on the right note by telling him that the father of an English captain serving at Tobruk had offered £10,000 for his head. The field marshal found that quite flattering.[103]

By 17 December Rommel had strung his forces along the Via Balbia from Nofilia to Sirte, a distance of about 120 kilometres. The Afrikakorps was at the front, behind them were two reconnaissance units, then the Panzergrenadier Regiment Africa, behind which stood the 90 Light Africa Division. The Young Fascist Division brought up the rear. The forward positions soon came under heavy attack as the British tried to outflank the Afrikakorps at Nofilia. It took some time before enough fuel was brought forward to enable the Afrikakorps and Reconnaissance Unit 33 to counterattack, destroying twenty British tanks, warding off the threat to the flank, keeping the Via Balbia open and enabling a further withdrawal.[104] The Panzer Army staff assumed that the British, having made several botched attempts to out-flank them, would now opt for a full-scale offensive on a broad front, but Rommel used the unlikely threat of 8th Army going round the Sirte and Buerat positions and going for Tripoli as an argument for further withdrawal.[105] The withdrawal proceeded while 8th Army regrouped at Nofilia and concentrated on trying to deal with the exceptionally hazardous mining of the coastal road between Agheila and Nofilia, which forced transport columns to find alternative routes through the desert. Rommel moved his headquarters behind the Buerat Line, so that he was 150 kilometres away from the Afrikakorps. Since radio contact was sporadic he gave the DAK full freedom of action to withdraw if threatened by an outflanking movement.[106] The next major difficulty for Rommel came in the afternoon of 19 December in the form of an order from Mussolini, couched in words that Rommel called 'pathetic': 'Resist to the utmost. I mean resist to the utmost with all the troops in the German–Italian Panzer Army in the Buerat Line.'[107]

Rommel promptly contacted Cavallero and asked him what he should do if the 8th Army marched past the Buerat Line to the south thus cutting off the Panzer Army, deviously claiming that intelligence reports suggested this was Montgomery's intent. Cavallero gave the Delphic reply that Rommel had to fight in such a manner so as not to allow the Italians to be sacrificed once again. Superlibia told Rommel that the Buerat position had to be held at all costs, but in the same breath added that it could not afford to lose another 30,000 troops. Rommel pointed out the obvious contradiction, ordering General Mancinelli to go to Bastico and ask him how he could possibly hold on to the Buerat Line, while making sure that the Italians were brought back safely. Rommel repeated his claim that captured papers and air reconnaissance indicated that Montgomery was intent on an outflanking movement. Bastico was unable to give an unambiguous answer.[108] Rommel quickly realised that he was in an equally awkward situation. Cavallero and the Comando Supremo were looking for an excuse to relieve him of his command, while were Libya to be abandoned, Bastico as governor would be out of a job. Rommel's constant fear at this stage was that the Allies would be able to cut off the German–Italian Panzer Army from 5 Panzer Army in Tunisia, the main threat coming from the Allied forces to the west. His only hope was that he could obtain enough fuel to move back before the Allies realised the operational need for such a move. Rommel told Bastico that the non-motorised troops had to be withdrawn to the Tarhuna–Homs position. The entire operation would take ten days, so it had to start at once. He said that he hoped to be able to remain at Homs for some time, but that this would be possible only if they started moving at once. Bastico refused to issue this order, which ran counter to his instructions from Mussolini and the Comando Supremo, even though he saw a certain logic in Rommel's argument.[109]

Rommel was also engaged in an acrimonious argument with Kesselring, who accused the Panzer Army of wasting fuel in the rear echelons, thus starving the armour of the fuel needed for a mobile defence.[110] Rommel insisted that 95 per cent of all the fuel that arrived in North Africa had been sent to the front, and that the only units that wasted fuel were from Kesselring's Luftwaffe, while the Panzer Army's trucks with their empty tanks littered the coastal road.

Westphal had done his best to improve the Buerat Line. Eighty thousand mines had been laid, tank traps had been built and the defences were strong enough to resist all but a massive attack, but none of this obviated the threat of an outflanking movement to the south. The Panzer Army simply did not have enough armour to counter such a move. The Long Range Desert Group constantly threatened the Panzer Army's supply lines, laid mines and destroyed telephone lines, further exacerbating the supply problem. It proved virtually impossible to find any effective method of countering these daring hit-and-run raids. Rommel repeatedly asked the Comando Supremo for instructions as to what to do to obviate the threat to his southern flank, but the only answer he received was a repetition of the Duce's order.[111]

The Panzer Army was saved for the moment by 8th Army's slow advance. They assumed that there would be no major attack for several days, giving them time to establish a base at Nofilia. On 21 December, 21 Panzer Division was sent to guard the southern extremity of the Buerat Line and placed on the alert for an eventual outflanking movement.[112] The major remaining problem was that Bastico still refused to give any clear answer as to what to do should 8th Army make a wide swing around the southern flank and head for Tripoli. Then on 23 December he blandly announced that such an operation across 400 kilometres of desert would give the Panzer Army ample time to react, either by attacking the flank or by moving at least one motorised Italian division from the rear defensive positions to meet the threat. Panzer Army's staff was appalled at this ludicrous suggestion. There simply was not enough fuel available to move armoured units over such vast tracts of desert. An Italian armoured division could not possibly halt a massive tank attack, while the Panzer divisions had been so reduced as to be incapable of taking on an overwhelmingly superior enemy. It was obvious that 8th Army was intending to attack with a huge force, against which the Panzer Army would be helpless. Rommel constantly repeated that once an attack began it would be too late to pull back the infantry divisions to the Homs–Tarhuna Line. That movement would have to begin at once.[113]

Meanwhile, the meeting between Ciano and Hitler on 18 December was inconclusive. It was a day that for Manstein, given the precarious situation at Stalingrad, was marked by a 'crisis of major significance', which must have cast a shadow over the proceedings.[114] Mussolini excused himself for health reasons. Hitler expressed his sympathy, for he too suffered from severe digestive problems due to a nervous condition caused by overwork. Rintelen had still not recovered from his plane crash and could not attend. Hitler rambled on about the struggle for existence, the deadly threat to the 'racial substance' should the Allies succeed in breaking through at any one front. Predictably he turned down Mussolini's suggestion to wind up operations in the east, and dismissed the threat of an Allied landing in the west, adding that he would welcome one. He then tried to reassure Ciano, who seemed to those present to be exceptionally calm and collected given the gravity of the situation, by the vain promise to send four crack divisions to North Africa. Hitler imagined that the main problem was transport across the Mediterranean. He therefore called upon the Italians to improve their naval escorts. The Italians replied by requesting additional support from the Luftwaffe. Since neither side did anything, the situation continued to worsen. Operations in North Africa were scarcely mentioned, but Hitler said that if he were in command in that theatre he would order Rommel to make a stand at the Buerat Line. Once again he insisted that Rommel had had no reason to withdraw so quickly at El Alamein, and argued that were he to retreat to the Tunisian border the British, with their overwhelming superiority, would break through as they had done at El Alamein. Hitler failed to see that this was precisely why Rommel was arguing for the need to withdraw from North Africa.[115]

Hitler had a second meeting with Ciano in Berlin on 20 December, along with Ribbentrop, the ambassadors Mackensen and Alfieri, Marshal Cavallero and Jodl. Here he spoke at some length about Italy's historical right to *Lebensraum* in North Africa. He also claimed that from a 'military-geographical point of view' North Africa was essential for the defence of Europe. It obliged the enemy to tie up its forces as well as its shipping in the region. On the basis of totally erroneous statistics, he claimed that the 'Anglo-Saxons' were only able to replace half the tonnage they were losing in the naval war, thus placing them in an exceedingly difficult situation. Hitler seemed to imagine that the Allies were denied access to the Mediterranean and thus obliged to send most of their shipping around the Cape, thus having to use a far greater number of ships. The United States was apparently running desperately short of gasoline, and the scarcity of rubber was 'catastrophic'. In conclusion, Hitler argued that North Africa was a 'decisive' theatre as far as the outcome of the war was concerned, and for this reason the transport problem had to be solved.[116]

On Christmas Eve the Panzer Army reported to OKW and OKH that Tripoli was closed to Italian shipping. All supplies had now to go via Tunis, but the railway from Tunis to Gabes had been bombed to smithereens and coastal shipping was totally inadequate. The Italians were quick to point out that this was quite untrue. Submarines had managed to bring 750 tons of fuel to Tripoli and there was more on the way. Furthermore, there were five supply ships docked in Tripoli. This should be enough to enable Rommel to remain at Buerat for some time.[117]

At 0700hrs on 24 December Rommel set out, accompanied by two Italian armoured cars, to inspect the southern flank. They passed through the ravines of the Wadi Zem-Zem and drove on to El Fashia where they found tracks indicating that the British had been there recently. Rommel hunted around in the hope of bagging a member of the Long Range Desert Group, but only ran across a group of Italians, along with a few German troops who had succeeded in capturing some British commandos the previous day. Rommel returned to his command post where he received the news that 4,500 British vehicles had been spotted south of Sirte. 15 Panzer Division, which was positioned near Sirte, was about to settle down to celebrate Christmas Eve, but was ordered to move immediately. Unperturbed, Rommel and Bayerlein took part in CO Company's Christmas celebrations at 1700hrs, during which Rommel was presented with a miniature oil barrel filled with coffee.[118] At 2000hrs Rommel invited his closest associates to a dinner of roast gazelle that had been bagged that morning. Most of the Army Group spent a miserable Christmas sheltering from the pouring rain.[119]

Rommel's composure and self-possession were due to the fact that he had quickly learnt that Montgomery had the mentality of a conservative banker: no advance without absolute security. Rommel was amply justified. On Christmas Day the 8th Army halted its advance and appeared to wait for further reinforcements, giving Rommel ample time to pull back 90 Light Africa Division and 580 Reconnaissance Group, positioned in the arrière-garde, behind the Buerat Line. But the Panzer Army Africa was now virtually immobile for lack of fuel, a sitting duck for the 8th Army.[120] Rommel made a careful inspection of the defensive positions, ordering a number of feint 88 positions to be made to attract the British artillery, which had done such damage to his antitank emplacements at El Alamein. By 29 December the entire Panzer Army was behind the Buerat Line, ready to meet an imminent attack.[121] Cavallero reported that Mussolini wanted the Buerat Line to be held as long as possible, but Rommel quickly pointed out that this order could not be carried out. The road from Tunis to Tripoli was very vulnerable. The sea route to Tripoli was virtually blocked. Transport aircraft were needed in Russia to relieve Stalingrad, and there was a desperate shortage of trucks that could not possibly be replaced. The same applied to railway rolling stock. Kesselring had ordered that eleven Tigers designated for the German–Italian Panzer Army be allocated to 5 Panzer Army in Tunis. Reconnaissance showed that 7th Armoured Division, 2nd New Zealand Division, 10th Armoured Division and 51st Highland Division were preparing for a massive attack on the thinly held Buerat Line once 8th Army's air support was ready for combat. The Panzer Army knew that it only had a few days' grace.[122] Bastico agreed with the Duce, insisting that a strong force be left on the Buerat Line so as to win time and prepare once again to go on the offensive. Rommel, appalled at such unrealistic talk from a man desperately trying to hang on to his job, and knowing that he had Cavallero's support, argued force-fully for a swift pull back to Homs, leaving minimal forces at Buerat to slow down the British advance.[123] Bastico argued that there was not enough transport available to bring the non-motorised troops back to Homs, and in any case there was no material available to build ade-quate defences along the Homs–Tarhuna Line. Furthermore, it would take at least two months to destroy the harbour facilities in Tripoli, and a withdrawal from the Buerat Line would give the British a number of excellent airfields close to the front. Rommel replied with the familiar argument that it would take ten days to withdraw the non-motorised troops with the transport available, so that it would be madness to wait until 8th Army commenced its attack to begin such a com-plicated move. Given such a sharp difference of opinion, clearly Mussolini would have to adjudicate, but he was temperamentally re-luctant to do so.

Montgomery's hesitancy in front of the Buerat Line astonished Rommel, giving him, as he put it, 'a stay of execution'. What was now needed was a repeat performance of Mersa el Brega. All units that were not motorised had to be pulled back to avoid being cut off. Bastico and Rommel once again discussed the situation on New Year's Eve. Bastico continued to argue that they had to stay put and think in terms of offensive operations from the Buerat Line. Rommel impatiently repeated that this was impossible, pointing out that the Comando Supremo had already ordered the Homs–Tarhuna position to be strengthened. Bastico countered with Kesselring's argument that if they abandoned the Buerat Line the British would take a number of valuable airfields, leaving the Italians, who had virtually no anti-aircraft guns, hopelessly vulnerable. Rommel trotted out his familiar argument that the British would attempt to outflank the Buerat posi-tion, just as they had tried at Mersa el Brega, Agheila, Wadi Matratin and Nofilia, this even though his staff agreed that Montgomery would now opt for a frontal assault. He continued to insist that if they stayed put, the Panzer Army would be destroyed, and that there was nowhere near enough fuel to carry out Comando Supremo's call for a mobile defence. Bastico began to waver. He realised that Rommel's argument was persuasive, but he had his orders from Rome, which he had to obey. For Rommel the main problem was that he had 45,000 immobile troops at Buerat and not nearly enough trucks to get them out quickly. If they did not start moving right away they would all be destroyed.

Bastico said that Cavallero wanted Rommel to hang on in Tripolitania as long as possible, suggesting that he was thinking in terms of at least a couple of months. To this end he proposed to stay on the Buerat Line until there was a real danger of a breakthrough, then retire. Rommel's reply was that the timetable would be set by Montgomery and not by Rome. If he waited for the British to attack before withdrawing his infantry it would be far too late.[124] To add to the confusion, as early as 29 December OKH had received an order from Mussolini to Rommel to withdraw step by step to the Gabes Line, but this does not seem to have reached him, possibly because it was contrary to thinking of Comando Supremo, through which it would have had to pass.[125]

This placed Bastico once again in a familiarly awkward situation. On the one hand he was, as Rommel was the first to admit, a fundamentally decent man, who clearly saw the military logic of Rommel's position, and was not afraid to make his views known. On the other hand he was under orders from the Comando Supremo to make Mussolini's assessment of the situation known and his orders followed, even though Cavallero sympathised with Rommel. Since it appeared that Rommel and Mussolini took diametrically opposed positions the result was an impasse, but Bastico gradually changed his mind and did what he could for Rommel. It was ultimately thanks to him that Tripolitania was eventually abandoned. The fundamental problem was one of command and communication. Hitler, OKW, OKH, Mussolini, Comando Supremo, Bastico, Kesselring and Rommel were so often at counter purposes, that a clear chain of command was impossible. By contrast, Montgomery was clearly in command. He managed to ward off Churchill's impetuous and counter-productive interventions, and did not have to fight all the time with Alexander or Brooke.

New Year's Day 1943 found the German–Italian Panzer Army still at the Buerat Line, but that day the Comando Supremo ordered it to retire as slowly as possible to the Gabes Line so as to give time to evacuate Tripoli. This by no means solved the essential problem. On 2 January Bastico ordered that the motorised units should ensure that the 8th Army was held to the east of Tripoli for at least six weeks. Rommel's staff was quick to point out that there was a blatant contradiction between the order 'to save the German–Italian Panzer Army from destruction' and pinning it down to an exact timetable. It was after all Montgomery who was calling the shots, not the Comando

Supremo in distant Rome. All Rommel could do was to hang on as long as possible.[126] It was now decided that the situation was so tense that Rommel should return to Germany and Bastico be replaced. A new Army High Command was to be formed under an Italian general. Mussolini announced that he would adjudicate between Rommel and Bastico as to the future course of action in North Africa. Kesselring reported to OKW that Mussolini was prepared to give Rommel permission to withdraw, provided that he took at least three weeks to go back to Homs, plus devote another three weeks to the eastern defences of Tripoli. Once they had reached Homs a decision could be taken as to which units could be withdrawn all the way to Gabes. Hitler gave his approval to Mussolini's plan.[127] The situation was still very confusing, with Bastico calling for a counteroffensive to win time and Rommel promising that he would do everything possible to launch an attack, even though he knew perfectly well that this was absolutely impossible.[128] On 2 January 1943 Bastico finally granted Rommel permission to move his infantry back to the Homs–Tarhuna Line, giving him 500 trucks to do the job. Rommel immediately passed on the order so that 10 and 21 Corps began to withdraw that night. The Young Fascist, Spezia, Pistoia and Trieste Divisions began their withdrawal during the night. The German troops stayed on the Buerat Line, including 164 Light Africa Division, which had been motorised, using vehicles from other divisions.[129] Comando Supremo continued to insist that the Panzer Army should keep the 8th Army east of Tripoli for at least six weeks. Rommel, furious at being tied down to a fixed timetable, continued to request freedom of action, assuring Bastico that he would hang on for as long as possible. By this time the British had an estimated seven to eight fully equipped divisions in front of the Buerat Line, behind which stood the rag-tag and exhausted remainder of the Panzer Army's German troops. Rommel's intelligence officers reckoned with a British offensive from 11 January, with the main weight to the south, in a battle that Montgomery hoped would be decisive.

On 6 January Cavallero, Bastico and Kesselring came to Rommel's headquarters to discuss the situation.[130] Rommel was adamant that he did not have the fuel to mount any sort of offensive action. The ever-optimistic Kesselring insisted that the Axis had air superiority owing to the fact the DAF's fighters could not support the bombers, because they did not have the range until new airstrips were built. Cavallero announced that Mussolini had agreed to a withdrawal to Tunisia

because of the intractable logistical problems. The Panzer Army was to
retire to Tunisia and prepare for the 'final victory'. Time remained of
the essence, with Rommel moving back as slowly as possible, allowing
at least two months for the position at Mareth to be prepared, the last
defensive position left to the Axis in Tunisia.[131]

On 10 January Rommel was informed by Cavallero that there
was an acute danger that the Americans or the British would succeed in
breaking through at Gabes, and he received an urgent request to detach
164 Light Africa Division. Rommel insisted that without the 164 Light
Africa Division he could not possibly hang on for two months before
he moved back to the Mareth Line. The Italian infantry lacked mobility
and were unsuited for an effective defence. He suggested that 21 Panzer
Division was far better suited for the fighting in Tunisia, where it could
act as an operational reserve at Sfax. 164 Light Africa Division, which
was still not fully mobile, was desperately undermanned and short of
equipment.[132] Even though Mussolini complained that Rommel was
disobeying orders, and insisted that there would be a breakthrough if
he made such a rapid withdrawal, OKW supported this suggestion. At
midnight on 12/13 January Mussolini fell in line, issuing orders that
21 Panzer Division move to Sfax. The division immediately began to
roll westwards, leaving the Buerat Line even more seriously depleted.
Its movement was painfully slow, owing to lack of fuel, and Rommel
insisted that it leave behind much of its heavy weaponry, so as not to
leave the Buerat defences desperately weak.[133] 164 Light Africa Division
was now added to the Afrikakorps as a replacement for 21 Panzer
Division. That evening Rommel ordered the withdrawal to Homs of all
Italian troops remaining in the Buerat Line. The Panzer Army Africa was
thus further deprived of armour and was rapidly becoming an immobile
defensive force. The situation improved somewhat the following day
when Comando Supremo, at Kesselring's request, ordered 21 Panzer
Division to hand over all its Panzer and heavy weapons to 15 Panzer
Division.[134] This left on the Buerat Line three weak German divisions,
15 Panzer, 90 Light and 164 Light Africa Divisions, along with one
German infantry brigade and six battalions of Italian infantry, the latter
with substantial artillery. The troops had only thirty-four Panzer and
fifty-seven Italian tanks as they awaited an attack by seven to eight
well-equipped divisions with 700 tanks.[135]

Kesselring had visited the Wolf's Lair on 12 January where
he told Hitler that 5 Panzer Army was quite capable of defending the

Tunisian bridgehead on its own, but according to his own account he confided in Göring that the front could not possibly withstand a major offensive without substantial reinforcements.[136] This was a tactic typical of Kesselring and other senior commanders. He told Hitler what he wanted to hear, regardless of the truth, in order to stay in his good books, while being slightly more candid with his immediate superior. In both instances he was clearly distancing himself from Rommel, who had fallen from grace. He told Göring that Rommel was cooking up excuses to retire, such as the withdrawal of the 21 Panzer Division to Tunisia, and insisted that the Mareth Line would not be ready for at least two months.[137] Ignoring what was happening in Stalingrad, and lacking the courage to confront Hitler, Kesselring remained the blindly obedient 'soldier until the last day', as in the title of his autobiography. With commanders like these, Germany was heading for a well-deserved disaster. Kesselring claimed that with 60,000 tons of supplies per month, the 107,059 men of 5 Army, of whom 30,735 were Italians, could hold Tunisia against the 367,531 Allied troops. They could do this alone, without the assistance of Rommel's Panzer Army. Hitler agreed, and later promised 150,000 tons of supplies per month. Once again it was all in vain. Less than one-fifth of the supplies Hitler had promised actually reached North Africa; the rest lay beneath the waves.[138] Mussolini still imagined that it would be possible to hang on at the Buerat Line for two months or so, until the Mareth Line was ready. Rommel repeated that all depended on the strength and determination of 8th Army's imminent attack. All he could do was to promise that he would do the utmost to stay put as long as possible.[139]

Comando Supremo now decided that the last-ditch stand should be made at the Mareth Line to the south-east of Gabes. These defensive positions had been built during the First World War, but had been partially destroyed by the Italians in 1940. Rebuilding had already begun and Rommel sent Lieutenant-General Fritz Krause, commander of the Panzer Army's artillery, to inspect the defences and ordered all non-motorised troops back to the area around Mareth.[140] On 13 January Bastico felt it necessary to repeat the Duce's orders that the Buerat Line should be held for at least two months, because it would take that amount of time to prepare the defences on the Mareth Line. Rommel truculently repeated that he would do everything possible to hold the line, adding that there was a distinct danger that the army would be 'annihilated' and that it was 'questionable' whether he could hold up the 8th Army for two months.[141]

Rommel's staff estimated that 8th Army's attack would begin on 16 January, so they were caught by surprise when it began at daybreak on 15 January, spearheaded by 7th Armoured and 2nd New Zealand Divisions.[142] Both attacked in the south, the New Zealanders with some eighty armoured cars that forced 33 Reconnaissance Unit back 15 kilometres, until they were halted by 3 Reconnaissance Unit. The main blow was delivered by 7th Armoured Division with 150 tanks and 100 armoured cars, against 15 Panzer Division. By now the Panzer Army had only 36 Panza and 57 Italian tanks against 8th Army's 650 tanks and 200 armoured cars. Nevertheless, 15 Panzer Division managed to withstand the attack, knocking out 33 British tanks, but Rommel ordered them back at 2000hrs when fuel and ammunition ran dangerously low. Once again the British failed to follow up, waiting for their artillery to move forward. The Italian 20 Corps was withdrawn in the direction of Homs, while 21 Corps with the bulk of the Young Fascist, Spezia and Pistoia Divisions was already in position on the Homs–Tarhuna Line. One-third of the Spezia and Pistoia Divisions guarded the approaches to Tripoli.

The Panzer Army was now positioned along the line from Sedada to Bir el Manga. The British attacked again during the afternoon of 16 January, pitching more than one hundred tanks against 15 Panzer Division, the Centauro Battle Group and 3 Reconnaissance Unit, while 51st Highland Division, backed up by a tank brigade, pushed along the Via Balbia and ran up against the 90 Light Africa Division. Both attacks were halted, in part owing to the effective use of the Luftwaffe and the Italian air force, and twenty British tanks were destroyed.[143] Mussolini relayed a message to Rommel telling him to hang on as long as possible, but Rommel told a group of Italian staff officers that this was utterly impossible. At first he thought that it might be possible to defend the Homs–Tarhuna Line for some time, but now he felt that two days would be the absolute maximum. It had taken two weeks to move the Italians back to Homs; they were still immobile and permanently short of fuel.[144]

The Panzer Army was now in an extremely awkward position with a wide gap between 15 Panzer and 90 Light Africa Divisions. Lacking the manpower to fill this gap, Rommel ordered the Panzer Army to retire to Beni Ulid and Bir Durfan, two important airfields to the south that were likely targets for Montgomery. This could only be a stopgap measure, so during the evening of 18 January the Panzer Army was withdrawn to the Homs–Tarhuna Line to the immediate east of Tripoli, in order to avoid being outflanked to the south.[145] 8th Army's attacks were losing momentum, thanks to difficult terrain, well-positioned minefields and effective roadblocks. Fuel had been brought up to the front, and the move back to Homs went according to plan.[146] This position could not possibly be held for long, so as soon as there were enough trucks available the Italian infantry, including the Pistoia, Spezia and Trieste Divisions, were moved back to Tripoli.

On 19 January 8th Army attacked the Homs–Tarhuna Line, once again concentrating its effort against the southern flank. The 7th Armoured and 2nd New Zealand Divisions were to outflank the Panzer Army to the south and push forward to Garian to the south-west of Tripoli, then swing north to trap it east of Tripoli. Grossly overestimating the strength of this left hook, Rommel concentrated all his remaining armour in the south, consisting of the twenty-three Panzer from 15 Panzer Division plus sixteen tanks in the Centauro Battle Group in the south, while he drew all the remaining infantry back, leaving the Homs–Tarhuna Line virtually undefended.[147] This was done in defiance of an order from Hitler that day that he should stand and fight for as long as possible, regardless of his logistical problems, because 'with regard to future operations it is essential to win as much time as possible'.[148] Rommel realised that he would be unable to hang on to the Homs–Garian–Tarhuna Line for more than a few days but Cavallero, who felt that he was being altogether too pessimistic, insisted that he should conduct a mobile defence, in order to comply with the dictators' orders.[149]

Mussolini was every bit as appalled as Cavallero when he heard of Rommel's move.[150] He had disobeyed the order to stand and fight so as to allow sufficient time to prepare the Mareth Line, and he agreed that he had greatly exaggerated the threat to his southern flank. They charged him with increasing the danger of a breakthrough by his precipitous westward dash. Rommel haughtily replied that the finest strategic plan was worthless if it was tactically impossible. In the afternoon of 20 January Cavallero, Bastico and Kesselring had heated discussions with Rommel, who said that the choice was between 'losing Tripoli and the army in a few days time, or losing Tripoli a few days earlier, while saving the army by moving back to Tunis'.[151] He demanded to be given clear instructions: was he to stay put east of Tripoli, fight to the last man and be destroyed, or bring the army back to the Mareth Line and soldier on? There were no other choices. Bastico had already issued an order the previous day to the effect that he should stand and fight, but Rommel did not receive this until the afternoon of the following day. In any case Bastico always added the rider that the 'annihilation of the army is out of the question'. Mussolini told OKW that Rommel should not 'retreat rapidly and virtually without a fight', as he had done in the previous few days, but that he left the final decision to Cavallero, who was on the spot. Cavallero shifted responsibility back on to Mussolini, telling Rommel that he first had to consult the Duce. His reply, worthy of a Solomon or a Pythia, came the following day: 'The Duce's guidelines remain unchanged. There can be no question of the army being destroyed, but as much time as possible must be won.'[152] The threat of a breakthrough during a withdrawal was such that Rommel had to stand and fight.[153] Hitler, who was absorbed with the fighting at Stalingrad where the situation had become desperate, showed no interest in North Africa, much to the German–Italian Panzer Army's relief.

Rommel ignored these orders, claiming that he was fighting a mobile defence, for which it was essential to move his non-motorised units back, and that there was a very real threat of the army being destroyed if there was no withdrawal. He insisted that his order to retreat was fully justified, in that he had thereby managed to avoid being outflanked. 90 Light Africa Division had had a tough time fighting off a powerful British force that attacked from the rear along the Via Balbia to the west of Homs, some of them landing on the coast. It had suffered heavy casualties, and this was taken as a serious warning of how vulnerable the Panzer Army was to a flank attack, until it retired to the Tunisian border.[154] Rommel continued to pull his army back, hotly pursued by 8th Army. In the course of fierce fighting he was indeed able to avoid being outflanked, but his supply lines were under constant attack from the air, while the Panzer Army was subjected to merciless artillery fire. At least by using up the entire reserves at Tripoli, there was now sufficient fuel. There could be no question of defending Tripoli, because of the continued threat to the southern flank, so on 22 January the Panzer Army withdrew to the Bianchi–Olivetti Line, 40 kilometres west of the town, taking with it vast quantities of fuel and supplies.[155] The last German had hardly left Tripoli before the first British troops arrived, three months after their victory at El Alamein. Once in possession of the town, 8th Army paused to rest, bring up supplies and reorganise. Once again the Italians complained that they had been left in the lurch, while the Germans drove off with all the available transport.[156] This was a gross distortion of the truth. By 26 January 1943 the bulk of the Italian troops had crossed the Tunisian border.[157]

Meanwhile, Kesselring told Cavallero that priority must be given to 'pumping' men and equipment into the Tunisian bridgehead, while the OKW's Command Staff (WFSt) argued that Rommel was acting perfectly correctly, and that priority had to be given to strengthening the defences at the Mareth Line and Gabes, which should be manned by the Italians, with the Panzer forming a mobile reserve. WFSt also insisted that the command structure in Tunisia should be settled as soon as possible. They felt that Rommel was the man for the job, while an Italian supreme commander was out of the question. Hitler disagreed for political reasons, so OKW passed on a message to this effect to Mussolini and the Comando Supremo, urging them to form an Army High Command for Tunisia as soon as feasible. Sending troops and equipment to North Africa was to be given the same priority as for the eastern front.[158]

This gave Rommel a welcome breathing space. Tripoli having been abandoned, the priority now was to move the 30,000 Italian infantrymen back behind the Mareth Line, while using the motorised units to hold up the 8th Army in western Tripolitania for as long as possible.[159] Montgomery gave Rommel ample time to carry out this operation. Some British units continued the pursuit west of Tripoli on 25 January, but 90 Light Africa Division was able to make a stand at Zuara until 29 January. The Afrikakorps continued to man the arrière-garde in Libya until 15 February, when 15 Panzer Division was finally withdrawn. By this time the defences of the Mareth Line were virtually completed.

Montgomery has been severely criticised for allowing Rommel to escape to Tunisia. Liddell Hart felt that he had had a 'magnificent opportunity' to destroy Rommel's tattered army, blaming him for 'caution, hesitation, slow motion, and narrow manoeuvre'. The British historian John Ellis described the Panzer Army as 'an army for the taking'.[160] Even Freddie de Guingand, Montgomery's chief of staff, 'thought he ought to have rounded up the enemy', insisting until his dying day that his 'Grapeshot' plan would have done the trick, had it not been sabotaged by his boss.[161] Montgomery's biographer, Nigel Hamilton, while absolving him from all blame, attributes the failure to trap Rommel to 8th Army's 'lethargy, confusion, lack of communication and administrative chaos' and to its subordinate commanders who lacked initiative and flair, with Lieutenant-General Sir Herbert Lumsden as the principal culprit.[162] In spite of all Montgomery's sterling efforts to lick the 8th Army into shape, and although he had done so much to restore morale, it was still very much an amateur army when compared with Rommel's Germans.

Rommel and his outstanding staff showed their true mettle during the retreat to Tunisia, which was one of the most brilliant retreats in the history of warfare. They were practically impossible to catch. Regardless of serious logistical problems they moved as fast as humanely possible, kept their heads, and fought their way ferociously out of any encirclements. Determined rearguard actions slowed down the British advance, while defensive positions were carefully prepared ready to make another stand, however brief. The Wehrmacht proved to be capable of astonishing feats when retreating. Rommel's example was to be followed in the Soviet Union, Sicily, Italy, Normandy and up the Rhône.[163]

The slow progress of 8th Army, and the leisurely build-up after the 'Torch' landings, resulted in Hitler sending substantial assets to Tunisia, where they would almost inevitably be lost. The Americans gained valuable battlefield experience, in the course of which they weeded out some second-rate generals and promoted Bradley and Patton. But it was Rommel's astonishing victories that, by landing the British in a perilous position, prompted Roosevelt to opt for 'Torch' as a rescue operation, in spite of the unanimous opposition of his senior military advisers and of the secretary of war, Henry Stimson. This led to an inevitable delay in the opening of a second front in Europe, which the Soviets were persistently demanding, and to a strengthening of Moscow's conviction that the Allies were fighting to the last drop of Soviet blood.

Rommel's astonishing performance after El Alamein serves also to show up his many weaknesses when he seized the initiative. His impetuosity bordered on foolhardiness. He flatly refused to cut his coat according to his cloth. He failed to ensure command and control. He lacked a clear strategic vision. His deplorable handling of allies and subordinates, coupled with his insolent attitude to most of his superiors, all suggest that they, including Halder and Rundstedt, were correct in insisting that he was unfit to command anything above the divisional level. The story was quite different when the tables were turned. Now he had to watch the enemy's every move, so he finally came to realise the vital importance of reconnaissance, which in his impulsiveness he had all too often overlooked. His recklessness was reined in when forced to react defensively. Logistical difficulties could no longer be simply ignored. Although determined to maintain the maximum degree of independence, he now showed far greater concern for his allies, and learnt to appreciate not only the extraordinary difficulties they had to face, but also the sterling quality of some of their units and commanders. By leading from the front and sharing all the hardships of his men, he maintained a high degree of morale, even though most of his men knew that they were doomed. He was disillusioned, his health was ruined, and he no longer had Hitler's all-important support, but perhaps this all served to slow him down, and sharpened his judgement. He was no longer hungry for glory and fame, but was solely concerned with saving what he could of an army with whom he had already earned his place in history.

12 ✠ TUNISGRAD

As the campaign in North Africa reached its final phase OKW, the Comando Supremo and Kesselring agreed that the time had come to recall Rommel. They failed to appreciate his exceptional skill in withdrawing from an overwhelming enemy with minimal casualties and argued that he had wilfully disobeyed Hitler and Mussolini's orders, had precipitously abandoned the Homs–Tarhuna Line, and was a mere shadow of his former self. Rommel was plunged into a deep depression, with the intrigues against him making it increasingly difficult to concentrate on his work. He knew full well that his days as commander of the Panzer Army were numbered.[1] On 26 January he received a radio message from Comando Supremo to the effect that once he had brought the Panzer Army back behind the Mareth Line he was to be removed from his command for health reasons, to be replaced by General Giovanni Messe. Messe had until November been the commander of the Italian forces in the Soviet Union, where he had learnt heartily to detest the Germans.[2] Rommel was given the right to choose when to hand over command to his successor. Feeling that he was once again being made a scapegoat for the incompetence of the Commando Supremo, Kesselring's blind optimism and OKW's refusal to accept unpleasant facts, he asked that General Messe be sent to North Africa as soon as possible to be put fully in the picture. Messe considered his appointment to be a typical backhanded blow by his rival Cavallero. He felt that he should have been put in charge of the Comando Supremo rather than Cavallero, whom he assumed must have known that the campaign in North Africa was irredeemably lost. He knew that he was doomed to failure, probably destined to end up in an Allied POW camp. Mussolini, on the contrary, was living in a fool's paradise, talking wildly of successes, offensives and recovery.[3]

On 26 January Rommel made his first visit to inspect the Mareth Line, which ran from the sea to the Marmata Mountains just south of Gabes. It consisted of a series of antiquated French bunkers that offered inadequate protection against artillery. The defensive battle would therefore have to be fought from positions between the bunkers. To the south the bunkers offered excellent protection against tanks. In the centre there was a steep-sided wadi that was impassable for tanks. There were salt marshes to the north, but tanks could be driven across them, provided the crews were well trained. There was high ground in front of the Mareth Line, which obstructed the artillery's view and gave the British excellent positions from which to control their artillery. Most serious of all, the French generals Catroux and Gautsch had shown in 1938 that the position could be outflanked to the south by motorised forces, thus rendering the entire position worthless. Rommel pointed this out to the Comando Supremo, and suggested that the stand should be made further west at Gabes, a position between the sea and the Chott Jerid that could not be outflanked.

On 28 January Comando Supremo repeated its orders to Rommel to hold the Mareth Line, appending an order from the Duce that he was to fight his way back as slowly as possible. Comando Supremo asked OKW to repeat this order to Rommel, to make sure that he got the message.[4] OKW replied to the Comando Supremo saying that the main aim of the operation was to build up a force in Tunisia that would soon be able to go on the offensive. To this end it would be sufficient to place three Italian and one German division on the Mareth Line, with one Panzer division and an Italian armoured division as a reserve. A mobile offensive group was to be made up of 10 and 21 Panzer Divisions and the Hermann Göring Division, along with various units from the German–Italian Panzer Army. For this reason OKW refused to second Comando Supremo's orders to Field Marshal Rommel.[5] OKW was thus blindly following Hitler's fantasy that it would soon be possible to mount an offensive from the Tunisian bridgehead, and was thus intent on pouring men and matériel into a trap that would soon be sprung by the Allied armies advancing from both sides. The Italians, who made a far more realistic assessment of the gravity of the situation, were now principally concerned about the defence of continental Europe.

Rommel called a meeting on 29 January to discuss how best to defend the Mareth Line. It was attended by Colonel Baron von

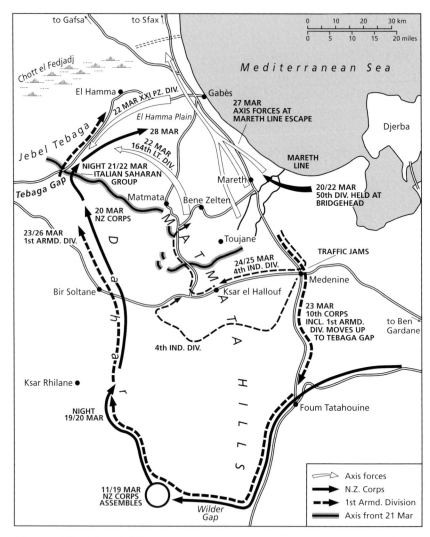

Map 22. The Mareth Line

Liebenstein, the commander of the Afrikakorps, Major-General Krause, commander of the artillery, Major-General Bülowius, the chief engineer and mine specialist, Major-General Franz, commander of 19 Anti-Aircraft Division, and Major-General Seidemann, the air chief in Africa. The Italian contingent was made up of Generals Navarini (21 Army Corps), Bitossi (20 Army Corps), Roncaglia (commander-in-chief of the Italian troops), Mannerini (Sahara Group), Stefanis (representing the Comando Supremo) and Mancinelli (Messe's designated chief of staff). Rommel stressed the importance of strengthening the southern and south-western flank, which he expected would have to bear the brunt of the attack. Mannerini's Sahara Group was to be placed to the south and could only be withdrawn when so ordered by Army Command. 164 Light Africa Division was to be placed between the Sahara Group and the Pistoia Division. It was to remain under the direct command of the Afrikakorps. The Roncaglia Group, made up of 7 Bersaglieri Regiment and three machinegun battalions, was to man the western flank. The main front was to be under Rommel's direct command and was to consist of the Pistoia, Spezia, Trieste, Young Fascist and 90 Light Africa Divisions; 15 Panzer Division was to act as a mobile reserve. The Centauro Division was to be placed behind the Trieste Division.[6] Rommel remained highly dubious that it would be possible to hold the Mareth Line for any length of time.

On 31 January both Bastico and Cavallero were relieved of their commands. Rommel had grown to appreciate Bastico, who had given him what support he could against the more senseless commands from Rome, and he gave him his due for the part he had played in helping to bring the Panzer Army back behind the Mareth Line with minimal casualties. By contrast, he was delighted to see the end of Marshal Cavallero, whom he regarded as incompetent. Cavallero was sacrificed as a scapegoat for the loss of Tripoli, accused of subservience to the Germans, excessive optimism and lack of national pride, and replaced by Ambrosio, the army's chief of staff.[7] Ambrosio was a highly regarded officer, who got on very well with Rintelen, who said of him 'by Italian standards he is remarkably calm'. The problem was that he had no experience of the all-important question of logistics, and had no say over the troops serving outside Italy.[8] Shortly afterwards, the Italian cabinet was shuffled with the replacement of nine ministers, among them Mussolini's son-in-law Ciano, whose removal was met with sighs of relief. Ambrosio, feeling, like most Italians, that Cavallero had been too submissive to the Germans, was determined to achieve a degree of independence. He came to the conclusion that Mussolini had a disastrous influence over the armed forces. The Duce was in serious psychological and physical decline, spending days on end in bed, and seldom leaving his apartment.[9] The mood in Italy after the loss of Libya was profoundly pessimistic, and the change in personnel did nothing to revive the regime's popularity. All hopes that the glorious Wehrmacht would turn the tide were dashed with Paulus' surrender at Stalingrad, and Ambrosio was soon to realise that it was in his country's best interests that the war should be ended before all was irrevocably lost.

General Messe arrived on 2 February putting on a show of optimism and bravado, which only served to strengthen Rommel's decision not to hand over command until the situation had stabilised somewhat. General Warlimont, who had been sent to North Africa by OKW to assess the situation, was less sanguine. He described the situation as 'a house built of cards'. He felt that given the shortages of men, matériel, fuel and transport, a large-scale offensive operation was out of the question for the foreseeable future. Most of 10 Panzer Division was tied down in defensive positions, 21 Panzer Division had yet to be replenished, while the Panzer-Grenadier battalions in both divisions were only semi-mobile; 15 Panzer Division could not be moved from its present position. It was highly unlikely that the Italian divisions would be able to withstand a major offensive. Warlimont also pointed out that the ports of Tunis, Bizerta and Sousse were still operating far below capacity.[10]

Rommel's considered assessment of the Mareth Line was that it presented 'an insoluble problem', given the relative strengths of the two sides. He thought that the Allies were most likely to attack to the south from Gafsa to Guettar and Gabes, or Maknassi and Sfax. He therefore ordered mobile reserves into the area around Gabes and began to think in terms of an attack on the Americans at Gafsa, so as to remove the threat of an attack on the Mareth Line from the rear. Messe was in full agreement.[11] Rommel's plan called for a concentric attack with 21 Panzer Division and units from 5 Panzer Army forming a northern group attacking from the northeast and east, and units from the German–Italian Panzer Army attacking from the south and southwest. The plan was sent to Comando Supremo for approval on 4 February 1943. Permission was granted two days later. Mobile forces from the German–Italian Panzer Army and 5 Army were to be placed under Rommel's command, but DIPA's staff pointed out that 15 Panzer Division could not be withdrawn from the front without a serious risk of a breakthrough. All they could spare was three motorised infantry regiments (one of them Italian), an artillery regiment, a Panzer unit and a reconnaissance group. The attack would begin on 11 February at the earliest.[12] Rommel discussed the operation with Kesselring and Arnim on 9 February at Seidemann's command post. Intelligence reports showed that the Allies had removed a large part of their force from Gafsa, so it would no longer be possible to strike a decisive blow against them. Rommel now had serious reservations about the Gafsa operation. He felt that the withdrawal of forces from the Mareth front would tempt 8th Army to attack, so that troops used for the Gafsa operation would have to brought back quickly to shore up the front. Furthermore, an advance at Gafsa would lengthen the front, making it all the more difficult to defend with the forces at hand. Once again Kesselring dismissed these concerns as unfounded, pointing out that they would now enjoy the benefits of fighting within inner lines. Warlimont also endorsed the Gafsa operation as vital to secure the Panzer Army's rear. OKW, which was growing increasingly frustrated with this lack of clear leadership, argued that given Rommel's state of health he should be withdrawn as soon as possible. Hitler agreed, but insisted that the staff of Messe's new Army Group should be made up largely of German officers from the Panzer Army.[13] Rommel's headquarters reported on the following day to OKW that the attack on Gafsa, code-named 'Morning Air' (*Morgenluft*), could not begin before 16 February at the earliest.[14] Meanwhile, Operation 'Beer Sausage' (*Bierwurst*), the withdrawal of 15 Panzer behind the Mareth Line, began on 12 February. Rommel soon came under attack from Comando Supremo, which accused him of pulling back his forward positions far too early and for no apparent reason. He replied that 8th Army was hammering away at the southern flank of the Mareth Line, while he had been preparing his attack on Gafsa to meet the threat from the rear. He asserted that 'holding the Mareth Line, which I previously described as an insoluble problem, has become even more difficult'. He concluded his riposte with the following words: 'I regard this as a totally unjustified accusation, which I herewith categorically reject.'[15]

On 11 February Rommel went with Warlimont to examine the Chott Line to the north of Gabes. They agreed that this was a far better position than the Mareth Line in that it was shorter, far more difficult to outflank and not threatened to the rear. The only major problem was that Comando Supremo had ordered that the Mareth Line was the final line of defence. Warlimont did what he could to persuade OKW that the Mareth Line could not be held for long.[16]

By this time OKH had come to the conclusion that the game was up in North Africa and that 'sooner or later' the Axis forces would be defeated. The main problem now was to find out where the Allies would launch an invasion. They bemoaned the fact that Allied counter-intelligence was so effective, their deception measures so skilful and their radio discipline so strict that OKH was left almost completely in the dark. As a result the Allies' next move was almost certain to come as a complete surprise. It was, however, reasonable to assume that they would choose a spot on the Channel coast where the distance by sea was relatively short, where they were likely to meet with little resistance and where they could rapidly gain a firm foothold. The Allies were doubtless aware that a large number of German troops had been withdrawn from western Europe, so they might well attempt a landing on the Channel coast, possibly combined with a feint attack on the west coast of France. It was generally considered far more likely that the Allies' next move would be against Italy, beginning with an aerial offensive against the mainland, followed by an invasion of Sicily. Sicily was not only an ideal springboard for an attack on the mainland; it also could be used to secure the sea lanes through the Mediterranean to Egypt. A landing in southern France was most unlikely, given the distance, the rugged terrain between Toulon and the Italian frontier, and the presence of German troops. OKH concluded that once the fighting was over in North Africa, the Allies would have complete operational freedom. Although an attack on Italy preceded by a landing on Sicily was the most likely next move, an invasion of northern France should not be ruled out.[17]

Warlimont returned from his trip to North Africa on the evening of 14 February, and reported to OKW the following morning. The picture he painted was far from encouraging. The Allied forces in Tunisia were poised for an attack on either Tunis or Bizerta, while to the east the 8th Army was expected to attack the Mareth Line between 16 and 18 February. It was assumed that given weather conditions and the phases of the moon, a massive joint offensive could be expected in mid-March. Warlimont repeated his description of the Axis position as 'a house of cards'. The Army Group was chronically deficient in all respects; 5 Panzer Army could not possibly withstand a serious attack. The Mareth Line could only be held if substantial amounts of men and matériel were brought up to the front; there were neither enough tank traps nor sufficient material to improve the fixed defences. The Italian units were poorly equipped and could not be relied upon to put up a serious fight. Warlimont stressed the serious logistical problems and posed the essentially rhetorical questions of whether the proposed offensive would bring any real advantage and whether, in the long run, the Tunisian bridgehead could be held. He insisted that full attention should now be paid to building up the defences in Italy and the Italian islands. Warlimont was able to give Hitler only a brief account of his trip, since he was about to leave for a visit to Army Group South in the Soviet Union. Kesselring, who was present at the meeting, ever mindful to play the role of Hitler's faithful vassal, argued that Warlimont's report was altogether too pessimistic and that the Gafsa operation should go ahead. Kesselring persuaded Göring that Warlimont's assessment of the overall situation was mistaken, but Hitler does not appear to have made any decision on this matter, so Warlimont felt obliged to repeat his concerns about the logistical situation at a conference of the Command Staff on 17 February.[18] The chain of command in North Africa was still undecided, but on 18 February Hitler ordered that Rommel should stay in command of the German–Italian Panzer Army until the completion of the present operation. Rommel was to remain nominally in command, even if he had to be withdrawn for health reasons, in order to deceive the Allies.[19]

Rommel now felt that the time had come for Messe to take over command of the Panzer Army, which was promptly renamed 1 Italian Army and given command over the Mareth front.[20] Rommel was put in command of the 'Assault Group North' made up of 10 and 21 Panzer Divisions and the Afrikakorps Battle Group. He was then given command over the 'Rommel Group', consisting of the 'Assault Group North' and the 1 Italian Army. On 23 February, 5 Panzer Army was added to form the Army Group Africa, otherwise known as Army Group 180, under Rommel's command. He also remained in direct command of the 'Assault Group North'. He remained at this post until 8 March.[21] None of this did anything to simplify the already hideously complicated chain of command.

The Panzer Army was a shadow of its former self. It had suffered severe losses at El Alamein, in particular to the Ariete Armoured Division and the Italian infantry. This was largely a result of Hitler and Mussolini's insistence that they stand and fight on 3 and 4 November. Further senseless orders obliged Rommel to attempt to ward off an overwhelming force with the battered remnants of an army that was bereft of supplies. He had managed to keep losses to a minimum by tactical brilliance and decisive leadership. None of this would have been possible without helping hands. In Fritz Bayerlein he had an outstanding chief of staff, a cool-headed officer of exceptional intelligence and operational guile.[22] In Montgomery he had an opponent whose methodical plodding gave him every opportunity, whenever he had the fuel, to make his characteristically swift and daring moves. He soon worked out a simple formula. His armour made a robust stand for one or two days while the infantry withdrew. Meanwhile, he did as much reconnaissance as possible to assess where the main weight of 8th Army's offensive could be expected, and how far the outflanking movement to the south had progressed. As soon as he estimated that the next blow would be delivered, he withdrew during the night to a new position, then to begin again. In spite of Montgomery's overwhelming superiority in men and matériel, and the enormous advantage afforded by Sigint from Ultra, Montgomery never succeeded in breaking through his front, or in outflanking him.

The Afrikakorps had the enormous advantage of acting according to the traditional tactics of the German army based on instructions (*Auftragstaktik*), whereas junior commanders had their hands tied by precise orders (*Befehlstaktik*). The Wehrmacht gave commanders all the way down to NCOs a high degree of flexibility to act as they saw best, within the framework of an overall tactical concept, whereas the British had to adhere to precise plans handed down from above. It was small wonder that in fast-moving armoured warfare the German approach proved to be superior.

In a sense Montgomery suffered from an *embarrass de richesse*. His powerful army needed immense logistical support. His lines of communication grew longer and longer the further he moved west, whereas Rommel moved ever closer to his bases. This meant that there were times when the Panzer Army was numerically superior to 8th Army's forces at the front. All it needed was sufficient fuel and ammunition to exploit the situation before the British could bring in reinforcements. Very rarely was this the case. The other problem was that Ultra provided an excess of information that had to be carefully sorted out and assessed in relationship to information gathered through reconnaissance. Furthermore, 8th Army knew of Rommel's expressed intentions through messages sent to OKW and Comando Supremo, but more often than not, knowing that such intentions were tactically impossible, he acted quite differently.

Although Rommel had many misgivings about the Mareth Line, he felt that for the time being it afforded him a degree of security against an attack by the 8th Army, at least until they had brought forward all their artillery. In his more optimistic moments he imagined that it might be possible to exploit the advantage of fighting on the inner lines, concentrate his armour in the west and attempt to push back the British and American forces from their positions from Gafsa to the sea. Having dealt with them he hoped to be able to mount at least a limited offensive against the 8th Army, thereby regaining an element of initiative.[23]

Having been replenished, 21 Panzer Division was loaned to Arnim. On 1 February it was ordered by 5 Army command to attack the poorly equipped Free French at the Faid Pass, a strategic point that controlled the Tunisian coastal plain. The operation was a success; the pass was taken, attempts by 1st US Armoured Division and the British Guards and paratroopers to retake it were repulsed, and a thousand Americans were taken prisoner. This still left the 'Rommel Group' in an awkward position with the Americans at Gafsa threatening the point where the 5 Panzer Army joined the 1 Italian Army. Rommel was determined to obviate this threat, and to this end ordered 21 Panzer Division to attack the flank of the American 2nd Armoured Division, while a Panzer Battle Group engaged the Americans to the front and another smaller force harassed them from the rear. The attack on 14 February was a carefully planned and skilfully executed attempt to turn the Allied southern flank in Tunisia, which caught the inexperienced Americans completely by surprise and in an extremely awkward tactical predicament. After an intense tank battle the Americans retreated in disarray, leaving more than seventy burnt-out tanks on the battlefield. Staff Sergeant Augustin's Tiger destroyed a Sherman from 2,700 metres distance, an awesome demonstration of its armament.[24]

5 Panzer Army was determined to pursue the Americans during the night so as not to give them time to regroup. But Lieutenant-General Heinz Ziegler, who had direct command over 21 Panzer Division, was somewhat slow in reacting. On 16 February Rommel left the Mareth Line defences to visit the battlefield, where he urged the men forward, but it was not until the night of 16/17 February that they were able to overtake the retreating Americans. By the morning they had reached Sbeitla, but the Americans had had time to organise and put up a determined and spirited defence. Their resistance was broken by evening after a fierce fight. 21 Panzer Division claimed to have taken 1,600 prisoners and destroyed 165 tanks and armoured cars, while its own losses

were minimal. This soon proved to be a gross exaggeration. Meanwhile, the Americans had withdrawn from Gafsa during the evening of 14 February before Rommel could launch his attack. The Afrikakorps Battle Group and the Centauro occupied the town on the following day. Encourage by this limited success, Comando Supremo sent a message to Rommel and Arnim claiming that the poor quality of the American troops gave them a favourable moment to score a decisive success in Tunisia. Rommel promptly issued orders to the Assault Group to push on.[25] The Americans had blown up the Citadel, in which they had stored their ammunition, resulting in the destruction of thirty houses with about as many dead and eighty reported missing. At this the inhabitants of Gafsa went on a plundering spree, gave vent to their hatred of the Americans, and welcomed the Axis troops as liberators.

From Gafsa the Battle Group moved southwest to Metlauoi in order to blow up the railway tunnel. On the way they picked up a substantial amount of fuel, as well as a number of railway cars. There was also a pile of 200,000 tons of phosphate that was badly needed in Germany, but there were no means of moving it. The Afrikakorps Battle Group under Major-General Baron Kurt von Liebenstein then moved on to Feriana, which fell on 17 February after a fierce fight. The Americans destroyed their supply dumps, and reconnaissance units reported that other depots were up in flames as the Americans retreated. The Afrikakorps pushed on to Thelepte where they found thirty aircraft in flames on the abandoned airfield.

In spite of these successes, Rommel knew that his situation was extremely precarious. The Allies had an overwhelming superiority in men and matériel and were they to use it with a degree of operational skill, by attacking the Rommel Group's extended flanks and cutting off its lines of supply, Rommel would be left high and dry. Rommel insisted they had to move immediately, while the Allies were caught off balance and fighting on a reversed front. He therefore argued for a rapid thrust towards Tebessa, a vital crossroads and supply point, and up to the sea at Bône. Colonel-General von Arnim strongly disagreed with Rommel, arguing that this was too risky an operation, which would interfere with his plans for an offensive in western Tunisia. He wanted to concentrate on a limited operation in his area of command. Rommel dismissed Arnim's objections as being due to his lack of experience of the deficiencies of Allied leadership, and forwarded his

proposal to the Comando Supremo and to Kesselring. He was counting on the excessively optimistic assessment of the overall situation in
North Africa by the Italians and Kesselring, as well as Mussolini's desperate need for a success, to be given the go-ahead.[26] Kesselring was
enthusiastic and promised to do all that he could to persuade Comando
Supremo to approve the plan. Rommel and his staff waited impatiently
for Comando Supremo's reply, but it did not come until 0130hrs on
19 February. It called for an advance further east, towards Thala and
Le Kef. Rommel was appalled. This would mean that the offensive was
far too near to the Allied front and would run into reserve units, but
there was no time to waste arguing about the details.[27]

The clashes between Arnim and Rommel were due in large
part to Rommel's ingrained dislike of aristocratic general staff officers,
whose cautious approach and traditional professionalism lacked any
flair. For his part, Arnim disliked Rommel's publicity-seeking antics,
his bravado and his penchant to go for broke. Both men realised that
the situation was hopeless; but while one stoically awaited the downfall,
the other preferred to go down in a blaze of glory.

The Afrikakorps was given the task of fighting its way through
the Kasserine Pass in Operation 'Frühlingswind' (Spring Breeze), opening the way up to Thala. 21 Panzer Division was to force its way
through a parallel pass to the right and to advance to Sbiba. 10 Panzer
Division was to be held to the rear, to be used to support either thrust
as needed. Meanwhile, the Allies had begun to withdraw forces from
northern Tunisia to meet the threat to the southwest. For the moment
Allied forces in the south were relatively weak. The pass was held by
2,000 ill-trained and inexperienced American infantry supported by
one battery of French 75s, and barely protected by a poorly placed
minefield, but this motley force gave the Axis a surprisingly unpleasant
welcome.

At first Rommel hoped that 3 Reconnaissance Unit would be
able to clear the Kasserine Pass with one bold stroke, but the resistance
was so strong that the attempt had to be abandoned. Otto Menton's
Panzergrenadier Regiment made a renewed attempt, but this too failed.
Rommel attributed this to the fact that the troops were used to fighting
in the desert, but now were in totally different terrain. Fighting through
a pass with heights of up to 1,540 metres was a quite different matter.
Menton had opted to move along the bottom of the pass so that his men

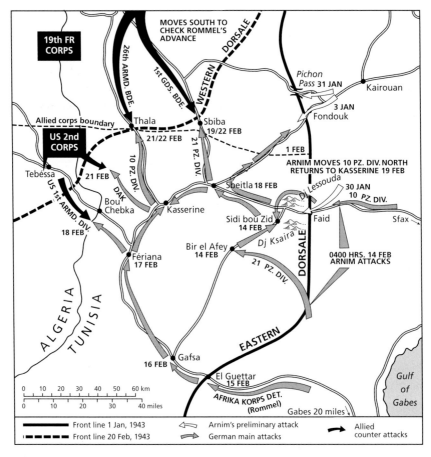

Map 23. Kasserine

were overlooked by American infantry and French artillery observers, rather than clearing out the high ground.

Rommel came up to the Kasserine Pass in the early afternoon on 19 February to examine the situation. He found the area littered with dead Americans and ruined vehicles, the victims of the air offensive. He promptly sent a battle group under General Bülowius into the pass, and then moved to see how 21 Panzer Division was doing.[28] It had made better progress, but had made slow work of it. Rains had made the roads very heavy going; the division ran into an extensive minefield and had been stopped in front of Sbiba. The slow progress up the passes gave the Allies time to bring up their reserves and prepare to block the Assault Group once it managed to fight its way through the passes.

Rommel was thus left uncertain where he should send 10 Panzer Division, but after careful consideration he felt that the Allied forces were weakest in the Kasserine Pass. At 0700hrs he returned to the pass to give General von Boich, the divisional commander, his orders. To his horror he found that Arnim had seconded part of the division for his operation to the north. There was considerable muddle and confusion as to which unit should lead the attack, so much valuable time was wasted, and Rommel became increasingly impatient. It was not until the afternoon that the attack could continue. Its success was in part due to the effective use of the Nebelwerfer rocket-launchers. It was the first time that they had been tried out in North Africa, and they spread panic among the raw 'hicks, Micks and spicks' in the American infantry. The pass was finally taken at 1700hrs. Menton's Panzergrenadiers had suffered heavy losses, and Rommel was full of admiration for the way the Americans had fought on the Kasserine Pass. They had suffered 2,000 casualties, but Rommel was well aware that his was only a tactical victory and that, unlike the Americans, the losses he had sustained were ones that he could not afford.

Once through the pass a fresh threat was presented by an American armoured unit in a pass to the left that was clearly on its way, intent on attacking. The Americans, who were no match for the experienced and battle-hardened men in 8 Panzer Regiment, were soon beaten back. A number of crews abandoned their tanks and made their way back on foot over the hills. Twenty tanks and thirty armoured vehicles, most of which towed 7.5cm anti-tank guns, were captured. Rommel now called a halt to prepare for a counterattack, but during the night forward units reported that the Americans had withdrawn. Seeing that the Americans had decided to fight their way back, Rommel opted for a deep thrust by 10 Panzer Division past Thala to Kalaa Djerda in order to cut off the roads and the railway. The Afrikakorps was to move through the pass to the northwest and advance to Tebessa; 21 Panzer was to remain in position, while 5 Panzer Army was ordered to engage the Allies as much as possible, tying them up and stopping them from sending reserves to the south.

Assuming that the Allies had suffered such losses in the Kasserine Pass that they would be incapable of mounting a counterattack, Rommel ordered 10 Panzer Division to advance in the direction of Thala at 1300hrs on 21 February, as he had been ordered to do by Commando Supremo. With the benefit of hindsight Kesselring later argued that this was a mistake, resulting from Rommel's lack of enthusiasm for the entire operation. He insisted that Rommel should have moved west towards Tebessa, thus outflanking the Allied position, rather than north to Thala and Le Kef. Rommel, however, who for once had followed orders, felt that he had delivered the Allies a humiliating defeat that had thrown their plans out of kilter, so he could now return to the Mareth Line and the serious business of dealing with the 8th Army's advance from Libya.

Progress was painfully slow against heavy opposition, including Mark VI Crusader tanks, now equipped with a powerful 7.5cm gun that had replaced the ineffectual 4cm model. The division, with Panzergrenadiers sitting on the Panzers' hulls, reached Thala at 1900hrs. A British battalion was overrun, with 700 men taken prisoner, but a counterattack by 6th Armoured Division and other Allied units, positioned on the high ground around the town, soon forced the Germans to retire. Rommel attributed this setback to Arnim's refusal to give him nineteen of the new Tigers, saying that they were all undergoing repairs. According to Rommel this subsequently proved to be untrue. Arnim simply wanted to keep them for his own operation. Whatever the truth of this accusation, Rommel unfairly blamed the failure of the offensive on Arnim's rivalry.[29] Arnim had every reason to want to hang on to his Tigers, which had proved most effective against the Americans. As one of his Panzer men, Major Luder of 501 Panzer Section, said: 'We must do all we can to put purebred Tiger units into action.'[30] The Tigers, which were first used in the North African campaign in Tunisia, and the newly introduced multiple rocket-launchers, the Nebelwerfer, helped boost morale. It now seemed that North Africa was no longer the 'Cinderella front' and that the German–Italian Army Group would at last be given the tools to do the job.[31]

Rommel left 10 Panzer Division in the late afternoon of 21 February to inspect the Afrikakorps. He found them under a heavy artillery barrage, unable to make any progress. The Americans had allowed the Germans to move along the pass and then attacked from three sides. Bülowius was unpleasantly surprised by the skill and accuracy of the American artillery which had knocked out a number of his Panzer. He was obliged to retire with the Americans in hot pursuit, inflicting severe casualties. The following morning Rommel returned to Thala, where he found that the Allied forces were now so strong that it was impossible to continue the offensive. At about 1300hrs Rommel discussed the situation at his command post with Kesselring, Seidemann and Westphal. There was general agreement that the offensive had to be called off. The enemy's strength, the heavy rain, the difficult terrain and the mounting threat to the Mareth front left them no alternative. Comando Supremo's permission to retire reached Rommel's command post at 2310hrs.[32] 10 Panzer Division and the Afrikakorps were pulled back during the night to the opening of the Kasserine Pass, while 21 Panzer Division remained at Sbiba. Thus by 22 February, with Rommel no longer able to conduct operational warfare, the initiative had irrevocably passed to the other side. The Army Group Africa could now merely react to the next Allied blow.[33]

Kesselring had asked Rommel whether he would like to take over command of the Army Group Africa. Although he was gratified that his 'defeatism' was now regarded as acceptable and that he was no longer to be seen as a *persona non grata*, Rommel refused. He knew that on 27 January 1943 Hitler had already decided that Arnim should have the post, so he could not expect full support from that quarter, and he did not intend to submit to the meddling by Comando Supremo down to the tactical level.[34] He also realised that the end was near. The Allies had recovered quickly from the initial shock and had shown great tactical skill in the defence. The Americans had such vast quantities of tanks and anti-tank weapons that there was little hope of success in mobile warfare. If only his battle group had moved fast enough, and if Arnim had not dragged his feet, Rommel might have be able to fight his way out into the open against little resistance, but now it was too late. Licking his wounds, he soon began to dream of a fresh offensive to be launched at the beginning of March that would break 8th Army's offensive capability.[35]

By 23 February all Rommel's units had withdrawn from the Kasserine Pass.[36] The weather had improved so that Allied aircraft were once again active, delivering blistering attacks that Rommel felt were even worse than those at El Alamein.[37] Whilst he brooded over the failure of the offensive, which he blamed largely on Comando Supremo and Arnim, Rommel was informed in the evening of 23 February 1943 that an Army Group Africa was to be formed under his command. It was up to him to decide when to hand over command to Arnim. Rommel was on the one hand pleased to be given command over all the forces, but on the other did not relish becoming once again OKW's, Comando Supremo's and Kesselring's whipping-boy. Rommel probably realised that with the failure of the operation, and with the Allies energetically counterattacking on his left flank, as well as stepping up the pressure on the Mareth Line, this was in operational terms the end of the campaign in North Africa.

In spite of Eisenhower's persistent prodding, General Lloyd Fredendall failed to deliver the *coup de grâce*. He preferred to shuffle papers in his bunker at Djebel Kouif 60 miles from the front, where he thundered on against 'Jews, Negroes and the British', rather than concentrating on finishing off the Axis forces. Major-General Ernest Harmon, commander of the US 2nd Armoured Division, frustrated by Fredendall's miserable performance, condemned him as a 'physical and moral coward'. Lieutenant-General Kenneth Anderson, although hardly in any position to make such a judgement, described him as incompetent, long before his miserable performance at Kasserine.[38] An exasperated Eisenhower replaced Fredendall with a very different type of soldier, the butt-kicking General George Patton, in March 1943. Fredendall was compensated with the award of a third star, welcomed home as a conquering hero and then shunted off to command a training army in Tennessee. Eisenhower could count himself lucky that he too was not sent home in disgrace.

Kesselring gave a rosy account of the recent operations in his report to OKW. He described the performance of Rommel's men as 'good' and often 'outstanding'. They had delivered such a devastating blow on the Americans and some British units that the Allies would be unable to mount another offensive for four to six weeks. The situation on the Mareth Line was such that motorised units would have to be withdrawn from northern Tunisia to act as a mobile reserve. This meant that there would have to be a withdrawal back to the starting line. The main object must now be to destroy 8th Army's forward units. Keitel was not taken in by 'Smiling Albert's' optimism, commenting in a marginal note on this report that he was 'deeply concerned' about the future of the Army Group in Tunisia. Nothing could be done without a radical improvement of the logistical situation. Regardless of these concerns, Hitler ordered a company of Tigers to be sent to Tunisia.[39]

On the following day Rommel discussed the proposed offensive by 5 Panzer Army at Medjez el Bab, to the north and due west of Tunis. Rommel agreed that an excellent opportunity presented itself, but did not agree that Arnim should withdraw his men once the operation was successfully completed. The Medjez el Bab plain was an excellent place for the Allies to deploy their forces for an attack on Tunis, which in Rommel's view was the most vulnerable point in the Axis bridgehead.

That evening Colonel Westphal, who had been Rommel's chief of operations (1a), but who was now Kesselring's chief of staff, arrived at Rommel's command post with details of a plan from Comando Supremo for an offensive by 5 Panzer Army towards Beja. This was the first Rommel had even heard of the place and he knew nothing of the plan. It seemed to him to be overly ambitious and ill timed. Beja was northwest of Thala, so the offensive should have been timed when 10 Panzer Division was at Thala, not after it had been withdrawn, quite apart from the fact that 5 Panzer Army did not have the manpower to carry out such an ambitious offensive.

The attack, with the curiously appropriate codename 'Blockhead' (*Ochsenkopf*), went ahead on 26 February, in spite of Rommel's misgivings, initially catching the Allies by surprise. A breakthrough was quickly achieved, but the Allies counterattacked and the Germans were hampered by bad weather from bringing up their heavy weapons, the Tigers becoming stuck in the mud. The fighting continued for a few days, the Germans unable to achieve their objectives, suffering greater losses than the Allies, and the battle degenerated into a slogging match. Fifteen of the nineteen Tigers were destroyed along with a number of other Panzer.

On his appointment to command the Army Group Africa on 23 February Rommel had ordered an offensive against the British positions at Medenine, where the 8th Army stood in front of the Mareth Line. It was a very risky operation, drawn up by General Messe, codenamed Operation 'Capri'; but he knew that if he did not at least try to disrupt 8th Army's preparations for a massive assault on the Mareth Line, all would be lost. The Germans had a tough time keeping the road open, but in a last desperate effort threw all their twenty tanks into a counterattack before being withdrawn during the night behind the Mareth Line. 5 Army's offensive meant that moving 10 and 21 Panzer Divisions to the Mareth Line would have to be delayed. Rommel's only hope was that the tried and tested 8th Army would not be firmly entrenched in its defensive positions and could be caught on the wrong foot.

Messe's plan for 'Capri' placed 21 Panzer Division to the left and 10 Panzer Division on the right. They were to attack from the high ground of the Matmata, while 15 Panzer Division attacked along the coastal strip. After further delays, during which 8th Army strengthened its positions, the attack began on the misty and overcast morning of 6 March with an artillery barrage at 0600hrs. Initially all went well for the Germans until they ran up against stiff opposition from 8th Army, which was well positioned in hilly country, protected by dense mine-fields and with carefully positioned anti-tank emplacements. Mont-gomery, who expected Rommel to attack, had repaired his defences to meet him wherever he chose to attack. He had 600 six-pounder anti-tank guns and 400 tanks, and his infantry were well positioned. Repeated attacks against this awesome defensive line were beaten back. The Stukas were brought in, but were met with a hail of anti-aircraft fire, the like of which had never been seen before. At 1700hrs Rommel ordered a halt. Once again he had missed the bus, and the British were ready for him. He had lost forty Panzer, but even worse was the realisa-tion that he had been unable to stop Montgomery's advance and now had to prepare for the final assault. His failure confirmed his belief that for the Army Group to remain in North Africa amounted to suicide.[40] Montgomery said of Rommel's attack in a letter to Sir Alan Brooke: 'It is an absolute gift, and the man must be absolutely mad.'[41] To oth-ers he complacently announced that 'the Marshal has made a balls of it.' Montgomery's success at Medenine and the American humiliation at Kasserine served further to bolster his already hypertrophic vanity, fanning his contempt for the Americans and worsening his relations with his allies. He had fought an effective defensive battle against an ill-considered attack, but he still had to fight his way through the Mareth Line.

At the end of February Rommel had asked his two army commanders, Arnim and Messe, for their candid assessment of the situation.[42] Both men agreed that it was untenable. The Army Group faced the virtually impossible task of defending a front of 625 kilometres – roughly the same as the western front in the first World War – with 120,000 fighting men and 150 Panzer against 210,000 Allied troops with more than 1,200 tanks.[43] This was no longer the familiar desert war. They now had to defeat one or other of the oppos-ing armies, but it was highly dubious whether they had the means to do so. They had to feed and supply 350,000 men, two-thirds of whom

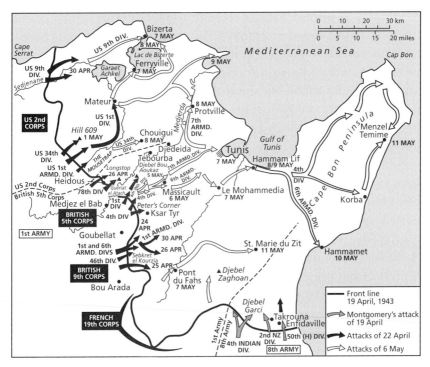

Map 24. Tunisia: the final act

were Italians. Of these only about one-third were at the front. The Army Group's defences were thin and lacked depth, with mobile reserves that were only capable of dealing with one breakthrough at a time. The two key questions were: were there sufficient mobile forces to beat one or other army, and could they be adequately supplied? These were to prove to be purely rhetorical questions. On behalf of 5 Panzer Army, Arnim said that the main danger was that the Allies would succeed in separating the two armies. The ports and lines of communication were under constant attack, while the Luftwaffe was left powerless. If supplies were completely cut off, which was a distinct possibility, Tunis could not be held beyond 1 July. The only hope was to deliver such a strong blow against one or other army, so as to put it out of action for at least six months, giving time to destroy the other. Here Arnim was clearly grasping at straws. His front was so long that he could in effect only post sentries along it, while his reserves were far too weak to stop a determined attack. It was therefore absolutely essential to shorten the front. Tunis was virtually without reserves of ammunition and food, and needed 140,000 tons of supplies per month to enable it to withstand a major offensive. This would clearly not be forthcoming. General Messe pointed to the poor quality of the new units and the overwhelming superiority of the Allies in the air. He anticipated attacks from the southeast, the southwest or the west and northwest, but thought it distinctly possible that the attack would come from all three directions. In that case the only hope was to withdraw behind a mobile defence.

On 1 March Rommel pointed out that the Army Group had to defend a front of about 625 kilometres, of which about 550 kilometres were either very thinly covered, or not at all. 5 Panzer Army was only partially defended by the mountainous terrain. Infantry could easily open up the weakly defended passes. There was a wide gap between the two armies either side of the Chott Jerid that was open to motor vehicles in the dry season. The only hope of hanging on for a while was to reduce the front to 150 kilometres and to ensure that it received at least 140,000 tons of supplies per month, which Rommel realised was virtually impossible.[44] The best he could do was to try to force the Allies to delay their offensive, but the blow would almost certainly come with the next full moon. If they did not withdraw in time this would result in the two armies being knocked off one by one.[45] He then sent a message to OKW, Comando Supremo and Kesselring asking them how they envisaged future operations in Tunisia, given that a massive Allied attack was imminent.

Kesselring, as an airman, argued that shortening the front would give the Allies valuable airfields that would be used to pound the Axis troops to pulp, thus further menacing the flow of supplies. The Axis air forces would then be left with nowhere to go. He still believed that the Army Group could continue to disrupt the Allies' preparations for an offensive, thus winning time to improve defences, particularly on the Mareth Line and the Chott, as well as to bring in reinforcements and supplies. Kesselring somehow imagined that it would be possible to move three new Panzer divisions as well as a light division to Tunisia, and give them full logistical support. With these forces the bridgehead could be secured and preparations made for offensive operations. Göring, who had long since written off Rommel as a waning asset, supported Kesselring's arguments when conferring with Hitler.[46] For the moment no one asked where these four new divisions were to be raised.

Rommel sent repeated memoranda calling for a shortening of the front, with Kesselring refusing to listen to any such suggestion. He was living in a fantasy world, but it was one shared by Hitler, who announced on 5 March that a shortening of the front would be 'the beginning of the end'. The Army Group should concentrate on disrupting the Allies by a series of limited attacks, while the remainder of the Hermann Göring Division, 999 Africa Division and 387 Regiment were brought to Tunis. To make all this possible supplies had to be doubled or even tripled. This would only be possible if shipping were better protected. On behalf of the Duce, Comando Supremo seconded the Führer's absurd assessment of the situation in Tunisia.[47] Keitel and Jodl were by now in full agreement with Rommel, but were helpless against Hitler's mulish obstinacy, which was reinforced by Kesselring's groundless optimism.

Unlike Rommel, who had no time for the political indoctrination of his troops, Arnim tried to spur on his men with tirades against the 'English'. In an army order of 5 March he complained that there was far too much talk about the 'fairness' of the English. This, he said, was pure rubbish. They treated their prisoners unfairly. They had started the war. They had stirred up the French, Norwegians, Belgians, Dutch, Greeks and Gaullists against Germany. They had forced the United States to enter the war. They had delivered Europe up to Bolshevism. For this they had earned the undying hatred of every good German. England is Germany's main enemy, so commanders must do everything possible to make their men hate the English. Anyone talking of the 'fairness' of the English is guilty of undermining the morale of the army and must be severely punished. This tirade appeared to do nothing to undermine the respect that Germans soldiers had for their opponents as the campaign entered its final phase; indeed it merely confirmed how widespread such feelings were, so Arnim felt compelled to return to the theme a few weeks later. He echoed his Führer's words by insisting that fighting spirit and the will for victory are the secret for success. All rumours must be instantly squashed. The enemy had neither been able to stop the two armies joining up, nor succeeded in breaking through to Bizerta and Tunis. They had failed to trap the southern army on the Mareth Line, and could not break through the Chott position. They could not cut off the Afrikakorps, or the southern army. The Army Group was inflicting severe damage on the Allies' lines of communication; the local population was against them and were raiding their rear echelons. The claim that Allies were suffering heavy losses fell on deaf ears. Two days later Arnim felt obliged to issue yet another order complaining of widespread defeatism. There was far too much talk that the supply situation was so serious that success was impossible. He more or less admitted that this was indeed true when he concluded by saying that the Führer and the Duce had ordered the Army Group to fight until the last round had been fired.[48] This was hardly enough to galvanise a demoralised army into making one last effort.

Meanwhile, Rommel waited impatiently for a reply. Eventually he heard from Kesselring that Hitler did not approve of his plan, appending an absurd set of statistics purporting to show that the Army Group was much stronger than Rommel claimed. He was now on his way out. On 7 March he said farewell to Ziegler and Bayerlein, who was appointed chief of staff to General Messe, much to Rommel's delight, for he had come greatly to appreciate this splendid staff officer.[49] He now decided that he would go once again to visit Hitler in a final attempt to persuade him to realise the gravity of the situation. On 9 March, having handed over the Army Group to Arnim at 0750 hrs in Sfax, he flew to Rome along with his trusted amanuensis, Berndt, and his personal physician, Professor Forster. The day before Hitler, Mussolini and Keitel had agreed that the fight in Tunisia must go on as long as possible, while German forces must be strengthened in preparation for an Allied invasion of Italy.

In Rome Rommel got the impression that the Italians assumed that he would not return to North Africa, and that Hitler would order him to take a lengthy cure. This was not at all what Rommel intended. He hoped to convince Mussolini and Hitler of his point of view and then return to his command. He had no luck with Mussolini, who seemed to think that sending another Italian division to Tunis would turn the tide. Rommel said that first of all the existing Italian units should be brought up to strength and properly equipped. Rommel quite liked Mussolini, who spoke to him in German, but said 'he was a great actor, like all Italians', who was too fond of the dramatic gesture, given to emotional outbursts and a hopeless optimist. He felt that he had done a great deal for his country, but now saw his dreams shattered.

In mid-March a half-hearted attempt was made to improve the protection of the convoys to North Africa, but it was too little, too late. Dönitz, the newly appointed commander-in-chief of the navy (ObdM) was sent to Rome, where it was agreed that the German navy would play a greater escort role. A German operational staff was attached to the Italian Naval Command (Skl), something that the Italians had hitherto resisted, but this made precious little difference. As part of the personnel changes, which Dönitz described as 'the big seal hunt', Weichold was removed from his post in Rome, charged with being overly pessimistic. These administrative changes did nothing to remedy the situation. The Axis forces needed at least 140,000 tons of supplies per month for an effective defensive in Tunisia. In March only 21,600 tons were delivered.[50]

Mussolini had repeatedly called upon Hitler to negotiate a separate peace with the Soviet Union, but Ribbentrop had brought a negative reply with him when he visited Rome at the end of February to discuss how best to counter partisan warfare. For Hitler decisions had to be reached on the battlefield, not at the negotiating table. Mussolini repeated his plea on 9 March and again on 25 March, but to no avail.[51]

Göring was in Rome at that time and suggested to Rommel that they travel together in his personal train to Hitler's 'Werewolf' headquarters at Winnitza. Rommel turned down the offer for fear that Göring would paint too rosy a picture of the situation in North Africa and set off on his own. He arrived at Hitler's headquarters in the afternoon of 10 March and saw Hitler in the evening, when he was regaled with tea and biscuits. Hitler was in a gloomy mood after the loss of Stalingrad, remarking that after a defeat one tended to see only the dark side of everything, and become seriously misguided. He was thus in no mood to listen to Rommel, whom he dismissed as a pessimist. He rejected Rommel's suggestion that the troops in North Africa be withdrawn to Italy, rearmed and replenished to be ready to meet the threat of an Allied invasion. Nor would he hear of shortening the front, insisting that this would make future offensive operations impossible. Rommel pleaded with him to allow him to return to his post and stay for a few weeks to see if the Americans would attack. Instead Hitler ordered Rommel to undertake a cure, after which he could return to North Africa to lead an offensive against Casablanca. The only positive outcome of the interview was that Hitler agreed to a withdrawal from the Mareth Line to Gabes. Hitler, who continued to fantasise about an offensive that would drive the Allies out of North Africa, soon countermanded the order when Kesselring visited his headquarters and gave a far more optimistic assessment of the overall situation.[52]

Göring arrived the following day full of blustering confidence, so that Rommel had no hope of getting Hitler to change his mind. The award of diamonds for his Knight's Cross with crossed swords was no compensation. Kesselring again insisted that the Mareth Line had to be held and claimed that Comando Supremo fully agreed. Comando Supremo had indeed accepted all of Kesselring's arguments, contending that recent offensive operations in western Tunisia had disrupted the Allies' preparations for an offensive. Similar attacks on the 8th Army would have the same effect, and in any case the Mareth Line was strong enough to withstand any offensive. In the meantime, while fresh troops poured into Tunisia, the Italians promised that they would do everything possible to increase the volume of supplies to 120,000 tons per month. They seem to have overlooked the fact that this was still 20,000 tons short of what Rommel and Arnim thought was an acceptable minimum.[53] Mussolini sent an urgent message to Hitler insisting that Tunisia be held at all costs, and that Rommel's plan to shorten the front would be disastrous. On the contrary the area under Axis control should be greatly expanded.[54]

Rommel, whose return to Germany was kept secret, did at least manage to persuade Hitler to modify his views somewhat. He convinced him that the Chott position should be greatly strengthened by the Pistoia and Spezia Divisions, so as to stop 8th Army from outflanking the Mareth Line. The Centauro Division was to relieve the 164 Light Africa Division, which was to move up to the Mareth Line. The Trieste Division was to be held in reserve east of Gafsa. The Luftwaffe was to step up its operations so as to delay an Allied offensive.[55] None of this did anything to tackle the fundamental problems.

Kesselring had demanded an extra infantry division for Tunisia on 7 March, but Armed Forces Command Staff at OKW said that this was eminently desirable tactically, but impossible given the logistical problems. They felt that transport and fuel should be given top priority. Troops without supplies were worse than useless, and in any case a considerable number of fresh troops were already on their way.[56] Some efforts were made in the following days to improve the protection of convoys, but they amounted to little more than organisational changes, the shuffling of various staffs, the exchange of views and discussions between Italian and German naval officers. Hitler had announced that the defence of Tunisia had top priority, and that logistics were the key to this, but the practical results of these discussions amounted to nothing.[57] Given the Allies' overwhelming superiority at sea and in the air, there was precious little that could be done.

Berndt, who travelled with Rommel, painted a grim picture of the situation in Tunisia to Goebbels. Although there were 75,000 German and 200,000 Italian troops in North Africa, they were desperately short of weapons, fuel and provisions. Only about 60 per cent of supplies actually got through. Rommel had told Hitler of all the problems he had with the Italians, complaining bitterly of the confusing command structure with Kesselring, Arnim, the Comando Supremo in Rome and the local Italian authorities, all anxious to assert their prerogatives. Berndt did not think it would be possible to hold the Mareth Line, and said that Rommel was correct in arguing for a withdrawal to Gabes, but that this was impossible because of resistance from various quarters. Goebbels, recognising that there was a distinct possibility that Tunisia would be lost, was fearful of the consequences in Italy.[58]

Montgomery's attack on the Mareth Line, Operation 'Pugilist', was a disaster.[59] Freyberg with 200 tanks and 27,000 men was sent on a wide left hook to the south of the Mamata Hills, intent on punching their way through the Italian infantry of General Giovanni Mannerini's Sahara Group (*Raggruppamento Sahariano*)[60] which was holding the front from the Mamata Hills to the Chott Jerid, while two divisions from Leese's 30th Corps attacked the northern end of the Mareth Line. The calculation was that the Axis forces would be unable to withstand two simultaneous attacks.[61] Ultra revealed that the Army Group Africa had spotted the movement of troops to the south, so that all elements of surprise had been lost, but Montgomery made little of this and by somewhat perverse logic argued that it would increase the element of surprise for the direct infantry attack on the Mareth Line. Surprise or not, the Mareth Line was a formidable obstacle, with the Wadi Zigzaou running along its front, offering extra protection. At some points it was up to 200 yards wide. The defences were manned by the German 90 and 164 Light Africa Divisions, both of which had been refurbished, and by four Italian infantry divisions; 15 and 21 Panzer Divisions were held to the rear. Leese's feint attack on the centre during the night of 16 March turned into a bloody attempt to break through the Mareth Line with the Grenadiers and the Coldstream suffering such heavy casualties in the dense minefield that they had to be withdrawn at dawn.

The main attack began at 2230hrs on 20 March 1943 with the biggest barrage since El Alamein. Messe, just as Montgomery predicted, was placed in an awkward quandary as to which attack was the more serious.[62] The attack on the Mareth Line was on too narrow a front, with insufficient force and inadequate armoured support. The Axis could concentrate its artillery and machinegun fire, while 15 Panzer Division prepared to strike back. The Geordies in 151st Brigade, led by Brigadier Beak VC, fought their way across the Wadi Zigzaou, only to find that it was impassable for wheeled and tracked vehicles as a result of heavy rain. Beak decided to halt until crossings had been secured. Freyberg's left hook made much better progress. By the morning of 21 March he had reached the minefields and Montgomery ordered him to press on to El Hamma and Gabes, then attack the Mareth Line from the rear, while Leese extended his bridgehead. The Geordies, who were now supported by a lone tank regiment of obsolete Valentines with their risible two-pounder guns, were unable to make much progress. Montgomery therefore sent in a brigade of Shermans from 7th Armoured Division to give the attack more weight. Ultra revealed that Arnim had ordered 21 Panzer Division to meet Freyberg, so that the only armour behind the Mareth Line was that of 15 Panzer Division.

On 22 March the British troops in the 2-kilometre deep bridgehead were being sorely tried, the attempt by 51st Highland Division to relieve the pressure by attacking to their left having failed to have much effect. The situation was chaotic, the Jocks' divisional commander, Major-General D. N. Wimberley, later remarking that 'at Divisional HQ the fog of war was thick!'[63] The Germans counterattacked with 15 Panzer Division, units from 90 Light Africa Division and the Ramcke Brigade. It was a brilliantly conducted operation with perfect co-operation between the Panzer and the infantry. The bridgehead was destroyed in a series of merciless attacks. Leese woke up Montgomery at 0200hrs on 23 March to announce that he had lost the bridgehead. De Guingand reported that this was one of the two occasions when Montgomery lost his composure. He turned to his chief of staff and asked: 'What am I to do, Freddie?'[64]

The next morning Montgomery wisely decided to call off the attack on the Mareth Line and to strengthen Freyberg's push to El Hamma. Freyberg had also became stuck in the minefield in the bottleneck between the Tebega and Mamata Hills, known to the British as the 'Plum'. Strengthening Freyberg would prove a lengthy business, for he was now 200 miles away, so Montgomery opted to use the Desert Air Force as an additional artillery weapon. This also took some time to arrange, giving Arnim time to bring up 15 Panzer Division and begin the withdrawal from the Mareth Line. The DAF, which had been licked into shape by its new and brilliant young commander, Harry Broadhurst, did the trick, in spite of a heavy sandstorm. Several squadrons of Kittyhawk fighter-bombers, a Spitfire wing and a tank-buster squadron blasted a gap through the Axis positions, through which 1st Armoured Division passed. With the breakthrough at 'Plum' and with General George S. Patton's 2nd US Corps attacking Gafsa from the west, the Axis troops were trapped, and Arnim began to feel that Rommel's assessment of the overall situation had been right after all. Alexander gave the Axis a break by ordering Patton to halt, so as not to stand in Montgomery's way as he advanced up the coast from Mareth to Tunis. In doing so Patton was denied the possibility of cutting off 1 Italian Army, for there was virtually nothing between him and the sea. This gave Arnim the chance to hit Orlando Ward's 1st US Armored Division north of Maknassy, but Patton made every effort to counterattack. 10 Panzer Division managed to ward off Patton, and a violent sandstorm on 26 March held up the New Zealanders, but by nightfall that day it looked as if the Axis was about to collapse. 15 and 21 Panzer Divisions were in disarray, 164 Infantry Division was falling apart, the way to El Hamma seemed open, but 21 Panzer made another hasty night-time retreat, thus winning the race. 10 Panzer Division held firm while Messe began moving his men to the protection of the Wadi Akirit to the northwest of Gabes.

The Axis troops took a terrible beating on the Mareth Line. Most of the artillery in 1 Italian Army was lost, leaving the Italians virtually unable to continue to fight. Rommel admired Montgomery's operational plan, even if it was poorly executed, because it forced the Army Group to improvise. That it managed to survive he attributed to the cool-headed staff work of Bayerlein, without whom Messe would almost certainly have been lost.

On 28 March the 8th Army was in full possession of the Mareth Line, but the Axis was now in position in the Wadi Akirit, a formidable obstacle. It remained to be seen whether Montgomery had learnt from his mistakes at the Mareth Line and would attack on a broader front with stronger forces, as some of his staff were urging.[65] With the

Americans to the west held up in a series of ill-coordinated and indecisive engagements, and with little chance of encirclement, the Akirit Line would have to be taken by frontal assault. Initially Montgomery thought that this could be done by two divisions from 30th Corps, but the divisional commanders baulked when they examined the terrain. A revised plan called for three divisions to punch a hole, through which the New Zealand Division and an armoured division would pass. Patton was urged to keep up the pressure to the Axis' rear.

On 29 March Arnim sent a desperate message to OKW: 'Supplies disastrous. Ammunition for 1–2 days, nothing left in the depot for heavy artillery. Petrol similar, major movements no longer permitted. No ships for several days. Supplies and provisions only for one week.'[66] Emergency measures such as distilling ersatz petrol from wine, making mines out of wooden boxes or spades from old ships' hulls could not possibly make up for these shortages. By this time even Kesselring had at last come to the conclusion that all was far from well, and that there should be at least a partial evacuation of North Africa. Comando Supremo called for a determined defence of the Wadi Akarit, but conceded that if this could not be held there should be a withdrawal to Enfidaville, provided that sufficient time was allowed to build up the defences.[67] Arnim reported to OKW on 31 March that there was no immediate danger on the western front from Guettar to Maknassy, and that as soon as there was enough fuel available 15 and 21 Panzer Divisions would launch a counteroffensive, but given the mountainous terrain this could only be strictly limited in scope. On the other hand it was doubtful whether the Akarit Line could hold out for long, but Arnim assured OKW that the Army Group would hang on until '5 minutes before 12'. He also pointed out that a withdrawal from Wadi Akarit would be exceedingly difficult, because of a gradual widening of the coastal plain that made it impossible to guard the flank.[68] It was this sober assessment that served to change Kesselring's mind, but OKW remained adamant, with Hitler ranting on in all too familiar tones of fighting to the last round. Faced with such opposition, Kesselring capitulated, calling for a fight to the bitter end.[69] On behalf of his Führer, Dönitz made futile demands on the Italians to increase the amount of supplies to Tunisia. They flatly refused to make this pointless sacrifice.[70]

The Italians began to crumble, thanks to the steady pressure on the Akarit Line. The initial night-time attack caught them by surprise, with 21 and 10 Panzer Divisions away in the west facing the Americans. By 5 April the Allied bridgehead was 3 kilometres deep and 10 wide, thus reaching a point where a breakthrough was imminent.[71] While the Axis squabbled with increasing acrimony, the main attack was launched in the pitch-black night of 6 April, achieving complete tactical surprise. Fighting was ferocious, with 51st Highland and 4th Indian Divisions taking severe casualties, but fighting magnificently. At 0930hrs Arnim felt constrained to move his 10 and 21 Panzer Divisions from Patton's front in the hopes of plugging the gaps in the Wadi Akirit. All this was to no avail. By dawn on 7 April the Wadi was in British hands, with the 8th Army moving along the coastal road to Sfax. The 88,000 Americans under Patton's command, who suffered heavy casualties as a result of their inexperience and lack of tactical skill, made no progress, in spite of the fact that the front had been denuded in a desperate attempt to staunch the haemorrhage at the Wadi Akirit.[72]

Sfax was taken on 10 April and the Axis army continued its withdrawal with 10th and 30th Corps in hot pursuit. A private soldier wrote home that day: 'We are once again experiencing a massive English attack and are retreating to the last defensive positions here in Africa. Hopefully we will be able to hold on.' He doubted very much whether this would be possible, owing to the lack of supplies. Major R. von D. serving in the harbourmaster's staff in Tunis saw that the end was near. He wrote: 'We do not know how long it will last here. For the second time in a war I am experiencing German inadequacy and the overwhelming strength of the others.'[73] Even OKW's laconic daily reports began to sound a note of pessimism, referring to 'a hard defensive battle against an enemy that is constantly replenished' and 'a retreat after a ferocious and bitter battle against an infinitely superior enemy'. This was the kind of language used as the Battle of Stalingrad drew to an end.[74] Those with any experience of reading between the lines knew that it would not be long before all was over.

Alexander attempted an attack on the flank of the retreating army by 9th Corps, but it was badly botched. The Americans in 34th Infantry Division had failed to capture the high ground covering the pass, but Alexander went ahead with the attack. In a fierce battle between 6th Armoured Division and 10 Panzer Division both sides suffered heavy casualties, but the Germans were able to limp back to Enfidaville where a defensive line had been built. 9th Corps' pursuit was far too slow, and the opportunity was lost. Eisenhower should have tried to separate the 1 Italian Army from 5 Panzer Army, instead of wasting time and suffering heavy casualties in the hills to the north-west. It would then have been relatively easy to knock out the Italians in cooperation with 8th Army.[75] By 12 April the bulk of 1 Italian Army had managed to fight its way back to the Enfidaville Line, while the Afrikakorps disengaged and retreated in an orderly fashion.[76] On the positive side, Montgomery was now able to cash in on a bet he had had with Eisenhower that if he reached Sfax by 15 April he would be given a B17 Flying Fortress with an American crew for his own personal use. The plane was duly delivered on 16 April, to Montgomery's unalloyed delight.[77]

The Afrikakorps and 1 Italian Army had fought their way back to the Enfidaville Line with determination and courage. In spite of 8th Army's overwhelming superiority, they had managed to knock out 123 tanks and a large number of sundry other armoured vehicles.[78] On 18 April American fighter pilots shot down twenty-four Ju52 transport planes and forced another thirty-five to crash land in the 'Palm Sunday Massacre'. Kesselring had been obliged to remove most of his air force to Sicily as the Allies overran the remaining airfields, so the low-flying transporters were left defenceless. The Axis lifeline was irrevocably severed.

For the Allies the final stages of the campaign in Tunisia were complicated by the face that they coincided with the preparations for 'Husky', the invasion of Sicily. Which units should be allotted to the invasion, and which were to finish off the job in North Africa? Was the British 1st Army, supported by US II Corps, or the British 8th Army to deliver the *coup de grâce*? On 19 April Horrocks' 10th Corps headquarters was given four divisions. With Freyberg's New Zealanders and 4th Indian Division in the centre, he attacked the Enfidaville Line, which was very thinly defended, thus tempting Arnim to bring in his armour. The initial attack was repulsed with heavy losses on both sides, but the Axis forces braced themselves for a renewed attempt.[79] The plan called for the Americans to attack on 22 April. Horrocks was then to break through, race along the coast and stop the Axis forces from retreating to the Cape Bon peninsula when pushed back by the Americans. Meanwhile Rommel, from his nursing home bed in Semmering, continued to demand that the remains of the Army Group be evacuated.[80]

Arnim acted as predicted, bringing up 90 and 164 Light Africa Divisions, as well as 15 Panzer Division. The Germans mounted fierce counterattacks on 20 and 21 April in an attempt to dislodge two divisions that had succeeded in capturing some commanding positions on the high ground at Takrouna.[81] 8th Army suffered heavy casualties, and was soon running short of ammunition, but by 22 April was in an excellent position to dash along the coastal road as soon as the Americans attacked. But to the north Alexander's Operation 'Vulcan', otherwise contemptuously known as the 'partridge drive', was a badly botched affair, as Montgomery suspected it would be. 1st US Army was dispersed along a broad front, so that there was, in Montgomery's words to Brooke, 'no depth and no "punch"'.[82] The problem was now that the Allies needed more weight, but could not afford to use divisions earmarked for 'Husky'. The Germans threw in all their reserves, moving 10 Panzer Division from the Afrikakorps' front to lend weight to a counterattack. On the British side the newly arrived 56th Division was thrown into the battle, but lacking any battlefield experience it fought badly, and by 29 April the attack was pronounced a failure.[83] An additional 11,400 German troops were sent to Tunisia in April and May, but without weapons and transport they were simply a drain on the grossly inadequate supplies, while 2,000 trucks destined for 10 Panzer Division, along with vast quantities of ammunition, fuel and heavy weapons, was still waiting on the docks in Italy.[84]

Montgomery, who had never liked 'Vulcan', calling it a 'dog's breakfast', now cabled Alexander, asking him to come to see him to discuss re-grouping. In the course of discussions on 30 April it was agreed that 8th Army should lend weight to 1st US Army, so as to be able to deliver one massive concentrated blow, a method that Montgomery insisted was the only way to beat 'the boche'. 5 Panzer Army was beginning to fall apart. It was desperately short of ammunition and fuel, and Colonel Hasso von Manteuffel's division was unable to plug the holes that were punched through the front. To the south the Afrikakorps and the Young Fascists were desperately trying to win back ground they had lost.[85] The Allies kept up a series of limited attacks, most of which were beaten off with heavy losses. Only in the north was any progress made, but Warlimont's staff at OKW described the situation as 'very serious'.[86] On 30 April Montgomery ordered Horrocks, always referred to as 'Jorrocks', to take the 7th Armoured Division (the famous 'Desert Rats'), Tuker's 4th Indian Division and 201st Guards Brigade from the Enfidaville front and join up with 1st Army to the north. He was then to be given command of 9th Corps, with orders to 'smash through to Tunis and finish the war in North Africa'.[87] Montgomery told Alexander that it would be unwise to leave the final push to Freyberg, a soldier whom he described as being 'a nice old boy, but a bit stupid'.

Horrocks' attack, known as Operation 'Strike', began at 0300hrs on 6 May and 'went like clockwork'.[88] The two infantry divisions punched a hole through 15 Panzer Division's defences, 6th and 7th Armoured Divisions began to pour through the gap at 0730hrs and by midday were trundling their way down the road to Tunis, thus splitting the Army Group Africa in two.[89] To the north 2nd US Army Corps seized Bizerta and Ferryville, the Germans having destroyed all the port installations. On 7 May the British entered Tunis. Among them was the irreverent chronicler of the Desert War, Spike Milligan, who observed that he was as much a prisoner of the British army as were the Germans and Italians, who were marched off to the pen without offering any resistance.[90] By 9 May, 5 Panzer Army, without fuel and having lost virtually all its anti-tank guns and artillery, ceased to exist. OKW received the following message: 'Army Group Africa. 5 Panzer Army HQ reports at 1523hrs. Documents and equipment destroyed. *Auf widersehen, es lebe Grossdeutschland und sein Führer.*'[91] Its last message read: 'Having done our duty, the last warriors of the 5 Panzer Army greet the homeland (*Heimat*) and our Führer. Long live Greater Germany.'[92] On 1 Italian Army's front it was reported that 'niggers from Senegal' from Leclerc's French 19th Corps had broken through 164 Light Division's lines, while the Afrikakorps was fighting for its life.[93] The most that now could be hoped for was that the Allies had suffered enough damage that they would have to postpone their final push for a few days.[94] Units from the Afrikakorps and 1 Italian Army managed to cut off the Bône peninsula and take up isolated positions in the high ground, but their situation was hopeless.

On 10 May Arnim received the following radio message from Hitler:

> *I offer my thanks and warm acknowledgement to you and*
> *your heroically fighting troops who, with their Italian*
> *brothers in arms, have defended every inch of African soil.*

*I, along with Germans, have followed the heroic
and awe-inspiring struggle of our soldiers in Tunisia. It is a
vital contribution to the overall success in the war.*
*The final effort and the attitude of your troops will
be exemplary for the armed forces of the Greater German
Reich, and will be seen as a gallant page in the military
history of Germany. Signed Adolf Hitler.*

Mussolini wrote in much the same vein:

*I watch with admiration and pride what the troops of the
Army Group Africa have achieved with stalwart resolution
and unbending heroism against the enemy's superiority in
numbers. History will pay tribute to these heroic acts. I
send my greetings to the officers and soldiers of the Army
Group Africa, who are the finest expression of the courage
of the peoples of the Axis. Signed Mussolini.*[95]

By 12 May the Allies managed to join forces, moving from
Enfidaville to the south and Bou Ficha to the north, thus completing
the encirclement of the Army Group Africa. At 0040hrs on 12 May the
Afrikakorps sent the following radio message to OKW:

*Out of ammunition. Weapons and vehicles destroyed.
According to orders the DAK has fought to the bitter end.
The DAK must be revived.*
Heia Safari! Signed: C-in-C DAK Cramer

The disrespectful use of the expression 'Heia Safari', the battle
cry of the Afrikakorps, in place of 'Heil Hitler', cannot have escaped
notice.

Later that day General Messe refused the Allies' demand that
his surrender should be unconditional, even though 1 Italian Army had
shot its last artillery round and spiked its guns.[96] OKW received its
last report from Tunisia on 13 May at 1220hrs when it was reported
that the parleying party with the 8th Army had not yet returned. They
complained bitterly that in spite of the ongoing armistice negotiations
'coloured troops' had once again attacked 164 Light Division.[97]

General von Rintelen reported from Rome that Italian morale was extremely low after the loss of Tunis. The general feeling was that the Italians had blindly followed the German lead in North Africa. Even at the best of times they had only been able to compare their disastrous failures with the Germans' spectacular successes. In doing so they effectively abandoned their pretensions to an Italian-dominated North Africa. Now the Comando Supremo was determined to stay in charge in Italy and not play second fiddle to the Germans.[98] Rintelen complained that the Italian army had been utterly ineffectual in the present war. Their weapons were useless, their officers were poorly trained, and the troops' morale was consistently low, because they did not believe that the war could possibly be won. The Italians would be totally incapable of defending their country against an Allied invasion, so a powerful German force would be absolutely essential for its defence.[99] OKH were uncertain as to the Allies' next move. They ordered the German troops in Sardinia, Corsica and Sicily, as well as the Peloponnese and Dodecanese, to go on maximum alert in anticipation of an Allied landing.[100] Hitler ordered preparations for Operation 'Alaric', the occupation of Italy, in the hope of keeping the Allies away from Germany's border. The significance of the codename cannot have been lost on the Italians as they contemplated changing their allegiance.

The Wehrmacht remained convinced that the defeat in North Africa was due to the overwhelming superiority of the Allies in matériel, and to the incompetence of the Italians. They continued to believe that their operational and tactical skills, combined with their superior training throughout all ranks, would in the end prevail. The fallacy of this argument was succinctly exposed by a cheery Tommy who, when a German in the back of a truck heading for a POW camp shouted out that the British army was no good, replied: 'Who put you in the fucking cattle truck?'[101]

The Germans lost 5,200 dead and 14,000 prisoners during the entire campaign in North Africa; 130,000 men from the Army Group were now taken prisoner. The atmosphere in Hitler's headquarters was extremely gloomy; following closely upon Stalingrad it was clear to many that the writing was on the wall.[102] Hitler admitted that Germany had suffered a serious defeat, and ordered complete silence on the propaganda front. He argued that any attempt to counter British reports on the poor quality of the German troops in North Africa would inevitably show the Italians in a poor light. Similarly, painting the Panzer Army as heroes, as the Italians had done, would end up making them look ridiculous. If blame were placed on logistical shortcomings this would also be attributed to the Italians' failures. Furthermore, it was obvious that the Germans had made serious mistakes during the campaign. The best was therefore to remain silent and fight on with renewed resolve, just as the victory at Kharkov, according to Hitler, had silenced all the talk about the defeat at Stalingrad.[103]

Goebbels did his best to turn defeat into victory, arguing that the heroic struggle in North Africa had given the Germans six months' grace to build the Atlantic Wall and to make all of Europe impregnable against invasion. He thus managed to persuade himself that the mission had been accomplished, but was forced to admit that the cost had been extremely high. After all, 130,000 Germans and 120,000 Italians had been taken prisoner in Tunisia, so this amounted to a 'second Stalingrad'. Hitler felt compelled to send ten divisions to the Balkans and seven to Greece in anticipation of an invasion, in addition to the seven already stationed in the region, so these divisions were also effectively lost thanks to 'Tunisgrad'. But this was not a decisive victory for the British. They had succeeded in driving the Germans out of Africa, but that was not part of Germany's *Lebensraum*. This was quite different from the Germans chucking the British out of Europe at Dunkirk, because maintaining the balance of power has always been the *sine qua non* of British politics. Goebbels, who still had full confidence in Rommel, argued that the most important thing now was to let the German people know where he was to be posted, for he was the best guarantee that the British and Americans would be frustrated in any attempt to invade the European continent.[104]

Hitler remained convinced that his decision to fight to the bitter end in Tunisia was absolutely correct. At the beginning of July he told a group of leading generals on the eastern front:

> *Naturally I have tried to decide whether the operation in Tunisia, which after all resulted in the loss of troops and matériel, was justified. I have come to the following conviction: the occupation of Tunisia resulted in us postponing an invasion of Europe by half a year. Even more important is the fact that thereby Italy has remained in the Axis. Otherwise Italy would definitely have left the*

*alliance. The Allies would have been able to land in Italy
without any resistance, and advance across the Brenner at a
time when, because of Stalingrad, Germany would not have
had a single man to spare to stop them. That would
inevitably have led to a prompt loss of the war.*[105]

It is impossible to know whether Hitler was parroting Goebbels, or whether the propaganda minister's ingenious spin on this shattering defeat was inspired by his Führer.

The war in the Mediterranean was lost, but the Germans still had two years of fierce fighting ahead of them. Tremendous victories had been won at Stalingrad and Tunis, both due to Hitler's obstinate refusal to permit a withdrawal, as well as his blind faith in willpower, fanatical commitment and unquestioning obedience. These, the first setbacks after a series of triumphs, weakened Adolf Hitler's astonishing charismatic hold over the German people, but it was not yet broken. For many it had diminished to the point that it became little more than a straw at which to clutch, but it was enough to ensure another two years of horrific bloodshed and destruction, owing to a refusal to see that all was lost, and fears that even worse was to come. Rommel, Hitler's favourite general, whose star had risen with him, was the first to fall. His faith had been shattered, for which apostasy he paid with his life.

NOTES

Chapter 1

1. Walter Baum and Eberhard Weichold, *Der Krieg der Achsenmächte im Mittelmeer-Raum. Die 'Strategie' der Diktatoren* (Göttingen: Musterschmidt, 1973) p. 19.

2. Adolf Hitler, *Mein Kampf* (Munich: F. Eher nachf., 1934) p. 699.

3. Ibid. p. 721.

4. Ibid. p. 709.

5. Joseph Goebbels, *Tagebücher*, ed. Ralf Georg Reuth, 5 vols. (Munich: Piper, 1992) vol. I, 15.2.1926.

6. On Mussolini see: MacGregor Knox, *Mussolini Unleashed, 1939–1941: Politics and Strategy in Fascist Italy's Last War* (Cambridge University Press, 1982). On the Mediterranean theatre see: Michael Howard, *The Mediterranean Strategy in the Second World War* (Cambridge University Press, 1966).

7. Adolf Hitler, *Hitlers zweites Buch; ein Dokument aus dem Jahr 1928*, ed. Gerhard L. Weinberg, Foreward by Hans Rothfels (Stuttgart: Deutsche Verlags-Anstalt, 1961) p. 176. See also: Andreas Hillgruber, 'Politik und Strategie Hitlers im Mittelmeerraum' in Andreas Hillgruber, *Deutsche Großmacht- und Weltpolitik im 19. und 20. Jahrhunderts* (Dusseldorf: Droste, 1977).

8. MacGregor Knox, *Hitler's Italian Allies: Royal Armed Forces, Fascist Regime, and the War of 1940–1943* (Cambridge University

Press, 2000). German troops were soon with bitter irony to call the Mediterranean 'Germany's Swimming Pool'.

9. Benito Mussolini, *Opera omnia di Benito Mussolini* (Florence: La Fenice, 1951) vol. XXVI, p. 233.

10. Baum and Weichold, *Krieg der Achsenmächte*, p. 20, quoting Italian army chief of staff Badoglio's memoirs.

11. For attempts to gain British support against an *Anschluss* see: D. C. Watt, 'Gli accordi mediterranei anglo-italiano del 16 aprile 1938', *Revista di Studi Politici Internazionale*, Vol. 26 (February–March 1959), 51 –76.

12. Count Galeazzo Ciano, *Ciano's Diaries* (London: Henemann, 1947) (hereafter *Ciano Diaries*) 21.4.1938.

13. For details see: Felice Guanieri, *Battaglie economiche tra le due grandi guerre* (Milan: Garzanti, 1953).

14. Knox, *Hitler's Italian Allies*, pp. 16, 38.

15. Percy Ernst Schramm (ed.), *Kriegstagebuch des Oberkommandos der Wehrmacht (Wehrmachtsführungsstab) 1940–1945*, 4 vols. in 7 (Frankfurt: Bernard und Graefe, 1961–5) vol. I, p. 234.

16. Enno von Rintelen, *Mussolini als Bundesgenosse. Erinnerungen des deutschen Militärattachés in Rom, 1936–1943* (Tübingen: R. Wunderlich, 1951) pp. 50 and 54–6. Siegfried Westphal, *Heer in Fesseln. Aus den Papieren des Stabschefs von Rommel, Kesselring und Rundstedt* (Bonn: Athenäum, 1950) pp. 157–9.

17. 'Faith' is preserved in the Malta Aviation Museum.

18. Franceso Rossi, *Mussolini e lo stato maggiore: Avvenimenti del 1940* (Rome: Regionale, 1951) p. 35.

19. Statistics taken from: Ralf Georg Reuth, *Entscheidung im Mittelmeer. Die südliche Peripherie Europas in der deutschen Strategie des Zweiten Weltkrieges 1940–1942* (Koblenz: Bernard und Graefe, 1985).

20. Figures from I. C. B. Dear and M. R. D. Foot (eds.) *The Oxford Companion to the Second World War* (Oxford University Press, 1995) pp. 585, 459, 1183.

21. Knox, *Hitler's Italian Allies*, p. 55.

22. Ibid. p. 57.

23. The mobility ratio was 1:40 in June 1940 and 1:38 in June 1943.

24. Pietro Badoglio, *L'Italia nella seconda guerra mondiale (memorie e documenti)* (Milan: A. Mondadori, 1946) p. 58. Actually by September the Italians had lost 1,247 dead and missing.

25. Rintelen, *Mussolini als Bundesgenosse*, p. 100.

26. Rintelen's report in *Mussolini als Bundesgenosse*. Jodl memo. Nürnberger Prozess, Vol. 28 (1947), pp. 301ff.

27. KTB OKW vol. I.1 7.8.40.

28. KTB OKW vol. I.1 9.8.40.

29. KTB OKW vol. I.1 14.8.40.

30. Rintelen, *Mussolini als Bundesgenosse*, p. 93.

31. Col.-Gen. Franz Halder, *Kriegstagebuch. Tägliche Aufzeichnungen des Chefs des Generalstabes des Heeres, 1939–1942*, ed. Hans-Adolf Jacobsen, 3 vols. (Stuttgart: W. Kohlhammer, 1962–4), vol. I 14.8.39.

32. KTB OKW vol. I, p. 64.

33. KTB OKW vol. I, p. 73.

34. PAAA R102974 Fremde Heere West to Foreign Office 22.10.40. A second memorandum is undated.

35. PAAA Fiche 2628 Stülpnagel for OKW 12.10.40.

36. Rintelen, *Mussolini als Bundesgenosse*, p. 95.

37. KTB OKW vol. I 30.8.40, p. 54.

38. Eberhard Weichhold, 'Die Deutsche Führung und das Mittelmeer unter dem Blickwinkel der Seestrategie', *Wehrwissenschaftliche Rundschau*, Vol. 9 (1959), 166.

39. Der Prozess gegen die Hauptkriegsverbrecher vor dem Internationalen Militärgerichtshof (14. November 1945 bis 1.

Oktober 1946). Amtlicher Text in deutscher Sprache, Vol. XXVIII, pp. 301ff.

40. Rintelen, *Mussolini als Bundesgenosse*, p. 101.

41. *Ciano Diaries*, 27.8.1940.

42. *Ciano Diaries*, 8.8.40.

43. *Ciano Diaries*, 19 and 20.8.40.

44. Halfaya Pass was a formidable obstacle. The RAF used to sing: 'If your engine cuts out over Hellfire Pass / You can stick your Browning guns up your arse.'

45. Gerhard Schreiber, Bernd Stegemann and Detlef Vogel, *Das Deutsche Reich und der Zweite Weltkrieg, Band III: Der Mittelmeerraum und Südosteuropa. Von der 'non belligeranza' Italiens bis zum Kriegseintritt der Vereinigten Staaten* (Stuttgart: Deutsche Verlags-Anstalt, 1984) p. 248.

46. *Ciano Diaries*, 14.9.40.

47. *Ciano Diaries*, 2.10.40.

48. Armistice negotiations with France continued in Wiesbaden until Vichy was occupied in November 1942.

49. Halder KTB vol. II, p. 125.

50. Bundesarchiv Militärarchiv (hereafter BAMA) RH 27–3/14; Rintelen, *Mussolini als Bundesgenosse*, p. 101.

51. *Ciano Diaries*, 12.10.40.

52. Halder KTB vol. II 3.10.40, p. 124.

53. Gerhard Engel, *Heeresadjutant bei Hitler, 1938–1943. Aufzeichnungen des Majors Engel*, ed. Hildegard von Kotze (Stuttgart: Deutsche Verlags-Anstalt, 1974) 28.10.40, p. 88.

54. Baum and Weichold, *Krieg der Achsenmächte*, p. 108.

55. Halder KTB vol. I 3.11.40.

56. DRZW vol. III, p. 421.

57. Halder KTB vol. II 20/21/23/24/25/26/27/28.10.40; KTB OKW vol. I.1 28.10.40.

58. KTB OKW vol. I, pp. 144 and 150.

59. Andreas Hillgruber (ed.) *Staatsmänner und Diplomaten bei Hitler*, 2 vols. (Frankfurt: Bernard und Graefe, 1967–70) vol. I, p. 230; Rintelen, *Mussolini als Bundesgenosse*, p. 101.

60. Halder KTB vol. II, p. 212.

61. KTB OKW vol. I, pp. 191, 194, 204 and 211; Halder KTB vol. II, p. 210.

62. Engel, *Heeresadjutant*, p. 88.

63. For further details see: Baum and Weichold, *Krieg der Achsenmächte*.

64. Reuth, *Entscheidung im Mittelmeer*, p. 26.

65. Enno von Rintelen, 'Operation und Nachschub', *Wehrwissenschaftliche Rundschau*, Vol. 1 (1951), 46–51; W. Warlimont, 'Die Insel Malta in der Mittelmeerstrategie des Zweiten Weltkrieges', *Wehrwissenschaftliche Rundschau*, Vol. 8 (1958), 421–36; Weichold, 'Die Deutsche Führung'; W. Warlimont, 'Entgegnung zu der Stellungnahme des Admirals Weichold', *Wehrwissenschaftliche Rundschau*, Vol. 3 (1959); M. Van Creveld, 'Rommel's Supply Problem', *Journal of the Royal United Services Institute for Defence Studies*, Vol. 119, No. 3 (1974).

66. Rintelen, *Mussolini als Bundesgenosse*, p. 96.

67. *Ciano Diaries*, 4.12.40.

68. Badoglio had been viciously attacked by Roberto Farinacci, a radical Fascist, whereupon he announced that if Farinacci did not retract his remarks he would hand in his resignation. Farinacci, certain of Mussolini's support, refused and Badoglio drew the consequences. *Ciano Diaries*, 23.11.40; Rintelen, *Mussolini als Bundesgenosse*, p. 115.

69. H. R. Trevor-Roper (ed.). *Hitler's War Directives, 1939–1945* (London: Pan, 1966) pp. 80–7. Text of Order Number 18 in KTB OKW vol. I 13.11.40, p. 187.

464 / Notes to Pages 33–9

70. 'Marita' is outlined in Order Number 20 of 13.12.40 in Trevor-Roper, *Hitler's War Directives*, pp. 90–2. 'Felix' in Order Number 18 as Note 69.

71. ADAP D XI, p. 538 10.11.40.

72. Rintelen, *Mussolini als Bundesgenosse*, pp. 112–13.

73. *Ciano Diaries*, 18 and 19.11.40; ADAP D XI 19.11.40 and 5.12.40.

74. *Ciano Diaries*, 20.11.40.

75. Reuth, *Entscheidung im Mittelmeer*, p. 31 quoting David Irving, *Die Tragödie der deutschen Luftwaffe. Aus den Akten und Erinnerungen von Feldmarschall Erhard Milch* (Frankfurt: Ulstein, 1970) p. 174.

76. Reuth, *Entscheidung im Mittelmeer*, p. 32.

77. Karl Gundelach, *Die deutsche Luftwaffe im Mittelmeer, 1940–1945*, 2 vols. (Frankfurt: Lang, 1981) vol. I, pp. 92ff.

78. 'Attila' was first considered in Order Number 19 of 10.12.40: Trevor-Roper, *Hitler's War Directives*, pp. 88–90; KTB OKW, p. 222. See also KTB OKW 4.2.41 and 20.1.41.

79. Trevor-Roper, *Hitler's War Directives*, pp. 98–100; KTB OKW vol. I, p. 261.

80. Rintelen, *Mussolini als Bundesgenosse*, p. 115. Ciano was deeply concerned about the effects of this defeat both at home and abroad. Graziani had lost four divisions and seemed at a loss to know what to do. Public opinion, already shaken by the startling failures in Albania and Greece, was further rattled. *Ciano Diaries*, 10 and 11.12.40.

81. *Ciano Diaries*, 12.12.40.

82. *Ciano Diaries*, 15.12.40.

83. For details see: Michael Salewski, *Die deutsche Seekriegsleitung, 1935–1945, vol. I: 1935–1941* (Frankfurt: Bernard und Graefe, 1970).

84. Gerhard Wagner (ed.) *Die Lagevorträge des Oberbefehlhabers der Marine vor Hitler, 1939–1945* (Munich: Lehmann, 1971) 8/9.1.41.

Chapter 2

1. KTB OKW vol. I 20.12.40.

2. Knox, *Hitler's Italian Allies*, p. 102.

3. *Ciano Diaries*, 21.12.40.

4. ADAP Series D, vol. IX, 2, vol. 4. II, p. 825; KTB OKW vol. I 28.12.1940.

5. Reuth, *Entscheidung im Mittelmeer*, p. 36.

6. For details see: Gundelach, *Luftwaffe im Mittelmeer*, and Alberto Santoni and Francesco Mattesini, *La partizipazione tedesca alla guerra aeronavale nel Mediterraneo, 1940–1945* (Rome: Edizioni dell'Ateneo and Bizzarri, 1980).

7. KTB OKW vol. I. 8.12.41.

8. Order Number 22 (11.1.41.) and 22b (20.1.41.); Halder KTB vol. II, p. 243; KTB OKW vol. I.1 9.1.41.

9. KTB OKW vol. I, p. 268.

10. KTB OKW vol. I, p. 270.

11. Klaus-Michael Mallmann and Martin Cüppers, *Halbmond und Hakenkreuz, Das Dritte Reich, die Araber und Palästina* (Darmstadt: Wissenschaftliche Buchgesellschaft, 2006) pp. 74–5. Woermann was given a seven-year sentence in the 'Ministers Trial' in 1949, but only served a few months. He died in 1979, aged ninety-one.

12. For Mussolini's visit to the Berghof see: Hillgruber, *Staatsmänner*, vol. I, 19 and 20.1.41.

13. Rintelen, *Mussolini als Bundesgenosse*, p. 25.

14. The Western Desert Force had been renamed 13th Corps shortly after the fall of Bardia. W. G. F. Jackson, *The North African Campaign, 1940–43* (London: Batsford, 1975) p. 71.

15. 'Sirte' refers to the town, 'the Sirte' to the surrounding district.

16. The use of 'Battle Groups', specialist teams designed for specific tasks, was one of the main secrets of Rommel's successes. The British

regimental system, by contrast, resulted in compartmentalisation and a chronic lack of co-ordination between different arms.

17. KTB OKW vol. I, p. 281.

18. Halder KTB vol. II 23.7.41.

19. M. van Creveld, 'Rommel's Supply Problem, 1941–42', *Journal of the Royal United Services Institute for Defence Studies*, vol. 119, No. 3 (1974), 68.

20. KTB OKW vol. I 1.2.41.

21. Engel, *Heeresadjutant* 1.2.41; Halder KTB vol. II, p. 265, 1.2.41.

22. Organisationally Halder, as chief of the general staff to Brauchitsch, the commander-in-chief of the army, was not responsible for Africa, which was the province of Keitel and OKW. OKH supervised the three Army Groups earmarked for the Soviet Union, as well as the Army Reserve. But Halder was also part of Hitler's headquarters staff. Hitler was commander-in-chief of the armed forces, and took over from Brauchitsch on 19 December 1941 as commander-in-chief of the army.

23. Halder KTB vol. II, p. 244, 16.1.41.

24. *Ciano Diaries*, 22.1.41. Ciano admitted later that there was nothing mysterious about it at all. General Annibale Bergonzoli commanded 23 Corps.

25. KTB OKW vol. I 3.2.41.

26. KTB OKW vol. I 4.2.41.

27. KTB OKW vol. I 5.2.41.

28. KTB OKW vol. I, p. 273.

29. Rintelen, *Mussolini als Bundesgenosse*, pp. 128–9; KTB OKW vol. I 6.2.41.

30. KTB OKW vol. I; Halder KTB vol. II, p. 272, 7.2.41. B. H. Liddell-Hart (ed.) *The Rommel Papers* (hereafter *Rommel Papers*) (London: Collins, 1953) p. 98.

31. Trevor-Roper, *Hitler's War Directives*, pp. 98–100; Halder KTB vol. II, p. 271, 3.2.41.

32. KTB OKW vol. I.1 3.2.41.

33. Westphal, *Heer in Fesseln*, p. 198.

34. Rintelen, 'Operation und Nachschub'.

35. Halder KTB vol. II, p. 272, 7.2.41.

36. Reuth, *Entscheidung im Mittelmeer*, pp. 47–8.

37. Ibid. p. 52.

38. KTB OKW vol. I 13.2.41.

39. The LRDG was to be nicknamed the Libyan Desert Taxi Service because it came to specialise in transporting commandos, the SAS, the SIG and other specialists in ungentlemanly warfare deep behind the enemy lines.

40. The monument was dedicated to two heroic Carthaginians, the Fileni brothers, who resisted the Greeks.

41. Artemis Cooper, *Cairo in the War, 1939–1945* (Harmondsworth: Penguin, 2001) p. 39.

42. KTB OKW vol. I, p. 308.

43. KTB OKW vol. I, pp. 321–2.

44. *Rommel Papers*, p. 100.

45. Ibid.

46. Messe's comment in *Ciano Diaries*, 4.6.42. On 27.2.41 Graziani had requested to be relieved of his command. Mussolini agreed. Gariboldi had previously commanded the Italian 5 Army. KTB OKW vol. II 27.2.41.

47. For the arrival of Rommel and the Afrikakorps in North Africa (Operation 'Sunflower') see: Adalbert von Taysen, *Tobruk 1941. Der Kampf in Nordafrika* (Freiburg: Rombach, 1976).

48. *Rommel Papers*, pp. 100–1.

49. Goebbels, *Tagebücher*, vol. IV: 1940–2, 22.2.41.

50. *Rommel Papers*, p. 101.

51. Schreiber *et al.*, *Zweite Weltkrieg*, vol. III, p. 602.

52. Halder KTB vol. II, p. 292, 25.2.41.

53. Von Wechmar was German ambassador to Britain from 1984 to 1989 and skilfully smoothed the prickly relations between Prime Minister Margaret Thatcher and Chancellor Helmut Kohl.

54. The Afrikakorps called the *khamsin* the 'Ghibli'.

55. Montgomery was to adopt the opposite tactic at El Alamein. He disguised his tanks as trucks.

56. Halder KTB vol. II 28.2.41.

57. Taysen, *Tobruk 1941*, p. 62.

58. These were metric tons.

59. Baum and Weichold, *Krieg der Achsenmächte*, p. 128.

60. *Rommel Papers*, p. 103.

61. Westphal, *Heer in Fesseln*, p. 165.

62. The pathetically diminished British forces in North Africa were soon to be renamed the 8th Army. Churchill, with typical imperial flourish, referred to it as the Army of the Nile.

63. Janusz Piekalkiewicz, *Rommel und die Geheimdienste in Nordafrika, 1941–1943* (Munich: Bechtermünz, 1984) p. 40.

64. F. H. Hinsley, *British Intelligence in the Second World War, its Influence on Strategy and Operations*, 2 vols. (London: HMSO, 1979 and 1981) vol. I, pp. 390–2. Neame had earned a Victoria Cross in the First World War.

65. Halder KTB vol. II 20.3.41.

66. KTB OKW vol. I 17.3.41.

67. F. W. von Mellenthin, *Panzer Battles: a Study of the Deployment of Armour in the Second World War*, trans. H. Betzler (London: Futura, 1977) p. 54.

68. The Clausewitzian concept of the *Schwerpunkt* was a key element in German military doctrine.

69. Taysen, *Tobruk 1941*, p. 65.

70. Halder KTB vol. II, p. 304, 7.3.41.

71. Halder KTB vol. II, p. 310, 12.3.41.

72. Halder KTB vol. II, p. 315, 16.3.41.

73. KTB OKW vol. I 18.3.41.

74. Halder KTB vol. II, p. 320, 17.3.41.

75. Halder KTB vol. II, pp. 323ff, 20.3.41; Erwin Rommel, *Krieg ohne Hass*, ed. Lucie-Maria Rommel and Generalleutnant Fritz Bayerlein (Heidenheim: Heidenheimer Zeitung, 1950) p. 20.

76. Goebbels, *Tagebücher*, 21.3.41.

77. It was not until 1995 that the Colonel-General Dietl Barracks in Füssen was renamed the Allgäu Barracks. Dietl was a swashbuckler who, unlike Rommel, was unconcerned about the heavy losses occasioned by the suicidal attacks he was fond of ordering. He died in a plane crash in June 1944 while on his way to Hitler's headquarters.

78. Taysen, *Tobruk 1941*, p. 70.

79. For further details see: Stephen W. Roskill, *The War at Sea, 1939–1945*, 4 vols. (London: HMSO, 1956) vol. I, pp. 421ff.

80. Gundelach, *Luftwaffe im Mittelmeer*, p. 101.

81. Hinsley, *British Intelligence*, vol. I, pp. 404–6.

82. Baum and Weichold, *Krieg der Achsenmächte*, pp. 118–24.

83. For the Battle of Matapan see: Roskill, *The War at Sea, vol. I: The Defensive*; Baum and Weichold, *Krieg der Achsenmächte*, pp. 124ff; Salewski, *Seekriegsleitung*, pp. 325–7.

84. Major-General I. S. O. Playfair, *The Mediterranean and Middle East*, vol. II: *The Germans Come to the Help of their Ally, August 1941* (London: HMSO, 1956) p. 55.

85. BZG 8.5.41. He made it on the second attempt and wrote this letter on his way up to the front at Tobruk.

86. Ibid. p. 54.

87. Ibid. p. 58.

Chapter 3

1. Schreiber *et al.*, *Zweite Weltkrieg*, p. 616.

2. Halder KTB vol. II, p. 341, 3.4.41.

3. Morshead had fought with distinction at Gallipoli. The nickname came from the villain in the Flash Gordon comics. He had the habit of crumpling his face and narrowing his eyes when faced with a problem. Rommel gave him frequent occasions to grimace in the months to come.

4. Barton Maughan, *Tobruk and El Alamein* (Canberra: Australian War Memorial, 1966) pp. 34ff and 47ff.

5. David Irving, *The Trail of the Fox: the Life of Field-Marshal Erwin Rommel* (London: Book Club Associates, 1977) p. 73.

6. Taysen, *Tobruk 1941*, p. 66.

7. Agedabia was the former centre of the Senussi sect, which had been outlawed by the Italians in 1923. The Senussi now supported the Allies.

8. Rommel, *Krieg*, p. 22.

9. Taysen, *Tobruk 1941*, p. 76.

10. Halder KTB vol. II, p. 344, 4.4.41.

11. *Rommel Papers*, p. 111.

12. Goebbels, *Tagebücher*, 9.4.41.

13. Taysen, *Tobruk 1941*, pp. 84–5.

14. *Rommel Papers*, p. 111.

15. Westphal, *Heer in Fesseln*, p. 163.

16. Halder KTB vol. II, p. 353, 7.4.41.

17. *Rommel Papers*, p. 118.

18. Baum and Weichold, *Krieg der Achsenmächte* p. 131.

19. Halder KTB vol. II, p. 357, 9.4.41. German generals often forgot that Hannibal won the battle at Cannae, but lost the war. Much the same was to happen to Rommel. Actually only four generals were captured, two of them at Derna. The other two 'generals' were brigadiers, a rank equivalent to brigadier-general in the German army.

20. Heinz-Werner Schmidt, *Mit Rommel in Afrika* (Munich: Argus Verlag, 1951) pp. 35–41.

21. Brigadier Combe had previously commanded the 11th Hussars.

22. Taysen, *Tobruk 1941*, pp. 92–3.

23. The Germans used the term Cyrenaica for the western part of the area. Eastern Cyrenaica they called Marmarica.

24. KTB OKW vol. I. 2 12–15.4.41.

25. Halder KTB vol. II, p. 361, 12.4.41.

26. Halder KTB vol. II, p. 364, 13.4.41.

27. In August 1941 the Overseas Organisation (AO) of the Nazi Party inaugurated a soldiers' home named after General von Prittwitz. It was financed by Nazi Party members living abroad. BAMA RH/19/VIII/47 28.8.41.

28. Notable exceptions are Jon Latimer, *Alamein* (London: John Murray, 2002) and Niall Barr, *Pendulum of War: the Three Battles of El Alamein* (London: Jonathan Cape, 2004).

29. Rommel, *Krieg*, p. 40; Taysen, *Tobruk 1941*, pp. 102ff. He court-martialled a tank battalion commander who burst into tears when his attack failed. Irving, *Trail of the Fox*, p. 97.

30. *Rommel Papers*, p. 124.

31. Taysen, *Tobruk 1941*, p. 103.

32. Ibid. p. 110.

33. Knabe and Behr were both mentioned in dispatches and were awarded the Knight's Cross. *Die Berichte des Oberkommandos der Wehrmacht, 1939–1945*, 5 vols. (Munich: Verlag für Wehrwissenschaften, 2004) vol. II, 1.1.1941–31.12.1941, p. 102 sec.

34. Großherzoglich Leib-Infanterie. In the summer of 1942 Herff, having been awarded the Knight's Cross for his achievements in 1941, was posted back to Germany to become head of the SS personnel department with the rank of SS-Obergruppenführer and General der Waffen-SS. He was arrested by the British in April 1945. He died in September of that year while still a prisoner of war, aged fifty-two.

35. *Rommel Papers*, p. 124, Letter dated 14 April 1941, 0300hrs.

36. *Rommel Papers*, p. 126.

37. Rommel, *Krieg*, pp. 44–5.

38. *Rommel Papers*, p. 128.

39. Rommel, *Krieg*, pp. 44–6. The Afrikakorps used to sing: *Kennst du den Avanti Schritt?/Ein Schritt vor und zehn züruck* ('Do you know the Avanti march?/One step forward and ten steps back').

40. Taysen, *Tobruk 1941*, pp. 114–15.

41. PAAA Fremde Heere West to Foreign Office 25.4.41.

42. Bibliothek für Zeitgeschichte (BZG) Afrikabriefe. The Germans almost always referred to British and Commonwealth troops as 'the English'. A. D. 30.4.41; S. K. 9.5.41; H. E. 22.5.41.

43. Stegemann in Schreiber *et al.*, *Zweite Weltkrieg*, p. 623; Playfair, *Mediterranean*, vol. II, pp. 37ff.; Taysen, *Tobruk 1941*, p. 113.

44. Maurice-Philip Remy, *Mythos Rommel* (Munich: List, 2002) p. 70.

45. Irving, *Trail of the Fox*, p. 103.

46. BAMA RH/19/VIII/110.

47. Halder KTB vol. II, p. 366, 15.4.41.

48. Halder KTB vol. II, p. 365, 14.4.41.

49. *Rommel Papers*, pp. 130–1, Schraepler to Frau Rommel, 22.4.41.

50. BZG Afrikabriefe Gfr. H. E. 22 and 25.5.41, Lt A. F. 28.5.41.

51. Playfair, *Mediterranean*, vol. II, pp. 93ff.

52. Reuth, *Entscheidung im Mittelmeer*, p. 58.

53. Kurt Student, *Generaloberst Student und seine Fallschirmjäger. Die Erinnerungen des Generaloberst Kurt Student*, ed. Hermann Götzel (Friedberg: Podzun-Pallas-Verlag, 1980) p. 198.

54. Stegemann in Schreiber *et al.*, *Zweite Weltkrieg*, p. 612.

55. Malta endured 154 days of bombing, compared with London's 57.

56. Reuth, *Entscheidung im Mittelmeer*, p. 60.

57. Halder KTB vol. II, p. 377, 23.4.41.

58. Ibid. p. 379, 24.4.41.

59. Stegemann in Schreiber *et al.*, *Zweite Weltkrieg*, p. 625.

60. He expressed this fear in a letter to his wife on 21.4.41. *Rommel Papers*, p. 129.

61. Taysen, *Tobruk 1941*, p. 124.

62. KTB OKW vol. I.2 25.4.41.

63. Taysen, *Tobruk 1941*, p. 128.

64. Ibid. pp. 128–9.

65. Irving, *Trail of the Fox*, p. 135; Wolf Heckmann, *Rommels Krieg in Afrika: Wüstenfüchse gegen Wüstenratten* (Bergisch Gladbach: G. Lübbe, 1976,) pp. 120ff.

66. Schmidt, *Mit Rommel in Afrika*, p. 53.

67. 'Sent for a camel ride' was Afrikakorps jargon for being sacked. This was not the resister Friedrich Olbricht.

68. Halder KTB vol. II, p. 385, 29.4.41.

69. Halder KTB vol. II 23.4.41; also in Wolf Heckmann, *Rommel's War in Africa*, trans. Stephen Seago (New York: Doubleday, 1981) pp. 166–7.

70. Heckmann, *Rommels Krieg in Afrika*, p. 120.

71. BAMA Oberkommando des Heeres/Generalstab des Heeres RH/2/594.

72. Halder KTB vol. II 8.5.41.

73. BAMA Oberkommando des Heeres/Generalstab des Heeres RH/2/594 orders of 28.4.1941.

74. Government Code and Cypher School picked up Paulus' report from Luftwaffe Enigma. It was read with relish in Whitehall and Cairo, further convincing the chiefs of staff that the Axis would not attempt to advance into Egypt. Hinsley, *British Intelligence*, vol. I, pp. 396–7; vol. II, p. 280. The report is in BAMA Oberkommando des Heeres/Generalstab des Heeres RH/2/594.

75. Paul Carrell, *Die Wüstenfüchse* (Munich: Herbig, 2003) p. 28.

76. For details see: Kirchheim, Heinrich Georg. '*Angriffgruppe Kirchheim am 30.4 und 1.5.1941 beim Angriff auf Tobruk. Kritische Untersuchung der Ursachen für das Scheitern des Angriffs (Juni 1948)*', typewritten manuscript at the Militärgeschichtliches Forschungsant (MGFA) D-350. Holtzendorff, *Angriff auf da Ras Mdauur*, MGFA D-087; Rommel, *Krieg*. The best overall account is in Taysen, *Tobruk 1941*.

77. Halder KTB vol. II, p. 392, 3.5.41.

78. Halder KTB vol. II, p. 392.

79. Halder KTB vol. II, p. 404, 8.5.41.

80. Baum and Weichold, *Krieg der Achsenmächte*, pp. 132–3.

81. Taysen, *Tobruk 1941*, pp. 155–7.

82. Van Creveld, 'Rommel's Supply Problem', p. 68.

83. Goebbels was of a contrary opinion. He greatly admired the way in which Rommel used propaganda, considering this proof that he was a truly modern general. Montgomery was to take a leaf from Rommel's book and soon became a master of self-promotion.

84. Heckmann, *Rommel's War*, p. 232.

85. This was an issue of lengthy debate at the protracted armistice negotiations in Wiesbaden.

86. For Paulus' report see: Walther Görlitz (ed.), *'Ich stehe hier auf Befehl'. Lebensweg des Generalfeldmarschalls Friedrich Paulus. Mit den Aufzeichnungen aus dem Nachlass, Briefen und Dokumenten* (Frankfurt: Bernard und Graefe, 1960) p. 46. BAMA RH/2/594. Rintelen, *Mussolini als Bundesgenosse*, p. 133.

87. Halder KTB vol. II, pp. 400 and 405, 7.5.41 and 9.5.41.

88. Halder KTB vol. II, p. 407, 11.5.41.

Chapter 4

1. *Rommel Papers*, p. 135; Halder KTB vol. II, p. 426, 22.5.41.

2. Cooper, *Cairo in the War*, p. 68.

3. Hinsley, *British Intelligence*, vol. I, pp. 395ff.

4. BZG Afrikabriefe Gefr. H. E. 6.6.41, Lt A. F. 28.5.41.

5. Cooper, *Cairo in the War*, p. 109.

6. Hinsley, *British Intelligence*, vol. I, p. 396; Winston S. Churchill, *The Second World War: the Grand Alliance* (New York: Houghton and Mifflin, 1950) p. 283.

7. Playfair, *Mediterranean*, vol. II, pp. 160ff.

8. Hinsley, *British Intelligence*, vol. I, p. 398.

9. *Rommel Papers*, p. 136.

10. Ibid. p. 138.

11. Halder KTB vol. II, p. 446, 7.6.41.

12. Halder KTB vol. II, p. 448, 7.6.41.

13. Mallmann and Cüppers, *Halbmond und Hakenkreuz*, p. 87.

14. BAMA Deutsch-Italienischen Panzerarmee (Afrika) RH19/VIII/52.

15. Almasy was later to feature in a somewhat different role in *The English Patient* by Michael Ondaatje.

16. In an operation codenamed 'Fleshpots' – a tribute to Eppler's proclivities.

17. Mallmann and Cüppers, *Halbmond und Hakenkreuz*, pp. 159–60; Cooper, *Cairo in the War*, pp. 204–8; John Eppler, *Operation Condor: Rommel's Spy* (London: Futura, 1977); Anwar Sadat, *Revolt on the Nile* (New York: Harper and Row, 1957) and *In Search of Identity* (New York: Harper and Row, 1978); A. E. W. Sansom, *I Spied Spies* (London: Harrap, 1965). The story inspired two novels: Leonard Mosley's *The Cat and the Mice* (1958) and Ken Follett's *The Key to Rebecca* (1985). Both were made into films. Some claim that the five-pound notes were forged. Whether this is true or not, it was the large quantity of these unusual notes that aroused suspicion. Sadat was later to become president of Egypt and win the Nobel Peace Prize.

18. Charles Eade, *Winston Churchill's Secret Session Speeches* (London: Cassell, 1946) pp. 58ff.

19. Hinsley, *British Intelligence*, vol. II, pp. 280–1.

20. BAMA KTB Anlage 19 E 14.2.42 (Aide memoire for Rommel for discussions with Führer and Duce.).

21. The Matilda had a power to weight ratio of 7.17hp/ton. The Panzer III 16.75hp/ton.

22. Hinsley, *British Intelligence*, vol. II, p. 278.

23. Hinsley, *British Intelligence*, vol. I, p. 399.

24. Taysen, *Tobruk 1941*, pp. 167–82.

25. Kümmel was to be awarded oak leaves to his Knight's Cross at El Alamein.

26. *Rommel Papers*, p. 144.

27. Ibid. p. 145; Halder KTB vol. II, p. 459, 21.6.41.

28. OKW estimated that the British had lost 180–200 tanks; KTB OKW vol. I.2, 18.6.41.

29. Playfair, *Mediterranean*, vol. II, p. 171 says that the Western Desert Force lost ninety-one tanks in 'Battleaxe'.

30. KTB OKW vol. I.2, 19.6.41.

31. Playfair, *Mediterranean*, vol. II, p. 173.

32. Heckmann, *Rommel's War*, p. 196.

33. *Rommel Papers*, p. 146. The Crusader was also plagued with mechanical troubles.

34. Trevor-Roper, *Hitler's War Directives*, pp. 130-4.

35. Goebbels, *Tagebücher*, 11.6.41.

36. BAMA RH19/VIII/5 OKW to Rintelen, *Mussolini als Bundesgenosse*, 7.6.1941.

37. Stegemann in Schreiber *et al.*, *Zweite Weltkrieg*, p. 640.

38. Hinsley, *British Intelligence*, vol. II, pp. 278-9.

39. BAMA RH2/631 2.7.41.

40. BAMA RH2/630 OKH 24.7.41.

41. Halder KTB vol. III, p. 39, 3.7.41.

42. BZG 27.6.41.

43. Halder KTB vol. III, p. 48, 6.7.41.

44. *Rommel Papers*, p. 149.

45. KTB OKW vol. I 13.7.41.

46. Reuth, *Entscheidung im Mittelmeer*, p. 89.

47. *Rommel Papers*, p. 148.

48. Halder KTB vol. III, p. 95, 19.7.41.

49. Baum and Weichold, *Krieg der Achsenmächte*, p. 168.

50. BAMA RH19/VIII/5; Halder KTB vol. III, p. 133, 30.7.41 and p. 140, 1.8.41.

51. The movement of U-boats to the Mediterranean is vividly shown in the film *Das Boot*.

52. Halder vol. II, pp. 412, 420.

53. BAMA Oberkommando des Heeres/Generalstab des Heeres RH/2/594 memorandum signed by Halder KTB vol. III 14.6.1942. Also: Stegemann, *Zweite Weltkrieg*, pp. 638-9.

54. Halder KTB vol. III, p. 58, 9.7.41.

55. Halder KTB vol. III, p. 48, 6.7.41.

56. Crüwell was a man of means, his father having made a fortune as a publisher of hymnbooks.

57. Rintelen, *Mussolini als Bundesgenosse*, pp. 134–5.

58. Mellenthin, *Panzer Battles*, p. 45. Mellenthin told the historian L. C. F. Turner, the editor of the English-language version of his book, that he felt that James Mason's portrayal of Rommel in *The Desert Fox* was 'altogether too polite'.

59. 'Muckefuck' is hardly a flattering appellation. It derives from a Rhenish dialect – 'Mucke' = brown earth and 'fuck' = rotten. An ersatz coffee made of various combinations of grains, acorns, figs, chicory, grape seeds and other similar ingredients, this disgusting potion continued to be served in the German Democratic Republic.

60. BZG Afrikabriefe 23.11.41.

61. ADAP D XIII.1 p. 335; Reuth, *Entscheidung im Mittelmeer*, p. 107.

62. BAMA RH2/632 OKH August 1941.

63. Reuth, *Entscheidung im Mittelmeer*, p. 90.

64. Baum and Weichold, *Krieg der Achsenmächte*, p. 169.

65. Ibid. p. 170.

66. Reuth, *Entscheidung im Mittelmeer*, p. 92.

67. The Italian expeditionary force in the Soviet Union comprised four divisions, rising to six. This meant that their forces in North Africa were far too weak for this to be the 'Italian theatre' as they claimed.

68. BAMA RH19/VIII/5 Wagner to OKW. 'When we get to Cairo' is in a marginal annotation.

69. A grisly example of these war correspondents' prose can be found in their joint work *Balkenkreuz über Wüstensand*, published by the Luftwaffe in 1943. See also: Hanns Gert von Esebeck, *Afrikanische*

Schickalsjahre. Geschichte des deutschen Afrikakorps unter Rommel (Wiesbaden: Limes Verlag, 1949).

70. Schmidt, *Mit Rommel in Afrika*, p. 87.

71. Goebbels, *Tagebücher*, 9.9.41.

72. Reuth, *Entscheidung im Mittelmeer*, p. 92.

73. Ibid. p. 93 quoting KTB DAK BAMA.

74. BAMA Oberkommando des Heeres/Generalstab des Heeres RH/2/599 13.8.41.

75. BAMA Oberkommando des Heeres/Generalstab des Heeres RH/2/599 2.9.41.

76. Reuth, *Entscheidung im Mittelmeer*, p. 94.

77. BAMA RH19/VIII/5 1.10.1941. The British continued to attack these facilities, but there is no indication that the Panzer Group took any deliberate retaliatory action.

78. *Rommel Papers*, p. 151, 29.9.41.

79. BAMA RH19/VIII/5 30.10.41.

80. Reuth, *Entscheidung im Mittelmeer*, p. 95.

81. Ibid. p. 108.

82. Trevor-Roper, *Hitler's War Directives*, pp. 130–4.

83. Baum and Weichold, *Krieg der Achsenmächte*, pp. 193–4.

84. Ibid. p. 172.

85. Hinsley, *British Intelligence*, vol. II, pp. 287, 324. Intelligence gained from Italian naval code C38m traffic showed that a minefield had been laid off Benghazi, but C-in-C Mediterranean does not seem to have relayed this information to K Force, whose commander was not an Ultra recipient. Furthermore, the Royal Navy considered it impossible to lay moored mines at 100 fathoms.

86. Reuth, *Entscheidung im Mittelmeer*, p. 111.

87. Goebbels, *Tagebücher*, 3.10.41.

88. KTB OKW 1 Doc. 105, Discussion on 24.10.41.

89. Reuth, *Entscheidung im Mittelmeer*, p. 112.

90. Rintelen, *Mussolini als Bundesgenosse*, p. 156.

91. Ibid. p. 155.

92. ADAP D XIII p. 584.

93. Mussolini's reply 6.11.41 in ADAP D XIII p. 613.

94. Wagner, *Lagevorträge*, 27.10.41.

95. Ibid.

96. Trevor-Roper, *Hitler's War Directives*, pp. 163–5; Albert Kesselring, *Soldat bis zum letzten Tage* (Bonn: Athenäum, 1953) p. 140.

97. Rintelen, *Mussolini als Bundesgenosse*, pp. 158–9.

98. Ibid. pp. 160–1.

99. Ugo Cavallero, *Comando Supremo. Diario 1940–43 del Capo di S.M.G.* (Bologna: Cappelli, 1948) p. 175.

Chapter 5

1. *Rommel Papers*, p. 152 12.10.41.

2. BAMA RH19/VIII/5 30.10.1941.

3. BAMA RH19/VIII/5 31.10.41.

4. Reuth, *Entscheidung im Mittelmeer*, p. 97 is also taken in by this deception. Hinsley, *British Intelligence*, vol. II, 319ff.

5. Baum and Weichold, *Krieg der Achsenmächte*, p. 191.

6. BAMA RH19/VIII/5 11.11.1941.

7. BAMA RH19/VIII/5 17.11.1941.

8. Stegemann in Schreiber *et al.*, *Zweite Weltkrieg*, p. 651.

9. Churchill, *The Grand Alliance*, p. 472; *Rommel Papers*, p. 156. The account of this incident was written by Lieutenant Fritz Bayerlein.

10. Carrell, *Wüstenfüchse*, p. 68.

11. Crüwell had been appointed to command the Afrikakorps at the end of August, with Bayerlein as his chief of staff. He replaced General Schaal, who had been pronounced unfit for duty in the tropics. Crüwell and Bayerlein were briefed at OKH on 31 August. Halder KTB vol. III, p. 208, 31.8.41.

12. Taysen, *Tobruk 1941*, pp. 197–201.

13. The gun, with a range of a mere 600 metres, only fired armour-piercing rounds.

14. Westphal, *Heer in Fesseln*, p. 165. British intelligence greatly overestimated these figures. It reported 244 Panzer ready for action; 70 Pzkw II, 149 Pzkw III and 35 Pzkw IV. It was also unknown that the Pzkw III and IV had greatly strengthened armour. This made the British overconfident at the beginning of 'Crusader'. Hinsley, *British Intelligence*, vol. II, p. 297.

15. Stegemann in Schreiber *et al.*, *Zweite Weltkrieg*, p. 659.

16. Janusz Piekalkiewicz, *Rommel und die Geheimdienste in Nordafrika, 1941–1943* (Munich: Bechtermünz, 1984), pp. 52, 145.

17. Hinsley, *British Intelligence*, vol. II, p. 298.

18. Taysen, *Tobruk 1941*, pp. 198–202.

19. John Bierman and Colin Smith, *The Battle of Alamein: Turning Point, World War II* (New York and London: Viking, 2002) p. 102.

20. Taysen, *Tobruk 1941*, p. 221.

21. Playfair, *Mediterranean*, vol. III, pp. 22–6.

22. Ibid. pp. 8, 38.

23. OKH estimated that the British had 630 Cruisers, 250 infantry support tanks and 775 light tanks and armoured cars in Egypt, making Rommel's predicament 'menacing'. Halder KTB vol. III, p. 269, 5.10.41.

24. BAMA RH/19/VIII/10; *Rommel Papers*, p. 158 (Bayerlein's account).

25. Taysen, *Tobruk 1941*, p. 205.

26. Mellenthin, *Panzer Battles*, p. 60. The Light Africa Division, soon to be called 90 Light Africa Division, was largely made up of former members of the French Foreign Legion. In November 1941 most of its heavy weapons were still in Naples.

27. Taysen, *Tobruk 1941*, p. 206.

28. Paulus reported to OKH on Rommel's plans for an attack on Tobruk on 8.11.41. Halder KTB vol. III, p. 284.

29. The Stuart required aviation fuel for its Pratt and Whitney aero-engine, which meant that it easily caught fire. But with a maximum speed of 40mph it was the fastest tank of all.

30. BAMA RH/19/VIII/10.

31. BAMA RH/19/VIII/10.

32. Taysen, *Tobruk 1941*, p. 219. A very detailed account of the fighting from 18 November 1941 to 6 January 1942 is in BAMA RH/19/VIII/10.

33. BAMA KTB Anlage 19E 14.2.42.

34. *Berichte OKW*, vol. II, 20–22.11.41.

35. Mellenthin, *Panzer Battles*, p. 63.

36. *Rommel Papers*, p. 159 (Bayerlein's account).

37. Mellenthin, *Panzer Battles*, p. 67.

38. Major General John Charles 'Jock' Campbell, the most famous of the Desert Rats, after whom the 'Jock Columns' (small combined arms mobile units) were named, won the VC for this action. He was appointed divisional commander in February 1942, but was killed shortly afterwards when his car overturned on the Halfaya Pass.

39. Goebbels, *Tagebücher*, 22.11.41.

40. Playfair, *Mediterranean*, vol. III, p. 48 erroneously says that the Germans claimed to have taken 267 prisoners.

41. The 'Mammoth' was a renamed Dorchester ACV, a huge armoured contraption the size of a bus that had been captured from

Lieutenant-General Gambier-Perry at Mechili. It was in this Dorchester that Rommel found the goggles that he wore on his cap and which, along with the scarf given to him by his wife, became his trademark.

42. *Rommel Papers*, p. 162 (Bayerlein's account).

43. OKH was kept pretty much in the dark about the battle, presumably to avoid any interference from above. Halder KTB vol. III, p. 316, 29.11.41.

44. Freyberg, known as 'Tiny', because he was over six feet tall, won the first of three DSOs at Gallipoli and the VC in France.

45. Westphal, *Heer in Fesseln*, p. 168.

46. Cooper, *Cairo in the War*, p. 146.

47. Mellenthin, *Panzer Battles*, p. 76.

48. Goebbels, *Tagebücher*, 25.11.41.

49. Irving, *Trail of the Fox*, p. 175.

50. *Rommel Papers*, p. 164 (Bayerlein's account).

51. Alex Bowlby, *The Recollections of Rifleman Bowlby* (London, 1999), quoted in Niall Ferguson, *The War of the World: History's Age of Hatred, 1914–1989* (London: Allen Lane, 2006), p. 524.

52. Playfair, *Mediterranean*, vol. III, p. 52.

53. Mellenthin, *Panzer Battles*, p. 79.

54. Taysen, *Tobruk 1941*, p. 263.

55. *Rommel Papers*, p. 168 (Bayerlein's account).

56. He had briefly commanded a battalion in 1938 in Jerusalem during the Arab revolt.

57. Alan Moorehead, *African Trilogy: the North African Campaign, 1940–1943* (London: Cassell, 2000) p. 229.

58. Playfair, *Mediterranean*, vol. III, p. 63.

59. Taysen, *Tobruk 1941*, p. 276.

60. Ibid. p. 283.

61. While still a prisoner in Alexandria he sent a warm letter of congratulation to Lieutenant-Colonel Jock Campbell, an elderly and exceedingly colourful warrior, for his VC won at Sidi Rezegh. Two other VCs were awarded at Sidi Rezegh, both of them posthumous.

62. Hinsley, *British Intelligence*, vol. II, p. 310.

63. Ibid.

64. Figures from Taysen, *Tobruk 1941*, p. 303.

65. Gambara was fond of remarking that there is a big difference between orders and their execution.

66. OKH considered the situation in North Africa to be 'serious' and discussed whether or not to withdraw to Gazala. Halder KTB vol. III, p. 328, 6.12.41.

67. Taysen, *Tobruk 1941*, p. 332.

68. BAMA RH19/VIII/5. Kesselring's title was somewhat absurd, since he was initially in command only of the two air corps in Sicily and southern Greece, not of the armed forces in the region. Rintelen, *Mussolini als Bundesgenosse*, p. 158.

69. Trevor-Roper, *Hitler's War Directives*, pp. 163–5.

70. Stegemann in Schreiber *et al.*, *Zweite Weltkrieg*, p. 676.

71. KTB OKW vol. I.2 12.12.41.

72. OKH understandably considered the situation at Sollum and Bardia to be worrisome, since the troops there were isolated. But the major danger was that the British would succeed in outflanking the Gazala Line. Halder KTB vol. III, p. 334, 8.12.41.

73. Hinsley, *British Intelligence*, vol. II, p. 314.

74. For the discussion in Berta on 16 and 17 December 1941 see: Rommel, *Krieg*, p. 90; Albert Kesselring, *Soldat bis zum letzten tag* (Bonn: Athenäum, 1953), pp. 161ff; Siegfried Westphal, *Erinnerungen* (Mainz: v. Hase und Koehler, 1975), p. 140; Cavallero, *Comando Supremo*, pp. 164ff.

75. BAMA RH19/VIII/5 22.12.1942.

76. KTB OKW vol. I.2 7.1.42.

77. KTB OKW vol. I.2 3/4.1.42.

78. Hence the Arab name for Sirte, 'Gasr Zaafrán'.

79. BAMA RH/19/VIII/10.

80. Bach was awarded the Knight's Cross for his gallantry. He died of pneumonia in December 1942 while a POW.

81. Carrell, *Wüstenfüchse*, p. 119.

82. Reinhard Stumpf, 'Der Krieg im Mittelmeerraum 1942/43: Die Operationen in Nordafrika und im Mitteleren Mittelmeer' in Horst Boog, Werner Rahn, Reinhard Stumpf and Bernd Wegner, *Der Gobale Krieg. Die Ausweitung zum Weltkrieg und der Wechsel der Initiative 1941–1943*, Das Deutsche Reich und der Zweite Weltkrieg (Stuttgart: Deutsche Verlags-Anstalt, 1990) pp. 573–4.

Chapter 6

1. Reuth, *Entscheidung im Mittelmeer*, p. 122. Rommel knew of these movements from his excellent intelligence.

2. Ibid. p. 123.

3. Ibid. p. 125.

4. For Germany's relations with Japan see: Bernd Martin, *Deutschland und Japan im Zweiten Weltkrieg. Vom Angriff auf Pearl Harbor bis zur deutschen Kapitulation* (Göttingen: Musterschmidt, 1969) and Reinhard Stumpf, 'Der Krieg im Mittelmeerraum 1942/43: Die Operationen in Nordafrika und im Mitteleren Mittelmeer' in Horst Boog, Werner Rahn, Reinhard Stumpf and Bernd Wegner, *Der Gobale Krieg. Die Ausweitung zum Weltkrieg und der Wechsel der Initiative 1941–1943*, Das Deutsche Reich und der Zweite Weltkrieg 6 (Stuttgart: Deutsche Verlags-Anstalt, 1990).

5. Salewski, *Seekriegsleitung*, vol. II, pp. 54ff.

6. BAMA KTB Anlage 19E 14.2.42.

7. See Cavallero's comments on his meeting with Rommel on 23 January 1942 in: Cavallero, *Comando Supremo*, 24.1.42. Rommel was fortunate to make the meeting. The day before, the Storch in which he and Westphal were travelling was badly hit.

8. Cavallero, *Comando Supremo*, 17.3.42.

9. Reuth, *Entscheidung im Mittelmeer*, p. 128.

10. Goebbels, *Tagebücher*, 20.1.42.

11. Knox, *Hitler's Italian Allies*, p. 74.

12. Salewski, *Seekriegsleitung*, vol. II, pp. 253–7.

13. KTB OKW vol. II.2, p. 1262.

14. It will be remembered that the Axis troops surrendered about a fortnight later.

15. ADAP I 29.12.41 doc. 62.

16. Hillgruber, *Staatsmänner*, vol. II, 3.1.42.

17. Ibid. vol. I, 28.11.41.

18. BAMA RH/19/VIII/14, Gause 22.2.1942 for AOK.

19. Reuth, *Entscheidung im Mittelmeer*, p. 134.

20. *Ciano Diaries*, 5.7.41.

21. ADAP Series E vol. I, pp. 141–2.

22. Ibid. pp. 166–7.

23. *Rommel Papers*, p. 180.

24. Baum and Weichold, *Krieg der Achsenmächte*, pp. 212–13.

25. BZG Afrikabriefe 12.1.42.

26. Stumpf, 'Krieg im Mittelmeerraum', p. 574; Mellenthin, *Panzer Battles*, pp. 83ff.

27. The message was relayed from Teheran on 15.4.41.

28. Mallmann and Cüppers, *Halbmond und Hakenkreuz*, p. 43. Schrumpf-Perron had a practice in Cairo, but later went to Berlin to work full-time for the Abwehr.

29. For details see: Łukasz Hirszowicz, *The Third Reich and the Arab East* (London: Routledge and Kegan Paul, 1966) pp. 232ff.

30. Rintelen, *Mussolini als Bundesgenosse*, p. 153.

31. Mallmann and Cüppers, pp. 123–4.

32. Rommel, *Krieg*, 390.

33. *Rommel Papers*, p. 179, Rommel diary entry 17.1.42.

34. KTB OKW vol. II.1 19.1.42.

35. BZG Afrikabriefe 23.1.42.

36. Hinsley, *British Intelligence*, vol. II, p. 331.

37. KTB OKW vol. II.1, 24.1.42.

38. *Rommel Papers*, p. 181.

39. Westphal, *Heer in Fesseln*, p. 173; Cavallero, *Comando Supremo*, 24.1.42, with splendid understatement reported back to Mussolini that 'Situazione presente non ancora ben delineata' (The present situation is not yet quite clear).

40. Rommel, *Krieg*, p. 98; Kesselring, *Soldat*, pp. 192ff; Westphal, *Erinnerungen*, pp. 149ff; Cavallero, *Comando Supremo* 23/24.1.42.

41. *Rommel Papers*, p. 182.

42. Goebbels, *Tagebücher*, 24.1.42.

43. KTB OKW vol. II.1 25.1.42.

44. KTB OKW vol. II.1 26–27.1.42.

45. Berndt toadishly claimed to Rommel that he had secured his promotion by appealing directly to Goebbels and Hitler. Irving, *Trail of the Fox*, p. 101.

46. Mellenthin, *Panzer Battles*, p. 91.

47. *Rommel Papers*, 22.1.42.

48. Hinsley, *British Intelligence*, vol. II, pp. 338–9.

49. Reuth, *Entscheidung im Mittelmeer*, p. 137.

50. *Rommel Papers*, p. 183; this latter comment by Bayerlein.

51. KTB OKW vol. II.1 30.1.42.

52. Stumpf, 'Krieg im Mittelmeerraum', p. 584.

53. KTB OKW vol. II.1 2.1.42.

54. That means western Cyrenaica, exclusive of the Marmarica.

55. *Ciano Diaries*, 4.2.42.

56. Details of the talks between Göring and Mussolini on 28.1.42 in ADAP series E, vol. I, pp. 320–36; Rintelen, *Mussolini als Bundesgenosse*, p. 161.

57. Reuth, *Entscheidung im Mittelmeer*, p. 138.

58. Rintelen, *Mussolini als Bundesgenosse*, p. 162.

59. Stumpf, 'Krieg im Mittelmeerraum', p. 587.

60. The Panzer Group Africa was renamed Panzer Army Africa on 22 January 1942.

61. BAMA KTB Anlage 19E 14.2.42. Between 18.11.41 and 15.2.42 the totals of killed, wounded and missing were 14,760 Germans (33 per cent) and 21,712 Italians (40 per cent). By far the largest category was 'missing', the vast majority of whom were presumably prisoners. The highest death rate was among German officers (7 per cent), the lowest among Italian other ranks (1.5 per cent).

62. BAMA KTB Anlage 19E 14.2.42, Aide memoire for discussions with the Führer and the Duce.

63. BAMA RH/19/VIII/13 15.2.1942; Reuth, *Entscheidung im Mittelmeer*, pp. 138–9.

64. Kesselring, *Soldat*, p. 148.

65. Reuth, *Entscheidung im Mittelmeer*, p. 141.

66. Scepticism about an attack on Malta was also widespread in Rome; *Ciano Diaries*, 13.5.41.

67. Hinsley, *British Intelligence*, vol. II, p. 359.

68. Reuth, *Entscheidung im Mittelmeer*, p. 144. Rost's racist prejudices did not impede his career with the Evangelical Church after the war, and then in the Press and Information Department of the Federal Government.

69. Wagner, *Lagevorträge*, 13.2.42.

70. PQ conveys were outward bound from the UK to Archangel and Murmansk. The return conveys were codenamed QP conveys.

71. Salewski, *Seekriegsleitung*, vol. III pp. 266ff.

72. Reuth, *Entscheidung im Mittelmeer*, p. 146.

73. Bottai had taken part in the March on Rome, had been minister of corporations and was to vote for Mussolini's deposition. Condemned to death, he joined the Foreign Legion after the war and was later amnestied.

74. ADAP series E, vol. I, pp. 456–64.

75. Wagner, *Lagevorträge*, 12.3.42.

76. Ulrich von Hassell, *Vom anderen Deutschland: aus den nachgelassenen Tagebüchern, 1938–1944* (Zurich: Atlantis Verlag, 1948) p. 253; these sentiments also recorded in Goebbels, *Tagebücher*, 30.1.42.

77. Carrell, *Die Wüstenfüchse*, p. 179.

78. Ibid.; Westphal, *Erinnerungen*, p. 155.

79. Halder KTB vol. III, p. 403, 19.2.42.

80. Trevor-Raper, *Hitler's War Directives*, pp. 178–83; Reuth, *Entscheidung im Mittelmeer*, pp. 150–1, who mistakenly numbers it Order Number 42.

81. Goebbels, *Tagebücher*, 20.3.42.

82. Wagner, *Lagevorträge*, p. 361, 12.3.42.

83. Reuth, *Entscheidung im Mittelmeer*, p. 156.

84. Hitler's fears of an invasion at this time are reflected in Order Number 40 of 23 March, concerned with costal defences, and Order Number 42, which revived 'Attila' and 'Isabella' – operations against Vichy France and the Iberian peninsula.

85. Reuth, *Entscheidung im Mittelmeer*, p. 152.

86. Winston S. Churchill, *The Hinge of Fate* (New York: Houghton Mifflin, 1979) p. 266. J. C. Drummond, principal scientific adviser to the ministry of food, was sent to Malta to advise on how best to survive on what little was available. Drummond was to be murdered in 1952 in the notorious 'Dominici Affair'. Fergusson, James, *The Vitamin Murders* (London: Portobello Books, 2007).

87. Dobbie was a devout member of the Plymouth Brethren, who many felt placed too much trust in God's help and too little in air-raid shelters and civil defence. Churchill, who so often displayed an astonishing lack of judgement, admired him greatly, referring to his 'Cromwellian' spirit and comparing him to General Gordon. Dobbie fell apart under the strain, to be replaced by Viscount Gort, the governor of Gibraltar, a more practical administrator, who was in Churchill's words 'a warrior of the truest mettle'. As commander of the British Expeditionary Force (BEF) he had presided over the Dunkirk fiasco, after which he had supervised the training of the Home Guard, before being sent to the Rock.

88. Jack Greene and Alessandro Massignani, *The Naval War in the Mediterranean, 1940–43* (London: Chatham Publishing, 1998), p. 224.

89. British Enigma decrypts in May indicated that 'A German offensive in Cyrenaica with the object of taking Tobruk...will probably be staged about 20 May. If this limited offensive meets with success an attempt will then be made to build up for a major attack on Egypt during the winter.' The attack began during the night of 26/27 May. Hinsley, *British Intelligence*, vol. II, p. 362.

90. BAMA RH/19/VIII/10 3.4.1942.

91. BAMA RH/19/VIII/13. Mussolini's orders of 18 March arrived at AOK on 23 March 1942. The Germans were very impressed by the

British use of armoured cars for reconnaissance, but felt that most of the information gleaned from this tallyho and dash was not put to particularly good use higher up.

92. BAMA RH/19/VIII/13 24.4.1942; Reuth, *Entscheidung im Mittelmeer*, p. 158.

93. BAMA RH/19/VIII/14 8 and 10.3.1942.

94. Reuth, *Entscheidung im Mittelmeer*, p. 159.

95. KTB OKW vol.II.1 15.4.42.

96. KTB OKW vol.II.1 13.4.42.

97. BAMA RH/19/VIII/13 28.4.1942.

98. Reuth, *Entscheidung im Mittelmeer*, p. 162–3.

99. BAMA RH/19/VIII/13 6.5.1942.

100. Mallmann and Cüppers, *Halbmond und Hakenkreuz*, p. 126.

101. Wagner, *Lagevorträge*, 13.4.42; Goebbels, *Tagebücher*, 26.4.42; KTB OKW vol. II.1 25.4.42.

102. KTB OKW vol. II.1 21.4.42.

103. Reuth, *Entscheidung im Mittelmeer*, p. 165.

104. Gerhard L. Weinberg, *A World at Arms: a Global History of World War II* (Cambridge University Press, 1994) p. 230.

105. ADAP series E, vol. II, pp. 271–4.

106. ADAP series E, vol. II, pp. 305–16; Reuth, *Entscheidung im Mittelmeer*, pp. 167–8; Hillgruber, *Staatsmänner*, vol. II, 29.4.42 and 3.5.42.

107. Rintelen's conclusions from these meetings in BAMA RH/19/VIII/13 1.5.1942.

108. It is difficult to agree with Reuth that 'When the top level conference ended at Kleßheim on 30 April, not only the Italian guests, but also the German generals still believed that "Hercules" would go ahead as planned in July, even though the summer offensive on the

eastern front would begin at the same time.' Reuth, *Entscheidung im Mittelmeer*, p. 168.

109. Rintelen, *Mussolini als Bundesgenosse*, p. 167.

110. KTB OKW vol. II.1 21.5.42; Walter Warlimont, *Inside Hitler's Headquarters, 1939–45* (New York: Praeger, 1964) p. 237.

111. Reuth, *Entscheidung im Mittelmeer*, p. 173.

112. *Ciano Diaries*, 16.5.42.

113. Crüwell had just visited Hitler's headquarters, but returned to North Africa on 20.5.42. Halder KTB vol. III, p. 445.

114. Kurt Student, *Generaloberst Kurt Student und seine Fallschirmjäger: die Erinnerungen des Generaloberst Kurt Student*, ed. H. Götzel (Friedberg: Podzun-Pallas-Verlag, 1980) p. 360; Reuth, *Entscheidung im Mittelmeer*, p. 170.

115. Rintelen, *Mussolini als Bundesgenosse*, p. 166.

Chapter 7

1. Rintelen, *Mussolini als Bundesgenosse*, p. 167.

2. BAMA RH/19/VIII/13 8.5.42. 'Gerede und Gequatsche.'

3. Mellenthin, *Panzer Battles*, p. 93.

4. Rommel's force at Gazala consisted of 90,000 men, 542 aircraft and 561 tanks, of which 228 were mediocre Italian models.

5. *Rommel Papers*, p. 195 with comments by Liddell-Hart.

6. From July 1941 the effectiveness of the Pak 38 was greatly reduced owing to the shortage of wolfram for the shell's core. Various alternatives were tested, but none was as effective.

7. 'Grant' was the British nickname for the American Lee.

8. BAMA RH/19/VIII/21 29.5.42.

9. *Rommel Papers*, p. 196.

10. Hinsley, *British Intelligence*, vol. II, p. 365.

11. John Connell, *Auchinleck: a Biography of Field-Marshal Sir Claude Auchinleck* (London: Cassell, 1959) p. 517.

12. Bruce Norman, *Secret Warfare: the Battle of Codes and Cyphers* (Newton Abbot: David and Charles, 1989) pp. 123–31. A different story, involving an Italian Mata Hari in Cairo, in: John W. Gordon, *The Other Desert War: British Special Forces in North Africa, 1940–1943* (New York: Greenwood Press, 1987) pp. 100–3. The British eventually turned this source, feeding it with misinformation, but it is unclear how they spotted the leak. Fellers was an Anglophobe, but was close to the mark when he complained that 'too many senior officers are sitting on their arses at GHQ.' He later joined the John Birch Society. Eisenhower said of him to Lady Ranfurnly: 'Any friend of Bonner Fellers is no friend of mine.'

13. Hinsley, *British Intelligence*, vol. II, p. 366.

14. Ibid. p. 367.

15. Ibid. p. 369ff.

16. Stumpf, 'Krieg im Mittelmeerraum', p. 600.

17. *Rommel Papers*, p. 206.

18. Wolz won the Iron Cross first class in the First World War, and a bar for his attack on the Maginot Line. He ended the war as military commander of Hamburg. With the agreement of Gauleiter Karl Kaufmann, who had secured his appointment against the wishes of OKW, he surrendered the city to the British on 3 May 1945.

19. Carrell, *Wüstenfüchse*, p. 177.

20. Stumpf, 'Krieg im Mittelmeerraum', p. 609 points out that this is not reported in 21 Panzer Division's KTB.

21. Playfair, *Mediterranean*, vol. III, pp. 223ff.; Barrie Pitt, *The Crucible of War, vol. II: Year of Alamein, 1942* (London: Jonathan Cape, 1982) p. 43.

22. Stumpf, 'Krieg im Mittelmeerraum', p. 612. OKW had not been informed of what was going on, but seemed well pleased with the operation so far. It was 'making excellent progress' and the

encirclement of Tobruk looked 'promising'. KTB OKW
vol. II.1 28.5.42.

23. Mellenthin, *Panzer Battles*, pp. 97ff; Kesselring, *Soldat*, pp. 170ff;
Westphal, *Erinnerungen*, pp. 160ff.

24. BAMA RH/19/21 30.5.1942.

25. Hinsley, *British Intelligence*, vol. II, p. 373.

26. BAMA RH/19/21 30.5.1942.

27. Heckmann, *Rommel's War*, p. 361.

28. *Rommel Papers*, p. 212.

29. Stumpf, 'Krieg im Mittelmeerraum', p. 619; *Rommel Papers*,
p. 218. On one occasion the Luftwaffe lost nearly forty Stukas in
one day. Most of the pilots who managed to bale out were
machine-gunned as they hung from their parachutes.

30. *Rommel Papers*, p. 213.

31. BAMA RH/19/21 5.6.1942.

32. *Ciano Diaries*, 6.6.42.

33. BAMA RH/19/21 Bastico to Rommel 4.6.42.

34. BAMA RH/19/21 orders for the attack 7.6.1942.

35. Schmidt, *Mit Rommel in Afrika*, p. 162.

36. Stumpf, 'Krieg im Mittelmeerraum', p. 619.

37. Marie-Pierre Koenig, *Bir Hacheim, 10 juin 1942* (Paris: Robert
Lafont, 1971) p. 329.

38. Ritchie had about 400 tanks available, Rommel only 130 Panzer
and some 100 Italian M13/40s, a thinly armoured and unreliable
weapon, totally unsuited to desert conditions. By June Ritchie had lost
more than half his tanks.

39. Colonel Ernst-Günther Baade, the group's commander, had the
singular misfortune to be killed by a low-flying aircraft on Armistice
Day, 8 May 1945, while serving as commander of 90 Panzergrenadier
Division in the vicinity of Faenza.

40. *Rommel Papers*, p. 220.

41. Koenig, *Bir Hacheim*, p. 350.

42. Miss Travers was also awarded the Légion d'Honneur. In 2000, at the age of ninety she published her memoirs: *Tomorrow to Be Brave*.

43. J. Mordal, *Bir Hacheim* (Paris: Amiot-Dumont, 1952); Jean Mathias, *Bir Hacheim* (Paris: Editions de Minuit, 1955).

44. In fact there were forty-four different nationalities among the prisoners with individuals from France (140 – mostly officers and NCOs), Spain (52), Italy (2), Switzerland (5), Poland (6), Czechoslovakia (3), Canada (1), Egypt (1), Indochina (6), Syria (27), Belgium (5), Sudan (1), Paraguay (1), Romania (2), Congo (4), Belarus (3), Greece (4), Turkey (4), Portugal (4), Mexico (2), Finland (1), Estonia (2), Bulgaria (1), Argentina (2), Oubangui (24), Madagascar (26), Holland (2), Iran (1), England (2), Tunisia (35), Yugoslavia (1), Luxemburg (1), Germany (1), Cuba (1), Alsace (19), Gabon (3), Cameroon (100), Hungary (5), New Caledonia (13), Tahiti (26), New Hebrides (5), Algeria (54), Morocco (26), Senegal (20). None were listed as Jewish, and there was only one German. PAAA R60747 report by Neurath to Foreign Office 14.7.42.

45. Bierman and Smith, *The Battle of El Alamein*, p. 170.

46. The quote is from the diary of Lieutenant Kämpf in: Stumpf, 'Krieg im Mittelmeerraum', p. 620. Baum and Weichold, *Krieg der Achsenmächte*, p. 221 indicates that there was a Jewish battalion at Bir Hacheim, but produces no evidence in support of this claim. There was a company of Jewish engineers serving with the King's West African Rifles, who began to lay a vast minefield near Bir Hacheim, and who were rescued by Koenig's men. Koenig ordered his Legionnaires to salute the Zionist flag as a tribute to their bravery.

47. Westphal, *Heer in Fesseln*, p. 196. The incident is mentioned in a book published in England during the war entitled *Above all Nations is Humanity*. The 'Commando Order' was in Directive Number 46a of 18 October 1942.

48. BAMA RH/119/VIII/26 22.8.1942.

49. BAMA Abwehr: RW5/v/684.

50. The *Prominenten* survived the war by persuading SS-Obergruppenführer Gottlob Berger, who was responsible for all prisoners of war, to surrender to the US army. Berger, a member of the NSDAP since 1922 and a slavish devotee of Himmler, was made head of the SS Main Office in 1940, in September 1944 was made responsible for the 'pacification' of Slovakia and in October 1944 was given responsibility for all POW camps. He was given a 25-year prison sentence in 1947, but was released in December 1951, in large part because of the intervention of the electrical engineering firm Bosch, for which he had done many favours. That he chose to surrender rather than have the *Prominenten* shot may also have acted in his favour.

51. *Rommel Papers*, p. 216. Liddell-Hart quoting from Auchinleck's dispatch.

52. Mellenthin, *Panzer Battles*, pp. 132–3.

53. Ibid. p. 49.

54. KTB OKW vol. II.1 16.6.42.

55. Ever ready with a sporting analogy, Cunningham's hasty move to the rear in November was known as the 'Matruh Stakes'.

56. Mellenthin, *Panzer Battles*, p. 112.

57. Connell, *Auchinleck*, p. 572.

58. *Rommel Papers*, p. 222.

59. Stumpf, 'Krieg im Mittelmeerraum', p. 625.

60. *Rommel Papers*, p. 225.

61. KTB OKW vol. II.1 18.6.42.

62. BAMA RH/19/21 AOK to OKH 19.6.1942.

63. For details see: Gundelach, *Luftwaffe im Mittelmeer*, vol. I, p. 372.

64. BAMA RH/19/22a for the plan of attack dated 18.6.1942.

65. KTB OKW vol. II.1 22.6.42 and 24.2.42.

66. Rintelen, *Mussolini als Bundesgenosse*, p. 168.

67. *Rommel Papers*, p. 232; also in BAMA RH/19/22a.

68. Carrell, *Wüstenfüchse*, pp. 254–5.

69. Heckmann, *Rommel's War*, p. 399.

70. Henry Picker, *Hitlers Tischgespräche in Führerhauptquartier* (Stuttgart: Seewald, 1976) p. 288, 27.6.42.

71. Leonidas E. Hill (ed.), *Die Weizsäcker Papiere, 1933–1950* (Frankfurt: Propyläen, 1974) p. 295, 29.6.42.

72. Mallmann and Cüppers, *Halbmond und Hakenkreuz*, p. 127.

73. Martin Gilbert, *Road to Victory: Winston S. Churchill, 1941–1945* (London: Heinemann, 1986) p. 128.

74. Churchill, *The Hinge of Fate*, p. 333.

75. A total of 50,000 M4s were built between 1942 and 1955, when the model went out of service. The chassis was also used for a number of other vehicles. The British named it the 'Sherman', just as they named other American tanks after famous generals. The name soon caught on in the USA.

76. See Rommel's complaints about the Sherman in BAMA RH19/VIII/35 22.11.42.

77. Gilbert, *Road to Victory*, pp. 137–41; Churchill, *Hinge of Fate*, pp. 340–55.

78. PAAA Fiche 2628 Schellenberg 7.6.42. Schellenberg was tried in the 'Ministers Trial' of 1949, served for a few months and then, it is said, worked for the British secret service. Rauff, who knew both men well, said of him that he was 'just as neurotically (*krankhaft*) ambitious as Heydrich'.

79. Stumpf, 'Krieg im Mittelmeerraum', pp. 633–5.

80. KTB OKW vol. II.1 22.6.42.

81. KTB OKW vol. II.1, p. 443 for an account by General Warlimont. 'Fredericus II' could mean both Frederick II of Hohenstaufen and Frederick the Great.

82. BAMA RH/19/22a.

83. BAMA RH/19/22a Rintelen to AOK 24.6.1942.

84. *Ciano Diaries*, 26.6.42 for the problems this caused.

85. *Rommel Papers*, p. 232.

86. Kesselring, *Soldat*, p. 172. Rommel was awarded diamonds for his Knight's Cross in March 1943.

87. *Rommel Papers*, p. 237.

88. KTB OKW vol. II.1 28.6.42.

89. BAMA RH19/VIII/22a.

90. *Ciano Diaries*, 23.7.42.

91. Stumpf, 'Krieg im Mittelmeerraum', p. 653; KTB OKW vol.II.1 27.6.42.

92. I am much indebted to Gabriel Gorodetsky for showing me extracts from his edition of the Maisky diaries in manuscript form. Entries for 29.6.42 and 2.7.42.

93. Barr, *Pendulum of War*, pp. 17–18.

94. Heinz Boberach (ed.), *Meldungen aus dem Reich. Auswahl aus den geh. Lageberichten des Sicherheitsdienstes der SS 1939–1944* (Herrsching: Pawlak, 1968) pp. 236, 238.

95. *Berichte OKW*, vol. III. 2.7.42.

96. *Ciano Diaries*, 26.6.42 for the background to this declaration.

97. Barr, *Pendulum of War*, pp. 19–21.

98. Rommel, *Krieg*, p. 180.

99. Mellenthin, *Panzer Battles*, p. 155.

100. *Rommel Papers*, p. 238.

101. Playfair, *Mediterranean*, vol. III, pp. 281ff.; Stumpf, 'Krieg im Mittelmeerraum', p. 640; Mellenthin, *Panzer Battles*, p. 129.

102. BAMA RH19/VIII/22a 30.6.1942.

103. Picker, *Tischgespräche*, p. 391, 28.6.42.

104. KTB OKW vol. II.1 30.6.42.

105. Mellenthin, *Panzer Battles*, p. 132.

106. *Rommel Papers*, p. 240.

Chapter 8

1. The three ridges run parallel to the sea between El Alamein and the Qattara Depression. From north to south they are: Miteiriya, Ruweisat and Alam Halfa.

2. Hirszowicz, *The Third Reich*, p. 240 for the full text of the Axis declaration.

3. BAMA RH19/VIII/22a AOK to OKH 30.6.1942.

4. Barr, *Pendulum of War*, p. 41. This was the last message to be decrypted. The Fellers leak had been stopped the day before.

5. Stumpf, 'Krieg im Mittelmeerraum', p. 656; Mellenthin, *Panzer Battles*, p. 128.

6. Barr, *Pendulum of War*, p. 74.

7. Hinsley, *British Intelligence*, vol. II, p. 329.

8. BAMA RH19/VIII/22a 1.7.1942 2215hrs.

9. Barr, *Pendulum of War*, p. 87.

10. BAMA RH19/VIII/22a 4.7.1942.

11. KTB OKW vol. II.1 7.7.42.

12. Mellenthin, *Panzer Battles*, pp. 132–3.

13. Hinsley, *British Intelligence*, vol. II, p. 396.

14. Mellenthin, *Panzer Battles*, p. 135.

15. BAMA RH/19/VIII/123 Report on the defensive battle in the El Alamein position 26.7.42.

16. BAMA RH19/VIII/22a AOK to 10, 20 and 21 Corps 11.7.1942.

17. On Seebohm and 621 Radio Intelligence Company see: Hans-Otto Behrendt, *Rommels Kenntnis vom Feind im Afrikafeldzug: Ein Bericht über die Feindnachrichtenarbeit, insbesondere die Funkaufklärung* (Freiburg: Rombach, 1980) p. 58.

18. BAMA RH/19/VIII/123 Report on the defensive battle in the El Alamein position 26.7.42.

19. BAMA RH19/VIII/22a AOK to OKH 12.7.1942.

20. Barr, *Pendulum of War*, p. 115.

21. BAMA RH19/VIII/22a AOK to OKH 15.7.1942. Mussolini confessed to Ciano that he had been scared of the ferocious-looking New Zealand POWs he had seen during his recent trip, and that he had made sure always to have a gun with him when anywhere near them. *Ciano Diaries*, 21.7.42.

22. KTB OKW vol. II.1 16.7.42.

23. Barr, *Pendulum of War*, p. 141.

24. BAMA RH19/VIII/22a AOK to OKH 15 and 16.7.1942.

25. BAMA RH19/VIII/22a AOK to OKH 17.7.1942.

26. BAMA RH19/VIII/22a AOK to OKH 17.7.1942; Mellenthin, *Panzer Battles*, p. 139.

27. BAMA RH19/VIII/22a Bastico to Rommel 17.7.1942.

28. PAAA R29863 Neurath to Ribbentrop 15.7.42.

29. KTB OKW vol. II.1 19.7.42.

30. KTB OKW vol. II.1 23.7.42; Mellenthin, *Panzer Battles*, p. 139. The commanding officer of 40th Royal Tank Regiment had said 'Let's make this a Balaclava, boys!'.

31. Barr, *Pendulum of War*, p. 159.

32. BAMA RH/19/VIII/123 Report on the defensive battle in the El Alamein position 26.7.42.

33. Playfair, *Mediterranean*, vol. III, pp. 347ff. and 353ff. for the naming of these battles. The New Zealanders call the second battle the 'Battle of El Mreir'.

34. Bierman and Smith, *The Battle of El Alamein*, p. 208.

35. Carrell, *Wüstenfüchse*, pp. 275–8.

36. BAMA RH19/VIII/22a AOK situational report 21.7.1942.

37. BAMA RH19/VIII/22a Rommel to Bastico and Bastico's reply 23.7.1942.

38. Correlli Barnett, *The Desert Generals*, rev. edn (London: Cassell, 1983) p. 223.

39. Mellenthin, *Panzer Battles*, p. 140.

40. KTB OKW vol. II.1; Lagebericht OKH 28 July 1942; BAMA RH19/VIII/22a AOK to OKH 27.7.1942.

41. Barr, *Pendulum of War*, p. 190.

42. KTB OKW vol. II.1 30.7.42.

43. *Rommel Papers*, p. 260.

44. Ibid. p. 261.

45. Ibid. p. 267; BAMA RH/119/VIII/26, 1a 6.9.1942. OKW to Panzerarmee 11.9.1942. The number of Italian troops was declining because men who had served more than two years in North Africa were relieved, but not replaced. The Brescia and Bologna Divisions were thus seriously below strength. Ibid. 18.9.1942. Playfair, *Mediterranean*, vol. III, pp. 390–1 gives very different figures from British sources.

46. Engel, *Heeresadjutant*, p. 88.

47. Rintelen, *Mussolini als Bundesgenosse*, p. 171.

48. *Ciano Diaries*, 2.7.42.

49. Mallmann and Cüppers, *Halbmond und Hakenkreuz*, p. 131.

50. PAAA R29863 Mackensen to Foreign Office 4.7.42.

51. PAAA R29863 Ribbentrop to Rintelen 17.8.42.

52. PAAA R29863 Wiehl 5.9.42.

53. Hirszowicz, *The Third Reich*, p. 247.

54. For German–Italian discussions on the future of Egypt see: ADAP, series E, vol. III pp. 71–2, 81–3, 94–5, 97–8, 105, 144, 514, and vol. IV, pp. 179–82.

55. PAAA R29863 Rintelen to Clodius 8.7.42.

56. PAAA R29863 11 and 12.7.42.

57. PAAA R29863 8.7.42.

58. Picker, *Tischgespräche*, p. 391, 28.6.42.

59. PAAA R29863 Woermann to Ritter 9.7.42.

60. Picker, *Tischgespräche*, p. 433, 9.7.42.

61. PAAA R29863 Ribbentrop 10.10.42. The Joint Commission was suggested by Ambassador Giannini to Clodius at a meeting in Brioni.

62. Details in John W. Eppler, *Geheimagent im Zweiten Weltkrieg. Zwischen Berlin, Kabul und Kairo* (Preußisch Oldendorf: Schutz, 1974) and *Rommel ruft Cairo. Aus dem Tagebuch eines Spions* (Gütersloh: S. Mohn, 1959).

63. Ronald W. Zweig, 'British Plans for the Evacuation of Palestine', *Studies in Zionism*, vol. 8 (1983); Daniel Silverfarb, 'Britain, the United States, and the Security of the Saudi Arabian Oilfields in 1942', *Historical Journal*, vol. 26 (1983).

64. KTB OKW vol. II.1 5.7.42 from a report from an agent named 'Hannibal'.

65. Picker, *Tischgespräche*, p. 391, 28.6.42.

66. ADAP E vol. III, p. 129; Mallmann and Cüppers, *Halbmond und Hakenkreuz*, pp. 134–5.

67. Barr, *Pendulum of War*, pp. 95–9.

68. Mallmann and Cüppers, *Halbmond und Hakenkreuz*, p. 118.

69. Joseph B. Schechtman, *The Mufti and the Führer: the Rise and Fall of Haj Amin el-Huseini* (New York: Thomas Yiseloff, 1965); Klaus Gensicke, *Der Mufti von Jerusalem, Amin el-Husseini und die Nationalsozialisten* (Frankfurt am Main: P. Lang, 1988).

70. PAAA R104 SD study 'Die Juden in Ägypten'.

71. Rauff ended the war in northern Italy. The church helped him to go underground and he managed to escape to Syria in 1949, whence he travelled to Ecuador in 1953 and Chile in 1958. He worked for the Gehlen Organisation, the forerunner of the post-war German secret service, and died in Santiago in 1972 aged sixty-six.

72. PAAA Fiche 2628 Rauff to AA 17.4.42.

73. PAAA R29863 Ribbentrop 29.5.42, with a draft memorandum by Schmieden.

74. PAAA R29863 Weizsäcker to Neurath 25.6.42.

75. PAAA R29863 Foreign Office memorandum 17.2.42.

76. PAAA R29863 Ribbentrop to Teheran 30.4.41.

77. PAAA R29863 7.3.42. The report came from the secretary of state in the Egyptian foreign ministry, Siri Omar Bei, who professed to be a great friend of Germany.

78. Schellenberg to Foreign Office 31.7.42.

79. PAAA R29863.

80. PAAA R29863 AOK PAA 1c to Foreign Office 8.4.42.

81. PAAA R29863 Report from German consulate in Bern (Köcher) 4.5.41.

82. The Germans, who were fully occupied with preparations for 'Barbarossa' and the invasion of Crete, were unable to send much support. The revolt was squashed and el-Husseini and al-Gailani fled. Both men arrived in Berlin in November 1941. They met Hitler before the end of the month. He told them: 'Germany stands for an uncompromising struggle against the Jews. This obviously includes the struggle against the Jewish settlements in Palestine, which are nothing more nor less than the nucleus of a state to promote the destructive aims of Jewish interests.' The aim of German policy was 'The destruction of Jewry in the Arab world, which is protected by British power.' Klaus-Michael Mallmann and Martin Cüppers, 'Das Einsatzkommando bei der Panzerarmee Afrika 1942', in Jürgen Matthäus and Klaus-Michael Mallmann (eds.), *Deutsche, Juden, Völkermord. Der Holocaust als Geschichte und Gegenwart*

(Darmstadt: Wissenschaftliche Buchgesellschaft, 2006) pp. 153–76.

83. Mallmann and Cüppers, *Halbmond und Hakenkreuz*, pp. 128–30.

84. Picker, *Tischgespräche*, p. 404. 2.7.42.

85. PAAA RR29863 3.7.42.

86. *Ciano Diaries*, 20.7.42.

87. ADAP series E, vol. III, pp. 212–13.

88. Picker, *Tischgespräche*, pp. 406–7.

89. PAAA R29863 OKM 30.6.42.

90. PAAA R27774.

91. ADAP series E, vol. III, pp. 262–6.

92. ADAP series E, vol. III, pp. 273–7.

93. ADAP series E, vol. III, pp. 304–7. Dietl, a professional soldier who had been a member of Ritter von Epp's Freikorps, had been close to Hitler since 1919 and had been in charge of the bouncers who protected his mass meetings. He had fought with extreme ruthlessness in Norway. He was killed in June 1944 when his plane crashed near Graz as he flew to visit Hitler at his headquarters. Hitler described him as 'a blind and uncompromising follower of my way of thinking (*Gedankenwelt*)'.

94. Churchill, *The Hinge of Fate*, pp. 393ff.

95. It is said that the nickname 'Strafer' came from the First World War German greeting: 'Gott strafe England!'.

96. Barr, *Pendulum of War*, p. 188.

97. 'Chink' Dorman-Smith was extremely clever, but his intellectual arrogance, mordant wit and taste for sleeping with other officers' wives made him widely unpopular. His intense dislike for Montgomery was mutual. He was also a friend of Ernest Hemingway and godfather to one of his sons. While watching the bullfights in Pamplona together, the idea struck him that the beret would be a

suitable headdress for tank crews. He managed to sell the idea to the War Office.

98. Lavinia Greacen, *Chink* (London: MacMillan, 1989).

99. Barr, *Pendulum of War*, p. 44.

100. For details see: Peter C. Smith, *Pedestal: the Convoy that Saved Malta* (Manchester: Crécy, 2002).

101. KTB OKW vol. II.1, p. 670 comment by Warlimont.

102. Details in BAMA RH/19/VIII/23.

103. Ibid.

104. Ibid.

105. Stumpf, 'Krieg im Mittelmeerraum', p. 670.

106. ADAP series E, vol. III, p. 212.

107. BAMA RH/19/VIII/23 Rommel to Bastico, Bastico to Rommel 23.7.42.

108. Stumpf, 'Krieg im Mittelmeerraum', p. 671.

109. Baum and Weichold, *Krieg der Achsenmächte*, p. 238; Kesselring, *Soldat*, p. 175; Cavallero, *Comando Supremo*, p. 292 19 July 1942 quoting Mussolini: 'La battaglia di Tobruk è chiusa; quali di domani sarà la battaglia del Delta' (The Battle of Tobruk is over; tomorrow's will be the Battle of the Delta). Cavallero noted on 5 September that 'if we neutralise Malta we will win all the battles in Africa. If we don't neutralise it, we shall lose everything.'

110. BAMA RH/19/VIII/26. On 2 August 1942 the Afrikakorps was desperately short-handed: 15 Panzer Division had 225 officers (full complement 310), 6,182 other ranks (10,216) and 65 Panzer (203); 21 Panzer Division had 290 officers (371), 8,706 other ranks (12,827) and 68 Panzer (216); 90 Light Africa Division had 133 officers (263) and 4,679 other ranks (9,257); 164 Infantry Division had 195 officers (391), 6,708 other ranks (11,277) and no transport. The anti-aircraft units had 114 officers and men, instead of 230.

111. BAMA RH/19/VIII/26.

112. Rommel drafted a memorandum for Keitel on 4 August, but sent it to Gause in Rome. He gave as the somewhat disingenuous reason for his change of mind his unwillingness to land Rintelen in trouble with OKW.

113. BAMA RH/19/VIII/26.

114. Piekalkiewicz, *Rommel und die Geheimdienste*, p. 73.

115. In fact there were 229 Panzer and 243 Italian tanks against about 700 in the 8th Army.

116. Mellenthin, *Panzer Battles*, p. 142.

117. BAMA RH/19/VIII/26.

118. BAMA RH/19/VIII/26.

119. BAMA RH/19/VIII/26.

120. BAMA RH/19/VIII/26. The battle, known in English as the Battle of Alam Halfa, is usually referred to as the Second Battle of El Alamein in German. The Afrikakorps cynically named the subsequent retreat the 'Six Day Race' after the famous annual indoor bicycle race in Berlin. Rommel, *Krieg*, p. 220; KTB OKW vol. II.1 2.9.42.

121. BAMA RH/119/VIII/26. Hitler's suggestion dated 24 August. Rommel said he would stay in command on the next day. *Rommel Papers*, p. 271 (note by Bayerlein); Remy, *Rommel*, p. 107.

122. BAMA RH/119/VIII/26; Rommel, *Krieg*; Westphal, *Erinnerungen*.

123. Footnote by Bayerlein, *Rommel Papers*, p. 275. At the end of 1943 Rommel said to Horster, 'The Führer is tired, he's finished. How do you imagine the war will end, Herr Professor?' Horster replied: 'May I remind you of your remark at the beginning of the "Six Day Race"?'

124. Barr, *Pendulum of War*, p. 224 quoting Nehring's account of the campaign.

125. Latimer, *Alamein*, p. 95. Montgomery's appointment of de Guingand as his chief of staff was a first in the British army. Hitherto a Brigadier General Staff at Army Headquarters had acted as a *primus inter pares*.

126. Hinsley, *British Intelligence*, vol. II, p. 408.

127. BAMA RH19/VIII/110 30.8.42. It is noticeable that Rommel usually referred to the 8th Army as his 'opponent' (*Gegner*) rather than as the enemy (*Feind*).

128. Mellenthin, *Panzer Battles*, p. 120.

129. BAMA RH/119/VIII/26.

130. *Rommel Papers*, p. 279.

131. BAMA RH/119/VIII/26.

132. Mellenthin, *Panzer Battles*, p. 144.

133. BAMA RH/19/VIII/25.

134. *Rommel Papers*, p. 279.

135. All details in BAMA RH/19/VIII/25.

136. Stumpf, 'Krieg im Mittelmeerraum', p. 685, quoting Grundelach, *Luftwaffe im Mittelmeer*, vol. I.

137. BAMA RH/119/VIII/26 2.9.42. The flight detection devices were known as 'FMG-T Geraeten'. Between 31 August and 4 September the Allies dropped 15,600 bombs on the Afrikakorps.

138. Mellenthin, *Panzer Battles*, p. 145.

139. BAMA RH/119/VIII/26 1a to OKH 5.9.42.

140. *Rommel Papers*, pp. 281–2. The 'Flying Kiwi' escaped four times from Italian POW camps, and was then sent to Germany where he also escaped four times. He eventually succeeded in avoiding recapture on his ninth attempt.

141. Bierman and Smith, *The Battle of El Alamein*, p. 259.

142. BAMA RH/19/VIII/14 1.4.42.

143. BAMA RH/19/VIII/14 1.4.42, p. 331.

144. BAMA RH/119/VIII/26 1a 6.9.42; OKW to Panzerarmee 11.9.42.

145. Mellenthin, *Panzer Battles*, p. 147.

146. BAMA RH/119/VIII/26 Rommel to OKW and OKH 11.9.42.

147. Baum and Weichold, *Krieg der Achsenmächte*, p. 249.

Chapter 9

1. Rommel, *Krieg*, p. 227.

2. Remy, *Rommel*, p. 111.

3. Weichhold, 'Die Deutsche Führung und das Mittelmeer', p. 173.

4. KTB OKW vol. II.1, p. 692.

5. Rintelen, 'Operation und Nachschub', p. 50.

6. See the letters to his wife 9 and 11.9.1942 in *Rommel Papers*, pp. 290ff.

7. *Rommel Papers*, p. 290; BAMA RH19/VIII/27 22.9.42.

8. Friedrich Paulus, *Ich stehe hier auf Befehl! Lebensweg des Generalfeldmarschalls Friedrich Paulus. Mit Aufzeichnungen aus dem Nachlass, Briefen und Dokumenten*, ed. Walter Görlitz (Frankfurt: Bernard and Graefe, 1960) pp. 186–7 and 192ff. Halder noted in his diary: 'Once again there is a campaign against the General Staff. The unfortunate Reichel incident . . . seems to have brought the problems that have been there for some time to boiling point. We'll have to wait and see when it blows up.' KTB vol. III, p. 464, 24.6.42.

9. Irving, *Trail of the Fox*, p. 51.

10. This latter trait was one of many that he shared with Montgomery.

11. Rommel, *Krieg*, p. 239; BAMA RH/19/VIII/25 and 27.

12. BAMA RH/19/VIII/27.

13. *Ciano Diaries*, 31.10.42.

14. BAMA RH19/VIII/27; AOK to OKH 22.9.42.

15. For details see Pitt, *The Crucible of War*, vol. II, pp. 236ff. Details of Axis reactions in BAMA RH/119/VIII/26.

16. BAMA RH19/VIII/26.

17. BZG Afrikabriefe 14.9.42.

18. Rommel, *Krieg*, 234.

19. Born in 1900, Kaufmann, a former unskilled labourer who had taken part in the Hitler Putsch, ran his own private concentration camp at Fuhlsbüttel and commanded another at Neuengamme. He was appointed Gauleiter of Hamburg in 1928 and State Governor (*Reichsstatthalter*) in 1933. After the war he was a prominent crypto-Nazi and member of the 'Gauleiter Circle'. He died in 1969.

20. BAMA RH/19/VIII/27 pp. 4ff and 26 pp. 328ff.

21. British tank men feared being given captured M13s. They boiled over every few miles and had to be cooled down by urinating into the radiator to save precious water.

22. 'Notes for a presentation to the Führer', 20.9.42 in BAMA RH/19/VIII/27.

23. A 'unit' of ammunition (*Ausstattung*) was the amount required for one day of heavy fighting. A 'unit' of fuel (*Verflegungssatz*, VS) covered the daily requirements of various vehicles under such conditions.

24. The 15-cm-Nbw.41 was a terrifying weapon, as the Allies were soon to discover in Tunisia. 'Nebel' (fog) did not refer to the weapons engineer Dr Nebel, but was a code name.

25. The fuel tank of 530 litres was enough for 60 kilometres across average terrain. Panzer Squadron 501 with six King Tigers arrived in Tunis in November 1942.

26. Rommel, *Krieg*, p. 237.

27. 'Notes on a presentation to the Führer' in BAMA RH/19/VIII/27.

28. Remy, *Rommel*, p. 116.

29. Ibid. p. 117.

30. BAMA RH/19/VIII/27 Stumme to Cavallero 3.10.42.

31. BAMA RH/19/VIII/27 Rommel to Stumme 5.10.42.

32. BAMA RH/19/VIII/25.

33. BAMA RH/19/VIII/27.

34. BAMA RH/19/VIII/27.

35. Baum and Weichold, *Krieg der Achsenmächte*, p. 255.

36. KTB OKW vol. II.2, p. 816.

37. KTB OKW vol. II.2 15.10.42.

38. KTB OKW vol. II.2 24.10.42.

39. ADAP series E, vol. III, pp. 113–14.

40. BAMA RH/19/VIII/25; KTB OKW vol. II.2 21.10.42. The Panzer Army had fuel for five and a half days' normal use (5.5 VS). The tanker *Panuco* with 3.5 VS, due to arrive in Tobruk on 20.10, had been torpedoed. There was sufficient food for three weeks, but on rations of 500 grams of bread per day.

41. BAMA RH/19/VIII/27.

42. Playfair, *Mediterranean*, vol. IV, p. 9.

43. KTB OKW vol. II.2 19.10.42; Playfair, *Mediterranean*, vol. IV, p. 30.

44. Marseille is often credited with 158 kills, but this is almost certainly an exaggeration due to reports from his wingmen. On one occasion he shot down six South Africans within the space of eleven minutes.

45. BAMA RH/19/VIII/27 30.9.42. Marseille had the Knight's Cross with oak leaves and diamonds, as well as the Medal of Honour (*Tapferkeitsmedaille*) in gold.

46. BAMA RH19/VIII/27 Stumme for Cavallero.

47. BAMA RH19/VIII/27 10.10.42.

48. BAMA RH19/VIII/27 20.10.42.

49. BAMA RH19/VIII/27 21.10.42.

50. BAMA RH19/VIII/27 20.10.42. The investigation was made two days later. An incident of a bomb landing on a dressing station killing

two and wounding ten, with the plane returning to strafe from a height of 5 metres, was reported on 31.10.42. It is not clear whether this was the same or a different incident. BAMA RH/19/VIII/33 31.10.42.

51. Montgomery had replaced Ramsden by Leese, a former pupil at the Staff College, curtly remarking: 'You're not exactly on the crest of a wave, Ramsden!' Barnett, *Desert Generals*, p. 268. Morshead was understandibly angry at once again having been passed over as corps commander, but Leese's affable personality soon won him over, along with Pienaar and Freyberg, all of them fiercely independent and difficult divisional commanders.

52. Details in Nigel Hamilton, *Monty, vol. I: The Making of a General* (London: Hamish Hamilton, 1981).

53. Baum and Weichold, *Krieg der Achsenmächte*, p. 257.

54. Cavallero, *Comando Supremo*, 22.10.42 and 24.10.42.

55. There is some confusion about the precise timing of the attack. According to the Germans it was at 2025hrs, but the British set their clocks one hour ahead so it was 2140hrs in the northern sector and 2125hrs in the south.

56. BZG Afrikabriefe Gefr. A.Sch. 606 Flak 15 Panzer Division 29.10.42.

57. BZG Afrikabriefe 6.6.41 and 2.10.42.

58. Rommel, *Krieg*, p. 246.

59. BAMA RH/19/VIII/31.

60. BAMA RH/19/VIII/31.

61. Barr, *Pendulum of War*, p. 329.

62. BAMA RH/19/VIII/31.

63. BAMA RH/119/VIII/27 25.10.42. The order to this effect at Panzer Army HQ referred to a 'General von Thomas'.

64. BAMA RH/19/VIII/110; BAMA RH/19/VIII/33 25.10.42. His was described by Rommel as a 'soldier's death' (*Soldatentod*).

65. Rommel, *Krieg*, p. 249.

66. KTB OKW vol. II.2, 25.10.42.

67. KTB OKW vol. II.2, 25.10.42.

68. BAMA RH/19/VIII/31.

69. BAMA RH/19/VIII/31.

70. The PzKpw VI Tiger I first went into production in August 1942.

71. ADAP series E, vol. IV, pp. 162–77. Alfieri had already told Weizsäcker that he had been surprised that Mussolini had not demanded Nice, Corsica and Tunisia. Mussolini had said that he was waiting for a 'wink' from Hitler in this respect, but Weizsäcker noted that Hitler had given Mussolini carte blanche to ask whatever he wanted.

72. *Rommel Papers*, p. 304.

73. Rommel, *Krieg*, pp. 247–9.

74. Barr, *Pendulum of War*, pp. 345–6.

75. It had recently been agreed between OKW and the Comando Supremo that, in order to emphasise the brotherhood in arms, the Panzer Army Africa should be renamed the German–Italian Panzer Army.

76. BAMA RH19/VIII/31.

77. BAMA RH/19/VIII/31 p. 28.

78. BAMA RH/19/VIII/31.

79. Rommel, *Krieg*, p. 253.

80. *Rommel Papers*, p. 310.

81. The British still continued to produce the two-pounders, with Oliver Lyttleton fatuously arguing in the House of Commons that to discontinue its production would reduce output.

82. Barr, *Pendulum of War*, pp. 360–1.

83. Rommel, *Krieg*, p. 255.

84. Hamilton, *Monty*, vol. I, p. 802.

85. 'Kidney Ridge' was marked on the map as such, but was in fact a depression. For this reason it is more accurately, though ambiguously, sometimes called the 'Kidney Feature'.

86. Hamilton, *Monty, vol. II: Master of the Battlefield* (London: Hamish Hamilton, 1984) pp. 14–19.

87. KTB OKW vol. II.2 29.10.42.

88. BAMA RH/19/VIII/33 Rommel 27.10.42.

89. BAMA RH/19/VIII/33 Rommel 28.10.42.

90. BAMA RH/19/VIII/33 Rommel to Rintelen 27.10.42.

91. BAMA RH/19/VIII/33 Rintelen to Rommel 29.10.42.

92. Rommel, *Krieg*, p. 259.

93. BAMA RH/19/VIII/33 Comando Supremo to Rommel 27.10.42. This doubtless increased the difficulties involved in supplying Paulus' army in Stalingrad.

94. BAMA RH/19/VIII/31.

95. BAMA RH/19/VIII/22 1.11.42; *Rommel Papers*, p. 316.

96. BAMA RH/19/VIII/31, pp. 73ff.

97. Bierman and Smith, *The Battle of El Alamein*, p. 318.

98. The 'Nono Bersaglieri' was an exceptionally fine unit that fought with great distinction.

99. BAMA RH/19/VIII/31 and RH/VIII/3.

100. *Rommel Papers*, p. 318.

101. BAMA RH/19/VIII/34a. Both reports dated 2.11.42.

102. BAMA RH/19/VIII/31 p. 84.

103. BAMA RH/19/VIII/31 2.11.42.

104. Cavallero, *Comando Supremo*, 30.10.42.

105. BAMA RH/19/VIII/34a 2.11.42.

106. Hitler's headquarters was divided into an inner circle (*Sperrkreis I*) and an outer circle (*Sperrkreis II*). Warlimont was in the latter. Hitler imagined that this was all part of a conspiracy by *Sperrkreis II* to frustrate the efforts of *Sperrkreis I*.

107. KTB OKW vol. II.2 3.11.42; Warlimont, *Inside Hitler's Headquarters*, pp. 268–70. There is no mention of these dramatic events in Engel's diary.

108. Knox, *Hitler's Italian Allies*, p. 124.

109. *Rommel Papers*, p. 320.

110. BAMA RH/19/VIII/34a 3.11.42. Hitler's message echoed that of Churchill to Auchinleck in June in which he said: 'Every fit male should be made to fight and die for victory.'

111. The order read: 'We have orders from the highest level to defend our present positions to the utmost. They may not be abandoned without my specific orders. The orders to withdraw to positions at the rear, issued in the radio message at 1340hrs on 10.11, are hereby cancelled.' BAMA RH/19/VIII/31 p. 89.

112. BAMA RH/19/VIII/34a 3.11.42.

113. BAMA RH/19/VIII/34; Rommel, *Krieg*, p. 269.

114. Arthur Bryant, *The Turn of the Tide, 1939–1943: a Study Based on the Diaries and Autobiographical Notes of Field Marshal the Viscount Alanbrooke* (London: Collins, 1957) p. 425.

115. BAMA RH/19/VIII/31 and 34; Rommel, *Krieg*, p. 267.

116. KTB OKW vol. II.2 5.11.42.

117. *Rommel Papers*, p. 348.

118. *Ciano Diaries*, 3–6.11.42.

119. BAMA RH/VIII/110.

120. Rommel, *Krieg*, p. 273.

121. BAMA RH/19/VIII/34b.

122. Heckmann, *Rommel's War in Africa*, pp. 480–2.

123. *Ciano Diaries*, 16.1.43. This was based on the intercept of a telegram. Ciano was convinced that this was true, because Thoma had said exactly the same thing to Bismarck during his last visit to Rome.

124. Latimer, *Alamein*, p. 303.

125. Rommel, *Krieg*, p. 273.

126. BAMA RH/19/VIII/31 p. 94.

127. Stumpf, *Krieg im Mittelmeerraum*, p. 708.

128. KTB OKW vol. II.2 6.11.42 OKH's situation report for 5.11.

129. BAMA RH/19/VIII/34.

130. *Rommel Papers*, p. 325.

131. BAMA RH/19/VIII/31 pp. 96–7.

132. Ibid. Rommel heard the news from Cavallero at 2045hrs and from Hitler five minutes later. The messages are in BAMA RH/19/VIII/34b.

133. Warlimont, *Inside Hitler's Headquarters*, pp. 297–8. Rommel remarked of Hitler's belief in willpower: 'Bombs kill men no matter how strong their belief.' Rommel, *Krieg*, p. 269.

134. *Rommel Papers*, p. 351, 14.11.42.

135. *Rommel Papers*, p. 327.

136. KTB OKW vol. II.2 7.11.42. The divisions were 1st, 7th and 10th Armoured Divisions, 1st South African, 2nd New Zealand, 9th Australian and 5th Indian Divisions, 44th London Division, and 50th and 51st 'Scottish' Divisions; 50th Division were in fact Northumbrians, the 51st Highlanders.

137. KTB OKW vol. II.2 9.11.42.

138. Warlimont, *Inside Hitler's Headquarters*, p. 267.

Chapter 10

1. Abetz was never formally the German ambassador to France, because the peace treaty was never signed, but he acted as such. He

was one of the few who admired Ribbentrop. He was an enthusiastic persecutor of French Jews and plunderer of art works.

2. Hinsley, *British Intelligence*, vol. II, p. 478.

3. KTB OKW vol. II.2 10.10.42.

4. Baum and Weichold, *Krieg der Achsenmächte*, pp. 270–1.

5. KTB OKW vol. II.2 4.11.42.

6. Walter Warlimont, 'Die Entscheidung im Mittelmeer 1942' in H.-A. Jacobsen and J. Rohwer, *Entscheidungsschlachten des Zweiten Weltkrieges* (Frankfurt: Bernard und Graefe, 1960) p. 262.

7. Ibid. p. 271; KTB OKW vol. II.2 6.11.42.

8. *Ciano Diaries*, 8.11.42.

9. Buttlar had won the Pour le Mérite in 1918 as commander of Zeppelin L-54. He ended the war as commander of 11 Panzer Division.

10. Warlimont, 'Die Entscheidung im Mittelmeer 1942', p. 277.

11. Ibid. p. 282.

12. Stumpf, 'Krieg im Mittelmeerraum', p. 713.

13. BAMA RW5/v./488 22.11.1942.

14. Douglas Porch, *The Path to Victory: the Mediterranean Theater in World War II* (New York: Farrar Straus and Giroux, 2004) p. 358.

15. ADAP series E, vol. IV, pp. 285–8.

16. *Ciano Diaries*, 11.11.42; KTB OKW vol. II.2 11.11.42.

17. KTB OKW vol. II.2 11.11.42. Hitler issued orders for 'Anton' at 2030hrs on 10 November.

18. Baum and Weichold, *Krieg der Achsenmächte*, p. 278.

19. KTB OKW vol. II.2, p. 927.

20. Baum and Weichold, *Krieg der Achsenmächte*, p. 283.

21. KTB OKW vol. II.2 10.11.42.

22. Baum and Weichold, *Krieg der Achsenmächte*, p. 281. For an overview see: Charles B. Burdick, *Germany's Military Strategy and Spain in World War II* (Syracuse University Press, 1968).

23. Eisenhower was well aware of the critical importance of Gibraltar for the 'Torch' landings; Harry C. Butcher, *My Three Years with Eisenhower* (New York: Simon and Schuster, 1946) p. 58.

24. *Ciano Diaries*, 9.11.42.

25. Rintelen, *Mussolini als Bundesgenosse*, p. 180.

26. *Ciano Diaries*, 18–20.11.42; Stumpf, 'Krieg im Mittelmeerraum', p. 720.

27. *Ciano Diaries*, 18–20.11.42; Hillgruber, *Staatsmänner*, vol. II, p. 196; Paul Schmidt, *Statist auf diplomatischer Bühne, 1923–1945* (Bonn: Athenäum, 1954) p. 578; ADAP series E, vol. IV, p. 257: Rintelen reported on 7 November that Mussolini was calling for a separate peace with the Soviet Union and that he intended to say this to Hitler.

28. BAMA RH19/VIII/358.

29. Robert O. Paxton, *Parades and Politics at Vichy: the French Officer Corps under Marshal Pétain* (Princeton University Press, 1996) for an admirable explanation of this intricate situation.

30. BAMA RH/19/VIII/358 Report by Nehring on military operations in Tunis 9–21 November.

31. BAMA RH/19/VIII/358.

32. BAMA RH19/VIII/358 Barré 18.10.42.

33. BAMA RH19/VIII/358 Rahn situation report 9–21 November 1942.

34. KTB OKW vol. II.2 13.11.42.

35. KTB OKW vol. II.2 p. 936.

36. Stumpf, 'Krieg im Mittelmeerraum', pp. 720–3; Rudolf Rahn, *Ruheloses Leben* (Dusseldorf: Diederichs Verlag, 1949). Rahn was interned for a couple of years and later ran a Coca-Cola bottling plant in Essen.

37. BAMA Oberkommando des Heeres/Generalstab des Heeres RH/2/602 18.1.43.

38. Rintelen, *Mussolini als Bundesgenosse*, p. 181.

39. BAMA RW5/v./488 23.11.42.

40. Hirszowicz, *The Third Reich and the Arab East*, p. 270. See report from Vichy signed Böhland dated 26.12.42 in BAMA RW5/v./489.

41. German Counter-Intelligence (*Abwehr*) found it very difficult to figure out who was on which side. They assumed that Estéva was undecided which way to turn and that Barré was loyal to Vichy. BAMA RW5/v./488 19.11.42.

42. BAMA RW5/v./488, p. 21, 27.11.42.

43. BAMA RW5/v./489 8.12.42. The report originated from an informant at the Abwehr office in Stuttgart attached to Army District (*Wehrkreis*) V.

44. PAAA Fiche 2213 German Consulate Tripoli 21.10.42.

45. Hirszowicz, *The Third Reich and the Arab East*, p. 277.

46. Hans-Gunther Stark, the Afrikakorps' veterans' archivist and editor of their magazine *Oase*, proudly claims that 'The Mediterranean was a barrier the SS never crossed.' Unfortunately this is not true, and it is only because the 8th Army defeated the Panzer Army at El Alamein that an unimaginable massacre was avoided. This remark is in Bierman and Smith, *The Battle of El Alamein*, p. 5.

47. Saevecke, who had served in an Einsatzgruppe in Poland in 1939, was later to serve in Italy where his brutality earned him the nickname the 'Hangman of Milan'. He was interned at Dachau after the war, but was soon employed by the CIA before joining the German Federal Police (BKA). He organised the notorious raid on the weekly magazine *Der Spiegel* in 1971. In 1999 he was condemned in absentia by a Turin court to lifelong imprisonment and died the following year aged eighty-nine. Best ended the war as a commander of the 'Werewolves' under the Senior SS and Police Chief (HSSPF) in Wiesbaden, where he meted out lynch justice. He was sentenced to fifteen years' imprisonment by an American military court, but only served

seven years. He then worked as a mechanical engineer in Mainz. Harder was killed while serving in Rauff's Einsatzkommando in Italy.

48. Helmut Mejcher, 'North Africa in the Strategy and Politics of the Axis Powers, 1936–1943', *Cahiers de Tunisie*, vol. 39 (1981), 629–48.

49. Mallmann and Cüppers, *Halbmond und Hakenkreuz*, pp. 203–8.

50. PAAA R102974 report to AA by one Dr Megerle 17.3.43 who complained that the French were not co-operating effectively with the Germans with propaganda for North Africa.

51. PAAA Fiche 2632 Rieth (Tangier) 29.3.42 and PAAA R27797 18.5.43. The camps were at Meknes and Bonarfa. The Spanish consul in Tangier reported that the British and Americans had been unable to investigate the charges that prisoners were being ill treated by the Free French.

52. PAAA R102974 report from Paris to AA 14.3.43.

53. Original in English.

54. PAAA R27332.

55. PAAA R27332 9.12.42.

56. PAAA R27332 Mackensen to Foreign Office 11.12.42.

57. PAAA R27827.

58. Mackensen to Foreign Office 7.12.42.

59. PAAA R27332 Report by Schnurre 26.6.43.

60. PAAA R102974.

61. Original in English.

62. PAAA R102974.

63. PAAA R102974; R27332.

64. Mallmann and Cüppers, *Halbmond und Hakenkreuz*, p. 212.

65. KTB OKW vol. II.2 7.12.42. The figure of five hundred is most likely grossly exaggerated by the Wehrmacht Command Staff.

66. Roger Faligot and Rémi Kauffer, *Le croissant et la croix gammée. Les secrets de l'alliance entre l'Islam et le nazisme d'Hitler à nos jours* (Paris: Albin Michel, 1990) pp. 146–8.

67. Ibid. for details.

68. BAMA RH19/VIII/358.

69. Hirszowicz, *The Third Reich and the Arab East*, p. 279.

70. There is an impressive memorial there to the almost 2,000 Commonwealth soldiers who died in the fighting between November and February.

71. KTB OKW vol. II.2, p. 1073, comment by Warlimont on Greiner's minutes of 3.12.42.

72. Porch, *The Path to Victory*, p. 357.

73. 5 Army comprised 10 Panzer Division from France, 334 Infantry Division, units from the Hermann Göring Panzer Division, the Barenthin Regiment and the Koch Assault Regiment (both parachute regiments), 501 Panzer Section, equipped with the new model Tigers, the Manteuffel Division, and some battalions of 47 Grenadier Regiment, some of which had fought in Crete.

74. KTB OKW vol. II.2, p. 1077.

75. Goebbels, *Tagebücher*, 18.12.42.

Chapter 11

1. BAMA RH/19/VIII/31, p. 99.

2. KTB OKW vol. II.2 7.11.42; BAMA RH/19/VIII/34b.

3. *Rommel Papers*, p. 340.

4. *Berichte OKW*, vol. III 9.9.42.

5. *Rommel Papers*, p. 343; BAMA RH/19/VIII/34b.

6. *Ciano Diaries*, 21.11.42.

7. *Rommel Papers*, p. 341.

8. Hamilton, *Monty*, vol. II, p. 15. De Guingand always felt that 'Grapeshot' should have gone ahead in order to round up the enemy. Liddell-Hart agreed. Rommel was amazed that the many opportunities offered were not seized. The answer lies not only in Montgomery's caution, but mainly in 8th Army's total inability to mount such an operation. Gott had baulked at the idea of a frontal attack at El Alamein for fear of heavy casualties, but Montgomery had no such compunctions. 8th Army suffered terrible losses in the resulting dogfight. In Montgomery's defence, in spite of his attempts to lick 8th Army into shape, he was in command of a very amateur army that had just managed to pull it off at El Alamein and was to bungle the pursuit.

9. Rommel, *Krieg*, p. 296.

10. BAMA RH/19/VIII/31, p. 116.

11. *Rommel Papers*, p. 345.

12. This would have included men from the Long Range Desert Force, whose courage and dash Rommel held in the highest regard.

13. KTB OKW vol. II.2 8.11.42 OKH situation report 7.11.42.

14. BAMA RH/19/VIII/34b 8.11.42.

15. BAMA RH19/VIII/35 Rommel to Kesselring 10.11.42.

16. BAMA RH19/VIII/35 90 LAD 1745hrs 11.11.42.

17. BAMA RH19/VIII/35 Cavallero to Rommel 10.11.42. OKW repeated this order to protect the non-motorised Italians on 11.11.42.

18. BAMA RH19/VIII/35 OKW to Rommel 11.11.42.

19. BAMA RH19/VIII/35 Rommel to Rome 1800hrs 11.11.42; Rommel, *Krieg*, p. 300.

20. Ralf Georg Reuth, *Rommel: the End of a Legend* (London: Haus Books, 2005) p. 187.

21. KTB OKW vol. II.2 11.11.42.

22. Goebbels, *Tagebücher*, 14.1.42.

23. KTB OKW vol. II.2, p. 957.

24. Baum and Weichold, *Krieg der Achsenmächte*, p. 304.

25. Ibid. p. 307.

26. BAMA RH/19/VIII/31, pp. 149–50.

27. BAMA RH/19/VIII/31, p. 154.

28. Hamilton, *Monty*, vol. II, p. 57.

29. BAMA RH19/VIII/35 AOK 1a 16.11.42.

30. KTB OKW vol. II.2 14.11.42.

31. *Rommel Papers*, p. 351.

32. BAMA RH19/VIII/35 Rommel to Comando Supremo 15.11.42.

33. BAMA RH19/VIII/35 Rommel to OKW and OKH 15.11.42.

34. KTB OKW vol. II.2 15.11.42 comments by Warlimont on Greiner's minutes.

35. KTB OKW vol. II.2, pp. 976–7.

36. KTB OKW vol. II.2, p. 978 for a comment by Warlimont.

37. BAMA RH19/VIII/35 16.11.42.

38. Rommel, *Krieg*, p. 302.

39. BAMA RH19/VIII/35 17.11.42.

40. BAMA RH19/VIII/35 16.11.42.

41. BAMA RH19/VIII/35 18.11.42.

42. BAMA RH19/VIII/35 19.11.42.

43. BAMA RH19/VIII/35 19.11.42.

44. For de Stefanis see: Westphal, *Heer in Fesseln*, p. 199.

45. BAMA RH19/VIII/35 20.11.42.

46. *Rommel Papers*, p. 357.

47. BAMA RH19/VIII/35 22.11.42.

48. BAMA RH19/VIII/35 23.11.42; Baum and Weichold, *Krieg der Achsenmächte*, p. 296; Stumpf, 'Krieg im Mittelmeerraum', p. 730.

49. *Rommel Papers*, p. 362; Rintelen, *Mussolini als Bundesgenosse*, p. 182.

50. BZG Afrikabriefe 31.1.43.

51. BAMA RH/19/VIII/31.

52. KTB OKW vol. II.2 27.11.42 Situation report of OHL for 26 November. Protocol in BAMA KTB Anl. Nr. 434/4.

53. BAMA RH/19/VIII/31, p. 207.

54. Rommel, *Krieg*, p. 312.

55. Rintelen, *Mussolini als Bundesgenosse*, p. 182.

56. *Rommel Papers*, p. 365.

57. BAMA RH19/VIII/36 Rommel to Comando Supremo 24.11.42.

58. BAMA RH19/VIII/36 Bastico to Rommel 26.11.42.

59. BAMA RH19/VIII/36 Rommel to Bastico 26.11.42.

60. BAMA RH19/VIII/36 Rommel to Bastico 26 and 27.11.42.

61. BAMA RH19/VIII/36 Interview with Private (Gefr.) Fitterling 27.11.42.

62. *Ciano Diaries*, 30.11.42.

63. Berndt prepared a position paper for Rommel: BAMA KTB Anl. Nr. 494/1.

64. The Mersa el Brega position was without water. The nearest source was at Nofilia, 150 kilometres to the west.

65. Rommel, *Krieg*, pp. 314–15; KTB OKW vol. II.2, p. 1041 for comments by Warlimont.

66. Heinz Linge, *Bis zum Untergang. Als Chef des persönlichen Dienstes bei Hitler* (Munich: W. Herbig, 1980) p. 21.

67. Warlimont, *Inside Hitler's Headquarters*, p. 308.

68. KTB OKW vol. II.2 1.12.42.

69. BAMA RH/19/VIII/31, p. 226.

70. BAMA RH19/VIII/36 AOK 29.11.42 Cavallero to Bastico 1.12.42.

71. *Ciano Diaries*, 1.12.42.

72. Rommel, *Krieg*, pp. 315–19.

73. Ibid. p. 317.

74. KTB OKW vol. II.2 1.12.42.

75. KTB OKW vol. II.2, p. 1068; 60,000 tons of shipping was sunk in November, 20,000 tons damaged. Contrary to the German navy's assessment the route to Tunisia was far from safe: 4,879 tons of fuel were landed, but 8,110 tons were sunk during this period.

76. *Ciano Diaries*, 2 and 3.12.42.

77. Hillgruber, *Staatsmänner*, vol. II: 18.12.42. Ciano makes scant mention of this encounter in his diaries, limiting his comments to describing Laval as 'the filthiest of Frenchmen' and mentioning Ribbentrop's faux pas. KTB OKW vol. II.2 18.12.42.

78. Westphal, *Erinnerungen*, p. 731.

79. Protocol in BAMA KTB Anl. Nr. 505/2.

80. BAMA RH19/VIII/36 AOK 4.12.42.

81. KTB OKW vol. II.2 6.12.42; BAMA RH19/VIII/36 4.12.42.

82. BAMA RH/19/VIII/31, p. 236.

83. BAMA RH19/VIII/37, p. 27.

84. BAMA RH19/VIII/37 Rommel to Kesselring and Bastico 6.12.42.

85. BAMA RH/19/VIII/31, p. 245.

86. KTB OKW vol. II.2 8.12.42.

87. KTB OKW vol. II.2 10.12.42.

88. KTB OKW vol. II.2, p. 1121.

89. The British refer to this phase as the Battle of Agheila.

90. BAMA RH/19/VIII/31.

91. BAMA RH19/VIII/37 12.12.42.

92. BAMA RH/19/VIII/31, p. 271.

93. BAMA RH/19/VIII/31, p. 264.

94. BAMA RH19/VIII/37 AOK to OKW and OKH, Rommel to Kesselring 14.12.42.

95. BAMA RH/19/VIII/31, p. 277.

96. Rommel, *Krieg*, pp. 323–4.

97. KTB OKW vol. II.2 17.12.42.

98. KTB OKW vol. II.2 16.12.42.

99. Hillgruber, *Staatsmänner*, vol. II, 18.12.42.

100. Goebbels, *Tagebücher*, 14.12.42.

101. The defensive position at Gabes runs along the Wadi Akarit, about 25 kilometres east of the town. The Germans sometimes referred to this as the Gabes Line, at others as the Akarit Line.

102. BAMA RH19/VIII/37 17.12.43; Stumpf, 'Der Krieg im Mittelmeerraum', p. 732; Rommel, *Krieg*, p. 325; *Rommel Papers*, p. 376.

103. BAMA RH19/VIII/37 17.12.43.

104. BAMA RH19/VIII/37 18.12.43.

105. BAMA RH19/VIII/37 AOK 19.12.43.

106. BAMA RH/19/VIII/31, p. 299.

107. Rommel, *Krieg*, p. 326.

108. BAMA RH19/VIII/38 20.12.43.

109. BAMA RH19/VIII/38 21.12.42.

110. BAMA RH19/VIII/38 Rommel to Kesselring 16.12.43.

111. Rommel, *Krieg*, p. 328.

112. BAMA RH/19/VIII/31, p. 304.

113. BAMA RH/19/VIII/31, pp. 309–10.

114. Erich von Manstein, *Lost Victories* (London: Methuen 1955) p. 362.

115. ADAP series E vol. IV, pp. 538–55; KTB OKW vol. II.2 19.12.42. Cavallero, *Comando Supremo*, 18.12.42 for reports on Ciano's visit.

116. ADAP series E, vol. IV, pp. 582–5.

117. BAMA RH19/VIII/38 AOK to OKW and OKH 24.12.42; discussions Rommel/Bastico 28.12.42.

118. OB (Oberbefehlhabers)-Kompanie was made up of the headquarters' staff of communications, drivers and clerks.

119. BZG Afrikabriefe. A letter home from a member of 334 Infantry Division 29.10.42.

120. KTB OKW vol. II.2 25.12.42.

121. Rommel, *Krieg*, pp. 328–30.

122. BAMA RH/19/VIII/31, p. 331.

123. BAMA Oberkommando des Heeres/Generalstab des Heeres RH/2/601 Cavallero 29.12.42; OKH Op. Ab. 2.1.43; BAMA RH19/VIII/38 Cavallero to Bastico 27.12.42.

124. BAMA RH19/VIII/38 Rommel/Bastico discussions 31.12.42.

125. KTB OKW vol. II.2 29.12.42.

126. BAMA RH/19/VIII/31, p. 343.

127. KTB OKW vol. III.1 2.1.43.

128. BAMA RH/19/VIII/38 Rommel to Bastico 2.1.43.

129. BAMA RH/19/VIII/31, p. 345.

130. BAMA RH/19/VIII/31, p. 355.

131. BAMA RH19/VIII/38 6.1.42.

132. BAMA RH19/VIII/39 Cavallero to Rommel via Bastico 11.1.43; Rommel to OKW and OKH.

133. KTB OKW vol. III.1 12.1.43. Cavallero relayed Mussolini's message to Rommel on 11 January 1943: BAMA Oberkommando des Heeres/Generalstab des Heeres RH/2/600.

134. KTB OKW vol. III.1 14.1.43.

135. KTB OKW vol. III.1 15.1.43; BAMA RH19/VIII/39 15.1.43.

136. KTB OKW vol. III.1 12.1.43; Kesselring, *Soldat*, p. 201.

137. Kesselring imagined that 164 Light Africa Division had been withdrawn, as originally intended.

138. The figures were: January 36,326 tons, February 32,966, March 29,267, April 23,017 and May 2,673; 129 Axis ships were sunk during this period, 9 were damaged. Alfred Gause, 'Der Feldzug im Nordafrika im Jahre 1943', *Wehrwissenschaftliche Rundschau*, vol. 12, No. 12 (1962), 720–8.

139. BAMA RH/19/VIII/31, p. 379.

140. BAMA RH/19/VIII/31, p. 374.

141. Stumpf, 'Krieg im Mittelmeerraum', p. 735. At this time Rommel had 36 German and 57 Italian tanks, 17 German and 16 Italian armoured cars, 111 German and 66 Italian anti-tank guns, and 72 German and 98 Italian guns against 8th Army's 650 tanks, 200 armoured cars, 550 anti-tank guns and 360 guns, according to Gause, 'Der Feldzug im Nordafrika im Jahre 1943'.

142. BAMA RH19/VIII/39 AOK 1a 15.1.43.

143. BAMA RH19/VIII/39 16.3.43.

144. BAMA RH/19/VIII/39 17.1.43. Among those present were Colonel Sedda (Chief of Staff 21 Corps) and Lieutenant-Colonel Cerri (1a Superlibia).

145. BAMA RH/19/VIII/32, p. 14.

146. BAMA RH/19/VIII/39 AOK 1a 18.1.43.

147. The New Zealanders had only fourteen tanks, 4th Light Armoured Brigade no heavy tanks, and 7th Armoured Division about thirty heavy tanks. Hamilton, *Monty*, vol. II, p. 117.

148. KTB OKW vol. III.1 19.1.43; BAMA RH19/VIII/39 AOK 1a 19.1.43.

149. BAMA Oberkommando des Heeres/Generalstab des Heeres RH/2/601 91.1.1943.

150. BAMA RH19/VIII/39 Cavallero to Rommel 20.1.43.

151. BAMA RH19/VIII/39 AOK 1a 21.1.43; Rommel, *Krieg*, p. 337.

152. BAMA Oberkommando des Heeres/Generalstab des Heeres RH/2/599 22.1.1943.

153. KTB OKW vol. III.1 22.1.43.

154. BAMA RH19/VIII/39 AOK 1a 22.1.43.

155. BAMA RH/19/VIII/32, p. 39.

156. *Ciano Diaries*, 22.1.43.

157. BAMA RH19/VIII/39 AOK 1a 26.1.43.

158. KTB OKW vol. III.1 22.1.43.

159. KTB OKW vol. III.1 24.1.43.

160. John Ellis, *Brute Force: Allied Strategy and Tactics in the Second World War* (London: André Deutsch, 1990) p. 283.

161. Hamilton, *Monty*, vol. II, p. 15.

162. Ibid. p. 37.

163. Porch, *The Path to Victory*, p. 324.

Chapter 12

1. *Rommel Papers*, p. 391.

2. *Ciano Diaries*, 4.6.42 Ciano added that 'everybody else who has had anything to do with the Germans' agreed with him. Messe added that the only thing to do with the Germans was to punch them in the stomach. See also BAMA RH/19/VIII/32, p. 58.

3. *Ciano Diaries*, 24.1.43.

4. KTB OKW vol. III.1 27.1.43.

5. KTB OKW vol. III.1 27.1.43.

6. BAMA RH/19/VIII/32, pp. 62–4.

7. *Ciano Diaries*, 30–31.1.43. Cavallero was arrested after the fall of Mussolini, released when the Germans occupied Rome, and committed suicide during the night of 12/13 September after an interview with Kesselring. He had manoeuvred himself into a hopeless situation, with Badoglio considering him to be a Fascist, the Fascists a traitor.

8. BAMA Oberkommando des Heeres/Generalstab des Heeres RH/2/594 30.1.1943.

9. Rintelen, *Mussolini als Bundesgenosse*, p. 187.

10. KTB OKW vol. III.1 7.2.43.

11. BAMA RH/19/VIII/32, pp. 78–82.

12. BAMA RH/19/VIII/32, p. 90.

13. KTB OKW vol. III.1 10.2.43.

14. KTB OKW vol. III.1 11.2.43.

15. BAMA RH/19/VIII/41 Rommel to Comando Supremo 15.2.42.

16. BAMA RH/19/VIII/32, pp. 106–9.

17. BAMA RH2/634 OKH Army General Staff, Foreign Armies West 8.2.1943.

18. KTB OKW vol. III.1 15.2.43.

19. KTB OKW vol. III.1 18.2.43.

20. BAMA RH/19/VIII/41 Rommel to Comando Supremo 19.2.43.

21. BAMA Oberkommando des Heeres/Generalstab des Heeres RH2/602 24.2.43. Further details in BAMA RH19/VIII/40 25.1.43 and 20.2.43 and RH19/VIII/32 27.1.43–23.2.43.

22. Bayerlein, who was previously the Afrikakorps chief of staff, was appointed army chief of staff on 7 December as a replacement for Westphal, who was seriously ill and had been sent back to Germany

for treatment. He was also given temporary command over 164 Light Africa Division, pending the arrival of a new commanding general. BAMA RH/19/VIII/31, p. 249.

23. Rommel, *Krieg*, p. 347.

24. Volkmar Kühn, *Mit Rommel in der Wüste. Kampf und Untergang des Deutschen Afrika-Korps 1941–1943* (Würzburg: Flechsig, 2006) p. 267.

25. BAMA RH/19/VIII/41 Comando Supremo to Rommel 18.2.43; Rommel to Assault Group 19.2.42.

26. BAMA RH/19/VIII/32, p. 136.

27. BAMA RH/19/VIII/32, pp. 139–40.

28. Bülowius, as Rommel's chief engineer, was responsible for the 'devil's gardens' that had caused 8th Army so many casualties.

29. Rommel, *Krieg*, p. 360. The PzKpfwVI Tiger 1 was a formidable weapon, first produced in August 1942. Armed with an 88mm gun and with 110mm armour it was the most powerful tank in the world. Weighing 55,000kg it was enormously heavy, slow and with a limited range. Virtually invulnerable from the front, it was highly vulnerable from the rear, and could be out-manoeuvred by more agile Allied tanks. The British first encountered the Tiger in February 1943 in Tunisia when they knocked out two of them at 500 yards with six-pounders. Fifteen of Arnim's nineteen Tigers were lost within a few weeks. Arnim may very well have been correct, because the tracks were too wide for road and rail transport, so they had to be fitted with narrower ones for such purposes. It also had overlapping road wheels that had to be removed when being transported. In addition it needed frequent maintenance and repair.

30. BAMA RH19/VIII/2364 16.2.1942.

31. BAMA RH/19/VIII/32, p. 147.

32. BAMA RH/19/VIII/41 21.2.43; *Rommel Papers*, p. 407.

33. KTB OKW vol. III.1 23.2.43. OKW does not seem to have been closely informed as to the operation.

34. KTB OKW vol. III.1 25.1.43 Telegram OKW/WFSt/Op. Nr. 6214/43 g.K. Chefs v, 28.1.43. The order was published on 28 January (see appendix to KTB OKW).

35. BAMA RH/19/VIII/32, p. 163.

36. BAMA RH/19/VIII/41 23.2.43.

37. Rommel, *Krieg*, p. 362.

38. Porch, *The Path to Victory*, p. 383. Anderson, a deeply religious and dour Scot, known to his men as 'Sunshine', claimed that 'serious setbacks at timely intervals' were 'good medicine for one's self-esteem'. He was to be given frequent doses without any noticeable palliative effect. His military career ended in North Africa, with the consolation of a knighthood and the governorship of Gibraltar.

39. KTB OKW vol. III.1 23.2.43.

40. Rommel, *Krieg*, p. 367.

41. Hamilton, *Monty*, vol. II, p. 169.

42. BAMA RH/19/VIII/41 26.2.43 AOK 5 Panzer Army.

43. Gause, 'Der Feldzug in Nordafrika im Jahre 1943'.

44. Ibid.

45. BAMA RH/19/VIII/41 Rommel 1.3.43.

46. Goebbels, *Tagebücher*, 2.3.43.

47. KTB OKW vol. III.1 5.3.43.

48. BAMA RH19/VIII/359 5.3.43, 12.4.43, 14.4.43.

49. KTB OKW vol. III.1 8.3.43.

50. Baum and Weichold, *Krieg der Achsenmächte*, pp. 315–17.

51. Rintelen, *Mussolini als Bundesgenosse*, p. 192.

52. *Rommel Papers*, pp. 419–20.

53. KTB OKW vol. III.1 9.3.43.

54. KTB OKW vol. III.1 14.3.43. The message was sent on 9 March.

55. KTB OKW vol. III.1 12.3.43.

56. KTB OKW vol. III.1 14.3.43.

57. KTB OKW vol. III.1 18.3.43.

58. Goebbels, *Tagebücher*, 17.3.43. Goebbels was eventually to lose confidence in Berndt, accusing him of gross exaggeration and deception. See diary entry for 6.6.44.

59. KTB OKW vol. III.1 22.3.43.

60. The Tripolitanian Military Command was renamed the Sahara Group on 26 January 1943 and placed under the command of the DIPA. It consisted of five infantry battalions, one of which was motorised, and ten batteries of 7.5 and 7.7cm anti-tank guns.

61. Hamilton, *Monty*, vol. II, p. 185.

62. Rommel, *Krieg*, p. 374.

63. Hamilton, *Monty*, vol. II, p. 190.

64. Ibid. vol. II, p. 192.

65. Ibid. vol. II, p. 207.

66. Gause, 'Der Feldzug in Nordafrika', p. 726.

67. KTB OKW III.1 30.3.43.

68. KTB OKW vol. III.1 31.3.43.

69. Kesselring, *Soldat*, p. 210.

70. Baum and Weichold, *Krieg der Achsenmächte*, p. 325.

71. KTB OKW vol. III.1 6.4.43.

72. KTB OKW vol. III.1, p. 297 Sonderorientierung des OKW/WFSt/Op. Nr. 01538/43g. für die Zeit vom 1.4.–7.4.1943.

73. BZG Afrikabriefe 10.4.43.

74. *Berichte OKW* vol. IV 10.4.43.

75. Rommel, *Krieg*, p. 375.

76. KTB OKW vol. III.1 12.4.43.

77. Hamilton, *Monty*, vol. II, pp. 221–3.

78. KTB OKW vol. III.1 p. 332 Sonderorientierung des OKW/WFSt/Op. Nr.01661/43g. für die Zeit vom 8.4.–14.4.1943.

79. KTB OKW vol. III.1 20.4.43.

80. Rommel, *Krieg*, p. 376.

81. KTB OKW vol. III.1 21.4.43.

82. Hamilton, *Monty*, vol. II, p. 233. 1st US Army comprised six US, two British and one French Corps, and soldiers from various Allied nations.

83. KTB OKW III.1, p. 400 Sonderorientierung des OKW/WFSt/Op. Nr.01904/43g. für die Zeit vom 22.4.–28.4.1943.

84. Gause, 'Der Feldzug in Nordafrika', p. 727.

85. KTB OKW III.1 1.5.43.

86. KTB OKW III.1, p. 436 Sonderorientierung des OKW/WFSt/Op. Nr.02011/43g. für die Zeit vom 29.4.–5.5.1943.

87. Hamilton, *Monty*, vol. II, p. 237.

88. Ibid. vol. II, p. 237.

89. KTB OKW III.1 7.5.43.

90. Spike Milligan, *Monty: His Part in My Victory* (Harmondsworth: Penguin, 1976) pp. 16–17.

91. BAMA Oberkommando des Heeres/Generalstab des Heeres RH2/629 9.5.43 (0930hrs).

92. KTB OKW III.1 p. 470 Sonderorientierung des OKW/WFSt/Op. Nr.02122/43g. für die Zeit vom 6.5.–12.5.1943.

93. KTB OKW III.1 8.5.43.

94. KTB OKW III.1 9.5.43.

95. *Berichte OKW IV Berichte OKW* 1.1.1943–31.12.1944, p. 121.

96. KTB OKW III.1 12.5.43.

97. KTB OKW III.1 13.5.43.

98. BAMA Oberkommando des Heeres/Generalstab des Heeres RH/2/594 von Rintelen 26.5.1943.

99. BAMA Oberkommando des Heeres/Generalstab des Heeres RH/2/600 6.5.1943.

100. BAMA RH2/634 OKH operations division 12.5.43.

101. Quoted in Porch, *The Path to Victory*, p. 414.

102. Goebbels, *Tagebücher*, 9.5.43.

103. PAAA R27797 Hewel to Foreign Office from the Berghof 25.6.43 reporting on his conversation with Hitler.

104. Goebbels, *Tagebücher*, 9.5.43. Goebbels published an article to this effect, 'Mit souveräner Ruhe', in *Das Reich* 23.5.43.

105. Gause, 'Der Feldzug in Nordafrika', p. 728.

BIBLIOGRAPHY

Archives

Bundesarchiv Militärarchiv (BAMA), Freiburg im Breisgau

Oberkommando des Heeres/Generalstab des Heeres RH2/
303K; 304K; 594; 595; 596; 597; 598; 599; 600; 601; 602; 603; 604;
605K; 606; 607; 608; 609; 610; 611; 612; 613; 614; 615; 616; 617;
618; 619; 620; 621; 622; 623; 624; 625; 626; 627; 628; 629; 630;
631; 632; 633; 634; 635; 1757; 1758K; 1894K; 1895K; 2557

Heeresgruppenkommandos RH19/VIII/
1; 2; 3; 4; 5; 6; 7; 8; 10; 12; 13; 14; 15; 20; 21; 22; 25; 26; 27; 31; 32;
33; 34; 35; 36; 37; 38; 39; 40; 41; 42; 46; 47; 48; 49; 50; 51; 52; 53;
54; 55; 56; 57; 65; 66; 68; 69; 71; 72; 74; 75; 76; 78; 79; 80; 81; 82;
83; 85; 86; 87; 88; 89; 91; 93; 94; 96; 97; 98; 99; 100; 101; 110; 126;
127; 130; 131; 132; 133; 135; 137; 138; 156; 158; 159; 160; 161;
162; 163; 164; 165; 166; 167; 168; 169; 170; 171; 172; 173; 174;
175; 176; 177; 178; 179; 180; 185; 238; 245; 246; 247; 248; 249;
250; 251; 252; 253; 254; 255; 256; 257; 258; 259; 260; 261; 262;
278; 289; 312; 322; 323; 324; 325; 326; 327; 328; 329; 330; 331;
332; 333; 334; 352; 352; 353; 354; 355; 356; 357; 358; 359; 360;
361; 363; 364

RH2/
133; 251; 252; 629; 630; 631; 632; 634

OKW/WFst./
526; 547; 657

N117/
4; 9; 10; 11; 12; 13; 14; 15; 16; 20;

Abwehr RW5/
86; 120; 121; 424; 488; 489; 675; 684; 739

Politisches Archiv Auswärtiges Amts, Berlin
R: 27324; 27325; 27326; 27332; 27353; 27772; 27797; 27827;

29533; 29863; 60675; 60747; 60748; 60770; 60771; 100752;

100753; 100860; 101022; 101023; 102974; 104776; 114022;

114023; 114024; 114025; 114026; 114027

Published sources

Aberger, Heinz-Dietrich, *Die 5. (lei.) /21. Panzer-Division in Nordafrika 1941–1943* (Reutlingen : Preussischer Militär-Verlag, 1994).

Aberger, Heinz-Dietrich and Taysen, Adalbert von Ziemer Kurt. *Nur ein Bataillon (The 8th Machine Gun Battalion)* (Essen: Selbstverlag Walter Barchardt, 1972).

Adès, Lucien. *L'aventure Algérienne, 1940–1944: Pétain-Giraud-DeGaulle* (Paris: P. Belfond, 1979).

Agar-Hamilton, J. A. I. and Turner, L. C. F. *Crisis in the Desert: May–July 1942* (Oxford University Press, 1952).

   The Sidi-Rezeg Battles (Capetown: Oxford University Press, 1957).

Agnelli, S. *We Always Wore Sailor Suits* (London: Weidenfeld and Nicolson, 1975).

Alanbrooke, Field Marshal Lord. *War Diaries, 1939–1945*, ed. A. Danchev and D. Todman (London: Weidenfeld and Nicolson, 2001).

Alexander, Field Marshal Viscount. *The Alexander Memoirs*, ed. J., Norton (London: Cassell, 1962).

   Despatch: the African Campaign from El Alamein to Tunis, 10 August 1942 to 13 May 1943, supplement to the *London Gazette*, 3 February 1948.

Alexander, G. *So ging Deutschland in die Falle* (Düsseldorf: Econ Verlag, 1976).

Alman, Karl. *Ritterkreuzträger des Afrikakorps* (Rastatt: E. Pabel, 1968).

Alsdorf, L. *Indien* (Berlin: Deutscher Verlag, 1943).

Alves, Dora. 'The Resupply of Malta in World War II', *Naval War College Review*, September–October (1980), 63–72.

Amery, J. *Approach March: a Venture in Autobiography* (London: Hutchinson, 1973).

Anchieri, Ettore. *Die deutsch-italienischen Beziehungen während des Zweiten Weltkrieges. Faschismus-Nazionalsozialismus. Ergebnisse und Referate der 6. Italienisch-deutschen Historiker-Tagung in Trier*, ed. Eckert von Georg and Otto-Ernst Schüddekopf, Schriftenreihe des Internationalen Schulbuchinstituts 8 (Braunschweig: A. Limbach, 1964).

'Das große Missverständnis des deutschen-italienischen Bündnisses', *Zur Aktenpublikation des römischen Außenministerium, Außenpolitik*, Vol. 5 (1954), 509–19.

'Italiens Ausweichen vor dem Krieg', *Außenpolitik*, Vol. 5 (1954), 653–62.

Anderson, J. A. and Jackett, J. G. T. (eds.) *Mud and Sand: the Official War History of 2/3 Pioneer Battalion AIF* (Sydney: 2/3 Pioneer Battalion Association, 1955).

Andò, E. and Bagnasco, E. *Navi et marinai italiani nella seconda guerra mondiale* (Parma: Albertelli, 1977).

Ansel, Walter. *Hitler and the Middle Sea* (Durham, NC: Duke University Press, 1972).

Arena, Nino. *Folgore: Storia del paracadutismo militare italiano* (Rome: Centro Editoriale, 1966).

Assmann, Kurt. *Deutsche Schicksalsjahre* (Wiesbaden: E. Brockhaus, 1950).

Deutsche Seestrategie in zwei Weltkriegen (Heidelberg: V. Vowinckel, 1957).

Atkinson, Rick. *An Army at Dawn: the War in North Africa, 1942–1943* (New York: Henry Holt, 2002).

Auchinleck, Field Marshal Sir Claude. *Despatch: Operations in the Middle East from 1 November 1941 to 15 August 1942*, supplement to the *London Gazette*, 13 January 1948.

Attard, Joseph. *The Battle of Malta* (London: Kimber, 1980).

Audet, R. 'La stratégie allemande en Méditerrannée', *Revue Défense Nationale*, No. 3 (1951), 483–94.

Auphan, Paul and Mordal, Jacques. *The French Navy in World War II* (Annapolis: United States Naval Institute Press, 1959).

Austin, R. J. *Let Enemies Beware! 'Caveant Hostes': the History of the 2/15th Battalion, 1940–1945* (McCrae: The 2/15th Battalion AIF Remembrance Club/Slouch Hat Publications, 1995).

Badoglio, Pietro. *L'Italia nella seconda guerra mondiale (memorie e documenti)* (Milan: A. Mondadori, 1946).

Bagnold, R. A. *Sand, Wind and War: Memoirs of a Desert Explorer* (Tucson: University of Arizona Press, 1990).

Baker, P. *Yeoman-Yeoman: the Warwickshire Yeomanry, 1920–1956* (Warwick: The Queen's Own Warwickshire and Worcestershire Yeomanry Regimental Association, 1975).

Baldwin, Hanson Weightman. *Battles Lost and Won: Great Campaigns of World War II* (New York: Harper and Row, 1966).

Barclay, C. N. *Against Great Odds: the Story of the First Offensive in Libya, 1940–1941* (London: Sifton Praed, 1956).

The History of the Sherwood Foresters (Nottinghamshire and Derbyshire Regiments), 1919–1957 (London: William Clowes, 1958).

On Their Shoulders (London: Faber, 1964).

Barkas, G. *The Camouflage Story* (London: Cassell, 1952).

Barker, A. J. *Afrika Korps* (London: Bison Books, 1978).

Barnett, Corelli. *The Desert Generals*, rev. edn (London: Cassell, 1983).

Barr, Niall. *Pendulum of War: the Three Battles of El Alamein* (London: Jonathan Cape, 2004).

Barrett, J. *We Were There: Australian Soldiers of World War Two* (Ringwood: Viking, 1987).

Barter, M. *Far Above Battle: the Experience and Memory of Australian Soldiers in War, 1939–1945* (Sydney: Allen and Unwin, 1994).

Barthel, Konrad. 'Die Kriegsziele der deutschen Imperialisten im Zweiten Weltkrieges', *Militärwesen*, Vol. 5 (1961), 934–52.

Bates, P. *Dance of War: the Story of the Battle of Egypt* (London: Leo Cooper, 1992).

Supply Company (Wellington: War History Branch, Department of Internal Affairs, 1955).

The Battle of Egypt: the Official Record in Pictures and Maps (London: HMSO, 1943).

Bauer, E. *La guerre des blindées*, 2 vols. (Lausanne, 1962). Published in German as *Der Panzerkrieg: Die Wichtigsten Panzeroperationen des Zweiten Weltkrieges in Europa und Afrika*, 2 Vols. (Bonn: Verlag Offene Worte, 1965).

Baum, Walter and Weichold, Eberhard. *Der Krieg der Achsenmächte im Mittelmeer-Raum. Die 'Strategie' der Diktatoren* (Göttingen: Musterschmidt, 1973).

Bayerlein, Fritz, Nehring, Walther, von Klimkowstroem, Graf and Caesar, Kurt. *Marsch und Kampf des DAK* (Munich: Karl Rohrig Verlag, 1945).

Beale, Peter. *Death by Design* (Gloucester: Sutton, 1998).

Beaton, Cecil. *Near East* (London: Batsford, 1943).

Beckett, D. *1/4th Essex Regiment: a Battalion of Eighth Army* (London: Wilson and Whitworth, 1945).

Beddington, W. R. *A History of the Queen's Bays (The 2nd Dragoon Guards), 1929–1945* (Winchester: Warren and Son, 1954).

Beesly, P. *Very Special Intelligence: the Story of the Admiralty's Operational Intelligence Centre, 1939–1945* (London: Naval Institute Press, 1977).

Begg, R. Campbell and Liddle, P. H. (eds.) *For Five Shillings a Day: Personal Histories of World War II* (London: HarperCollins, 2000).

Behrendt, Hans-Otto. *Rommel's Intelligence in the Desert Campaign* (London: William Kimber, 1985).

Rommels Kenntnis vom Feind im Afrikafeldzug: Ein Bericht über die Feindnachrichtenarbeit, insbesondere die Funkaufklärung, Einzelschriften zur militärischen Geschichte des Zweiten Weltkrieges 25 (Freiburg: Rombach, 1980).

Bekker, Cajus. *Angriffshöhe 4000* (Oldenburg: Gerhard Stalling, 1964).

Einzelkämpfer auf See (Herford: Koehler, 1968).

Hitler's Naval War, ed. and trans. Frank Ziegler (London: MacDonald, 1974).

The Luftwaffe Diaries (London: MacDonald, 1967).

Verdammte See (Frankfurt: Ullstein, 1971).

Die versunkene Flotte (Hamburg: Gerhard Stalling, 1967).

Belot, Raymond de. *La guerre aéronavale en Méditerrannée, 1939–1945* (Paris, 1949). Published in English as *The Struggle for the Mediterranean, 1939–1945* (Princeton University Press, 1951).

Below, Nicolaus von. *Als Hitlers Adjutant, 1937–45* (Mainz: Hase und Koehler, 1980).

Bender, Roger James and Law, Richard D. *Afrikakorps: Uniform, Organization and History* (San Jose, CA: James Bender, 1973).

Bennett, Ralph. 'Intelligence and Strategy: Some Observations on War in the Mediterranean, 1939–1945' in Ralph Bennett (ed.) *Intelligence Investigations: How Ultra Changed History* (London: Frank Cass, 1996) pp. 93–115.

Ultra and Mediterranean Strategy, 1941–1945 (London: Hamish Hamilton, 1989).

Bensel, Rolf. *Die deutsche Flottenpolitik 1933 bis 1939. Eine Studie über die Rolle des Flottenbaues in Hitlers Außenpolitik* (Berlin: E. S. Mittler, 1958).

Bergo, Erwan. *The Afrika Korps* (London: Alan Wingate, 1972).

Die Berichte des Oberkommandos der Wehrmacht, 1939–1945, 5 vols. (Munich: Verlag für Wehrwissenschaften, 2004).

Bernotti, Romeo. *Storia della guerra nel Mediterraneo, 1940–1943*, I Libri del Tempo 10 (Rome: V. Bianca, 1960).

Bernstein, B. L. *The Tide Turned at Alamein: Impressions of the Desert War with the South African Division and the Eighth Army, June 1941–January 1943* (Cape Town: Central News, 1944).

Bharucha, P. C. *The North African Campaign, 1940–1943*, Official History of the Indian Armed Forces in the Second World War, 1939–1945 (London and New Delhi: Combined Inter-Services Historical Section (India & Pakistan), 1956).

Biagini, Antonello and Frattolillo, Fernando (eds.) *Verbali delle riunioni tenute dal capo di Stato Maggiore Generale*, 4 vols. (Rome: Stato maggiore dell'Esercito, Ufficio storico, 1983–5).

Biagini, Antonello and Gionfrida, Alessandro (eds.) *Lo Stato Maggiore Generale tra le due guerre: verbali delle riunioni presiedute da Badoglo dal 1925 al 1937* (Rome: Stato maggiore dell'Esercito, ufficio storico, 1997).

Bidlingmaier, G. *Der Einsatz der schweren Kriegsmarineeinheitein im ozeanischen Zufuhrkrieg* (Neckargemünd: K. Vowinckel, 1963).

'Die strategischen und operativen Überlegungen der Marine, 1932–1942', *Wehrwissenschaftliche Rundschau*, Vol. 13 (1963), 312–31.

Bidwell, S. 'After the Wall Came Tumbling Down: a Historical Perspective', *Journal of the Royal United Services Institute for Defence Studies*, Vol. 135 (1990).

   Gunners at War (London: Arrow Books, 1972).

Bierman, John and Smith, Colin. *The Battle of Alamein: Turning Point, World War II* (New York and London: Viking, 2002).

Bingham, J. K. W. and Haupt, W. *North African Campaign, 1940–1943* (London: MacDonald, 1968).

Birkby, C. (ed.) *The Saga of the Transvaal Scottish Regiment, 1932–1950.* (Cape Town: Timmins, 1950).

Birkenfeld, W. *Der Synthetische Treibstoff, 1933–1945* (Göttingen: Musterschmidt Verlag, 1964).

Bishop, T. *One Young Soldier: Memoirs of a Cavalry Man*, ed. B. Shand (Norwich: Russell, 1993).

Blackburn, G. *The Guns of War* (London: Constable and Robinson, 2000).

Blair, S. G. *In Arduis Fidelis: Centenary History of the Royal Army Medical Corps* (Edinburgh: Scottish Academic Press, 1998).

Blamey, A. E. *A Company Commander Remembers* (Pietermaritzburg, 1962).

Blumenson, Martin. *Kasserine Pass: Rommel's Bloody, Climatic Battle for Tunisia* (New York: Cooper Square Press, 2000).

Boberach, Heinz. (ed.) *Meldungen aus dem Reich. Auswahl aus den geh. Lageberichten des Sicherheitsdienstes der SS 1939–1944* (Herrsching: Pawlak, 1968).

Boehm, H. and Marschall, W. 'Zur deutschen Seekriegführung 1939–1940', *Marine Rundschau*, Vol. 69 (1972), 41–79.

Böhme, Hermann. *Der deutsch-französische Waffenstillstand im Zweiten Weltkrieg. Erster Teil: Entstehung und Grundlagen des Waffenstillstandes von 1940* (Stuttgart: Deutsche Verlags-Anstalt, 1966).

Bolitho, H. *The Galloping Third: the Story of the Third The King's Own Hussars* (London: John Murray, 1963).

Borgiotti, Alberto and Gori, Cesare. *La guerra aerea in Africa Settentrionale, 1940–1941: Assalto del cielo*, Collezione Storica del Risorgimento e dell-unità d'Italia, Documenti e testimonianze 1 (Modena: STEM, 1973).

Borthwick, A. *Sans Peur: the History of the 5th (Caithness and Sutherland) Battalion, The Seaforth Highlanders, 1942–1945* (Stirling: Eneas Mackay, 1946).

Bottai, Giuseppe. *Diario, 1935–1944*, ed. Giordano Bruno Guerri (Milan: Rizzoli 1982).

Bowyer, C. *Men of the Desert Air Force, 1940–1943* (London: William Kimber, 1984).

Bowyer, C. and Shores, C. *Desert Air Force at War* (London: Ian Allen, 1981).

Bracher, K. D. *Zeitgeschichtliche Kontraversen: Um Faschismus, Totalitarianismus, Demokratie* (Munich: Piper, 1976).

Bradford, Ernle. *Siege: Malta, 1940–1943* (Harmondsworth: Penguin, 1987).

Bragadin, Marc'Antonio. *Il dramma della marina italiana, 1940–1945* (Milan: A. Mondadori, 1966).

The Italian Navy in World War II (Annapolis: US Naval Institute, 1957).

Brander, M. *The 10th Royal Hussars (Prince of Wales' Own)* (London: Leo Cooper, 1960).

Brant, E. D. *Railways of North Africa: the Railway System of the Maghreb: Algeria, Tunisia, Morocco and Libya* (Newton Abbott: David and Charles, 1971).

Bredt, Alexander (ed.) *Weyer's warships of the world* (Annapolis: Nautical & Aviation Publishing Company of America, 1968).

Brennecke, J. *Das große Abenteuer: Deutsche Hilfskreuzer, 1939–1945* (Herford: Koehler, 1958).

Haie im Paradies: Der deutsche U-Bootkrieg in Asiens Gewässern, 1939–1945 (Preetz: E. Gerdes, 1961).

Schwarze Schiffe – Weite See: Die geheimnisvollen Fahrten deutscher Blockadebrecher (Herford: Koehler, 1958).

Bright, J. (ed.) *The Ninth Queen's Royal Lancers, 1936–1945: the Story of an Armoured Regiment in Battle* (Aldershot: Gale and Polden, 1951).

Brookes, S. (ed.) *Montgomery and the Eighth Army: a Selection from the Diaries and Correspondence and Other Papers of Field Marshal the Viscount Montgomery of Alamein, August 1942–December 1943* (London: Bodley Head, 1991).

Brown, A. G., Dodwell, K. C. E., Hanniball, F. E. and Hopkinson, G. C. *A History of the 44th Royal Tank Regiment in the War of 1939–1945* (Brighton: 44th Royal Tank Regiment Association, 1965).

Brown, R. *Desert Warriors: Australian P-40 Pilots at War in the Middle East and North Africa* (Maryborough, Queensland: Banner Books, 2000).

Brownlow, D. G. *Checkmate at Ruweisat: Auchinleck's Finest Hour* (North Quincey, MA: Christopher Publishing House, 1977).

Bruna, Micheletti and Poggio, Pier Paolo (eds.) *L'Italia in guerra, 1940–1943* (Brescia: Fondazione Luigi Micheletti, 1991).

Bryant, Sir Arthur. *The Turn of the Tide, 1939–1943: a Study Based on the Diaries and Autobiographical Notes of Field Marshal the Viscount Alanbrooke* (London: Collins, 1957).

Buckley, Christopher. *Five Ventures: Iraq, Syria, Persia, Madagascar, Dodecanese* (London: HMSO, 1954).

Bungay, Stephen. *Alamein* (London: Arum Press, 2002).

Burdick, Charles B. *Germany's Military Strategy and Spain in World War II* (Syracuse University Press, 1968).

Unternehmen Sonnenblume (Neckargemünd: Vohwinckel, 1972).

Burdon, R. M. *24 Battalion* (Wellington: War History Branch, Department of Internal Affairs, 1953).

Büschleb, Hermann. *Feldherrn und Panzer im Wüstenkrieg: Die Herbstschlacht 'Crusader' im Vorfeld von Tobruk, 1941* (Neckargemünd: Vohwinckel, 1966).

Butcher, Harry C. *My Three Years with Eisenhower* (New York: Simon and Schuster, 1946).

Buttlar, H. 'Gedanken über die italienisch-deutsche Kriegsführung in mittleren Mittelmeer, 1940–1942 und über die mit ihr zusammenhängende operative Probleme', *Wehrwissenschaftliche Rundschau* (1951).

Caccia-Dominioni, Paolo. *Alamein, 1939–1963: an Italian Story* (London: Allen and Unwin, 1966).

Calvocoressi, Peter, Wint, Guy and Pritchard, John. *The Penguin History of the Second World War*, 2nd edn (1st edn published as *Total War*) (London: Penguin, 1989).

Cameron, I. *History of the Argyll and Sutherland Highlanders 7th Battalion* (London: Thomas Graham and Son, no date).

Carrell, P. *The Foxes of the Desert* (London: MacDonald, 1964).

Carrell, Paul. *Die Wüstenfüchse* (Munich: Herbig, 2003).

Carver, Field Marshal Lord Michael. *Dilemmas of the Desert War: a New Look at the Libyan Campaign, 1940–1942* (London: B. T. Batsford, 1986).

El Alamein (London: B. T. Batsford, 1962).

Second to None: the Royal Scots Greys, 1919–1945 (Doncaster: Military Publishers, 1998).

Tobruk (Philadelphia: Dufour Editions, 1964).

Catroux, Georges. *Dans la bataille de Méditerrannée: Egypte–Levant–Afrique du Nord, 1940–1944* (Paris: Juillard, 1949).

Cavallero, Ugo. *Diario 1940–1943*, ed. Giuseppe Bucciante (Rome: Ciarrapico, 1984).

Comando Supremo. Diario 1940–43 del Capo di S. M. G. (Bologna: Cappelli, 1948).

Cave-Brown, A. *Bodyguard of Lies* (London: William H. Allen, 1986).

Ceva, Lucio. *Africa Settentrionale, 1940–1943* (Rome: Bonacci, 1982).

La condotta italiana della guerra: Cavallero e il Comando Supremo, 1941–1942 (Milan: Feltrinelli, 1975).

Le forze armate (Turin: UTET, 1981).

'La guerra italiana in Africa Settentrionale, 1940–1943', *Revue d'Histoire Militaire*, Vol. 39, No. 1 (1978), 1–44.

Chalfort, A. *Montgomery of Alamein* (London: Weidenfeld and Nicolson, 1976).

Chaplin, H. D. *The Queen's Royal West Kent Regiment, 1920–1950* (London: Michael Joseph, 1954).

Churchill, Winston S. *The Second World War: the Grand Alliance* (New York: Houghton and Mifflin, 1950).

The Hinge of Fate (New York: Houghton Mifflin, 1979).

Ciano, Count Galeazzo. *Ciano's Diaries.* (London: Heinemann, 1947).

Diario, 1937–1943 (Milan: Rizzoli, 1968).

Ciano's Diplomatic Papers (London: Odhams, 1948).

Citino, Robert M. *Death of the Wehrmacht: the German Campaigns of 1942* (Lawrence: University of Kansas Press, 2007).

Clarke, D. *The Eleventh at War* (London: Michael Joseph, 1952).

Clarke, R. *With Alex to War: From the Irawaddy to the Po, 1941–1945* (Barnsley: Leo Cooper, 2000).

Clay, E. W. *The Path of the 50th.* (Aldershot: Gale and Polden, 1950).

Clayton, Aileen. *The Enemy is Listening* (London: Hutchinson, 1980).

Clayton, Tim and Craig, Phil. *The End of the Beginning: From the Siege of Malta to the Allied Victory at El Alamein* (New York: Free Press, 2003).

Clifford, A. *Three against Rommel: the Campaigns of Wavell, Auchinleck and Alexander* (London: Harrap, 1943).

Clifton, G. *The Happy Hunted* (London: Cassell, 1952).

Cody, J. F. *21 Battalion* (Wellington: War History Branch, Department of Internal Affairs, 1953).

28 (Maori) Battalion (Wellington: War History Branch, Department of Internal Affairs, 1953).

New Zealand Engineers, Middle East (Wellington: War History Branch, Department of Internal Affairs, 1961).

Combe, G., Ligertwood, F. and Gilchrist, T. *The Second 43rd Australian Infantry Battalion, 1940–1946* (Adelaide: Second 43rd Battalion AIF Club, 1972).

Comité d'Histoire de la Deuxième Guerre Mondiale. *La Guerre en Méditerrannée, 1939–1945: Actes du Colloque International Tenu à Paris du 8 au 11 Avril 1969* (Paris: Éditions du Centre National de la Recherche Scientifique, 1971).

Connell, J. *Auchinleck: a Biography of Field Marshal Sir Claude Auchinleck* (London: Cassell, 1959).

Auchinleck: a Critical Biography (London: Cassell, 1959)

Wavell: Soldier and Scholar (London: Collins, 1964).

Cooper, Artemis. *Cairo in the War, 1939–1945* (Harmondsworth: Penguin, 2001).

Cooper, M. *The German Army, 1933–1945: Hitler's Political and Military Failure* (London: MacDonald and Jane's, 1978).

Corvaja, Santi. *Hitler and Mussolini: the Secret Meetings*, trans. R. L. Miller (New York: Enigma Books, 2001).

Craig, N. *The Broken Plane: a Platoon Commander's Story, 1940–1945* (London: Imperial War Museum, 1982).

Craven, W. F. and Cate, J. L. (eds.) *The Army Air Forces in World War II, vol. II: Europe: Torch to Pointblank, August 1942 to December 1943* (Chicago: University of Chicago Press, 1949).

Crawford, R. J. *I was an Eighth Army Soldier* (London: Gollancz, 1944).

Creveld, M. Van 'Rommel's Supply Problem', *Journal of the Royal United Services Institute for Defence Studies*, Vol. 119, No. 3 (1974).

Creveld, Martin Van. *Supplying War: Logistics from Wallenstein to Patton* (Cambridge University Press, 1977).

Crew, F. A. E. *The Army Medical Services, Campaigns, vol. II: Hong Kong – Malaya, Iceland and the Faroes, Libya 1942–1943, Northwest Africa* (London: HMSO, 1957).

Crimp, R. L. *Diary of a Desert Rat* (London: Pan, 1974).

Crisp, R. *Brazen Chariots: an Account of Tank Warfare in the Western Desert, November–December 1941* (London: Frederick Muller, 1959).

   The Gods Were Neutral (London: Frederick Muller, 1960).

Crookenden, A. *The History of the Cheshire Regiment in the Second World War* (Chester: Cheshire Regiment, no date).

Cropper, A. *Dad's War* (Thurlstone: Anmas, 1994).

Cruickshank, C. *Deception in World War II* (Oxford University Press, 1979).

Cunningham, Admiral Sir Andrew. *A Sailor's Odyssey* (London: Hutchinson, 1951).

D'Avossa, Gianalfonso. 'Una strategia par continenti: Mediterraneo e vicino oriente nella concezione tedesca nella seconda guerra mondiale', *Rivista Militare* (1970).

De Guingand, F. *Generals at War* (London: Hodder and Stoughton, 1964).

   Operation Victory (London: Hodder and Stoughton, 1947).

Di Fortunato, Minniti. 'Aspetti organizzativi del controllo sulla produzione bellica in Italia', *Clio*, Vol. 4 (1977).

   'Il "Diario storico del Commando Supremo": Considerazioni e ipotesi sul ruolo del capo di Stato Maggiore Generale nee'estate del

1940', *Storia Contemporanea*, Vol. 18, No. 1 (February 1987), 171–90.

Di Sambuy, Vittorio. *Match pari tra due grande flotte. Mediterraneo, 1940–1942* (Milan: Mursia, 1976).

'Un Segreto Svelato – Il Segreto "Ultra"', *Rivista Marittima*, Vol. 109, No. 1 (1976), 103–8.

Das, D. *India from Curzon to Nehru and After* (New York: John Day, 1970).

Dawnay, Brigadier D. (ed.) *The 10th Royal Hussars in the Second World War, 1939–1945* (Aldershot: Gale and Polden, 1948).

Dear, I. C. B. and Foot, M. R. D. (eds.), *The Oxford Companion to the Second World War* (Oxford University Press, 1995).

Delaforce, P. *Monty's Highlanders: 51st Highland Division in World War Two* (Brighton: Tom Donovan, 1997).

Monty's Marauders: Black Rat and Red Fox: 4th and 8th Independent Armoured Brigades in World War Two (Brighton: Tom Donovan, 1997).

A View from the Turret: 3 RTR in World War II (Brighton: Tom Donovan, 2000).

Dessouki, M. K. 'Hitler und der Nahe Osten', dissertation, University of Berlin, 1963.

Detwiler, D. S. *Hitler, Franco und Gibraltar: Die Frage des spanischen Eintritts in den Zweiten Weltkrieg* (Wiesbaden: Steiner, 1962).

Detwiler, D. S., Burdick, C. B. and Rohwer, J. (eds.) *World War II German Military Studies, vol. XIV, Part IV: The Mediterranean Theatre* (New York: Garland, 1979).

Deutsch, Harold C. 'Commanding Generals and the Uses of Intelligence', *Intelligence and National Security*, Vol. 3, No. 3 (1988), 194–260.

Dinardo, Richard L. *Germany and the Axis Powers: from Coalition to Collapse* (Lawrence: University of Kansas Press, 2005).

Documents Relating to New Zealand Participation in the Second World War, 1939–1945, 3 vols. (Wellington: War History Branch, Department of Internal Affairs, 1949).

Doherty, R. *A Noble Crusade: a History of Eighth Army, 1941–1945* (Staplehurst: Spellmont, 1999).

Only the Enemy in Front: the Recce Corps at War, 1939–1946 (London: Tom Donovan, 1996).

Domarus, Max. *Mussolini und Hitler: Zwei Wege – gleiches Ende* (Würzburg: M. Domarus, 1977).

Doronzo, Rafael. *Folgore! Diario di un Paracadutista* (Milan: Gruppa Murcia, 1995).

Douglas, Keith. *Alamein to Zem-Zem*, ed. Desmond Graham (London: Faber and Faber, 1992).

Drevon, Capitaine de Corvette. 'Malte dans la guerre en Méditerrannée, 1940–1943', *Revue de Défense Nationale* (1954), 326–35.

Dülffer, Jost. *Hitler, Weimar und die Marine: Reichspolitik und Flottenbau, 1920–1939* (Dusseldorf: Droste, 1973).

Duncan, T. and Stout, M. *New Zealand Medical Services in the Middle East and Italy* (Wellington: War History Branch, Department of Internal Affairs, 1956).

Dupuy, Col. Trevor. *A Genius for War* (London: MacDonald and Jane's, 1977).

Durand de la Penne, Luigi. 'The Italian Attack on the Alexandria Naval Base', in *US Naval Institute Proceedings*, Vol. 82 (1956).

Eade, Charles. *Winston Churchill's Secret Session Speeches* (London: Cassell, 1946).

Edwards, Jill (ed.) *Al-Alamein Revisited: Proceedings of a Symposium held on 2 May 1998 at the American University in Cairo: the Battle of Al-Alamein and its historical Implications* (Cairo: The American University of Cairo Press, 2001).

The Eighth Army: September 1941–January 1943 (London: HMSO, 1944).

Elath, Eliahu. *Haj Amin al Husseini: Mufti of Jerusalem* (Jerusalem: Reshafim, 1968).

Ellis, John. *Brute Force: Allied Strategy and Tactics in the Second World War* (London: André Deutsch, 1990) p. 283.

Engel, Gerhard. *Heeresadjutant bei Hitler, 1938–1943. Aufzeichnungen des Majors Engel*, ed. Hildegard von Kotze (Stuttgart: Deutsche Verlags-Anstalt, 1974).

Eppler, John W. *Geheimagent im Zweiten Weltkrieg. Zwischen Berlin, Kabul und Kairo* (Preußisch Oldendorf: Schutz, 1974).

Operation Condor: Rommel's Spy (London: Futura, 1977).

Rommel ruft Kairo. Aus dem Tagebuch eines Spions (Gütersloh: S. Mohn, 1959).

Esebeck, Hanns-Gert von. *Afrikanische Schickalsjahre. Geschichte des deutschen Afrikakorps unter Rommel* (Wiesbaden: Limes Verlag, 1949).

Das Deutsche Afrikakorps (Munich: Heyne, 1980).

Helden der Wüste (Berlin: Heimbücherei, 1943).

Faldella, E. *L'Italia e la seconda guerra mondiale* (Bologna: Cappelli, 1959).

Faligot, Roger and Kauffer, Rémi. *Le croissant et la croix gammée. Les secrets de l'alliance entre l'Islam et le nazisme d'Hitler à nos jours* (Paris: Albin Michel, 1990).

Farndale, Martin. *History of the Royal Regiment of Artillery: the Years of Defeat, 1939–1941* (London: Brassey's, 1996).

Farran, Roy. *Winged Dagger: Adventures in Special Forces* (London: Collins, 1948).

Favagrossa, C. *Perchè perderemo la guerra* (Milan: 1947).

Fearnside, G. H. (ed.) *Bayonets Abroad: a History of the 2/13th Battalion AIF in the Second World War* (Swanbourne: John Burridge, 1993).

Fechter, Helmut and Hümmelchen, Gerhard. *Seekriegsatlas Mittelmeer – Schwarzes Meer, 1940–1943. Mit 42 Haupt- und*

34 Nebenkarten, davon 2 dreifarbig (Munich: Lehmann, 1972).

Ferguson, Niall. *The War of the World: History's Age of Hatred, 1914–1989* (London: Allen Lane, 2006).

Fergusson, B. *The Black Watch and the King's Enemies* (London: Collins, 1950).

Fergusson, James. *The Vitamin Murders* (London: Portobello Books, 2007).

Fernyhough, A. H. *A History of the RAOC, 1920–1945* (London: William Clowes, 1958).

Ferrari, Dorello. 'La mobilitazione dell'esercito nella second guerra mondiale', *Storia Contemporanea*, Vol. 18, No. 6 (1992), 1001–46.

Fioravanzo, Giuseppe. 'Italian Strategy in the Mediterranean, 1940–1943', *United States Naval Institute Proceedings*, Vol. 84, No. 9 (September 1958), 65–72.

'Der Kriegführung der Achse im Mittelmeer', *Marine Rundschau*, Vol. 55 (1958), 17–24.

'Situazione e impiego della Marine Italiana nel periodo compreso tra lo sbarco in Africa Settentrionale' in *Centro di Alti Studi Militari*, 3rd Session (Rome, 1951–2).

'Studi e progetti per la presa di Malta', *Rivista Marittima* (July 1954).

Fletcher, David. *The Great Tank Scandal: British Armour in the Second World War*, part 1 (London: HMSO, 1989).

The Universal Tank (London: HMSO, 1993).

Fletscher, A. *Afghanistan: Highway of Conquest* (Ithaca: Cornell University Press, 1965).

Fleury, A. 'La Subversion Allemande en Inde à partir de l'Afghanistan pendant la deuxième guerre mondiale', *Relations Internationales*, Vol. 3 (1975), 133–52.

Forty, George. *Afrika Korps at War, vol. I: The Road to Alexandria* (Shepperton: Ian Allen, 1978).

Afrika Korps at War, vol. II: The Long Road Back. (Shepperton: Ian Allen, 1978).

The Armies of Rommel (London: Arms and Armour Press, 1997).

Desert Rats at War (Shepperton: Ian Allen, 1975).

Foster, R. C. G. *History of the Queen's Royal Regiment, Vol III: 1924–1948* (Aldershot: Gale and Polden, 1990).

Fraser, D. *Alanbrooke* (London: Collins, 1982).

Knight's Cross: a Life of Field Marshal Erwin Rommel (London: HarperCollins, 1993).

French, David. *Raising Churchill's Army* (Oxford University Press, 2000).

Funke, Manfred (ed.) *Hitler, Deutschland und die Mächte: Materialien zur Außenpolitik des Dritten Reichs* (Dusseldorf: Athenäum, 1978).

Gabriele, Mariano. *Operazione C3: Malta* (Rome: Ufficio storico della Marina militare, 1965).

Gallagher, J., Johnson, G. and Seal, A. (eds.) *Locality, Province and Nation: Essays on Indian Politics, 1870–1940* (Cambridge University Press, 1973).

Garello, Giancarlo. *Regia aeronautica armée de l'air, 1940–1943* (Rome: Bizzarri, 1981).

Gause, Alfred. 'Der Feldzug im Nordafrika im Jahre 1941', *Wehrwissenschaftliche Rundschau*, Vol. 12, No. 10 (1962), 594–618.

'Der Feldzug im Nordafrika im Jahre 1943', *Wehrwissenschaftliche Rundschau*, Vol. 12, No. 12, (1962), 720–8.

Generalkommando des Deutschen Afrikakorps. *Marsch und Kampf des Deutschen Afrikakorps* (Berlin: Mittler, 1994).

Gensicke, Klaus. *Der Mufti von Jerusalem, Amin el-Husseini und die Nationalsozialisten* (Frankfurt am Main: P. Lang, 1988).

Giannini, Amadeo. 'L'accordo italo-germanico per il carbonne (1940)', *Rivista di Studi Politici Internazionali*, Vol. 21 (1954), 462–8.

Gilbert, Adrian. *The Imperial War Museum Book of the Desert War* (Swindon: Book Club Associates, 1992).

Gilbert, Martin. *Road to Victory: Winston S. Churchill, 1941–1945* (London: Heinemann, 1986).

Giorgerini, Giorgio. *Da Matapan al Golfo Persico: La Marina militare italiana dal fascismo alla Repubblica* (Milan: A. Mondadori, 1989).

Glaesner, H. 'Das Dritte Reich und der Mittlere Osten: Politische und wirtschaftliche Beziehungen Deutschlands zur Türkei 1933, zu Iran 1933–1941, und zu Afghanistan 1933–1941', dissertation, University of Würzburg, 1976.

Glasneck, J. and Kircheisen, I. *Türkei und Afghanistan: Brennpunkte der Orientpolitik im Zweiten Weltkrieg* (Berlin: Deustche Verlag der Wissenschaften, 1968).

Glenn, J. G. *Tobruk to Tarakan: the Story of a Fighting Unit* (Adelaide: Rigby, 1960).

Goebbels, Joseph. *Tagebücher*, ed. Ralf Georg Reuth, 5 vols. (Munich: Piper, 1992).

Goldsmith, R. F. K. 'The Eighth Army at Bay, July 1942, Part I', *The Army Quarterly*, Vol. 104 (October 1974), 552–60.

'The Eighth Army at Bay, July 1942, Part II', *The Army Quarterly*, Vol. 105 (January 1975), 67–75.

Gooch, John (ed.) *Decisive Campaigns of the Second World War* (Ilford: Frank Cass, 1990).

Goodhart, D. (ed.) *The History of 2/7th Australian Field Regiment* (Adelaide: Rigby, 1952).

(ed.) *We of the Turning Tide* (Sydney: F. W. Preece, 1947).

Goralski, Robert and Freeburg, Russell. *Oil and War: How the Deadly Struggle for Fuel in World War II Meant Victory or Defeat* (New York: Morrow, 1987).

Gordon, John. *The Other Desert War: British Special Forces in North Africa, 1940–1943.* (Westport: Greenwood, 1987).

Görlitz, Walther (ed.) *'Ich stehe hier auf Befehl'. Lebensweg des Generalfeldmarschalls Friedrich Paulus. Mit den Aufzeichnungen aus dem Nachlass, Briefen und Dokumenten* (Frankfurt am Main: Bernard und Graefe, 1960).

Goutard, A. 'La réalité de la "menace" allemande sur l'Afrique du Nord en 1940', *Revue d'Histoire de la Deuxième Guerre Mondiale*, Vol. 13, No. 43 (1963), 1–20.

Graham, A. *The Sharpshooters at War: the 3rd, 4th and 3/4th County of London Yeomanry, 1939–1945* (London: Sharpshooters Regimental Association, 1964).

Graham, F. C. C. *History of the Argyll and Sutherland Highlanders 1st Battalion (Princess Louise's)* (London: Thomas Graham and Son, 1948).

Grant, R. *The 51st Highland Division at War* (Shepperton: Ian Allen, 1977).

Grassi, Gaetano and Legnani, Massimo (eds.) *L'Italia nella seconda guerra mondiale e nella Resistanza* (Milan: Franco Angel, 1988).

Gravino, Igina. *Le Tre Battaglie di Alamein* (Milan: Longaresi, 1971).

Greacen, Lavinia. *Chink* (London: MacMillan, 1989).

Greene, Jack and Massignani, Alessandro. *The Naval War in the Mediterranean, 1940–1943* (London: Chatham Publishing, 1998).

Greiner, Helmuth. *Die Oberste Wehrmachtführung, 1939–1943* (Wiesbaden: Limes Verlag, 1951).

Greiner, Helmuth and Schramm, Percy Ernst. *Kriegestagebuch des Oberkommandos der Wehrmacht*, 4 vols. (Frankfurt: Bernard und Graefe, 1961–5).

Grigg, John. *1943: the Victory that Never Was* (Harmondsworth: Penguin, 1999).

Griselis, Waldis. *Das Ringen um den Brückenkopf Tunesien 1942–1943: Strategie der 'Achse' und Innenpolitik im Protektorat*, Europäische Hochschulschriften 3, 67 (Frankfurt: Lang, 1976).

Groehler, Olaf. 'Die Rolle Nordafrikas in der Kriegführung des deutschen Imperialismus während des zweiten Weltkrieges', *Militärwesen*, Vol. 7 (1963), 412–28.

Gruchmann, Lothar. 'Die "Verpassten Strategischen Chancen" der Achsenmächte im Mittelmeerraum, 1940–1941', *Vierteljahreshefte für Zeitgeschichte*, Vol. 18, No. 4 (1970), 456–75.

Guanieri, Felice. *Battaglie economiche tra le due grandi guerre* (Milan: Garzanti, 1953).

Guedalla, P. *Middle East, 1940–1942: a Study in Air Power* (London: Hodder and Stoughton, 1944).

Guerri, Giordano Bruno. *Galeazzo Ciano: una Vita, 1903–1944* (Milan: Bompiani, 1979).

Guiot, P. *Combats sans espoir: Guerre navale en Syrie, 1941* (Paris: Couronne Littéraire, 1950).

Gundelach, Karl. *Die deutsche Luftwaffe im Mittelmeer, 1940–1945*, 2 vols., Europäische Hochschulschriften 3, 136 (Frankfurt: Lang, 1981).

Günther, H. O. *Indien und Deutschland: Ein Sammelband* (Frankfurt: Europäische Verlagsanstalt, 1956).

Halder, Franz. *Kriegestagebuch. Tägliche Aufzeichnungen des Chefs des Generalstabes des Heeres, 1939–1942*, ed. Hans-Adolf Jacobsen, 3 vols. (Stuttgart: W. Kohlhammer, 1962).

Halstead, E. *Freyberg's Men* (Auckland: Heinemann Reed, 1985).

Halton, M. *Ten Years to Alamein* (London: Lindsay Drummond, 1944).

Hamilton, Nigel. *The Full Monty* (London: Penguin, 2001).

   Monty, 3 vols. (New York: McGraw-Hill, 1981–6).

Hamilton, Stephen D. *50th Royal Tank Regiment: the Complete History* (Cambridge: Lutterworth Press, 1996).

Hamilton, Stuart. *Armoured Odyssey: 8th Royal Tank Regiment in the Western Desert 1941–1942, Palestine, Syria, Egypt 1943–1944, Italy 1944–1945* (London: Tom Donovan, 1995).

Handel, Michael. *Intelligence and Military Operations* (Ilford: Frank Cass, 1990).

'Intelligence and Military Operations', *Intelligence and National Security*, Vol. 5, No. 2 (1990), 1–95.

Strategic and Operational Deception in the Second World War (London: Frank Cass, 1987).

Handel-Mazetti, P. Frhr von. 'Der Britische Flugzeugangriff auf die Italienischen Flotte im Hafen von Tarent in der Nacht 11/12 November 1940', *Marine Rundschau*, Vol. 50 (1953).

Harding, John. *Mediterranean Strategy, 1939–1945* (Cambridge University Press, 1960).

Harrison, Frank. *Tobruk: the Great Siege Revisited* (London: Arms and Armour Press, 1997).

Harrison, Mark (ed.) *The Economics of World War II: Six Great Powers in International Comparison* (Cambridge Univesity Press, 1998).

Hassell, Ulrich von. *Vom anderen Deutschland: aus den nachgelassenen Tagebüchern, 1938–1944* (Zurich: Atlantis Verlag, 1948).

Hastings, R. H. W. S. *The Rifle Brigade in the Second World War, 1939–1945* (Aldershot: Gale and Polden, 1950).

Hauner, Milan. 'Did Hitler Want World Dominion?', *Journal of Contemporary History*, Vol. 13, No. 1 (1978), 15–32.

India in Axis Strategy: Germany, Japan and Indian Nationalists in the Second World War (Stuttgart: Klett-Cotta, 1981).

'India's Independence and the Axis Powers: Subhas Chandra Bose in Europe during the Strategic Initiative of the Axis Powers' in S. C. Bose (ed.) *Netaji and India's Freedom* (Calcutta: Netaji Institute for Asian Studies, 1975) 235–261.

'Indien und Nationalsozialistisches Deutschland' in M. Funke (ed.) *Hitler, Deutschland und die Mächte* (Kronberg: Athenäum, 1978) 430–53.

'One Man Against the Empire: the Faqir of Ipi and the British in Central Asia on the Eve of and During the Second World War', *Journal of Contemporary History*, Vol. 16, No. 1 (1981), 183–212.

'The Place of India in the Strategic and Political Consideration of the Axis Powers, 1939–1942', dissertation, University of Cambridge, 1972.

'Les Puissances de l'Axe et la Lutte de l'Inde pour l'Independence', *Revue d'Histoire de la Deuxième Guerre Mondiale*, Vol. 24, No. 96 (1974), 37–66.

Haupt, W. and Bingham, J. K. W. *Der Afrika Feldzug* (London: MacDonald, 1968).

Heckmann, Wolf. *Rommel's War in Africa*, trans. Stephen Seago (New York: Doubleday, 1981). Originally published as *Rommels Krieg in Afrika: Wüstenfüchse gegen Wüstenratten* (Bergisch Gladbach: G. Lübbe, 1976).

Heckstall-Smith, A. *Tobruk: the Story of a Siege* (London: Anthony Blond, 1959).

Henderson, J. 22 *Battalion* (Wellington: War History Branch, Department of Internal Affairs, 1958).

RMT: Official History of the 4th and 6th Reserve Mechanical Transport Companies (Wellington: War History Branch, Department of Internal Affairs, 1954).

Henrici, E. 'Die deutsche Kriegführung und das Mittelmeer in den Jahren 1940 bis 1943', dissertation, University of Heidelberg, 1954.

Herington, J. *Australia in the War of 1939–1945: Air War Against Germany and Italy, 1939–1945* (Canberra: Australian War Memorial, 1954).

Herwig, Holger. 'Tobruk: the Limit's of Rommel's Reach', *MHQ: The Quarterly Journal of Military History*, Vol. 12, No. 3 (2000), 86–95.

Hildebrand, K. *Vom Reich zum Weltreich: Hitler, NSDAP und koloniale Frage, 1919–1945* (Munich: W. Fink, 1970).

Hill, Leonidas. E. (ed.) *Die Weizsäcker Papiere, 1933–1950* (Frankfurt: Propyläen, 1974).

Hillgruber, Andreas. *Hitlers Strategie: Politik und Kriegführung, 1940–1941* (Frankfurt: Bernard und Graefe, 1965).

'Politik und Strategie Hitlers im Mittelmeerraum' in Hillgruber, *Deutsche Großmacht- und Weltpolitik im 19. und 20. Jahrhunderts* (Dusseldorf: Droste, 1977).

(ed.) *Kriegestagesbuch des Oberkommandos der Wehrmacht* (Frankfurt: Bernard und Graefe, 1963).

(ed.) *Staatsmänner und Diplomaten bei Hitler*, 2 vols. (Frankfurt: Bernard und Graefe, 1967–70).

Hillson, Norman. *Alexander of Tunis* (London: W. H. Allen, 1952).

Hingston, W. G. and Stevens, G. R. *The Tiger Kills: the Story of the Indian Divisions in the North African Campaign* (London: HMSO, 1944).

Hinsley, F. H. *British Intelligence in the Second World War, its Influence on Strategy and Operations, vols. I and II* (London: HMSO, 1979 and 1981).

Hinsley, F. H. and Stripp, Alan (eds.) *Codebreakers: the Inside Story of Bletchley Park* (Oxford University Press, 1993).

Hirszowicz, Łukasz. *The Third Reich and the Arab East* (London: Routledge and Kegan Paul, 1966).

Hissmann, Josef. *Insh'Allah.* (Bochum: Pöppinghaus, 1968).

Hitler, Adolf. *Hitlers zweites Buch; ein Dokument aus dem Jahr 1928*, ed. Gerhard L Weinberg, Foreward by Hans Rothfels (Stuttgart: Deutsche Verlags-Anstalt, 1961).

Mein Kampf (Munich: F. Eher nachf., 1934).

Hitti, P. K. *History of Syria Including Lebanon and Palestine* (London: Macmillan, 1951).

Hoffmann, Peter. 'The gulf region in German strategic projections, 1940–1942', *Militärgeschichtliche Mitteilungen*, No. 2, (1988), 61–73.

Hooton, E. R. *Eagle in Flames: the Fall of the Luftwaffe* (London: Arms and Armour Press, 1997).

Horrocks, Lt.-Gen. Sir Brian. *A Full Life* (London: Collins, 1960).

Howard, Michael. *British Intelligence in the Second World War, vol. V: Strategic Deception* (London: HMSO, 1990).

   The Mediterranean Strategy in the Second World War (Cambridge University Press, 1966).

Howarth, T. E. B. *Monty at Close Quarters* (London: Leo Cooper, 1985).

Howe, George F. *The Mediterranean Theatre of Operations: Northwest Africa: Seizing the Initiative in the West* (Washington, DC: Office of the Chief of Military History, US Army, 1955).

Hubatsch, Walther. *Der Admiralstab und die Obersten Marinebehörden in Deutschland, 1848–1945* (Frankfurt: Bernard and Graefe, 1958).

   Hitlers Weisungen für die Kriegführung, 1939–1945 (Koblenz: Bernard und Graefe, 1983).

Ilari, Virgilio. *Storia del servizio militare in Italia*, 4 vols. (Rome: Centro Militare di Studi Strategici, 1989–91).

Irving, David. *Hitler und seine Feldherren* (Frankfurt: Ullstein, 1975).

   Rommel: the Trail of the Fox (London: Clib Associates Book, 1977).

   Die Tragödie der deutschen Luftwaffe. Aus den Akten und Erinnerungen von Feldmarschall Erhard Milch (Frankfurt: Ulstein, 1970).

Jablonski, David. *The Desert Warriors* (New York: Lancer Books, 1972).

Jackson, W. G. F. *Alexander of Tunis as Military Commander* (London: Batsford, 1970).

   The North African Campaign, 1940–43 (London: Batsford, 1975).

Jacobsen, Hans-Adolf. *Deutsche Kriegführung, 1939–1945* (Hanover: Niedersächs, Landeszentrale f. Politische Bildung, 1961).

Jacobsen, Hans-Adolf and Rohwer, Jürgen. *Entscheidungsschlachten des zweiten Weltkrieges* (Frankfurt: Bernard und Graefe, 1960). Published in English as H. A. Jacobsen and J. Rohwer (eds.) *Decisive Battles of World War II: the German View* (London: André Deutsch, 1965).

James, Malcolm (Malcolm Pleydell). *Born of the Desert: With the SAS in North Africa* (London: Greenhill Books, 1991).

Jellison, Charles A. *Besieged: the World War II Ordeal of Malta, 1940–1942* (Hanover, NH: University Press of New England, 1984).

Jensen, W. G. 'The Importance of Energy in the First and Second World Wars', *Historical Journal*, Vol. 11, No. 3 (1968), 548.

Jewell, Derek (ed.) *Alamein and the Desert War* (London: Sphere Books, 1967).

Jog, N. G. *Churchill's Blind-spot: India* (Bombay: New Book Company, 1944).

Johnson, R. B. *The Queen's in the Middle East and North Africa* (Guildford: Queen's Royal Surrey Regimental Museum, 1997).

Johnston, M. *At the Front Line: Experiences of Australian Soldiers in World War II* (Cambridge University Press, 1996).

Fighting the Enemy: Australian Soldiers and their Adversaries in World War II (Cambridge University Press, 2000).

Jones, A. F. *The Second Derbyshire Yeomanry: an Account of the Regiment during the War, 1939–1945* (Bristol: White Swan Press, 1949).

Jong, L. de. *The German Fifth Column in the Second World War* (Chicago: University of Chicago Press, 1956).

Juin, Alphonse. 'La Campagne de Tunisie', *Miroir de l'Histoire*, Vol. 8, Nos. 86/87 (1957), 186–99/312–24.

Kahn, D. *The Codebreakers: the Story of Secret Writing* (London: Weidenfeld and Nicolson, 1968).

Kay, R. *27 (Machine-Gun) Battalion* (Wellington: War History Branch, Department of Internal Affairs, 1958).

Kemnade, Friedrich. *Die Afrika-Flotille: Chronik und Balanz. Der Einsatz der 3 Schnellbootflotille im Zweiten Weltkrieg* (Stuttgart: Motorbuch Verlag, 1978).

Kemp, P. K. *The Middlesex Regiment (Duke of Cambridge's Own), 1919–1952* (Aldershot: Gale and Polden, 1956).

The Staffordshire Yeomanry (Queen's Own Royal Regiment) in the First and Second World Wars, 1914–1918 and 1939–1945 (Aldershot: Gale and Polden, 1950).

Kennedy-Shaw, W. B. *Long Range Desert Group: the Story of its Work in Libya, 1940–1943* (London: Collins, 1945).

Kesselring, Albert. 'Der Krieg in Mittelmeerraum', in *Bilanz des Zweiten Weltkrieges: Erkenntnisse und Verpflichtungen für die Zukunft* (Oldenburg: Stalling, 1953).

Soldat bis zum letzten Tag (Bonn: Athenäum, 1953).

Khadduri, M. 'General Nuri's Flirtation with the Axis Powers', *Middle East Journal*, Vol. 16, No. 3 (1962), 328–36.

Independent Iraq, 1932–1958 (London: Oxford University Press for the Royal Institute of International Affairs, 1960).

Independent Iraq: a Study of Iraqi Politics since 1932 (London: Oxford University Press, 1951).

King, M. *New Zealanders at War* (Auckland: Heinemann, 1981).

Kippenberger, Maj.-Gen. Sir Howard. *Infantry Brigadier* (Oxford University Press, 1949).

Kirchheim, Heinrich Georg. 'Angriffgruppe Kirchheim am 30.4 und 1.5.1941 beim Angriff auf Tobruk. Kritische Untersuching der Ursachen für das Scheitern des Angriffs (Juni 1948)'.

Kirk, George. *The Middle East in the War* (London: Oxford University Press for the Royal Institute of International Affairs, 1952).

Klein, H. *Springboks in Armour* (Cape Town: Purnell, 1968).

Knox, MacGregor. '1940: Italy's Parallel War, Part 1: From Non-belligerence to the Collapse of France,' dissertation, Yale University, 1976.

Common Destiny: Dictatorship, Foreign Policy and War in Fascist Italy and Nazi Germany (Cambridge University Press, 2000).

Hitler's Italian Allies: Royal Armed Forces, Fascist Regime, and the War of 1940–1943 (Cambridge University Press, 2000).

Mussolini Unleashed, 1939–1941: Politics and Strategy in Fascist Italy's Last War (Cambridge University Press, 1982).

Koch, Karl W. jr. 'The Luftwaffe and Malta: a Case of "Hercules" Chained', *Aerospace Historian*, Vol. 23, No. 2 (1976), 94–100.

Koenig, Marie-Pierre. *Bir Hacheim, 10 juin 1942* (Paris: Robert Lafont, 1971).

Kramer, Hans. 'Die italienische Luftwaffe vor dem Zweiten Weltkrieg und der italienische Luftkrieg, 1940–1941' in Rudolf Neck and Adam Wandruszka (eds.) *Beiträge zur Zeitgeschichte: Festschrift für Ludwig Jedlicka zum 60 Geburtstag* (St. Pölten: NÖ Pressehaus, 1976).

'Über den Seekrieg Italiens 1940–1943', *Zeitgeschichte*, Vol. 2 (1974–5), 257–65.

Krecker, L. *Deutschland und die Türkei im Zweiten Weltkrieg* (Frankfurt: V. Klostermann, 1964).

Kühn, Volkmar. *With Rommel in the Desert: Victories and Defeat of the Afrika Korps, 1941–1943* (Westchester, PA: Schiffer, 1991). Originally published in German as *Mit Rommel in der Wüste* (Würzburg: Flechsig, 2006).

Kurowski, Franz, Cioci, Antonio, Kayser, Herbert and Lucas, James S. *Der Afrikafeldzug: Rommels Wüstenkrieg, 1941–1943* (Leoni am Starnberger See: Druffel, 1986).

Lacey, P. *Fascist India* (London: Nicholson and Watson, 1946).

Laffin, J. *Middle East Journey* (Sydney: Angus and Robertson, 1958).

Lamb, R. *Mussolini and the British* (London: John Murray, 1997).

Landsborough, G. *Tobruk Commando* (London: Cassell, 1956).

Latimer, Jon. *Alamein* (London: John Murray, 2002).

Leach, B. *Massacre at Alamein?* (Upton upon Severn: Square One, 1996).

Lebucois, Jean. *Notre Première Victoire: La 1ere IDF à Bir Hacheim* (Paris: Éditions Colbert, 1945).

Leifer, W. *India and the Germans* (Bombay: Shakuntala Publishing House, 1971).

Leighton, Richard M. 'Overlord versus the Mediterranean at the Cairo-Tehran Conferences (1943)' in Kent Robert Greenfield (ed.) *Command Decisions* (New York: Center of Military History, United States Army, 1959).

Les Lettres Secrètes Échangées par Hitler et Mussolini (Paris: Éditions du Pavois, 1946).

Lewin, Ronald. *The Chief* (London: Hutchinson, 1980).

    Hitler's Mistakes (London: Leo Cooper, 1984).

    The Life and Death of the Afrika Korps (London: Batsford, 1977).

    Rommel as Military Commander (London: Batsford, 1968).

    Ultra Goes to War (London: Hutchinson, 1978).

Lewis, P. J. and English, I. R. *8th Battalion The Durham Light Infantry, 1939–1945* (Newcastle upon Tyne: J. and P. Beals, 1949).

Licheri, Sebastiano. *L'arma aerea italiana nella seconda guerra mondiale: 10 Giugno 1940–8 Settembre 1943* (Milan: Mursia 1976).

Liddell Hart, Sir Basil Henry. *The German Generals Talk* (New York: William Morrow, 1948).

    History of the Second World War (Swindon: Book Club Associates, 1973).

    'How Hitler Missed in the Middle East', *Marine Corps Gazette*, Vol. 40, No. 11 (1956), 50–4.

    The Other Side of the Hill (London: Pan, 1983).

The Tanks: a History of the Royal Tank Regiment and its Predecessors, 2 vols. (London: Cassell, 1959).

(ed.) *The Rommel Papers* (London: Collins, 1953).

Lindsay, T. M. *Sherwood Rangers: the Story of the Nottinghamshire Sherwood Rangers Yeomanry in the Second World War* (London: Burrup and Mathieson, 1952).

Linge, Heinz. *Bis zum Untergang. Als Chef des persönlichen Dienstes bei Hitler* (Munich: W. Herbig, 1980).

Llewellyn, S. P. *Journey Towards Christmas (1st Ammunition Company)* (Wellington: War History Branch, Department of Internal Affairs, 1963).

Lloyd, H. P. *Briefed to Attack: Malta's Part in African Victory* (London: Hodder and Stoughton, 1959).

Lohmann, Walter and Hildebrand, Hans H. *Die deutsche Kriegsmarine, 1939–1945: Gliederung-Einsatz-Stellenbestzung*, 3 vols. (Bad Nauheim: Podzun, 1956).

Long, Gavin. *Australia in the War of 1939–1945, Series 1, Army Vol. I: To Benghazi*, Australian Official History (Canberra: Australian War Memorial, 1952).

Longrigg, S. H. *Oil in the Middle East* (Oxford University Press, 1961).

Lucas, James *Panzer Army Africa* (London: MacDonald and Jane's, 1977).

Rommel's Year of Victory (London: Greenhill Books, 1998).

War in the Desert: the Eighth Army at Alamein (London: Arms and Armour Press, 1982.).

Lucas, L. *Malta: the Thorn in Rommel's Side: Six Months that Turned the War* (London: Stanley Paul, 1992).

Lucas-Phillips, C. E. *Alamein* (London: Pan, 1965).

Luck, Hans von. 'The End in North Africa', *MHQ: The Quarterly Journal of Military History*, Vol. 1, No. 4 (1989), 118–27.

Luftwaffe War Reporting Company. *Balkenkreuz über Wüstensand* (Oldenburg: Gerhard Stalling Verlag, 1943).

Lugol, Jean. *L'Égypte et la Deuxième Guerre Mondiale* (Cairo: Imprimerie E. and R. Schindler 1945).

Lushington, F. *Yeoman Service: the Kent Yeomanry, 1939–1945* (Aldershot: Gale and Polden, 1947).

McGregor, J. *The Spirit of Angus: the War History of the County's Battalion of the Black Watch* (Chester: Phillimore, 1988).

McGuirk, Dal. *Afrika Korps: Self Portrait* (Shrewsbury: Air Life, 1992).

    Rommel's Army in Africa (Shrewsbury: Airlife, 1987).

Macintyre, Donald. *The Battle for the Mediterranean* (New York: Norton, 1964).

McKee, Alexander. *El Alamein: Ultra and the Three Battles* (London: Hutchinson, 1981).

Macksey, Kenneth. *A History of the Royal Armoured Corps, 1914–1975* (London: Newton, 1983).

    Kesselring: German Master Strategist of the Second World War (London: Greenhill, 1996).

    Kesselring: the Making of the Luftwaffe (London: B. T. Batsford, 1978).

    Rommel: Battles and Campaigns (London: Arms and Armour Press, 1979).

    (ed.) *The Memoirs of Field Marshal Kesselring* (London: Greenhill, 1988).

McKinney, J. B. *Medical Units of 2 NZEF in the Middle East and Italy* (Wellington: War History Branch, Department of Internal Affairs, 1952).

Maclean, Fitzroy. *Eastern Approaches* (London: Pan, 1956).

McLeod, J. *Myth and Reality: the New Zealand Soldier in World War II* (Auckland: Heinemann Reid, 1986).

Majdalany, F. *The Battle of El Alamein* (London: Weidenfeld and Nicolson, 1965).

Maione, Giuseppe. *L'Imperialismo straccione: Classi sociali e finanza di guerra dall'impresa etiopica al conflitto mondiale, 1935–1943* (Bologna: Il Mulino, 1979).

Mallmann, Klaus-Michael and Cüppers, Martin. 'Das Einsatzkommando bei der Panzerarmee Afrika 1942', in Jürgen Matthäus and Klaus-Michael Mallmann (eds.), *Deutsche, Juden, Völkermord. Der Holocaust als Geschichte und Gegenwart* (Darmstadt: Wissenschaftliche Buchgesellschaft, 2006).

   Halbmond und Hakenkreuz. Das Dritte Reich, die Araber und Palästina (Darmstadt: Wissenschaftliche Buchgesellschaft, 2006).

Mancinelli, Giuseppe. *Dal fronte dell'Africa Settentrionale, 1942–1943* (Milan: Rizzoli, 1970).

Manstein, Erich von. *Lost Victories* (London: Methuen, 1955).

Maravigna, Pietro. *Come abbiamo perduto la guerra in Africa, 1940–1943* (Rome: Tosi, 1949).

Marcus, E. 'The German Foreign Office and the Palestine Question in the Period 1933–1939', *Yad Vashem Studies* (1958), 179–204.

Martin, A. C. *The Durban Light Infantry, 1854–1960, vol. II* (Durban: HQ Board, Durban, 1960).

Martin, Bernd. *Japan im Zweiten Weltkrieg. Vom Angriff auf Pearl Harbor bis zur deutschen Kapitulation* (Göttingen: Musterschmidt, 1969).

Martin, H. J. and Orpen, Neil. *South Africa at War: South African forces in World War II, vol. VII*, South African Official History (London: Purnell, 1979).

Masani, M. R. *The Communist Party of India: a Short History* (Bombay: Bharatiya Vidhya Bhavan, 1954).

Masel, P. *The Second 28th: the Story of a Famous Battalion of the 9th Australian Division* (Perth: 2/28th Battalion and 24th Anti-Tank Company Association, 2000).

Mason, Phillip. *A Matter of Honour* (London: Jonathan Cape, 1974).

Mather, Carol. *When the Grass Stops Growing* (Barnsley: Leo Cooper, 1999).

Mathias, Jean. *Bir Hacheim* (Paris: Éditions de Minuit, 1955).

Mattesini, Francesco. *La battaglia aeronavale di mezzo agosto* (Rome: Edizioni dell'Ateneo, 1986).

 La battaglia di Punta Stilo (Rome: Ufficio Storico della Marina, 1990).

 Il giallo di Matapan: Revisione di giudizi (Rome: Edizioni dell'Ateneo, 1985).

Mattesini, Francesco and Cermelli, Mario (eds.) *Le direttive tecnico-operative di Superareo*, 2 vols. (Rome: Stato Maggiore Aeronautica, Ufficio Storico, 1992).

Matthäus, Jürgen and Mallmann, Klaus-Michael. (eds.) *Deutsche, Juden, Völkermord. Der Holocaust als Geschichte und Gegenwart* (Darmstadt: Wissenschaftliche Buchgesellschaft, 2006).

Maughan, Barton. *Australia in the War, 1939–1945: Tobruk and El Alamein* (Canberra: Australian War Memorial, 1966).

 Tobruk and El Alamein (Canberra: Australian War Memorial, 1966).

Maule, Henry. *Spearhead General: the Epic Story of Sir Francis Messervy* (London: Odhams, 1961).

May, S. 'Strangling Rommel: British Submarine Commanders in the Mediterranean, June 1940 to September 1943', *Mariner's Mirror*, Vol. 88, No. 4 (2002), 456–68.

The Mediterranean Fleet: Greece to Tripoli: the Admiralty's Account of Naval Operations, April 1941 to January 1943 (London: HMSO, 1944).

Mejcher, Helmut. *Die Politik und das Öl im Nahen Osten* (Stuttgart: Klett-Cotta, 1990).

Mellenthin, F. W. von. *Panzer Battles: a Study of the Deployment of Armour in the Second World War*, trans. H. Betzler (London: Futura, 1977).

Merewood, J. *To War with the Bays* (Cardiff: 1st The Queen's Dragoon Guards, 1992).

Messenger, Charles. *The Unknown Alamein* (Shepperton: Ian Allen, 1982).

Migliavacca, Renato. *Ventiquattr'ore a Tobruk, 13–14 Settembre, 1942* (Milan: Longanesi, 1972).

Milligan, Spike. *Monty: His Part in My Victory* (Harmondsworth: Penguin, 1976).

Rommel? Gunner Who? (Harmondsworth: Penguin, 1976).

Ministero della Difesa. *La Prima Controffensiva Italo-Tedesca in Africa Settentrionale (15 Febbraio–18 Novembre 1941)* (Rome: Stato Maggiore dell' Esercito, Ufficio Storico, 1974).

Ministero della Difesa, Stato Maggiore Esercito – Ufficia Storico (ed.) *Seconda Offensiva Britannica in Africa Settentrionale e Ripiegamento Italo-Tedesco nella Sirtica Orientale (18 Novembre 1941–17 Gennaio 1942)* (Rome: Esercito, Corpo di Stato Maggiore, Ufficio Storico, 1949).

Mitcham, Samuel W. jr. *Rommel's Desert War: the Life and Death of the Afrika Korps* (New York: Stein and Day, 1984).

Rommel's Last Battle (New York: Stein and Day, 1983).

Triumphant Fox: Erwin Rommel and the Rise of the Afrika Korps (New York: Stein and Day, 1984).

Mitcham, Samuel and Mueller, Gene. *Hitler's Commanders* (Maryland: Scarborough Books, 1993).

Montanari, Mario. *L'esercito italiano alla vigilia della seconda guerra mondiale* (Rome: Stato maggiore dell' esercito, ufficio storico, 1982).

Le operazioni in Africa Settentrionale, 4 vols. (Rome: Stato Maggiore dell'Esercito, Ufficio Storico, 1984–93).

Montgomery, Field Marshal Viscount. *El Alamein to the River Sangro* (London: Hutchinson, 1946).

The Memoirs of Field Marshal Montgomery (London: Collins, 1958).

Moore, William. *Paner Bait: With the Third Royal Tank Regiment, 1939–1945* (London: Leo Cooper, 1991).

Moorehead, Alan. *African Trilogy: the North African Campaign, 1940–1943* (London: Cassell, 2000).

The End in Africa: a Personal Account of the African Campaign from El Alamein to the Fall of Tunis (London: Hamish Hamilton, 1943).

Montgomery (London: Hamish Hamilton, 1946).

Mordal, J. *Bir Hacheim* (Paris: Amiot-Dumont, 1952).

Moritz, Erhard. 'Planungen für die Kriegführung des Deutschen Heeres in Afrika und Vorderasien', *Militärgeschichte*, Vol. 16 (1977), 323–33.

Morris, G. A. *The Battle of El Alamein and Beyond* (Lewes: Book Guild, 1993).

Moseley, Leonard. *Gideon Goes to War* (London: Arthur Barker, 1955).

The Reich Marshall (London: Weidenfeld and Nicolson, 1974).

Moses, H. *The Faithful Sixth: a History of the Sixth Battalion, The Durham Light Infantry* (Durham: County Durham Books, 1995).

Motter, T. H. V. *The Persian Corridor and Aid to Russia* (Washington, DC: Office of the Chief of Military History, Dept. of the Army, 1952).

Müller, Klaus Jürgen. 'Französisch-Nordafrika und der deutsch-französische Waffenstillstand von 1940', *Wehrwissenschaftliche Rundschau* (1957), 687–99.

'Strategie et Logistique Allemandes en Afrique du Nord', *Revue Historique des Armées*, No. 1 (1983), 20–9.

Muraise, Eric. 'La Campagne de Libye (1940–1943)', *Revue Militaire Générale*, Nos. 4/5 (1969), 451–66/689–709.

Mure, D. *Master of Deception* (London: William Kimber, 1980).

Practise to Deceive (London: William Kimber, 1977).

Murphy, W. E. *2nd New Zealand Division Artillery* (Wellington: War History Branch, Department of Internal Affairs, 1966).

The Relief of Tobruk (Wellington: War History Branch, Department of Internal Affairs, 1961).

Murray, Williamson. *Luftwaffe: Strategy for Defeat* (London: Allen and Unwin, 1985).

Mussolini, Benito. *Opera Omnia di Benito Mussolini* (Florence: La Fenice, 1951).

Nehring, W. *Der Feldzug in Afrika* (Pretoria: University of South Africa War Histories, 1948).

Neillands, Robin. *The Desert Rats: 7th Armoured Division, 1940–1945* (London: Weidenfeld and Nicolson, 1991).

Nicolson, Nigel. *Alex: the Life of Field Marshal Earl Alexander of Tunis* (London, Weidenfeld and Nicolson, 1973).

Nightingale, P. R. *A History of the East Yorkshire Regiment (Duke of York's Own) in the War, 1939–1945* (York and London: William Sessions, 1952).

Nofi, A. A. 'The Desert Fox: Rommel's Campaign for North Africa, April 1941–December 1942', *Strategy and Tactics*, No. 87 (1981), 4–15.

Norman, Bruce. *Secret Warfare: the Battle of Codes and Ciphers* (Newton Abbott: David and Charles, 1973).

North, John (ed.) *The Memoirs of Field Marshal Earl Alexander of Tunis* (London: Cassell, 1962).

Norton, F. D. *26 Battalion* (Wellington: War History Branch, Department of Internal Affairs, 1952).

Oakes, B. *Muzzle Blast: Six Years of War with the 2/2 Australian Machine Gun Battalion, AIF* (Sydney: 2/2 Machine Gun Battalion War History Committee, 1980).

Oetting, Dirk. *Auftragstaktik: Geschichte und Gegenwart einer Führungskonzeption* (Bonn: Report Verlag, 1993).

Orange, Vincent. *A Biography of Air Chief Marshal Sir Keith Park* (London: Methuen, 1984).

Orgorkiewicz, R. M. *Armour* (San Antonio: Steves and Sons, 1960).

Orpen, N. *The Cape Town Highlanders, 1885–1970* (Cape Town: The Cape Town Highlanders History Committee, 1970).

 South African Forces in World War II, vol. III: War in the Desert (Cape Town: Purnell, 1971).

Orpen, N. and Martin, H. J. *Salute the Sappers* (Johannesburg: Sapper Association, 1981).

Otway, T. B. H. *British Airborne Forces* (London: Imperial War Museum, Facsimile Reprint, 1990).

Overy, Richard J. *The Air War, 1939–1945* (London: Europa Publications, 1980).

 Why the Allies Won (London: Pimlico, 1995).

Owen, Roderic. *The Desert Air Force* (London: Hutchinson, 1948).

Pack, Stanley Walter Croucher. *The Battle of Matapan (1941)* (London: Batsford, 1961).

 Seapower in the Mediterranean: a Study of the Struggle for Seapower in the Mediterranean from the 17th Century to the Present Day (London: Barker, 1971).

Packenham, T. *The Scramble for Africa* (London: Weidenfeld and Nicolson, 1991).

Packenham-Walsh, R. P. *History of the Corps of Royal Engineers, vol. III: 1938–1948* (Chatham: Institution of Royal Engineers, 1958).

Padoan, Gianni. *La guerra nel Mediterraneo* (Bologna: Capitol, 1978).

Palla, Marco. 'La Fortuna di un documento: il diario di Ciano', *Italia Contemporanea*, Vol. 33, No. 142 (1981), 31–54.

Palumbo, Michael Vincent. 'The Uncertain Friendships: Hitler–Mussolini, 1922–1939', dissertation, University of New York, 1979.

Parkinson, Roger. *The Auk: Auchinleck, Victor at Alamein* (St Albans: Granada, 1977).

Pastorelli, Pietro. 'La politica estera fascista della fine del conflitto etiopico alla seconda guerra mondiale' in Renzo de Felice (ed.) *L'Italia fra Tedeschi e Alleati* (Bologna: Il Mulino, 1973) pp. 103–14.

Paulus, Friedrich. *Ich stehe hier auf Befehl! Lebensweg des Generalfeldmarschalls Friedrich Paulus. Mit Aufzeichnungen aus dem Nachlass, Briefen und Dokumenten*, ed. Walter Görlitz (Frankfurt: Bernard and Graefe, 1960).

Paxton, Robert O. *Parades and Politics at Vichy: the French Officer Corps under Marshal Pétain* (Princeton University Press, 1996).

Payton-Smith, D. J. *Oil: a Study of War-time Policy and Administration* (London: HMSO, 1971).

Peniakoff, V. *Popski's Private Army* (London: Reprint Society, 1953).

Perrett, B. *The Valentine in North Africa, 1942–1943* (London: Ian Allen, 1972).

Petacco, Arrigo. *Le battaglie navali del Mediterraneo nella seconda guerra mondiale* (Milan: Mondadori, 1977).

Phillips, C. E. Lucas. *Alamein* (Boston: Little, Brown, 1963).

Picker, Henry. *Hitlers Tischgespräche in Führerhauptquartier: Vollständig überarbeitete und erweiterte Neuausgabe mit bisher unbekannten Selbstzeugnissen Adolf Hitlers. Abbildungen, Augenzeugenberichten und Erläuterungen des Autors: Hitler wie er wirklich war* (Stuttgart, Seewald, 1976).

Piekalkiewicz, Janusz. *Rommel and the Secret War in North Africa, 1941–1943* (West Chester, PA: Schiffer, 1992). Originally published as *Rommel und die Geheimdienste in Nordafrika, 1941–1943* (Munich: Bechtermünz, 1984).

Pimlott, John (ed.) *Rommel in his Own Words* (London: Greenhill, 1994).

Pirelli, Alberto. *Taccuini, 1922–1943* (Bologna: Il Mulino, 1984).

Pirrone, Giorgio. 'La Brigata Corazzata speciale in Africa Settentrionale', *Rivista Militare*, Vol. 102, No. 3 (1979), 105–12.

Pitt, Barrie. *The Crucible of War, vol. I: Western Desert, 1941* (London: Jonathan Cape, 1980).

  The Crucible of War, vol. II: Year of Alamein, 1942 (London: Jonathan Cape, 1982).

  The Crucible of War, vol III: Montgomery and Alamein (London: MacMillan, 1986).

  'Monty's Foxhounds', *War Monthly*, Vol. 9, No. 3 (1981).

Pitt, R. W. *Royal Wilts: the History of the Royal Wiltshire Yeomanry, 1920–1945* (London: Burrup and Mathieson, 1946).

Pitt-Rivers, J. A. *The Story of the Royal Dragoons, 1938–1945* (London: William Clowes and Son, no date).

Playfair, Maj.-Gen. I. S. O. *History of the Second World War, UK Military Series; The Mediterranean and the Middle East, vol. I: The Early Successes against Italy (to May 1941)* (London: HMSO, 1954).

  History of the Second World War, UK Military Series; The Mediterranean and the Middle East, vol. II: The Germans Come to the Help of their Ally (August 1941) (London: HMSO, 1956).

  History of the Second World War, UK Military Series; The Mediterranean and the Middle East, vol. III: British Fortunes Reach their Lowest Ebb (September 1941–September 1942). (London: HMSO, 1960).

  History of the Second World War, UK Military Series; The Mediterranean and the Middle East, vol. IV: The Destruction of the Axis Forces in Africa (London: HMSO, 1966).

Porch, Douglas, *The Path to Victory: the Mediterranean Theater in World War II* (New York: Farrar Straus and Giroux, 2004).

Potter, E. B. and Nimitz, C. W. (eds.) *The Great Sea War: the Story of Naval Action in World War II* (Englewood Cliffs, NJ: Prentice-Hall, 1960).

Prasad, A. *The Indian Revolt of 1942* (New Delhi: S. Chand, 1966).

Preti, Luigi. *Impero Fascista, Africani ed Ebrei*, Testimonianze fra cronaca e storia (Milan: U. Mursia, 1968).

Puttick, Sir E. *25 Battalion* (Wellington: War History Branch, Department of Internal Affairs, 1960).

Puttkamer, Karl Jesco von. *Die unheimliche See: Hitler und die Kriegsmarine* (Vienna: K. Kühne, 1952).

Quereshi, M. I. *The First Punjabis: History of the First Punjab Regiment, 1759–1956* (Aldershot: Gale and Polden, 1958).

Quilter, D. C. *No Dishonoured Name: the 2nd and 3rd Battalions Coldstream Guards, 1939–1946* (London: William Clowes and Son, 1974).

Rahn, Rudolf. *Ruheloses Leben* (Dusseldorf: Diederichs Verlag, 1949).

Rainero, Romain. *La rivendicazione fascista sulla Tunisia* (Milan: Marzorati, 1980).

Rainero, Romain H. and Biagini, Antonello. *L'Italia in guerra* (Rome: Commissione Italiana di Storia Militare, 1991–6).

Rainier, P. W. *Pipeline to Battle* (London: Hamish Hamilton, 1944).

Raspin, Angela. *The Italian War Economy, 1940–1943* (New York: Garland, 1986).

'Wirtschaftliche und politische Aspekte der italienischen Aufrüstung Anfang der dreißiger Jahre bis 1940' in Fritz Blaich (ed.) *Wirtschaft und Rüstung im 'Dritten Reich'* (Dusseldorf: Schwann, 1987) 202–21.

Reed, Rowena. 'Central Mediterranean Sea Control and the North African Campaigns, 1940–1942', *Naval War College Review*, Vol. 32, No. 4 (1984), 82–96.

Reid, H. M. *The Turning Point: With the New Zealand Engineers at El Alamein* (Auckland: Collins, 1944).

Remy, Maurice-Philip. *Mythos Rommel* (Munich: List, 2002).

Reuth, Ralf Georg. *Entscheidung im Mittelmeer. Die südliche Peripherie Europas in der deutschen Strategie des Zweiten Weltkrieges, 1940–1942* (Koblenz: Bernard und Graefe, 1985).

Rommel: the End of a Legend (London: Haus Books, 2005).

Rhodes-Wood, E. H. *A War History of the Royal Pioneer Corps, 1939–1945* (Aldershot: Gale and Polden, 1960).

Richard, Denis and Saunders, Hilary St George. *Royal Air Force, 1939–1945, vol. II: The Fight Avails* (London: HMSO, 1954).

Ring, Hans and Girbig, Werner. *Jagdgeschwader 27* (Germany: Motorbuch Verlag, 1971).

Ring, Hans and Shores, Christopher. *Luftkampf zwischen Sand und Sonne* (Stuttgart: Motorbuch Verlag, 1969).

Rintelen, Enno von. *Mussolini als Bundesgenosse. Erinnerungen des deutschen Militärattachés in Rom, 1936–1943* (Tübingen: R. Wunderlich, 1951).

'Mussolinis Parallelkrieg im Jahre 1940', *Wehrwissenschaftliche Rundschau*, Vol. 12, No. 1 (1962), 16–38.

'Operation und Nachschub', *Wehrwissenschaftliche Rundschau*, Vol. 1 (1951), 46–51.

Risio, Carlo de. 'El Alamein: cinquantesimo anniversario della battaglia', *Rivista Militare*, Nos. 4/5 (1992), 102–19/106–24.

Rissik, D. *The Durham Light Infantry at War* (Brancepeth Castle: The Durham Light Infantry Depot, 1952).

Rissotto, Sergio. 'Der Flugzeugträger *Giuseppe Garibaldi*', *Marine Rundschau*, Vol. 80, No. 10 (1983), 450–3.

Roberts, G. P. B. *From the Desert to the Baltic* (London: William Kimber, 1987).

Robinson, Derek. *A Good Clean Fight* (London: HarperCollins, 1994).

Robinson, James R. 'The Rommel Myth', *Military Review*, Vol. 77, No. 5 (1997), 81–9.

Rochat, Giorgio. *L'esercito italiano in pace e in guerra* (Milan: RARA, 1991).

'Mussolini Chef de Guerre', *Revue d'Histoire de la Deuxième Guerre Mondiale*, Vol. 25, No. 100 (October 1975), 59–79.

'Una ricerca impossibile: le perdite italiane nella seconda guerra mondiale', *Italia Contemporanea*, Vol. 201 (1995), 687–700.

Rohwer, Jürgen. 'Bericht aus der Forschung: Literaturverzeichnis zum Krieg im Mittelmeer, 1939–1943', *Wehrwissenschaftliche Rundschau*, Vol. 8, No. 8 (1958), 461–9.

'Der Einfluss der Alliierten Funkaufklärung auf den verlauf des Zweiten Weltkrieges', *Vierteljahrshefte für Zeitgeschichte*, Vol. 27, No. 3 (1979), 325–69.

'Der Nachschubverkehr zwischen Italien und Libyen von Juni 1940 bis Januar 1943', *Marine Rundschau*, Vol. 56 (1959), 105–20.

'Vorläufige Bemerkungen zur Frage der Sicherheit der Deutschen Schlusselmittel', *Marine Rundschau*, Vol. 72 (1979), 527–33.

Rommel, Erwin. *Krieg ohne Hass*, ed. Lucie-Maria Rommel and Generalleutnant Fritz Bayerlein (Heidenheim: Heidenheimer Zeitung, 1950).

Roskill, Stephen W. *The War at Sea, 1939–1945*, 4 vols. (London: HMSO, 1956).

Ross, A. *23 Battalion*. (Wellington: War History Branch, Department of Internal Affairs, 1959).

Rossi, Franceso. *Mussolini e lo stato maggiore: Avvenimenti del 1940* (Rome: Regionale, 1951).

Routledge, N. W. *History of the Royal Regiment of Artillery: Anti-Aircraft Artillery, 1914–1955* (London: Brassey's, 1994).

Royal Air Force Middle East Review, vol. II. (London: HMSO, 1944).

Ruge, Friedrich. *Sea Warfare, 1939–1945* (London: Cassell, 1957).

Rust, K. C. *The 9th Air Force in World War II* (Fullbrook, CA: Aero Publishers, 1970).

Sadat, Anwar. *In Search of Identity* (New York: Harper and Row, 1978).

Revolt on the Nile (New York: Harper and Row, 1957).

Sadkovich, J. J. *The Italian Navy in World War II* (Westport, CT: Greenwood, 1994).

'Of Myths and Men: Rommel and the Italians in North Africa, 1940–1942', *The International History Review*, Vol. 13, No. 2 (1991), 221–440.

'Understanding Defeat: Reappraising Italy's Role in World War II', *Journal of Contemporary History*, Vol. 24, No. 1 (1989), 27–61.

Sairigné, Gabriel de. 'Bir Hakeim', *Revue Historique des Armées*, No. 1 (1981), 166–84.

Salerno, Reynolds M. *Vital Crossroads: Mediterranean Origins of the Second World War, 1935–1940* (Ithaca: Cornell University Press, 2002).

Salewski, Michael. *Die deutsche Seekriegsleitung, 1933–1945*, 2 vols. (Frankfurt and Munich: Bernard and Graefe, 1970–5).

Salmad, J. B. *The History of the 51st Highland Division, 1939–1945* (Edinburgh and London: William Blackwood and Sons, 1953).

Samwell, H. P. *An Infantry Officer with the Eighth Army* (Edinburgh and London: William Blackwood and Sons, 1945).

Sansom, A. E. W. *I Spied Spies* (London: Harrap, 1965).

Santoni, A. *Il vero traditore* (Milan: Mursia, 1981).

Santoni, Alberto. 'Der Einfluß von "Ultra" auf den Krieg im Mittelmeer', *Marine Rundschau*, Vol. 78, No. 9 (1981), 503–12.

'Il servizio informativo inglese nel Mediterraneo alla viglia delle ostilita, secondo documenti britannici inediti', *Rivista Marittima*, Vol. 113, No. 10 (1980), 77–82.

Santoni, Alberto and Mattesini, Francesco. *La partizipazione tedesca alla guerra aeronavale nel Mediterraneo, 1940–1945* (Rome: Edizioni dell'Ateneo and Bizzarri, 1980).

Santoro, Giuseppe. *L'aeronautica italiana nella seconda guerra mondiale*, 2 vols. (Rome: Edizioni Essi, 1957).

Schechtman, Joseph B. *The Mufti and the Führer: the Rise and Fall of Haj Amein el-Husseini* (New York: Thomas Yoseloff, 1965).

Schinzinger, Francesca. 'Kriegsökonomische Aspekte der deutschen-italienischen Wirtschaftsbeziehungen, 1939–1941', in Forstmeier, Friedrich and Volkmann, Hans-Erich (eds.) *Kriegswirtschaft und Rüstung* (Dusseldorf: Droste, 1977) pp. 164–81.

Schmider, Klaus. 'The Mediterranean in 1940–1941: Crossroads of Lost Opportunities?', *War and Society*, Vol. 15, No. 2 (1997), 19–41.

Schmokel, W. W. *Dream of Empire: German Colonialism, 1919–1945* (New Haven: Yale University Press, 1964).

Schmidt, H. B. 'The Nazi Party in Palestine and the Levant, 1932–1939', *International Affairs*, Vol. 28 (October 1952), 460–9.

Schmidt, Heinz-Werner. *Mit Rommel in Afrika* (Munich: Argus Verlag, 1951).

  With Rommel in the Desert (London: Constable, 1987).

Schmidt, Paul. *Statist auf diplomatischer Bühne, 1923–1945* (Bonn: Athenäum, 1954).

Schnabel, R. (ed.) *Tiger und Schakal: Deutsche Indienpolitik, 1941–1943. Ein Dokumentarbericht* (Vienna: Europa Verlag, 1968).

Schramm, Percy Ernst (ed.). *Kriegstagebuch des Oberkommandos der Wehrmacht (Wehrmachtsführungsstab), 1940–1945*, 4 vols. in 7 (Frankfurt: Bernard und Graefe, 1961–5).

Schreiber, Gerhard. 'Italien im Machtpolitischen Kalkul der Deutschen Marine Führung, 1919 bis 1945', *Quellen und Forschungen aus Italienischen Archiven und Bibliotheken*, Vol. 62 (1982), 229–69.

  'Der Mittelmeerraum in Hitlers Strategie 1940', *Militärgeschichtliche Mitteilungen*, Vol. 28, No. 2 (1980), 69–99.

  'Reichsmarine, Revisionismus und Weltmachtstreben' in K.-J. Müller (ed.) *Militär und Militarismus in Weimarer Republik* (Dusseldorf: Droste, 1978) 149–76.

Revisionismus und Weltmachtstreben: Marineführung und deutsch-italienische Beziehungen, 1919 bis 1944, Beitrage zur Militär und Kriegsgeschichte 20 (Stuttgart: Deutsche Verlags-Anstalt, 1978).

'Die Seeschlacht von Matapan', *Marineforum*, Vol. 50 (1975), 332.

'Les structures stratégiques de la conduite de la guerre de coalition Italo-Allemande au cours de la deuxième guerre mondiale', *Revue d'Histoire de la Deuxième Guerre Mondiale*, Vol. 30, No. 120 (1980), 1–32.

'Sul teatro mediterrano nella seconda guerra mondiale: inediti punti di vista della marina germanica del tempo', *Rivista Marittima* (1987).

'Thesen zur Ideologischen Kontinuität in den Machtpolitischen Zielsetzungen der Deutschen Marineführung, 1897 bis 1945' in *Militärgeschichte: Probleme – Thesen – Wege*, Im Auftrag des Militärgeschichtlichen Forschungsamtes aus Anlass des 25 jährigen Bestehens ausgewählt und zusammengestellt von Manfred Messerschmidt, Klaus A. Maier, Werner Rahn und Bruno Thoss, Beiträge zur Militär und Kriegsgeschichte 25 (Stuttgart: Deutsche Verlags-Anstalt, 1982) pp. 260–80.

'Zur Kontinuität des Groß- und Weltmachstrebens der Deutschen Marineführung', *Militärgeschichtliche Mitteilungen*, Vol. 27, No. 2 (1979), 101–71.

Schreiber, Gerhard, Stegemann, Bernd and Vogel, Detlef. *Das Deutsche Reich und der Zweite Weltkrieg, Band III: Der Mittelmeerraum und Südosteuropa. Von der 'non belligeranza' Italiens bis zum Kriegseintritt der Vereinigten Staaten* (Stuttgart: Deutsche Verlags-Anstalt, 1984).

Schröder, Bernd Philipp. *Deutschland und der Mittlere Osten im Zweiten Weltkrieg*, Studien und Dokumente zur Geschichte des Zweiten Weltkrieges 16 (Göttingen: Musterschmidt, 1975).

Schutt, Werner. 'Der Stahlpakt und Italiens "Nonbelligeranza", 1938–1940', *Wehrwissenschaftliche Rundschau*, Vol. 8, No. 9 (1958), 498–521.

Scoullar, J. L. *Battle for Egypt: Official History of New Zealand in the Second World War* (Wellington: War History Branch, Department of Internal Affairs, 1955).

Serle, R. P. (ed.) *The Second Twenty-Fourth Australian Infantry Battalion, Ninth Australian Division: a History* (Brisbane: Jacaranda, 1963).

Seth, Ronald. *Two Fleets Surprised: the Story of the Battle of Cape Matapan* (London: G. Bles, 1960).

Shankland, Peter and Hunter, Anthony. *Malta Convoy* (London: Collins, 1961).

Sheppard, E. W. 'The Campaign of El-Alamein, 1942' in E. W. Sheppard, *The Study of Military History* (Aldershot: Gale and Polden, 1952).

Shore, P. *Mud and Blood: 'Albury's Own' Second Twenty-Third Australian Light Infantry Battalion, Ninth Australian Division* (Perth: John Burridge Military Antiques, 1991).

Shores, Christopher; Cull, Brian and Malizia, Nicola. *Malta: the Hurricane Years, 1940–1941* (London: Grub Street, 1987).

Malta: the Spitfire Year, 1942 (London: Grub Street, 1991).

Shores, Christopher and Ring, Hans. *Fighters over the Desert* (London: Neville Spearman, 1969).

Showalter, Dennis. *Patton and Rommel: Men of War in the Twentieth Century* (New York: Berkley Caliber, 2005).

Siebert, Ferdinand. *Italiens weg in den Zweiten Weltkrieg* (Frankfurt: Athenäum, 1962).

Silverfarb, Daniel. 'Britain, the United States, and the Security of the Saudi Arabian Oilfields in 1942', *Historical Journal*, Vol. 26 (1983).

Simpkins, A. *The Rand Light Infantry* (Cape Town: Howard Thomas, 1965).

Simpkins, B. G. *Rand Light Infantry* (Cape Town: Timmins, 1947).

Smith, Kevin D. 'Coming into its Own: the Contribution of Intelligence at the Battle of Alam Halfa', *Military Review*, Vol. 82, No. 4 (2002), 74–7.

Smith, Peter C. *Massacre at Tobruk* (London: William Kimber, 1987).

Pedestal: the Convoy that Saved Malta (Manchester: Crécy, 1999).

Sokol, E. A. 'Seapower in the Mediterranean, 1940–1943', *Military Review* (August 1956), 12–27.

Spick, Mike. *Luftwaffe Fighter Aces* (London: Greenhill Books, 1996).

Spooner, A. J. *In Full Flight* (London: MacDonald, 1965).

Supreme Gallantry: Malta's Role in the Allied Victory, 1939–1945 (London: John Murray, 1996).

Warburton's War (London: William Kimber, 1987).

Staffens, Hans von. *'Salaam', Geheime Kommando zum Nil* (Neckargemünd: K. Vohwinckel, 1960).

Stark, F. *The Arab Island: the Middle East, 1939–1943* (New York: Knopf, 1945).

Stark, Warner. 'The German Afrika Korps', *Military Review*, Vol. 45, No. 7 (1965), 91–7.

Stato Maggiore dell' Esercito. *La guerra in Africa Orientale (Giugno 1940–Novembre 1941)* (Rome: Ufficio Storico, 1971).

In Africa Settentrionale: la preparazione al conflitto, l'avanza su sidi el Barrani (Rome: Ufficio Storico, 1955).

La prima offensiva britannica in Africa Settentrionale (Ottobre 1940–Febbraio 1941), vol. I: Narrazione e Allegati (Rome: Ufficio Storico, 1964).

La terza offensiva britannica in Africa Settentrionale (Rome: Ufficio Storico, 1961).

Stevens, G. R. *Fourth Indian Division* (Toronto: McClaren and Son, 1948).

Stewart, Adrian. *Eighth Army's Greatest Victories: Alam Halfa to Tunis, 1942–1943* (Barnsley: Leo Cooper, 1999).

Stewart, Norman. 'German Relations with the Arab East, 1937–1941' dissertation St Louis University, MO, 1975.

Stitt, G. *La campagne de Méditerrannée, 1940–1943*, sous le commandement de l'amiral Cunningham, grand officier de la Légion d'honneur (Paris: Payot, 1946).

Strawson, John. *The Battle for North Africa* (New York: Bonanza Books, 1969).

El Alamein: Desert Victory (London: Dent, 1981).

Student, Kurt. *Generaloberst Student und seine Fallschirmjäger. Die Erinnerungen des Generaloberst Kurt Student*, ed. Hermann Götzel (Friedberg: Podzun-Pallas-Verlag, 1980).

Stumpf, Reinhard. 'Der Krieg im Mittelmeerraum 1942/3: Die Operationen in Nordafrika und im Mitteleren Mittelmeer', in Horst Boog, Werner Rahn, Reinhard Stumpf and Bernd Wegner, *Das Deutsche Reich und der Zweite Weltkrieg, vol. VI: Der Globale Krieg. Die Ausweitung zum Weltkrieg und der Wechsel der Initiative 1941–1943* (Stuttgart: Deutsche Verlags-Anstalt, 1990).

Sullivan, Brian R. 'The Italian Armed Forces, 1918–1940' in Alan R. Millet and Williamson Murray (eds.) *Military Effectiveness, vol. II: The Interwar Period* (Boston: Unwin Hyman 1988).

Sünderman, Helmut and Sudholt, Gerd. *Tagesparolen: deutsche Presseweisungen, 1939–1945: Hitlers Propaganda und Kriegsführung* (Leoni: Druffel Verlag, 1973).

Sweet., J. J. T. *Iron Arm: the Mechanization of Mussolini's Army, 1920–1940* (Westport: Greenwood, 1980).

Sym, J. M. *Seaforth Highlanders* (Aldershot: Gale and Polden, 1962).

Synge, W. A. T. *The Story of the Green Howards, 1939–1945* (Richmond: The Green Howards, 1952).

Taysen, Adalbert von. *Tobruk 1941. Der Kampf in Nordafrika* (Freiburg: Rombach, 1976).

Tedde, Antonio. *Fiamme nel deserto: da Tobruk ad El Alamein* (Milan: Istituto Editoriale Cisalpino, 1962).

Tedder, Marshal of the RAF Lord. *With Prejudice* (London: Cassell, 1966).

Terraine, John. *The Right of the Line* (London: Sceptre, 1988).

Thierfelder, Franz. 'Deutsch-indische Begegnungen 1926–1936', in H. O. Günther (ed.) *Indien und Deutschland: Ein Sammelband* (Frankfurt: Europäische Verlagsanstalt, 1956) pp. 146–57.

Thomas, E. W. *Ambulance in Africa* (New York: Appleton, 1943).

Thompson, Julian. *War Behind Enemy Lines* (London: Imperial War Museum/Sidgwick and Jackson, 1998).

Thompson, R. W. *Generalissimo Churchill* (London: Hodder and Stoughton, 1973).

The Montgomery Legend (London: Allen and Unwin, 1967).

Tillman, Heinz. *Deutschlands Araberpolitik im Zweiten Weltkrieg*, Schriftenreihe des Instituts für Allgemeine Geschichte an der Martin Luther Universität Halle-Wittenberg 2 (East Berlin: Deutscher Verlag der Wissenschaften, 1965).

Timpson, Alistair, with Gibson-Watt, Andrew. *In Rommel's Backyard* (Barnsley: Leo Cooper, 2000).

Tobler, D. H. *Intelligence in the Desert: the Recollections and Reflections of a Brigade Intelligence Officer* (Victoria, BC: Morriss Printing, 1978).

Todd, A. *The Elephant at War: 2nd Battalion Seaforth Highlanders, 1939–1945* (Auckland: Pentland, 1998).

Toscano, Mario. 'Le conversazioni militari italo-tedesche alla viglia della seconda guerra mondiale', *Rivista Storica Italiana*, Vol. 64 (1952), 336–82.

Trevor-Roper, H. R., *Hitler's War Directives, 1939–1945* (London: Pan, 1966).

Trigellis-Smith, S. *Britain to Borneo: a History of 2/32 Australian Infantry Battalion* (Sydney: 2/32 Australian Infantry Battalion Association, 1993).

Trizzino, Antonio. *Di verratene Flotte: Tragödie der Afrikakämpfer* (Kiel: Arndt, 1957).

Truchet, André. *L'armistice de 1940 et l'Afrique du Nord* (Paris: Presses Universitaires de France, 1955).

Trye, R. *Mussolini's Afrika Korps: the Italian Army in North Africa, 1940–1943* (Bayside, NY: Axis Europa Books, 1999).

Mussolini's Soldiers (Shrewsbury: Airlife, 1995).

Tuker, F. *Approach to Battle* (London: Cassell, 1963).

Tungay, A. W. *The Fighting Third* (Cape Town: Unie-Volkspers, 1947).

Tute, W. *The North African War* (London: Sidgwick and Jackson, 1976).

Ufficio Storico della Marina Militare. *Le azioni navali in Mediterraneo dal 10 giugno 1940 al 31 marzo 1941* (Rome: Ufficio Storico della Marina Militare, 1971).

Efficienza all'apertura della ostilità (Rome: Ufficio Storico della Marina Militare, 1982).

L'organizzazione della marina durante il conflitto (Rome: Ufficio Storico della Marina Militare, 1972).

Underhill, Major D. F. *Queen's Own Royal Regiment The Staffordshire Yeomanry: an Account of the Operations of the Regiment during World War II, 1939–1945* (Stafford: Staffordshire Libraries, Arts and Archives, 1994).

Valentin, Rolf. *Ärtze im Wüstenkrieg* (Koblenz: Bernard und Graefe, 1984).

Váli, Ferenc A. *Bridge across the Bosphorus: the Foreign Policy of Turkey* (Baltimore: The Johns Hopkins University Press, 1971).

Vere-Hodge, Edward. *Turkish Foreign Policy, 1918–1948* (Ambouilly-Annemasse: Impr. Franco-Suisse, 1950).

Verney, G. L. *The Desert Rats: a History of 7th Armoured Division* (London: Hutchinson, 1954).

Voigt, Johannes H. 'Hitler und Indien', *Vierteljahrshefte für Zeitgeschichte*, Vol. 19, No. 1 (1971), 32–63.

Indien im Zweiten Weltkrieg, Studien zur Zeitgeschichte 11 (Stuttgart: Deutsche Verlags Anstalt, 1978).

Vulliez, Albert. *Analyse des conférences navales du Führer* (Paris: Grandes Éditions Françaises, 1949).

Wagner, Gerhard (ed.) *Die Lagevorträge des Oberbefehlhabers der Marine vor Hitler, 1939–1945* (Munich: Lehmann, 1971).

Wake, Sir H. and Deeds, W. F. (eds.) *Swift and Bold: the Story of the King's Royal Rifle Corps in the Second World War* (Aldershot: Gale and Polden, 1949).

Walker, R. *Alam Halfa and Alamein: Official History of New Zealand in the Second World War* (Wellington: War History Branch, Department of Internal Affairs, 1967).

Ward, S. P. G. *Faithful: the Story of the Durham Light Infantry* (London: Thomas Nelson and Son, 1962).

Ward-Harvey, K. *The Sapper's War: With Ninth Australian Division Engineers, 1939–1945* (Neutral Bay, NSW: Sakoga/Ninth Division RAE Association, 1992).

Wardrop, J. *Tanks across the Desert: the War Diary of Jake Wardrop*, ed. G. Forty (London: William Kimber, 1981).

Warlimont, W. 'Entgegnung zu der Stellungnahme eds Admirals Weichold', *Wehrwissenschaftliche Rundschau*, Vol. 3 (1959).

Im Hauptquartier der Deutschen Wehrmacht, 1939–1945 (Frankfurt: Bernard und Graefe, 1964).

'Die Insel Malta in der Mittelmeerstrategie des Zweiten Weltkrieges', *Wehrwissenschaftliche Rundschau*, Vol. 8 (1958), 421–36; Vol. 9 (1959), 173–6.

Inside Hitler's Headquarters, 1939–45 (New York: Praeger, 1964).

Warner, Geoffrey. *Iraq and Syria, 1941* (London: Davis-Poynter, 1974).

Warner, P. *Alamein* (London: William Kimber, 1979).

Auchinleck: The Lonely Soldier (London: Buchan and Enright, 1981).

Warner, Philip. *The Special Air Service* (London: William Kimber, 1971).

Watt, D. C. 'Gli accordi mediterranei anglo-italiano del 16 aprile 1938', *Revista di Studi Politici Internazionale*, Vol. 26 (February–March 1959), 51 –76.

Wavell, A. P. *The Good Soldier* (London: MacMillan, 1948).

'We Were Monty's Men': With the Green Howards of the 50th Division from Gazala to Tunis (Richmond: Green Howards Museum, 1997).

Weal, John. *Junkers Ju 87: Stukageschwader of North Africa and the Mediterranean* (London: Osprey, 1998).

Weber, Frank G. *The Evasive Neutral: Germany, Britain and the Quest for a Turkish Alliance in the Second World War* (Columbia: University of Missouri Press, 1979).

Weichold, Eberhard. 'Die Deutsche Führung und das Mittelmeer unter den Blickwinkel der Seestrategie', *Wehrwissenschaftliche Rundschau*, Vol. 9 (1959), 164–73.

Weinberg, Gerhard L. 'German Colonial Plans and Policies, 1938–1942' in W. Besson (ed.) *Geschichte und Gegenwartsbewusstsein: Festschrift für Hans Rothfels zum 70. Geburtstag* (Göttingen: Vandenhoeck and Ruprecht 1963) pp. 462–91.

A World at Arms: a Global History of World War II (Cambridge University Press, 1994).

West, F. *From Alamein to Scarlet Beach: the History of 2/4th Light Anti-Aircraft Regiment, Second AIF* (Gerlong: Deakin University Press, 1987).

Westphal, Siegfried. *Erinnerungen* (Mainz: v. Hase und Koehler, 1975).

The Fatal Decisions (London: World Distributors, 1965).

'Der Feldzug in Nordafrika 1941–1943', in *Schicksal Nordafrika* (Döffingen: Europa-Contact Verl.-Ges. 1954) pp. 137–265.

The German Army in the West (London: Cassell, 1951).

Heer in Fesseln. Aus den Papieren des Stabschefs von Rommel, Kesselring und Rundstedt (Bonn: Athenäum, 1950).

Weygand, General Maxime. *Recalled to Service* (London: Heinemann 1952).

'What We Have We Hold!': a History of 2/17th Australian Infantry Battalion, 1940–1945 (Loftus, NSW: 2/17th Battalion History Committee/Australian Military History Publications, 1998).

Wheatley, D. *The Deception Planners* (London: Hutchinson, 1980).

Whiting, C. *The Poor Bloody Infantry* (London: Guild, 1987).

Wilkinson-Lotham, J. *Montgomery's Desert Army* (London: Osprey, 1977).

Wilmington, M. W. *The Middle East Supply Center* (London: University of London Press, 1971).

Wingate, J. *The Fighting Truth* (London: Leo Cooper, 1971).

Winterbotham, F. W. *The Ultra Secret* (London: Weidenfeld and Nicolson, 1974).

Wilmot, Chester. *Tobruk* (Sydney: Angus and Robertson, 1945).

Winston, John. *Cunningham: the Greatest Admiral since Nelson* (London: John Murray, 1998).

Woodman, R. *Malta Convoys* (London: John Murray, 2000).

Woolcombe, Robert. *The Campaigns of Wavell, 1939–1943* (London: Cassell, 1959).

Yergin, Daniel. *The Prize: the Epic Quest for Oil, Money and Power* (London: Simon and Schuster, 1991).

Yisraeli, David. 'The Third Reich and Palestine', *Middle Eastern Studies*, Vol. 7 (October 1971), 343–53.

Young, Desmond. *Rommel: the Desert Fox* (London: Fontana, 1955).

Young, M. and Stap, R. *Trojan Horses: Deception Operations in the Second World War* (London: Bodley Head, 1989).

Zamagani, Vera (ed.) *Come perdere la guerra e vincere la pace: L'economia italiana tra guerra e dopoguerra, 1938–1947* (Bologna: Il Mulino, 1997).

Ziegler, Philip. *Mountbatten* (New York: Knopf, 1985).

Zweig, Ronald W. 'British plans for the Evacuation of Palestine', *Studies in Zionism*, Vol. 8 (1983).

INDEX